Josephine P. Bree

CICERO: A BIOGRAPHY

CICERO

A Biography

By

Torsten Petersson

Biblo and Tannen

New York

1963

BIBLO and TANNEN
BOOKSELLERS and PUBLISHERS, Inc.
63 Fourth Avenue   New York 3, N. Y.

Library of Congress Catalog Card Number: 63-10768

Printed in U.S.A. by
NOBLE OFFSET PRINTERS, INC.
NEW YORK 3, N. Y.

TO

IVAN MORTIMER LINFORTH

> Quid dulcius quam habere quicum omnia
> audeas sic loqui ut tecum ?

PREFACE

The purpose of this book is to give as comprehensive an account of Cicero as a single volume will permit. It endeavors to keep a proper proportion between his political activities and his accomplishments as an orator and a writer of essays and letters. It aims to present the Roman background, which alone can make the narrative intelligible to any but the special student; to determine and to make clear the Roman attitude toward a man's work in the world, the political atmosphere of Rome, the spirit in which the orators spoke, and the Roman view of rhetoric, philosophy, and authorship. Above all, it seeks to give a narrative of Cicero's life as it unfolded from one period to another, and to convey a little of the spirit that animated him.

The manuscript of this book has been read, completely or in part, and assistance of various kinds has been given me by several of my colleagues. Professor J. T. Allen and Professor A. W. Ryder have offered many helpful suggestions; Professor M. E. Deutsch has placed a number of lecture notes at my disposal; Professor O. M. Washburn, who as Manager of the University Press has skillfully supervised the printing of the book, has suggested numerous improvements; and Professor R. F. Scholz, now at the University of Washington, has given me the benefit of his knowledge of Roman history and politics. Professor I. M. Linforth has practically acted as editor, and has read the entire manuscript with great care; there is scarcely a page in the book which has not profited by his keen and sympathetic criticism. To Professor G. R. Noyes, finally, I owe perhaps most. His thorough scholarship, his eminent literary gifts, and, more than all else, his generous appreciation and encouragement, have been of priceless value to me in more ways than can readily be described. It gives me great pleasure to express here my heartfelt gratitude to these gentlemen.

Torsten Petersson.

February, 1919.

CHAPTER I

INTRODUCTORY

Marcus Tullius Cicero was born in Arpinum, a small town about sixty miles from Rome, on the third of January, 106 B.C. While still a boy, he was taken to Rome, where he lived almost continuously for the rest of his life. He began to plead cases in the forum when he was about twenty-five, rose to considerable prominence within a year or two, and at the age of thirty-six was recognized as the most eminent pleader at the Roman bar. Meanwhile he had entered upon his career as a magistrate, and at forty-two was elected to the consulship, the highest office in Rome. As consul he suppressed the Catilinarian conspiracy, and was thus led to take a leading part in Roman politics. The formation of the first triumvirate caused his exile, in 58 B.C.; but he was recalled the following year. During the rest of his life he gave much of his time to study and writing, though he continued to be active in politics and, especially, in the courts. After the assassination of Caesar he directed the opposition against Antony in an effort to save the republican government. He was murdered in the proscriptions of the second triumvirate on the seventh of December, 43 B.C.

More is known about Cicero than about any other person of the ancient world. His prominence in his own day as an orator, statesman, and writer, and, above all, the great popularity of his numerous works, made him loom large in the Roman consciousness. He was one of the great Romans, and was much imitated and discussed. Quintilian, in his work on oratory, frequently refers to him, and advises his readers that they can measure their own progress by their appreciation of Cicero. Pliny the Younger, who like Cicero was an orator and a man of letters, set about consciously fashioning his life after that of

Cicero. He made no secret of his ambition to emulate his great predecessor, frequently instituting modest comparisons between Cicero and himself, and publishing a collection of letters addressed to his friends, the contents and phraseology of which are largely due to Cicero. The orations of Cicero were early used as text books for the teaching of oratòry, and the events of his life became the subject of declamations in the rhetorical schools. The historians of the empire discuss him as a statesman. Other writers of almost every kind refer to him, and commentaries were written on several of his works. In addition to this, Cicero's own freedman, Tiro, wrote a biography of his patron, which undoubtedly contained much information of an intimate and gossipy nature. This biography has been lost. Finally, Plutarch wrote a life of Cicero, still extant, in which he gathered together much of this information. He fused the true and the false without critical judgment, but his account contains many things which would not otherwise have been known to us, and his view of Cicero is substantially correct.[1]

All this writing about Cicero, however, which culminated as it were in Plutarch's life of him, as well as the scattered references and opinions in the following few centuries, gives scarcely more than is known about any one of several prominent Romans. Our unique knowledge of Cicero comes from his own extant writings, which have an aggregate extent materially greater than that of Gibbon's *History of the Roman Empire*. In addition to numerous fragments of various kinds, both in prose and in verse, and sometimes of considerable length, the extant works of Cicero consist of fifty-eight speeches, about two thousand pages of philosophy and rhetoric, and some eight hundred letters. Much of this would naturally be impersonal, since it is concerned with other people's affairs or with the discussion of abstract subjects, but in the case of Cicero even the most impersonal of his works are largely autobiographical. This is due in some degree to Cicero's personality, but far more to the character of the times.

---

[1] See Gudeman.

The speeches, delivered either in the courts, before the senate, or in the forum, are not confined to impersonal arguments or discussions. Public life in republican Rome had a man-to-man attitude. The personal character and influence of a pleader in a lawsuit, for instance, was of immense importance, and was looked upon as one of the strongest arguments for the client. If the upright Cato was willing to vouch for a man by taking his case, much was gained even before the trial began. As a result, Cicero in his legal speeches frequently explains how he came to take the case and what his relations were both to his client and to the latter's opponent. Often a speech for another man becomes a defense of Cicero's own political activity, since the opposing speaker tried to weaken Cicero's side by attacking Cicero himself; all of which was quite according to accepted standards. The personal element in the orations delivered before the senate or the people would naturally be even greater, as the character and position of the speaker were often of as much importance as the subject under discussion. The orator said not merely that such or such a line of action was preferable; he dilated on his own unselfish motives and on the wisdom and honesty of his past career, incidentally showing little consideration for his opponent's.

There was, however, still another circumstance that makes for self-revelation in these speeches. When published, they took the place of modern newspaper reports and interviews. They were intended not merely to spread the author's professional reputation and to give to the public his view of an important case or public question, but also to set before the Romans the kind of picture of himself that he wished them to have. Cicero often describes the manner in which his words and those of his opponents were received; he gives expression to his hopes and his fears about the future, and his opinions about the past and the present; he even talks about his friends and his family.

Nothing seems too personal for inclusion. The speeches suggest at times the orations, after-dinner talks, personal reminiscences, and revelations of family intimacies that are poured out during an American presidential campaign. And they are scarcely more trustworthy. It was recognized that an orator was pleading for his client or for himself. Some speakers did not publish. their orations, in order to escape the charge of inconsistency. Cicero, like most of the orators, published; and laughingly admits that he may have changed his mind, or that the opinions expressed in a former speech may have been colored by circumstances.

Of Cicero's writings on rhetoric and philosophy, the essays, six are concerned with the art of pleading and public speaking; the others are philosophical. Among the latter are two on political science, which the ancients classed as a branch of philosophy. In the three most important rhetorical essays Cicero sets forth his view of oratory. One discusses the aims of an orator and his training; another contains a history of oratory, including something about Cicero himself; the third gives a picture of the ideal orator. All this, though containing much of the rhetorical science of the time, is based on Cicero's own thought and experience, and is permeated with his personality. The philosophical essays— except the *De Officiis,* on Duty—are less personal. Their chief aim is to introduce the Romans to Greek philosophy and Greek political thinking; they are, therefore, largely in the nature of adaptations from Greek works; but all of them nevertheless reveal something, now more and now less, of Cicero's own opinions. He had read about matters philosophical and political, but he had also thought about them and lived with them.

These essays were intended for a smaller, more select public than the orations, and therefore contain the private opinions of Cicero even when these ran contrary to the current beliefs that governed Roman public life. Thus, in the matter of religion, the educated Romans, whether pious or not, usually did not believe in Jupiter, Minerva, and the other gods of the Roman

pantheon, but as state officials they observed a decent regard for them, and were glad to hold priesthoods. Caesar, though a thoroughgoing sceptic, was for a large part of his life pontifex maximus, the head of the Roman state religion; the office was important politically. Cicero was on the board of augurs, whose duty it was to practise divination, but he did not believe that the gods vouchsafed to mortals a view into the future. This belief of his is set forth in the *De Divinatione*, where he not only makes his attitude perfectly clear, but represents his brother Quintus as calling attention to the discrepancy between his public utterances and his private opinions. "Why did you make such a moving appeal to Jupiter while you were speaking in the forum, when you don't believe that Jupiter helps us?" And Cicero's reply makes it obvious that the father of the gods had his statues about the city for the sake of the dear public.

The essays have various external characteristics that offer an opportunity for personal revelations. The manner in which the dialogue form is used in the *De Divinatione* has just been indicated. It was used in the same way in the other dialogues; and most of the essays are dialogues. Sometimes Cicero himself is the chief speaker; at other times the conversation is carried on by personal friends of his, many of whom clamored for this kind of publicity; at still other times the speakers are men of past ages, but in these cases Cicero usually makes one of them his mouthpiece. The dialogues have ordinarily somewhat extended introductory scenes, undoubtedly founded on reality. Not that any particular conversation need be supposed to have taken place under the exact circumstances described, but something similar had happened. They are *Dichtung,* but also *Wahrheit;* and often reveal matters otherwise unknown. The only extant description of his childhood home is such a scene. And finally, whether dialogues or not, the essays are addressed to a definite individual, purporting to answer some special need or request of his. Although this does not always have any influence, its effect is sometimes very marked, as in the work on Duty, addressed to Cicero's son. In this essay, and in some others, it gives to the writing a definite point of view, which makes for clarity and power, and imparts to it a warmth rarely if ever found in modern essays, which are addressed to nobody in particular. But the most direct, and perhaps the most valuable and interesting, personal revelations in the essays are found in the prefaces that introduce several of them. These are occasionally of considerable length. They resemble the old-fashioned epistles to the gentle readers of a century or two ago, in explaining Cicero's aim and attitude as a writer; but they also contain singularly frank comments on persons and events that had particularly influenced him. They are his meditations; the only avowedly, and at the same time intimately, autobiographical parts of his writings. There is nothing quite like them in the rest of ancient literature.

The third large group of Cicero's extant writings consists of his correspondence. There are about eight hundred letters written by him, and one hundred addressed to him by various people. They were published posthumously, some of them long after his death. He had had an intention, never carried out, of publishing a selection from his correspondence; if he had done so, he would certainly have held back many of the letters that we now have. He wrote a great many more than are extant. Twice as many are supposed to have been actually published, and some may have been suppressed, to shield certain persons, such as Emperor Augustus. The suppression was not made for the benefit of Cicero, as is clear from the most casual reading; nor is it at all likely that there was any revision. The letters come as unchanged from the hands of Cicero and his correspondents as copying would allow.

The correspondence of an ancient Roman was naturally different from ours. He had no newspapers, no telegraph, and no telephone. When away from the city, he would receive all his political and financial news through letters. His own reports would be in the form of letters to the senate, in character much like the reports of a modern representative in a foreign country; but if he wished to advertise his doings for political purposes, this had to be done in letters to friends, who would read these in the senate, or in other ways let them be known. When in or near the city, a Roman would also make more extensive use of letter writing than is the case with us. Cicero in a suburb and Atticus in Rome exchanged frequent notes, whereas, under modern conditions, they would have used the telephone.

Since letter writing filled a larger place in ancient than in modern life,[2] it received unusual attention. The Greek rhetoricians, always prompt to make any current practise a subject for instruction, and always thorough and systematic, taught the art of correspondence under various subdivisions. The Roman boys learned to write letters of news, letters of exhortation, letters of a pleasant, chatty character, in which, according to proper teaching, wit was the important ingredient. And the Romans in after life did not forget the teaching. Good letter writing was a sign of good breeding. In the early empire letters had become a recognized form of literature, so that Pliny the Younger published a voluminous correspondence about his own thoughts and experiences, just as he might have published a collection of lyric poems. Letters were by that time a sort of inoffensive autobiography. But even Cicero and his friends wrote many letters that would not have been written today, which were solely the expression of their cultivated tastes.

It is not to be supposed that all Romans were good letter writers—some of the epistles sent to Cicero indicate the contrary —but Cicero himself possessed the necessary qualities in a very unusual degree.[3] He had wit, grace, a vivid imagination, and an open eye. He had the artist's vanity of wishing to please,

[2] See especially Peter, *Der Brief etc.*

[3] On Cicero in his letters, see particularly Boissier, pp. 1–23.

and he understood his correspondents. He wrote briefly to those who were chary of words; he was serious with the serious and jocose with the wits. The great majority of his letters are so perfectly adjusted to the addressees that these can be recognized without the superscription. Cicero is infinitely varied and adaptable. His replies to letters of criticism or enmity, in the few cases where they can be put side by side with the latter, are veritable object lessons in diplomacy and good manners. The compliments he addresses to his friends seem to be of the very kind that they would have liked. His letters of recommendation, of which there are many, are varied and graceful, even when they necessarily contain but little. Cicero had the gift of saying nothing or next to nothing with urbanity and charm; but he also had an even greater ability of giving expression to deep feeling. He was a man of strong emotions. He hated whole-heartedly, though rarely, and could express his hatred with a concentrated fury or a malicious sarcasm that would be difficult to parallel. But his love for people was greater than his hatred. His affection and admiration for his brother Quintus and for Atticus was profound and unwavering. It is only on rare occasions[4] that these feelings would find direct expression in the course of a frequent correspondence, but when this happens, Cicero writes with such ardor, self-abandonment, and gratitude for the gift of these men's love that the reader feels himself blessed as with a benediction. It is a source of gladness to know that such friendships have existed.

The letters to Quintus and to Atticus contain the most intimate revelation of Cicero. Of these the letters to Atticus are by far the more important, for those to Quintus are much less numerous and were written within a period of seven consecutive years. During that time, furthermore, Quintus was far away from his brother, so that the interchange of letters took considerable time; consequently Cicero did not write almost daily, as he did at

---

[4] *Att.* 1, 17, is the best example.

times to Atticus, and the letters do not give a picture of his moods as they changed from day to day. Quintus was during a part of this period with Caesar in Gaul, and it is clear that some of the letters were intended to be shown, at least in part, to Caesar. The letters to Atticus, on the other hand, extend over a period of twenty-five years, and were not intended for a second reader.

The character of Atticus has been debated, but one thing is certain: Cicero loved him sincerely, and never had any doubts about his loyalty. No letters from Atticus have been preserved, so that only one side of their relations is revealed to us. The letters from Cicero to Atticus constitute about one half of his whole correspondence. Their frankness is unparalleled. He reveals his every weakness and fear as well as his every source of strength and hope. Everything that gives him pleasure, everything that flatters his vanity, is put down. He writes when he has something to say and when he has not. He urges, cajoles, scolds, in order to get more letters from Atticus, though obviously he received a great many—if Atticus has nothing to write about, he might at least write to tell Cicero of his lack of news.

Cicero is constantly deferring to his friend and asking his advice. Sometimes Atticus fails to offer suggestions, and Cicero complains of this; at other times Atticus does advise, and if things turn out badly, Cicero complains of the advice. Atticus has been stupid, but no more so—and that is the keynote of their friendship—than Cicero himself. The two are like parts of the same body. It is inconceivable to Cicero that one could ever wilfully hurt or even neglect the other. Cicero's letters have the character of an intimate conversation far more than that of ordinary letters. His need of writing to Atticus was great. He sits down, pen in hand, and rambles on as if he were actually talking. Even when he is to see Atticus in a few hours, he writes a hurried note to express his joyful expectation.

The very impulsiveness and frankness of these letters, however—as has of late been noted, though frequently ignored—may easily lead to misunderstanding on the part of the reader. They give the thoughts and emotions of a moment; things that most persons would keep within their own breasts, and certainly never write. The fact that Cicero did write them is in danger of endowing them with an importance altogether unwarranted. Cicero wrote as a modern person might possibly talk, but then only to a very trusted friend or to a wife. He was thinking aloud. His judgments of people and events, his expressions of joy or pride, of sorrow or chagrin, are not the result of deliberate thought or well-settled convictions; they are in their very essence evanescent, real while lasting, but often as unsubstantial as the shadow of a cloud on a hillside.

The beliefs and ideals by which Cicero governed his life are not expressed. They were known to Atticus. They formed, in Atticus' mind, a background against which he read aright every word that came from Cicero's pen. He knew what Cicero would do and what he would not do. When Cicero discussed a proposed course of action, balancing, perhaps, one selfish consideration against another, Atticus attributed this to a clearness of vision that saw all sides of a question, and he was not misled into supposing that Cicero's final decision would run counter to his patriotism or his loyalty to friends. In fact, the complaints of Atticus, when he made any, were invariably to the effect that Cicero had acted with too little thought of himself, often pursuing an ideal that seemed to Atticus unnecessary and visionary. When Cicero does decide to think of his own advantage or safety, Atticus, we learn, has for a long time been urging him to do so.

The letters of Cicero thus fill out and give living warmth to the picture that we have of him in the other writings. The orations were intended for the public at large. In them Cicero records the words he had uttered and draws his own portrait as a man of affairs, revising and adding according to the practise of his time. The essays are the result, as it were, of his intellectual life, and also afford to a smaller circle of contemporaries a view of his private beliefs and his inmost yearnings. They are frank, but not spontaneous; they contain nothing that Cicero wished to hide. In the letters there is no thought of an audience, whether large or small. Cicero merely lives his life as it comes into relation with others, and we watch him.

There is one circumstance of vast importance, however, that should be noted in connection with this large amount of information. Our knowledge of Cicero is confined almost exclusively to the last twenty years of his life, the period subsequent to his consulship; even the parts of his writings that have reference to the earlier years were written after 63 B.C.

The exceptions to this statement are only apparent. One of the essays was composed in his youth; but it is a treatise on Invention, a division of rhetoric, and as impersonal as a graduate student's thesis, which, indeed, it very much resembles. There are only twelve letters, out of the nine hundred and more, which belong to the years 68–64 B.C. Of these, eleven were written by Cicero, and one—really a treatise on electioneering—by his brother. Apparently it was not until Cicero had attained a prominent position that it occurred either to him or to his friends to keep his letters. Nor is the correspondence large for some years after 63 B.C.; due in part, very likely, to the burning of Cicero's house in 58, which doubtless caused the destruction of any copies he may have had, for we know that he made copies of important letters. There are no letters from the year of his consulship; about fifty from the year 51 B.C.; after that they increase rapidly. Half the correspondence belongs to the last four years of his life, after Caesar had overthrown the republic and established himself as dictator.

With the orations the case is somewhat different. Fifteen, of the total of fifty-eight, come from the years 81–66 B.C., and some of these are both long and important. They give a pretty complete idea of Cicero as an orator during this period; or at least as a pleader, for all but one were delivered, or written as if delivered, in the courts. Though containing much self-revelation that would not be found in modern speeches of the same kind, they are, nevertheless, very deficient in this feature when compared with the orations of the later period. Cicero was as yet only making his way, politically. He had not yet attained a prominence that could be used, in typically Roman fashion, as an argument in the courts. Neither directly nor indirectly were the cases his own. All this was changed with the year 63. As a consular, and still more as the one who had suppressed the Catilinarian conspiracy, Cicero was one of the chief men in Rome. Everything that has already been said about the personal element in legal and forensic oratory applies now with full force. In addition, he often spoke directly in his own behalf, justifying his past actions, explaining or eulogizing them, attacking his enemies, and defending his friends, or proposing measures for which he alone was the sponsor.

It is, therefore, true that Cicero is known to us very intimately, from strictly contemporary sources, only after he had attained the consulship, the goal of Roman ambition. Such late knowledge in the case of any man would tend to distort our view of him; in the case of Cicero there is an especial danger that this may happen. Under normal Roman conditions the attainment of the consulship would have ended the strenuous part of his career; an ex-consul pleaded in the courts when he so desired, took a grave and influential part in senatorial debate, was honored by all, and, for the rest, with the full approval of everybody, devoted his time to his own private pursuits. He was entitled to a dignfied leisure, *otium cum dignitate*. Cicero had earned these privileges, but suddenly, through no fault of his own, he found himself face to face with political anarchy. Partly from choice and partly from necessity he entered the strife. He had personal triumphs and momentary successes, but he was on the losing side. He fought for the retention of the existing government; for his country, as he saw it; wisely or not, according as men will judge; without selfishness; and the government was doomed. He was also growing old; nearly all his friends died, most of them by violence; his daughter died; and he had other domestic afflictions. The manner in which he conducted himself in the midst of all these troubles fills nearly our whole record of his life; he was being weighed in the balance, and, it seems, not found wanting, but he had little reason for being either hopeful or happy, though even in these respects he can still be an inspiration. He was living through the tragic ending, long drawn out, of a long drama.

It thus becomes needful to remember the forty years during which he grew into the personality that is later revealed to us in the unequal struggle. During these years he won his position as the leader of the Roman bar; acquired immense influence both in Rome and in many other cities in Italy and elsewhere; gained the friendship and admiration of statesmen, financiers, literary men, and philosophers; became the idol of the young men of ambition; and attained the consulship—all in spite of his equestrian birth. During this time, too, he married, and his two children were born, one of whom, Tullia, was dearer to him than any other person in the world. These were years of very hard work, but of great hopes and uninterrupted success, and, undoubtedly, of a large amount of happiness. They are by no means entirely unknown to us; but there are, after all, only eleven letters from this period. Though these are filled with matters of business, plans for the future, and happy references to Tullia, they are, nevertheless, a very insignificant part of the whole correspondence.

CHAPTER II

THE POINT OF VIEW

When Cicero was a candidate for the consulship, in the year 64 B.C., his brother Quintus addressed to him an essay, in the form of a letter, on the proper behavior of a man seeking the highest office in Rome. The essay takes note of the circumstances peculiar to Cicero's candidacy, so much so, indeed, that it may have been helpful as a political pamphlet, but Quintus hopes that with a few changes it may be useful to others as well. He wants it to be a handbook of electioneering, *commentariolum petitionis*. Brother Quintus was not a great politician, for he was too hot-tempered and made enemies; and he was not a great orator, thinking that one orator was glory enough for one family. He fought well under Caesar in Gaul; he wrote poetry—four tragedies, once, in sixteen days; despite his irascibility he was rather submissive to his wife; and altogether he seems to have been an easy-going, lovable gentleman. He had a great admiration for brother Marcus' talents and successes, but twitted him with working too hard, and liked to give him advice. On this occasion, among various other things, both shrewd and impudent, he cautions his older brother—four years older—not to forget that he is a New man, that he is seeking the consulship, and that the place of his canvass is Rome. As Marcus went down into the forum, which would happen almost daily, he was to turn these thoughts over in his mind: *novus sum, consulatum peto, Roma est.*

Perhaps Marcus needed this advice, although he had for seventeen years been a speaker in the forum and had already held the three offices that usually preceded the consulship. The modern student who follows his life in his extant works needs the advice much more. Every time he reads a page, he may profitably murmur to himself that this is Rome, the republican

Rome of Cicero, Caesar, and Pompey, which came to an end nearly two thousand years ago, and was in many ways very different from anything that has existed since.

Montaigne has a story that is applicable in this connection. There was once a country woman, according to him, who was very fond of a little calf and carried it constantly in her arms; when the calf grew to be a great ox, she still carried him in her arms. It had become a habit. In the same way the Romans of this period had their habits. They all carried their oxen; but we see only Cicero and his burden clearly. Compared with him, his great contemporaries are like phantoms. We get a glimpse here and a glimpse there; we see one side of a man's character, but the rest is hidden; we follow him—never from day to day, and never very closely, as we follow Cicero—but we nevertheless follow him, for a few months or even for a few years; and then he is swallowed up in the darkness, perhaps to reappear later, perhaps not. The details known about men like Caesar and Pompey are numerous, and often extremely important, and yet they are not sufficient to enable us ever to recreate a living and abiding figure. We see only the barest outline of their Roman oxen; and, as a result, we are in constant danger of forgetting them, and of imagining that Cicero, like Montaigne's woman, was the only one who carried an ox.

This failure to take Cicero's contemporaries into account in our judgments of Cicero himself can readily be illustrated. Suetonius gives a long list of Caesar's mistresses, ranging from the wives of political friends or opponents to foreign queens and barbarian ladies in Gaul. Cato, the Stoic of the time, and perhaps of all times, allowed his wife Marcia to live with the wealthy orator Hortensius, and took her back after the latter's death. Pompey, at the urging of Sulla, put away one wife and married another, although the latter, already married, was expecting soon to become a mother. The reasons for such marriages, divorces, and illegitimate relations, which could easily be cited in great

numbers, were love, lust, ambition, and greed.   Cicero, after a
married life of thirty years, divorced Terentia.   We do not know
very much about Terentia.   It is clear, however, that she had
a very decided mind of her own, and that Cicero, after the
divorce, had doubts about her honest intentions even when she
promised to remember their son in her will.   She had rheumatism,
which probably did not improve her temper, and her general
health seems to have been rather poor, in spite of the fact that
she managed to continue her precarious existence for one hundred and three years, possibly contracting a second marriage,
and even a third or fourth.   After the divorce, Cicero, being in
need of money, married a young lady of wealth, his own ward,
whom he presently sent back to her mother.   Tullia, his beloved
daughter, had died, and he wished to be alone.   Incidentally,
the departure of the young wife involved the repayment of
the dowry she had brought, so that Cicero relinquished the
pecuniary advantages of the marriage.   Whether or not his
behavior toward his two wives is defensible according to modern
standards, it can be judged by them, and is by that much
superior to the actions of Caesar, Cato, and Pompey.   Cicero
partly explained the reasons for his divorce from Terentia in a
letter to a friend; Caesar, according to report, divorced one of
his wives with the proud statement that Caesar's wife must be
above suspicion, and he remained the political associate of
Clodius, her alleged seducer.   Clodius was useful to him politically.   And yet the marital delinquencies of Cicero, if such they
were, have been much argued about; admirers of his character
have grieved over them and enemies have sneered.   Those of his
three great contemporaries, on the other hand, might as well have
happened in Mars; they form no real part of our estimate of
the men.

Similarly, we are informed—and have no reason to doubt
the information—that Caesar more than once in his campaigns
refused to accept the surrender of hostile towns in order that

he might capture them by arms, and thereby be able to apply the laws of war in all their rigor, pillaging the temples and private homes, and selling the inhabitants into slavery. His cruelty and greed make no emotional appeal to us. We know nothing of the subsequent fate of the enslaved townspeople; there is no description of the Roman legionaries breaking into private dwellings; and Caesar has not debated the right and the wrong of his act with a trusted friend. The whole thing is a mere matter of record, another detail to be filed with the rest of our information. Caesar is still the great general, and rightly.

With Cicero the case is again different. On an occasion of great stress, moved by a suspicion that proved only too true, he opened some letters not addressed to him. A packet of letters from Quintus to various friends had accidentally come into his hands. After he had forwarded some of them, he learned from the recipients that the letters were filled with bitter attacks on himself. He therefore opened the letters still in his possession, and, writing to Atticus about the whole matter, wondered whether they should be forwarded. They could easily be resealed, he said, as Quintus' wife no doubt had a seal ring belonging to her husband. All this happened in the midst of the civil war between Caesar and the Pompeians. Cicero's sin against morality and good manners, if a sin it was, has sunk far more deeply into the modern consciousness than Caesar's looting of towns and enslaving of whole populations. The personality of Cicero is so vivid in our minds that this new bit of information becomes a living fact, to be remembered and pondered. Hearing it about Cicero is like hearing it about a neighbor.

It is by no means on every occasion, however, that parallel words and acts among Cicero's contemporaries can be cited as criteria for judging him. The intimacy of our knowledge raises many questions that can be answered only indirectly. Sometimes he received praise or blame, which indicates the contemporary point of view; but far oftener there is no hint to guide us, beyond the manner in which he mentions a thing to a correspondent, particularly to Atticus. The moral attitude and the numerous conventions of the times, in great matters and small, have to be reconstructed almost entirely from Cicero's works. It is a delicate task, and can not always be solved with absolute certainty.[1]

We are also especially tempted to neglect both the obvious parallels and the hidden indications. The Romans were not like the Fiji Islanders, who are supposed to eat their own wives and children. On the contrary, they had countless resemblances to us. They had jury trials and parliamentary debates, knowing something of filibustering; they dined with discrimination and knew all about the luxuries of hot baths; they often married for love and they educated their children; they meditated on the immortality of the soul, free will, and providence; and they cremated their dead. Spiritually, indeed, they are a link in the long chain that stretches from the Greeks to modern Europe and America; materially, they laid in many places the foundations on which we are still building. And so, since most of their words and thoughts and actions are like ours, we take for granted, unconsciously as a rule, that we can understand them, or Cicero, rather, without effort; and we apply to him our own standards of morality or convention. But this leads to frequent misapprehension.

Cicero, as we have seen, was an augur, one of whose duties it was to observe the omens; but he did not believe in omens, and said so. He governed a province once, and thought he did well because he was personally honorable and tried to curb the rapacity of others; and yet he instituted no permanent reforms, and took no great interest in the provincials. In his speeches he was often violent, egotistical, and irrelevant. He frequently won cases by his wit or his pathos, ignoring the law.

---

[1] This has been attempted on a large scale by Schneidewin. See also Fowler, *Social Life etc.*

He published speeches that had not been delivered, giving them the appearance of verbatim reports. He wished that his authorship of a certain troublesome speech might be denied.[2] He wrote an epic poem about his consulship, quoted it in later writings, and followed it up with another epic on his further political vicissitudes. In these poems the muses appeared, giving him sage counsel, and approving his deeds. He asked Lucceius, a friend, not only to write about his political career but to do it in a spirit of enthusiasm rather than of truth. He dictated to the copyist of Atticus a letter in praise of their good friend Caelius, which he thereupon read to the latter as having come from Atticus. He asked Atticus to write letters of thanks for him to various people. He wrote countless letters of recommendation, and sometimes marked those that were to be taken seriously. He seems to have taken a more lenient view of gladiatorial combats than we do of prize fights; on one occasion, at any rate, planning to go to them, to please his daughter Tullia; and yet he could write a fine letter about the inhumanity of such amusements. He was always buying things with borrowed money. Once he returned home from dinner in a suspiciously genial mood—*bene potus,* he calls it—though he was able to verify an intricate matter of law, which he and a friend had discussed over their cups. He was much given to jesting; sometimes untranslatably and sometimes out of season, by our standards. The grandmother of Atticus died after a life of piety. Cicero, who knew that his Epicurean friend would not be overwhelmed by the news, announces the poor lady's demise without a word of solemnity, and apparently attributes it to her fear lest the next Latin festival fall below its oldtime grandeur. He not only came near committing suicide before deciding to go into exile, but he also wrote later, both to Atticus and to his family, that he wished he had not clung to life. And

---

[2] See *Att.* 3, 12. Tyrrell (I², 42) discusses this letter.

he did other things that would shock Mrs. Grundy, and better people than she.

Nevertheless, Cicero was the admired friend of the most cultured and the most powerful men of Rome. From the Roman point of view his standard of personal morality was unimpeachable. He was not affected by the widespread licentiousness of his age, but filled his life with hard work, laboring when others played. He borrowed money, but lent it with the same readiness. He did not practise usury, as did many of the great and lesser Romans; and he did not take his money from the provinces, which was an almost universal practise. In an age of systematized bribery, he did not bribe. He wrote better letters than his correspondents. He was a good conversationalist; his wit was renowned. He was affectionate and sensitive. He could hate well, as could other Romans; but he loved more, and was ready to forgive even friends. He was generous, not only with his means but in his recognition of other men's deserts. Young men imitated and loved him; his servants were devoted to him. Those who knew him best loved him most, and they remained his friends for life. He was intensely ambitious; but his love of Rome was greater than his ambition, for he refused to join the triumvirate; it was also greater than his human fears, for he died for her. He was by no means a paragon of all the virtues; he had faults; but he had also the saving grace of a sense of humor that embraced himself.

It can probably be maintained with an exceptionally high degree of likelihood that if the great Romans of his day had taken a vote to decide which one among them stood highest as a representative of unselfishness in public service, of culture, and of good breeding, the outcome would have been the same as at the time when the colleagues of Themistocles took their famous vote. Each one, like a true son of Romulus, might have put himself in the first place, but he would have given the second place to Cicero.

VIRTUES

21

If such a committee of Romans had cast this vote and had thereupon announced the result in the senate, probably Cicero would have conducted himself very much as he did on a notable occasion in the year 61 B.C.[3] Crassus had made an extremely laudatory speech about Cicero, explaining with great emotion how it was to Cicero's consulship that he owed his position as senator and citizen, even his freedom and life, and how the sight of his wife, his home, and his country never failed to make him gratefully conscious of his debt to the great consular. Cicero, in the course of the further proceedings, made a fiery speech of his own; and later he wrote an account of the happenings to Atticus. "O ye gods," he wrote, "how I exulted before my new auditor Pompey! Then, if ever, did I make use of well-rounded periods and other rhetorical devices. There was great applause. I talked about the dignity of the senate, the favorable attitude of the knights, the unanimous spirit of all Italy, the dying remains of the Catilinarian conspiracy, the present low cost of living, and peace. You know what a noise I can make on subjects like these. But I can be brief in my description, for you must have heard my thunders even in Epirus."

[3] *Att.* 1, 14.

CHAPTER III

ARPINUM

Though it was in Rome that Cicero won his triumphs, he was not a genuine Roman, in that he came from the little town of Arpinum among the Volscian mountains. He has given a sketch of his home, with a few hints about his family, in the introductory scenes to his dialogue on the Laws. This treatise was begun some ten years after his consulship, and was well under way in 52 B.C. The conversations of which it consists are also supposed to have taken place after the consulship, though no exact date is indicated. Cicero, therefore, had reached his high place in Roman life, and was outlining for his Roman readers the background against which he wished to appear.

The speakers of the dialogue are Marcus Cicero himself, his brother Quintus, and his dearest friend Atticus, the brother-in-law of Quintus. As Cicero was three years younger than Atticus and four years older than Quintus, they may be thought of as in their forties, or early fifties. Atticus, obviously by poetical license, is represented as visiting the home of the Ciceros for the first time; his knowledge of it is derived from Cicero's writings, particularly a youthful poem entitled *Marius*, known to us only by fragments. Marius, also an Arpinate, was one of Cicero's earliest inspirations; he had brought the war against Jugurtha to a successful close in the year of Cicero's birth, and had conquered the Cimbri and Teutones within the next five years. His fame, great in Rome, could not have been less in Arpinum.

The three friends are sauntering along the wooded banks of the river Liris. According to the custom of Ciceronian interlocutors, they keep an eye open for a shady nook. In the meantime the conversation is desultory.

"Ah," says Atticus, "this must be the grove and that famous oak of which I have read so often in Marcus' poem. If that oak is still in existence, this is surely the one. It is certainly old enough."

This was the oak near which Marius had had some vision or other of an eagle, "the tawny messenger of Jove, a wonderful sight," as young Marcus had expressed it.

"Oh, yes," says Quintus, the poet; " that oak will never die. Trees planted by poets have longer lives than those set out by farmers."

"What do you mean, Quintus? Poets planting trees? Aren't you thinking a little of yourself, though you seem to be singing your brother's praises?"

"Possibly."

And Quintus explains that the sacred olive in Athens will always flourish. The palm tree in Delos, which Ulysses in the Odyssey saw, is still pointed out to visitors. So, naturally, the oak of Marius will be green long after it has fallen a prey to wind and weather.

Atticus thinks this possible, but, banker and level-headed man that he is, wants to know the facts. He turns to Marcus.

"Was there really such an oak? Or are you alone responsible for it?"

Marcus evades the question. "Is it true," he asks, "that after Romulus had disappeared, he was found walking near your house in Rome, and told Proculus that he had become a god and wanted a temple built in his honor in the neighborhood?"

"What are you talking about?"

"Well, such things are merely matters of tradition."

"Yes, but there are a good many stories about Marius, and you ought to know the truth."

Marcus confesses that he does not wish to be considered lacking in veracity; but what about Numa and Egeria? Did they really enjoy their reputed rendezvous? Did an eagle pick the cap from the head of Tarquin?

"I understand," says Quintus. "The laws of history and of poetry are not the same."

Marcus concurs, reminding his companions that even Herodotus, the father of history, did not disdain to introduce improbable stories in his work.

This conversation introduces the first dialogue, which fills the first book of the *Laws* and extends over about fifty pages.

At the beginning of the second book, Atticus thinks it would be pleasant to find another place for the continuation of their conversation. Marcus has been practically the sole speaker and needs new inspiration.

"Let us go and find seats on the little isle in the Fibrenus. I suppose that is Fibrenus over there."

The Fibrenus was a tributary to the river Liris. The friends apparently crossed the Liris and followed the Fibrenus toward the isle.

"Yes," said Marcus, "I am very fond of the place. I go there often, when I wish to read or write or think."

Atticus is charmed with the scenery, and begins to speak slightingly of costly villas with marble floors and paneled ceilings.

He is particularly impressed by the masses of rushing water in the Fibrenus.

"Those fellows," he says, "dig little ditches and call them the Nile or the Euripus. It is laughable to any one who has seen this place."

From the orations and poems of Cicero he had received the idea that Arpinum was nothing but rocks and hills, and he had been in the habit of wondering why Cicero ever went there. Now, with the hills in the distance, with one stream behind him and another on his left, with greensward under foot, and trees all about, he wonders how Cicero can ever go anywhere else when he is away from Rome.

Cicero explains that it is hard to get leisure for many days at a time. He comes to Arpinum whenever possible, especially in the hottest part of summer, for Arpinum then is a cool and pleasant refuge.

He calls Atticus' attention to a farmhouse, probably on their left, and situated between two of the arms into which the Fibrenus divides before it empties into the Liris. This is the house in which Marcus and his brother were born. It has been the home of the family for generations. Cicero's father, who was somewhat of an invalid and fond of books, lived there nearly all his life. He enlarged the house and gave it a smarter appearance. At the time of Cicero's birth, when his grandfather was still living, it was an old-fashioned farmhouse, just like the well-known Curiana, in the Sabine country, from which, as the reader of the *Laws* knew, M. Curius Dentatus, like Cicero the first consul of his family, issued forth to defeat Pyrrhus, two centuries and a half earlier.

Atticus gracefully expresses his delight at becoming acquainted with Cicero's native heath. He is always peculiarly fascinated, he says, by places that remind him of people he likes or admires. Atticus, as we know, had lived a large part of his life in Athens, was extremely fond of the city, and even derived from it his name Atticus, the Athenian. His real Roman name had been Titus Pomponius until the year 58 B.C., when he was adopted by a millionaire uncle, and became Quintus Caecilius Pomponianus. He admired the splendid works of art in Athens, he now said, but he took an even keener delight in the memories that haunt the former homes and lecture halls of departed great men. He liked even to search for their gravestones and read their epitaphs. He will grow very fond of Arpinum, now that he can think of it as Cicero's birthplace.

In the course of the further conversation, he recalls a public utterance of Pompey the Great to the effect that Rome had special reasons for gratitude to the little town because it was the home of two of its saviors, Marius, who had defeated the barbarians, and Cicero, who in his consulship had withstood Catiline and his fellow-conspirators. And presently the friends arrive at the isle in the Fibrenus.

Nothing could be prettier. It lies in midstream, cutting the current as with the beak of a trireme. The waters rush past on either side, leaving a place just big enough for comfortable rest and conversation, and then, coming together with a swirl, they dash madly forward on their way to the Liris. The water is cool and pleasant. Atticus, however, thinks it is the coldest he ever saw, though he has looked upon many streams. He would rather not dip his foot in it, despite the classic precedent of Socrates and Phaedrus, who, some three hundred and fifty years earlier, had taken pleasure in wading through a shallow pool in their inevitable search for a shady nook.

Marcus acknowledges the beauty of the place, but he has heard enough from brother Quintus to know that nothing can excel the stream Thyamis in Epirus, where Atticus has a villa. Quintus agrees with this, mentioning the plane trees and the amaltheum on his brother-in-law's estate.

At the suggestion of Quintus, the three friends, like Socrates, find seats in the shade, so that they may continue their discussion, which again is mainly a monologue on the part of Marcus.

"I thought I had escaped," he says; but Quintus orders him to begin.

"We'll consecrate the whole day to you."

The discussion lasted through that summer's day, and is supposed to have filled six books. Only the first three of these have been preserved. The speakers seem to have moved from place to place on the estate, for a sentence is quoted from the fifth book which shows that they had been sitting under some trees of recent growth until the early afternoon sun drove them to the alders on the bank of the Liris.

There is not much to add to this account of Cicero's home. Like his father before him, he made additions to the villa.[1] As early as the year 61 B.C., less than two years after his consulship, he is writing to Atticus about an amaltheum that he wishes to build in Arpinum, somewhat after the model of the one on his friend's estate in Epirus. Atticus is to inform him about furnishings and wall paintings. An amaltheum was probably a shrine in honor of Amalthea, with which was connected a garden house. The mythological Amalthea herself was either the goat that suckled the infant Jupiter, or else a nymph that took care of both Jupiter and the famous goat. As a nymph she was symbolic of the creative forces in nature, and had her shrine by running water. The wall paintings of Atticus' garden house represented various incidents connected with the Amalthea myth, and also had descriptive verses. Of all these things Cicero wants an account from Atticus. Since the place was intended for reading, a sort of modern library, it contained statues of famous men, with inscriptions. Atticus had such a statue of Cicero, but this was perhaps not so very surprising, since statues seem to have been nearly as common as modern portraits.

At the end of the next year Atticus inspects Cicero's amaltheum, while the latter is himself in Rome. Atticus finds the windows too small. Cicero replies that the architect had explained that a view through small windows is particularly pleasant. Evidently the architect did not agree, he says, with the Epicurean philosophers—and Atticus was an Epicurean— who believed that sight is caused by very thin, film-like images that are constantly traveling from the object seen to the eyes of the observer, for in that case the poor images would find it difficult to get through the narrow windows. As for any other criticisms Atticus may feel inclined to make, Cicero will be glad to hear them, provided they involve no expense.

---

[1] On Cicero's home and villas, see Schmidt, *Ciceros Villen*. Schmidt gives complete references.

The villa was probably both commodious and costly, as a result of the additions and alterations made by Cicero and his father. In the year 54 B.C., when Quintus was with Caesar in Gaul, Marcus visited his brother's estates in Arpinum, where alterations were in progress. As it is likely that Marcus and Quintus built in very much the same way, the things mentioned in his letter to Quintus may well have had a counterpart in his own villa. There were big rooms with pools of water; rooms for summer and for winter use; a suite of bathrooms heated from below; vaulted ceilings; fresco paintings; and columns of polished marble, which, by the way, it was difficult to place absolutely perpendicularly and at equal distances from each other. There were graveled paths and pillared walks. Water and trees were plentiful on the grounds. There seems to have been a formal garden with trees cut in geometrical figures. Ivy added grace and softness, climbing over the walls and pillars, and even covering the statues as with a mantle. The latter, Cicero says, looked as if they had become addicted to fancy gardening and were advertising the merits of ivy.

The estate itself was, nevertheless, a real farm, not one of those suburban country houses of the Romans to which vegetables were brought from the city, as Martial laments. The land was divided into sections and rented to tenants, so that at least a part of the family income was derived from it. This arrangement is mentioned by Cicero in a letter of the year 45 B.C., and may have been introduced by his invalid father; the grandfather would have scorned both vicarious farming and ivy-clad statues.

This grandfather is the first member of the family about whom anything is known. The Ciceros, however, though not descended from the ancient Volscian king Tullus Attius—as some would have it, according to Plutarch—were autochthonous in Arpinum and had a good position. They were rich enough to be counted among the knights, who possessed at least 400,000 sesterces, from $16,000 to $20,000; but they are not known to have engaged in provincial business, as did the more prominent among the knights. Apparently they had farmed until Cicero's father broke the family tradition.

The grandfather was a man of strong personality, conservative and outspoken. Living at the time of Scipio the Younger and Laelius, when the Greek influence was establishing itself in Rome, he set his face against the new ideas. The Romans, he was in the habit of saying, were like Syrian slaves; the more Greek they knew, the worse they were. He was opposed to changes of any kind. When his brother-in-law Gratidius attempted to introduce a new election law in Arpinum, the old Marcus fought him, and even carried the fight to Rome. The matter came before the Roman consul, who gracefully lamented because a man of Marcus' ability and courage confined his activities to a small municipality like Arpinum, instead of taking part in the central government.

Cicero's father was cast in a different mould; indeed, Cicero himself seems to be a combination of the two. The father was an invalid and a student. But he was not indifferent to the great world. He had a house in Rome, where he must have lived part of the time, and he was on friendly terms with several of the most prominent public men. He was interested in politics, discussing with his son the doings of former statesmen. Cicero quotes him to this effect both in an oration and in one of his philosophical essays. It was evidently he who decided that the two boys, Marcus and Quintus, should be educated in Rome, and so be given the opportunity of making a career in the capital. He lived long enough to see Marcus as one of the leaders at the Roman bar, and possibly, though probably not, as a candidate for the consulship. He seems to have died in the year 67 B.C.[2]

Cicero's mother, on the other hand, must have died in his youth. She is not mentioned in his writings. Even her name, Helvia, comes to us from Plutarch. Only one trait of her char-

---

[2] *Att.* 1, 6, 2, and Tyrrell's note. See below, p. 204.

acter has been recorded, and this one was not inherited by her famous son. She was thrifty. Quintus, in a letter to Marcus' favorite freedman, Tiro, written as late as 44 B.C., mentions a practise of hers that he himself remembered. When bottling wine, she sealed not only the jars that had been filled but also those that were empty. This was to prevent thievish slaves from emptying a full jar, and then pretending that it had never been filled. Perhaps she needed to have an eye for details, since her husband read books and modernized the farmhouse. She, too, was well connected, for a sister of hers was married to the famous jurist Aculeo, an intimate friend of the great orator L. Crassus.

Cicero's family, despite its aristocratic connections, was humble in the eyes of the Roman world, but he was never inclined to make any excuses for it. The grandfather, the father, the home in Arpinum, occur frequently, both in his orations and in his other writings. Plutarch says that, when Cicero was on the point of entering public life, he was advised to change his name, but he replied that he would endeavor to make his name even more glorious than that of the Scauri and the Catuli. Perhaps Plutarch has only invented an appropriate story, though his information may have come ultimately from Tiro's biography. Cicero was called a foreigner by the people who considered that all genuine Romans came from the city or its immediate environs; but he laughingly reminded his detractors that it was a favorable circumstance to be such a foreigner, for the men from small towns like Arpinum had votes, which they gave to their fellow townsmen. It was of no assistance, he said, to come from Tusculum, where consuls were numerous. He more than once publicly instituted comparisons between the simplicity of country life and the luxury that flourished in the city, not to the advantage of the latter. One of these occasions was the trial of Plancius, in the year 54 B.C., and as Cicero seems to have begun his treatise on the Laws shortly after this date, his praise of the country districts during this trial may well have led him to place the scenes of the *Laws* near his own home.

These scenes contain the whole story. He has two countries, he says, Arpinum and Rome. He gives the greater loyalty to Rome, but he is proud of the long and honorable tradition of his farming ancestors, and of the little town, whose inhabitants classed him with Marius. The Arpinates, as he says elsewhere, were certain to tell any chance visitor among them of Marius, and probably also of Cicero. Arpinum, according to the *Laws*, was a place richly blessed with beauty of scenery, in which dreams could be dreamed and noble aspirations fostered. Great men of the past had come from just such places. Here Cicero could meditate, read, and write, and also entertain his dearest friends.

Cicero's letters indicate that although he could not often find time to leave Rome long enough to go to Arpinum, where he was cut off from direct connection with politics, he always retained a peculiar affection for his paternal estate. He also kept in touch with the Arpinates. The town of Arpinum owned land in Gaul, from which it derived its only income as a municipality. As the collecting of the rent from this land could be facilitated or made difficult by the governor of the province, Cicero's influence with men of power was of material assistance. Two letters are extant in which he recommended the interests of Arpinum to the good will of the governor; and inasmuch as this governor was M. Iunius Brutus, the pupil and admirer of Cicero, the recommendation was undoubtedly heeded. On another occasion he caused his own son and the son of his brother Quintus to be chosen chief magistrates of Arpinum, which not only was a compliment to the Arpinates, but also seems to have been a means of bringing order into their tangled affairs.

But the most inspiring thing to Cicero about Arpinum was the fact that it was the home of Marius. The families of Cicero and Marius were not related, and yet there was a sort of connection. Marius had adopted a distant relative of Cicero's, to be scrupulously exact, the son of the brother-in-law of Cicero's paternal grandfather. Though this remote connection may have meant nothing, Cicero had grown up in an atmosphere filled with the praise of Marius; he was also the fellow student of Marius' son; and, as he was twenty years old when Marius died, he had seen the old warrior often and had very likely heard him speak in the forum. Cicero's thoughts about him were not exhausted with the youthful poem. In agreement with the other Arpinates, Cicero naturally looked upon himself as the companion in fame of Marius.

Two men could scarcely be more unlike. Marius was rough, uneducated, opposed to the patricians, and careless of human life. Cicero was always striving for spiritual growth, he was devoted to Greek culture, he became in time the leader of the patricians, and he abhorred war. But they were alike in their ambition and their will power, and they had both to make their own way politically. Throughout his career Cicero frequently refers in public to Marius; and when he is driven into exile, he again thinks of him as one who had suffered a similar fate. At that time he even had a dream about the old Arpinate.[3] Having fallen asleep toward morning, after a restless night, he dreamed that he had lost his way in a solitary place and was roaming about dejectedly. Marius, in the garb of a triumphator and accompanied by his lictors, met him, and inquired about the reason for Cicero's condition. When told that Cicero had been expelled from Rome, Marius took him by the right hand, asked him to be of good cheer, and directed one of his lictors to accompany him to a certain temple erected by Marius himself. There Cicero would find help.

Cicero was not superstitious, but he accepted the dream as a good omen.

[3] *De Divin.* 1, 59; 2, 140.

CHAPTER IV

ROME

Not much is known about Cicero before his twenty-sixth or twenty-seventh year, when he pleaded his first case. Coming early to the capital, he received his education[1] there, with the exception of some elementary instruction in Arpinum, and it was likewise in Rome that he was from boyhood affected by the influences that shaped his whole life.

Cicero had ambition, talents, and self-confidence; he wished from the beginning to make a mark in the world, he knew that he could do it, and he was willing to pay the full price of ceaseless industry. His conscience was that of the true artist, for he scorned shoddy work. This may be a kind of pride, but it is not the pride that goes before a fall. Standing, like Hercules, at the parting of the ways of Pleasure and of Virtue, it chooses that of Virtue. It is a better preservative of character than a host of negative excellences, which are always battling against temptation, and must yield occasionally, if only to get a little rest. Cicero never needed to fight against the ordinary temptations of pleasure, or greed, or envy, or idleness; he was so filled with his ambition and his devotion to good work that nothing antagonistic to these made any appeal to him.

Talents and a disposition like Cicero's usually lead to success, and it may not be necessary to inquire whether a man is to be praised for the possession of them. They are a gift of the gods, and the gods are partial. In Cicero's case, according to Plutarch, the good gods even went to the trouble of sending a vision to his nurse, in which it was foretold that the child in her arms would be of great benefit to Rome. And as a boy in school, still according to the veracious Plutarch, he acquired such

---

[1] For Cicero's training, see below, pp. 343–351, 373–412.

a reputation that the fathers of his schoolmates came to see the prodigy. Like modern fathers, however, some of them were too enamored of their own offspring to enjoy the sight; they became angry when their children received young Cicero "with respect into the middle place." Perhaps the boys were not conscious that they were doing Cicero an honor. Plutarch's fine phrase seems to be borrowed from the habits of mature men; but probably it only indicates that Cicero was already a good talker.

What Cicero might have become in an age like ours is a matter for speculation. Nothing now seems quite to require or reward the particular combination of gifts that he possessed. He was a student of law, political science, philosophy, and literature, as well as of the art of speaking, which we no longer cultivate; he was one of the foremost stylists that the world has ever seen, combining the minor delicacies of language, ordinarily supposed by literary critics to be the qualities of a good style, with the forcefulness and the humor that constitute the far greater quality of genuine popularity, for he was a man first, and only secondly a writer; he spoke at least as well as he wrote; he desired and knew how to mingle with busy men. Among us, it seems, he would have cultivated one or another talent to a higher degree than he actually did, but to the exclusion of the others. In Rome they could all be used for the one thing that the most ambitious Romans cared about, namely, a political career.

Rome was a city entirely devoted to politics. In former times, as Cicero read in his books, the Roman people had been a nation of farmers, who were always ready to leave the plough to go to public meetings or to war. Their first duty had been to their country. They had been lawmakers and soldiers, earning their living by farming. They had been free men, selling their personal services to no man. And now, in the time of Cicero, when farming had almost disappeared, and the land of Italy was largely in the hands of the rich, who used it for

cattle raising, the tradition still remained that a Roman could
be honorably employed—gloriously and profitably, one fears, is
more exact—only in connection with service to his country. He
must be a soldier—a general, that is, and not a private—or an
officeholder, preferably both. Money-making, except on a large
scale, is not for him. The question of earning a living does not
exist for him. He either has sufficient inherited wealth to live
on, as Cicero had, or else his problems in life are of too humble
a nature to come under the consideration of those who think and
philosophize about life.

To them the situation is clear, and capable of easy demonstration. Cicero expresses it in his essay on Duty,[2] which is
addressed to his son Marcus. Gainful occupations, he says, are
almost always debasing to the character. Collectors of harbor
duties—who belonged to the publicans of the New Testament—
usurers, and others whose business naturally attracts the hatred
of their fellow-men, are most to be despised. It is unsuitable
for a free man to engage in work where he is paid for his manual
labor rather than for his skill, for his wages are a contract by
which he binds himself to the activities of a slave. Retail dealers
are sordid. They buy only to sell, and can not prosper without
lying. Mechanics and handicraftsmen are base; there can be
nothing noble in a workshop. Dealers in salt fish or fresh,
butchers, cooks, and sausage-makers; those who sell perfumes;
dancers and vaudeville players; and all others who minister
to the pleasures of men—are not to be approved. Work that
requires more than ordinary skill or that is useful, such as
medicine, architecture, and teaching, is honorable enough for
certain classes of society. Merchants who traffic from port to
port are a base lot if their business is on a small scale. If they
carry large cargoes and supply many people, without cheating,
their activity is not so very discreditable; and they are even to
be highly respected if they give up their business after they

[2] *De Off.* 1, 150–151.

have made a competency, and retire to the life of a farmer. Farming, indeed, is of all occupations the one most suitable to a free man—like Cicero's sturdy old grandfather, for instance.

The passage contains a line from Terence, about the dealers in fish and their like, but it is, nevertheless, serious. Cicero never wrote a more serious work than this one on Duty, nor one into which he put more of his own thought about life. The attitude is given as traditional; it still prevailed in Cicero's time, and was shared by him. The ethical charge is not to be pressed. Cicero was capable of recognizing virtue among his slaves and freedmen, and treated them with consideration, at times even with respect and affection. But slaves and even freedmen—doctors, architects, and teachers were usually Greek freedmen—had other problems than those of the prominent Roman; they and the Roman citizens of their social position were not the ones for whom Cicero was writing. The philosophers, Greeks themselves, were in accord with him; and no doubt found an ethical reason for the worldly attitude. The Stoics—and Cicero based this work principally on Panaetius, the great Stoic of the preceding generation—said that all men are citizens of a world state, and so, presumably, equal. The Stoics preached about providence; but they preached to the Romans who sat, or expected to sit, on curule chairs, and not to those who brawled in the forum. And the latter, most likely, would have taken a very cheerful attitude toward this disparagement of gainful occupations, if by any chance it had reached them. An overwhelming majority among them had only one gainful occupation, that of selling their votes, and this was not mentioned by Cicero; they also had only one demand, or perhaps two, free food and free amusements.

It was not that the great Romans were expected to refrain from money-getting. Though the mere amassing of wealth was never in Rome an Open Sesame to the high places, and was indeed held in contempt if pursued as an end in itself, still, even men of the greatest renown engaged in activities which were fabulously lucrative. But they did this as stockholders in the large companies that farmed the taxes in the provinces, as lordly lenders of gold to foreign princes, who spent the money in Rome to gain political advantages, or as employers of their own or other people's slaves, whose work ranged all the way from the copying of books to fighting as gladiators. But these activities were not under the necessity of petty cheating and lying, and above all they did not involve a slavish dependence on some one else. The physician must come at a moment's notice; the architect must humor his customer, and the teacher his pupils, or their fathers. These Romans humored no one. They no longer farmed, but their forefathers had done so; and it is no disgrace to be dependent on wind and weather.

Preserving their personal freedom, the Roman politicians must not use it selfishly; they must be inspired by a lofty patriotism.[3] Love of one's country, says Cicero, voicing the ideal, includes and transcends that for parents, children, relatives, and friends. Every man should be willing to die for his country. There are many who will sacrifice their lives as well as their possessions for her, though they will not give up their own personal glory, as they should do. A friend is the greatest blessing that can come to a man, greater than political honors, wealth, or pleasures, but even a friend must not be cherished to the detriment of the state. It is the duty of every one who can to seek public office. And—with a glance at the plebeians— though there are some who should govern and others who should obey, it is the duty of all to live for their country.

A few men in Rome challenged this exalted view of civic duty, and insisted on a man's right to devote his energies to study and meditation, provided he did not debase this occupation by selling his services. If a man had the means, inherited or otherwise honorably procured, of obtaining leisure, he would not

---

[3] See esp. *De Rep.* 1, chaps. 1–8; and *Dc Off., passim*, esp. 1, 70–73.

serve his reputation by indulging in banquets and depraving pleasures; but why should he not devote himself to intellectual interests? He ennobled his character, which might not always be maintained of the politician, and, if he meditated and wrote on the management of the state, he also did a real service to his country.

This ideal of scholarly leisure, though unintelligible to the nation as a whole, and, in its real essence, even to the average aristocrat, had a peculiar fascination for Cicero. It was due to the influence of things Greek, intellectual as well as artistic; and Cicero would be the last man to deny his debt to the Greeks. It was adopted, furthermore, by men of great personal charm, some of them the most intimate friends of Cicero, as, for example, Atticus; and Cicero could not have loved Atticus if he had not sympathized strongly with his tastes. Friendship, as Cicero himself wrote,[4] consists in a complete agreement about all things, human and divine, to which are added good will and affection. At times, in moments of speculative and moral enthusiasm, Cicero sets philosophical studies above all things else; most strikingly, perhaps, when he quotes[5] the opinion of Pythagoras to the effect that life is like a great public festival. Some come to win glory in the athletic contests, others to make money by buying and selling, but a third group, and this the most talented, come merely to observe and to meditate. So, too, in life: some struggle for glory, others for wealth, but those who have wisdom scorn these lesser pursuits and give themselves up to thought and study. In Cicero's whole life, however, and in nearly all of his writings, he opposes the ideal of Atticus. Cicero was neither pugnacious nor given to propaganda in his personal relations. "The only difference between you and me," he writes to Atticus, "is that we have chosen different roads in life." He was, nevertheless, very clear in his own mind, and could

---

4 *De Amic.* 20.
5 *Tusc.* 5, 9.

draw arguments from the very philosophy to which his studious friends were devoted. Man, he says, is naturally gregarious and finds his highest activity in his relations with his fellow-men. His intellectual life, if divorced from action, is a maimed and incomplete thing. The man who shrinks into solitude might as well be dead. He is like one wandering in desert places. His greatness of soul is almost brutish and inhuman.

Some men may have an excuse for not engaging in public life. They may be weak in health, as was Cicero's father, or they may have very unusual gifts for intellectual pursuits, which was scarcely true of Atticus; and each person should of course heed his natural bent in choosing his life work. They may have other cogent reasons. But let these men of leisure, these *otiosi,* remember that the life of a student is easier and safer than that of a public servant, and that it is less exposed to envy. Philosophers are wrong if they profess to look down upon political activity and the fame it brings. Though their contempt for fame may be praiseworthy, they may find, if they look into their own hearts, that they are not actuated by this lofty feeling but by a desire to avoid hard work and the ignominy of possible failure. Even the philosophers who write in favor of despising glory do not forget to put their names on their books.[6] Those, therefore, who can should seek magistracies, for thus they will assist in managing the state properly, and will also have an opportunity to show their greatness of soul.

A politician, far more than a philosopher, needs largeness of vision and philosophic calm, if he is not to be forever worried and inconsistent. Nor should a man engage in politics only when the state is in special need of honest endeavor. Such impromptu saviors of the state are like men who refuse to learn navigation when the weather is calm, but wish to stand at the helm when the storm is raging. It is well to write about the government of states, but even the seven wise men of Greece performed their civic duties.

---

[6] *Pro Arch.* 26.

Nevertheless, when Crassus bought elections, he had not lain awake nights planning for the welfare of his country. Cicero himself was as nobly devoted to Rome as any one, but his life was not governed merely by unselfish devotion. The objectors to politics had some truth in them; they were doubtless lazy and timid, but they saw that men rushed into political life, talked, bought, or fought their way into it, because it offered not only an opportunity for service but also for personal prominence, great wealth, and excitement.

Rome was at this time the most powerful country on the Mediterranean. The larger and richer part of this region was directly under Roman rule, while in the rest her influence was paramount. Where two countries bordered upon one another, and thus were natural rivals, Roman diplomacy, aided by Roman arms, had ordinarily established her in the position of an arbiter. When a people was divided into warring parties, Rome usually stepped in, usually to her own advantage.

Moreover, she had no rivals, scarcely even a serious enemy. The half-civilized tribes to the north were frequently a source of uneasiness and trouble, occasionally defeating Roman armies and threatening to break into Roman territory. But the effect of their attacks was temporary, and confined to a small portion of the Roman dominion. As yet they did not constitute a very serious menace. The same was, on the whole, true of the nations in the East. The Parthians, in the old country of the Medes and Persians, were a vigorous and warlike people, but their interests did not often bring them into collision with Rome. They lived in a world of their own, satisfied, on the whole, to keep their territory intact. Though the Romans in their proximity suffered from inroads, Rome as a nation paid slight heed to the Parthians, and looked upon them as a people to be conquered in the course of future expansion. The kingdoms east of the Roman possessions in Asia Minor were more troublesome. At least one great ruler, Mithradates, arose among them, who in his ceaseless hatred of Rome waged a long and at times a successful war; but Mithradates was conquered and his country became part of a Roman province.

The Romans and the peoples among whom they were dominant looked upon themselves as practically constituting all of the world that really mattered. They worked out their own problems and took little cognizance of any country not contiguous to the lands around the Mediterranean. Alexander the Great had gone to the borders of India, to be sure; but India and China, the other two great centers of civilization in ancient times, were known only through the picturesque accounts of chance travelers. To a Roman statesman they were as unreal as the country of the Amazons or of the Lotus-Eaters. The Romans, therefore, rightly considered themselves the rulers of the world. A Roman citizen was a privileged person wherever he happened to be; foreign monarchs were the clients of Roman senators.

It was not by meekness that the Romans had inherited most of the earth, and were taking the rest. They did not set themselves off from all others as a different people, whether intellectually and artistically, as the Greeks had done, or with reference to religion, as did the Jews. The Roman state did not readily interfere with the religion or the institutions of a dependent people. Admitting in practise that others were like themselves, they employed their services and rewarded them with Roman citizenship.

But the Romans did feel, and made no effort to hide their feeling, that they were incomparably superior in those qualities that make for political supremacy. The Carthaginians, in their eyes, were treacherous, or had been, for the Carthaginians were no more. The Gauls, though good fighters, were boastful, and had no reverence for religion. The Jews were abjectly superstitious. The Greeks—and to them the Romans yielded precedence in many things—the Greeks lied, they talked too much, they flattered, they had no gift for self-government. No one of these peoples had at the same time as good soldiers and as good statesmen as the Romans. As a physician or a philosopher a Roman might not be able to rival a Greek, nor did he seriously attempt to do so; but as a commander of armies or a director of states he could have no peers outside of Rome.

And other nations—some of them in subjection to, or alliance with, Rome; others fearing or desiring one or the other of these alternatives—tumbled over each other in their eagerness to pay court. Barbarian kings schemed against one another for the favor of influential Romans, sending gifts to senators, and entertaining generals with the obsequiousness of humble subjects, who, nevertheless, ventured to present their Roman majesties with jewelry, money, tables, chairs, and bedsteads of gold, and beautiful slaves. Especially did the Greeks practise this adulation; and there were Greeks, or people educated in the Greek manner, in all the Mediterranean countries. They were found at great distances from its coasts, for King Artavasdes in far-off Armenia wrote Greek tragedies, histories, and orations, and celebrated the marriage of his daughter with recitations from the *Bacchae* of Euripides. Most of the Greeks themselves were poor in gifts, preferring to receive them; but they could write epics and shout in processions. And the Romans, sauntering through Greek lands, on their way home from foreign conquests or on their way from Rome when the political situation had made a temporary absence desirable, even while they were in exile, basked in the sunshine of popular and scholarly fawning. Indeed, it was the Greeks who made supremacy especially sweet to the Romans in the matter of world fame, for, as Cicero said,[7] Greek was read in almost all countries, whereas Latin was confined within its natural narrow boundaries. In Rome, even the scholars and poets of Greece, at times, were little better than private tutors to the children of the aristocrats, although they were treated with

[7] *Pro Arch.* 23.

consideration and outward deference, as are private tutors. In their own cities, the Greeks gave what they had to the visiting masters; Romans of high rank were entertained by the wealthiest, for some were still wealthy; those of low rank or no rank at all became the guests of ordinary citizens.[8]

It is not necessary to cite many illustrations of this attitude; the life of every prominent Roman abounds in them. Cicero had his share of adulation in the city, and even out of it, though he never left Rome except under compulsion, and added no provinces to the empire. In Sicily as quaestor and in Cilicia as governor, he lacked nothing that the provinces could give. Even as a young man, when traveling in Greece and Asia Minor for his health, and also for instruction, he was escorted from place to place by the most prominent rhetoricians. These were among the leaders of thought, so that a modern parallel could be found only if the professors of Oxford and Cambridge should journey about England with a young stranger from America, giving him instruction in the things he wished to know. And yet Cicero was at that time of no great consequence; he had pleaded for two years in the forum, in only one case of importance, and he had held no office. Nor was he a born aristocrat, through whom the Greek professors might pay reverence to an influential family.

Cicero's experiences, however, scarcely contain a hint of the real circumstances. A better indication is found in a story that Cato used to tell. Once, during the time that Pompey was fighting in the East, Cato was traveling in Syria and came to Antioch. As he and his companions were approaching the city, they saw a large throng outside the city gates. There were young men on one side of the road and children on the other, all in holiday attire; there were also magistrates and priests, dressed in white and wearing garlands. Cato thought they had come out to meet him. He had sent some servants to the city, evidently to make

---

[8] *In Verr.* II, 1, 65. See below, p. 145.

preparations, and was angry because they had not prevented this outburst of civic enthusiasm. For the greater honor of the foolish Antiochians, he made his companions dismount from their horses—he was walking himself—and so proceeded toward the throng. The leader of the latter, an old man, with a staff and a garland in his hand, approached Cato and asked where he had left Demetrius, and when the latter could be expected. Now, Demetrius was only a freedman of Pompey's. The philosophical Cato murmured something about the unfortunate city, while his companions laughed. In later years Cato, too, could laugh at the people of Antioch awaiting the great general's favorite.

The Greeks of Antioch no doubt had their reward. It is, at all events, told of the victorious Pompey, who soon afterward wended his slow way toward Rome, that he made Mytilene a free city, in honor of the Greek Theophanes, who was singing his exploits. The poets of this city, it may be pertinent to note, were holding one of their regular contests during Pompey's presence, and made him the theme of all their warbling. In Rhodes, Pompey attended the lectures of all the philosophers, giving each of them a talent, or about one thousand dollars. Posidonius, the most famous Greek scholar of the period, here held a discussion with the rhetorician Hermagoras on the rhetorical subject of Invention for the amusement and instruction of Pompey, later publishing the disputation; but we are not informed how the disputants were rewarded. At Athens, Pompey encouraged the local philosophers with the generosity he had shown at Rhodes, and also gave the city fifty talents for repairs and beautification. Young Demetrius, incidentally, did not suffer because of Pompey's generosity to others; he is said to have left an estate of four thousand talents, about four million dollars. And yet the services of an untrained slave could be had for twelve asses a day, about ten cents.

It is in Rome, however, and not in the provinces, that we are to look for the influences that moulded Cicero and his prominent contemporaries. Even a great general like Pompey lived most of his life in Rome; neither he nor any one else who had ambitions would ever have thought of making his home at any considerable distance from the city, provided he could stay there in safety.

The whole power of the Roman people, and consequently of the Roman world, was centered in Rome.[9] The senators lived in the city or its vicinity. The people, who in their assemblies made the laws and elected the magistrates, and who filled the forum, consisted almost entirely of the Roman populace. Shortly before the time that Cicero entered public life the Roman franchise had been obtained by the Italians, who thus with the inhabitants of the city and the Roman citizens living outside of Italy, especially in favored communities, constituted the Roman nation; but the seat of government was in Rome, and there was no system of representation. In order to vote, a citizen must be in the capital. The enfranchised Italians frequently came to Rome for important elections. Cicero could count upon the support of his admiring fellow-townsmen of Arpinum, and indeed his political success, in so far as it was not due to the knights, depended mostly on his influence among the Italians. As a statesman he also had them constantly in mind. It seems, nevertheless, that although the Italians occasionally had a steadying influence on the Roman populace, they did not materially affect the character of public life in Rome. An influence by no means steadying was exerted by the veterans, who lived away from Rome on land given them by the state. They, too, gathered to the polls in large numbers to give their vote for a former commander, and they were occasionally

---

[9] No attempt is here made to give an account of Roman political institutions. See Greenidge, *Roman Public Life,* Botsford, *The Roman Assemblies etc.,* and Abbott.

responsible for the lawlessness in the city; but, though their influence was sometimes paramount, they did not form a constant part of the people. Under normal conditions the populace of Rome ruled the assemblies.

Rome, in the time of Cicero, was a city of small extent, covering a little less than five square miles, which is not quite one quarter of the Borough of Manhattan of New York City. It was also a hilly city. But the population was large. Estimates necessarily differ considerably, but one million two or three hundred thousand seems a reasonable supposition. While this makes the density of population more than twice that of Manhattan, and considerably greater than in the most crowded parts of London, it is by no means impossible, for perhaps a third of the population consisted of slaves, whose quarters were at best very small; and almost all of the people comprising the other two thirds were exceedingly poor and crowded together in large tenement houses on very narrow streets. The climate of Italy, furthermore, allows of much outdoor living, so that the dwellings of many were probably little more than places in which to eat and sleep.

The people of Rome, exclusive of the slaves and some seventy thousand foreign residents, who did not possess the franchise, were sharply divided into three classes. The first class was the nobles, a small group of families, the founders of whom had held high office. Below them were the knights, who possessed a minimum of four hundred thousand sesterces, between sixteen and twenty thousand dollars. These two classes, the political and the financial aristocracy, had a unity of education and financial means that set them off at an almost immeasurable distance from the rest of the people. Numbering only about ten thousand altogether in a city of a million, which itself was the center not only of Italy but of the world, the nobles and the knights formed a very small minority, but they are the only ones about whom much is known. They wrote the books, the orations, and the letters of the period. In the big spectacle of the last century of the republic every great individual who moves across the stage is a noble or a knight, while the immense third class, the *plebs urbana,* performs the necessary office of the mob, indifferent or threatening as the case may be, but always present. They are like an indistinct background against which are seen the figures of generals, orators, financiers, and students.

Though the *plebs urbana* liked to think of themselves as the Roman people, large numbers were foreign slaves who had been manumitted, and a still larger number had none of the qualities that had made Rome the mistress of the world. There must have been among them a great many who earned an honest living as artisans, small tradesmen, and laborers of various kinds; but there were many circumstances that made them as a class no better than an ordinary city rabble. Much of the work that they might have done was performed by the thousands of slaves in the city. It is not likely that the nobles or the knights made extensive use of the services of free citizens. Slave labor was cheap, and in many ways more efficient, for the slaves could be given a training not accessible to the poor free man. Slaves performed not only the ordinary menial tasks; many of them were educated and acted in such capacities as copyists and binders of books, private secretaries, and physicians. Though many of them were manumitted, they remained in the service of their former masters, precluding the employment of free citizens. Foreigners, too, especially Greeks, were largely employed in positions requiring unusual skill or education. Nor did the free citizens perform all the tasks that pertained to their own lives. They did not, for example, always build their own houses. The big tenement houses in which they lived were erected by slaves. Crassus, we are told, had five hundred slaves so employed. As early as 103 B.C., three years after the birth of Cicero, there were only two thousand people in Rome who owned property.

It is not probable that the great majority of the populace wished to work. As the sovereign people of the world they expected the world to feed them. And the world did feed them; or rather the Roman state, which in its turn drew its income almost exclusively from conquered territory. In 5 B.C., thirty-eight years after Cicero's death, there were in Rome three hundred and twenty thousand people who received from the state a gratuity of sixty denarii, about ten dollars. This number probably included all the free citizens and their sons. During the lifetime of Cicero the state sold bread to the free citizens at a reduced rate, or gave it to them for nothing; one result of which was that a large number of bankrupts, loafers, and adventurers flocked to Rome, who further increased the poverty and unruliness of the plebs.

This class, however, was not a serious problem merely because of their presence in the city; they had considerable political power. Theoretically they were almost supreme. Organized into assemblies, with different rules of procedure and under different presidencies, they were the law-making and electoral body. In regard to law-making, however, they were strangely hampered both by the senate and the magistrates, and neither they nor their leaders made any real effort to assert the rights of the people as the seat of power in the republic. The struggle between the people and the aristocracy belonged almost entirely to the past. In the time of Cicero the leaders of the so-called democratic party were nearly all generals, or supporters of generals, who rebelled against the domination of the senate in their efforts to secure power for themselves, not men who tried to establish a democratic republic.

These ostensible leaders of the plebs, as well as other politicians seeking office, needed the support of the populace as electors, and the latter, in consequence, received from the state not only most of their livelihood but also their amusements. The public games, with circus and theatrical performances, were given for their benefit, normally occupying some seventy-six days of the year. These were in charge of public officials, who found it advisable to spend large sums of their own or their supporters' money in addition to the state allowance. The demand for these amusements on the part of the plebs was so great that a magistrate who had treated the public shabbily was very likely to fail of election to higher offices. The spending of money in this way was well established by tradition, and was recognized by thinkers as one of the duties of public life, provided it did not deteriorate to ruinous extravagance. It was also traditional to feast the people and give them gifts of money in connection with triumphs, funerals of prominent men, and any other extraordinary occasions.

But the demands of the plebs resulted in a still graver situation. Bribery at elections became almost universal. Laws were passed to check the evil, but there was no real public sentiment behind them. Though charges of bribery were frequently brought before the courts, they rarely aimed at raising the moral level of elections, but were merely political weapons in the hands of defeated candidates. And as the political disintegration progressed, the plebs were ready to be organized into gangs that obstructed or carried through elections and legal action, filling the streets, the Campus Martius, and the forum with shouting, spitting, stone-throwing, and bloodshed. Indeed, the situation seems to have been this, that the *plebs urbana* as a class was a thoroughly unworthy wielder of large political power, demanding flattery and concessions of every kind, and contributing consciously and unconsciously to the destruction of the Roman social order; while there were numerous political leaders, belonging to the aristocracy and not to the plebs, who were ready to make full use of the opportunities thus offered.

Above the populace was the order of the *equites*, or knights, to whom Cicero belonged. They were the well-to-do people of Rome. Some of them cultivated their farms, as Cicero's grandfather had done; others, like his father, lived a life of studious leisure; still others, like Atticus, were bankers and private business men. Above all, however, they were the financiers of Rome, who directed the big enterprises. The common people did not have money enough for this, and the aristocracy were forbidden to engage in business, at least outside of Italy. The knights formed large stock companies, in which aristocrats often owned shares, and these companies farmed many of the taxes of the provinces. In return for a fixed sum to be paid into the state treasury, which thus constituted the tax in question so far as the government was concerned, the knights received the right to collect from the provincials as much as the legal conditions of taxation allowed them. These companies became in this way an important, though unofficial, part of the government. Much of the money that poured into Rome was in the form of booty, and with this the companies of the knights had nothing to do; but as practically the entire regular income of Rome was derived from the provinces, the knights were justly called by Cicero the mainstay of the whole social fabric. Their influence was enormous. Since the aristocracy, through the senate and the magistracies, had almost complete charge of the provinces, so that the letting of the contracts for taxation as well as the facilities for actually collecting the taxes depended on them, the knights were brought into very close contact with them, often in a spirit of coöperation, but still more often by way of opposition. Between them, these two classes controlled the revenues of the state.

Socially the knights held a high place. In matters of education and personal friendships the son of a knight seems often to have had the same advantages as the son of a consul. This was true to a very remarkable degree of Atticus; and it was almost equally the case with Cicero. Lucius Crassus, the greatest orator during Cicero's youth, guided the education of young Cicero and his brother, and even admitted them to his home. Marcus Antonius, the other great orator of the period, was another friend. An uncle of Cicero's had accompanied him to Cilicia—which Cicero himself later governed—where Antonius had fought against the pirates; and later the uncle and Antonius had together attended philosophical and rhetorical lectures in Athens. The uncle often spoke of his experiences during this time. Besides the two eminent orators, the great family of the Scaevolas were friends of the Ciceros. When Marcus, probably at sixteen, had assumed the *toga virilis,* the external sign of maturity, he became one of the young men who were initiated into public life by Scaevola, the augur. The latter, who was about seventy-one years old at the time, was one of the greatest of the Romans, and his home was crowded with prominent men. Despite his advanced age, he was the first to arrive in the senate-house for the meetings. Like other members of his family, he was a great jurist, and Cicero was allowed to be present in his house when he gave legal advice to his numerous consultants.[10] This was his way, a common one, of giving instruction in law to his young protégés; he did not teach formally. At the death of the augur Cicero attached himself to the latter's kinsman, Scaevola, the pontifex maximus, also an old man. The pontiff was said by Lucius Crassus to be the best orator among the jurists and the best jurist among the orators.

Cicero's connection with the Scaevolas was not limited to an apprenticeship for public life. One of the Scaevolas seems to have taken sufficient interest in his early literary efforts to have praised his poem on Marius. Cicero was also received in the family, and speaks of the ladies, who were women of uncommon accomplishments and character. The augur's wife, Laelia, was the daughter of Laelius, the friend of Scipio Africanus. Cicero was thus brought into close spiritual connection with the so-called Scipionic Circle and the period of the Roman republic which was considered, both by him and by later writers, as its culmination.

[10] *De Amic.* 2. A very attractive scene.

The influence on Cicero of these great nobles was deep and lasting, and can be traced at all periods of his life. They are often speakers in his dialogues; their opinions are frequently quoted, always with reverence and approval; anecdotes about them are scattered through his writings; and their ideals, both political and spiritual, were largely his, though in politics he remained at heart a knight, with a broader view than that of the typical aristocrat. Above all, these nobles, as friends of his family, introduced him at an early date to the throbbing, brilliant political life of Rome, in which they themselves were leaders, and so guided his ambition, if indeed it needed guidance after he had once come to the capital.

But the opportunities of Cicero, or of any other young knight, were merely social and financial; they were not political. A member of the equestrian rank might be elected to the lower magistracies, though even that, as Cicero more than hints, was not accomplished without opposition; if he became a candidate for high office, he was certain to have arrayed against him the concerted influence of the aristocracy, strengthened by the envy of less successful knights and by the conviction of the common people that the highest magistracies were the prerogatives of the nobles.

The nobles, *nobiles,* constituted the highest social order. They consisted almost exclusively of a comparatively few families, who either belonged to the patricians of early Roman history or had become members of the aristocracy because an ancestor had held at least the curule aedileship, the second lowest office. Election to the curule aedileship would admit a person to the nobility, and as election was dependent upon the will of the whole people, almost any politician could become a noble. But within the nobility he held no position of consequence unless he attained the highest offices, and, as a matter of actual practise, the nobility exercised so great an influence in elections that it was extremely difficult for any one but a noble by inheritance to

attain these offices. Even when these New men, as they were
called, had reached the pinnacle of the magisterial career, they
were not full-fledged nobles, and were readily looked down upon
and antagonized by the genuine aristocrats. The sons of these,
on the other hand, were destined for the consulship while they
still lay in their cradles, Cicero says, truthfully enough, though
with bitterness, for he was then struggling toward the high
places himself. A defeated candidate could claim superiority
over his successful rival on the ground that his own family
was the nobler of the two, and do this without exciting surprise.
In the atrium, the chief room or reception hall, of a noble were
kept the portrait masks of his ancestors, and these were carried
in the funeral processions of the family. Only noble ancestors
received this curious canonization. The funeral ceremonies were
held in the forum, where an oration, a eulogy—*laudatio funebris*
—was delivered, setting forth the virtues of the deceased and
calling attention to the services to Rome of his whole family.
These eulogies thus constituted a history of the family; and
these family archives, taken together, contained nearly all that
was known of early Roman history.

Belonging to a hereditary nobility, the individual aristocrat
was not always rich; and even if he possessed considerable means,
the lawful expenses connected with elections and public games,
and the practise of bribery, which at times assumed incredible
proportions, frequently impoverished him before he reached the
highest offices. But these offices, though no salaries were connected with them, more than made good his losses. There were
many ways in which this was accomplished. Foreign kings sent
gifts to influential politicians to secure favorable senatorial
action; individuals and communities outside Rome did not practise parsimony in their relations to the senator who was their
representative; rich clients in Rome seem to have paid their
advocates well, despite the law that there should be no legal fees;
and wealthy men, whether Romans or foreigners, were in the

habit of willing moneys to well-known political leaders, thus.
honoring themselves and their families by association with
greatness. But the two great avenues to wealth were war and
the government of the provinces. It was through war that such
men as Caesar, Pompey, and Lucullus amassed their huge fortunes; but great and successful generals were necessarily few.
The ordinary aristocrats relied on the less martial feat of despoiling the provinces. Even the honest propraetor or proconsul
made large sums. Cicero, after his one year in Cilicia, found
himself the possessor of 2,200,000 sesterces, from 88,000 to
110,000 dollars; and yet he was scrupulously honest, not taking
even what the law allowed him, and restraining his subordinates
to the point of causing complaint. But the great majority of
provincial governors were not honest. *Innocentia*—innocence,
but interpreted as referring to self-restraint in reference to
other people's property—was in the eyes of honest men one
of the greatest virtues that a governor could have, but few of
them had it. The provinces were on the whole fair game. It
is not likely that every governor practised extortion with the
skillful thoroughness of Verres in the rich island of Sicily, who
stole silver from the tables of hosts who entertained him, and
carried off marble pillars from the temples, employing artists
to help him decide what was worth stealing; but extortion was,
nevertheless, prevalent. Trials of home-coming governors—
de repetundis rebus, for the recovery of property, as the Romans
frankly put it—were so common that the returning official nearly
always faced the unpleasant possibility of having his record
investigated. Convictions, however, were rare. The trials, like
those for bribery, became weapons to be wielded by one politician
against another; honesty and the just claims of the provincials
were scarcely considered. Argument in their favor scarcely
went further than this, that they should not be made so hostile
to Rome that they would cause trouble, nor so poor that they
could not pay the taxes.

Politically, the nobles were identical with the senate, and so constituted the so-called senatorial order, even though not every noble actually entered politics and had a seat in the senate. Through a law of Sulla, whose great changes took place immediately before Cicero's entrance upon a public career, the quaestorship had become the stepping-stone to the senate. After this time the senate consisted normally of six hundred members, but it was dominated by the old noble families both because of the large number of senators that belonged to them and because the leaders of the senate were the men who had held the consulship, and these were almost without exception nobles by inheritance.

The senate was the sovereign power in the Roman state. This had come about through a long series of events and had reached completion a century before Cicero's birth. It was legally recognized, as well as extended, by the legislation of Sulla. Theoretically the senate lacked many powers which belonged to the assemblies and to the magistrates, but in practise the influence of the senate was felt everywhere. The great nobles in the senate dominated the elections to the magistracies, as has already been mentioned. The assemblies, and not the senate, made the laws; but the assemblies could vote only on a motion put before them by their presiding officers, and these were magistrates. The two assemblies of the greatest importance in Cicero's time were the *comitia centuriata* and the *comitia tributa.* The consuls presided in the former; and the consuls were almost always members of the aristocracy, and therefore devoted to the interests of the senate. The *comitia tributa* was presided over by the tribunes of the plebs, and since these, whether nobles or not, were often opposed to the aristocracy, it was in this assembly, and practically in this only, that the senate did not exercise their domination. But although the senate did not make the laws, and although the decrees of the senate had to be approved by the people before they became laws, these decrees were often carried out before the assembly had an opportunity to vote on them, so immediate was the senate's hold on the executive power; and many decrees were binding without the approval of the people. The magistrates, furthermore, on taking office, issued so-called edicts, in which they set forth the rules by which they intended to govern themselves during their year of office. The edicts of the praetors, who presided in the courts, had a far-reaching influence; taken together, they practically formed a code of laws, and the praetors were thus, in practise if not in theory, lawmakers. A governor of a province issued a similar edict; he was either an ex-praetor or an ex-consul. The people had the power of declaring war and making peace. But since the foreign relations of Rome were practically in the hands of the senate and since the generals of the Roman armies were ex-magistrates, assigned to their positions by the senate, wars were made and peace terms were settled very much according to the wishes of the senate. The finances of Rome were controlled by the senate; the people, who were not taxed, had nothing to say about the expenditure of money. The senate, as a body, had no part in jurisdiction. The assemblies and some of the individual magistrates had certain powers, which need not be described, but all cases of importance came before the standing courts. These, however, were presided over by the praetors, who possessed discretionary powers that often determined the outcome of a lawsuit. The jurors had been knights in the period before Sulla, but he gave the courts to the senators, and when this was changed, some ten years later, the senate retained one third of the jury, while the other two thirds went to the knights and to a certain high class of plebeians. The influential advocates in the courts, finally, were almost without exception magistrates or ex-magistrates.

It was through the magistrates that the senate exercised much of its authority; and this was possible because the magistrates themselves were often little else than the servants of the

senate. Though their legal and executive powers were considerable, they were used under normal conditions for the interests
of the nobility that composed the senate. This state of things
had been brought about by a variety of circumstances, only one
or two of which it is necessary to mention. The powers of the
individual magistrates conflicted. Two consuls, eight praetors,
and ten plebeian tribunes held office at the same time, and each
one of these not only exercised the same powers as his respective
colleagues but he had the same rights of intercession or veto,
by which he could nullify the action of a colleague; yet such a
veto could not itself be vetoed. Out of the inevitable conflict
and confusion which resulted from the rival position of the
magistrates there had arisen the need of some central authority,
and the senate had supplied this need. The interests of the
individual magistrates, furthermore, were bound up with the
senate. All the magistrates had seats in the senate, and here the
new magistrate came under the influence of the experience and
greater age of his senatorial colleagues. He held office for only
one year, whereas he remained a senator for life. If he desired
the usual political reward of a province, his appointment depended on the senate. He would, therefore, have to be an
extraordinarily original and brave man to strike out on a course
opposed to the desires of the senate; in most cases he had not
even the wish to do so.

The senate thus practically ruled Rome during the later
republic, and Rome ruled the world. In the senate itself the
greatest influence was wielded by the ex-consuls, or consulars.
They had the highest rank and the most varied experience, and
they were also aided by the rules of procedure. They were first
called upon to express their opinion in debate. After them,
the praetors and ex-praetors were invited to speak, and then
the word was given, in proper order, to the holders or ex-holders
of the other offices. But since all things were decided by open
debate and since the senate was a large body, the right of the

consulars always to speak first made them the leaders of the senate. A Roman, therefore, who had filled the various magistracies through the consulship and had thereupon become one of the leaders of the senate, thus enjoyed a position to which the modern world offers no parallel. He was the very incarnation of worldly success, having attained the only thing worth striving for. In modern society there are many roads that lead to wealth or to fame, and no one would maintain the superiority of one kind of activity over all others, though popular applause may be given in one country to men of wealth, in another to soldiers, and in still another to artists or writers. A man chooses his work, or drifts into it, allowed, on the whole, to follow his own particular bent; and he may achieve success in one field though he would have failed in another. In Rome the way to success was the same for all; only one kind of talent was richly rewarded. But for that reason the reward was the greater.

As an influential statesman, furthermore, the Roman surpassed his modern counterpart in the variety and range of his activities. He was, or had been, a lawgiver, a soldier, an executive; he often pleaded in the courts, and he had presided in them. Very few could attain eminence in all of these activities, but an ex-consul had engaged in all of them at one time or another, and was therefore in touch with every branch of public life. He was the shaper of large commercial undertakings inasmuch as most Roman business had to do with the provinces, and consequently depended ultimately on the attitude of the senate. He was the honored representative at Rome of whole communities, whose material well-being might depend entirely on his ability. And, finally, he and his peers were the rulers of the world.

This unique eminence was greatly enhanced by the manner of life in Rome. The prominent statesman was in daily contact with the people. In the morning he held a reception, *salutatio*, at his home; then he went, or descended, as the Romans said, for his residence was probably on the Palatine Hill, to the forum, accompanied by a large crowd of clients and supporters of every kind. In the year of his magistracy he also had with him a bodyguard of lictors, twelve if he was a consul, two if a praetor; and he wore a toga with a purple border. If he was a candidate for office, his toga was chalked; and the crowd about him was as large as he could muster, in order to make display of his influence. Even after he had retired from office, his dress as a senator differed from that of an ordinary citizen, and his followers were numerous.

The forum, not a very large place, was filled with slaves, freedmen, foreigners, ordinary citizens, knights, senators, and magistrates. It was a busy, swirling place, alive with applause and condemnation. Nearly all public business was conducted there. The courts were held in plain view, so that the crowd surged around to listen. They did not listen silently, but shouted approval in the midst of a cross-examination, loudly ridiculed discomfited speakers or witnesses, and if a speaker failed to interest them, they went elsewhere in search of better entertainment. The different points of a case were discussed before and after trials, and the persons concerned were freely congratulated, sneered at, or condoled with.

The meetings of the senate were not open to the people, but the latter were always outside the senate-house or the temple in which the meeting was held; and they did not conceal their presence, often being noisy enough to disturb the debates. Immediately after the meeting, if anything of unusual interest had been under discussion, the consul, or a prominent senator, frequently addressed the people, informing them of the senate's action.

The people were always being addressed. Public meetings, *contiones,* presided over by magistrates but extremely informal nevertheless, preceded the sessions of the assemblies and were also called in reference to everything of importance. They were most often held in the forum. It is on record that a magistrate might address the people every day during his whole year of office. On holidays the people also had the Circus and the plays, where popular favorites were applauded and popular scapegoats hissed. If a verse in an old tragedy could be interpreted as referring to political conditions, the actor might be called upon to repeat it interminably for the glory or discomfiture of the person concerned. These expressions of popular opinion were so noisy and carried so much weight that the politician who was for the moment unpopular rarely ventured into their presence.

It was an intimate, vociferous life, this life in Rome, which tried a man severely, and then rewarded or punished him. Probably every senator of prominence was known to the whole people; they had all heard him speak. If he was unsuccessful and stayed away from the forum, his absence was remarked. If he was successful, the crowd surged around him. He was always meeting friends or foes. During the time of elections or important events, the prominent politicians would be constantly among the people, speaking with individuals or addressing crowds, arguing and persuading; but even when there was no unusual excitement, the well-known senators, each accompanied by his large retinue, sauntered back and forth, exchanging greeting or repartee, for which there was always an audience; and the repartee was sometimes of a kind not suitable for repetition before modern readers.[11]

But life in the forum did not consist merely of oratory and repartee at the time Cicero was growing up. In 107 B.C., the year before Cicero was born, his townsman Marius attained the consulship. His election broke the aristocratic tradition. He was a plebeian, and had been put into office to carry on the war against Jugurtha. In the following year he brought the Jugurthine war to a successful conclusion, and for several years after that he was kept almost constantly in office as a general, so that

---

[11] See *Att.* 2, 1. 5.

he was holding his sixth consulship at the time Cicero was six years old. Marius, who was a poor politician, became involved in trouble with his own party and was out of politics for about ten years, returning in 90 B.C., in the early part of which year Cicero probably assumed the *toga virilis*. During these years conditions in Rome had been comparatively quiet, though acts of violence had not been lacking and the knights had made extensive and scandalous use of their power in the extortion courts. Late in the year 91 B.C. Lucius Crassus had died, and Cicero had shortly thereupon begun to attend Scaevola, the aged augur. From this time on, Cicero, who now, in the man's toga, could go about unattended and also seek instruction wherever he chose, was constantly in the forum. In the year 89 B.C., however, probably from the spring to the fall, he was in the army doing his military service. The Social War, waged by the Italian allies against Rome, to secure Roman citizenship, had begun in 90 B.C., and lasted two years. Nothing is known of Cicero as a recruit; not even as to whether or not he took part in any fighting. The only incident recorded is that he was present at a conference between his general and one of the rebel leaders. The former was Pompeius Strabo, the father of the Pompey who was soon to be called the Great; and Cicero may have met the latter in camp. Pompey was nearly eight months younger than Cicero.

The end of the Social War did not bring peace to Rome. The next years were filled with anarchy by Marius, Sulla, and their factions. In 88 B.C., while Sulla was consul, a tribune of the plebs, P. Sulpicius Rufus, brought forward various laws in favor of the people, one of which assigned to Marius the command against Mithradates, although this had already been given to Sulla by the senate. In order to prevent legislation, the consuls proclaimed a public holiday, during which no public business could be transacted; but Sulpicius armed his followers and drove the consuls from the forum. The holiday proclamation was withdrawn and the laws were passed. Sulla thereupon marched

upon the city with an army; all democratic resistance yielded;
Marius and Sulpicius fled, the former, after picturesque adventures, to Africa and the ruins of Carthage; and Sulla carried
some laws that increased the aristocratic power. He also
secured the Mithradatic command, and departed for the East
the following year.

After Sulla's departure, Cinna, one of the consuls, revived
the proposals of Sulpicius. His aristocratic colleague fell upon
the voters with an armed force, and the forum was heaped high
with the bodies of the slain. Cinna fled, but to the legions.
Partisans joined him from many directions, and Marius returned
from Africa. The senate prepared to defend themselves, but
were forced to yield, after a short resistance. Cinna and Marius
entered Rome with their army; terrible massacres followed.
Marius' desire for vengeance was insatiable. Men were cut
down, says Plutarch, if Marius neglected to return their greeting; maimed and headless corpses were thrown about and
trampled upon in the streets. Among the numerous nobles who
lost their lives in this reign of terror was Marcus Antonius, the
great orator who had befriended Cicero. Many circumstances
connected with his death are reported. After he had been murdered, his head was brought to Marius, who was banqueting
with friends, and later it was fastened to the rostra in the forum.
Marius and Cinna had had themselves elected consuls for the
next year, 86 B.C.; it was Marius' seventh consulship, but he
died a few weeks after entering upon office. Thereupon Cinna
ruled Rome for three years, 86–83 B.C., during which time constitutional government was practically suspended.

In the year 83 B.C., however, Sulla landed in Italy with an
army of 40,000 men and a large number of nobles who had fled
to him. Civil war blazed up anew and lasted for two years.
Among those slain by the popular faction was Scaevola, the
pontifex maximus, who was butchered before the image of the
goddess Vesta. In 82 B.C. Sulla entered Rome, and presently

proclaimed himself dictator. Sulla's victory was signalized by proscriptions and massacres, which were not limited to the city of Rome. The conditions in Rome and Italy were more terrible, if possible, than under Marius and Cinna, for system was added to cruelty. The proscribed are said to have numbered 4700, including 2600 members of the equestrian order, who had sided with Marius. Cicero's kinsman, the adopted son of Marius, was among those killed. His murderer was Catiline. Quintus Cicero, in his pamphlet on electioneering, written in 64 B.C., described the circumstances, for Catiline was running against Marcus Cicero for the consulship. According to Quintus, Catiline flogged Gratidianus, the kinsman of Cicero, through the streets of Rome, tortured him horribly, and finally cut off his head; the blood flowed in streams between the fingers of his left hand, with which he had seized the hair of his victim.

The assassinations and proscriptions nevertheless came to an end, and Sulla restored order. Everything was done to insure the predominance of the aristocrats. Two measures were especially important. One of these related to the plebs. The power of the plebeian tribunes was limited. As champions of the people, they had the right of vetoing any proposal whatsoever, and of putting a stop to parliamentary discussion. This immensely powerful weapon was taken away, and, although the tribunate had thus been shorn of all real power, election to this office was also made a disqualification for further officeholding. The other measure was directed against the knights. The extortion courts were taken from the latter and given to the senators. While remaining a democracy, Rome was thus made definitely a democracy in which one class was endowed with so much power that the other classes were certain to rebel. But even more important than this was the fact that Sulla, partly following the example of Marius, had taught the Roman politicians to rely on the army. Rome was a military power; her whole life depended on the success of her armies. While the nation was inspired by patriotism and a feeling of unity, the power of Rome could be wielded by the civil government, wherever the armies were and by whomsoever commanded; but with the nation divided, each party fighting for supremacy, the armies would unavoidably be brought into the conflict by some individual, or individuals, who could command their loyalty. And it was inevitable that the soldiers, who sometimes served for long periods in foreign countries or in the provinces, should become exceptionally devoted to their general. His success was their success; complacency on his part meant license to plunder for them; and when they returned to Rome, it was he who had to secure for them their reward from the state, which usually consisted of free land. For more than half a century generals, when away from Rome, had been growing less and less amenable to senatorial dictation. Now Marius and Sulla had introduced the soldier into politics.

The reason for these momentous changes is not to be sought in the character of any particular persons. Everything was wrong in Rome. The nobles and the knights had too much money, as is indicated by Pompey's gifts to Athens and to Demetrius; the majority of the plebs had no money at all, and lacked both the desire and the opportunity to earn any. The three social classes were constantly in collision, their weapons being bribery, violence, and even murder. Below them were the innumerable slaves, drawn from many nationalities, who performed the menial labor of Italy, and so might be looked upon as the basis of society. They were treated fairly well in the city and on the small farms and in the vineyards; but on the great estates of the nobles, which were scattered over nearly the whole country, they were no better than beasts of burden, held in check by armed overseers. They often revolted. In no department of life was there a sound public opinion to serve as a check. The rich indulged in almost incredible extravagances, and were often immoral; they had lost their old religion and in its stead had substituted Greek philosophy, many carrying their philosophic speculations just far enough to prove that morality was a matter for clever debate. The poor, on the other hand, earning little and having no responsibility, lived for the day, constantly making impudent demands for support and entertainment. Religion and morality can scarcely be discussed at all in connection with the Roman populace, for they had little of either. And even in the other cities of Italy and in the country districts, where the Roman people was at its best, falsification of wills, ruinous extravagance, divorce, and murder frequently failed to call forth the right kind of public censure, and, when legally punishable, escaped in the courts.[12] This whole social fabric, finally, was supported by money stolen or extorted from hostile countries or from the provinces; both enemies and provincials, despite their fawning, hated Rome with unceasing hatred, and with good reason.

This national deterioration, due to Rome's world-power, had been going on for a century before the birth of Cicero. It can be traced most readily in the numerous laws passed during these hundred years. There were laws in favor of the different social orders, and in their disfavor, all tending to break up the nation. There were laws to check bribery, to drive out the Greek philosophers, to establish courts for the trial of provincial governors, to restrain private expenditure. These laws were passed, but they were not obeyed. Things went continually from bad to worse. And yet Rome not only retained her rule over the Mediterranean world, but she was destined to retain it for centuries, even extending her boundaries beyond those set by Pompey and Caesar. Her foreign enemies and her discontented provincials did not break her power; in fact, they scarcely even tried to do so. In Italy she had civil wars of many kinds, some of which brought her to the very edge of the precipice, but she was not hurled into the abyss. By victory or by wise yielding, she constantly

---

[12] This appears most glaringly in Cicero's defense of Cluentius. See below, p. 120.

emerged from her throng of difficulties, strong as before, or even stronger. She was like another Antaeus who, when thrown, bounded from the ground with renewed strength.

This inexhaustible resilience was due to the one quality that the Romans had not lost, the will to rule. They spent their ill-gotten money basely, or at least foolishly, and they disobeyed every law that they made for themselves; but in the face of danger, whether from within or without, they always rallied in some inscrutible way, so as to remain masters both of themselves and of others. The less difficult mastery to retain was that over others, the provincials and the foreign nations. These were morally no better than the Romans; in some ways, far worse. Indeed, Rome's deterioration was largely due to contact with the decadent Hellenized world; and she had not yet allowed the bad influences to destroy her ability to make her commands effective. In her dealings with others, she resembled an unscrupulous but successful business man, doing much that was cruel and illegal, but always seeing to it that the business continued. The greater difficulty consisted in retaining her mastery over herself. There was enough strength left in the nation to accomplish this. There were unselfish lovers of Rome among the upper classes; and there must have been, though rarely visible to us, a large body of decent and strong men in the cities of Italy, the real Roman nation, from which the armies came, and men like Cicero. The government, however, was beyond redemption, and had to be overturned.

The revolution which changed Rome from a republic to a monarchy was not accomplished in a generation, nor was it due to the foresight or agitation of any individual or any class of citizens. Perhaps the change was too gradual and too aimless to be called a revolution. It may be said to have lasted from the attack leveled against the aristocracy by Tiberius Gracchus in 133 B.C. until the battle of Actium in 31 B.C., and was a period of constant unrest, of almost continuous law-breaking, and of frequent bloodshed. It was a Hundred Years' War with the characteristics of the French Revolution. There was no time for extended efforts to improve Rome; only temporary measures to meet pressing difficulties could be attempted. While perhaps no one, with the exception of Mark Antony toward the end of the period, strove consciously to make himself sole ruler, men of ambition got themselves into positions where they must secure supreme power in order to make themselves safe.

Cicero's whole life fell within the limits of this protracted anarchy, and was conditioned by it. Born in the year of Marius' second consulship, he was twenty-four years old when Sulla became dictator and twenty-seven when Sulla resigned, and he died twelve years before the battle of Actium. The constitution of Sulla had legalized and extended the power of the aristocrats. The goal of Cicero's ambition might, therefore, be a position of eminence like that of Lucius Crassus or the Scaevolas, but even if he could overcome the disadvantages inevitably connected with his equestrian birth, he could not hope to rise in Rome even under such comparatively peaceful conditions as had surrounded the early life of his great inspirers. The outlook was one of peril. Atticus left Rome in the year 86 B.C., or about that time, while Cinna was master, and did not return until twenty years later. But while Atticus was in Greece, evolving his philosophy of a meditative and safe abstention from politics, Cicero turned all his energies to the winning of public distinctions. The republic was tottering, but it had not yet fallen. Cicero could hope to gain glory from the grandeur of Rome as Themistocles had gained glory from the grandeur of Athens. Once, as Cicero tells us in his essay on Old Age,[13] a man from the little island of Seriphus insisted that Themistocles owed his great reputation to the fame of Athens and not to his own deserts. Themistocles admitted part of the charge. "I should not have been famous if I had been a Seriphian, but you would not have attained fame even if you had been an Athenian." Rome was like the Athens of old, and Cicero was a Roman.

---

[13] *De Sen.* 8.

CHAPTER V

IN THE COURTS

I

IMPORTANCE OF ORATORY

The means of entrance into public life, fortunately for Cicero, who never thought of becoming a soldier, was not military ability; and this in spite of the fact that the Romans lived by war. Nor was a soldier's reputation necessary for advancement to the highest honors. In the case of Marius, ability as a soldier had won for him the public support that put him into high office; he had begun life in the army and had come from it to public life. But Marius was an exception, favored by very unusual circumstances and equally unusual military ability. To many other men who sought high office, a good record in the army was an exceedingly strong recommendation, but they did not make their first appeal to the electors as soldiers. The only person who secured the consulship not only as a military leader but also without holding the other offices, was Pompey; and he did so by means of intimidation. He had made his start as a lieutenant of Sulla during the civil wars; his election to the consulship was revolutionary. Political life was civil; the means of success consisted presumably of the activities of a peaceful citizen.

To have slept in an aristocratic cradle, however, was far and away the most useful qualification for official honors; in practise, almost the only one; but Cicero's first bed had been less soft. He had no smoke-begrimed busts, as he calls them, of noble ancestors, which could be paraded through the streets; and he had not an inherited body of clients and friends, who would shout and vote for him as the flourishing scion of ancient worthies. Neither did he possess a large fortune, to be judiciously

expended among the proud sons of Romulus; if he had possessed
one, he would have used if for better purposes. Nor does he
seem to have busied himself as a political retainer, although
there must have been many little ways, scarcely to be more than
surmised by us, in which an ambitious Roman of non-aristocratic
birth and of no great wealth could make himself useful and
pleasing to the ordinary electors or to men of influence. Political
life was a busy, intriguing thing. Voters had to be persuaded;
bribery required men of caution, with a kind of thieves' honor;
there was need of shouting and enthusiasm; clubs and societies
of many complexions had to be won over; and country districts
had to be visited. Indeed, there were agents and organizers of
every conceivable sort, not to mention breeders of violence and
perpetrators of crime, when the occasion so required. The
account of electioneering by brother Quintus indicates this, as
do the letters of Cicero, which describe the political doings of
later years. As ambitious youths began to take part in the life
of the forum at the age of twenty, although they could not be
elected to the quaestorship until they were thirty, there was a
long period that could be devoted to these activities, if it was
not spent in the army. And it must have been used in this way,
for other men of humble birth besides Cicero attained official
honors, and these men must have gained personal influence in
some way. They were not all orators, like Cicero, or at least
their oratorical ability was of an indifferent kind. Quintus
climbed high on the official ladder, without any considerable
oratorical gift. He was probably assisted by his elder brother;
but every one did not have an elder brother.

It was through oratory that Cicero expected from the beginning to succeed. Ability to speak was the greatest weapon in
public life, dwarfing into insignificance every minor activity.
Everything in Rome was decided by debate in the senate and
in the forum. The gift of swaying the excitable populace was
the most valuable asset of a politician, even in times of threat-

ened violence. But the man who had not held office did not belong to the senate and he had no opportunity to address the people, for the *contiones* were presided over by the magistrates, and only magistrates or prominent men were invited to speak. In another sphere, however, the beginner could speak, often to a large audience. The courts, as has already been noted, were open to the public. In them a speaker, when pleading, could not only demonstrate his potential ability as a debater on public questions, but he could also entertain the speech-loving citizens, and even take a direct part in matters political, since the majority of the important cases were connected with politics. And if he published his orations, he could influence public opinion in many directions, or at least express it, and so wield the power of the modern newspaper man.

The aristocrats and the knights recognized the necessity of oratorical ability, for nearly all education at Rome—and, in general, only these two classes educated their children beyond the elements—had for its aim to make speakers. In the earlier stages, where literature was taught, the instruction was directed largely toward the formation of a good style, fit for oratory. The boys thereupon were taken in hand by the rhetoricians, the professional teachers of speaking. And even the philosophers, who completed the education if it were not already considered complete, gave much of their time to oratory, being, indeed, determined rivals of the rhetoricians and claiming to do the work better. Young men, scarcely more than boys, were taken to the forum, as was Cicero, and there they were constantly listening to speeches. When the young aristocrat was considered old enough to begin life seriously, at about twenty, he often made his bow before the people by prosecuting some prominent politician. The charge was usually maladministration in a province, bribery at an election, or some other law-breaking on a large scale. In such a case the ardent beginner, fresh from the declamations of his teachers, could talk about momentous questions in a fine moral way; and that seems to have been nearly all that was expected of him. One is almost tempted to imagine that such prosecutions were looked upon as the peculiar training ground for young talent. The young orator rarely secured a conviction; but he had an opportunity to show his mettle and to give an earnest of future usefulness in political strife.

Cicero had received as careful a training in oratory as any aristocrat; and he had added to this, perhaps in a higher measure than any one else, constant practise in declamation, both by himself and with his friends, as well as an almost daily attendance in the forum, where he observed the various speakers with a view to improving his own method. In the *Brutus,* written some seventeen years after his consulship, he has given a list of all those who spoke in the forum during the long years of the Marian and Sullan struggle, and has characterized these speakers. Nothing was neglected by him that could contribute to masterful speaking. One reason for this was his early realization, doubtless due in part to the influence of Crassus and his other aristocratic exemplars, that oratory would be his one means of success. He also had a shrinking from appearing in public with insufficient preparation. In later years he was not a comfortable opponent to the ambitious youths who gave loud voice to their ill-digested thoughts in the phraseology, as he puts it, that they had copied from their rhetorical textbooks. Speaking with the experience of over thirty years in the forum, he says that when he began to plead, he was fully prepared, both because of his age and because of his long studies, and had no need to learn his art by actual practise.

It was not due solely to forethought that his preparation had been long and many-sided. Conditions in Rome had made it impossible or distasteful for him to begin his oratorical career in his early youth. At times no courts were held; at other times public speaking centered entirely around violent party politics. Plutarch has it that he thought during this period of devoting

himself to less practical studies; and Cicero tells us himself that
in the year 88 B.C., after the tribune Sulpicius had been murdered and Sulla had taken Rome, he devoted himself entirely
to philosophy. These philosophical studies, his omnivorous reading, much of which was in history, and his interest in poetry, of
which he wrote a considerable amount in these years, all these
became of great assistance to him in speaking. Pleading in
court was not very different from public speaking; it was part
of the same uproarious life; and such speaking would gain by
anything that widened his vision, clarified his thoughts, and
increased his vocabulary. He could have begun pleading during
the years 86–84 B.C., when there was peace in Rome under Cinna,
so that the outward circumstances were not the only reason for
his complete preparation. It was complete, however, when Sulla
became dictator.

Cicero did not begin his pleading like a young aristocrat, by
prosecuting some prominent politician. A knight by birth, he
had no tradition to serve; and his main aristocratic supporters,
the four who have been mentioned, were dead. Crassus died
before Cicero had assumed the *toga virilis;* Scaevola the augur
seems to have died in 87 B.C., some three years after Cicero began
to frequent his house; Antonius and Scaevola the pontifex had
been murdered. Cicero was therefore alone. He had received
aristocratic inspiration and educational assistance, but he had
no powerful friend under whom he could enter public life. A
prosecution of the usual kind would at the least have been a
useless display; it might have attracted enmities, which he could
ill afford. Cicero, furthermore, was about twenty-five when he
took his first case. In view of the fact that these prosecutions·
were considered suitable training for the young, he had in this
an additional reason for avoiding them.

His first cases would necessarily be concerned with unimportant matters of business and with private disagreements,
which could attract no very great attention. By means of them,

however, Cicero built up a following among the people, bound
to him by actual services. That this was important can be seen
in the case of a man like Crassus, who later became one of the
triumvirs. Crassus was an aristocrat by birth, he had won a
great reputation as a general, and he had the means and the
willingness to bribe profusely, and yet he always held himself
ready to take the cases of insignificant clients. Cicero, indeed,
established for himself the reputation of being a protector of the
humble; he often claimed this position in his speeches; and he
no doubt found it serviceable.

With success, his horizon widened. During his second year
in the courts he pleaded in a criminal case of considerable importance and won it. After that he could have any case that
he chose to accept. His task was to make himself useful to the
greatest number of people, belonging as far as possible to the
various social classes, and to establish himself as one of the great
entertainers and potential political speakers in the forum. How
well he succeeded in this, may be gathered from the description
given by Quintus of his position during his consular candidacy. He then had the favor of all the farmers of the public
revenue, or publicans, of nearly the whole equestrian order,
of many individuals defended by him in court, of men of every
order, of some clubs or colleges, political or otherwise, of very
many young men bound to him by their love of oratory, and of
a large crowd of friends, who gathered about him daily in the
forum.

There was nothing original in Cicero's recognition of the
importance of oratory, though his devotion to it was probably
as unique as was his success. In one respect, however, he took
an attitude, which, if not new, he nevertheless maintained with
a persistence that was novel. Throughout his career, except in
one case, he pleaded only for the defense; and the exception, the
prosecution of Verres, was of such a nature that it proves the
rule. There was no public prosecutor in the city of Rome. The

tribunes of the plebs often undertook prosecutions, but, on the whole, the righting of wrong was left to individual citizens. But an individual will be readier to avenge an outrage on the public conscience if the perpetrator is his own enemy; and he may even profess to have discovered moral obliquity where none exists. Prosecution in large matters was recognized as a political weapon, provided a man had a good reason, and a personal one was sufficient. In much unimportant litigation, on the other hand, spite and personal enmities were apparently often at work; and even greed, for the state offered rewards for the detection of crime. Apparently prosecution in such cases was looked down upon, or at least raised the suspicion that an orator was actuated by improper motives. There seems, indeed, to have been a class of pettifoggers, of no political and very little social standing, who made almost a profession of minor prosecutions.

Cicero avoided both kinds of prosecution. He may thus have foregone some opportunities for personal influence and aggrandizement, but his decision was nevertheless wise. Defense was safer than prosecution, as he himself says; and it secured a more devoted following, for the person who had been protected would be more grateful than the man who had used Cicero as a means of attack on somebody else. Defense was also praiseworthy. At a time when personal enmities were violent and litigation was endless, it was undoubtedly a noble office to protect those who were in peril. In his treatise on Duty[1] he gives this as one of the most glorious services of oratory; and in his earliest extant speech[2] he attacks the prominent orator Hortensius for "using his great talents to injure men and not, as formerly, to save them."

---

[1] De Off. 2, 49–51.

[2] Pro Quinc. 33. It is interesting to find Polybius saying of the young Roman politicians of his time that "they could not win praise unless they brought harm to some one of the citizens, for this is the natural result of forensic activity" (Polyb. 32, 15).

II
Beginnings

Cicero began pleading in the courts after order had been restored with the establishment of Sulla's dictatorship. Probably his first case was tried in the year 81 B.C. Though he accepted clients throughout his public career, his legal activity, like the rest of his life, was sharply cut into two periods by the consulship. During the earlier period his chief aim was to gain personal influence for the sake of political advancement. Later he pleaded either from political necessity or from choice. Having attained the consulship, he would have been allowed by public opinion to retire from the courts, to a considerable extent at least; but he had established so large a reputation that it was difficult to withdraw. Many of the cases belonging to the later years were connected with politics, and were consequently necessary; others were private, but he took them, as he says himself, to preserve his influence by the same means by which he had gained it. His oratorical manner changed from one period to the other. After the consulship he possessed that typically Roman *auctoritas,* or personal influence due to public position, which was of all perhaps the most powerful argument in favor of a client. Before the year 63 B.C., on the other hand, he argued entirely from the merits of the case, as these were understood by the Romans. To Cicero himself, therefore, the early period was his time of pleading; in the later years the courts yielded to the forum. He has indicated this in the *Brutus* by limiting the account of his activity at the bar to the years before 63 B.C.

The cases of these years were very numerous and varied. Cicero was undoubtedly the busiest pleader in Rome, and published a larger number of orations than any one else.[3] Nevertheless, the extant speeches, complete or nearly complete, repre-

---

[3] *Or.* 108.

sent only eight cases. Several others are known by name, or
even from fragments and comments, but many of them have
been entirely forgotten. For instance, Cicero won the support
of all the farmers of public revenue, as Quintus phrases it, and
yet there is not a single case, with the possible exception of the
prosecution of Verres in 70 B.C., in which he can be said even
indirectly to have defended the interests of the equestrian order.
The range of his activity can, therefore, only be inferred from
the following that he won. His manner,[4] on the other hand, is
amply illustrated in the seven hundred pages of legal oratory
belonging to this period.

Cicero's beginnings, as has already been observed, were necessarily small. We know nothing about his first lawsuit. The
earliest extant speech, delivered in the year 81 B.C., is his defense
of Quinctius, *Pro P. Quinctio.* The case was trivial, and came
to Cicero only because the orator who had until then had charge
of it was absent from Rome. Cicero describes the occasion. The
famous actor Roscius, who had assisted Cicero in his oratorical
training, asked him to take the case; the defendant Quinctius
being the brother-in-law of Roscius. Cicero refused, on the
ground that the opposing lawyer was Hortensius, already a
leader of the bar. It would be as impudent for a beginner, said
he, to appear against Hortensius, as for an ordinary actor to
rival Roscius. When Roscius is on the stage, nobody else seems
worthy of attention. Roscius, in reply, gave several reasons
why Cicero should defend Quinctius, explaining finally that all
Cicero would have to prove was that no man can walk seven
hundred miles in two or three days. "You surely are not too
bashful to say that much, even against Hortensius?" asked
Roscius; and when Cicero admitted his possession of that amount
of temerity, Roscius made clear how the case hinged upon the
improbable walk.

---

[4] For analysis and criticism of Cicero's orations, see esp. Cucheval,
Cicéron orateur etc.

The matter was not quite so simple as that. Two praetors had already given decisions in the case adverse to Quinctius. An investigation of the whole situation, however, would be long and unprofitable, nor would it lead to any great certainty, for the points in dispute had been manipulated by various lawyers, and the speech, furthermore, has suffered in transmission. It seems more than likely, however, that Cicero managed his side of the case with skill and with a thorough grasp of the law.

On the face of it, justice should have been on the side of Quinctius. Four years before this trial he had inherited the property of his brother, who had been the partner of the present plaintiff, Naevius. Quinctius had attempted to dissolve the partnership which had thus devolved upon him, but Naevius so juggled matters that he now laid claim to Quinctius' property.

Naevius was a business man and had influence; Quinctius, unskilled in business, was without influence and already about sixty years old. This situation is seized upon by Cicero. Again and again he pits the old, friendless Quinctius against the rich and influential Naevius. And he does not spare the latter. Naevius was an auctioneer. Cicero sneers at the bawling profession, and, recalling Naevius' claim that he had shown consideration for the old Quinctius, he gives an impressive picture of the timidity and retiring disposition ordinarily found in people who manage public auctions; their modesty is like that of innocent young girls. It is therefore perfectly credible, suggests the sarcastic orator, that the vocal Naevius could not bring himself to wound even the ears of his old partner. And yet he is now trying to deprive him of his civic status!

As for poor Quinctius, he was a man of serious mind, taking no part in the gay life of the city. He had no wealth, and did not imagine that he was eloquent—as auctioneers might do. He lacked the finer graces, he did not saunter about the forum, he neither gave nor received invitations to fine dinners. But he was an honest man, fond of his wife and children, loyal to his friends, thrifty in the management of his property. And this poor old man, so unlike the brilliant, successful Naevius, had been driven from pillar to post; he had with tears entreated his assailant for mercy; and now, in his sixtieth year, too poor even to give his marriageable daughter a suitable dowry, he had been hailed to court, where an attempt was made to strip him of that reputation for honesty which he had maintained throughout his long life.

The peroration, only a part of which has just been suggested, is long and ecstatic. Cicero was young, enthusiastic, and impassionable; his twenty-five years may very possibly have looked upon the advanced age of Quinctius as something very piteous. But he might also have been vividly conscious of the rhetorical rules that counseled emotional perorations; there is a certain obviousness in the last chapters which can not be reproduced without quoting rather fully; the rhetorical machinery peeps through, as it were. Two pages from the end, Cicero says: "Now that I have given the peroration"—although he is still in the midst of it—"it seems to me that the very circumstances of the case and the magnitude of the threatening danger will force Quinctius to address you, O judge, and the men who sit with you in judgment, praying and entreating you by his old age and his desolate condition for this one service, that you obey the promptings of your kind hearts. Thus, since justice is on his side, his helplessness will more readily move you to pity than the resources of Naevius will tempt you to cruelty."

The juxtaposition of pity and cruelty—that is, anger toward the defendant, which would lead to cruelty—as well as other things in this passage, short as it is, recall the admonitions of the rhetorician. And yet, there is also underneath it the impressionable personality of the speaker, laboring toward expression. It is the first appearance, and in Cicero's first oration, of that element of pathos which was at all times one of his chief characteristics, contributing most powerfully to his immense success at the bar. A public expression of emotion, especially when prepared beforehand, as a lawyer's plea must be, is a mixture of sincerity and artistry, and in Rome this was especially likely to be the case because of the long rhetorical training of the orators. The listener, and even more, the reader, must give his sympathies free rein, allowing the orator, as he would allow a poet, to take him whither he wills. It is proper to forget, and Cicero's Roman audience was very ready to forget, that the quarrel between Quinctius and Naevius was merely one of business, after all—the inability of two partners to dissolve their partnership amicably.

We do not know whether Cicero won the case. His speech was undoubtedly well received, otherwise he would not have published it. But perhaps he had also another reason for publication. This was the first time that he had opposed Hortensius, and we know from later utterances that Cicero formed an early ambition to emulate him. Probably the great Hortensius was loftily unconscious of the rivalry, but to Cicero this first encounter was a real adventure. He hints at it in the brief dialogue with Roscius, and he takes care, there and elsewhere in the speech, to compliment his great opponent. But he is not entirely overawed. He criticises Hortensius for engaging in prosecution, and once he turns directly to him with the statement that he, like Hortensius, will distribute his argumentation under proper headings. "You always do this, for you have always the ability to do it; I shall do it in this case, for here I think I shall be able to do it"—and Cicero very likely held up his hand and counted off the points on his fingers, not altogether to the glory of the systematic Hortensius. But despite the contest with Hortensius, the case was unimportant, and is interesting to us mainly because it is the first.

In the following year, however, Cicero had a real opportunity. A certain old man, Roscius, had been murdered one evening on the streets of Rome as he was returning home from a dinner party. Though living in the capital, he was a citizen of Ameria, some fifty-six miles away, where he possessed considerable property. At Ameria lived his wife, his son—a man past forty, who managed the family estate—and numerous relatives. Among the latter were two nephews, with whom the murdered man had for a long time been on hostile terms. On the morning after the murder, news of it was brought to Ameria; not, however, to the widow or the son, nor to any of the friendly relatives, but to one of the nephews. The messenger, an intimate friend of his, had driven the fifty-six Roman miles—about fifty-two English miles—in ten hours, and at night. Four days later the murder was reported to Sulla's young Greek freedman and favorite, Chrysogonus, together with a word about the wealth left by the late Roscius. All this happened in the year 81 B.C. Though it was after the time allowed for posting names on the Sullan proscription lists, the name of Roscius was posted, which made his property forfeit to the state. It was thereupon sold at public auction for 2000 sesterces—somewhat less than one hundred dollars—though its value was estimated at three hundred times that amount. There were thirteen farms, of which one of the nephews took three, while the other, acting in the name of Chrysogonus, took the rest. Obviously the influential freedman had seen to an early auction, and had also done the bidding, in person or by proxy, inevitably without a rival.

But this was not all. The nephew of the ten farms carried things in a very high-handed manner. He ejected the son of the murdered man before the latter had completed arrangements for his father's funeral. He transferred to his own house, openly or secretly, as suited his convenience, every movable thing that took his fancy; the rest he gave away or sold. The treatment of the son caused such a scandal that the townsmen of Ameria sent a deputation of ten men to Sulla; but when these arrived in Sulla's camp, they were met by the plausible Chrysogonus, who urged them not to bother the great man with the matter, and promised to do anything about it that they wished. The ambassadors, persuaded that the dead Roscius' name would be taken from the proscription lists and his son restored to his property, returned home.

Restitution was delayed on one pretext or another, and traps were in the meantime set for the son. At last the latter's position became so dangerous that he fled to Rome, where he was received and protected by a woman of noble birth, an old friend of his father. When the destitute son had in this way escaped the danger of direct physical violence, he was suddenly accused of being his father's murderer.

The accuser was a certain Erucius, one of the orators who made a business of prosecutions. The trial attracted a large crowd, many of them able and famous orators, for the Roscii were connected with some of the most prominent aristocratic families in Rome. It was the first time a man had been tried for murder since the bloody days of the proscriptions, and it was felt that the jury would be likely to return a verdict of guilty, if only to check the prevalent lawlessness.

Before the proceedings, it was observed that Erucius, looking over the notable assembly, inquired of his friends whether this or that famous and influential speaker was going to argue for the defense, but none of the notabilities had avowed any such intention. Evidently they were held back by the universal recognition that Chrysogonus was behind the prosecution, desirous to get the son, Roscius, out of the way, so that his possession of the Roscian estate might never be called into question. Among the men present was also Cicero, now twenty-six years old and with one year of pleading to his credit, but Erucius did not take the trouble to ask questions about him; the young Arpinate had pleaded only in unimportant cases of a private character.

Relieved at having no opponent of consequence, Erucius launched jauntily into his speech for the prosecution. His case

was not a good one. Roscius, the accused, had lived all his life
in the country. He had none of the graces of city dwellers, but
also none of their vices. He had been in Ameria at the time of
the murder. Professional assassins were plentiful in Rome, but
Erucius could not produce, did not even try to produce, the
name of any one of these, or of anybody else, hired by Roscius to
commit the murder; he made no attempt to fix the deed on any
individual. His contention that Roscius the son was ultimately
responsible was founded on the fact that he had lived in the
country while his father stayed in Rome. If there had been the
proper relation between them, they would have lived together.
As the father had chosen not to have his son with him, they
must have been enemies. The father had had another son, who
had lived with him in Rome. When this son died, why did not
the father have his other son come to the city? The latter had
not been in Rome for years, and never for more than three days
at a time; he never received any invitations. Therefore the
father disliked this son, and the latter had caused the murder.

In spite of the weak argument, Erucius was completely at his
ease. He acted with the casualness of a man alone in his own
house. He sat down in the middle of his speech; he walked back
and forth; he stopped and summoned his slave for a silent con-
sultation as though he were giving orders for dinner. At last
he arrived somehow at his peroration, and then, certain of success,
he took his seat. His case was clear; there was no orator for the
defense.

Cicero arose. Erucius took a breath of relief;[5] he had been
correct in his surmise that nobody—that is, no one of consequence—would oppose him. He turned to his friends and whispered something humorous. Cicero mentioned the name of
Chrysogonus, and Erucius sat up to listen. Cicero mentioned
Chrysogonus a second time, and a third time; and presently
messengers were hurrying back and forth, no doubt, as Cicero

---

[5] These details come from the oration. See below, p. 95.

conjectures, to inform Chrysogonus that there was a man who dared to speak against him, that the trial was not being conducted as had been expected, that the sale of Roscius' property was revealed, that the conspiracy was brought to light, that no thought was given to Chrysogonus' great power, that the jurors were listening attentively, and that the people seemed to think that a great crime had been committed.

There was no difficulty in disproving the charge against Roscius; a mere relation of the facts would accomplish this. To strengthen his position, Cicero amplifies, as the rhetoricians would say, on the high state of morality prevailing in the country as opposed to the city, since Roscius lived in the country, whence Cicero also had come; and he indulges in commonplaces about parricide. A man like Roscius could not conceivably be guilty of such a crime. Cicero also hints that it was a compliment to Roscius to be left in the country as manager, and this may be so; but the truth is obviously that the elder Roscius liked dinner parties and the son did not, which could not have increased their mutual admiration. No enmity between them, however, had been demonstrated. Erucius had asserted that the father intended to disinherit his joyless son, but of that there was no proof. The questionable nephews, on the other hand—and Cicero shows that their reputations might easily have been better—had gained immensely by the murder, so that if any one was interested in finding the assassin, he would know where to look.

But Cicero's main task was not to prove Roscius innocent. He had to persuade the jury that it would be safe to acquit the defendant, and that it was their duty to do it. Chrysogonus was behind the prosecution; behind Chrysogonus was Sulla, who was all-powerful, and not gentle. The wounds which he had inflicted on the state were still bleeding. It was not surprising that men of prominence had refused to plead, says Cicero; and he explains his own willingness to do so by calling attention to his humble position in the world. The other men were eloquent and

courageous, but their eminence would have endowed their words
with a significance beyond the trial. On the other hand, Cicero
had no eloquence; he was young and obscure. He could safely
say anything he pleased, and nobody would pay much attention
to it. And he had been urged to plead by men whose requests
he could not ignore.

Having cleared his way, he attacks the principal difficulty
by separating Chrysogonus from Sulla, insisting that the latter
knows nothing, and could not be expected to know anything,
about the matter. Sulla takes thought for the past and for the
future, for peace and for war; all look to him, and he rules
everything. He is so busy that he scarcely has time to breathe
—Cicero's own expression, despite its modernness. But there
are many men watching Sulla, ready to go about their evil deeds
as soon as he looks away. He is truly fortunate, *felix*, but no
one can be so fortunate as not to have among his numerous slaves
at least one who is a rascal. Cicero, further, professes approval
of Sulla's rule, on the ground that it had led to aristocratic
supremacy, and he even claims that he himself, though not with
arms, had in his small way assisted the Sullan aristocrats in their
struggle with the plebeians.

These sentiments about Sulla are of course due to the
occasion. Cicero hated the dictator, just as he hated Cinna and
the Marians, who had murdered his aristocratic supporters. Nor
could his partisanship in the factional struggle have gone much
beyond a silent prayer; and the Romans—least of all, a man
like Cicero—did not have recourse to silent praying. It almost
seems as if this assertion about giving aid to the Sullans is
introduced in sarcastic bravado. Sarcasm seems also to be grin-
ning at the all-powerful ruler when Cicero reverts to his statement about Sulla's inability to know everything, and compares
him to Jupiter Optimus Maximus. The latter rules the world
by his nod. He gives us all our blessings; from him come the
light of day and the air we breathe. But Jupiter has too much

to look after. Harm is frequently done to men, to cities, to the crops, by violent storms, by excessive heat or cold. This is not a part of Jupiter's intention; it is due to an unavoidable inadvertence. So it is with Sulla. It is not strange that he is unable to watch everything and everybody, unless it be strange that human power fails to accomplish that which is beyond the power of the gods.

The sarcasm may have existed only in Cicero's soul. Sulla was an intensely superstitious man, and was endowed with a firm belief in his divinely directed career; and the Romans themselves were not strangers to deifications and had none too high an opinion of their fallible gods. In any case, after Cicero had proclaimed that a crime had been committed through governmental influence, and that Sulla could have known nothing about it, it did not seem likely that Sulla would assert omniscience in order to exculpate his guilty freedman. Chrysogonus was left alone, facing the senatorial jurymen and the Roman audience, who could have nothing but the strongest aversion for the subtle young Greek. Favorites like him were a constant and irritating reminder to the Romans that Sulla was king and they were his subjects. Chrysogonus is the forerunner of the Greek freedmen who wielded power during the Roman empire; versatile, unprincipled, and thoroughly hated. The more contemptuous and scathing Cicero could make his attack, the more likely were the jurors to free Roscius. And Cicero, who no doubt shared the general feeling, was perfectly capable of giving it suitable expression.

He refers to Chrysogonus' residence on the Palatine, where the nobility lived, and to his villas and farms, all excellent, and situated near the city so that they may give him the needed mental relaxation. His house in Rome is filled with works of art, some of which are alone worth the price of a farm. He has silverware, tapestries, paintings, statues, and things of marble. His house is crammed with costly possessions, stolen from great families during the present reign of terror. His slaves are innumerable; not only ordinary ones, like cooks, bakers, and litter-bearers, but also men of parts, of musical training; the neighborhood resounds both night and day with their voices, their stringed instruments, and their flutes. The daily expense of all this is incredible. The house of Chrysogonus, with its nightly banquets, is not properly a house; it is a laboratory of vice and a caravansary for evil. And when the young beau himself, frizzled and pomaded, flits through the forum, he is accompanied by a large retinue of Roman citizens. He looks down on everybody, he thinks no one else has elegance and refinement, he considers himself alone a man of wealth and power.

And this charming gentleman of golden name—Chrysogonus is derived from the Greek word for gold—now comes before the jury, says Cicero, with a very unimportant little request, that they convict Roscius. While the latter is alive, Chrysogonus is troubled and does not sleep of nights. Let the jurymen free him from this annoyance; he can then fully enjoy his ill-gotten gains. But, Cicero concludes, let the jurymen remember that the granting of Chrysogonus' request, small as it may seem to him, is fraught with the gravest danger; it will lead to slavery and oppression of the worst kind.

Cicero won the case. The result of the trial may not indicate a very material victory, for, though the life of Roscius was saved, his property remained in the hands of Chrysogonus and the nephews, so far as we know, and no attempt was made to punish the assassins or to clear the reputation of the elder Roscius by removing his name from the proscription list. But in the light of contemporary conditions the victory was considerable. Cicero had won it by his skill, and, above all, by his courage. After that, as he wrote in the *Brutus* some thirty-five years later, he was chosen to plead in the most important cases. He had become one of the leading Roman orators, and he was only twenty-six years old.

III

Publishing

In addition to pleading, Cicero published the more important of his orations, and, to judge from those extant, some that were not important. The practise seems to have been rather common, though not universal. Some orators found the editing of speeches for publication too irksome; others, who spoke better than they wrote, preferred not to diminish their oratorical glory by inferior writing; and still others were averse to recording their opinions, lest these be quoted against them in case they changed their minds.[6] M. Antonius, one of Cicero's greatest models, had refrained from publication; Crassus, perhaps the greatest of them, had published speeches in his youth. Cicero, according to his own statement, published more orations than any one else. Having no powerful supporters, he needed to avail himself of every means for success; and he had the ability to write as well as he spoke.

The reasons for publication were manifold. The professional value of it, which was the most important, has already been indicated;[7] the published speeches, like modern newspaper reports, advertised the orator and give publicity to the case.[8] The demand for such reports was apparently considerable. Speeches connected with noteworthy cases were occasionally taken down in shorthand by persons in the audience, and then circulated, but such publication could rarely satisfy the orator. Both the rhetorical form and the content might suffer. To obviate this, the speaker did his own publishing; and there was no convention that caused this to seem egotistical.

The published speeches had also another use; they served as patterns for the young. Cicero himself, having studied exclu-

---

[6] *Brut.* 91–93; *Pro Clu.* 140.

[7] See above, pp. 3–4.

[8] Cicero seems to have published the speech in defense of King Deiotarus to please the old king (*Fam.* 9, 12, 2).

sively under Greek rhetoricians, had been trained on Greek oratory, but he had also read Roman speeches privately, some of which were quite neglected by his less ambitious contemporaries. His own speeches, in their turn, were actually used in the rhetorical schools. It was considered creditable for an orator in this way to assist his younger contemporaries. He was doing practical service. Indeed, he might even write a little about oratory in a technical way, as M. Antonius had done and as Cicero later did, without derogating from his position, however eminent this might be. It is obvious that Cicero did not publish his earlier speeches for this didactic purpose, but as his fame increased, this would become the case. Probably he had not pleaded many years before the young men who came to listen wished also to read and learn what he wrote.

In a certain sense, finally, the publication of orations might be looked upon as a literary activity. The Greek orators had published voluminously. In the field of oratory, therefore, the Romans could rival the Greeks without departing from their own practical concerns. This was a motive with Cicero. He thinks of his orations as literary monuments, as for instance when he decides to publish the orations of his consulship together, in a sort of series; he compares the oratory of Rome with that of Greece, to the advantage of Rome, and such comparison was necessarily based mainly on published orations; and he actually called his speeches connected with his struggle against Antony, *Philippics*, in this way setting them side by side with those of Demosthenes directed against Philip of Macedon. The great attention paid to the rhetorical form of published orations also made them very much like literature; they gave pleasure to older readers, of whom Cicero had many, for these had been trained in oratory. It would nevertheless be a mistake, it seems, to consider oratorical publication as primarily literary. It involved art, but it was not art for art's sake. That had not yet come into being among the Romans of position. They wrote poems, descriptive and otherwise, and also other things, for their cultured friends, to show that they had taste and culture; but such writing was an avocation. The Roman of Roman ambitions would have scorned to give his best powers to writing for the amusement, or even for the instruction, of any public, small or great; and he had not yet arrived at the psychological complexity which prompts vain self-revelations. In publishing his orations, nevertheless, Cicero was unconsciously fitting himself for his later authorship in less practical fields.

All these motives, working together, led to the publication of speeches that had never been delivered. Five of Cicero's orations against Verres are of this kind. The defendant threw up the case before the proceedings had been concluded, whereupon Cicero, both for glory's sake and no doubt for professional and political reasons, worked his material into five long orations. These have in every way the form of his other speeches; there is no suggestion that they had not been delivered. The exordia and perorations are managed with the same care that was observed in the forum. Verres is pictured as present in the court; even his impudence in appearing there is attacked, and the effect on him of Cicero's words is described. And yet every Roman reader knew that the situation depicted was the result of Cicero's imagination and literary skill.

There was only one further convention possible, and the Roman's adopted it: to publish political pamphlets in the form of speeches. Cicero's so-called *Second Philippic*, perhaps his best ''oration,'' is of this character. The Romans were so fond of the oratorical form, with its aesthetic appeal and its suggestion of public life, that such a fictitious speech must have seemed perfectly natural to them.

This cheerful convention of throwing political pamphlets into the form of speeches, with a complete reproduction of the rhetorical manner characteristic of actual speaking, will naturally raise the supposition that the published form of a real oration was a thing by itself, possibly differing widely from its professed original.[9] Under the assumption that Cicero, at the time of publication, introduced changes at will, his occasional defiance of men in power, his praise and attack, his political forecasts, all his important expressions of opinion, can be relegated to a later period, and so lose their force. As a revelation of Cicero's attitude toward men and things, the orations will thus become very untrustworthy. And it will also be impossible to ascertain the manner in which he spoke. The rhythm, the imagery, the verbal details of style, and the flights of eloquence may be later additions. The question of the relation between the spoken and the published oration is not a moral one; there is no reason for thinking that Cicero's changes, whether great or small, were different from those of other orators. It is, however, important; and some attempt should be made to answer it. Unfortunately, no answer can be given that is absolutely certain or absolutely complete.

Two orations of Cicero are particularly noteworthy. On his return from exile, in the year 57 B.C., he addressed the senate. The occasion was of extreme importance; his speech was practically a political manifesto. He therefore not only wrote it beforehand, but resorted to the very unusual practise of reading from his manuscript, whereupon he published the speech, probably at once. He did all this in order that he might later refer to particular statements in the oration without any one raising a question as to whether the published version recorded exactly what he had said. This speech was one of the very few that could be completely prepared beforehand. The visible precautions with which Cicero, even in the case of such a speech as this, secured literal accuracy in the published copy and guarded against suspicions to the contrary, are in themselves a sufficient indication that the Romans did not expect complete identity between the spoken and the written word even in the rare cases where this was easily attainable.

---

[9] Laurand, *Études etc.*, pp. 1–17.

This attitude is also illustrated in the history of the speech delivered in defense of Milo, in the year 52 B.C. During the trial Cicero was interrupted and intimidated by the gangs of Clodius, and was unable to speak as he had wished. His words were taken down in shorthand by one of the auditors, and put into circulation. Cicero also issued the customary edited version. There were thus two speeches professing to represent the same oratorical effort; and the Romans read both without moral comments on the orator. Their comments, however, do indicate that the differences between the two versions were considerable, and had to do mainly, if not entirely, with the form. Cicero's broken delivery, as reproduced in the reported version, neither satisfied his own aesthetic sense and that of his readers, nor, perhaps, did it give proper force to the arguments he had used. The case, however, was highly exceptional, for the trial had been turbulent even beyond the usual wide limits. This, moreover, is the only recorded instance of two such versions. They existed side by side for a very long time; but, and this is worth noting, the version finally preserved is the one edited by Cicero.

The published version was thus ordinarily a thing by itself. From Cicero's letters, which belong to the later period of his life, we learn that he took great care with these versions; and this must have been the case in the early part of his career as well. After writing a speech, he made all the minor corrections of detail and little improvements in style that a modern speaker would make before publication; he even submitted his draft to his friends for criticism. The exact nature of several of these alterations are known; they aim at making the published version neither more nor less like the spoken original, but are made as if on an entirely new work. It has furthermore been shown, by careful analysis of the speeches,[10] that they contain parallel passages. Evidently Cicero experimented to find the most suitable expression, just as he did, or any other careful writer might

---

[10] Norden, *Aus Ciceros Werkstatt*, pp. 6–12.

do, in other literary works; and these experiments found their
way into the published form. Not all the extant speeches would
have the same finish; neither, of course, had all the delivered
speeches. But it is not certain that the roughnesses discernible
in the published versions correspond to those heard by his
listeners in the forum. Cicero was often pressed for time. The
weaknesses of the published versions may be due to rapid composition quite as much as to an unpolished original. Speaking
extemporaneously, he might have attained a very high degree
of stylistic finish; writing the oration later, in haste, he may
have been quite unable to reproduce it. The conclusion of the
whole matter seems to be, provided the oration was not prepared entirely beforehand, which could not happen often, that
the spoken and the written speech were two different things;
and yet there are many indications that it was possible for Cicero
to make the printed version a close reproduction of the speech
he had delivered, and that he actually did this.

The manner in which he prepared himself before speaking
enabled him later to reproduce his spoken words with considerable accuracy. Always an ardent believer in writing as an aid
to speaking, Cicero seems to have composed and memorized any
passages that he would be likely to use. Since much of an
oration, even in an intricate matter of law, consisted of generalizations and emotional appeals, much could be foreseen.[11]
Patriotism, the sanctity of human life, personal attack and
defense, these and many other matters could be written beforehand; Cicero might not know exactly in what part of his speech
they could best be introduced; but, having them ready, he would
use them, with slight alterations, as occasion offered. The character of the exordium and the peroration could also be foreseen
with considerable detail. As a result, much of a speech even
in court, and still more in the forum and the senate, was com-

---

[11] Norden, *op. cit.*, pp. 12–32.

posed beforehand; and Cicero could use all this in the published oration. As for the rest of the speech, Cicero made all sorts of notes before the trial, and doubtless during it. Tiro published at least thirteen books of them. These notes, any assistance he cared to make use of from the stenographic reports, and his own very excellent memory could give him at least the thought of the passages not prepared beforehand; and probably not a little of their style.

The degree of exactness attainable depended very much on the time at which Cicero published his speeches. It has been thought, but never proved, that his speeches against Catiline were written three years after their delivery; the question can not be settled from the available evidence. Some of the other speeches, on the other hand, are known to have been in circulation within a short time after they were spoken, so that Cicero must have prepared them for publication almost at once. In general, it is probably beyond doubt that the speeches were published as soon as possible after they had been delivered; only the circumstances that produced the speech would make publication worth while. An oration published long after its delivery would have only a historical or literary interest; to many Roman readers it would be as dull as a campaign speech after the election.

Prompt publication would also necessitate the highest degree of exactness attainable. Many of the readers, perhaps the majority of them, had heard the speech; and the political circumstances at the time of publication and delivery would be the same. The orator would therefore find it neither possible nor desirable to make important changes. The extant orations bear this out. They have many characteristics that must have come from the spoken originals. Only one of them, perhaps the most significant, need be mentioned: the difference between orations on the same subject addressed to the senate and to the people respectively. Cicero said to either audience things that he could not very well say to the other, and it might be expected that the published versions, accessible to all, would not show these differences; but such is nevertheless the case. As this extends even to very small matters of expression, it becomes an argument not only in reference to the content but also to the style. It may, therefore, be assumed that the extant orations reproduced the opinions Cicero had actually uttered, alterations being rare and unimportant, and that even the style preserved its distinctive qualities.

Something more may be said as to the question of style. Some whole speeches, and at least long passages in most of the others, were extemporized. Cicero's own notes and memory, even when aided by promptness of publication and stenographic reports, could scarcely have availed to procure an absolute reproduction of his extemporization, and it is clear that his editing aimed at good writing and not at reproducing his delivered speech. And yet the result must have contained few deviations. For this belief there are many reasons. The style of any extant oration is on the whole uniform, so that the characteristics of rhythm and expression found in the portions prepared beforehand are also found in the rest of the speech. The written orations were used by students in oratory. Rhetorical science, which undertook to teach actual oratory, gave rules that are observed by the published orations. Cicero was in later life criticised by rival orators for some of the very stylistic qualities that are found in these speeches, even as to matters of rhythm, and it is inconceivable that the critics were attacking his publication and not his actual performance. But it is not necessary to give further reasons for thinking that the style of the orations represents the actual delivery; the Romans could scarcely have arrived at a convention which sanctioned in published speeches a style not actually found in the forum.

And it is very likely, finally, that Cicero had the ability to extemporize on the same high level as he wrote. He, like other Roman orators, had received much training in extemporaneous speaking—speaking suddenly, as he calls it—and he declaimed constantly, long after he had made his mark in the forum. In discussing writing as a means of oratorical training, he makes a remark that perhaps throws some light on the matter. He says[12] that if the orator has prepared himself by writing, he will go on in the same manner when he has to depart from that which he has prepared; he will go on from his own impetus, as a boat does after the rowers stop rowing. His own extemporizations, therefore, were probably finished enough in expression to leave upon the audience the same impression that was later received from the published form, which he had carefully revised.

Certain obvious changes, however, were made, with a view to making the speeches interesting and self-explanatory. The published form was the shorter, as is expressly stated by Cicero in several places, especially in the *Brutus*. This was accomplished by the abbreviation or omission of lengthy arguments. The readers apparently cared less for a complete statement of the proofs, provided these were indicated, than for the oratorical form, as, indeed, the judges often did. Cicero mentions it as extraordinary that an orator once published a verbatim report of a speech; doubtless referring to a failure to make these omissions. In the speeches of Cicero there are frequent headings to indicate what has thus been omitted.

The orator also made certain additions. He introduced descriptions of his opponent's behavior, such as the very detailed account of Erucius in the speech for Roscius, and references to the number and the character of the audience, and to their expressions of approval or disapproval. Bits of repartee are also found in Cicero's speeches, which very likely had not been a part of his set plea, but of his cross-examination of witnesses, for which he was famous. One of his orations, *In Vatinium*, is entirely directed against a witness, and was probably based on an altercation between Vatinius and Cicero himself. It is also possible, though by no means certain, that two of his Catilinarian

---

[12] *De Or.* 1, 152–153.

speeches, the first and the fourth, contain what he said both when laying the subject of debate before the senate and when he later took part in the discussion. But all these additions and alterations were woven so skillfully into the texture of the published oration that it is rarely possible to say with much confidence that any particular passage was not a part of the set speech; the detailed character and the large number of such passages are the main reasons for supposing that they were introduced later. The reader's impression is that the orator intended not only to reproduce his actual speech, omitting dull portions, but also to include anything else of interest that he uttered during the proceedings, as well as to give at least a hint of the proceedings themselves. The Roman, listening at his ease to a trained slave reading from the manuscript, during dinner, perhaps, would in this way experience anew the pleasures of the forum; the little volume performed the office both of literature and of a newspaper.

IV

VACATION

Cicero's frequent pleading in the courts, the labor of publishing, and his constant study and oratorical practise were gradually enfeebling his health.[13] For a year after his victory over Chrysogonus he pleaded in various cases, none of which are represented by extant orations, and then he found it necessary to take a vacation. He had had two unusually successful years in the courts, and was very unwilling to go away. Having begun his career late, five years or more later than was customary, he had no time to lose. But his friends and his physicians, as he wrote more than thirty years afterward, in the *Brutus*, even feared for his life, and insisted that he take a rest. Cicero, yielding to them, found some consolation in the thought that a

---

13 For this section, see particularly *Brut.* 301–324.

prolonged stay in Greece would not only restore him to health but might also improve his way of speaking, for he would of course study oratory and practise declamation under the famous Greek rhetoricians. A vacation without work would have seemed inconceivable to him. And he had never visited Greece, although his whole intellectual life, like that of other Romans, had been derived very largely from Greek books and Greek teachers.

Cicero was not robust in his youth, as we learn from Plutarch, who no doubt relied directly or indirectly on Tiro's biography. His inheritance from his father was not good. Cicero's digestion troubled him; he had to be careful about his food, and rarely had anything to eat before the day's work was done. By means of regular walks, however, and rubbings, as Plutarch calls them, he not only kept out of sickness, but even hardened himself to endure every kind of exertion. He was not an invalid, and we are not to think of him as anxiously tinkering with his health; he was too normal a person for that. His correspondence rarely refers to his physical condition. It indicates that he had a regular time for walks, though it is impossible to imagine Cicero as a devoted pedestrian. In some letters he excuses himself from one thing or another by pleading indisposition; and at times during the later part of his life he was ill, once from overeating at a vegetarian dinner. He was a temperate man. If his attitude can be inferred from his occasional references in his philosophical works and in his letters,[14] he cared but little for food and drink, preferring good conversation. Apparently his unceasing mental activity, aided by common sense, overcame any inherited weakness with which he was affected. He needed little sleep, often writing at night; when past sixty, at a time when there was little to do in the forum, he stopped working at night, and even began to take naps at noon. Much study had weakened his eyes; they were sometimes inflamed, and troubled him so that he had to dictate

[14] See below, p. 615, note 13; p. 664, note 36.

his letters. But we have it on the authority of the acrimonious Asinius Pollio,[15] that both nature and good fortune had favored Cicero; even in old age—after sixty, perhaps, for he died at sixty-three—he was handsome[16] and enjoyed excellent health.

Before leaving Rome, he was very lean and frail, with a long, thin neck. He was nervous and excitable, shouting his speeches in a high monotone and making violent gestures. He was away for two years, 79–77 B.C. When he returned, he was a changed man. He had studied with several rhetoricians; chief among them Molo, who had previously given him instruction in Rome. Now Molo was at Rhodes. He exerted himself particularly in restraining Cicero's youthful exuberance; with the result that Cicero learned to manage his voice; his oratory, in his own phrase, no longer effervesced; he became strong, and his frame filled out.

Cicero speaks of the instruction under Molo as marking an epoch in his development. Previously his oratory had been like an untamed river overflowing its banks; Molo checked it, or rather, he endeavored to check it. But it was not to be done. Fullness of expression and an impassioned rush had been, and remained, one of Cicero's characteristics as a successful orator. Readers of Cicero can discover a difference in style between the two earlier and his later orations only by a minute attention to rhetorical figures or other matters of detail.[17] As Cicero continued speaking or writing, he changed as other men change, but his style remained essentially the same.

Of course, he became a more finished artist. The speech in defense of Quinctius seems to contain traces of a somewhat mechanical obedience to rhetorical rules, as has been pointed out. And Cicero himself quotes[18] a high-flown commonplace about the

---

[15] Sen. *Suas.* 6, 24.

[16] For ancient busts of Cicero, Bernouilli, pp. 132 ff.

[17] The development of Cicero's style is discussed in Norden, *Die Antike Kunstprosa*, 1, 225–234.

[18] *Or.* 107.

punishments of parricides from the speech for Roscius. "What is so common," Cicero had declaimed, "as breath to the living, the earth to the dead, the sea to those who are on the waves, and the shore to the shipwrecked? They"—parricides—"live while they can, but in such a way that they do not breathe the air of heaven; they die, but so that the earth does not touch their bones; they are tossed about by the waves, but so that these do not wash them; they are finally thrown forth, but so that in death they find no rest even on the rocks." "And the rest of it," he adds, for there was more. He says, truly enough, that the passage is youthfully innocent of experience, but he does not seem altogether displeased with it. He recalls the applause it evoked, hints that it contained promises for the future, and immediately after the quotation, he refers to a passage from a speech written fourteen years later, which is very much of the same kind. And similar passages could be quoted from nearly every one of his speeches, whenever written. The speech for Roscius, furthermore, as Cicero goes on to say, was not all in one strain any more than were his later speeches; it showed the variety of tone that he later claimed as his peculiar merit.

Passion had been rather lacking in the orators who pleaded during the early part of Cicero's career.[19] Cicero, seeing the value of passion, made much use of it from the very beginning; he took incredible pains with its management, to use his own words, and he never deserted it. He was in this guided by a true appreciation of the character of Roman jurors. The passage in the speech for Roscius has more fire than real meaning, and it does not add much to the argument, for nobody needed reminders of the heinousness of parricide in order to look upon Roscius as innocent; in later orations, Cicero's passionate outbursts have more intrinsic meaning and they are used as real arguments. It is probably this increased adroitness in managing a weapon that might easily turn to bombast which Cicero

---

[19] *Or.* 106. On Roman oratory before Cicero, Cucheval, *Histoire etc.*

wishes to attribute to the teaching of Molo. The latter had opened his eyes, and he was thereafter a more conscious artist. It is also to be remembered that a change of style will seem far greater to the writer himself than to the listener or the reader; the author's consciousness that he is working with a new view of his art will not always lead to easily discernible changes in his writing.

It is very likely that the main improvement due to Molo was in Cicero's manner of delivery. It became better adapted to the varying moods of his words. Cicero looked upon a proper delivery as the most important part of oratory. He is said by Plutarch to have received instruction from Aesop and Roscius, the two most eminent actors of the time. He took considerable pains with his voice. He praises the grace of Crassus' delivery with so much ardor that he must himself have had a reputation for the same quality. The change from the monotonous, high-pitched enunciation and the violent gestures of his early years probably transformed his oratory. Plutarch has it that Cicero's delivery contributed not a little to render his eloquence persuasive, and remarks that Cicero was in the habit of ridiculing loud speakers, saying that they shouted because they could not speak, just as lame men go on horseback because they can not walk. Cicero seems to have had an expressive face, which reflected his thoughts faithfully. His voice, his face, and his gestures doubtless were a mirror of the style of his orations; and this is conversational, sarcastic, witty, declamatory, soothing, irate, or trembling with lofty passion.

Cicero came to have a great power over his audiences, swaying them in one direction or another according to his wish, playing upon them as a great musician plays on an organ; and he could do this because, whenever speaking, he had himself the feelings with which he wished to inspire others. It is not surprising, he says in this connection,[20] that an orator feels anger,

---

20 *De Or.* 2, 190 ff.; *Or.* 132.

sorrow, or any other emotion natural to his subject even though he be speaking in behalf of another person; he need not resort to trickery and feigning; his own words, though addressed to others, move the speaker himself; he is stirred both by thoughts about his own success and by the eventual risk to his client. Actors often feel the emotions which they are expressing, and yet their business is with something unreal and imagined. Poets can not write unless they are moved by a divine frenzy. It is likewise with orators.

In a passage of the *Tusculan Disputations*[21] Cicero seems to contradict this opinion. Orators should neither feel nor simulate anger, he says; will they write out their orations, after the trial is finished, under the impulse of anger? Is Aesop angry on the stage, or Accius when he writes his tragedies? Emotions are well enough for those who lack reason, but not for the wise. And Cicero himself utters these words in the dialogue. But he is speaking in a philosophical sense; Pickwickian, it might be called. The wise man referred to is that Stoic paragon, studiously apathetic, who never existed in the body. It may be that the depths below the depths in an orator's or actor's soul are not stirred; his attitude, as he confronts the great verities, may be Olympian; but Cicero had nothing of that when he was pleading. In the *De Divinatione*,[22] to quote a single passage, Quintus is allowed to say that both Cicero and Aesop, the actor, who had given him lessons in delivery, were often so excited as to seem quite beside themselves; and as for Aesop, it is related that once, while taking the part of King Thyestes, he struck a slave so hard with his sceptre that the blow proved fatal; realism could scarcely go farther. The passages previously referred to about these sympathetic emotions, furthermore, come from his rhetorical works, in which he gives his own opinions and not those of Greek writers.

---

[21] *Tusc.* 4, 55.
[22] *De Divin.* 1, 80.

But Cicero, according to his own repeated confession, did not slip at once into this excited state; he was always embarrassed when he began to speak; seized with a great fear, as he expresses it.[23] This embarrassment, which followed him through life, throws perhaps the strongest light on his manner of delivery. In spite of his success, he never became the pompous popular favorite that thinks it necessary only to open his mouth in order that people shall listen with all their ears; nor did he acquire an inartistic uniformity of manner which could be used at all times because it had once proved successful. Each occasion for speaking presented to Cicero a new problem; he was always apprehensive that he might not do justice to his subject.

V

MANNER OF PLEADING

Cicero's manner of pleading has perhaps been sufficiently indicated already, and yet something should be added. He has been accused of praising himself, of declaiming, and of talking beside the point—serious charges, indeed, were it not for the fact that he won his cases. The critics have forgotten that they were not criticising an aesthetic performance, which may be bad art, though popular, but a practical profession, the only test of which is practical success. And Cicero had success; greater than that of any other pleader in Rome. It is not necessary to defend him; but it may be worth while to show briefly how he pleaded very much like other lawyers, differing from them only in degree. His weapons were like theirs, but sharper and wielded with more skill.

The difference between him and his colleagues, too tame a term for Roman pleaders, has been stated by Cicero himself in the *Brutus*.[24] He has been giving a brief account of his rhetorical

---

23 Examples are found in *In Caec.* 41–42, *Pro Clu.* 51, *Pro Rege Deiot.* 1.
24 *Brut.* 322.

studies and of his professional career, and then, coming to the time of his consulship, he says that he had earned this by his constant care and industry in pleading and by the fact that men were attracted by his new style of oratory. It seemed, he continues by way of explanation, that, except for Cicero himself, no orator had more than an ordinary acquaintance with literature, which is the very fountain-head of perfect eloquence; that no one devoted himself to philosophy, the mother of good deeds and good speaking; that no one had acquired a knowledge of civil law, which is an essential to a pleader in private cases, giving him the necessary grasp of his subject; and that no one knew Roman history, from which, at need, most reliable witnesses may be raised, as it were, from the very dead. Nor, to take up more personal characteristics, did there seem to be any one who could entangle his opponent in a mesh of terse and exact reasoning, and then relieve the strain on the jurors' attention by lapsing into fun and laughter; no one who could rise from the narrow bounds of the immediate subject in hand to a larger vision; in other words, no one who knew the full value of generalization; no one who gave pleasure by timely digression, who stirred the judge to exceeding wrath against the other side, who could draw tears from his audience, or who attained the one great aim of all pleading, to force the judge into agreement with the arguments set forth.

Cicero did not intend to claim that he was the sole possessor of each one of the qualities mentioned. His characterizations of other orators, in the earlier parts of the book, contain every single characteristic here claimed for himself, often assigned to them in a very high degree; and Cicero furthermore qualifies his whole statement by representing it as the popular opinion— *videretur*. His intention was to point out the things which, as the source of his success, seemed worthy to be striven for.

It is not possible to test Cicero's statement by actual comparison, for the orations of every other orator have been lost.

The rhetorical declamations of later times as well as the speeches in Roman historians, written by the latter in accordance with definite literary conventions, would not be useful in this connection. His claim to the creation of a new style must therefore be taken on faith, externally supported only by his phenomenal success. It is possible, however, to discover that his manner was of the same kind as that of the other pleaders. The rhetorical declamations and the rules of rhetoric point to this; so also do the speeches in Roman histories, the indications in Cicero's own orations of the arguments used by his opponents—and these indications are very numerous—and, above all, the reports of many famous cases that have come down to us.

These reports contain perhaps the most instructive as well as the most interesting evidence; they read like accounts of Cicero's own cases. One of the trials most fully described is that of Norbanus, which took place in the year 95 B.C., when Cicero was eleven years old. During the war with the Cimbri a proconsul, Caepio, had by his insubordination brought a serious defeat upon the Romans. On returning to Rome, he was deprived of his proconsulship, expelled from the senate, and, finally, Norbanus and another tribune of the people proposed a special commission to inquire into his behavior in Gaul. Caepio was condemned to death, but the intervention of another tribune succeeded in commuting the sentence to exile. In connection with the struggle between the tribunes a riot took place, in which Norbanus was involved. This happened in 103 B.C. Eight years later Norbanus was accused of high treason for having taken part in the riot; and M. Antonius, Cicero's older friend, defended him.

It was a famous case. Cicero frequently refers to it, giving in one place a pretty complete account of Antonius' speech.[25] Antonius is represented as describing the trial; he addresses himself particularly to Sulpicius, who had conducted the prosecution.

---

[25] *De Or.* 2, 197 ff.

"You had stirred up the people,' says Antony, "not only by your words, but by the vehement sorrow and excitement you displayed, so that I scarcely knew how to begin. Everything was on your side. You had spoken of violence, stone-throwing, and the cruelty of the tribunes toward Caepio. It was well established that stones had been hurled at the leader of the senate; nobody could deny that a consul and a tribune of the people had been driven from the temple when they tried to interfere; and you yourself were a young man speaking with great dignity against these disorders in the state, whereas I, already a censor, could scarcely with honor, it seemed, undertake to defend such doings. The jurors were prominent men and the forum was filled with honorable citizens. My only excuse for appearing in the case, and that a feeble one, was that Norbanus had been my quaestor, so that I might well look upon him as my son.

"I spoke of all kinds of civil discord, gathering them from our whole history, to show that, although riots had always been a source of trouble, some of them had nevertheles been justified, and almost necessary. The expulsion of the kings, the creation of the tribune's office, the frequent limitations imposed on the consular power, the right of appeal to the people, which is the very bulwark of our liberty—all these were due to dissensions among the nobles. And if these dissensions and riots had benefited the state, it would be unjust to conclude offhand that Norbanus' participation in a riot made him punishable for high treason. If the Roman people had ever been justified in resorting to violence—and they had been so justified—then never had there been a better reason for violence than in this riot of Norbanus and his friends.

"Thereupon I approached my task from another side. I inveighed against Caepio's flight in Gaul and I bewailed the destruction of our army, thus stirring up the old sorrow of those whose friends and relatives had been slain. I also aroused anew

the anger of the knights against Caepio by reminding them how
he had been instrumental in taking the courts out of their hands.

"Having in this way won the favor of the people, by talking
about calamities to the state, private grief, and political hatred,
I lowered my tone to one of great gentleness. I reminded the
jurors that from time immemorial a quaestor had been looked
upon as the son of his superior magistrate, and that therefore
they must decide with a thought of me and my reputation.
Nothing could harm my standing more nor cause me greater
sorrow than that I, who had often helped strangers, should be
unable to help my own friend. I asked the jurors to consider
my great age, the offices I had held, my honorable record; they
could see that my sorrow on behalf of Norbanus was just, and
they knew also that I had always pleaded in behalf of my friends,
and never for myself.

"In such a case as this," Antony continues, "the theorists
would have had me define the crime of high treason and discuss
the law under which Norbanus was accused; but I merely
touched upon this point. Instead, I was very severe in attacking Caepio and very gentle in preferring my own claims, with
the result that the jurors were greatly excited, though I had
not told them much about the case itself; and my client was
acquitted."

This case was won by Antony's appeal to the civic and private
emotions of his auditors and by the use of his own *auctoritas*.
Another famous trial reported by Cicero[26] illustrates how the
people were amused and stirred by a mingling of comedy and
pathos, all of it entirely irrelevant to the facts before the court.
The successful pleader in this case was L. Crassus, Cicero's
second great exemplar; his opponent was a certain Marcus
Brutus.

Brutus, in speaking against Crassus, had two secretaries
beside him, who read alternately at his bidding, one from a

---

[26] *De Or.* 2, 223 ff.

speech in which Crassus had attacked the senate, the other from a speech in which he had defended the senate and attacked the knights. Crassus, speaking later, had three secretaries beside him, to each of whom he handed one of the three books on civil law written by Brutus' father. Brutus, incidentally, was a notorious spendthrift and had wasted his large patrimony. Evidently the law books were in the nature of a dialogue between Brutus the father and Brutus the son.

Crassus' first secretary, therefore, read from book one: "It so happened that my son Marcus and I were at my estate in Privernum." "You see, Brutus," said Crassus, "that your father has given proof that he left you an estate in Privernum." The second secretary read: "We were in my estate at Alba, my son Marcus and I." After which Crassus observed: "Evidently the wise man realized the character of his spendthrift son, and was afraid people might think he had not left him anything, since Marcus has nothing." The third secretary read from the end of the third and last book: "We happened to be sitting in my place at Tibur, my son Marcus and I." And Crassus: "Where are the estates which your father left you, as he indicates by these public documents?" As Brutus had also sold some baths inherited from his father, Crassus goes on to remark that if Brutus had not then been too old to bathe in company with his father, Brutus senior would have composed a fourth book, representing himself and his son as having just bathed, in order to show that the son had also inherited these baths.

It happened, while the trial was in progress, that the funeral procession of the aged Iunia, a relative of Brutus, was passing through the forum. Crassus seized the opportunity. Fixing his eyes on the luckless Brutus and threatening him with violent gestures, he launched into a new attack. His utterance, says Cicero, was rapid; his words grave. "Why are you sitting here, Brutus? What message do you wish this old lady to take to your father? To all those ancestors of yours whose images you see in the procession? What shall she say to L. Brutus, who freed this nation from the tyranny of the kings? What shall she report that you are doing? To what business, to what ambition, to what manly virtue shall she say you are devoted? Are you engaged in increasing your inherited wealth? But business is not worthy of an aristocrat, so I will let that go. Still, you have nothing left of your property; it has been wasted in vicious living. Are you a student of civil law? Such was your father. But she will say that you have sold your houses and have not reserved even a place for your father's chair. Are you a soldier? You who have never seen a camp! Are you an orator? You lack the ability; the little natural equipment of voice and speech that is yours you prostitute in making a base trade of prosecutions. How can you dare to appear in public? To face these men? To be seen in the forum, among your fellow-citizens? Do you not tremble before the corpse that is being taken to burial, before the very images of your ancestors? You have not left yourself an opportunity for imitating them; no, not even an atrium in which you can set them up.''

The cases of Norbanus and Brutus are only two of the many that could be cited to show that pleading partook to an astounding degree of the intensely personal, man-to-man attitude of public life. This situation, particularly as it concerns Cicero, has been referred to in previous chapters. One or two features, however, may be added.

Both the plaintiff and the defendant, but especially the latter, brought their friends and supporters, whether of high degree or low, to the courts, to lend moral and often verbal support. Deputations, to testify to the defendant's noble character, would arrive from his home town, if he lived out of Rome; from clubs and societies to which he belonged; and from provinces that he had governed. Parents, brothers and sisters, often little children were present, rarely to testify, but always to enhance the pathos of the situation; and these as well as the defendant himself, at times even large bodies of citizens, dressed in mourning. The juries, and important trials were by jury, were large; varying, however, with different cases. And around this concourse of people, more or less directly interested in the proceedings, was the inevitable crowd of loungers and sight-seers, who rarely felt constrained to observe silence.

The trial itself, whenever possible, reached beyond the point at issue. It became an investigation not merely of a definite alleged act but of the whole life of the accused. His behavior as son, brother, and father; his public acts long before the period immediately under discussion; his past and even his probable future value to the state, in case he should be spared—all these matters were suitable for discussion. So also were the deeds and character of the members of his family, whether still living or long dead.

The general scrutiny, as has been stated, included the plaintiff and the lawyers on either side; even the witnesses were not exempt. No free man was obliged to give testimony. Witnesses, therefore, were naturally looked upon as friends or foes according to the nature of their depositions; and were treated as such. What reason had a certain witness for giving condemnatory evidence? The defendant had never injured him or any friend of his. The witness was known to be a liar; how could he be telling the truth now? And the offending witness was at times put through a cross-examination only less comprehensive than the trial of the defendant.

The spirit of these proceedings was, indeed, that of Roman public life, intensely, almost elementally, human. Exaggeration and outspokenness were the dominant notes. Superlatives of eulogy and superlatives of insult crowded each other. Men did not hide their lights under bushels, nor those of their friends; and they did not draw a discreet veil of forgiveness over the shortcomings of their enemies. Insults were hurled at a man because of his parents, his low station, his poverty, his personal

appearance, and his private habits. Crassus was considered a
model of propriety as a speaker, and yet he dragged the aged
Iunia's funeral into his abuse of Brutus. It was a medley of
tragedy and comedy. The air was filled with shouts, jeers,
laughter, and tears. The defendant, his children and his relatives, wept; if he remained unmoved, his behavior might be noted
as remarkable. The counsel of course wept; the old warrior
Marius, we are told, wept at the trial of a friend, and thus
moved the jurors to an acquittal; even the presiding magistrate
and the jurors wept, when they did not laugh.

But it was not all personal. Like Antony, other orators
discoursed about the grandeur of Rome and about her troubles.
General truths about life and death, virtue and vice, were constantly given utterance, for the pleasure or agitation of the
people present. Even the gods had their share in this excited
performance. It was not that many of the orators or perhaps
the majority of the ordinary citizens believed in the gods as
very real or personal divinities; but the gods and goddesses were
the outward symbols of Roman religious consciousness; they were
the most important part of the state religion; and they had
temples and statues in the forum. They were, therefore, constantly apostrophized in glowing terms, and oratorical hands
were raised to them. Jupiter Optimus Maximus, the guardian
of the city, must have been a very patient god indeed, and a
very busy one, if he listened attentively whenever a Roman
orator called upon him for help or vengeance.

VI

LAW

All this impassioned commotion left but small room for law
and its precise interpretations. Cicero noted it as exceptional
that he knew law, and obviously the general feeling among

pleaders was to the effect that such knowledge was not essential to success. Antony, speaking for them in the *De Oratore*,[27] says that wit is more important than the most minute acquaintance with statutes and senatorial decrees, and that the orator can make the stones weep by raising a dead father from the grave and giving a picture of him as he with tears embraces his son; so that quotations from the Twelve Tables, the very essence of Roman law, would seem like meaningless formulae learned from an inexperienced teacher. Antony himself professes never to have needed law. He admits that it may be useful, but other things, such as the proper management of voice and gesture, are of far greater assistance. And this he had shown to be true in the trial of Norbanus.

The interpreters of law, he says, frequently disagree, and in those cases eloquence wins the day. An orator has so much else to learn that he can never know enough law to settle difficult points; let him consult a jurisconsult. The latter will supply the spear, as it were, and the orator's mighty hand will hurl it. And yet it is not proper to consider the knowledge of law as merely the handmaiden, the servant, of eloquence, he adds, thus distinguishing between the professions of the jurisconsult and of the orator, with the implication that it is not possible, and would not be desirable, for a man to excel in both.

Cicero was in direct opposition to the opinion he voices through Antony. In his various works on oratory he argues frequently for legal knowledge as essential to a well-equipped orator. In the *De Oratore*, particularly, he discusses the question from both sides. Antony's arguments, representing the opposition, have already been given. Cicero's side is voiced through Crassus.[28]

The latter refers to several cases in which the decision turned on a question of civil law. He recalls how on one occasion two

---

[27] *De Or.* 1, 234–262.
[28] *De Or.* 1, 166–203. See also *Brut.* 214, 322; *Or.* 120.

orators, eloquent enough, too, bawled against each other in court, each clamoring for something which he erroneously conceived to be advantageous to his side of the case. Crassus speaks of the ridicule such performances drew from men who knew law, and says that legal ignorance is due to nothing but laziness, as the facts are easily accessible, which they had not always been, and that it is the height of impudence to plead without knowing the technical basis of the discussion. He gives a list of legal terms evidently of frequent occurrence in the courts, and while admitting that cases turning on them are usually of comparative insignificance, he expresses his firm opinion that men who cannot manage small matters should not be entrusted with great ones; the man who is lost in a rowboat would be quite at sea in the Argo. Cases of wills, of the sale of houses, and of questions relating to a man's civic status, according to Crassus, were also common, and some of these were of considerable importance. Turning from the mere necessity of knowing civil law, Crassus speaks of the honorable character of the study, and finally remarks that public law, *publica iura,* relating to the state as a whole, is useful in many public cases as well as in political discussions in the forum.

The indifference to law on the part of the pleaders, as shown in the discussion between Antony and Crassus, is the more remarkable as the Romans were the best lawmakers of the ancient world, and took pride in their achievement. Their civil law seems to have been the direct outgrowth of their own administrative genius; they asserted that very little had been borrowed from others, and they held the laws of other nations in contempt, singling out the Greeks for especial derision. The study of law, furthermore, had been ardently pursued for generations before the time of Cicero, and was considered worthy of a place of honor beside the activities of the soldier and the orator. In Greece those who knew law were called *pragmatici,* men versed

in business; they had no social standing, and sold their knowledge
to orators for small pay.[29] In Rome the legal scholar, *juriscon-
sultus,* jurisconsult, was consulted like an oracle, or even more
reverently, for oracles were by this time of doubtful inspiration;
his house was crowded with people seeking advice; he was
admired and revered by the young. He gave advice about cases
submitted to him, conducted legal actions, and drew up legal
instruments of various kinds. He also wrote on law, and much
had already been written, though the law had not yet been
completely systematized nor brought into a form suitable for
instruction.

There were many circumstances that drew Cicero to legal
studies. The importance of law, just indicated, in the structure
of Roman society, stronger in the past than in Cicero's own
anarchic times, was one motive, for Cicero was at all times
zealously devoted to everything thoroughly Roman, with the
exception of war. The Scaevolas and other legal students among
those who had befriended him in his youth, like his uncle Aculeo,
but particularly the Scaevolas, offered him an early opportunity
for learning, and doubtless fostered in him a realization that law
was the basis of society. It was only through law that any
orderliness could still be attained in Rome; and Cicero, naturally
just and a man of peace, was ever a champion of orderliness and
justice. He was an inquiring spirit, furthermore, reaching out
in all directions; desiring to know not only that a thing was so,
but also the why of it. A categorical reply from a jurisconsult
would not have satisfied him. Professionally, too, a knowledge of
law was very helpful, according to his own well-considered opinion, though not an absolute essential; and Cicero's ambition was
not likely to neglect anything of possible use. He had had time
both for thought about these things and for actual study during
his long period of preparation.

---

[29] *De Or.* 1, 198 ff.

The extent of Cicero's legal information is not ascertainable, whether as an absolute or a relative quantity. Many of his orations have been lost; those concerned primarily with legal matters were least likely to be published; and even in the extant speeches arguments have been omitted. As for his relative knowledge, the use of law made by his opponents can only be inferred, and with much uncertainty, from Cicero's orations, so that we must on the whole fall back on his statement that he, and not his rivals, knew law. It is inconceivable that toward the end of his career he should have insisted on legal studies unless he had been known as an exponent of them. His letters, furthermore, are filled with legal puns and allusions, especially when addressed to his legal friends. Cicero wrote on law. Although the treatise entitled the *Laws* is largely philosophical, being a continuation of the work on the State, it contains much detail. wielded with the ease that comes from mastery. He thought of writing more; not collections of statutes with notes, for many were doing this, but a short systematic treatise, which would give the prospective pleader a grasp of the field, by dividing the laws into well-defined groups. Such a treatise is outlined in the *De Oratore* by Crassus, who speaks for Cicero; and Cicero may have carried out the intention, for there are references in later writers to a work of his entitled *de iure civili in artem redigendo,* a Systematic Treatise on Civil Law. In later life the suggestion was made to him that he give consultations as a jurisconsult, a suggestion that he laughingly rejected. And he prepared his cases with great care; even making a public claim to it in so early a speech as the *Pro Quinctio.* He had been called to speak at such short notice, he says regretfully, that he had not had sufficient time for mastering the details according to his usual wont.

A belief in the completeness of Cicero's legal equipment need not rest entirely on general grounds. Four of his orations have been exhaustively studied from this point of view, and the investigator[30] has been led to declare that Cicero was a consummate jurisconsult, who, without ever losing sight of practical details, had the ability to grasp underlying principles, as well as to foresee and favor legal reforms that had become necessary and were later carried out, as evidenced by the *Digest;* that, in short, he was in every way a worthy successor of the Scaevolas themselves, at all periods of life giving of his time to jurisprudence as he gave to philosophy. This statement is probably somewhat extravagant. The augur Scaevola wrote a work on civil law in eighteen books, and is often quoted, with honor, in Justinian's *Digest.* Sulpicius, most prolific of jurisconsults, is said to have written some 180 books on his subject; he wrote critical notes to Scaevola's systematic work and a commentary on the Twelve Tables, and was the founder of a juristic school. Cicero did not rival these men. But he certainly knew law well; he had studied it more than was necessary for his pleading, which itself was of a kind to make more than an ordinary use of law.

This greater reliance on law was necessitated by Cicero's aims as a pleader. He was the lawyer of the knights, the business men of Rome, and has even been called a corporation lawyer; he also constituted himself at an early date the defender of ordinary men. In both of these last capacities he needed law to a far greater extent than in the more spectacular cases with political connections. That he pleaded often in the more technical trials is shown, among other things, by the fact that the four cases referred to constitute just one half of those extant from the years

---

[30] Gasquy: *Pro Quinc., Pro Rosc. Com., Pro Caec., Pro Tull.*
Greenidge, *The Legal Procedure etc.,* treats fully of the law involved in Cicero's orations. The four cases mentioned are discussed by him, pp. 530–568. It is usually said, though no attempt is made to prove it, that Cicero was not well versed in law. This opinion seems to be based on his ''human'' arguments, which have already been shown to be necessary, and on the fact that he often ridicules legal knowledge. The best instance of such ridicule is found in the *Pro Murena;* for which see below, pp. 257 ff. Cicero, though at bottom a very earnest man, was never blind to the human comedy; he made merry with his own love of fame, his political eminence and accomplishment, his sincere interest in philosophy, and his oratorical manner.

before his consulship. Two of them, those for M. Tullius and Caecina, have to do with real estate transactions; the *Pro Quinctio,* already discussed, was concerned with a business contract; the fourth, in defense of the actor Roscius, was the result of an old quarrel about an alleged debt. It would be a lengthy matter, *longum* as Cicero says, to attempt an explanation of the details involved in these trials. Like the case of Quinctius, they had been tried before; lawyers had made them intricate, however simple they may have been in the beginning. And as the speech for Tullius is very fragmentary, while the beginning and the end of the defense of Roscius have been lost, these two cases can not be made out with much completeness.

The speech for Caecina is noteworthy. More than twenty years after its publication, Cicero in the *Orator* refers to it, with the true observation that it is concerned entirely with defining a legal formula. It was obviously intended as an advertisement of Cicero's legal ability, with little thought of the young men who wished to learn oratory or of the older men who read for amusement. One passage in it generalizes about the value of civil law as the great stabilizer of the social order, the only thing that can put a stop to the misuse of irresponsible power. This is Cicero's proclamation of attitude and of his claim to legal knowledge, but it is also a reply to his opponent. The latter, evidently in fear of Cicero's greater skill, had voiced the complaint, common enough in Rome, it would seem, as among us, that legal technicalities lead to injustice. After eulogizing the civil law, Cicero shows that in this particular case it is his opponent, and not he, who is trying to hide behind a harmful literalness of interpretation. Cicero, with the claim that he is pleading on the side of equity, insists that the court must try to arrive at the obvious intention of the lawgivers and not be bound by any failure on their part to attain exactness of expression. He thereupon turns suddenly on his opponent with the assertion that the law, even when literally interpreted, is in

Cicero's favor; and then follows a rather long argument as to whether the word whence, *unde,* means only *out of* a place, as Cicero's opponent would have it, or also *from* a place, as Cicero contended.

But Cicero has not forgotten the wisdom of Antony. The auditors must not be wearied; or, as he himself put it in the *Brutus,* it is necessary to entangle the opponent in a mesh of terse and exact reasoning, and then to relieve the strain on the jurors' attention by lapsing into fun and laughter. Latin, he says, though less briefly, is a poverty-stricken language; it has not enough words to express everything. But neither has any other language. And words are not necessary when we have once comprehended the meaning for the sake of which the words exist. No law, no senatorial decree, no public document of any kind, and no private document, can be made to yield an indubitable meaning if we look only at the words. Everyday speech will fall to pieces if we go fowling for vocables. The discipline in a house would collapse if every slave were allowed to obey our words only, with a disregard for the sense behind them. So it is in law. There is a legal formula beginning with the words, "when I see you here in court." Would the honorable opponent maintain that this formula could not be used by Appius Claudius the Blind? No, words have been invented to reveal our wishes, not to hide them.

VII

Professional Standard

Cicero's professional standard can not be absolutely determined. Many of his cases have been completely forgotten, leaving no trace, and many others are known to us only by name, by references which contain little information, or by equally insufficient fragments. Even in connection with the cases which are represented by extant orations it is not infre-

quently difficult to decide whether he had justice on his side.
The speeches of his opponents have all been lost; their arguments
can be inferred only from Cicero's manner of meeting them, and
he gives it as his opinion that an orator should say nothing, or
as little as possible, about the strong points of the opposition.
His own statement of the case, one-sided at best, as it should be,
is not always clear to us. The laws to which he refers are
frequently unknown; the text of his speeches has suffered;
arguments have been omitted. After he had reached eminence,
furthermore, he was at times only one of several orators on his
side, always pleading last, because of his unusual ability in
influencing the jury. He therefore touches only the main points
of the evidence, sometimes not even all of these. And, finally,
his arguments are Roman, seeming weak from the modern point
of view, although they were strong in the forum.

Something can nevertheless be known in reference to Cicero's
professional attitude. His projected defense of Catiline, which
apparently did not take place, is perhaps most to be condemned.
In the year 65 B.C. he writes[31] to Atticus that he is thinking of
defending Catiline, that the jurors are the kind of men he wants,
and that the prosecutor is well-disposed, meaning, of course, that
he will not press the prosecution. Both Catiline and Cicero were
at that time intending to run for the consulship; and Cicero adds
the hope, that, if acquitted, Catiline will not work against him;
if Catiline is condemned, Cicero will have to bear it as a man.
The matter is referred to incidentally, in a few very brief sentences; it is treated as a thing in which Atticus might possibly
be interested, and there is no attempt made either to excuse or
to explain it. Though the trial did not take place, Cicero was
ready to undertake the defense, having made all the arrangements mentioned, and it is not likely that he supposed Catiline
innocent.

Another trial of unusual interest is Cicero's defense of
Cluentius, which occurred in the year 66 B.C. Eight years

---

[31] *Att.* 1, 2, 1.

earlier Cluentius had accused his stepfather Oppianicus of attempted murder. Cluentius' first legal step had been the prosecution of a freedman, Scamander, who, it was alleged, had brought both the bribe and the poison to the slave of Cluentius' physician, who was to commit the crime. Scamander was easily proved guilty, but Oppianicus escaped. The trial of Oppianicus, who was as consummate a rascal as even Rome in the time of Sulla could produce, caused a great scandal; Cluentius, it was said, had attempted to secure his stepfather's conviction by the most shameless use of bribery. Cicero had defended Scamander. In the year 66 B.C., after Oppianicus was dead, Cluentius was accused of having murdered him. Cicero now defended Cluentius. When the earlier trial was cited against him, he replied that he had not known the facts in connection with Scamander, a statement that may have been true; but since he himself had in the meantime referred to some of the jurors in the trial of Oppianicus as having taken bribes, one of them indeed from both sides, and had published the animadversion, the prosecutor of Cluentius also quoted from Cicero's published speeches. "It is a weighty authority you are appealing to," rejoined Cicero with mock pomposity.[32] "I don't remember the oration in question, but I still admit that it was a disgraceful trial, because of Oppianicus, however. It would be a mistake, nevertheless, to quote from an oration as if it were the deposition of a witness; I was echoing the general opinion. An orator speaks with an eye to his case, not for the purpose of revealing his own real opinions or those of his client. If lawsuits could speak for themselves, there would be no need of lawyers." And then he mentioned how Antony did not publish his speeches, so as not to be confronted with them later; and told the humorous story of Crassus and Brutus with their secretaries. In reference to the trial of Cluentius, Cicero is also said to have boasted that he threw dust in the eyes of the jurors, poured darkness over the case, as the Latin expresses it.

---

[32] *Pro Clu.* 138–142.

It should be added that the speech for Cluentius makes it practically certain that he was not guilty. The accusation was the last act in an interminable family feud, which had been characterized by divorces, murders of grown people and children, falsification of wills, robbery, and almost every other conceivable crime. Cluentius' mother, who was the sixth wife of her foul husband and a very fit partner for him, had caused her son to be accused, and although in her attempt to secure evidence she had tortured her slaves with extreme cruelty, she had not been able to produce any convincing proofs. Cicero was thus justified in defending Cluentius, and his courage in doing so, after opposing Cluentius in the earlier trial, is greatly to his credit. When Cicero said that he had thrown dust in the eyes of the jurors, he could not have been referring to the main accusation, but was speaking only of one phase of the trial. Cluentius' alleged bribery in the earlier trial had at that time made him very unpopular. His mother now attempted to revive this unpopularity in order to turn the jury against him. Cicero's discussion of this phase of the question is so long and so involved and so contradictory that he very likely succeeded in confusing the jurors. In all probability both Cluentius and his stepfather had bribed at the earlier trial. The stepfather could not have escaped without using bribes; and if his character was what Cicero represented it to be, Cluentius could have had no hope of winning the case unless he resorted to the same means.

Cicero's statements about his professional attitude, however, his defense of Scamander, which displayed carelessness even if it was not a conscious attempt to pervert justice, his willingness to defend the guilty Catiline, and the further fact that in later years, for political or personal reasons, he defended men who were guilty, do not seem to indicate a very high sense of moral responsibility. But human morality is not a perfect, unchangeable Platonic idea. Cicero was not an impossible Sir Galahad in search of a Holy Grail; he was a very successful Roman advocate, who sought political advancement or victory, or defended his political or personal friends. The question in reference to his professional standard should perhaps be, not whether his clients were always in the right, but whether Cicero as an advocate stood on as high a level as his contemporaries, or possibly on an even higher level.

The fact that Cicero published so large a number of orations would seem to prove that he was at least not desirous of making a secret of his professional methods. Not all orators had the frankness to publish, as Cicero himself observed. Neither does he seem ever to have shocked the moral sensibilities of his contemporaries. While a rival lawyer might effectively point out that Cicero was not always consistent, we find that this very speech for Cluentius was not only published by Cicero but that the Romans of the next generation studied and admired it. The honest Quintilian, who mentions the confusion of the jurors, quoted the speech more than forty-five times, as some one has counted, and he has many complimentary things to say about it. Indeed, a modern lawyer of the best standing might well plead in a case similar to that of Cluentius. He would not have undertaken the defense of Catiline, however, nor would he have resorted to Cicero's measures to insure success. But Cicero, who had no pressing reason for revealing his conduct to Atticus, reveals it, and this revelation, as well as his gossipy manner, precludes the supposition that either Atticus or Cicero himself saw anything in the matter which deserved criticism. The threatened prosecution of Catiline, no less than the later trials in which Cicero's clients were guilty, belonged to political life. The prosecutor in trials like these was not desirous of punishing wickedness, but to undo the defendant for personal or political reasons; and the moral question involved for the defending lawyer was not concerned with the innocence or guilt of his client but with his own political or personal relations with him. It became, broadly speaking, a question of prudence or wisdom.

A Roman advocate's professional standard is thus, in the great majority of his cases, to be judged as a part of his political life; and as a politician Cicero had a reputation for unimpeachable honesty, which indeed was one of the chief reasons for his success. The charges that could be brought against him as a pleader could be brought against such men as his great exemplars, Crassus and Antony, who were among the noblest of their generation. There can be no doubt that Cicero lived on a far higher moral level than the great majority of his contemporaries; when he made frank admission of employing a legal trick, the Romans might have thought him boastful, but scarcely iniquitous. And in one respect he set his professional standard above that of his fellows, in refusing to prosecute. This was good policy no less than honesty, as has already been pointed out; but it was moral elevation nevertheless, and made him even as a pleader a power for betterment. That he showed courage in his efforts to stem malicious prosecutions, is attested by his defense of Roscius of Ameria. His appearance in behalf of Cluentius required not a little moral courage; and his only prosecution, that of Verres, was undertaken largely to bring justice to the Sicilians. In this trial the prize of success was great, but the likelihood of defeat, as will be presently shown, was equally great.

But whether Cicero pleaded in a case with political ramifications, as usually happened, or in as strictly private a case as could occur in Rome, like the trial of Cluentius, his standard was very much what it would have been if he had pleaded in an ideal state of the Stoics, the most severe moralists of his time. "To defend a man, provided he is not personally immoral, even when guilty," Cicero wrote in his work on Duty,[33] "accords with the laws of society, with tradition, and with the dictates of humanity. It is for the judge to decide about the truth; the pleader can be satisfied with something less. And this I should not dare to write in a book on philosophy, if it were not also the opinion of Panaetius, the strictest of the Stoics."

[33] *De Off.* 2, 51.

CHAPTER VI

THE PROSECUTION OF VERRES

I

THE TRIAL

The prosecution of Verres, which took place in the year 70 B.C., when Cicero had held only one office, the quaestorship, has already been mentioned in various connections. There are several reasons why it deserves a somewhat extended treatment.[1] It was Cicero's most important legal victory, establishing him as the undisputed leader of the Roman bar; indeed, it was, if not the most important, certainly the best known case of antiquity. It was Cicero's only prosecution. Five of the seven orations published as an account of it had not been delivered; and these five contain a picture of Roman public morals, particularly as displayed in the long-suffering provinces, that has no parallel either for wealth of material or vividness of treatment.

Verres had governed Sicily as propraetor in the years 73–71 B.C. His original appointment had been for a single year, according to the prevailing custom, and his successor had been chosen in due time, but the latter had been needed for command against the rebelling Spartacus. Verres, therefore, remained undisturbed. His deeds, however, were becoming known. Sicilians, impoverished and ill-treated, fled to Rome for protection; Romans doing business in the rich island lodged complaints; the behavior of Verres was discussed in the senate; the consuls took a hand, and the tribunes of the plebs, Cicero speaking before the latter on one occasion. Finally, in the year 70 B.C., a successor to Verres was sent to Sicily, and immediately afterwards ambassadors representing all the Sicilian communities, except Syracuse and Messana, came to the city to accuse him of extortion.

---

[1] See Cowles, in bibliography.

Sicily was the oldest of the Roman provinces; it was also one of the two richest, the other being Asia. The Sicilians, therefore, had patrons among several of the noblest families in Rome, but they entrusted their case to Cicero, now thirty-six years old. Cicero had been quaestor in Sicily in 75 B.C.; he had been honest and courageous; when leaving the province, he had promised to give assistance if the need should arise. Though he was their youngest patron, he was an orator of the first rank; and he had no aristocratic connections that might tempt him to neglect his clients for the sake of the old prerogative of extortion.

The Sicilians needed a prosecutor who was both absolutely honest and possessed of great ability. Verres was well connected. He secured Hortensius, still the first orator of Rome, and at this time a candidate for the consulship, to manage the defense; and he had among his *advocati*, or moral sponsors, various men of high standing. Noticeable among the latter were the family of the Metelli, relatives of Verres, three brothers, one of whom was a candidate for the consulship, another for the praetorship, while the third was the very man who had succeeded Verres in Sicily. Verres was also extremely generous with his money, attempting to bribe even Cicero. The money, the skill, the influence on the side of Verres were able to wage a long and energetic battle, which very nearly thwarted the prosecution.

The first step was an attempt to eliminate Cicero from the case. Provincials, seeking redress in Rome, could not choose their own lawyer; the latter had to be appointed by the court. Cicero, supported by the wishes of the Sicilians, applied for such appointment. Under normal circumstances this would probably have been granted at once; it was the obvious and the fair thing to do; but in this case a rival aspirant appeared, and the matter was argued before a jury. This part of a trial was called a *divinatio,* divination, because the jurors were not called upon to decide about submitted facts but to look forward into the future, as it were; so, at least, the ancients themselves explained the name.[2] Cicero's speech on this occasion, also called a divination, is extant, the first of the seven; and is directed against Caecilius, who would gladly manage the prosecution for the Sicilians, although the latter did not want him. He was a Sicilian by birth, and thought it suitable that they should be defended by a fellow-islander; he had been quaestor under Verres, and consequently was in a position to know the facts; he also claimed, a wonderful claim but characteristically Roman, to be the personal enemy of Verres, who had insulted him; and he was of course too honorable to take bribes, intending to push the prosecution with the utmost vigor. The only flaw in his assertions was that Verres wished him to prosecute.

Cicero's speech, the only divination extant, made short work of Caecilius. One of Cicero's arguments related to the desires of Verres in the matter; another made the inevitable comparison between Caecilius and himself. This, however, was done cleverly. Though Cicero's speech, as published at any rate, and probably at the delivery, hints at his own successful career and his devotion to oratory, he says far less about his own ability than about Caecilius' shortcomings. Caecilius, he indicates, would have a very uncomfortable time with the great Hortensius. Cicero has pleaded both against the latter and on the same side several times, and knows what he is talking about; Caecilius, on the other hand, though older than Cicero, has had no forensic experience. There is much more in the oration, most of it to the undoing of Caecilius, so that one may surmise that Caecilius would gladly have faced Hortensius in order to escape the sarcastic Arpinate. But Verres would not have been convicted. The jury decided for Cicero, not even allowing Caecilius to appear as an assistant prosecutor, though he had asked for that.

---

[2] Aul. Gellius, 2, 4, 3.

The *divinatio* took place early in the year, almost certainly in January.[3] Cicero now handed his charge against Verres to the praetor and asked for one hundred and ten days in which to gather evidence. The case would thus be called, probably, at the end of April. Suddenly, however, an accusation for extortion in Achaia was lodged against a former governor of Macedonia; the prosecutor desired one hundred and eight days for the gathering of evidence.

The whole question of this Achaian trial is somewhat obscure. Cicero charged that it was a trick of the defense, to gain time. Any postponement would be an advantage to Verres, giving him new opportunities for bribery; and if the trial were postponed until the following year, Verres would undoubtedly be acquitted. In that year Hortensius and one of the Metelli would probably be consuls, as actually did happen; the other Metellus would be praetor; several of the present incorruptible jurors, now candidates for office, would in case of election be by law incapacitated from serving on the jury, and their places would be taken by other men, who might prove more amenable. It certainly appeared as if the Achaian trial was intended to cause a delay. The one hundred and eight days, two less than Cicero's, would just give it precedence; with careful management it might be made to last a considerable time. And there was another reason for suspecting it; the prosecutor did not go to Achaia for his evidence. In this he resembled some other prosecutors, but his laxness showed a lack of interest in his case, and made the one hundred and eight days seem very suspicious.

It is not known whether the Achaian trial ever took place; but the trick, if a trick it was, succeeded, partially at least. Verres' case was not called until August, and Cicero makes the statement that three months had been stolen from him. He may, however, have thwarted his opponents' plans to some extent,

---

[3] The chronology of this trial can not be determined with certainty. The latest and clearest discussion of it is given by Cowles, pp. 192–204, who summarizes the theories of previous scholars.

for he gathered his evidence in Sicily in fifty days, and he refers
to his celerity in the matter as though it had enabled him to
present the case in time. Whether or not the trial against 'the
governor of Macedonia was a trick, and whether or not the trial
took place, May, June, and July were somehow lost to Cicero;
July was probably given to the elections, but the loss of May
and June seems to have been due to the Achaian prosecution.

The fifty days in Sicily are noteworthy. Cicero and his
cousin, Lucius Cicero, traveled over the whole island, visiting
towns and villages, and even talking with individuals in "their
huts and by the plough."[4] Though Cicero might have enjoyed
the public hospitality of the various communities as a Roman
senator and a former quaestor of the island, he preferred to stay
with friends; complaining, however, that the Mamertini did not
give him a public invitation, an unprecedented insult to a Roman
senator. He secured a very large number of letters, both from
cities and from individuals, numerous public records and decrees,
and very many witnesses. Finally, in his need of a prompt
return to Italy, he left Sicily in a small boat, though it was in
the winter, when the sea was rough; his safety being threatened,
besides, by fugitive slaves, the remnants of the war with Spartacus, by pirates, and by the emissaries of Verres.

Most of the Sicilian communities received him as their savior.
At Henna, so he tells us, he was met by the priests of Ceres with
chaplets and sacred boughs. A meeting of citizens was held, as
happened in the other cities as well. While Cicero was speaking,
there was so much weeping and groaning that the whole city
seemed to be filled with the most bitter grief. Henna was entirely
devoted to the worship of Ceres; the city was like a shrine,
its inhabitants like priests and temple attendants. Now they
exclaimed that they would utter no complaint about unjust taxes
and injuries of every other kind inflicted by Verres; only one
thing they could not forgive: Verres had desecrated the temple

---

[4] *Pro Scauro* 23–26. Other details are given in the Verrine orations.

of Ceres, sacred to all Sicily, and had carried off the statue of the goddess herself. He had come like another Pluto; for, as the god of the infernal regions had stolen Proserpina, the daughter, so Verres had stolen Ceres, the mother.

Everywhere there were bereaved mothers, sisters, and wives. Cicero arrived at Heraclea in the night. All the matrons of the town, carrying torches, came to meet him. Their leader, calling Cicero her savior and Verres her destroyer, fell at Cicero's feet; uttering the name of her murdered son, as though Cicero could raise him from the dead. And this scene was repeated, Cicero continues, in other cities; by aged mothers, and even by small children, who had suffered.

But Cicero also encountered obstacles. Verres had friends, both individuals and a few communities, who, according to Cicero, had prospered by unworthy means, or at least had not suffered as much as others, under Verres. The new governor also tried to prevent Cicero from securing evidence. On first arriving in Sicily, Metellus had abolished many of the evil practises instituted by his predecessor, had righted many wrongs, and had sent damaging reports to Rome. It seemed, in Cicero's words, as if he were less intent upon performing his own duties as praetor than upon undoing the deeds of Verres. But when Cicero reached Sicily, all this had changed. Two days previously a certain messenger had arrived from Rome, with letters; after that, Metellus had proclaimed himself the friend and relative of Verres. When possible, he forbade the delivery to Cicero of public documents; he dissuaded, even forcibly prevented, witnesses from going to Rome; and he commanded communities to send embassies to support Verres at the trial.

Cicero's experiences at Syracuse are the most instructive; they are also related with most detail. The people of Syracuse had many reasons, so Cicero had been led to believe, for being friendly to Verres; they had not joined in the prosecution and had even sent a laudatory embassy. Cicero, therefore, expected nothing from them and did not ask for permission to examine their public records. Instead, he had recourse to the Roman citizens resident in Syracuse; examining their books and getting evidence about the injuries they had sustained. When he had been in the city for some time, often busy in the forum, Heraclius, a leading Syracusan, approached him with a request that he and Lucius attend a meeting of the local senate; he had come, he said, at the bidding of the senators who were gathered together in large numbers. After some hesitation, Cicero and Lucius followed Heraclius. As they entered the senate-house, the senators arose, to do them honor; the presiding magistrate thereupon asked them to be seated.

The first speaker was a certain Diodorus, foremost in "authority, age, and experience." The Syracusans, he said, were grieved and disappointed because Cicero had neglected them, whereas he had offered his services to all the other Sicilian communities, receiving from them letters and other kinds of evidence. Cicero replied that when the Sicilian embassies met in a body at Rome to ask him to undertake the prosecution, the ambassadors from Syracuse had not been present. He added that he was not asking that any decree be passed against Verres in a senate-house which was adorned with a gilt statue of the former propraetor. The assembly cried out as they looked toward the statue. Many stood up, one after the other, and described how the city and the shrines had been despoiled. The statue, they said, had not been set up by the city; it was the work of a few individuals, accomplices of Verres, who were now in Rome as the representatives of Syracuse. It was not surprising that these men had failed to join the other embassies.

When it had become clear from numerous speeches that Syracuse had suffered more, and not less, than the other cities of Sicily, Cicero promised help. He referred to a public commendation of Verres that had come from Syracuse; the senators explained that it had been passed within the last few days, under coercion; at Cicero's suggestion, they expressed their desire to rescind it. First, however, they brought out the public records, which had been kept hidden in the public treasury, a sacred place. In these were told the misdeeds of Verres; more numerous than Cicero could make use of in the trial. Verres' thefts were classified in this way: things stolen from the temple of Minerva; of Jupiter; of Bacchus. Cicero arranged to have the records sealed with the seal of the city and taken to Rome.

The Syracusan commendation of Verres had come about in this manner. Shortly before Cicero's arrival, letters had been received from Verres, asking for it; but nothing had been done. Later, when some of Verres' friends urged the matter, there had been shouting and disorder in the senate, but no decree was passed. Still later, immediately before Cicero reached Syracuse, Metellus ordered that a commendation be passed. In the debate that ensued every device was used to avoid passing the laudatory decree; no one was willing to move it; in spite of the fact, as Cicero recalls, that the senate-house contained a statue of Verres and a statue of his little son, in the nude. At last, by coercion, the commendation was decreed. But its wording was satirical. Verres was praised because he had had nobody flogged, "struck with the rods," implying that he had caused men to be executed, "struck with the ax;" he had administered the province with watchful care, but the watchfulness, or wakefulness rather, had been due to riotous nights; and he was commended for keeping the pirates from the island, though everybody knew that they had been received by him into the island.

When Cicero had learned all these things, he and Lucius left the senate-house, so that the senators might pass whatever decrees they wished. First they made Lucius the guest-friend of the city, because he had evinced the same spirit toward it as Cicero; this decree they not only wrote out, but they had it inscribed on a bronze tablet, which was given to the Ciceros. Thereupon it was voted to rescind the commendation of Verres.

This vote had already been set down in the minutes when a former quaestor of Verres hurried off to summon Metellus; and the latter ordered the senate to adjourn.

As a result, a large crowd, senators first and then ordinary citizens, made their way to Cicero, exclaiming that their rights were being destroyed; and the Roman citizens of Syracuse gathered around him, evidently as a protection against any attempt of violence on the part of the praetor. The excitement was intense, directed especially at the quaestor who had called in Metellus; and it was only with great difficulty that Cicero succeeded in restraining the crowd from inflicting summary punishment on the offending quaestor. After this disturbance Cicero went before the praetor, who was sitting in judgment; but the latter rose hurriedly from his curule chair and departed, giving Cicero no opportunity to state his business. As evening was by this time coming on, the crowd left the forum.

On the following day, in the morning, Cicero again appeared before the praetor, requesting that the decree against Verres be given to him. Metellus said no, adding that on the previous day Cicero had acted without the proper Roman dignity, in that he had addressed the Syracusan senate in Greek. At the advice of the townspeople, Cicero tried to get the decree by force. A riot ensued, for, as Cicero remarks, Verres had friends in Syracuse. One of these was a certain Theomnastus, nicknamed Theoractus, which means "smitten by god;" "the kind of man that children follow on the street;" mad, Cicero says, though perhaps he was not so mad after all, having once been elected to the priesthood of Jupiter, by the grace of Verres.[5] Theoractus, mad or not, laid hold of the tablets that Cicero was trying to carry off; foaming at the mouth and glaring insanely, he shouted that Cicero was hurting him. Neither let go his hold of the documents; and thus "chained together," they went to the praetor. Cicero demanded that the tablets be sealed and

---

[5] See below, pp. 152–153.

given to him. The praetor said no. They quarreled. Cicero quoted the Roman law that entitled him to gather evidence. Metellus, getting angry, said that he had nothing to do with such laws. Cicero threatened, pointing out the penalty of the praetor's disobedience. Finally he secured the decree. After that, Theoractus—or Theomnastus, on this occasion, for he no longer acted like a madman—produced a book that he gave to Cicero; it contained a list of the Syracusan thefts of Verres. Cicero, however, had already secured information about these.

After the fifty days had thus elapsed, whether they came at the beginning or at the end of the one hundred and ten, which is uncertain, Cicero returned to Rome. It was time for selecting the jury. A rumor had been spread abroad, for the discouragement of the Sicilian witnesses, that Cicero had accepted a bribe, and consequently would be but an indifferent prosecutor. He proved his honesty, however, by the manner in which he objected to the doubtful members of the jury panel; and an honest jury was secured.

The elections for the next year presently took place. The higher magistrates were chosen first; Hortensius and Metellus were made consuls-elect; the other Metellus secured the praetorship, also receiving in the allotment charge of the extortion court. Some of the present jurors were also elected to office, so that they would be unable to serve if the trial should go over to 69 B.C. The hopes of the supporters of Verres had been justified, and there was open rejoicing. When Hortensius, after his election, was returning with a great multitude from the Campus Martius, a certain C. Curio happened to meet the throng; seeing also Verres, he greeted him with a loud shout, embraced him, and told him to lay aside all worry. "You have been acquitted by this election," he cried, loudly enough for many to hear. And the praetor-elect Metellus, when allotted charge of the extortion court, was so delighted that he sent slaves ahead to his house to announce the good news to his wife.

The election of aediles was fast approaching, at which Cicero would be a candidate. Moneys arrived from Sicily, as Cicero learned from friends; and Verres one night called together the agents of electoral bribery, *divisores,* of all the tribes. One of them came that very night to Cicero and reported what had taken place. Verres reminded the agents how generously he had treated them during his own canvass for the praetorship, as well as during the recent elections when Hortensius and the Metelli had secured their offices; and he promised to pay any sum for the defeat of Cicero. Some said they did not dare to attempt it; others thought it impossible; but one of them promised to do it for 500,000 sesterces. After that, a few others agreed to assist him. But it all came to nothing. Cicero was elected, and unanimously.

The magistrates on Verres' side were not wearied. Just before Cicero's election, Hortensius had summoned the Sicilian envoys to his house, but, on learning what he desired, they had refused to come. Later the other consul-elect, Q. Metellus, summoned the ambassadores; a few obeyed the summons, inasmuch as L. Metellus, his brother, was governor of Sicily. Q. Metellus pointed out to the envoys that measures had been taken for the acquittal of Verres; the Sicilians could not hope to accomplish anything against the three brothers Metelli, a consul, a praetor, and a propraetor.

Metellus took for granted that the trial would not be concluded until the next year; and there was every likelihood that this would happen. The case was called on August fifth. The ordinary procedure would be for Cicero to make a complete exposition of Verres' crimes in a set speech, which probably would last some days; the defense would reply; and not until later would the witnesses be introduced for examination by Cicero as well as by Hortensius. This set speech would be Cicero's great oratorical triumph; he had prepared for it during months of labor, in the midst of intrigues and opposition of every kind; it would be the utter undoing of Hortensius, his only rival. But such a speech at this time would mean the acquittal of Verres. Ten days after the opening of the case the so-called votive games would begin; and other games would follow, so that the opposition would not make its retort until after a holiday of some forty days, in itself an inauspicious circumstance. Other games and holidays nearly filled the rest of the year; it would not be difficult for the defense to waste the few remaining days; and once the tenth of December had arrived, when the new tribunes of the plebs took office, two of whom were jurors, Verres' acquittal would be a certainty.

Cicero, therefore, reversed the ordinary procedure, not entirely without precedent, thus relinquishing, for the moment at least, his own desire for oratorical fame and the confusion of Hortensius. The trial began at the eighth hour, about two o'clock in the afternoon. Cicero made a short speech, setting forth the intrigues of the opposition, and then made his charges very briefly, introducing the witnesses at once to substantiate them. His only hope of success was to make so strong an impression on the jury, before Hortensius could launch into dilatory oratory, that a verdict would be practically assured.

For nine days the stream of witnesses passed before the jurors, and documents were read. The first hour, as Cicero later describes it, cut off Verres' hope of bribing the jury; on the first day it became clear to the Roman people—and there were unusually large crowds in Rome at the time because of the recent elections, the census which was being taken, and the impending games—that an acquittal would mean the overturning of all order in the state; on the second day the friends and supporters of Verres relinquished all hope of victory and even lost their willingness to argue in defense; on the third, Verres pretended to be sick, so that he might not have to make reply to his prosecutor. Hortensius sat speechless during most of the proceedings, rarely questioning a witness, though that was his right. Probably it was during these days that he made an impatient remark about one of Cicero's allusions, which is quoted by Plutarch. "I cannot guess riddles," said Hortensius; and Cicero: "You nevertheless have a sphinx in your house," referring to a gift the orator had accepted from Verres. Sometimes Hortensius objected to the violence of the witnesses, maintaining that they were behaving like accusers and not like witnesses. The popular excitement was intense; the praetor more than once had to close the proceedings, fearing, according to Cicero, that the people, driven to fury by the revelations of Verres' cruelty, would take vengeance then and there; and Cicero claims to have withheld testimony for the same reason.

The trial, according to law, was to consist of two parts, *actiones*, separated by a period of two days. Verres, however, went into voluntary exile, not waiting for the second part of the trial; and Hortensius threw up the case. The court confirmed Verres' voluntary exile, and ordered that his possessions should be sold publicly, to secure restitution to the Sicilians. This would be either the actual amount alleged to have been stolen, or two and one half times as much.

Before going to Sicily, Cicero had estimated Verres' thefts at 100,000,000 sesterces; now, after a careful evaluation, he gave 40,000,000 as the sum.[6] Verres, however, had succeeded in taking away much of his wealth; indeed, he was proscribed in the year 43 B.C. by Antony, who desired some of his Corinthian bronzes.[7]

Cicero, as Plutarch cleverly observes of the great speaker, had won his case by refusing to speak; and it may be added that Cicero made the same statement in introducing his undelivered

---

[6] This is a disputed matter. For a brief statement of the facts, see Cowles, pp. 177–8.

[7] Pliny, *Natural History*, 34, 6; Sen. *Suas.*, 6, 24.

orations: "I do not wish Hortensius to say that the defendant has been overwhelmed because the prosecutor said nothing about him, and that nothing is so dangerous to an innocent defendant as silence on the part of his opponents; nor do I wish that Hortensius should damn me with faint praise, saying that if I had made a speech, he would have defended his client, but that he lost his case because I kept quiet."

The discomfiture of Hortensius, Cicero's ancient rival, was a large part of Cicero's success, and meant the primacy of the Roman bar. For some years subsequently Hortensius very nearly abandoned pleading. Cicero refers to this situation some twenty-four years later in a passage of the *Brutus*,[8] which has already been quoted in part. Cicero's explanation is characteristically polite. Hortensius, he says, was consul in 69 B.C.; after attaining this honor, he felt justly that he could ignore the claims of orators below him in rank, while among the consulars nobody rivaled him. He grew indifferent to the passionate ambition that had inspired him from very boyhood; he became lax, imagining that he was leading a more enjoyable life. The first year, the second, and the third, each took away something from his former splendor; it was like the fading of the colors in an old picture; so that finally he became utterly unlike his old self. Neither an ordinary listener nor a trained and critical observer could have recognized him. Every day diminished Hortensius' ability. All his oratorical qualities suffered, especially the rapidity of his delivery and his grace of style, for which he had been famous. Cicero, on the other hand, continued his practise in the forum and his oratorical exercises. When he, too, had attained the consulship, Hortensius bestirred himself; after which they often pleaded together, each professing to consider the other the greater orator. But Hortensius did not recover his old excellence. He had been greater in his youth. One reason for this was that he had relaxed his training; the

8 *Brut.* 320 ff.

---

other, that his peculiar gifts, fluency and the refinements of style, were less suited to a more advanced age than to youth.[9]

Cicero's praise of Hortensius, and Cicero always praises him in his oratorical works, scarcely conceals the fact that even in the later period Cicero was popularly held to be the greater orator; a thing easily proved from other circumstances; and it shows very clearly that the first recognition of his superiority was due to the prosecution of Verres. Hortensius may have been conscious of a hidden struggle with a rival even during the trial, when he observed that he could not guess riddles. Cicero, certainly, had it very definitely in mind. There is much about Hortensius in the *divinatio,* as there is also in the later Verrine orations. Cicero speaks of Hortensius' great influence in the courts, calling him an autocrat, and of his practise of dividing his speeches systematically, matters that Cicero had mentioned in earlier orations as well, but he also more than hints that he has no fears. Much of Hortensius' previous success, Cicero says, has been due to the inferiority of his opponents; he has played with them; he would play with Caecilius; but not with Cicero, and Cicero indicates how he can use the very devices on which Hortensius is accustomed to rely.

The juxtaposition of Cicero and Hortensius was to some extent inevitable in the *divinatio,* and Cicero took care to emphasize it; equally inevitable, or even more so, was praise of himself as an orator. A *divinatio* was by its very nature a self-laudation. Cicero, as has been indicated, managed the matter well; rather pointing out what Caecilius lacked than what he himself possessed; but the inference to be drawn was not hidden. The speech became thus not merely a defiance of Verres, but also a statement of Cicero's claims as an orator. His own honesty, his

---

[9] The passage from the *Brutus* (320 ff.) contains much of our knowledge about the Asiatic style. See Wilkins, pp. 45–46, for a brief statement; also Schanz, 207 ff. This oratorical tendency, however, is of less importance for our appreciation of Cicero than for a knowledge of the history of ancient oratory. But see Norden, *Die Antike Kunstprosa*, 1, 229 ff. See also below, pp. 438 ff.

long training, his past career are set forth, directly or indirectly; and are set forth with a view not merely to the case itself but to the more distant future. Cicero was well aware that this was his one great opportunity at the bar; that it was, indeed, the final test of his fitness for the highest offices.

Professionally, a prosecution was a departure from his previous record; but it might not have been entirely unsuitable to indicate to the Romans that Cicero could attack as well as defend. Brother Quintus, in the much quoted electioneering pamphlet, counsels Cicero to threaten with prosecution any competitor who resorts to bribery; attack was a strong political weapon, and Cicero was approaching the political heights. In 67 B.C., three years hence, he might stand for the praetorship; and the preliminaries for the canvass would begin much earlier. On the other hand, this prosecution, as Cicero repeatedly asserts, was not of the ordinary kind. He was not, at least when first undertaking the case, a personal enemy of Verres; he was acting as a patron of the Sicilians; as their defender, in fact. He had already appeared before the tribunes in behalf of one of these very Sicilians; and at that time he could have had no thought of launching a prosecution against Verres. The enormity of Verres' crimes, too, gave this prosecution a nobler character, made it a defense, as Cicero claims, not merely of the plaintiffs but also of the dignity and welfare of Rome. Cicero insists on these thoughts, eager to make clear that his professional attitude has not changed; and he returns to the question at the very end of the seventh oration. His last words are to the effect that he may be allowed in the future to defend the good rather than to punish the wicked; and this wish is introduced after a long apostrophe to the gods, which, in calling down vengeance on Verres, might with much more oratorical propriety have ended the oration.

Cicero was, indeed, maintaining the highest level of his professional standard, that of protecting the weak. The progress of the case through its many weary months is sufficient proof that the Sicilians could not have secured any redress without his assistance. Cicero might not have taken the case if he had had no hope of winning it, and if victory had not meant great professional advancement, which latter is inconceivable; but he did run a very grave risk. Defeat was never far off; his opponents as well as outsiders expected it. It is not too severe a strain on the imagination, therefore, in view of Cicero's own considerate and upright behavior toward provincials at the time when he himself became a governor, to suppose that he was genuinely stirred by the atrocities of Verres. He had been in Sicily, and he knew many of the men who had suffered under Verres. When he breaks into eloquent appeals to the humane feelings of the jurors, he voices a real emotion. As provincials, the Sicilians mattered to the Romans only in so far as they might be useful; and Cicero's arguments, if carefully scrutinized, will be seen not to rise much higher. He also puts far greater emphasis, too great, it seems, on the sufferings of the comparatively few Romans who had encountered Verres, for he was addressing a Roman jury. But as human beings, the Sicilians mattered to Cicero much more, probably, than to the majority of his contemporaries.

Much is said in these speeches, or at least written, which might indicate that Cicero was not only building up his oratorical reputation but also more or less definitely allying himself with the knights and the people in their fight against the aristocrats. This was the important year, 70 B.C., when the popular tribunes regained the power of which Sulla had deprived them, and when the public courts, at the end of the year, after the Verrine trial, were taken from the nobles; the jurors were henceforth equally divided between them, the knights, and the so-called *tribuni aerarii,* who seem to have been plebeians rich enough, or almost rich enough, to belong to the knights. Cicero inveighs against senatorial corruption in the courts; he attacks the aristocratic exclusiveness, which would keep all others from high office. The whole case was a blow at the nobility, and may have been of considerable assistance in bringing about the reform of the courts; the fact that the jury decided justly did not weaken the argument against the nobles, for everybody was acquainted with Cicero's long fight before he could even get the case tried.

But Cicero was not allying himself with the opponents of the aristocracy.[10] His professional and humanitarian reasons for taking the case were quite sufficient. His attacks on the aristocrats in the course of the trial are to be interpreted, not as the expression of his political opinions, but as an effort to win a verdict, an interpretation which Cicero himself four years later, in his defense of Cluentius, frankly suggested for anything he might say in court. Nor is it likely that his prosecution of an extortionate governor could have marked him as a foe to the nobles, for in the very next year he defended a certain Fonteius, who was accused of malversation in Gaul. The trial of Verres was in one respect a bid for popular favor, but it appealed to the people as a demonstration of Cicero's oratorical and legal ability, and to the provincials as a blow struck in their behalf.

It would be interesting to know whether Verres was, after all, an exception among Roman governors. Cicero would naturally try to make his listeners and readers believe it; he cites many of his deeds, quite cruel enough for any age or circumstances, as similar to those of others, and then invariably describes something worse as peculiar to Verres; but it may nevertheless be doubted whether Verres was either more cruel or more greedy than very many of his contemporaries.[11] He was condemned, and they were not; but the condemnation was en-

---

10 Cf. Heinze. Heinze discusses Cicero's cases before the consulship, and briefly those of the consulship. His view, shared by others, that Cicero must be looked upon mainly as an orator before the year 63 B.C. seems to me indubitable, but I can not agree with his contention that in these years Cicero was at heart an aristocrat, opposed only to the excessively conservative few.

11 For Sulla in Asia, see below, p. 184.

tirely due to Cicero's skill; several of Verres' worst crimes had
been perpetrated before he went to Sicily, and had not been
punished. It is also very unlikely, and no further arguments
need be given, that the aristocrats, including Hortensius, a man
of good reputation, would have defended Verres so persistently,
even recklessly, if his actions had really seemed monstrous to
them; aside from other considerations, they could have served
their aristocratic cause better by refusing to protect him. The
question is important for our view of Rome; but, like many
others; it can not be settled definitely. The scant evidence seems
to point to this: that Verres' character and methods were not
revoltingly low in Roman eyes, but his opportunities and his
skill had been unusual. The career of Verres becomes thus one
of the most serious indictments against republican Rome.

II
The Facts

The account of Verres' crimes is given in the five unspoken
orations. The two speeches that Cicero delivered had not contained it. As published, the *divinatio* has almost nothing
about Verres; and the oration of August fifth, which was
called *actio prima* after the name of this part of the trial, is
merely an introduction, devoted almost entirely to the ineffectual
chicanery, tergiversations, and knavery of the defense. The
witnesses, the documents, and some of the sufferers, for even
bereaved children were brought into court, had told the story
effectively enough in the course of their nine days; but of all
this there was no impressive record. In publishing the facts,
Cicero creates a picture of a second session, *actio secunda;* such
as would have taken place if Hortensius had not abandoned the
case. He represents himself as delivering a long speech; the
very speech, in fact, which Hortensius had hoped Cicero would

begin with on the fifth of August and which, at that time, would have spoiled the prosecution. It is divided into five books, called the five orations of the *actio secunda*.

All the motives for the publication of orations, professional, literary, and pedagogical, were active in this case; increased by the fact that this was Cicero's only prosecution, and that during the trial he had had no opportunity for eclipsing Hortensius as an orator. Cicero had won the case by every kind of skillful and courageous activity that could be employed by a Roman lawyer, but he had missed the purely oratorical part of it, by far the best part both to the pleader and to his public. The published orations supplied this want. Apparently their effect was as great as if they had been actually delivered; Cicero and students of oratory used them for illustrations in matters oratorical exactly as they used the other orations, Cicero saying[12] that they contained every kind of oratory useful in prosecution. They are scarcely too long to seem the report of actual speeches; a Roman orator, like a modern lawyer, might speak for several successive days. Thus, in the trial of the tribune Cornelius, in 65 B.C., Cicero spoke for four entire days, and then published his plea in two books, now lost except for fragments; and yet the Cornelian case was one of high treason, where the facts were relatively few, whereas the facts in the Verrine trial were almost innumerable.

Verres gave early proof of his criminal inclinations, according to Cicero, but the speeches have no account of his boyhood and youth. This is to save time, a true reason; and also for the sake of decency, a consideration that the orator seems to have forgotten as he proceeded. It is hinted, however, that Verres, even in his early years, was not a stranger to late hours, procurers, and gamblers.

The review of his life begins with his quaestorship under Carbo, at the time of the civil war between Sulla and Marius. Verres would not ally himself openly with either party, though

---

12 *Or.* 131.

he is said to have been a Marian. He went to Gaul, Carbo's province, with the money sent by the state; but at the first opportunity he absconded. His report of his stewardship was remarkable. He stated, without items, but down to seventeen sesterces, what he as quaestor had been called upon to spend, and then added that six hundred thousand sesterces, not accounted for, had been deposited for safekeeping in Ariminum, a very safe place for Verres since Ariminum had been destroyed in the civil war, before anybody had an opportunity to count Verres' deposit. Thereupon he suddenly joined the Sullan party. Sulla, who ought to have been delighted with this new partisan, did not send him to the army, where, if loyal, he might possibly have been of some use, but ordered him to stay at Beneventum; the men in power there, thoroughly devoted to Sulla, would see that Verres did no harm to the aristocratic cause. At the end of the civil war Verres was liberally rewarded, for leaving the Marian side, with property confiscated at Beneventum.

Afterwards he became quaestor to Dolabella, the governor of Cilicia. On his way to the province with Dolabella, to mention, says Cicero, only the crimes that would seem incredible if charged against some one else, Verres demanded money from the magistrate of Sicyon; this sort of thing others had done, but Verres, when the magistrate refused to pay, shut him in a small room where a fire was made of green wood. The magistrate was almost choked to death. In Achaia Verres stole pictures, which are not specified; in Athens, a large amount of gold from the temple of Minerva. Proceeding on his way, he came to Delos. Here, at night, he removed from the temple of Apollo several exquisite and ancient pieces of sculpture, and had them loaded on a transport. A storm arose, doubtless through the influence of the outraged Apollo; Dolabella could not depart from the island; it was dangerous even to stay in the city. Verres' transport was stranded, and broken up; and Apollo's art treasures were scattered over the beach. Here they were found, and Dolabella had them replaced in the temple; after which the storm ceased, and Dolabella left the island.

At Chios Verres forcibly carried off a number of art treasures; so at Erythrae and Halicarnassus. In Tenedos, in addition to extorting money, he stole the statue of the patron god of the town; in Samos he pillaged the famous temple of Juno. Cicero had seen these spoils when he came to seal Verres' house as part of the legal proceedings; these art works were found in all parts of Verres' residence, even in the gardens; but, Cicero asks, where are they now? Verres was saving them for Antony.

Aspendos was a famous old city in Pamphylia, filled with works of art. Here Verres did not steal only this statue or that; he did not leave a single one in the whole town. From temples and public places, with the townspeople looking on, everything was carted away in vans. Among the things stolen here, for Cicero stops to specify, was the well-known lyre-player of Aspendos; famous enough to be the source of a Greek proverb, of which scholars give varying interpretations. This statue was with Verres in Rome; very suitably, for the proverb,[13] in some way or other, had reference to doing things for one's own sake, whether it be playing or stealing. At Perga, too, Verres continued his robberies; despoiling the ancient shrine of Diana and seizing the temple treasure.

Other Romans, Cicero remarks, carried away treasures and works of art from conquered cities; but surrendered them to the Roman state, carefully listing them in their reports; such statues may now be seen throughout the city of Rome and its temples, as well as in all parts of Italy. Verres, on the other hand, stole things from friends and allies of the Roman people, and kept them for himself and his friends. On one occasion, as Verres boasted, he adorned the forum and the rest of the city. Cicero admits remembering it, but he also remembers that am-

---

[13] *In Verr.* II, 1, 53: *quem omnia intus canere dicebant.*

bassadors from Asia and Achaia had wept at the sight of their stolen treasures. "Sometimes I bought these things," says Verres. Cicero has examined all of Verres' books, and those of his father, but finds no record to that effect.

Theft and robbery were not Verres' sole occupation. He was also lascivious. In every town that Verres visited were girls and married women who had been wronged by him. But crimes of lust are often little known, says Cicero, and can be denied. He therefore singles out from the many one that was notorious, and gave indication of Verres' cruelty as well.

On the Hellespont, opposite modern Gallipoli, was the city of Lampsacus, rich and famous, devoted to the arts of peace, and entirely friendly to the Roman people. Verres, in his many journeyings back and forth, had occasion to pass through Lampsacus. Here he stayed at the house of a certain Ianitor, a guest-friend, while his retinue were entertained by various people. As soon as he had arrived, he ordered his men to find out if there was in Lampsacus any girl or woman for the sake of whom it might be worth his while to tarry a little in the city. Rubrius, the worst of his companions, presently made report. Philodamus, so Rubrius had learned, a man of high station and great wealth, the foremost citizen of Lampsacus, had a very beautiful daughter; she was unmarried and lived with her father; her character and reputation, unfortunately, were unblemished. Verres immediately announced that he would move to the house of Philodamus. Ianitor, his host, was alarmed, thinking something in the entertainment had been amiss, and urged Verres not to leave him. Verres yielded, but decided to send Rubrius to Philodamus. The latter, informed of the impending visit, called on Verres, to object; he often entertained traveling Romans, he said, but only those of praetorian or consular rank; it was not his duty to receive the servants of a praetor's legate. Verres, for reply, gave orders that Rubrius should be installed in Philodamus' house, by force, if necessary.

Philodamus had a reputation for hospitality and friendship toward the Romans. When he saw that he must open his house to Rubrius, he resolved to do it with an appearance of willingness. He prepared a costly banquet to celebrate Rubrius' arrival; and asked the latter to choose his own guests. If agreeable, Philodamus would keep a place for himself, but for no one else. He sends his son, a young man, to dine with a relative.

The guests come early; which means that the dinner will be long. There is talk; and toasts are given in the Greek manner. Philodamus is a pleasant and generous host; the guests call for larger goblets, and the drinking proceeds gaily; every one joins in the conversation. Presently Rubrius inquires of his host why he does not summon his daughter. The old man is struck speechless by the Roman's impudence, and when the latter insists, he replies that it is not the custom for Greek women to join in the revels of men. The Romans begin to shout; such an explanation is intolerable; let the girl be called. And at the same time Rubrius orders his slaves to shut the door and take their stand by it. Philodamus orders his slaves to pay no attention to him, but to protect his daughter if the Romans should resort to violence; he also sends one of his slaves to find the son. The slaves of Rubrius and of Philodamus come to blows; the others presently take part. Philodamus is jostled; Rubrius pours a pitcher of hot water over him. In the meantime the son arrives, to do what he can; it is already getting dark; a crowd of townspeople gather at the house. In the fight that ensues, Cornelius, one of Verres' lictors, is killed; he had been present, ostensibly as a guard, but in reality to carry off the girl. Some slaves are wounded; Rubrius himself gets a scratch or two. And Verres, when all this is reported to him, thinks that he had better leave Lampsacus, if he can get away.

In the morning the citizens of Lampsacus hold a public meeting, all agreeing that the Roman people will not make them suffer if they take justice into their own hands; in any case, actions like those of Verres can not be endured. The crowd surges to the house of Ianitor, where Verres is staying. They batter down the door with rocks, put armed men around the place, and prepare to burn the house, with Verres in it. The Roman residents of Lampsacus now intervene; Verres is bad, they say, but, after all, he has failed in his design, and he will never come back; the people of Lampsacus had better respect his position as a Roman legate. And the provincials, in fear of distant but powerful Rome, allowed themselves to be persuaded, and Verres escaped.

He returned presently, however; though the long story need not be retold. The end of it was that Philodamus and his son were executed for the murder of the lictor Cornelius; so that Verres continued his official career without the regret that provincials had balked him with impunity.

But it would be utterly impossible, and perhaps not desirable, to recite even briefly the numerous deeds chronicled by Cicero. The account already given is a summary of twenty-one chapters of the first undelivered oration. This oration has sixty-one chapters; the five together have three hundred and seventy-six, nearly eighteen times the twenty-one that take Verres through the execution of Philodamus. The five orations are by themselves a big book, crammed with grim information.

Cicero's manner of narrating the facts has been indicated in the brief summary. Sometimes he gives a long series of crimes, one after the other, almost without vivifying details, though to the Roman reader the mere mention of cities, large or small, of famous temples, of works of art known throughout the world, might be vivid enough. At other times he stops to give a picture; there is a wealth of concrete detail; the scene of the action is sketched, often minutely, and the actors themselves are described in such a way that we can almost see and hear them. He is usually in terrible earnest, for the things reported are not amusing; but occasionally there is an opportunity for a different treatment. Verres was vain and pretentious; his satellites, Greeks as well as Romans, were a mean lot, and quarreled among themselves; a few of the crimes were so petty, relatively at least, or so ingenious that they are entertaining; and Verres was himself tricked once in a hundred times.

Cicero also interrupts his narrative with digressions. He describes places and things; he recalls historical events; he defies Hortensius, exults over the cringing Verres, exhorts and praises the jurymen; he moralizes about virtue and vice; and he turns in apostrophe to many dead worthies and to nearly all the gods and goddesses. These digressions, paralleled in other orations, are a necessary part of forensic oratory, even when published; the Roman reader expected them and was moved by them. The less excitable modern reader, particularly if he be in search of facts, might find them uninteresting, and certainly irrelevant, in these speeches as in others; but here they have, after all, a value even for him. The sight of much cruelty, Cicero says elsewhere, makes men callous. The deeds of Verres are so numerous that no amount of variation in the narrative could prevent the reader from becoming a little indifferent; even as it is, he is tempted to check off one crime after another in a rather impassive way. This is prevented, at least to some extent, by the digressions. They do not stir him, perhaps, as they stirred the ancient Roman; but, like some of the Greek choruses, they give him time to think, keeping his mind for a moment on the thoughts engendered by some impressive bit of narrative, before he passes on to something else.

Verres had many adventures after leaving Lampsacus. He had secured the conviction and execution of Philodamus through the assistance of his chief, Dolabella; the latter also screened him, not entirely for unselfish reasons, one may guess, on many subsequent occasions; and afterwards, when Dolabella was in due time accused of extortion, Verres turned against him and gave damaging evidence. The relation of a loving son and father, supposed to exist between a quaestor and his superior, had no weight with Verres; and this was bad, says Cicero; but, he adds, there was a certain appropriateness in one villain turning against another.

And so Verres became praetor in Rome. His actions during his year of office, 74 B.C., were what might have been expected, dictated by cruelty, lust, and greed. He could not treat the Romans like provincials, but he was contemptuous of ordinary people and had at least one person flogged, a man who had been introduced at a *contio* by a tribune of the plebs. In presiding in court, he issued various edicts, or rules of procedure tantamount to laws, which were different from anything used before in Rome, and were not applied even by Verres himself in Sicily. Nor did he obey them in Rome, except when convenient. Some of them were retroactive. All this was for the purpose of instigating litigation, particularly in reference to wills, which would bring profit to the praetor. His injustice caused his colleague Piso to nullify many of his decrees, and became so notorious that people made malicious puns on the name Verres. *Verres*, with a small letter, means pig; *ius Verrinum* is justice as practised by Verres, but it is also pork-broth. Poor puns, says Cicero, finding an excuse for his repetition of them in the fact that they indicated Verres' reputation, which followed him to Sicily.

The person who had most influence with Verres during this year was a courtezan, called Chelidon, which is Greek for swallow. The Swallow was faithful to Verres, after her kind, for she made him her heir. Her sway over him was considerable. Litigants in his court, according to Cicero, found her advice far more helpful than that of jurisconsults; her house was crowded with people counting out bribes and signing papers. Sometimes, when Verres had decided between two litigants, the Swallow would whisper in his ear, and he would forthwith recall the departing consultants and change his decision. The strange sounds of barbarous tongues, incidentally, was by the Greeks likened to the twitter of swallows.

But Chelidon was not always successful, as was seen in a case which had to do with some temple repairs. Verres, whether or not by special appointment, had charge of the maintenance of temples and other public buildings. This he made a second important source of income, the other being his management of cases of inheritance. On this occasion a certain P. Iunius had by contract had charge of the large temple of Castor, but had died before his work had been approved by the magistrates. As the son of Iunius was a minor, the situation seemed to offer an opportunity to Verres; he was always enriching himself, says Cicero, at the expense of wards. The temple, however, was in good condition; the contract of Iunius had been fulfilled. Verres goes to inspect the building, and can find nothing amiss. One of his men suggests that the pillars are not absolutely true to plumb, carefully explaining the point to Verres, who at first did not understand. If we are to believe Cicero, pillars in ancient times were rarely perfectly vertical; nor was the matter mentioned in Iunius' contract. Verres, however, decides that the building is not in a fit condition for acceptance by the state.

The guardians of young Iunius go to Chelidon. She receives them very affably, as was to be expected of a courtezan, Cicero remarks, and promises to speak to Verres. The guardians, worthy Roman citizens, a little ashamed of having recourse to her, return on the next day, and are informed that Verres will not yield. There is too much money involved, Chelidon explains. Verres thereupon manages, through a series of devices which need not be recounted, to give a contract for alterations to one of his own henchmen, Habonius, for the sum of 560,000 sesterces, though the guardian of Iunius had offered to do the unnecessary work for 80,000. Habonius takes down some of the pillars, and puts them up again, using the same drums; the rest he leaves as they were. Verres had frightened off other bidders for the contract by requiring the work to be done in two and one half months; but Habonius,. once the contract had been awarded, was allowed to let the matter drift. His work was not finished and approved until four years later.

It was this young Iunius whom Cicero brought into court at the Verrine trial. Hortensius objected to the presence of the child, and it is interesting to find that Cicero justifies it on the ground that the boy was not the son of a prominent man.

The praetorship and the events preceding it are described in the first of the five orations, which is named from its most important part, *de praetura urbana.* The arrangement is chronological, except in the account of the praetorship, which treats first of Verres' administration of justice and then of his inspection of public buildings. The other four orations are devoted to his rule in Sicily. Here a chronological arrangement would have resulted in chaos, for Verres made one journey a year through various parts of the island and his misdeeds did not change their character from year to year. Cicero, therefore, divides the immense material into groups, as he had done in describing the praetorship in Rome; there are four large divisions, though each is not concerned exclusively with one subject. Verres' administration of justice, his supervision of Sicilian elections, and his demand for statues as a testimony to his upright character, are treated in the first of these orations, the second of the *actio secunda.* This is called *de praetura Siciliensi,* a praetor's or propraetor's main function being that of a judge; or, more explicitly, *de iudiciis.* The next oration is devoted to Verres' management of the tithes and other matters connected with grain, *oratio frumentaria.* Thereupon, in the fourth oration of the five, follows an account of his thefts of works of art, *de signis.* And finally, in the last oration, Cicero describes Verres' measures, or lack of them, for the military protection of the province, and the cases in which he inflicted capital punishment upon Roman citizens. The importance of the last section gives the name to the oration, *de suppliciis.*

Everything that Verres had done before, he now repeated, but on a far larger scale and without the slight restraint which previous conditions had imposed on him; he was now the sole ruler of a rich province, while Roman courts were far off and probably for sale. As he said himself, he would use the proceeds of one year to pay his lawyers and defenders, and of another, the third and most profitable, to buy the jury; the remaining year would yield quite enough for his own needs. Cicero finally estimated his thefts, "the money that he had taken out of Sicily contrary to the laws," at forty million sesterces, between two million and one million six hundred thousand dollars; but even that sum seems too small. It is not likely that Cicero appraised all the statues, rugs, table silver, and other household articles that Verres stole; some of them were too precious to have any market value at all; nor could Cicero have established the value of the others in court by means of witnesses and documents, and it is with such evidence that he undertakes to prove the amount stolen. Forty million sesterces is a huge sum, and may be all that Verres acquired; but Cicero himself made two million two hundred thousand in a single year in Cilicia, a very poor province when compared with Sicily; and Cicero did not steal.

As a dispenser and supervisor of justice, Verres reversed previous judgments, expressed publicly his willingness to entertain any accusation against those who had opposed him, changed the old Sicilian laws and those made for the province by the Romans themselves, sold magistracies and priesthoods. One man he deprived of an inheritance of three million sesterces, keeping most of it himself; from two brothers whose father had died twenty-two years before, he secured four hundred thousand sesterces in connection with the father's will. And he had a sense of humor. There was a law relating to the election of the priest of Jupiter in Syracuse which required that as many lots be placed in an urn as there were candidates, the lot drawn to determine the election. At this time there were three candidates. Verres had three lots put in the urn, and the lot drawn proved to contain the name of Verres' candidate: he had put the latter's name on all three. The new priest was Theomnastus, the Theoractus, smitten by god, who later fought with Cicero. Another occasion, also an election to a priesthood, was managed with almost greater cleverness. It was to take place on the first of March. The candidate, who had not secured Verres' support, arrived for the election by the middle of February; in ample time, as he thought; but he found that his rival had been elected a whole month before. Verres had consulted the stars, and discovered that the calendar needed adjustment; a matter of six weeks.

Several cases are described with considerable detail. A few words may be said about that of a certain Sthenius of Thermae, to illustrate how information about Verres was sometimes brought to Rome. A charge of having falsified the town records had been trumped up against Sthenius, who had a right to be tried by his fellow-citizens. When Verres insisted on hearing the case himself, Sthenius fled to Rome. Verres, who was ignorant of the flight, took his seat on the curule chair at three in the afternoon, and when the defendant did not appear he sent men to find him, his presence being necessary for the trying of the case. Verres' messenger searched the house of Sthenius and then, on horseback, visited his farms and scoured the surrounding country, but in vain. Verres in the meantime shivered on his official chair, for it was winter. For six hours he stayed there, till nine in the evening, and then he dismissed the court.

On the next day, contrary to legal procedure, he pronounced Sthenius guilty, imposing a large fine; and shortly afterwards he found a man to bring a capital charge against him. Such a charge involved the loss either of life or of civic status. This trial was set for the first of December. Verres summoned Sthenius from Rome, at the least a doubtful procedure; and the consuls brought the matter before the senate, at the same time revealing a long list of persecutions to which Sthenius had been subjected by Verres. The sentiment was strongly in favor of Sthenius, but Verres' father succeeded in getting a filibuster under way, so that the matter did not come to a vote. Before the next session of the senate he had persuaded the friends of Sthenius not to press the matter; he would write to his son, he said, and all would be well. Letters were sent to Verres both by his father and by others, but Verres would not listen. The trial took place as scheduled, in the absence of the defendant, and of the accuser, too, as it happened. Sthenius was pronounced guilty.

Again the matter was agitated in Rome. The tribunes of the people took it up, this being the occasion when Cicero appeared before them. Verres was informed of the indignation at the capital, and, in fear, had the minutes of the trial altered in the records.

How some of Verres' trials were conducted is indicated by the experiences of Sopator of Halicyae. He had been tried on a capital charge before Verres' predecessor, and had had no difficulty, according to Cicero's claim, in securing an acquittal. The charge was revived when Verres came to Sicily, and Sopator was cited to appear in court. Sopator had good reasons for confidence. The trial would take place in Syracuse, as before; the praetor's assessors, *consilium*, would be the same; no new evidence had been secured; and Sopator's lawyer was a well-known Roman knight. Timarchides, however, a Greek who managed such things for Verres, came to Sopator: the latter had better not trust overmuch to the merits of his case or to the previous decision; his enemies intended to give money to the praetor. But Verres, Timarchides knew, would prefer not to reverse the former judgment, if properly induced. Sopator decided to think the matter over. He consulted his friends and at their advice he paid Timarchides the bribe; only 80,000 sesterces, as he was then in serious financial difficulties.

The case came to trial, but the proceedings were not finished at that time. Again Timarchides called on Sopator. The accusers had promised a handsome bribe; much more than Sopator had given; what would he do? Sopator was incensed. "Do what you like," he exclaimed, "I shall not pay any more." This reply seemed proper to Sopator's friends as well. After all, Verres would be unable to find a pretext for reversing the judgment.

When the trial was about to begin, Verres announced that, inasmuch as Petilius, one of his assessors and a Roman knight, was at that time in charge of a private case, Verres would be willing to dispense with Petilius' services, so that he might attend to the case in question; nor would Verres retain any other members of his *consilium* who might wish to accompany Petilius. They all left the court, so that Verres had only his own friends about him. This would seem a sufficient reason for postponing the trial; and so thought Minucius, Sopator's lawyer. Verres, however, ordered him to make his plea. "To whom?" said Minucius. "To me," Verres replied, "if I seem fit to sit in judgment over a Sicilian and a Greekling." "You are fit enough, but I wish those men were here who have been present before and who are familiar with the facts of the case." "They can not be present," said Verres; "speak!" "By Jove," exclaimed Servilius, "neither can I be present. Petilius wants me, too, to help him." And he started to leave the court.

Verres threatened, but Minucius answered that he would not plead without a *consilium;* and departed. For some time Verres seemed uncertain what to do. He turned this way and that. There was a large crowd present, waiting in silence for the outcome of the proceedings. Timarchides, it was observed, bent forward several times and whispered to Verres. At last Verres ordered Sopator to state his case. The latter begged for a trial with a regular *consilium.* Verres, ignoring him, ordered the witnesses to be called; one or two of them spoke briefly, and

there was no cross-examination. The herald announced that the
pleadings were at an end. Verres, hurriedly, lest Petilius and
the other assessors should return, took the votes of his friends,
a secretary, a physician, and a soothsayer, and thereupon pronounced Sopator guilty.

As a testimony to such proceedings as this, holidays in Verres'
honor had been established in Syracuse and Messana, and statues
had been erected both there and in other places; not entirely
without suggestion from Verres himself. The statues in Syracuse have already been mentioned. Here not only Verres and
his son were commemorated, but also his father, a touching sign
of filial affection, Cicero observes. Statues were set up in public
buildings, in market places, even in alleyways; all over Sicily
and in Rome; and most of those in the island, by the way, were
thrown down as soon as Verres had left the province.

But Verres had not thought merely of praise. Contrary to
all custom, he had himself extorted the money for the statues
from the Sicilians; a large sum, possibly three million sesterces;
and had of course not used all the money for statues. It was
an innovation, says Cicero, not to allow admiring provincials to
place their own contracts for the making of statues.

As Verres had secured the friendship of some Sicilians by
unfair means, so he had won the favor of the *publicani;* and these
had voted in formal meeting to remove from their books any
statement which might reflect upon Verres. In some of their
books, consequently, there figured a large creditor by the name of
C. Verr-ucius. The last letters had been written on an erasure;
there was no such person as Verr-ucius, and the propraetor's
name was C. Verr-es.

The fabulous Verrucius is the climax of the second oration.
The third oration, concerned with Verres' management of the
tithes on the produce of the soil, and his buying and valuation
of the grain, is far less spectacular than his performances in the

open courts, but it contains, on the whole, the most serious part of the entire accusation. Cicero himself recognized this, but placed his account in the middle of his charge; it was of necessity filled with numerous exact statements about measures and values and would not serve either as a pleasant introduction or as a stirring conclusion.

Tithes were levied by the Roman government on all the produce of Sicilian soil; on wine, oil, and fruits, as well as on grain; but the latter was the most important. The state was also in the habit of buying grain from Sicily at a price fixed by the Roman government; some twelve million sesterces were appropriated for this purpose during the three years of Verres' praetorship. And, finally, grain was allowed for the maintenance of the governor's household; usually not paid in kind, but by commutation of its value in money. It would require altogether too long an account of Roman provincial administration to explain the numerous devices employed by Verres for the purpose of extortion. Old laws were abrogated and new laws were passed. Two or three times the lawful amount was exacted; sometimes even more was demanded than had actually been produced during the year. When money was to be paid instead of grain, Verres valued the grain at four times the price that obtained in any other part of the island. Money sent him from Rome for the purchase of grain he invested for his own gain, at twenty-four per cent. And all his new rules and demands were enforced by violence or threats of violence.

The exploitation extended to every part of Sicily. Farmers had to leave their farms; others, who could have stayed, refused to till the soil. Both individuals and whole communities were made to suffer. One man, at the bidding of Verres' agent, was hung on an olive tree in the market place of Aetna, where he was left until the agent, Apronius by name, thought he had been chastised sufficiently. Many Sicilians went into exile; others hanged themselves. Regions that had been extraordinarily fertile at the time of Cicero's quaestorship, were deserted when he returned four years later to gather evidence. Sicily was one of the chief granaries of Rome, but the exploitations of Verres had brought things to such a dangerous pass that Metellus, Verres' successor, sent letters to Sicily, before he himself went there, entreating the farmers to cultivate their land and promising that the old laws would again be enforced. These letters Cicero produced in court.

Nor did Verres' agent make a secret of the fact that the praetor himself was the spoiler behind the new regulations. Apronius, chief among the agents, said openly that the smallest part of the gains went to him, and called Verres his partner, *socius*. A certain Rubrius, therefore, maintained in the market place of Syracuse, in the presence of Verres, that Apronius had called the praetor his partner; and offered a wager on the truth of his assertion, the question to be settled in court. But Verres, without denying the charge, smoothed the matter over. Later a Roman knight, Scandilius, offered a similar wager, to the amount of five thousand sesterces, and the proper legal steps were taken. Verres, however, said that he could not entrust a question relating to his own honor to any but his friends; instead of taking the judges from the usual panel, he appointed them from his own retinue. Scandilius then suggested that the question be taken to Rome, but Verres would not allow this; and when Scandilius finally offered to let the whole matter rest for the present, he was ordered forthwith to pay the five thousand to Apronius.

Apronius and Timarchides were the most notorious of Verres' numerous *canes venatici*, dogs of the chase, as Cicero calls them; with the qualities of pointers as well as retrievers. Members of the same pack, these two seem to have given each other assistance or advice as the occasion demanded. Timarchides, the wily Greek, sent a letter in his own hand to Apronius, suggesting how the latter might gain the good will of the new governor, Metellus, when Verres had passed from the scene; and Cicero found the letter in Apronius' house in Syracuse, and read it later, with appropriate comments, to the jurymen in Rome.

The insertion of such letters as this one from Timarchides varies the monotony of the *oratio frumentaria,* but this speech, the longest of them all, is nevertheless rather heavy. By way of relief, Cicero proceeds in the next oration, the fourth, to Verres' passion for works of art. In this, Verres the connoisseur is always in evidence, and his methods of acquisition are often amusing. From individuals who entertained him, Verres asked for gifts, or borrowed without returning. From cities he made frank demands, and if the local senate proved obstinate, he sometimes raised the taxes, at other times punished the leading citizens. Sopator, noted for other misfortunes as well, was thus tied naked to the equestrian statue of Marcellus, which stood in the market place; and here he was left, although it was in the middle of winter, very cold, and raining heavily, until Verres' request was granted. His requests were always granted ultimately. He also sent slaves in the night to steal things from temples. According to his own assertion, he bought his works of art, though a governor was by law forbidden to purchase anything but necessaries in a province.

Verres' tastes were catholic, embracing everything made for use or ornament; for homes, temples, and public places. He gathered articles of silver, gold, and other metals; jewels, paintings, tapestries, and statues; goblets, mixing bowls, and vases. Some things were too cumbersome to carry away, and it is on record that he left a certain large statue; but he removed the ornaments from temple gates and carried off pillars. He overlooked nothing because it was small. A certain man wrote him a letter and had the misfortune of using a beautiful seal ring; Verres at once sent for it.

In Messana the citizens built a ship to carry his treasures to Rome, and were rewarded in various ways. In Syracuse he had a factory in which for eight months skilled workmen were busy remaking or remodeling things; all vases made there were of gold. Verres, in an easy dishabille, passed considerable time in this factory, at which Cicero cries, "O tempora, o mores," the famous phrase used later by him in the first Catilinarian.

Verres also had with him two brothers, Greeks from Cibyra and temple robbers, a painter and a sculptor, who supplied professional guidance. Sometimes they deceived him. A citizen of Libybaeum, already robbed of a precious ewer of silver, an heirloom, had been ordered to bring Verres two goblets which he was known to possess. He arrived when the praetor was taking a nap, but the two brothers were in attendance. They asked to see the goblets, which were ornamented with beautiful figures. When the owner complained that he was being robbed of everything, they suggested that he pay them one thousand sesterces, a small sum considering the value of the goblets, and this he promised to do. Verres presently awoke. While he was examining the drinking vessels, the brothers remarked that they had been misinformed about the artistic workmanship; in fact, the goblets were very ordinary, quite unworthy of being added to the praetor's collection. Verres said that he thought so too; and the man from Lilybaeum returned home with his precious silverware.

In this incident and elsewhere, Cicero represents Verres as quite ignorant of art, his passion for collecting being merely greed and a desire for display. Verres, however, did not sell his statues and bronzes; he gave some of them to his friends, but the large majority he kept with him, clinging to them through every adversity, until they caused his death. Similarly, Cicero himself affects considerable lack of knowledge at the very time when he gives much minute information. He professes to have learned the names of the most famous artists of antiquity as part of his preparation of the case. He hesitates as if in doubt before giving a name. And this, it has been thought, was due to his desire of seeming indifferent to art as the old-fashioned Romans had been and as no doubt many Romans still were, especially the uneducated. But if ignorance was to Cicero's credit, it could scarcely be much to Verres' discredit. Cicero, as revealed in his letters, was an intelligent lover of art; and Verres may have been like him. But Verres as a pretender and Cicero as an ignoramus were amusing, especially to the reader who knew them both; and that would be sufficient reason for Cicero's attitude. The reader, like the auditor, must be entertained; a rule that Cicero observes whenever possible.

The most conspicuous of Verres' victims in the matter of art was the young prince Antiochus of Syria. Antiochus, who had been in Rome on political business, was returning by way of Sicily. Verres immediately sent him generous gifts of wine, oil, and wheat; and invited him to dinner. The decorations at the banquet were exquisite; there was a large display of silver dishes. The young prince was pleased, and gave a dinner in return, no less magnificent. There were many things of silver; not a few goblets of gold, set with previous stones, "as is the habit of kings," Cicero says, "especially in Syria;" and, most remarkable of all, a wine ladle made from a single gem, with a handle of gold. Verres is deeply impressed. He takes each dish and cup in his hand, admires and praises it; and the boyish prince is well satisfied with his entertainment.

A little later Verres asks to borrow the most beautiful pieces, wishing to show them to his engravers; and the unsuspecting Antiochus is glad to send them; even the cup made of the single gem, which Verres asked for particularly, as it had not been sent at first. But Antiochus had in his possession something still more valuable; a large golden candlestick of wonderful workmanship, set with precious stones. He and his brother had brought it to Rome as a gift for Jupiter Optimus Maximus; but as the latter's temple had not been completed, Antiochus was taking back the candlestick, intending to send it later. Verres had heard of the candlestick. Might he not see it? He would show it to nobody. And Antiochus sends this too. His men uncover it in Verres' presence; and the latter exclaims that it is indeed worthy of the Syrian kingdom and of the great Jupiter. When Verres has admired it for some time, the servants of Antiochus prepare to take it away; but Verres has not yet looked his fill. They must leave it, so that he may enjoy it at his leisure.

Antiochus suspected nothing at first. One day passed, another, several days, and still the candlestick is not returned. The prince sends a message that the praetor would please return it, and Verres tells the messengers to come back later. This seems strange, and Antiochus sends word a second time. Finally he goes himself to Verres. The latter asks for the candlestick as a gift. Antiochus replies that it is a sacred object; many nations know about it; it can not be given to any one but Jupiter. Verres begins to threaten, and when Antiochus refuses to yield, Verres orders him to leave Sicily before nightfall. There has come report, he says, that pirates are on their way to the province from Syria; which, presumably, would prove Antiochus hostile to the Romans, as possibly in league with the pirates, and so unfit to remain in Roman territory.

Antiochus leaves the praetor, but goes to the forum. Here— and the matter was well known, for it happened in Syracuse, amid a large crowd—Antiochus, with tears and with entreaties to gods and men, describes how he has been robbed, and publicly dedicates the candlestick to Jupiter. But that this prevented Verres from retaining it is very doubtful, for Cicero asks in another oration whether a gift intended for the Capitol should be placed side by side with things inherited from Chelidon.

In the fifth oration, the last, Cicero takes up Verres' behavior as the military protector of Sicily and his cruelty toward Roman citizens. These topics, except insofar as they involved the execution of certain Sicilians, were not part of the Sicilian accusation, for, on the one hand, the province had not suffered to any considerable extent because of Verres' laxness in managing the navy, and, on the other, the fate of Roman citizens and Roman knights was no concern of the Sicilians. They were important accusations in the eyes of a Roman jury, nevertheless; the most important, in fact. In introducing the first oration of the five, Cicero had divided his accusation into three parts; or rather, he had said that he would accuse Verres of extortion, cruelty, and sacrilege as governor of Sicily, and of peculation as a quaestor. If that accusation should fail, Cicero would accuse Verres of having freed the enemies of the Roman people, even keeping a pirate chief in his own house in Rome; and these were matters connected with Verres' activity as commander of the Roman navy in Sicily; in reality a charge of high treason. And if this accusation, too, should prove unavailing, Cicero would maintain that Verres had imprisoned, tortured, and executed Roman citizens; questions connected with liberty and the rights of citizenship; and from this charge the Roman people would not let him escape.

Hortensius had intended, Cicero says, to found the defense mainly on Verres' services as a military man. This intention had doubtless been given wide circulation in the forum both by Hortensius and by the other supporters of Verres; nothing else would make so strong an appeal to the imperialistic Romans. Hortensius did not use his opportunity at the trial to give a picture of Verres the great general, and he did not afterwards publish a speech for this purpose; probably there was little to Verres' credit that Hortensius could tell; but Cicero takes up this chief weapon of the defense, and turns it against Verres.

The latter was supposed to have kept Sicily free from harm in connection with the Slave War in Italy, recently ended. To this Cicero devotes very little time, only pointing out that the slaves in Italy had no boats with which to go to Sicily and that the slaves in Sicily itself were in no condition to start a revolt. Instead of dwelling on this point, which was unimportant, Cicero gives a picture of Verres' personal habits, and these were certainly not those of a vigilant commander.

Verres spent the winters in Syracuse, for there, as the saying went, the sun shone every day even in the worst of seasons. He lay on his couch. The short days were given to banquets; the long nights to worse things. At the coming of spring, which Verres dated, not from the first blowing of the west wind or from the position of the stars, but from the blooming of the rose, Verres made ready for the labor of official travel. He never mounted a horse, but reclined in a litter, like a king of Bithynia; the bearers were eight; there was an exquisite pillow filled with rose leaves; Verres had one wreath on his head and another around his neck, though even banqueting Romans were satisfied with the wreath on the head; and, as he was carried along, he occasionally raised to his face a fine-meshed linen bag filled with rose leaves. Arriving at the end of his journey, in some city, he was taken, still in the litter, directly to a bedroom, and here the Sicilian magistrates as well as the Roman knights of the community were allowed to consult him. He listened, without witnesses, to their errands; his decisions were later announced in public. After giving some time to the official business, at which decisions were always for sale, he considered himself entitled to devote the rest of his sojourn in the city to the worship of Bacchus and of Venus. In every Sicilian community where he held court some woman had been chosen to make him welcome. Some of these joined openly in his banquets; others avoided publicity. The banquets themselves were not characterized by the usual decorum of Roman state affairs; there was shouting, quarreling, and even fighting; after all was ended, men lay fallen as after the battle of Cannae.

The summers were ordinarily used by governors in Sicily for official trips through the province; but not by Verres. He pitched his camp in Syracuse, with tents and awnings of the finest linen; near the beach, at the entrance to the harbor. Here he stayed. Nobody was admitted except his companions and ministers in lust; Timarchides chiefly, and his own son, who was beginning to imitate his father, though nature had intended differently. But if there were no men present except Verres and his son and an occasional boon companion, the ladies of Syracuse were not excluded. Cicero mentions several by name. There was the daughter of a mime, whom Verres had stolen from a flute-player. She caused a disturbance one day because objection to her presence had been made by the other ladies, all of noble birth. One of the latter was Pipa, wife of a certain Aeschrion; verses had been composed about her, which were known, sung perhaps, in all parts of Sicily. Another was Nice, a famous beauty, the wife of Cleomenes; the latter loved his wife, but dared not oppose the wishes of Verres. And the praetor himself, most often without male companion, lolled about in a flowing robe of purple and a tunic that reached to his heels. He rarely went to the forum to sit in judgment, and of this men were glad; his absence was like the absence of cruelty and violence.

Verres, in purple robe and slippers, was a new kind of military man, says Cicero. The revolting slaves had given this fine general no opportunity to show his prowess; but such was not the case with the pirates. These had for years infested the whole Mediterranean, cutting off Roman grain ships, making travel insecure, and practically paralyzing commerce. They frequently raided the coasts, and made prisoners of prominent Romans or their sons, whom they held for ransom. They were foes worthy of Verres' steel.

And he did capture one of their ships. It had run aground near Syracuse, and there his men found it, crew and all, and brought it to the famous camp by the Syracusan harbor. Verres and his friends spent a whole night superintending its unloading;

which must have been a picturesque sight. The ship was filled
with beautiful young slaves, with silver vessels and silver coin,
and with costly tapestries. The pirates, as outlaws, should have
been executed. Verres executed the old among them; he spared
those who were young and those who had any unusual accomplishments, so that they would be valuable as slaves. Most of
these he kept for himself; others he gave to his son, his secretaries, and his friends; six musicians he sent to a friend in
Rome.

Crowds gathered both from the city of Syracuse and from
other places to see the pirates punished; they were public
enemies, their captain especially being greatly feared by the
Syracusans. To satisfy the public desire for revenge, Verres
caused the execution, as already mentioned, of those pirates
whom he could not use; and when their number was too small
to give perfect satisfaction, he substituted Roman citizens whom
he had had imprisoned. These were led to execution with their
heads covered. When some of them nevertheless were recognized,
Verres explained that they had been partisans of the revolting
Sertorius in Spain, or that, after being captured by the pirates,
they had made common cause with the latter. Nobody in Syracuse
saw the pirate captain. Verres had sent him to another city,
where he was guarded, though well supplied with everything.
Later Verres sent him to Rome, with one other captain.   The
popular suspicion, that Verres had been bribed to spare the life
of the captain, was obviously true. When, during the trial,
Verres was asked why he had a pirate living in his house, he
explained that he had not executed him in Sicily, because the
people, in their enmity, would have claimed that Verres had
taken bribes and then executed some one else; now, on the other
hand, the pirate was still available—a wonderful explanation,
both in what it proved and in what it failed to prove.   The
two pirate captains had been in Verres' house for a year; at
the request of Cicero they were taken into custody.

But the pirates did not always run aground. The Roman fleet in Sicily consisted of seven ships, contributed by the island communities. Cleomenes, the cuckold husband of the beautiful Nice, had been appointed admiral by Verres; a thing contrary to all precedent, for Verres had legates and other Romans from whom to choose; but it was convenient both to reward Cleomenes and to have him out of the way. The seven ships made a brave showing as they sailed out of the harbor of Syracuse; past Verres, who, slippered and in his purple robe and long tunic, was standing on the shore, leaning on one of his mistresses. But the ships lacked equipment, had an insufficient number of rowers, and were not even supplied with food for the scanty crews; Verres having taken money from the Sicilians instead of men and material.

Presently it was rumored that a pirate vessel was in the neighborhood. Cleomenes, who had the swiftest boat and the largest number of rowers, flees; the other ships follow, each as it is best able. The pirates take two of them; but the others reach shore, where they are deserted by their crews. The pirates, coming up shortly afterwards, set the ships on fire, and then sail for Syracuse.

A messenger had reached the city in the dead of night; the people had also seen the glare of the burning ships, a new kind of beacon, says Cicero, for it was customary to announce the presence of pirates by beacons along the coast. The people of Syracuse go to Verres, and he comes forth to meet them as the day is dawning; but he is not sober enough to take charge. The citizens, therefore, arm themselves, and occupy the market place, and also the island, a part of the city reserved for the dwellings of the resident Romans, since it dominated the rest of Syracuse and could easily be defended.

The pirates, on arriving, first visit Verres' wonderful camp on the beach, which they find deserted; thereupon, with their four small boats, they sail into the harbor. The city was built around this, so that the pirates, as they sail back and forth, come very close to the market place. They make no attempt to land, but fling to the shore some roots of the edible dwarf palm, which they had found in the Sicilian ships, gathered for food by the ill-supplied sailors. After a while they depart, unmolested, as they had entered; and yet, Cicero exclaims, it was in this very place that the three hundred ships of Athens had come to grief.

As the captains of the ships, sons of prominent Sicilian families, say everywhere that the disgrace was due to lack of food and equipment and to the flight of Cleomenes, their admiral, Verres, in self-defense, decides that the captains must be executed. Only Cleomenes is to be saved and, for the sake of appearances, though only for the present, the captain who had been in command of Cleomenes' ship. The trial is held in the forum of Syracuse; Cleomenes sits by the side of Verres; the jury consists of the friends of the praetor. The parents and relatives of the youthful defendants are present, begging for mercy; the trial itself, foreshadowing its outcome, is one of noise and violence. One of the speakers for the defense dares to attack Cleomenes, and the lictors almost tear the clothing from his back; one of the defendants, realizing that the verdict has already been settled, accuses Verres himself in a speech, which he later, in prison, committed to writing. It was read everywhere in Sicily.

The defendants are condemned, including a captain who because of eye trouble had been on leave at the very time of the flight from the pirates. The punishment is to be death.

While the condemned are in prison, nobody can secure permission to see them except by bribing the jailor. Timarchides, too, is on hand, selling favors and promises. He suggests to the captain of Cleomenes' ship that he must not trust overmuch in the fact that he has not been arraigned; he is in danger of being flogged to death, and should know how best to protect himself. The parents of the young men pass the night outside the prison.

Only through Timarchides can they send food to their sons, or be sure that the executioner will despatch his victims with a single blow of the ax, or that the corpses will be given decent burial and not be thrown to the wild beasts. Everybody in Syracuse, says Cicero, heard of Timarchides' bargains about the burials while the condemned were still living.

On the following day the young captains were led forth, in chains, and beheaded.

The execution of the Sicilians at Syracuse closes the list of Verres' crimes against the provincials. Cicero thereupon turns to Verres' treatment of Roman citizens, the climax of his whole charge.

One old man, a trader, was beaten by six lictors before the very tribunal of the praetor; his eyes and his face were struck with a cane, and when he had fallen to the ground, blows were still showered upon him. He died shortly after he had been carried away. Many Roman traders who touched at Sicily with rich cargoes, were arrested and their property confiscated; they were accused of being in league with the pirates, or with the slaves of Spartacus, or of sympathizing with Sertorius. These Romans were huddled together in the quarries of Syracuse, which were known throughout the world and which were used for criminals from all parts of Sicily. When the quarries could hold no more, the prisoners were executed, in batches. Among the Romans confined here had been the men who were beheaded in place of the pirates.

A certain P. Gavius had escaped from the quarries, and reached Messana, the modern Messina, on his way to Rome. When he was actually embarking on the ship that was to take him to Italy, he uttered threats against Verres; he would be in Rome, he said, to meet the praetor when the latter returned from his province. The people of Messana, friends of Verres, arrested Gavius, and as the governor on that very day happened to come to Messana, Gavius was brought before him. Verres at once takes his seat on the tribunal and orders the lictors to get ready their rods. Gavius cries that he is a Roman citizen, *civis Romanus sum,* which would entitle him to a trial in Rome. Roman citizenship, says Cicero, was a protection in every country; a man threatened with violence among the Persians or even in distant India would have appealed for protection to nothing else, for the rights of a Roman citizen lay at the very basis of Roman world rule. But Verres pays no heed. It has been discovered, he replies, that Gavius is a spy from the revolted slaves; let the lictors flog him; after that, he is to die on the cross.

In Messana the place for crucifixions was behind the city. Verres decides to have the cross erected on the shore, in sight of the mainland; Gavius will thus be able to look toward Italy and his home, since he claims to be a citizen. And the cross was erected, Cicero concludes, as Verres had ordered; in sight of all the ships that pass back and forth through the strait; a monument to Verres crimes.

With the picture of the Roman citizen hanging on the cross at the straits of Messina, Cicero comes to the end of the long list of Verres' crimes. Cicero then turns to the gods in solemn invocation, and, as a last word, he expresses the hope that it may be his fortune never again to have to engage in a prosecution, but that he may be enabled to devote his energies to the defense of the oppressed.

CHAPTER VII

IN POLITICS

I

MAGISTRACIES

The account of Cicero as a pleader has been long, though by no means exhaustive. Oratory was Cicero's main, almost his exclusive, business during the years before his consulship; and even after 63 B.C., when he was caught in the political whirlwind and directed his thwarted energies either toward saving the state or toward making conditions better, oratory was his chief weapon. The Romans of later generations called him Cicero the Orator even when they did not forget his political and literary activities.

The ultimate goal of his pleading was the consulship, the road to which lay through the minor offices. This had always been the custom; Sulla had made the custom a law in so far as it applied to the quaestorship and the praetorship. The aedile-ship, while not required legally, was extremely useful, since the aediles, as supervisors and practically givers of public games, had an extraordinary opportunity for winning popular favor. One other office there was, the plebeian tribunate, but the latter had by Sulla been made a disqualification for further office-holding; and although this limitation was removed in the year 75 B.C., the tribunes had been shorn of so much of their power, not restored until 70 B.C., that the office did not during these years attract really able men. Tribunician activity, moreover, was distinctly political, the very thing eschewed by Cicero. He, therefore, did not stand for the tribunate. He held the other offices, each at the earliest age allowed by law; but his official doings, like everything else during these years not connected with his oratory, are very imperfectly known.

He was quaestor in 75 B.C. His election attested his early popularity, for the vote in his favor was one of the largest secured by the twenty successful candidates. Of these twenty quaestors, the regular number since Sulla, eight were employed in Rome, while twelve were sent to the provinces. Cicero was one of the two assigned to Sicily, where he seems to have spent practically the whole year. He was stationed at Lilybaeum, in the western part of the island; the propraetor and the other quaestor were in Syracuse. He had charge of the public funds and revenues, which included the buying of grain. This was a year of dearth; food was high in Rome; but Cicero showed himself a good provider, sending large cargoes of grain to the city. Though the provincials groaned at first under the unusual burdens, Cicero won their confidence by his fairness and integrity; he even cut off the customary perquisites of the clerks and other subordinates of his office. The Sicilians, in return, paid him extraordinary honors, so that he could say in court,[1] twenty-one years later, that no quaestor in Sicily had reaped more glory from his office than had he. When leaving Lilybaeum, he spoke to the citizens, promising them his support, a promise that the Sicilians were glad to remember when desirous of prosecuting Verres. They had had an opportunity of observing Cicero as an orator, for he had appeared before the propraetor as counsel for some young Romans who had been accused of misconduct in military service, and had secured their acquittal.

His return from Sicily is better known than his whole year of residence; at least, two events are later described by him in considerable detail. The first of these took place in Syracuse. As a center of Greek life in the west, and Cicero says that it was the most famous and formerly the most learned of Greek cities, Syracuse offered much of interest to Cicero. He doubtless saw everything, including the notorious quarries, which dated back some thrée centuries to Dionysius, the tyrant of Syracuse,

---

[1] *Pro Planc.* 64.

for he has much to say about the latter in a passage of the *Tusculans,*[2] obviously reminiscent of this time. The reminiscence, however, is concerned with an archaeological discovery, the first notable event of his return, in which he took considerable satisfaction to the very end of his life, the *Tusculans* being written about two years before his death.

The grave of the great mathematician Archimedes was supposed to be in Syracuse, but the Syracusans had neglected it, did not know where it was, and even denied its existence. Cicero was familiar with a description in verse of the tomb, to the effect that it contained a globe and a cylinder. In company with some prominent citizens of Syracuse, he went to a burial place by one of the gates, and there, after some search, he found a small column with a globe and a cylinder. It was almost covered with weeds. When these had been removed, the verses remembered by Cicero were found on the front of the pedestal, but only the beginnings of the lines were still legible. "To think," exclaims Cicero, with the amateur's delight, "that I, an Arpinate, should find the grave of Archimedes, the most famous citizen of Syracuse, when his fellow-citizens knew nothing about it!" In a small way, the incident is indicative of a greater movement; the Greeks were yielding their places to the Romans in nearly every sphere; in the next generation, largely as a result of Cicero's literary activity, Rome would produce authors far superior to their Greek contemporaries. As for Archimedes, Cicero seems to have studied mathematics and may have had some faint understanding of his greatness.

The other event is even better known. Cicero stopped at Puteoli, the fashionable watering place on the bay of Naples. He was thirty-two and enthusiastic. Having sent large grain supplies to hungering Rome, he was convinced that the busy capital was resounding with his praises; the Roman people would be ready to do him all kinds of honor. Some acquaintances met

---

[2] *Tusc.* 5, 57 ff.

him at Puteoli. "What is the news from Rome?" they asked. Rome! As if Cicero had just come from Rome! The question almost prostrated him. "I am on my way from my province," he said. "Oh, I remember. From Africa?" "No, from Sicily," corrected Cicero rather scornfully, for he was getting irritated. A third person intervened. "Why, don't you know that M. Tullius has been quaestor in Syracuse?" He thought himself well informed! And Cicero had sent grain ships from Lilybaeum! There was nothing further to do. Cicero forgot his irritation, and joined the crowds that "had come to the waters."

There was a moral to this little scene. Cicero tells the story in the *Pro Plancio*,[3] in the year 54 B.C. He is addressing a young prosecutor, Laterensis, who found it unjust that the electors had passed him by in favor of Plancius. The latter had spent his life in the forum, whereas Laterensis had been much away, doing good service in the East. But service abroad, Cicero explains to his youthful opponent, is not the way to win popular favor. Cicero had discovered as much at Puteoli; a discovery that was far more useful to him than any praise could have been. The Romans, he continues, are dull of hearing, but they have very sharp eyes. Cicero had therefore been daily in the forum; and Laterensis ought also to have been there. The Romans do not often hear about events in the provinces—unless, he might have added, Cicero is a prosecutor and Verres the defendant.

While Cicero was exerting himself to bring Verres to trial, he was also a candidate for the curule aedileship. He was elected, as has been mentioned, despite the opposition of Verres and his supporters; and even secured more votes than the other successful candidate, two curule aediles being elected every year. This office made him a member of the nobility, with the right of transmitting his portrait bust to his descendants. His duties were manifold, all connected with the external life of Rome; he had charge of the temples, public buildings, markets, and streets.

---

[3] *Pro Planc.* 64–67.

He also gave public games on three different occasions. In later years he speaks[4] with approval of a decent outlay in connection with the games, to secure popular favor; but he adds that he spent little himself. Cicero's success depended upon service to the people and not on sumptuous entertainments. The Sicilians, grateful for Verres, sent him gifts of all kinds, and Plutarch, who mentions it, says that Cicero used them to reduce the price of food. But this year, 69 B.C., is after all even more of a blank than that of the quaestorship, at least so far as Cicero's official deeds are concerned. It was in 69 B.C., probably, that he defended Fonteius.

The praetorship, in 66 B.C., is somewhat better known. The magisterial elections in 67 had been turbulent and were twice interrupted; and there seems to have been unusual bribery, for Cicero in a letter to Atticus says that the candidates for office were harassed more than ever by all manner of unreasonable demands, and these demands must have come from electioneering agents. He was not troubled about his own prospects. There had been some thought, it seems, of Atticus coming to Rome to assist in the canvass, but Cicero writes to him not to come; he also adds that, since their friends might naturally expect Atticus to be present in the capital, he has himself warded off criticism by explaining to them that it is more important for Atticus to attend to his own business and that he is consequently staying away at Cicero's own urgent request. And Cicero's confidence proved well founded. Though the praetorian elections were twice interrupted, they were carried far enough to indicate that Cicero was in the lead; and this lead he maintained when the elections were finally brought to a valid conclusion.

As praetor, Cicero was allotted charge of the extortion court; the very court in which he had secured the conviction of Verres. Only one of the cases that came before him is mentioned, that of Licinius Macer, who is better known as an annalist than as

---

[4] *Pro Mur.* 39, and esp. *De Off.* 2, 57–59.

a robber of provincials. His province is not named. Macer,
who was supported by Crassus, later one of the triumvirs, had
expected an easy acquittal, but he was unanimously pronounced
guilty; a matter, says Plutarch, which brought much credit to
Cicero. The latter refers to this trial in a letter to Atticus.[5]
Though the interpretation of his words is somewhat doubtful,
it seems clear either that he had been unfair to Macer or that
he might have favored him in such a way as to save him. The
people, he continues, had very markedly approved of his management of the case, so that he had gained far more from this
approval than anything that could have come to him from
Macer, if acquitted. Cicero, in spite of his truly Roman coolness
in estimating the result of the trial, had probably acted justly:
the people approved, and yet Macer was one of the people's
party.

It was not Cicero's triumphant election, however, nor even
the trial of Macer that makes his praetorship noteworthy, but
the fact that during this year for the first time he took a direct
part in the shaping of public policy. In the past he had kept
himself free from political entanglements, winning his way
entirely as an orator. He had made use of political conditions
when favorable to his cases, as was inevitable, but he had
remained independent, accepting cases from people of very different political complexions. Now, however, he supported the
bill of the tribune Manilius, which proposed that the command
against Mithradates be given to Pompey.

II
POMPEY

The years since Sulla's death in 78 B.C. had witnessed the
gradual but certain rise of Pompey to a position of dominance
that, while not a dictatorship, had nevertheless not been par-

---

[5] *Att.* 1, 4, 2.

alleled even by Sulla himself. Pompey's emergence or, at least, the emergence of some powerful general, was natural. Sulla had through arms established the nobles as a ruling caste, but these did not have the arms to maintain their preëminence. They had their wealth, tradition, and capacity, the latter largely military and still considerable, but their rule depended on the laws of Sulla, and laws at this time were made to be broken quite as much as to be obeyed. The nobles did not have a standing army, but were a civil and not a military aristocracy. If trouble should arise, whether within the state or without, some military leader would have to be found, and the latter, whether a noble or not, would be very unlikely to forget the lessons of Marius and Sulla.

There were troubles everywhere, calling for military inter- ference. Spain was in the possession of the Marians, headed by Sertorius, who had gone thither in 83 B.C. The rebel power in Spain was like that of a hostile nation. Macedonia was con- stantly raided by the barbarians; Egypt teemed with endless possibilities of complications; the pirates lorded it in every nook of the Mediterranean; and Mithradates, in spite of triumphs celebrated in Rome to commemorate victories over him, was as determined and ready an enemy as ever. Within Italy as well there was imminent danger. Sullan veterans, settled on other people's lands, were attacked by former owners, as at Faesulae in Etruria, later famous as a Catilinarian center; and this attack at Faesulae is only one little bubble in the whole seething sea of Italy, where such careers as that of Oppianicus were possible. Rome itself was like an overcharged engine, ready to explode whenever Sulla should be gone. He died in 78 B.C., and the trouble began at once. The consuls quarreled about his funeral, continuing their disagreements through the year, and in the following year one of them, at the head of an army, began what was virtually a civil war.

All this gave Pompey his opportunity. There was no noble who could be sent against the rebellious ex-consul. Pompey had even as a stripling been praised by Sulla for his great military gifts; he was only a knight and still young, born the same year as Cicero, but he was sent to stop the civil war. This he accomplished, and then, since the danger of Sertorius was growing greater, he was entrusted with a command in Spain. The fighting here was not all to the glory of Pompey, for Sertorius had ability and good soldiers, but Pompey was ultimately successful, largely through treachery in Sertorius' camp, which led to his murder in 72 B.C. When Pompey returned to Italy, he was the most popular and successful general in Rome.

He was not the only military leader, however, who rose to distinction during the first years after Sulla's death. Crassus became prominent through the Slave War, which began in 73 B.C. Spartacus, said to have served in the Roman army, was the leader of the revolting slaves; the band numbered seventy at first, but had reached seventy thousand at the end of the year; a formidable army, for many of the slaves were trained gladiators. The government levied armies, one after another, but they were defeated until Crassus, while praetor in 71 B.C., finally put an end to the war. The devastation of Italy, carried to an almost incredible extent during the Social and civil wars of Cicero's youth, became even greater; when the struggle was finished, crosses with the rotting corpses of slaves could be seen along the roads.

The wars against the Marians in Spain and the slaves in Italy came to an end about the same time, 71 B.C., Verres' last year in Sicily. Crassus had not conquered unaided, for M. Lucullus, returning from Macedonia, gave him real assistance; and Pompey, on his way from Spain, had the good fortune to fall in with a band of slaves who were fleeing to the north. He cut them to pieces and could later claim that he, and not Crassus, had really stamped out the rebellion. Pompey, no less than Sulla, ought to have been called Felix, the lucky one, for he was always reaping where others had sowed. This had been true in Spain as it was now in Italy, and as it would be again in the East. He was undoubtedly a great general, but his reputation was even greater; and at this time, when he was pitted in popular estimation against Crassus, he easily got the lion's share of applause. Crassus was not a popular favorite. He had made his money through the Sullan proscriptions; he was hard-hearted and grasping; and although he gave much of his time to pleading in the courts in behalf of ordinary people, he was not a great orator like Cicero. Nevertheless he was a capable pleader, as well as the richest man in Rome, and, after defeating the slaves, the leader of a victorious army.

Matters came to a head toward the end of 71 B.C. Crassus and Pompey, each in command of an army, were among four generals encamped before Rome demanding triumphs. Crassus, at this time as well as always later, envious of his great rival, nevertheless made overtures to him; and they joined in demanding the consulship for the next year. This demand was illegal. Crassus had held the offices prescribed by Sulla, but he was still praetor, and the law required two years to elapse before he could hold the consulship. This, however, was not a very serious objection. Pompey, on the other hand, was still a knight; he had held no offices, and, at thirty-five, was far below the legal age for the consulship. Not having been praetor, he also lacked the official requirement for celebrating a triumph, though he had already, under Sulla, celebrated one triumph. The senate refused the joint demand, imagining that their bulwark of Sullan laws was stronger than the army of the two generals.

Pompey's reputation as a general and the opposition of the aristocrats would have been enough, perhaps, to enlist popular support. He made this support whole-hearted by promising that if he was elected he would restore the tribunician power.

Agitation for its restoration had begun in the very year of
Sulla's death and had been going on ever since. Macer, later
convicted in Cicero's court, had been much occupied with it;
and Caesar, who had begun his political career by two unsuccessful prosecutions of extortionate nobles, had made himself something of a popular leader by agitating in favor of a reëstablished
tribunate. In making his promise, therefore, Pompey allowed
himself to be identified with the popular party, as its leader, of
course; but he was not interested in city politics. His only
connection with the people's party consisted in the fact that he
was for the moment opposed to the nobility.

He also made an alliance with the knights. These had for
years been clamoring against the senatorial juries, wishing for
a return of the happy days when they themselves sat in judgment over ex-governors and could consequently expect favorable
treatment in the provinces at the hands of governors still in
office. The knights had nothing in common with the plebs except
that they were all in opposition to the nobles. For the time
being these two orders formed one party, and the tribunes
ranted against senatorial jurors just as they shouted for more
power. It is not likely that Pompey made any definite promise
about the courts, but his election would weaken the aristocrats
and might lead to the desired reconstruction of the juries.

Pompey and Crassus were elected. The people's party had
helped, and also the knights, but the armies had been the great
argument. It was also in the shadow of the army that the
proposed measures were carried. The tribunate was restored
in all its power for good and evil, mostly evil. The knights did
not get back the courts, but they secured one third of the jury,
as has been shown earlier; the nobles retained one third; and
the rest was given to the plebs, though to the richest of them,
who stood closest to the knights. The struggle about the courts
was long, and was doubtless influenced by the Verrine trial.
This year, 70 B.C., completed the destruction of the Sullan con-

stitution, but the nobles were scarcely in a worse position than they had been before the time of Marius and Sulla. They were, in fact, in a better position, because they retained part of the courts. The violent rivalry between the orders would continue.

Pompey, however, now dominated Rome. He could have made himself an absolute ruler, had he so chosen, but that was not what he desired. His wish was to be recognized as Rome's most eminent citizen; to be applauded when he appeared in public—and his favors toward the plebeians had contributed toward this; to be in Rome, as it were, or above it, but not of it. He therefore served his year as consul, and then, scorning the usual reward of a province, retired ostentatiously to private life. His relation to Roman politics was not unlike that of a modern money king to the stockmarket: others might gamble for small gains, not so small perhaps if we recall Verres, but Pompey would bestir himself only in larger matters, such as great wars, which by adding new provinces to the empire actually opened virgin fields in which the little politicians might show their greed and cleverness. He was waiting for some such great opportunity, and Crassus followed his example; but Crassus had to wait so long that he found it advisable to ally himself closely with the plebeians and finance their most promising politician, Caesar. Caesar had genius; he also had great need of money to win popular support; he was quaestor in 69 B.C., when Hortensius was consul and Cicero aedile.

Pompey's golden hour presently arrived. The pirates were becoming daily more insolent and more of a public danger. They had no close union, each captain scouring the sea independently, but still they formed a sort of brotherhood, acting together when necessary. They also had strongholds and fortified cities on the southern coast of Asia Minor and elsewhere in the eastern Mediterranean. Their ships were swift and well manned, many of the crews being composed of Romans who had been driven from Italy during the civil wars or who had left Spain after the defeat of the Marians. They terrorized the whole Mediterranean, kidnapping children and adults to be sold into slavery or held for ransom, attacking and looting cities, and, most important of all, waylaying the grain ships that fed Rome. It was the Romans who suffered most, for although the pirates favored nobody—they made a bargain with Spartacus, the enemy of Rome, and then cheated him—their depredations brought the greatest injuries to Rome, who ruled the world. Food prices soared aloft in the city; the knights and other investors in the provinces lost their money; even Roman armies, so Cicero says, possibly with some exaggeration, could not be transported from Brundisium across the narrow Adriatic except in the middle of winter. The constant menace of the pirates is shown by the practise in Sicily, doubtless followed elsewhere, of lighting beacons along the coast at their approach.

Their insolence was monumental. It has already been mentioned how they sailed into the landlocked harbor of Syracuse and jeered at the armed citizens gathered together in the forum. But they came even nearer to Rome. The naval station at Caieta, near Formiae, not many miles from the capital, was laid waste before the very eyes of a Roman praetor. Ostia, the seaport of Rome at the mouth of the Tiber, was surprised, the ships burned, and everything stolen or destroyed. Roman ambassadors were captured and held for ransom; two praetors were captured; so were the children of the very man in command against the pirates, says Cicero, perhaps referring to the daughter of M. Antonius, to be mentioned presently; even the Appian Way, one of the great Roman thoroughfares, was unsafe. Among the most notable captives were Clodius, later the most unruly tribune of these unruly times, and Caesar, who had been fighting a little and studying rhetoric in the East. Plutarch's account of Caesar's captivity describes how he stayed with the pirates for thirty-eight days, joining in their games and even reciting verses and speeches to them, with taunts at their illiteracy when they failed of the proper enthusiasm. He also threatened to come back to hang them after he had been ransomed, and this he did.

The piratical nuisance had lasted for generations, dating much farther back than the Roman claim to world rule. It had been growing constantly worse; many Romans had been sent against them, two commanders especially having within the last few years received large powers for this purpose. One of these was Servilius, a consul in 79 B.C., who opposed them very successfully for three years, successfully enough at any rate to celebrate a triumph in 75 B.C., but without really doing much good. After him the war against them was entrusted to M. Antonius, noteworthy mainly as the son of the great orator who befriended Cicero. Antony was given general command of the sea and the coasts, to be effective in the provinces wherever necessary, but he was a miserable failure. He attacked the pirates in Crete and was apparently defeated; the Romans in consequence dubbed him Creticus.

It was therefore an immensely popular bill that Aulus Gabinius, the tribune of the plebs, brought forward in the year 67 B.C., namely, to appoint an ex-consul—by which was meant Pompey—for a period of three years, with supreme power on the waters of the whole Mediteranean and on a coast strip all around it to a depth of fifty miles. In Crete, at this time, one of the family of the Metelli was doing good work against the pirates, but everywhere else they were unchecked. The bill, an extension of the powers of Antony, was favored by the people, who wanted food; by the knights, who wanted safety for their extensive provincial business; and apparently by many nobles, who were not insensible to pecuniary opportunities. Aside from any selfish considerations actuating this class or that, the proposed measure was a necessity of the times. The bill was opposed by the staunch aristocrats, among whom Catulus, the leader of the senatorial party, and Hortensius, its greatest orator, were conspicuous. But these could accomplish nothing.

Pompey's appointment caused an immediate lowering of prices in Rome; his success was almost instantaneous. In forty days, during the first half-year, he cleared the western seas; after which he made a short visit to the capital, to bask in his new popularity. In another forty-nine days he completed the even greater task of driving the pirates from the sea in the eastern Mediterranean and of conquering their strongholds on the coast of Asia Minor.

But Pompey's good fortune was preparing even greater things for him. Mithdradates, the consistent enemy of Rome, had fought the so-called First Mithradatic War in 88–84 B.C., and had been defeated by Sulla; he had fought the Second Mithradatic War in 83–82 B.C. successfully, against a lieutenant of Sulla; finally, in 75 B.C., he began new hostilities. L. Licinius Lucullus, who stood very high in the nobility and who was consul in 74, took the field against him. He was eminently successful; by the middle of 70 B.C. he had brought all of Mithradates' ancestral kingdom, Pontus, under Roman rule. The king sought and obtained assistance from his son-in-law, the king of Armenia, whereupon Lucullus invaded Armenia. But in Rome the tide was going against the aristocrats; one result of which were machinations for Lucullus' recall. The popular agitators were joined by the knights. Sulla had oppressed the province of Asia in a manner worthy of Verres in Sicily. Though Asia was, with Sicily, the richest province in the Roman realm, cities had had to sell their property in order to satisfy Sulla, and citizens had been forced to give their sons and daughters into slavery. Lucullus put an end to this fearful condition, by various arrangements, and actually cleared the province of debt in four years. But this meant great loss to the knights. Lucullus was a very strict disciplinarian, which did not endear him to his soldiers. Some of these, moreover, had been in foreign service for eighteen years, and wished to return home. In the winter of 69–68 B.C., therefore, there was a mutiny.

When news of the political movement in Rome for Lucullus' recall reached the army, enhanced by agitators, of whom Clodius was one, discipline went entirely to pieces; not only the ordinary soldiers, but even the officers, refused to obey the general. Mithradates, aided by his Armenian ally, regained nearly all he had lost; and in 67 B.C. one of the consuls of that year was appointed to a governorship in the East, practically to supersede Lucullus. He went to his province, but did not take the field against Mithradates; the latter was not an enemy to be lightly opposed, but it may be that the ex-consul was in the East mainly to prepare the way for Pompey by his own obvious incapacity.

In 66 B.C., while Pompey was still in the East making final disposition of the pirates, many of whom he settled in widely scattered communities, Manilius, also a tribune, brought forward a bill. Pompey, without surrendering any of the powers granted him the year before, was to be entrusted with the war against Mithradates, having absolute authority to conclude alliances and to make peace; in short, while he already commanded the whole Roman navy and the more important parts of the provinces, he was now also to be made the irresponsible head of Rome's largest army. No power like this had ever before been entrusted to a Roman.

The bill was as usual discussed in a *contio*. Cicero's speech, still extant under the title *De Imperio Cn. Pompei,* is an enthusiastic and eloquent statement of what was obviously the general opinion in Rome. After dwelling for a moment on the fact that this was his first appearance in a discussion of public policy, a situation which he had avoided until now when he was a praetor and forty years old, he introduces his plea by exclaiming that it will be easier to begin than to end a speech about Pompey.

He discusses first the character and importance of the war against Mithradates; how it involves the glory of Rome, the safety of her allies, the revenues from the provinces, and the possessions of numerous citizens, reminding his auditors, among many other things, how twenty-three years earlier Italian men, women, and children to the number of eighty thousand had in one day been massacred at the command of Mithradates, who still remained unpunished. Mithradates, moreover, had sent legates and letters to the Marians in Spain, thus planning to attack Rome from two sides; he had allied himself with the pirates; and, when forced to flee from his kingdom, he had scattered his treasures in many places, in this way causing his greedy Roman pursuers to delay while they gathered his gold, just as Medea had scattered on the sea the limbs of her murdered brother, so that her father might stop his pursuit in order to collect the fragments of his son for burial.

Cicero thereupon eulogizes Pompey; his military ability, his courage, his reputation at Rome and abroad, and last of all his good luck, for Pompey, like many military men, was a man of destiny. Cicero's praise, though excessively high, was very likely the sort of thing often heard in the forum during these years; and Cicero does not fail to pay fine compliments to the ability of Lucullus, who, however, had been unable to finish the war. In reviewing Pompey's record, Cicero makes much of the war against the pirates, already won though not yet fully completed; and adduces, as a further argument in Pompey's favor, that he is already in the East and that Mithradates has shown fear at his approach.

Catulus and Hortensius, speaking for the unyielding aristocrats, as they had also done the year before, had dragged forward their old idol of precedent. No man had ever been given so much power as was now proposed for Pompey, they had argued; it was contrary to every tradition. So it was, but their idol had been much battered of late. Many men, Cicero reminded them, had been allowed privileges never heard of before; especially had this been the case with Pompey throughout his career; even the sturdiest aristocrats themselves had voted for unprecedented honors in his behalf. And as for this particular situation,

Catulus and Hortensius had voted against the Gabinian law: what would have become of Roman power if Pompey had not conquered the pirates? The opponents of Pompey's command have been wrong once, and are wrong again; and even they admit that if such sweeping legislation is to be passed in favor of any man, that man should be Pompey. Cicero, however, does not antagonize Catulus and Hortensius, but praises them highly, as he had praised Lucullus, pointing out in the meantime that other great nobles support the new bill.

The argument against Catulus and Hortensius was an excellent one, and it is still a reply to the modern critics of the speech. These remember that great military commands brought about the destruction of the republican form of government and that Cicero's political aim from the year 63 onward was to maintain this very government; consequently, according to them, he shows an utter lack of political insight in supporting the Manilian law. This criticism would be valid if Manilius had been the originator of such commands, but he was not. Marius and Sulla had begun the tradition, and this tradition itself was the result of numerous conditions which no single individual could modify. If the command against Mithradates had not been given to Pompey, it would have been given to somebody else; and that somebody else would either have lost the war, to the undoing of Rome's power, or else, winning it, he would have returned to Rome with an army that could either have made him dictator and king if he so chose, or under any circumstances a serious enough rival to Pompey, returning from the vanquished pirates, to render civil war possible. The question resolves itself, therefore, into a choice between Pompey and somebody else; and Pompey was obviously the most suitable man of the times. He did win the Mithradatic war, and after winning it he did not use his immense power to erect an autocracy. Pompey never had the ambition to rule; he wished merely to be the idol of Rome.

But speculations as to the ultimate result to Rome of great military commands are natural only to the modern student, who can see the whole course of Roman history; they could scarcely have occurred to Cicero and his contemporaries. Even Catulus and Hortensius, in maintaining that so great a command should be given to no man, were arguing speciously and only with an apparent largeness of vision; their objection was directed against Pompey because he was not a supporter of the nobility; the staunchest nobles themselves had found nothing amiss in Sulla's great military power. If it is conceivable that any one in Rome could have looked forward, as the modern student can look backward, then it is equally conceivable that Cicero foresaw the real harmlessness of Pompey. In the year 71 B.C. Pompey had been satisfied with election to the consulship, and after the consulship he had voluntarily retired to private life; he had made no effort to rule Rome. It may be that Cicero had drawn the correct inference from these years; at a later period Pompey's essential harmlessness was understood not only by Cicero but also by the nobles when they had to choose between Pompey and Caesar.

The bill became a law, but it can not be supposed that this was due in any considerable degree to Cicero's speech. The supporters of Pompey, including Caesar as spokesman of the plebs, comprised nearly all the voters in Rome: the plebeians, the knights, and even some of the aristocrats. These had passed the bill of Gabinius without the aid of Cicero; they would even more easily have passed that of Manilius, for Pompey had in the meantime conquered the pirates. He could well be expected also to conquer Mithradates, and this was needful if the Romans were really to profit by the victory over the pirates; it would be of little avail to have an open sea if the rich province of Asia as well as the rest of Asia Minor were taken by the king of Pontus; the open sea was useful only for bringing food and money from the provinces. The bill would therefore have passed under any circumstances. Cicero, to be sure, had a large following, but it was personal, and useful only for election to offices. He had not taken part in politics, and could not have effectively opposed Manilius, had he tried. His speech was an eloquent expression of the prevailing mood, and as such added no doubt to the enthusiasm in the forum. It was, however, a little more. Politics were carried on largely by lawsuits, and Cicero was the leading pleader. Manilius would certainly be accused of something or other by the defeated aristocrats. Cicero, therefore, promises him his aid, and we learn that Manilius was actually indicted and that Cicero was ready to take his case. Other matters intervened, however, so that the trial never took place.

Cicero's canvass for the consulship, if he became a candidate at the earliest possible moment, would begin the following year. The electors had therefore a good reason for expecting him to take sides in the great political questions of the day, or at least to show what he could do as a deliberative orator; and this was probably his chief motive for appearing at this particular time. Otherwise he might have supported the bill of Gabinius. He enrolled himself among those who believed in Pompey. This might be useful, but not to any great extent. The supporters of Pompey were so numerous that the individual would be lost in the crowd; they were also of very different political persuasions. Cicero could not expect any real assistance from Pompey, who would be in the East during Cicero's candidacy; nor did he get any assistance, except the very negative one of being known as a candidate whom Pompey did not oppose.[6] The speech, however, is the first public expression of Cicero's admiration for the successful general; an admiration which was to continue for the rest of Pompey's life, though at times it was dimmed by Pompey's faithlessness and political incapacity. It was, on the whole, an unprofitable admiration, bringing Cicero much disappointment, though it also did him and Rome some

[6] *Comment. Petit.* 5.

good. Cicero was a man of peace; in later years he insists[7] that the victories of peace are as great as those of war, perhaps greater; but he was enough of a Roman to think very highly of military gifts and of foreign conquests. Perhaps his infatuation for Pompey, for such it really was, had begun when he himself was a recruit in the camp of Pompey's father. It was certainly nourished by Pompey's unparalleled military career.

Advocacy of Pompey, who stood above political parties, did not commit Cicero to the program of the selfishly progressive plebeian party or to opposition to the equally selfish aristocratic conservatives. At the end of the speech he announces that he will try to earn further preferment by the means by which he had so far succeeded, his pleading. In this statement he voices his political detachment, and he maintained it. He opposed the most conservative aristocrats by supporting Pompey. In the next year he pleaded for the tribune Cornelius, whom the nobles attacked; but Cornelius from all reports was a good citizen; and it is in the very year of the Manilian law that, as praetor, he allowed Macer, with Caesar the leader of the plebeians, to be found guilty. It is also in this year, while speaking for Cluentius, that Cicero makes the remarkable statement that his references to politics in his orations are to be taken in a Pickwickian sense. The only class that he avowedly supported in urging Pompey's command was the knights. As he says, they were receiving daily letters from Asia about the critical situation; his close connection with their order had led them to remind him of the condition of the Roman state and of the danger that threatened their own possessions. This avowal is almost tantamount to a declaration that Cicero is pleading for the knights; but the knights represented the business interests of Rome and so, in Cicero's eyes, its prosperity.

---

[7] *De Off*. 1, 74–79.

III

Consular Canvass

Cicero began his canvass for the consulship on the sixteenth day before the Kalends of August, or July 17, in the year 65 B.C.; at least, writing to Atticus[8] earlier in the year, he gives it as his intention to begin then. It was the time of the tribunician elections and there would be great crowds in the Campus Martius. This was not to be the heavy part of the canvass, only the insinuating preliminaries, the so-called *prensatio,* in which prospective supporters were "laid hold of." Six other candidates appeared on the horizon at the time of Cicero's writing; and Catiline would be a seventh, if he could weather a prosecution which was hanging over him. One of the candidates had begun his *prensatio* too early, the result of which was to show that the men approached were in favor of Cicero.

From September to the end of the year, because of the numerous holidays, which had already played their part in the trial of Verres, there would be little to do in the courts. Cicero therefore intended to go to Cispadane Gaul, to stay until the following January, for the purpose of enlisting the municipalities and country districts. It is not known whether or not he carried out this plan, but he was very active during these days and took every precaution. One incident is reported. Atticus' wealthy uncle Caecilius, who later left his nephew ten million sesterces, had a business quarrel with a certain Satyrus, and asked Cicero to take the case. Satyrus, however, had been useful politically both to Cicero himself and to Quintus, and might still prove helpful. Cicero explained to the uncle that he would have taken the case if Caecilius had been the only accuser, but there were several of them, including two very blue-blooded aristocrats, so that Caecilius could easily get justice without Cicero's aid;

---

[8] *Att.* 1, 1.

this was no time for Cicero to jeopardize the friendship of trusted supporters, a thing Caecilius ought to consider. The uncle refused to consider the point, and ceased coming to Cicero's house; his visits, Cicero adds, had begun only a few days earlier and so, by implication, had been due to the disagreement with Satyrus. Cicero hopes Atticus will see the matter in the right light, for adverse judgment against Satyrus would have led to *infamia,* a serious matter; he certainly wishes Atticus to be considerate, but if he be inclined to grumble, why, then Cicero can only reply with a line of Homer about Achilles and Hector:[9]

> No vulgar prize they play,
> No vulgar victim must reward the day;
> Such as in races crown the speedy strife:
> The prize contended was great Hector's life.

Atticus had been expected in Rome in July of the preceding year, and had even promised to come earlier to assist in Quintus' canvass for the aedileship, to which Quintus was elected that year, 66 B.C. But Atticus did not allow anything to interfere with his numerous business engagements. Now, in 65 B.C., Cicero tells him to be in Rome without fail in January of 64 B.C., the time when Cicero would return from his campaign in Cispadane Gaul, and it is likely that Atticus arrived shortly before this time.

Atticus could win the interest of Pompey's followers; he might even do something with them while still in Greece. Incidentally, Cicero gives him permission to inform them, or the great general himself, who was busy with his wars in the East, that Cicero will not feel affronted if Pompey does not appear at the election; an innocent little joke that has been interpreted as a sign of monumental conceit; as if Cicero could ever have thought that Pompey would leave his campaigns and travel across the Roman empire to solicit votes in the forum. Atticus was

---

[9] *Iliad* 22, 159. Pope's translation.

also, and more importantly, to help in securing the support of the nobles, with whom as a class he seems always to have had intimate relations. At the beginning of the canvass their attitude had been somewhat doubtful, but with the passing of the months it had become clear, in 65 B.C., that they would oppose Cicero's candidacy; nearly every one thought so, Cicero says.

There is good reason for believing that Cicero was an efficient canvasser, quite at his ease in the babbling, intriguing Campus and forum. He made enemies occasionally, for he lived up to his reputation for saying sharp things. Thus, during this canvass, as Plutarch tells us, he once became thirsty, from talking doubtless, and stopped at a fountain. There was a crowd around him. "You have reason to fear the displeasure of the censor," he observed, "since I drink water." The censor, as every one knew, was a great lover of wine. But Cicero also made numerous friends, who kept him informed of the tricks of the other candidates. This was the case even as far back as the year 70 B.C., when he was a candidate for the aedileship. Verres at that time, it will be remembered, called together the professional electioneering agents to see if bribery might not keep Cicero out, and Cicero learned about the meeting in detail.

He had set about equipping himself for practical politics early in his career.[10] Ordinarily a Roman politician had a slave, the *nomenclator,* whose business it was to know the names of as many people as possible; an excellent arrangement no doubt, and not limited to ancient politics, but nevertheless not the best. Cicero, who had a prodigious memory, decided to acquire this knowledge himself, and to increase it. He learned the names of all the prominent citizens, where they lived, what lands they possessed, what people they employed in their political life, and with whom in their neighborhood they were on a friendly footing. When he traveled on any road in Italy, he could point

---

[10] Plut. *Cic.* 7. References to Plutarch will ordinarily be omitted. The passages can easily be found, since Plutarch's *Life of Cicero* is chronological in arrangement.

out the houses and estates of any one of his acquaintances. He was well prepared, therefore, to carry on a successful canvass. What was actually expected of him as a candidate may be gathered from his reported doings and from much that has already been said about the forum and the courts, but only in its ruder aspects, after all; the finer touches are supplied by Quintus in his excellent *Handbook of Electioneering*.

The winning of friends and supporters, says Quintus, is of course the main object. Every one under obligation to the candidate must be strongly impressed with the fact that this is the time for adequate acknowledgment; now or never. The candidate must not be narrow in his interpretation of the term friendship; he must take a generous view of it, for it is quite proper during a canvass to give the name of friend to persons of whose friendship at any other time in life he would be ashamed. He must discover what men are of importance in their various neighborhoods, and cultivate these, not wasting his time on the rest. Men from the country are flattered to find themselves known by name to a candidate for high office, but the latter must not be a mere *nomenclator;* he should endeavor to seem a real friend; Cicero, says Brother Quintus, was naturally affable, and had therefore a distinct advantage over his rivals; but a little simulation would not be out of place, nor even a little flattery, though disgraceful at other times. People in any way connected with the candidate's household and likely to have intimate knowledge about him, men of the same tribe, neighbors, clients, freedmen, and slaves, would be particularly useful, for they give the tone to the gossip in the forum; and it is of course desirable that the ears of as many as possible be filled with good reports about the candidate. Young men are excellent partisans; they are naturally given to enthusiasm and know how to bestir themselves.

A canvass must be a period of display, tempered with the proper dignity. The candidate should always have a large

crowd about him. There are three kinds of adherents, of varying degrees of devotion. Very many come to the *salutatio,* or
reception, in the morning; these are the most numerous, for some
of them go from one politician's house to another. Their service
is not very great, but the alert candidate will not fail to take
note even of this amount of attention; he will never ignore a
caller, but will express gratitude for the call both to the man
himself and to the latter's friends. These *salutatores,* in the
course of their migrations, will observe what candidate is most
appreciative, and reward him with their vote. Even when such
a caller is not to be relied upon, the candidate will do well to
have the appearance of believing in his sincere intentions. More
valuable than the ordinary morning visitors, however, are those
who stay to escort the candidate to the forum. He must, therefore, be additionally grateful to them, for it is important to enter
the forum with a large retinue; and he will wisely assist their
devotion by making it a point to start from his house at the same
time every morning. But not all of these *deductores* remained
with the candidate after he had reached the forum; some drifted
away in the crowd. There was a third class, the *adsectatores,*
who formed a permanent retinue. Some of these act entirely
from friendliness, and should be correspondingly encouraged;
others, whose duty it is always to be near the candidate because
of benefits they have received, should have it pointed out to them
that either they must come themselves, or, if they are prevented
by business or old age, they must make their friends come. Most
helpful of all *adsectatores* are those who have been successfully
defended by the candidate.

Banquets should be given both by the candidate and by
his friends, in the tribe and everywhere. The candidate must
keep open house; he must be accessible at all times, day and
night. He must have a friendly, open countenance; open as his
doors, otherwise he might as well close the latter. Men will exact
promises of future service. The adroit candidate will give his

promise in a spirit of willingness, never grudgingly; if he has to refuse, he will make clear his grounds and express sorrow at his inability, so as to win the petitioner's good will, if possible. Some orators have been known to gain more favor by their manner of refusing to take a case than others by actually undertaking it. For a philosopher, a reader of Plato, like Cicero, Quintus observes, it may be unseemly to make a promise he thinks himself unable to fulfill; but C. Cotta, consul in 75 B.C., a master in the art of canvassing, used to say that he promised everything. He had observed that when the occasion arrived for fulfilling his promise, he often had more time than he had expected, or that the petitioner frequently had no need of his services; indeed, many people make requests merely for the satisfaction of receiving a promise of future assistance, with no thought of ever using it. In any case, it is better to disappoint the few who eventually require the service that you cannot render than to disappoint the many. People are more irritated by a refusal that refers to the future than by the later breaking of a promise, provided the orator's inability to serve at that time is satisfactorily explained.

The canvass must be carried on systematically; each friend must be shown exactly what he has to do. All the electors are to be approached; nobody is to be given a chance to say afterwards that he was not asked for his vote. The canvass must embrace the senators, the knights, who are very numerous, the other orders, the whole city, and all of Italy. The same argument is not to be used everywhere. The nobles should be told that Cicero's previous advocacy of Pompey is not a sign that he advocates the people's side; since Pompey is all powerful, Cicero spoke in his behalf merely to win his support, or at least to avert opposition. The people, on the other hand, must be reminded that Pompey is Cicero's friend. In fine, the senate should be impressed with the idea that Cicero will uphold their power; the knights and the men of wealth, with a belief in him as a man of peace; and the people, with a conviction that he will do nothing contrary to their interests. Evidence for all these assertions can be found in Cicero's past record, and should be sought there, for a canvass is the proper occasion for calling attention to the candidate's past acts.

Marcus is to remember, every day as he goes down into the forum, that he is a New man, that he is seeking the consulship, and that the place of his canvass is Rome. In reference to Cicero's "newness" and his consular ambition, the electors must be reminded that an orator who has been held worthy to defend men of consular rank, is not himself unworthy of consular honors. Cicero's chief claim to election is his record as a pleader, his eloquence, says Quintus, who thereupon gives an impressive list, which has already been quoted, of his brother's numerous and varied supporters. But Cicero also has opponents. There are three kinds of these. Some have been injured by Cicero, who has pleaded against them; they are to be told that circumstances made Cicero's course necessary, but that he will assist them in the future. Others merely happen not to approve of Cicero, and they are to be won over. The third class are devoted to the rival candidates. If their support can not be gained, Cicero can intimate to them that he is well disposed to his rivals. It is useful, however, to cause the circulation of bad rumors about them; and Quintus immediately launches into vituperation of Antony and Catiline, who were Cicero's chief competitors.

Rome is a wicked city, says Quintus at last; men are tricky, deceitful, vicious, arrogant, stubborn, malevolent, proud, tiresome, and vexatious. Marcus is to make it clear that he will prosecute those who resort to bribery; not that he is to go about flourishing this threat, but only to let them know that they are being watched. They will thus fear Cicero's diligence and his power as a speaker as well as the evident support given him by the knights. After all, no election is so corrupt but that some tribes vote in all honesty, free from bribery; vigilance can therefore put a stop to the corruption arrayed against Cicero.[11]

As the time of the election approached, it became clear that Catiline and Antony were Cicero's only serious rivals. Their position was peculiar, and can be understood only in the light of the political movements of the years that immediately preceded. With the departure from Rome of Pompey less important politicians, particularly Caesar and Crassus, began to maneuver for position. Pompey was certain to return in a few years, probably at the head of a victorious army. Before that happened, Caesar and Crassus must have established themselves as leaders of the plebeian party, if they were to remain prominently in the political arena; otherwise the people would immediately fall into line behind the great general. There was need for a sort of balance of power, something to hold the military argument in check; and, as this was desired by the nobles no less than by the democratic leaders, we find the two parties acting together on occasion, though never with very great concord. They were after all natural enemies. The events of these years are not very clear, but it cannot be far from the truth that Caesar and Crassus were always in the background of political events. Each schemed for himself, though he also assisted the other, Caesar with political capacity and Crassus with money. Smaller men were put forward to do violence or to gain office; but Caesar and Pompey were the plebeian bosses.

---

11 For Quintus' authorship of this letter, see Tyrrell I², pp. 110–121. Quintus' purpose in writing it has been much discussed. It seems on the whole most likely that he wrote in the spirit of a literary man, expecting the letter to be circulated mainly among the intellectuals of Rome. The pamphlet also has certain qualities which must have been well suited to further Cicero's canvass. The attack on Catiline and Antony is in line with the usual practise. The cynical account of electioneering morals would indirectly call attention to Cicero's personal honesty; Quintus suggests the use of flattery, but says that he hesitates to offer such counsel to his brother, a pupil of Plato. The various interpretations of Cicero's relation to Pompey, which have led to the assertion that publication of the letter at this time is "quite unthinkable," would serve a purpose: they pointed out that advocacy of Pompey meant nothing in city politics, for many politicians hitched their little wagons to Pompey's star, and that Cicero was an independent candidate, whose real merit was to be sought in his oratory.

Violence and corruption flourished during this period even more than before. The cat was away and the mice played. In addition to the traditional bribery and riots, against which laws were passed in increasing numbers, there was introduced the use of hired gangs to enforce party desires; violence became systematized, and was to remain so until the fall of the republic. In the year 67 B.C., when Cicero was elected praetor, many meetings were broken up and one of the consuls was mobbed. Things were no better in 66 B.C. The consuls elected in that year, for 65 B.C., had made such notorious use of bribery that they were prosecuted and unseated; whereupon a new election was held and their defeated rivals were successful. This led to a conspiracy, which gave a promise of assistance to Catiline.

The details of this conspiracy, the First Catilinarian, are by no means certain. The plan was to murder the consuls of 65 B.C. on the first of January, when they took office. After this plan had miscarried, the attack on the consuls was set for the early part of February, but in this plan, too, the conspirators failed. The intention had been to get the rejected consuls-elect reinstated, and as these were the creatures of Caesar and Crassus, these two seemed to have been behind the whole project; if it succeeded, they would be the rulers of Rome. Catiline has been given as the leader in this conspiracy, which can scarcely be true, but he must have played a prominent part. He had been praetor in 68, had governed Africa in 67, and had returned to Rome in 66 B.C., to stand for the consulship. A threat of prosecution for provincial extortion had prevented his candidature; this and his naturally unscrupulous character would be incentive enough for his participation, in the hope that something would come of it.

Catiline is known to us mainly from Cicero's orations of the year 63. There can be no doubt of Catiline's very great guilt during this year; Cicero, though speaking against him, is not more severe than Sallust, who wrote some twenty years later and could have had no reason for making Catiline the wicked

hero of his historical monograph if this had not been warranted
by Catiline's reputation. This reputation he also kept in later
Roman histories. But it is founded on the year 63 B.C., which
has given its color also to the preceding years, notably in Sallust.
Catiline's record during the earlier years was by no means good.
He had been greedy and cruel during the Sullan proscriptions,
one of his victims being Cicero's kinsman Marius Gratidianus.
He was not impeccable in his private life; in 73, Fabia, a Vestal
Virgin and the half-sister of Cicero's wife, had been brought
to trial for accepting Catiline as her lover. Fabia had been
acquitted, but the trial indicates Catiline's reputation. Popularly he was charged with various immoralities that need not be
repeated. As governor of Africa, finally, he seems to have
practised unusual extortion.

But all these blots on his character can be paralleled in the
case of many of his contemporaries. He probably was very much
of the typical politician and man about town. It has already
been noted that Cicero in 65 B.C. thought of defending him.
Cicero did not do this, but his mere intention is important, for
he could scarcely have planned to associate himself with a
notorious criminal. Many years later, in 56 B.C., Cicero gives
a picture of Catiline. Without contradicting his earlier statements about Catiline's crimes, he describes how Catiline was a
man of many gifts, both for good and evil, how he gathered
young men about him, how he associated not merely with bad
but also with upright citizens, and how, before the conspiracy
of 63 B.C., he even tempted Cicero to think well of him. Cicero
was speaking in defense of his friend Caelius,[12] who had been
one of the supporters of Catiline's candidacy in 63 B.C.; but
he was probably giving a fair estimate of Catiline as he had
appeared during the period of Cicero's canvass.

Catiline's partner was C. Antonius, whose chief recommendation to the people of Rome was the fact of his being the son

---

[12] *Pro Cael.* 10–16.

of the great orator, who had befriended Cicero. He was a dissolute man, deeply in debt, unprincipled, and ready to take any road that might lead to success. If elected, he would be a very amenable colleague to Catiline. The canvass was financiered by Crassus, and the candidates gave themselves the appearance of representatives of the people, though their support was not limited to the plebs. If they succeeded, Crassus and Caesar, or, better still, Caesar and Crassus, would be the real masters. But both Antony and Catiline were patricians, whereas Cicero, their only opponent, was equestrian by birth. Cicero's letter to Atticus has already shown that the nobles were unwilling to vote for him. In the meantime they had small ground for confidence in the other two candidates. Catiline seems to have been raising a body of gladiators, for a friend, it was reported, but not very convincingly. Antony, more openly, was boasting that although poor he had enough slave-herdsmen to seek redress if defeated at the polls.

The situation came to a sudden head a few days before the election. The bribery in favor of the two partners had been carried to such an extent that more law-making seemed desirable. The bill was being debated in the senate when one of the tribunes interfered. Cicero saw his advantage. He sprang to his feet and delivered a crushing invective against the two rascals. The speech, later known as *In Toga Candida,* because Cicero wore the white toga of a candidate for office, has come down only in fragments, together with an ancient commentary; but these show that Cicero not only attacked the private and public life of his rivals, as was natural, even hinting at Catiline's alleged connection with Fabia, but also struck at the adroit manipulation of the canvass. During the preceding night, he said, Antony and Catiline had had a meeting with their corrupt agents at the house of a certain noble, well known in the "profession of bribery," which noble, as the old commentator observes, was either Crassus or Caesar. Antony and Catiline replied to Cicero, but their retort amounted in the main to this, that Cicero was a New man; nothing very novel, for others had reminded the electorate of that, calling him a mere sojourner in the imperial city. The nobles were won for the side of Cicero. His triumph at the election was complete. Antony came in a bad second, and Catiline fell a few votes behind his partner.

Whether the sudden change on the part of the nobles determined the election can not be ascertained. Perhaps Cicero's natural following would have been large enough even without the aristocrats, for he proved so popular when the time came for voting that the electors did not cast their ballots, each in his own *century*, according to the usual procedure, but proclaimed him consul by acclamation. He carried every one of the thirty-five tribes. With a very doubtful exception, in the year 72 B.C., Cicero was the first New man to attain the consulship since the time of Marius; and he was the only New man who had ever secured the various offices, one after the other, at the earliest age allowed by law.

CHAPTER VIII

IN PRIVATE LIFE

It is hardly more than a glimpse that we get of Cicero as a private citizen during the twenty odd years of his activity in the courts and his official rise. There are for our information only eleven letters, and a bit of narrative written in the year 44 B.C., which describes one of his early days in Athens. This second stage of his life, however, ended with his election to the consulship, and it is perhaps desirable to stop a moment for the little knowledge that is attainable.

The eleven letters are all addressed to Atticus, who was still in Greece, traveling back and forth in his pursuit of wealth, but staying a good deal in Athens. The first letter belongs to the year 68 B.C., but many letters had preceded it and a great many followed. In the very first, Cicero is giving excuses for his delay in writing, which are repeated in some of the other letters, and in this, too, he signs himself "with brotherly affection": "be persuaded," as the Latin has it with only apparent formality, "that I love you as a brother." They had not met since Cicero was in Greece, ten years before. The eleven letters obviously owed their preservation to chance, but some reason for it may be found in their content, since each one mentions some commission entrusted to Cicero or asked for by him, so that Atticus may have kept his friend's papyrus sheets for reference.

That these are only a few of many letters exchanged is shown by their whole spirit, and also perhaps by their occasional brevity of detail. In three lines of the first letter, for example, Atticus is informed that Cicero is expecting Quintus to arrive in Rome any day, that Terentia, Cicero's wife, has had a bad attack of rheumatism, that she is much devoted to Atticus, as well as to Atticus' sister and mother, and that both Terentia and Cicero's

little daughter Tullia are adding hearty greetings at the end of
the letter. This brevity has at times scandalized modern readers;
particularly when Cicero, in the same year, says that his poor
father died on the 28th of November, enclosing this announcement between a surmise about Quintus' relation to his wife
and a statement that this is all Cicero has to write about. The
brevity is easily explained if we realize that Cicero wrote
frequently to Atticus, so that the latter was kept constantly
informed of the daily events in Cicero's home. It may easily
be, too, that in this particular case Atticus had inquired about
the date.[1]

Cicero is less brief in apprizing Atticus of the death of
Lucius Cicero, the writer's cousin; and naturally, for Lucius
would not be mentioned often in a frequent correspondence.
This cousin was the son of Cicero's paternal uncle, the friend
of the great orator M. Antonius. Being younger than Marcus,
he looked upon the latter as his model. He accompanied Cicero
to the East, and also assisted him in gathering evidence against
Verres in Sicily. The two men were bound together by ties of
very close affection. In this letter[2] Cicero mentions the similarity of their tastes, and refers to Lucius' sterling character
and professional usefulness; the younger man had been to
Cicero all that a friend could be, and his death, Atticus therefore
would understand, was a great blow.

Cicero's love for Lucius, as it happens, received more explicit
mention than his relations to the rest of his family. Tullia,
however, is referred to, and with the affection that never
wavered. We do not know when she was born. If Cicero's
marriage, as seems likely, took place shortly after his journey

---

[1] Asconius says that Cicero's father died at the time of his son's canvass
for the consulship, but this statement is open to suspicion. Cicero's expression has been interpreted to mean, not that the elder Tullius had departed
this life, but that he had departed from Rome. See Tyrrell, I[2], 130 (note
on *Att.* 1, 6).

[2] *Att.* 1, 5.

to Greece, the year of her birth may have been as early as 76 B.C. In 70 B.C., while speaking against Verres, whose novel edicts made inheritances uncertain, Cicero says that his abhorrence of Verres' behaviour was natural since he himself had a daughter of whom he was very fond. It is in his first extant letter, two years later, that Tullia adds her greetings to Atticus; probably scrawling her little message at the bottom of the page, the Latin word about it being *ascribit*. Atticus could not have seen her at this time, unless he had made an unrecorded visit to Rome, but he is sending gifts to her, or at least promising to send them. He was still a bachelor, and perhaps forgetful. Tullia has her father remind him, in 67 B.C., and the reminder is later repeated. She thinks her father ought to make good his friend's negligence, but Cicero says he will repudiate the debt rather than pay for Atticus. Cicero calls her his little Tullia and his sweetheart, *Tulliola, deliciae meae,* and is already making plans for her future. In 67 B.C. he betrothed her to Calpurnius Piso Frugi, a member of a prominent patrician family. Tullia would then be somewhat less than ten. The marriage took place during Cicero's consulship or shortly before,[3] and brought happiness both to Tullia and to her father. Piso, at any rate, stood staunchly by his father-in-law during the years of trouble, even to opposing some other Pisos; he died during Cicero's exile. Whether Tullia at the time of her early betrothal had already begun to resemble her father, we cannot say; in later years she was his very image, she talked like him and shared his tastes.[4] She also, in her fond father's eyes, was affectionate, modest, and talented. It has been thought, because of her resemblance to her intellectual father, that she was something of a bluestocking. Of that we have no means of judging; but it should be recalled that as a widow she fell deeply in love with Dolabella, who was younger than she, and fascinating, but very little else.

---

[3] *In Cat.* 4, 3.

[4] *Ad Q. Fr.* 1, 3, 3.

About Cicero's relations to Terentia[5] during these years the letters contain no enlightenment. Her unfortunate rheumatism —pain in the joints, in Latin phrase—had become severe even in 68 B.C.; in the same year she is reported as fond of Atticus' sister and mother; and two years later the son Marcus is born, Terentia doing well, as the father laconically puts it. The marriage came to a sad end many years later, after much had intervened. But that is no reason for supposing that in the beginning it was unhappy, or even merely decorous, as has been maintained. Terentia possessed certain worldly advantages, to be sure, which may have appealed to Cicero as a young advocate; she belonged to a patrician family, quite unknown except for her half-sister, the Vestal of undeserved ill repute; and she had some money. The dowry she brought her husband is estimated by Plutarch at one hundred thousand drachmae, about eighteen thousand dollars; she also owned a piece of wooded land and several houses in Rome. It is not known, on the other hand, that her family was of any assistance to Cicero, who already had patrician friends; nor does her wealth seem to have been considerable when compared with Cicero's expenditures and probable income; the house he bought on the Palatine in 62 B.C. cost nearly one hundred and fifty thousand dollars, which is more than eight times Terentia's dowry.

Cicero could not have been an ardent lover. He was not altogether lacking in appreciation of female beauty, for at the age of sixty-one, when various ladies had been suggested to him for matrimonial consideration, he writes to Atticus[6] about one of them that he had never seen anything homelier; and there was a rumor, no longer verifiable, that Terentia was jealous of Clodia, who had designs on her husband. A certain Caerellia, moreover; is mentioned by him as a great friend. She was rich and cultivated; apparently lent Cicero money on one occasion;

---

[5] See Schmidt, *Cicero u. Terentia.*

[6] *Att.* 12, 11.

interested herself in his second marriage; and carried on a correspondence with him, now lost. Their relation, however, could scarcely have been romantic; Caerellia was apparently several years older. The only fact known about her, except those mentioned, is that she made a copy for herself of Cicero's *De Finibus,* having borrowed the work from Atticus' copyists without Cicero's knowledge. But neither Caerellia's admiration nor Cicero's fastidiousness at sixty-one indicates that Cicero ever uttered the sharp cries of passion of a Catullus, or that he charmed the aristocratic ladies of Rome as did Caesar. Women seem, on the whole, to have played a very small part in his life; both in his youth, as he tells us, and later he was always busy, engaged with his public affairs, his books, or his political and literary friends. In 56 B.C., while defending the gay youth of his friend Caelius, he has some clever and considerate things to say about the necessity of sowing wild oats; but he had sowed none himself. When he stopped at Puteoli, on his return from Sicily, he was thinking of his ambition, and not of the gaieties by the seashore. He was essentially a man's man. His probable lack of intense interest in the other sex and his certain indifference to ordinary amusements are, indeed, the only respects in which his widely appreciative and enthusiastic personality can be said to have failed of completeness.

But Cicero was very affectionate and sympathetic; he found it easy to get along with people; and he was communicative. Terentia's nature is largely unknown, as has already been mentioned; very probably it can be summed up in the reputed remark[7] of Cicero that she was more likely to interfere with his political life than to allow him an opinion about the management of the house. She was ambitious, however, taking a keen interest in her husband's success; and she seems to have been a good manager, which Cicero was not. In their early years, for a great many years, indeed, they may well have had a very

[7] Plut. *Cic.* 20.

happy and affectionate home life. His first extant letters to Terentia, written during the exile, are aglow with love and appreciation, only part of which could have been due to his desolate condition; and he writes at the same time to Quintus[8] that he has been singularly fortunate in his brother, his children, and his wife.

Besides mentioning events in his own household in these letters, Cicero also sends an occasional word about the members of Atticus' family, who were living in Rome. Here was Caecilius, the uncle, an irritable gentleman whom nobody could endure except Atticus.[9] The latter's complaisance, so comprehensive as scarcely to be admirable, was rewarded with an inheritance of ten million sesterces. In Rome lived also Atticus' mother, not known to us; and the grandmother, who died of pious worry about the Latin festival.

And here, above all, was Pomponia, the sister of Atticus, whom Quintus is said to have married at the advice of Marcus. Whether or not responsible for the unfortunate union, Cicero both now and later sent bulletins to Atticus about Pomponia and Quintus. The date of the marriage is not known, but things had already begun to go wrong. Cicero finds it encouraging, on one occasion, that they are actually together on one of Quintus' estates in Arpinum; at another time, future agreement seems to be heralded by the expectation of a child in the family. Quintus, however, was hot-headed, though good at heart, if we may believe his brother, and with very winning ways; and Pomponia did not possess her brother's easy disposition. She was of as strong a mind as Terentia herself, and no great love seems to have been lost between these two ladies; it is at least suspicious, considering the temperaments of the sisters-in-law, that Cicero should go out of his way to mention Terentia's affection for Pomponia. Nor does Pomponia seem to have been

---

8 *Ad Q. Fr.* 1, 3, 6.
9 Nepos, *Atticus* 5.

very obliging to Cicero himself. She did not always inform him when a messenger was starting for Atticus in Greece, a kind of service extended in Rome even to friends of no great intimacy; so that her neglect, coupled with the uncertainty of Atticus' movements, was partly responsible for Cicero's failure to write as often as Atticus expected. And once, perhaps from design, she forwarded to Cicero at Tusculum a letter from her brother, sending word at the same time that a messenger would leave for Greece in the afternoon. Cicero gives this as his reason for brevity, though, if we look closely, the letter of that day is one of the three longest among the eleven.

Pomponia and Quintus found no harmony through the son that came to them. In the following years Cicero often has to explain to Atticus that Quintus is not the only one at fault; and to Quintus he gives some brotherly advice. Quintus and Atticus, too, had disagreements, which Pomponia apparently made no efforts to adjust, and may have caused. The marriage ended in divorce; a very clear case of incompatibility, a plea which was not invoked in Rome as often as in modern society.

One little scene, occurring as late as the year 51 B.C., may be worth recalling. It is described by Cicero,[10] Atticus having raised the old question about his brother-in-law's behavior. Cicero was visiting his brother at Arpinum, and, taking occasion to speak of Atticus, found Quintus' feelings perfectly satisfactory both toward Atticus himself and Pomponia. He also behaved in a very kindly way toward his wife; if he was provoked about expenses, a matter referred to only in this letter, he did not show it. Thus the day passed. On the following day, at Arcanum, another estate belonging to Quintus, the latter's tenants were to be entertained. He therefore said to Pomponia that he would invite the men if she would ask the women. Quintus' request seemed to Cicero in no way unusual, and both his words and his expression had been eminently gentle.

---

[10] *Att.* 5, 1, 3–4.

But Pomponia flared up, in the presence of her brother-in-law.
"I am a stranger in my own house," she cried. The reason for
her irritation, as Cicero could gather, was that Quintus' favorite
freedman had made the preparations for the meal. Quintus
turned to Marcus. "This is what I have to put up with every
day," he said. "You will say," Cicero interjects to Atticus,
"that it was no great matter. But you should have seen and
heard your sister." Cicero, however, gave his sister-in-law no
sign of his annoyance. Pomponia, in the meanwhile, stayed
away from the table, and when Quintus sent food to her room,
she refused it. There were also various other happenings, which
Cicero forbears to relate, things that vexed Cicero himself even
more than Quintus, who through it all behaved most exemplarily.
"So you may tell Pomponia from me," Cicero ends his account,
"that on that day she did not act like a lady"—was lacking in
humanitas, he writes. "I have written in greater detail than
is perhaps necessary, but you will understand that you, too,
might profitably offer a little advice."

Cicero was not merely observing the deportment of Quintus
for the information of Atticus; he was also attending to numerous
matters of business, some of which required considerable patience
and delicacy. Not everybody loved Atticus despite his pleasant
ways. Cicero is also entrusting errands to Atticus. Between
friends, as Cicero observes in his essay on Friendship, dedicated
to Atticus, there should be no weighing of services. Atticus was
useful to Cicero in many ways. He was an excellent literary
critic and an equally excellent man of business. He revised
Cicero's manuscripts, after coming to Rome; and he rarely
failed to attend to the numerous and often confused money
matters with which Cicero entrusted him, for Cicero was careless
in this respect, though always honorable. He was also helpful
in Cicero's connection with the aristocrats. Altogether, it may
seem that Atticus gave more than he received; but Cicero must
have been very useful to him, in matters of real importance,

because of his relations with provincial governors and large business corporations. Atticus must also have derived some profit from the publication of Cicero's orations and essays, which was usually entrusted to him.[11] Nor did Cicero ask for services that interfered with his friend's plans; he did not insist on Atticus' presence in Rome during the canvass for the praetorship, as has been mentioned, and there were many later occasions when Atticus seems to have forgotten promises, or half promises, to Cicero, in order to attend to his own affairs.

In the year 68 B.C., it seems, Cicero had recently acquired his Tusculan villa, to the annoyance of his aristocratic neighbors, on which he later commented;[12] and is enthusiastically planning for its adornment. Atticus is to buy works of art for it; statues of one kind and another, some of Pentelican marble with bronze heads; he is to follow his own taste, and Cicero, we read, is always pleased with the purchases. The position of art in Greek life and the Roman interest in it have been amply illustrated in the orations against Verres. Many Greek artists were settled in Rome; there were dealers in art and curios. As with us, the old masters quite outdistanced their later rivals in their appeal to the connoisseurs. Cicero shared this artistic enthusiasm, and seems to have had an intelligent appreciation.[13] Aside from the knowledge of art displayed in his prosecution of Verres, he constantly refers to pieces of sculpture and to paintings in his other works, especially in his oratorical writings. He wishes to have beautiful things about him, caring on the whole most for painting,[14] which at this time was largely devoted to portraiture.

[11] Exclusively, it would seem, from the middle of the year 45 B.C.; see *Att.* 13, 12, 2. On the interpretation of this passage, as to whether it refers to publishing or advertising, see Tyrrell's note on the passage, and Birt, p. 310, and esp. p. 320.

[12] *Att.* 4, 5, 2.

[13] Bertrand, *Cicéron artiste.* An interesting companion volume is Bertrand's *Cicéron au theatre.*

[14] *Fam.* 7, 23, 3.

He also was eager to own a library, but books, like works of art, were expensive. In the year 68 B.C. Atticus had a collection of books that he was willing to sell, and Cicero begs him not to let any one else have it; in the following year he is "hoarding his savings" for the purchase; the books are to be the comfort of his old age. We do not know whether Cicero secured this collection; while hoping to do so, he says that books are his greatest joy, and that he hates everything else—which seems to have been written in the midst of the political disturbances in 67 B.C. If he obtains the books, he will consider himself richer than Crassus; he will care nothing for the latter's houses and lands.

Cicero did not often hoard his savings, nor, for that matter, did he pay close attention to his finances. Like his contemporaries, he borrowed and lent money extensively;[15] differing from some of them in that he never charged usurious interest, if any at all. All his transactions were for purposes other than increasing his income. He frequently lent money to friends and acquaintances about whose solvency he knew next to nothing. When they did not or could not pay, and he needed money either for an old debt or for some purchase, he borrowed from some one else. He frequently had no conception of his own situation, leaving his business affairs in the hands of slaves, freedmen, and clients, as did others, and particularly of Atticus, who took infinite pains.

Once, to quote a single example of Cicero's carelessness, he had become guarantor for a debt of a certain Cornificius.[16] The creditor, Iunius, applied to Atticus, and the latter wrote to Cicero. This was in the year 45 B.C. Cicero replied that Cornificius himself was rich, but he wished Atticus to find out about the matter from some agents; there were two Cornificii, father and son, and Cicero did not know for which one he had become

---

[15] See esp. Boissier, pp. 83–93; Tyrrell, I², 34, 38; and Fruechtl.

[16] *Att.* 12, 14, 2; 12, 17; 12, 19, 2.

involved. When informed that the guaranty reached back more than twenty-five years, he wrote to Atticus that he had had no business dealings with Cornificius before his own aedileship, twenty-four years previously, but that of course he might be mistaken. It is not known how the matter was finally adjusted.

Cicero was not wealthy by Roman standards. Pompey enriched the Greek philosophers and made one of his freedmen a millionaire. Lucullus, after his campaigns against Mithradates, had retired to private life; he had several dining rooms, the cost of dinner varying with the room; in the "Apollo" it was fifty thousand drachmae, some nine thousand dollars. Cicero was not a rival of these men and many others like them, some of whom were of no great prominence in Rome. He did not build or entertain as they did, and, more important still, he did not win his way politically or try to influence legislation by the enormous legal and illegal expenditures of a Crassus or a Caesar. But he was nevertheless by no means a poor man, even for a prominent Roman. His carelessness in matters of detail frequently involved him in temporary embarrassment, and the exile caused him very serious difficulties, which very probably were never quite cleared away; but even toward the end of his life, when he was least prosperous, he was able to give his son Marcus as large an allowance for his stay in Athens as that of the noblest aristocrats.

During the time before his exile he spent a good deal of money. Some of his expenditures are known. His tour to Greece, Asia, and the Aegean islands lasted two years, and must have involved considerable expense even if he did not reward his Greek instructors after the manner of Pompey. Before the consulship he acquired two villas, at Formiae and at Tusculum; both are mentioned in the eleven letters; and later he made further purchases, so that he owned eight villas, including the paternal estate at Arpinum, and four lodges, in which he could stop over night while traveling from one place to another. The value of these villas and the expenditures connected with them are a matter of surmise. We do know, however, that when the villas at Formiae and Tusculum had been destroyed, a result of his exile, and he was later to be reimbursed, the senate allowed half a million sesterces for the Tusculanum and a quarter of a million for the Formianum, and that Cicero considered these amounts too small. Mosaics, marble columns, and ornamental gardens were costly, and so were paintings and other works of art. In the year 67 B.C. he paid 20,400 sesterces, about 1000 dollars, for marble statues for the Tusculan villa; "trust in my strongbox," he writes to Atticus about that time. But the largest sum mentioned in this connection is the three million and a half of sesterces, approximately one hundred and fifty thousand dollars, which he paid for his residence on the Palatine. As things went, this was not a very big price; we are told, for instance, that the mansion of Scaurus was sold to Clodius for 14,800,000 sesterces. The Palatine, none the less, was the most expensive residence section in the capital, the Olympus of the blue blooded Romans; so that Cicero caused many worthy heads to shake in condemnation of his extravagance, and doubtless also of his temerity in intruding among the great.

He had at all times a very lively appreciation of what was becoming to a man in high office, even discussing this with philosophical gravity in his work on Duty.[17] Young Marcus, to whom this treatise is dedicated, needed no urging in this direction; Cicero's remarks, as often, are addressed to the larger public. A man of prominence, he says, should live in a house befitting his position. Though his *dignitas,* a conception very dear to the Romans, should not be derived from his dwelling, it should be properly supported by it; there must be room for the various clients and other callers. On the other hand, nothing is more ridiculous than a huge mansion to which no crowds come,

---

[17] *De Off.* 1, 138–140.

particularly if it has been the resort of admiring multitudes under its former owner; in such a case, passers-by may well address the empty house in the words of the poet:

> *O antiqua domus, heu quam dispari*
> *dominare domino!*[18]

People frequently have occasion to speak thus at this time, Cicero continues, and then he goes on to say that magnificence in building, for those who are justified in owning palaces, must not become ruinous extravagance—a bit of advice that apparently was not allowed to interfere in an undue degree with his own undertakings.

The sources of Cicero's wealth are not very well known. He certainly made most of his money himself. His patrimony, though large enough to start him in life and no doubt sufficient for the expenses of an ordinary citizen, must have been comparatively small. Besides any ready money he may have inherited, of which we have no knowledge, he received from his father only the estate at Arpinum and a house in Rome; and the house he seems to have given Quintus at the time he bought the residence on the Palatine. And Terentia's eighteen thousand dollars, with her timber land and her houses in Rome, could not have enabled him to live as one of the great Romans.

Writing to Quintus during his exile, when he says that he had been fortunate in his family relations, Cicero says also that he had been fortunate in the very nature of his possessions. This is a reference to the honorable means by which he secured his large income. He did not lend money for gain, whether to Romans or to foreign kings and states, and he did not enrich himself as the governor of a province. In fact, he did not undertake a governorship until the year 51 B.C., when, contrary to his

---

[18] "O good old house, alas! how different
The owner who now owneth thee!"

The translation is by Walter Miller, in the Loeb series; the Latin poet is unknown.

own desires, he was assigned to Cilicia. His perquisites there
were large, despite his rigid honesty, but the 2,200,000 sesterces
from Cilicia, deposited in Ephesus, may have been taken by
Pompey during the Civil War;[19] in any case, they came late in
Cicero's life and did not affect the period of his prosperity.
Only at one time is there a hint that he may have received part
of the proceeds of provincial government.[20]

An important source of Cicero's income must have been his
fees as a pleader. Gifts they should be called, for there was a
law a century and a half old prohibiting orators from charging
fees, a measure ostensibly democratic in that it secured equal
legal assistance for all, but really aristocratic because it made the
profession of an advocate possible only for those who had independent means. This ancient law, like other restrictions of
recent date, spoke doubtless with a very small voice in the Roman
forum, for Quintus in his electioneering pamphlet can say that
the people defended by Cicero ought to be especially eager to
assist him since their defense had cost them nothing. Cicero,
and in all probability many others, refrained from charging fees,
but that did not prevent the acceptance of grateful gifts. The
Sicilians showed their gratitude after the conviction of Verres,
and others—foreign states and individuals perhaps even more
than Romans, but Romans too—must have done the same. Thus
a loan, which perhaps Cicero was not expected to repay, is mentioned in connection with the purchase of his house on the Pala-

---

[19] See Tyrrell IV, p. xlii, note, and I[2], p. 36, note.

[20] *Att.* 1, 12, 1–2; *Fam.* 5, 5; *Att.* 1, 13, 6. For political reasons he
yielded his consular province to his colleague Antony, and when the latter
was busy collecting the sesterces, he let it be known that part of them were
going to Cicero. The whole matter is very obscure, involving the identity
of a certain Teucris, who may have been the agent of Antony and who
certainly paid Cicero some money. If anything came from Antony to
Cicero, it may, however, have been in consideration for political assistance
in Rome, but even that is far from certain; Cicero did defend Antony when
charged with maladministration, but there were political reasons for doing
this, and he had previously had considerable hesitation about assisting his
worthless colleague. The whole situation is further involved by a letter
from Cicero to Antony in which the orator speaks as one who would neither
ask for nor accept favors.

tine. He borrowed two million sesterces from Sulla, and in the same year defended him against a charge of conspiring with Catiline. It is inconceivable, finally, that Cicero's intimate relations with large business corporations were entirely unprofitable.

Large sums of money seem to have come to Cicero through bequests. The testamentary eccentricity of the Romans has already been mentioned; it contributed directly to the glory of the politically great, and was certainly in Cicero's mind when he told Quintus that he had made his money in an admirable way. In the year 44 B.C., Antony, the triumvir, taunted Cicero with having received no bequests. Cicero replies[21] that he wished he could say the same of Antony, for then some of Cicero's dearest friends would still be alive, and he asserts that he has inherited more than twenty million sesterces, nearly one million dollars. It is not possible to decide whether this statement is exaggerated; it would surely not fall below the truth; but it may be substantially correct inasmuch as the gifts from people defended seem often to have taken the form of bequests. Plutarch[22] tells us that early in his life Cicero had been willed ninety thousand drachmae, which would equal nine tenths of Terentia's dowry. A bequest from a banker Cluvius yielded Cicero at first eighty thousand and later one hundred thousand sesterces a year, which would approximate four and five thousand dollars respectively.[23]

---

[21] *Phil.* 2, 40.

[22] Plut. *Cic.* 8.

[23] There is necessarily much uncertainty in all references to money; a slight change in a Latin statement as it has come down to us may decrease the sum one hundred times. Thus the Stoic philosopher Diodotus, who had lived for many years in Cicero's house, died in 59 B.C., and made Cicero his heir. Cicero writes to Atticus that Diodotus had left him ''perhaps ten million sesterces,'' nearly half a million dollars. The words are *HS fortasse centiens.* If *centiens* be changed to *centum,* the sum is one hundred thousand sesterces, about five thousand dollars; and this sum seems by far the more likely. Philosophers resident in Roman families could not have been extremely rich, nor would Cicero have made merely a passing reference to an inheritance of half a million. See *Att.* 2, 20, 6, and Tyrrell, I², p. 35.

But Cicero as well as most of his contemporaries, Atticus and Crassus excepted, would have been greatly astonished at these minute guesses about his expenditures and his income. These estimates are far removed from the spirit of his life, whether he happened to be in Rome or in one of his villas. The forum is typical of his public activities; his private occupations, on the other hand, are suggested by the villas, with their works of art, their books, and their shaded walks and amaltheums. Cicero was too ambitious and temperamentally too active a man to give much of his time even to mental pleasures; but when his Roman conscience allowed it—when others were noisily celebrating public holidays, giving dinners of many courses, gambling, or playing ball[24]—he sought a change in Arpinum, if he had time for the journey, or else in Tusculum or Formiae. He was not always alone; the introductory scenes to his dialogues are a reflection of conversations with congenial friends, and we are told, and can also readily infer, that he had many such friends, both Greeks and Romans. Nor were these talks and Cicero's private reading entirely divorced from practical life, for there was much declaiming and study of oratory; but the spirit of it all was that of the student and the artist.

It was during his two years in Greece and Asia that he enjoyed without distraction the leisure for things intellectual and spiritual which he hoped to make later an *otium cum dignitate*. He studied rhetoric, declaimed, listened to philosophical lectures, and strolled with his friends in the sunshine of Attica. He stayed six months in Athens and then went to Rhodes. He visited Delphi, and asked what he should do to become famous, the Pythia answering that he must guide his life by his own genius and not by the opinion of the many. It was a strange advice to a prospective candidate for office, and the naïve Plutarch remarks that it dampened Cicero's enthusiasm. He was also with Atticus initiated into the Eleusinian Mysteries,

---

[24] *Pro Arch.* 13.

which for centuries had given at least an indirect answer to the question, what shall I do to be saved? It was not as if either Delphi or Eleusis were of any practical value to him. Apollo had lost much of his reputation for veracity; he had been prophesying too long and frequently with too keen an eye to worldly conditions, and the frenzied Pythia had on one occasion made the mistake of raving in a Latin hexameter, though she was Greek, and had even spoken in acrostics.[25] Nor was the Eleusinian salvation a matter of great concern to Cicero and his friend. Atticus was an Epicurean and did not believe in a future life, and Cicero, though more spiritual, had no anxiety about Charon and Tartarus. But Delphi and Eleusis, no less than Athens, were holy ground to lovers of the Greek past; there they could dream. The journey in the East was the only vacation that Cicero ever had; it gave him in full draughts the things that he could find in Rome only during his rare hours of leisure.

In the beautiful pages that introduce the fifth book of the *De Finibus,* Cicero, Quintus, their cousin Lucius, Atticus, and M. Pupius Piso Calpurnianus, a Roman noble, are represented as being together in Athens during Cicero's six months there in the years 79–78 B.C. The essay was written in 45 B.C. and many things had happened in the interval. Lucius had died. Piso, with whom Cicero in his youth had practised declamation, had become a strong supporter of Pompey, and as such had antagonized Cicero. To Atticus, in 51 B.C., Cicero had written many bitter things of him; among them, that no good could come to the state from Piso because he was unwilling to do anything, and no harm because he was afraid. But in 45 B.C., after the death of Pompey and probably of Piso as well, Cicero recalls the old times before political enmities had set in. To the Roman reader the thoughts of the past with its bitter struggles and its deaths lay like a thin veil of sadness over scenes like this, and the modern reader can still discern it; but Cicero's actual words are

---

[25] *De Divin.* 1, 38; 1, 79; 2, 115–118; 2, 111.

instinct with the joyousness of the occasion he describes. A brief account of the passage will therefore most fittingly conclude this incomplete account of Cicero in his private life.

In the forenoon the friends had attended a lecture by the philosopher Antiochus. The young Romans agreed to walk to the Academy in the afternoon, for the gardens would at that time be deserted by the crowds. They meet at Piso's house, and walk the six stadia, about two thirds of a mile, from the Dipylon gate to Pláto's old school. First they discuss the wondrous quickening of the imagination which comes from visiting places where great men have lived and worked. Piso speaks of Plato and other philosophers connected with his school, adding, for he was a politician, that the old senate-house in Rome always made him think.of Scipio, the Elder Cato, Laelius, and his own grandfather, who was called Frugi. Being a student of oratory, like Cicero, he says that the rhetorical system of mnemonics is correct in aiming to develop the student's ability to visualize; an innocent little remark that must have reminded Cicero's first readers of many wearisome hours spent in making mental pictures of their own and other people's orations.[26] Quintus agrees with Piso's observation, but, poet here as in the *Laws*, he has been thinking of Sophocles. The sight of Colonus has recalled to him the opening lines of *Oedipus Coloneus*, in which the blind old king addresses his daughter:[27]

> Antigone, child of a blind old man,
> What lands are these, or what the folk whose gates
> We have attained? Who shall receive today
> With stinted alms the wanderer Oedipus?

Atticus is reminded of his abused idol Epicurus, both by the latter's garden and by the pictures of the philosopher which the Epicureans have in their homes and even on their drinking cups and their signet rings; but he prefers to obey the old saying that

---

[26] See *Ad Herennium*, 3, chaps. 16–24.
[27] Young's translation.

one should think of the living. To him, in modern phrase, a live dog is better than a dead lion. He was to speak differently when visiting Arpinum; and Cicero surmises that his friend Pomponius, obviously destined to be called the Athenian, has been so long in Athens that his flippancy can be excused.' Atticus, to whom the local appeal was an old story, was playing host. As for Cicero himself, he has been thinking of Carneades, whom he can almost picture to himself as actually speaking in his lecture room, the more as the features of the old sceptic were still known.

Young Lucius, modest, as a Roman student should be, has so far contributed nothing. He was an aspirant in oratory. When questioned by Piso about his impressions, he blushes most becomingly, and then replies that he has been to the beach where Demosthenes of old declaimed to the waves; he has also visited the tomb of Pericles, on whose lips persuasion dwelt, as old Eupolis said; but every place, so it seems to him, is historic ground. The suggestion is presently made that Piso set forth the teaching of Antiochus in reference to the supreme good, for the benefit of their young companion, and Lucius "timidly, or modestly rather" expresses his eagerness to learn; he has been unable to reach a decision by himself. Piso at last begins, prefacing his discourse by the remark that he would never have believed that he would one day talk philosophy in the Academy; no, not even if a god had prophesied it.

CHAPTER IX

THE CONSULSHIP

I

CAESAR'S SCHEME

Cicero's year as consul was not like a quiet afternoon in the gardens of the Academy, but a time of almost continual battle. As things turned out, he had to fight first against the leaders of the plebs, mainly Caesar, and later against Catiline; the two very dissimilar encounters dividing the year into practically equal portions. That a struggle of some sort was before him had been evident even before his election. As a candidate, he had not been the representative of any political party, but had stood clearly for the peaceful desires of the knights and of the citizens of Italy; he had once given his open support to Pompey, and he was also popular, through his oratory, with the less orderly elements of the city. Though not a political partisan, he was known as an opponent of violent measures; and as such he had secured the support of the nobles. His election as well as his own character and reputation thus made him the champion of the existing order; it was his duty to wage defensive warfare against threatening attacks, whether they should prove to be along the lines of revolutionary legislation or of brute violence.

The proposals for new legislation came first; as usual, casting their shadows across Rome long before it was time to act. Cicero has described the situation briefly, but at sufficient length to suggest the mixture of mystery, pompousness, and theatricality that characterized the performance.[1] After the elections in 64 B.C., hints began to be heard that the tribunes were preparing an agrarian law. This was in itself a reason for great excitement; it would mean gifts of land to the poor of Rome,

---

[1] In the speeches *Against Rullus*.

and there had been no such law proposed since that of Livius
Drusus, twenty-eight years before, in the stormy days that preceded the Social War. Cicero, now consul-elect, made advances
to the tribunes; he and they were to be magistrates in the same
year, he said, and ought to work together for the state; if the
law was a good one, really advantageous to the plebs, he would
support it, even sponsor it. The reply to his representations was
that he was not the kind of man who would favor any gifts to the
people; and Cicero desisted from further offers of coöperation.
The tribunes continued their legislative confabulations; they held
conferences with private citizens; they met mysteriously at night
and in out-of-the-way places; all of which greatly increased the
anxiety and suspense in Rome.

On the tenth of December the tribunes took office, three weeks
before the other magistrates; this gave them an opportunity to
propose legislation to be acted on during the coming year and to
prepare the public mind. P. Servilius Rullus now came into
prominence as the proponent of the new law; it was announced
that he would address the people at a *contio*. While the whole
city was eagerly looking forward to the meeting, Rullus assumed
a behavior suited to the seriousness of the situation. The expression of his face changed, the tone of his voice, his manner of
walking; he dressed in old clothes, did not wash, did not trim
his hair and beard. He was more stern than the other tribunes;
his unkempt condition seemed to bid the Romans beware of the
tribunician power, to utter threats against the state. At last
the meeting was held, attended by multitudes. Rullus made a
long speech, with a great many fine words, but nobody in the
large crowd could make out what he was talking about, says
Cicero, adding, however, that the more acute among the auditors
did surmise that Rullus was saying something or other about an
agrarian law. Whether from design or oratorical incapability,
Rullus gave no information about his intentions; but some time
later, probably at the end of the year, the bill was finally published. Cicero at once sent several men to copy it.

The elaborate mummery of Rullus had been commensurate with the far-reaching provisions of his bill. The poor citizens were to be settled on land in Italy; each to have his own farm, which was to remain the inalienable possession of his family. As the public land in Italy was utterly inadequate for such extensive colonization, a huge sum for the purchase of additional land was to be raised by the sale of state property. This would include many of the state's possessions in Italy, particularly the land acquired by Sulla during his consulship in 88 B.C., after the Social War; and nearly everything in the provinces, even in those recently conquered by Pompey. The power of sale embraced farms, vineyards, forests, meadows, roads, buildings, and everything movable and immovable; it made specific mention of almost countless communities and tracts in every portion of the Roman empire, and had general expressions that could be made to embrace still more. As there would not be purchasers enough for all this property, the bill provided for taxes on what was not disposed of by sale, the money to be added to the colonization fund. Money and booty, finally, which had been obtained in the recent conquests, or would so be obtained in the future, Pompey's excepted, were also to be used for the same purpose. The execution of this gigantic plan was to be in the hands of ten commissioners, who were to be elected by a majority of seventeen tribes, chosen by lot. The commissioners would decide what was state property and what was not, make all the arrangements for the sales, choose the land to be purchased in Italy, and have an armed force to make their decisions effective. They would have the rank of propraetors and hold office for five years. All candidates for the commission were to apply in person.

Cicero was opposed to the bill. He was opposed to agrarian legislation of any kind.[2] The city of Rome would undoubtedly

---

[2] The most complete examination of Cicero's political attitude is found in Cauer. Cauer reviews the opinions of previous scholars. To Cauer should be added Heinze. See also below, pp. 290 ff., 454 ff.

have profited if the pauper population could have been made to leave for the country; such an exodus would have purified politics and relieved the treasury. Italy, too, would have been changed for the better by the cultivation of deserted land and by the transformation of the large grazing districts into real farms. The advantages of the proposed colonization seem so great that the bill of Rullus might almost be looked upon as dictated by very farsighted statesmanship. But the prospective farmers consisted unfortunately of the Roman populace. It can not be known whether they would have adapted themselves to their new conditions, for no agrarian legislation intended to benefit them was carried out during Cicero's life except the two laws passed by Caesar in the year 59 B.C., and these seem to have affected Pompey's veterans to a far greater extent than the common people of Rome. We learn, however, of no improvement either in the city or in Italy as a result of Caesar's laws. But it is not likely that Rullus could have made even passable farmers of the plebs. The veterans of Sulla who had been settled on free land had not improved Italian farming.[3] They had lived like little lords on their new estates while their money lasted, and then, impoverished and unwilling to work, they were ready to take up the sword again, either in foreign or civil war. They had added to Roman politics a new group of malcontents and dangerous trouble-makers, and had even spoiled the character of the farmers among whom they lived. The idlers of Rome would scarcely have done better. The veterans had at least been accustomed to work and discipline of a kind, whereas many of the paupers in the city had never worked regularly, had been largely supported by the state, and had been kept amused into the bargain. The lazzaroni would have found farming very exacting and very lonesome when they thought of the idleness, the pleasures, and the excitement of the capital.[4]

---

[3] *In Cat.* 2, 20. See below, pp. 240–241.

[4] See below, pp. 229–230.

But Cicero did not object to the bill of Rullus chiefly on general grounds, however sufficient these may have been. The tribune's proposal was, after all, only a bait dangled before the plebs to win their support in carrying out the real purpose of the bill; and this purpose was revealed in the provisions for collecting the huge sum which was to be expended for farms. These provisions are known only from the orations of Cicero, who quotes or professes to quote directly from the bill, which of course every one had an opportunity to read. Cicero would not be inclined to present the provisions favorably, but he could not have misstated them to any considerable extent; when all possible deductions and adverse interpretations have been made, the chief facts still remain. And they show that the aim of the bill was to create a new power in the state, opposed both to the existing government and to Pompey; in fact, to all stable elements of the social order. The board of ten was to be entrusted with practically the entire wealth of the Roman people; they were to sell anything in the provinces and buy anything in Italy that they chose, entirely without responsibility, thus having infinite opportunities for indulging in favoritism, persecutions, and political jobbery of every conceivable kind. This unlimited legal power was to be supported by arms; the commissioners, as propraetors, would resemble provincial governors in commanding armies, and a door was opened even for the creation of a large army, for Egypt was indirectly included among the countries to be disposed of.

The matter of Egypt is important. This country was still independent, but it was ruled by a worthless monarch, not a legitimate member of the royal house and not recognized by Rome, and the Romans made a claim that the kingdom had been willed to them by the previous ruler. If Egypt, for the purpose of the proposed sales, was declared a province, some one of the commissioners would have to take it with an army, and this would create a military power in the East, to balance that of Pompey, who was excluded from the commission by the requirement that all candidates must apply in person. Crassus, as censor in 65 B.C., two years previously, had actually proposed to declare Egypt a province and a bill had been prepared to send Caesar there, but this attempt had come to nothing. Now it was revived, though less openly. The powers of the commission, legal as well as military, were to last for five years; before the termination of which Pompey could have finished his campaign in the East and his army would have been disbanded—if he acquiesced. The bill, therefore, so Cicero understood, and rightly, did not aim to improve the condition of the plebs; it was an all-embracing bid for power, along legal lines, and, inasmuch as the commissioners were to be chosen by the tribes of the people, the choice would inevitably favor the leaders of the so-called popular party, and these were above all others Caesar and Crassus.

The obscure and unkempt Rullus with his veiled threats and his disquieting lack of intelligibility thus drops out of sight, and his place is taken by Caesar and Crassus, really by Caesar, for he was obviously the strategist behind the daring attack. Crassus stood to gain something, of course; but he does not seem to have had the brains to conceive so insidious and vast a project, and he had not the popular following that might give promise of success, nor was he in such a position of political desperation as Caesar. Crassus was a consular and the wealthiest man in Rome; Caesar had so far held only the aedileship and he had no money.

Though Caesar must have known that the proposed measure could bring no good to Rome, and might bring very serious trouble, he is scarcely to be criticised for playing the game of the selfish, hand-to-mouth politics that had prevailed since the days of the Gracchi. Cato did not play it, nor did Cicero, each one of these seeking the good of Rome in his own way; and there were other men of less prominence whose ambition was moderate; but the great majority of politicians were as reckless as Caesar.

He was in the opposition, furthermore, and had a very special reason for his daring attempt in that Pompey was nearing the end of the Eastern war and would soon be in Rome. Pompey's absence had made possible the extravagant politics of the last few years; his return would place Rome in his hands, if he chose to take it. Most likely he would not seize all the power; he had not done so in the year 70 B.C.; but he would be the dominating figure. If Caesar was to gain an independent political position, he must gain it at once; otherwise he could do no better than to conciliate Pompey, and for many weary years play second fiddle —*secundas partis agere*, as the Romans said, very much with the modern turn of phrase.

II
AGAINST RULLUS

Cicero delivered four orations against the bill, the last of which has been lost. The first of them is addressed to the senate. The Rullan proposal had been so cleverly designed to win popular support that the senate might well have doubts as to Cicero's courage and ability to oppose it. Cicero took his first opportunity to calm their anxiety. It was customary for a consul on the very day of his accession to office, the first of January, to address the senate on the policies according to which he intended to be governed. Cicero, in his inaugural address, expressed his determination to oppose the bill by every means in his power. He discussed its objectionable and dangerous features, the chief of which have already been given; less it seems, for the purpose of proving the undesirability of the bill, a matter the senate would have taken on faith, than to show how he would fight the measure. Cicero's display of his mastery of offensive weapons was also intended to discourage the supporters of the bill; and he actually turned directly to the tribunes, urging them not to follow the lead of Rullus and his declared supporters. As for the latter, Cicero asserted that he, and not they, was truly devoted to the interests of the people; and that if the bill was not dropped, he would call a public meeting, and there show the people themselves what the proposed law really meant. Further to indicate his lack of fear of the tribunes, he revealed that he did not intend to take a province after his consular year, nor seek any other reward, and would thus deprive the tribunes of every opportunity of agitating against him.

Rullus and the far more important men behind him did not abandon the fight, and Cicero carried out his threat of holding a *contio*. Here his real difficulty appeared. He had to persuade the plebs that distribution of land to them, traditionally their chief desire, the one unanswerable argument on which popular leaders could always rely, that this distribution was not for their good. To do this, Cicero needed all his skill as the foremost pleader in Rome, and also the moral courage of jeopardizing his popularity and appearing as a mere tool of the prosperous members of the community, with whom the plebs were always at war.

Cicero was well aware that he was addressing a gathering the large majority of whom had no interests beyond their own unearned food and amusements, but he cleverly takes for granted that his auditors are the true Roman people, unselfishly eager for the grandeur and safety of the state. His arguments are therefore the very ones that he had used to the senate. The state treasury would be depleted, for all moneys would come into the hands of the commissioners. If the latter failed to find sufficient available land for purchase, they would have to force people to sell, and this would mean ruinous prices; and if the commissioners did not buy, they would retain the money for their own uses, since no provision had been made for its return to the treasury. Their power would be unlimited, and Cicero names the places in which they were directed by the bill to operate; a dazzling list, covering the Roman empire from Spain to the Black Sea. The commissioners could hold their auctions anywhere, so that the Roman people would have no opportunity to watch them; nor would watching do much good, for they could not be brought to trial during their five years of office, and these five years would be sufficient to establish them firmly in power. They would indeed be, not benefactors of the people, but kings. No such power had been entrusted to Cato, Philus, Laelius; and Cicero's auditors are invited to consider whether the men who would probably be chosen equaled those he had named.

Cicero does not forget that he is pleading before the idlers of Rome. The irresponsible commission, he suggests, may for private reasons buy land that is arid or pestilential. How would the free citizens of Rome like to have Rullus lead them off to such places? If they are wise, they will retain their freedom, their votes, the forum, the games, the festal days, and all the other blessings of the city. The thought is not pressed, for it was scarcely complimentary to Cicero's auditors, but, once mentioned, it would linger in the minds of these free electors, who listened to Cicero's real arguments with the solemnity of conscious patriots.

Cicero also pointed out that the creation of the powerful commisison might lead to opposition on the part of Pompey, particularly if a commissioner were established in Egypt at the head of an army. This would mean civil war. But Cicero did not make the mistake of naming the popular leader, Caesar, as the one who would go to Egypt, nor did he charge Pompey with reprehensible ambitions. Pompey was the idol of the people; he had restored the tribunician power and he was now winning great wars. Cicero therefore merely assured his worthy audience that Pompey would do anything the people desired, but if any one should attempt to force them to endure the unendurable, he would defend their rights. And the people, in their turn, should protect Pompey. His rights as general in the East would be infringed upon if some one else were sent to Egypt, Cicero said. Rullus, to be sure, had proposed that the booty of Pompey's present campaigns should not go into the colonization fund, but he had not made this provision out of friendship for the great general, for the customs of the Eastern conquests would be swallowed up, which Pompey had the right to make arrangements for; and, most important of all, the new possessions would be sold, and by such men as Rullus. This insignificant fellow will write a letter to the great general. He will neglect to give Pompey his name *Magnus,* the Great, and will say curtly: "Meet me at Sinopa and give assistance while I, in accordance with my law, sell the land which you have won by your labors." And thereupon he will set up his spear, the sign of a public auction, between the camps of Pompey and the enemy, and knock down the immense territories of Mithradates to the highest bidder.

Rullus, however, was a tribune, and the tribunes had always been the champions of the plebs; whereas Cicero, who opposed his bill, was a consul, the natural spokesman of the senate. Fortunately for Cicero, Rullus had overdone his acting while the bill was under preparation; and Cicero can make his audience laugh at the long-haired, glowering tribune; and laugh or shout with anger at the thought of his impudent letter to Pompey. Rullus' father-in-law owned some undesirable land he wished to dispose of. The indefatigable and lynx-eyed consul had discovered this, and informed his audience. In some haughty moment, furthermore, Rullus had said, at least so Cicero represents, that the *plebs urbana* had too much power, and ought to be drained out of the city; expressing himself, Cicero observes, as though he were speaking of bilge water and not of honorable citizens. Such words could not come from a true friend of the people!

And as for Cicero himself—but it would be a misrepresentation of Cicero's attitude to mention his references to himself in the same breath as his malicious thrusts at Rullus.   There is much of a specious character in this great oration, for Cicero was fighting fire with fire; he was in Rome, and had to do as the Romans did; but the speciousness is only on the surface; it is the honey on the edge of the cup of bitter medicine, as the Romans were fond of saying.   The arguments that he uses are in their essence both honest and true, though they have to be presented at times in a manner to appeal to his auditors, and of these arguments perhaps the strongest was his own personality. He is not speaking with strict truthfulness when he claims not to be opposed to agrarian legislation as such; though his opposition was justified; or, perhaps, when asserting that, though a consul, he is not unwilling to praise the Gracchi, "for they had accomplished much"—and yet in this very year he said[5] frankly that the Gracchi had deserved death for their agitation.   But he is not feigning when he says that he is not an aristocrat; and he quotes himself correctly to the effect that he had proclaimed in the senate—not the most suitable place for such an announcement—that he would be truly a *popularis*, devoted to the interests of the whole people.

He reminds his auditors that it was the Roman people who had advanced him from one office to another, until finally they had elected him consul with acclamation; and he recalls the condition of Rome at the time he assumed the consular insignia. Rome then, he says, had been full of fear and anxiety; there was no evil that the law-abiding citizens, the *boni,* did not dread and the wicked did not hope for; plans had been formed to injure the state and to put an end to peace; commercial credit was no longer to be found in the forum, having been driven away, not by any sudden calamity, but by suspicion and disturbances in the courts; and it was becoming clear that men were aiming at new powers, at the sway of monarchs and not the authority of magistrates.   It was to check such things that he had been elected.

---

[5] *De Lege Agr. (Contra Rull.)* 2, 10; *In Cat.* 1, 29.

These remarks open the speech. Nothing, says Cicero, is so much for the benefit of the people as peace, at home and abroad, and liberty; these he will give them. And at the end of the speech he returns to the same thought, announcing finally that he and Antony, his colleague, are acting in unison; they are not pursuing different aims, as his enemies had hoped they would do.

Though Cicero was arguing against the ostensible advantages of the plebs, his words were received with more enthusiasm than had been given to the arguments of any orator who favored an agrarian law; he had accomplished the impossible. Perhaps it was, as some would have it, his greatest oratorical triumph. Rullus, however, did not yield at once. He was too wise to argue against Cicero, but at a later *contio* he discussed certain minor points in the law, and secured some following. Cicero answered him in the *Third Agrarian Oration;* and may have been called upon to answer him again, for there was a fourth speech, also short, the content of which is unknown. The people finally sided with Cicero, and the bill was dropped. Cicero had secured one of the tribunes to veto the bill if it should come to a vote, but there was no need of this common but questionable maneuver.

III
CONSTANT ACTIVITY

The defeat of the bill of Rullus was, next to Cicero's suppression of the Catilinarian conspiracy, the most important event of his consulship; but there were other difficulties that he had to meet. Most of them are not important. Together, they show how he successfully pursued his aim of safeguarding the state and of performing his duties for the benefit of all classes. Three bills, all of which might have led to trouble or to further agitation, were abandoned by their sponsors at the intercession of Cicero. One of them proposed the remission or reduction of debts; the details are not known, but Cicero could later say with satisfaction that he had maintained the credit of Rome unimpaired. Another bill was for the restoration to the senate of the two consuls-elect for 65 B.C. who had been unseated for the use of bribery; and we are told that one of the two men himself acquiesced in the withdrawal of the bill. The third bill would restore to full citizenship the sons of those proscribed by Sulla, who had disqualified them for public office. In itself this demand was just; there was no reason why these men should suffer; but as the bill was an attack on the Sullan constitution, and consequently threatened the unstable equilibrium of the state, it might lead to mischief, and Cicero found it necessary to oppose it. He delivered a speech about it, now lost. Quintilian, however, speaks of this speech, marveling at Cicero's ability in winning approval for his course of action even from those who were to be benefited by the bill. By explaining that the state could not endure if the Sullan laws were broken, Cicero made his opposition to the bill seem to be a service even to the disfranchised.

In this passage[6] Quintilian calls Cicero *ille tractandorum animorum artifex,* an artist in his ability to sway the souls of men; an appellation that Cicero earned more than once during this difficult year. One further occasion is worth recording. In the year 67 B.C. a certain Otho had carried a law that assigned the first fourteen rows in the theater behind the seats of the senators to the knights. At one performance, when the great Roscius was acting, the people hissed Otho when he entered the theatre; the knights applauded him; words of insult were hurled back and forth, and the theater was in a tumult. Cicero was informed. He came to the theater and asked the people to go with him to the temple of Bellona. Here he scolded them roundly for their behavior, and thereupon sent them back to the play in such good humor that they vied with the knights themselves

---

6 Quintil. 11, 1, 85.

in doing honor to Otho. The speech was published, but has been lost; even if extant, it would probably have given us only a very dim reflection of Cicero's marvelous mastery over the people.

The non-partisan character of Cicero's official acts appears with almost arithmetical distinctness. In opposing Rullus Cicero had rendered a very great service to Pompey; he had shown how the proposed law would harm the absent general and had used the latter's claims as an argument against the bill. This, coupled with Cicero's earlier support of the Manilian law, might stamp him as a Pompeian. And yet it was mainly through Cicero's instrumentality that Lucullus was enabled this year to celebrate his triumph over Mithradates. But Lucullus was the most pronounced rival in Rome of Pompey, whose adherents had succeeded in preventing the triumph for three long years. Cicero's support of the noble Lucullus was a service to the aristocracy. He also defended Piso, another noble, when the latter was accused of extortion as governor of Narbonensian Gaul and of the unjust execution of a man from beyond the Po. The trial had been due to Caesar. In the meantime, Caesar had earned the enmity of Catulus as well, the leader of the senatorial party, by successfully rivaling him for the position of chief pontiff. But when Piso and Catulus, during the Catilinarian conspiracy, tried to induce Cicero to accuse Caesar of complicity, he refused to do so, in spite of the money and influence of Caesar's two enemies.[7] Cicero also acted in opposition to the interests of the senators when he attempted to abolish the so-called free embassies, *legationes liberae*. If a senator had business in the provinces, it was customary to appoint him a "free legate"; he had no duties, but traveled at public expense, borne mostly by the long-suffering provincials. Cicero drew up a bill to put a stop to this practise, but a tribune was found to veto it; a law was passed, however, limiting "free" embassies to a single

---

[7] See below, p. 278, note 25.

year. They had formerly extended for an unlimited time.
The marvelous thing about Cicero's proposal, if we are to believe
his own statement in the *Laws,* written some ten years later, was
that he secured the support of the senate at a meeting which was
extremely well attended—*senatu frequentissimo.*

In the early part of the year Cicero also defended Rabirius;
a trial of no great intrinsic importance, but significant because
it brought Cicero into almost direct opposition to Caesar, and
still more because the question really at issue was later to be
raised in Cicero's own case. During the sixth consulship of
Marius, in 100 B.C., riots and violence on the part of the tribune
Saturninus had led the senate to place the city under what might
be called martial law. In the fighting that ensued Saturninus
had been killed. Now, thirty-seven years later, Caesar had one
of his adherents, the tribune Labienus, later famous in the Gallic
wars, accuse Rabirius of the murder of Saturninus, and, with
Roman thoroughness, of some other things as well. Rabirius
was an old senator of no political consequence, nor did Caesar
care about him; and there had been so much violence in Rome
during the last seventy years that to single out a comparatively
innocent man nearly forty years after the alleged crime had
been committed, while notorious criminals like Catiline were
aiming at the consulship, was scarcely an attempt to have justice done. The real question at issue was not one of murder.
Rabirius had acted, as it were, within the terms of the martial
law which had been proclaimed, and the death of Saturninus
might therefore be interpreted as an execution. But a Roman
citizen who had been condemned to death had the right of appeal
to the assembly of the people; the people alone could legally take
away a man's life. Caesar, in prosecuting Rabirius, was therefore pleasing the people and worrying the senate by upholding
the right of appeal; and, since this right had been ignored, and
always was ignored, by the proclamation of martial law, Caesar
was attacking the senate for declaring martial law.

The accusation was for high treason, *perduellio,* the accused was tried before two judges chosen by lot, and, as the gods were favorable, Caesar and a kinsman of his were chosen. Rabirius was condemned, and appealed to the people. His strongest argument, according to Suetonius, was the open hostility with which Caesar had conducted the previous trial. It was in connection with Rabirius' appeal that Cicero spoke; he and Hortensius. Cicero's speech is extant, though fragmentary; when published, it was obviously enlarged, for at the appeal the tribune had so arranged it that Cicero had only half an hour for his plea. The proceedings came to an abrupt end, for which Cicero was probably responsible. In former times it had been a custom to keep a red flag on the Janiculum, which was pulled down whenever the hostile Etruscans approached the city gates, as a sign for the popular assembly to disperse and take up arms. The lowering of this flag had remained as a signal for ending the deliberations of the people; and on this occasion it was lowered by the augur Metellus Celer, a friend and supporter of Cicero. Labienus, that is Caesar, could have taken up the appeal at a later meeting, but he did not do so. Apparently Rabirius was not further molested.

To call the senate's action a proclamation of martial law is not strictly accurate. The senate had passed the so-called "last decree," *senatus consultum ultimum,* which called upon the consuls, or the consuls and other magistrates, or, indeed, upon any magistrate who for the time being was exercising the consular power, if the consuls were not in Rome, "to defend the state and see that it suffered no harm." In other words, the consuls, or persons acting in their stead, were requested by the senate to assume practically the powers of a dictator. But the senate had no legal right to make this request, and the consuls had no right to obey it. The "last decree" had nevertheless been passed, though not acted upon, in the year 133 B.C., and it had been passed and acted upon in 121 B.C., in 100 B.C., in 83 B.C., and

perhaps on one or two other occasions; always at a time of imminent danger, for it had become the senate's way of meeting an
extraordinary revolutionary crisis.[8]   Like many other prerogatives assumed by the senate, it might therefore be considered, not
legal, but constitutional, for the Roman method of government,
like English common law, was the result of precedents.   The
opponents of the senate seem practically to have admitted the
senate's right to pass the decree.   Caesar was at this time
worrying the senate by his attack, but a few years later he wrote
in the *Civil War*,[9] in reference to the "last decree" which had
been passed against him, that the senate had not formerly had
recourse to it except when the city was almost in flames or when
everybody despaired of safety; thus indirectly admitting the
senate's right to pass the decree, by his complaint that they had
"rushed" to it when he had given them no proper cause.   And
Sallust, who was never a friend of the senate, though perhaps
not much of a friend to anybody, states explicitly that according
to tradition, *more Romano,* which governed all things, the senate
had the power to pass this decree; to direct the consul to levy an
army, to carry on war, to check allies and citizens by every
means, and to exercise at home and abroad absolute military and
judicial powers; and that except for this decree the consul
possesses none of these powers unless they be given him by the
people.[10]   Sallust is speaking of the occasion in the year 63 B.C.
when the senate entrusted this power to Cicero for the purpose
of resisting Catiline.   Though Cicero, in defending Rabirius,
made the ordinary plea for his client on the ground of his piteous
old age, and though he also shocked the people by asserting that

---

[8] The most complete account of the "last decree" is Plaumann's *Das
sogenannte senatus consultum ultimum etc.* (Klio, 1913, pp. 321–386).
Plaumann seems on the whole to ignore the extraordinary character of the
decree, the very thing on which Caesar based his complaint.

[9] Caesar, *Bell. Civ.*, 1, 5.

[10] Sall., *Cat.*, 29. As Sallust's brief account of the conspiracy is
arranged chronologically, it will not be necessary to refer his various statements to their respective sections.

Rabirius would have been justified in killing Saturninus, which he had not done, as had been proved by Hortensius, Cicero nevertheless insisted that the question of the "last decree" was the matter really to be decided; he asserted that Marius was right and that he himself under similar conditions would have acted in exactly the same way.

Cicero's words were prophetic of the future, and may even have contained a warning to Catiline. The exact date of the speech for Rabirius is not known, but the publication could not have occurred until after the outbreak of the conspiracy. It may therefore be supposed that Cicero never uttered these words, but added them later as an assertion of his own attitude toward the "last decree." The point can not be settled. If the supposition of a later addition be true, the effect of it has no bearing on the constitutionality of the decree, which is indicated by Caesar and Sallust; it only shows that Cicero had not expressed himself on the question and that he was not a prophet.

The same spuriousness of prophecy, and for the same reason, may be imputed to another statement in this oration. Cicero says that no one acts praiseworthily and with courage in the midst of dangers to the state unless he be moved by thoughts of future fame. The human soul, he continues, is of divine origin; there are many reasons for believing this, but none more convincing than the fact that good men always look beyond the time of their own lives, their eyes fixed on eternity.

This was the thought that guided Cicero in the troublesome years that followed; it is his expression for unselfish service, found more than once in his later writings. If he uttered the words while speaking for Rabirius, he was already conscious of the approaching struggle with Catiline and knew how he would meet it.

IV
BEGINNING OF THE CONSPIRACY

The conspiracy of Catiline filled the last months of Cicero's consulship. It was a natural result of the conditions which for three quarters of a century had brought upon Rome civil wars, proscriptions, and personal violence of every conceivable kind. There had been men like Marius, Cinna, Sulla, Chrysogonus, and Verres; the conspiracy against the consuls of 65 B.C. had remained unpunished. Personal ambition was a fruitful source of crime, but money, the possession of it or the lack of it, was even more pernicious. Immense wealth had flowed into the country, but it was very unevenly distributed; the rich were extravagant and the poor were idle; some were poor because they had no financial opportunities, and others because they had spent their patrimony or their gains; and finally, all social classes, though not all individuals, had acquired the habit of making illicit demands.

That greed or culpable poverty lay at the bottom of Catiline's attempt to overturn the state is indicated by Cicero's description of the conspirators. Addressing the people after the conspiracy was well under way, Cicero divided the malcontents into six classes.[11] First there were men of wealth, possessed of fame, honors, silverware, slaves, and everything else; but they were greatly in debt and refused to pay. While respectable in appearance, because of their money, they hoped that a revolution would free them from their creditors and yet enable them to retain their possessions unimpaired. Then there were the political failures, also tottering under debt, who thought that somehow they might emerge into prominence through a state of anarchy. The third class consisted of the old soldiers settled in colonies all over Italy by Sulla. Coming into sudden riches, they had

---

[11] *In Cat.* 2, 17–23.

lived riotously for a while, imitating the great; and now, unwilling and perhaps unable to farm, they wished to get rid of their huge debts and to acquire new wealth. Living in the country, though many of them came to Rome, these veterans had acquired influence among their poor neighbors, who were now ready to follow their lead. Fourthly, there was both in Rome and in the rest of Italy a motley crowd of debtors, who were very numerous, lazy, bad managers, and extravagant. After them came the murderers, cutthroats, and criminals of every description, whom no prison was large enough to hold. And finally, in the sixth place, were the special favorites of Catiline; young men, who took great care with their hair and understood the use of cosmetics. They either shaved carefully or had well-trimmed beards; their tunics, like that of Verres on the Syracusan beach, had long sleeves and reached to the heels; they were draped in filmy stuffs instead of wearing togas. Banqueting, gambling, adultery, dancing, and singing were their occupations, but they could also brandish daggers and administer poison.

Sallust, who was a young man of twenty-three at the time of the conspiracy, and who wrote a dramatic account of it twenty years later, describes the conspirators in the same terms, but he adds another class, the women, and thus throws a further light on the moral depravity of Rome. Some of the women, he says, had been won over by Catiline; they would be useful for stirring up the slaves in the city and for setting fire to houses; they would gain their husbands for Catiline, or kill them. Their reason for joining the conspiracy was the same as that of nearly all the others—namely, debt. Among them was a certain Sempronia. She was of noble birth, with an assured position in Roman society; her husband had been consul in 77 B.C. and her son was the Decimus Brutus who afterwards conspired against Caesar. She had beauty, grace, and wit. She knew Greek as well as Latin; wrote verse, sang and danced better than befitted

a good woman. She was versatile, and could appear modest or
gentle or saucy, as the occasion demanded. But she had an evil
reputation; extravagance, debt, immorality, even murder were
mentioned in connection with her name. In fact, there was
nothing to which she gave less thought than to what people
said about her.

Catiline had made himself the leader of all these malcontents.
He had the ability to attract men of every kind and of every
age, by ministering to their vices, and involving them in crime.
He was brave to recklessness, had great physical strength, and
was as crafty as he was unprincipled. He was ruined, and had
been disappointed in his political ambition. After taking part
in the plot against the consuls of 65 B.C., he had himself sought
the consulship. First he had been prevented from becoming a
candidate, then he had been defeated by Cicero, and finally,
in 63 B.C., he again became a candidate.

The canvass was unusually disorderly and corrupt. Laws
were passed both against the hiring of gangs to escort a candidate and against bribery. Cicero himself drew up the latter
law, thus giving it his own name. Exile for ten years was added
to the former penalty. As Catiline was the only candidate
not of the conservative party, these laws were largely directed
against him, but he took no notice. He was constantly accompanied by large crowds of voters, many of whom had come
from the country districts, especially from Faesulae, where the
Sullan veteran Manlius was reported to be preparing a revolution; and he came freely to the meetings of the senate. Cato
once attacked him and threatened prosecution, to which Catiline
replied that if any conflagration was started against him, he
would put it out, not by water but by *ruina*—the tearing down
of houses.[12] There were many reports of Catiline's sayings
bruited about in the city at that time. At a meeting of his
accomplices he was supposed to have said that the only protector

_____
[12] *Pro Mur.* 50–52.

of those who were wretched was the man who was himself wretched; let them hope for nothing from the promises of those who were unhurt and fortunate; their leader and standard-bearer must needs be a man entirely without fear and deeply unfortunate.

While such rumors were being circulated, Cicero, on the day before the date set for the consular election, persuaded the senate to postpone the election in order that these matters might be discussed; and on the following day, at a large meeting, he called upon Catiline for an explanation. Catiline, according to his wont, made no excuses. He said there were two bodies in the state; one weak, with a shaky head; the other strong, but without a head; and that as long as he lived, this strong body would not lack a head, if it acted as it should. It was an obvious reference to the conservative minority with Cicero or the consuls, but really only Cicero, at their head, and the large indefinite host of poor citizens, ready for a revolution, the number of whom Catiline was glad to exaggerate. The senate groaned, says Cicero, but took no adequate measure; some of them fearing nothing and others fearing too much; and Catiline strode triumphantly from the senate-house. Shortly after, the election was held,[13] Cicero presiding. He was surrounded by an armed guard and wore a cuirass, "broad and conspicuous;" the shining cuirass was intended to inform the law-abiding citizens of the dangers that threatened the consul. Catiline had plotted against Cicero's life both before and after Cicero entered upon office. Whether or not Catiline had planned to use violence in the Campus Martius in this year, he made no attempt against Cicero; and the election was conducted without interference, to the defeat of Catiline.

---

[13] The date of the postponed election is not known. The usual time would have been in July, and the election may have taken place late in that month. It has been put as far back as the twenty-eighth of October. If that is correct, though it does not seem very likely, then Catiline had before that date come to realize that he would fail at the polls and had by his actions caused the senate to pass the "last decree."

Catiline and his adherents were now reduced to desperation, and turned definitely to violence. Since Rome had no garrison, she always offered an opportunity for revolutionary measures, but in this year the likelihood of a successful attack on the government seemed especially great. One of the consuls, Antony, was Catiline's old friend; Cicero, on the other hand, was a New man, and it could scarcely be expected that he would be able to marshal against Catiline, who was an aristocrat, the united support of the citizens. Nor did Catiline have any time to lose. Pompey and his victorious army would soon return from the East, and after that Catiline could have no hope either of becoming consul or of succeeding as a conspirator. Caesar and Crassus, who had supported Catiline as a candidate in 64 B.C., and possibly even in this year,[14] would no longer lend their assistance to a man who could not be useful in a city dominated by the presence of Pompey; and as Catiline had already failed of election despite their support, he was now doomed never to reach the consulship. Pompey's army would prevent Catiline from using violence. While Pompey was still away, however, Catiline could at least make an attempt to overturn the government. If he succeeded, there would be a few months of pandemonium in Rome, during which he and his accomplices might enrich themselves; after that, they would have to leave Rome or submit to Pompey. That a possible bargain with Pompey may have flitted through the mind of Catiline is suggested by the report that Lentulus, who later guided the conspiracy in the city, planned to except Pompey's children from the universal massacre, and hold them as hostages against the great general's arrival.

The burden of watching over the state fell entirely upon Cicero; this year might indeed have been called the consulship of Tullius and Cicero, just as 59 B.C. was called the consulship

---

[14] Since Catiline spent a great deal of money before the election, it is not impossible that Crassus was assisting him.

of Julius and Caesar, for Cicero's colleague did nothing. He was quiescent; perhaps all that could be expected of him. Cicero had won him to inactivity, probably before the year began, by yielding to him the province of Macedonia, which had been assigned to Cicero for the year 62 B.C. Antony wished for nothing but money, and this could be secured in Macedonia. But he had been known as an intimate of Catiline. Cicero therefore had announced to the senate on the first of January that he himself would not go to a province; an announcement that some senators may have interpreted as a sign of agreement between the consuls; and he told the people a few days later that he and Antony were acting together, contrary to the expectation's of Cicero's enemies. Still later in the year Cicero informed the people at a *contio* that he would not take a province; afterwards publishing the speech, which has been lost. In the list of his consular orations it immediately precedes those against Catiline, and may therefore have been delivered at a time when the fear of Catiline was already abroad in Rome; virtually it may have been an assertion not merely that Cicero's administration had no taint of self-seeking, but that Antony no longer supported his former political associate.

Cicero's long experience in the intriguing political life of Rome enabled him to keep a close watch on Catiline. In Sicily Cicero had himself tracked Verres on every devious path, unearthing letters, accounts, conversations, and the minutest details of the governor's private life. In Rome, during the same year, his influence among the electioneering agents, though he himself did not bribe, kept him informed even of the sums offered by his opponents to keep him out of the aedileship. Cicero had countless political and personal friends both in Rome and in the rest of Italy, who at this time undoubtedly brought him every bit of news that they could gather. Folly and treachery among Catiline's following also played their part. A certain Curius, formerly expelled from the senate, had joined the conspirators. He had had an old intrigue with Fulvia, a woman of noble birth, but when his money was spent, Fulvia lost her interest in him. Suddenly he began to boast, promising "seas and mountains," and finally he revealed that a conspiracy was on foot, which would enrich him. Fulvia could not keep the secret; and a little later both she and Curius were in the pay of Cicero, who thus had at least one spy within the conspiracy itself. Fulvia and Curius are the only persons mentioned as Cicero's informants, but it does not seem improbable that there were others, considering the large number of the Catilinarians and the many places in which they were active.

Catiline realized that Cicero was his chief opponent, and set all manner of traps for him, but Cicero was not lacking in astuteness. To ward off violence, he surrounded himself with a bodyguard of friends and clients; men came secretly from the country districts to protect him; a group of young men from Reate is mentioned by Cicero himself, though it is not certain when Cicero summoned them. He was using them for various purposes later in the year. His own consular lictors would have been quite insufficient for protection if a riot had been started. We hear of no attack on Cicero during these months, but his fears of it were doubtless well grounded. Catiline was equal to the attempt and Roman politics offered countless precedents. It was also part of Cicero's aim to rouse the population of Rome to a realization of the danger to the city, and this could be done by his own obvious precautions against violence, as was seen at the election.

Cicero's information about Catiline, however, and his measures for his own safety could do nothing to prevent the threatened outbreak unless he could persuade the senate to pass the "last decree." Only thus would he be able to levy an army. There was no military force in Rome. Meanwhile, the people were being agitated by strange omens, which always appeared at critical times; and horrifying rumors were circulated. It was said that Catiline and his accomplices had pledged themselves to crimes by drinking wine mixed with human blood, that Manlius was collecting armed men in Etruria, and that other emissaries of Catiline were busy in other parts of Italy. In addition to an uprising of hostile citizens, there might be a repetition of the horrors under Spartacus, though we are told that Catiline was unwilling, from first to last, to have rural slaves enlisted. Nevertheless the senate refused to act, from blindness, cowardice, and treachery. It would seem that such threats as those already reported about Catiline would have stirred the senate, but they were too familiar with invectives and altercations to heed the warning; Cato's denunciation of Catiline meant little, for Cato denounced everybody who was not as pure as a Stoic. The senators, furthermore, were unwilling to choose Cicero for their leader; he was probably the first New man who had presided over them for nearly forty years; very few of them had had so humiliating an experience before. Let him take care of himself. As for Catiline, he was after all an aristocrat; he, and Antony too, had been lavish in threats the year before, and nothing had happened.

On the twenty-first of October Cicero stated in the senate that Manlius would raise the standard of revolt on the twenty-seventh and that on the following day there would be a massacre of the *optimates* in the city. An ex-praetor also reported that soldiers were collecting in Etruria and that Manlius, with a large force, was going from city to city. Still another event may have occurred on this day. After the senate had convened that morning, at the summons of Cicero, the latter informed them that he had been wakened about midnight by Crassus and two other very prominent nobles, and had been told how after dinner Crassus had received from his porter a packet of letters, which had been left at the house by a stranger. One of the letters was addressed to Crassus; the others to various men. Crassus opened his, which he found to be anonymous; it warned

him of a terrible massacre to be started by Catiline, and advised
him to leave the city. Crassus went at once to Cicero with the
letters; he was overcome by the danger to the state and also
desirous to free himself of any suspicion that he was acting with
Catiline. Cicero now, in the senate, produced the unopened
letters and handed them to the addressees, requesting them to
read the missives aloud. All the letters contained the same
warning.[15]

The senate now passed the "last decree." Two generals,
who had returned from foreign service, were at that time outside
the city waiting for triumphs; evidently they had some troops
with them. These two, as well as two praetors, were sent to
various parts of Italy to quell disturbances; with orders to levy
soldiers for their need. A good beginning was thus made towards
checking any rising outside the city; and we are informed that
Manlius did declare against the government on the twenty-
seventh, as Cicero had foretold. Rome itself was patrolled both
night and day; the Palatine was amply protected; the knights
and others, either at once or presently, guarded the meetings
of the senate; and Cicero's own armed followers seem to have
been increased, for it is reported that after the declaration of
martial law they almost filled the forum. The gladiators in the
city, trained fighters and therefore most likely to become dangerous allies of Catiline, were sent to Capua and other municipalities.
Rewards were offered for information about the conspiracy.
Slaves were to receive their freedom and one hundred sestertia,
about five thousand dollars; free men, impunity and double that
sum. Many prominent men left Rome either as soon as the
"last decree" had been passed, or, at any rate, before the twenty-
eighth, the date set for the massacre—"not so much to save
their own lives as to thwart Catiline's plans," as Cicero dis-

---

[15] It has been surmised, apparently with reason, that Cicero sent these
letters in order to influence the senate and to force Crassus to choose between
the state and Catiline. Crassus was suspected of being one of the conspirators. See below, p. 278.

creetly put it. The effect on the city was profound. The old
happy life ceased; people no longer dared to loiter in public
places; everywhere there was distrust and apprehension; the
women were terror-stricken; and private citizens protected their
houses with guards. The law-abiding members of the community
now recognized Cicero as their champion, whether they were
senators, knights, or ordinary citizens; and it may be said that
a beginning had been made of a new party, as it were, which
included men from every class. There was what Cicero called a
great *consensio* among all good men, *boni;* the senate had at last
bestirred itself, acting through the consul.

V

THE FIRST AND SECOND CATILINARIANS

Very much had thus been gained, but not everything.
Though Manlius raised the standard of revolt and even wrote a
long letter of defiant explanation to the Roman general sent to
Etruria, Catiline and his fellow-conspirators had not been caught
in an overt act. The day set for the massacre in the city passed
without accident; Cicero had obviously succeeded in averting the
slaughter, but Catiline was also enabled to retain his appearance
of innocence. A similar situation arose in connection with
Praeneste, a town twenty miles from Rome, strategically one
of the most important places in Latium. Catiline had planned
to seize it on the first of November; he abandoned his attempt
when he found that Cicero's men already held the town in sufficient force; and, as a result, no new evidence was furnished.
At this time, a certain L. Paulus threatened to prosecute Catiline
for public violence, and Catiline at once made use of this opportunity to pose as a harmless citizen suffering from unjust persecution. He offered himself for voluntary arrest, first to an
ex-consul, then to Cicero, then to one of the praetors, all of whom

refused to take him into their houses; and at last, successfully, to a certain Q. Metellus, whom Cicero calls Catiline's boon companion.

Cicero's position was one of great difficulty. There were still men in the senate who supported Catiline, as Cicero himself told that body in his *First Catilinarian,* a few days later; and nobody could know, not even Cicero, how many of the people were ready to join a sudden outbreak. By virtue of the "last decree" Cicero might have punished Catiline by exile or by death, and some demanded this; but such a course of action would have been perilous in a city honeycombed with treachery, the more because of Catiline's adroit voluntary detention, which in effect proclaimed that he was innocent and ready to stand trial. A trial, however, was out of the question; the city was seething, and Cicero could not have produced witnesses of a reputation much above that of Curius, the expelled senator, and Fulvia, his notorious mistress. Nor was Catiline the only problem in the city. As subsequent events showed, there were enough desperate men in Rome to attempt murder and arson even if Catiline were eliminated. Nothing, therefore, was left for Cicero to do except to keep a close watch and to prevent actual violence: either Catiline and the other conspirators would grow weary and perhaps leave the city, after which they could readily be disposed of in the open field, or else they would commit some act that would brand them as public enemies.

To Catiline the situation was becoming unbearable; he decided to leave the city and join Manlius. It is conceivable that he thought he might best advance his cause by taking command of the forces in Etruria, though Manlius was an old fighter; but it seems more likely that he found himself so watched and hampered by Cicero that he despaired of accomplishing anything in Rome. His plan included an attempt to set the city on fire, and it is at least very suggestive that Catiline, who had thus far directed the conspiracy within the capital, should suddenly decide to go away at the very moment when the great blow was to be struck. Though under arrest, he moved about according to his needs. He held a meeting of some of his accomplices on the night between the sixth and seventh of November, at the house of a certain Laeca in the scythemakers' street. He explained that he intended to join Manlius at once, and chose the men he would take with him; he indicated to what other places in Italy certain other conspirators were to go; and he made final plans for burning the city. All this could be made effective if the state was first thrown into confusion by the murder of Cicero; Catiline therefore said he would leave Rome as soon as Cicero was out of the way. The conspirators were staggered by the difficulty of the proposed assassination; fear was expressed, and hesitation. Two men, however, volunteered to go to Cicero's house before daybreak on that very morning, accompanied by armed associates, and, joining in the crowd of early callers, at the *salutatio,* to fall upon the consul; "to despatch me in my bed," says Cicero dramatically, "before the very eyes of my wife and children."

Cicero learned of the plan, through Fulvia, almost before the meeting at Laeca's came to an end. He increased the guards at his house and even had time to inform some prominent men of the plot against his life. When the assassins arrived, they were refused admittance; and it seems probable that Cicero's prominent friends were present to witness their discomfiture.

The senate met on the eighth, though there is some reason for thinking it was on the seventh, possibly in the afternoon. The results of this meeting were such as nobody could have foreseen. There had been many meetings for the purpose of discussing Catiline; serious accusations had been hurled at the conspirator, and he still went about unmolested. The senate were gathered in the temple of Jupiter Stator; outside were knights and other citizens, some of whom, at least, served as a guard. Shouts were heard from these, and presently Catiline and some of his friends entered the senate. It is not known whether the proceedings had already begun, nor exactly what took place throughout the meeting. There was a hush when Catiline entered; his colleagues did not greet him; and after he had taken his seat, those in his vicinity drew away, noticeably all the men of consular rank. It would seem that his presence had not been expected; possibly he had avoided the senatorial meetings of late. Perhaps, too, Cicero had already had time to describe the meeting at Laeca's house and its results. Something, whatever it may have been, had changed the attitude of the senate, at least for the moment. Sallust informs us that Catiline's appearance filled Cicero with fear or with anger; he does not know which; and that Cicero then "delivered that oration, an excellent one and useful to the state, which he later wrote out and published"—the *First Oration against Catiline*. Sallust also describes the reply that Catiline made, interrupted by the senators; whereas Plutarch makes it appear that Catiline attempted to defend himself before Cicero spoke, but was silenced with shouts. Cicero's own speech refers to certain demands of Catiline, as though the latter interrupted the consul, but such references are sometimes found in Cicero's orations without a foundation in actual fact; they may have been added at the time of publication. In all probability, the meeting was one of much confusion. Catiline more than once interrupted Cicero in an attempt to clear himself, but Cicero finally secured the attention of the assembly and delivered an attack on Catiline.

Cicero spoke under the impulse of a sudden and very strong emotion. It could not have been fear, for there was nothing about Catiline's presence in the senate to inspire fear; it was anger, a wrathful consternation at Catiline's impudence and an angry impatience with the stupidity and the treachery among the senators that had for so long made Catiline's brazen speciousness possible. Cicero turns first against Catiline, passionately demanding to what lengths he thinks he can go and declaring that both precedent and the existing circumstances justify his death, for which many have long clamored. Then he begins to review Catiline's various revolutionary attempts; but suddenly he breaks off to exclaim against the traitors sitting before his very eyes, whom he knows to be worthy of death, and against whom nevertheless he has not until the present moment uttered even an angry word.

When Cicero began to speak, he probably did not know exactly what he would say; but as he proceeded, the resolve grew within him that he would make a supreme attempt to dispel the atmosphere of mystery, treachery, and threats under which the city had so long labored, that he would present the issue with such clearness and such force that it would admit of no further evasions. He declares open war against Catiline and his secret supporters; and he does not even give the latter an opportunity for debate. "Lay the matter before the senate," Catiline had said; but Cicero replies that he will not lay the matter before the senate. Without a formal reference to them, he will make clear to Catiline what the senate thinks; and he orders Catiline to leave the city, thus forcing the treacherous senators either to interrupt him for the purpose of defending Catiline, which they did not have the courage to do, or else forever after to say nothing in his favor. Cicero does not, as consul, formally send Catiline into exile, as he might have done, for that would have given Catiline's supporters an opportunity to represent the latter as a victim of persecution. But he tells Catiline that there is no room for him in Rome. Let him go into exile, if he wishes to rouse the people against Cicero; or let him go to Manlius, as he had prepared to do—and Cicero gives a minute account of Catiline's plans that must have astounded and terrified both Catiline and his friends. If Catiline had gone into voluntary exile, that would have been an admission of defeat, and the conspiracy would probably have melted away; but Cicero did not expect this. If Catiline should leave to join Manlius, Cicero's revelations of the completeness with which the conspirators were watched would perhaps lead them to accompany Catiline, and the city would be free; in the field, they would not be nearly so dangerous. This was what Cicero aimed at: to force the senate into uncompromising opposition to Catiline, and to get the conspirators to leave the city and openly declare themselves to be enemies of the state.

One of these aims was accomplished at once, the unification of the senate. Sallust says that Catiline, rising to reply, spoke first like one unjustly accused: he was of a noble family and had always looked forward to a career worthy of a patrician; both he and his family had served the nation well; let no one think that he, a man of high birth, had need for the sake of advancement to bring destruction upon the state and that its defense must be undertaken by M. Tullius, a sojourner in the city. This was the old rag of an argument which had been used against Cicero at the consular election and which had doubtless served many times since then to make the senate hesitate. But for the moment it had lost its appeal; when Catiline tried to add further insults, the senators drowned his voice with their shouts, calling him a public enemy and the assassin of his country. Then, still according to Sallust, he became enraged and, rushing out of the temple, shouted that since his enemies were recklessly pushing him on, he would extinguish the conflagration started against him by tearing down the houses about their ears—*ruina*. Though these words have already been quoted from Catiline's altercation with Cato, he may well have uttered them again; they expressed the attitude he was assuming, that he was forced into conspiring; and a violent parting threat was in accordance with his character. Cicero wrote in the *Orator*, some seventeen years later, that Catiline was struck dumb by his attack, but the word used by Cicero, *obmutuit*, is too vague to be pressed; Catiline argued no further. Whatever may have been the nature of Catiline's departure from the senate, the senators were now as unanimously behind Cicero as this captious body ever could be behind any one. There was now in Rome a union of the orders—*concordia ordinum.*

One thing else was accomplished. Late that night Catiline left Rome with a few followers, still watched by Cicero's men, who saw him take the Aurelian road, which led to Etruria; he had sent soldiers ahead to wait for him at Forum Aurelium, fifty miles out of Rome.[16] The conspirator did not go as he had planned, at his own volition and with the government thrown into confusion by the murder of the consul. To the people of Rome it was evident that Catiline had been outmaneuvered; they might hope that Cicero had the conspiracy well in hand.

But the large body of conspirators were still in Rome, left by Catiline to do what they could. This was the thought uppermost in Cicero's mind when he addressed the people on the following day; in the *Second Oration against Catiline.* He gives an extremely vivid picture of the expelled criminal: he now lies prostrate; he knows that he has been overwhelmed and is undone; often he turns his eyes toward Rome, grieving because it has been torn from his jaws. It is the description of a baffled wild beast, suggestive to the English reader of Milton's lines about Satan:

> ... he with his horrid crew
> Lay vanquished....
> ... round he throws his baleful eyes,
> That witnessed huge affliction and dismay
> Mixed with obdurate pride and steadfast hate.

Cicero also describes, briefly, the meeting in the senate on the previous day; justifies his seeming leniency toward Catiline and reveals his knowledge of the conspiracy, as he had done to the senators, pointing out that Catiline is now an open enemy—

---

[16] Three hundred men accompanied Catiline when he left Rome, according to Plutarch, who may have been thinking of the soldiers at Forum Aurelium.

unless he should go into exile, as his friends still maintained, but which Cicero declares to be inconceivable. The conspirators still in Rome, however, are his chief topic. He divides all the followers of Catiline into the six classes already mentioned, characterizing each, and shows how they are all bankrupts or criminals, not to be compared to the might of Rome; but he nevertheless asks the people to remember that those who have not gone with Catiline are very dangerous, more so than his army. They still flit about the forum; surround the senate-house, and even enter it; they shine with ointments and are brilliant in their purple cloaks. They are not a match for the law-abiding Romans —and yet let them go out! The gates are open, and no one will hinder their departure. Catiline has gone by the Aurelian road and is only a little way ahead; they can overtake him before evening if they hasten. If they remain, let them beware; for the city has patriots to apprehend them and a prison to hold them. As for the peaceful citizens, they must still guard their houses. But the conspirators remained.

Catiline, in the meantime, was traveling northward. He sent letters to most of the consulars, in which he complained that he had been falsely accused and was going to Massilia as an exile. Catulus, however, the leader of the senate, read to that body another kind of a missive, which he claimed to have received from him. In that, Catiline expressed his determination to champion the cause of the many, inasmuch as he himself had been cheated out of his well-earned honors by the election of unworthy men—the old cry about the sojourner in Rome! After a few days, Catiline surrounded himself with the lictors of a consul and assumed the other consular insignia; with them he entered the camp of Manlius. This meant war. The senate declared Catiline and Manlius public enemies, and directed the consuls to levy an army; Cicero was to stay in Rome, while Antony set out to meet the rebels. The state's pardon was offered to those who would lay down their arms by a certain day, unless they had

already been condemned for a capital crime; but no one left
Catiline's camp. Some joined it, who had not previously been
in the conspiracy; the son of a senator, who attempted to reach
Catiline, was brought back and executed at the bidding of his
father. But possibly the proclamation of amnesty was not
entirely fruitless. In the *De Finibus*[17] Cicero says that many
came and confessed voluntarily during his consulship; they must
have been Catilinarians.

VI

MURENA

The first real encounter with the conspirators had thus come
to an end; Catiline was out of the city; he and Manlius had
been declared public enemies, and armies had been despatched
against them. It was a substantial victory for Cicero and the
government. The importance of it is indicated by the publication of the first two orations against Catiline, for it is worth
noting that Cicero published none of the many speeches against
Catiline that he must have delivered during the preceding
months; not even the one which led to the declaration of martial
law. Cicero obviously felt that the first real blow was struck
when he drove Catiline into open warfare; the "last decree,"
as he said, had until then been like a sword in its scabbard. But
the victory was not decisive. There was little fear in Rome of
the rebel army, at least so Cicero represents, but there was much
fear of the conspirators who were still in the city. In the meantime Cicero had to meet a new danger.

Sulpicius, the jurisconsult, who has been mentioned as one of
the gretest lawyers of Rome, had been a candidate for the consulship during the recent campaign. He was an honorable man.
Finding that things were going against him, largely because of
bribery, he announced even before the election that he would

---

[17] *De Fin.* 1, 50.

prosecute his successful rival, Murena; and Cato, ever just, seconded him. Now, in November, the case came to trial. The situation was extremely serious, for a verdict of guilty would mean a new election with all that that implied of campaign oratory, the activities of clubs, and possibly of armed gangs, and every other kind of excitement, all of which would have given an excellent opportunity to the lurking conspirators. Sulpicius and Cato should have seen this, but the honest Sulpicius was smarting under his defeat and was, indeed, at no time a very forceful or clear-sighted public servant, as later years showed, and Cato, in his virtuous rigidity, was always stalking in where angels feared to tread. Crassus, perhaps anxious to prove himself a champion of order and stability, was one of the speakers for the defense; the others were Hortensius, naturally enough as an aristocrat, and Cicero, who again, as in the early months of his consulship, had to fight the legal battles of the state while he was also its executive and guardian against violence.

Cicero's position was disagreeable. He was a friend of Sulpicius and had supported his candidacy, while he was on no terms of intimacy with Murena; he had framed the latest law against electoral corruption; and he had himself won advancement honorably, as Sulpicius and Cato insisted that it should be won, pointing out, in the manner of Roman litigants, that this was no case for Cicero. It is also practically certain that Murena had bribed, though this can only be inferred from the honesty of the prosecutors; Cicero spoke last and did not go deeply into the facts of the bribery, which had been discussed by the other speakers, nor does Cicero's oration contain even the little that he said. That part of the speech is represented by headings.

It is not possible to go into the details of this wonderful oration. The trial was not one of the most important or most difficult in which Cicero pleaded, and the speech is therefore not one of his greatest; but it is one of his best. It is witty, sarcastic, serious, and impassioned; it exemplifies, perhaps, every one of his purely oratorical qualities except those of burning denunciation, dramatic narrative, and great pathos; and it contains numerous observations that throw light both on the persons concerned in the trial and on Roman circumstances and conventions. One of the latter should be mentioned. The prosecutors had attacked the private life of Murena, as was incumbent on them, but, finding little to criticise, they had said that he danced. It is a grave accusation, Cicero observes, to say that a Roman consul dances; nobody dances if he is sober unless he be insane, and nobody dances when he is by himself or at an inoffensive gathering. And more to the same purpose.

Cicero's sarcasm is never better than when it is directed against his friends; it then seems to suggest what his daily conversation may have been. He was fond of Sulpicius and he remained fond of him till the end, but he had good reason for annoyance with his friend's inopportune honesty, which was willing, when prompted by personal disappointment, to expose the state to confusion and anarchy.

Sulpicius was a great jurist and Murena was a soldier. Cicero therefore informs his friend that nobody is so popular with the people as a military man; a jurist is nowhere. He gets up early to give replies to clients, the general to set out with his army; he is wakened by the roosters, and the soldier by the trumpet; Sulpicius draws up documents, and Murena draws up battle lines. And in many other ways they differ. Now, the only one that can be compared with a soldier is an orator, but by no means a jurisconsult. Indeed, it is well known that in Rome some people who have failed in oratory are actually devoting themselves to the study of law.

Nor is law a difficult subject to master; Cicero himself, if hard pressed, might do it in a day or two. There is not much to it; it is a thin sort of science, mostly words and punctuation. For a long time the chosen few kept it to themselves, and were consulted by the people as if they were wise men from the East, Chaldaeans, interpreters of dreams, and that sort of thing. Then an ordinary scribbler—Cn. Flavius was his name, a sharp fellow —told the people on what days it was right to go to the courts, and he also made some notes from observation of actual trials; so he stole the whole legal science and made it accessible to everybody. And what did the jurists do? They set to work to make things intricate, so that nobody should undertake cases without their aid. For instance, if two men should lay claim to the same Sabine farm, one might say plainly: It is mine; and the other might retort: No, it is mine; and then they could go before a judge. Now, however, after the jurists have been at it, one must say: This farm, which is in the country which is called Sabine, I, in accordance with the legal rights of a Roman citizen, claim to be mine, and for that reason I call you from the praetor's tribunal to join hands with me on the said farm; to which the other, prompted by the jurisconsult as if he were a singer in the theater accompanied by a flute-player, must reply: For the same reason as you called me from the praetor's tribunal to join hands with you, for that same reason I call you in turn. And the poor praetor has no chance for a little eloquence, if he should happen to think of something clever; he must say—but it is not necessary to go through the whole scene, which Cicero doubtless acted with flawless skill.

Sulpicius might object that he had at least stayed in the forum, whereas Murena had been away; but Cicero, though admitting the value of keeping within the vision of the electors, confesses that people get tired of looking at a man; Cicero himself has overcome their weariness by working hard for them, and so perhaps has Sulpicius; but it is none the less true that it would not have hurt either of them to be missed a little—a remark that should be put side by side with Cicero's account of the lesson he learned at Puteoli, which has been made the subject of many solemn observations.

Murena had fought under Lucullus in the East, and Cato had said that fighting against Mithradates was like fighting against women; which gave Cicero the opportunity for a few remarks about the services of Lucullus, who was present in court, and about Pompey. Thereupon Cicero turns to Cato, prefacing his remarks with the statement that he is less afraid of Cato's charges than of his reputation for honesty. He does not dare, he says, to find fault with his adversary, but there is perhaps one respect in which Cato could be improved. Since he is not speaking before the untutored many, or before a gathering of farmers, he will say a few words, somewhat rashly, about the studies to which both Cato and Cicero himself have devoted themselves. There are people called Stoics, he then explains. They say that a wise man is never influenced by gratitude or a desire to please, *gratia,* and that he never pardons a wrong; that pity is found only in those who are stupid or of no great account; that a real man can not be bent from his purpose; that only wise men, however distorted, are beautiful; however poor, rich; if they are in slavery, still they are kings; that the rest of us, who are not wise, are no better than runaway slaves, exiles, enemies, and madmen; that all wrongs are alike, every little peccadillo a heinous crime, so that he who kills a chicken, when there is no need of it, is as guilty as the man who chokes his own father to death; and finally that the wise man, since he knows, does not opine, regrets nothing, makes no mistake, never changes his mind.

After this account of the Stoic wise man, Cicero observes that Cato has not learned their doctrines for the purposes of debate, but to live by. Cicero admits that he, too, turned in his youth to philosophy, distrusting his intuitions, but that his teachers, the followers of Plato and Aristotle, are moderate men; Cato might have listened to them, and yet have been brave and just. But it is to be hoped, Cicero concludes, that experience and added years will have a mellowing influence. Cato was eleven years younger than Cicero, thirty-two at this time; but he never changed.

Sulpicius lost his case, but not solely because of the consul's pleasantries. These had served to remind the jurors that the prosecutors, though honorable men, were too fond of moral hair-splitting, a thing that had no place in the excited forum. While the jurymen were still merry, Cicero suddenly sobered them by turning to the dangers they had just escaped, through the expulsion of Catiline, and the dangers that were still threatening from the conspirators in the city. The thought had never been far away during the earlier parts of the oration, giving substance to Cicero's jests, but now it rises to ringing eloquence. Cicero's year of service is nearly ended; let them not throw the state into the anarchy of a new election. The opposition to law and order, while mostly crouching in the dark, has the effrontery even to utter its shouts of subversion in the forum. On the very day before Murena's trial, Cicero recalls to his hearers, a tribune of the people had dared to preach sedition at a public meeting, and had been opposed by several champions of order, among them Cato himself.

VII

THE THIRD CATILINARIAN

Meanwhile the conspirators in the city were making detailed plans. One of the tribunes was to hold a *contio,* in which he would attack Cicero as the cause of the terrible war impending between Catiline and the state. Indeed, it had already begun, for conspirators in various parts of Italy, "acting individually and in madness," had already resorted to hostilities and had been checked by Metellus Celer and the consul-elect's namesake C. Murena; but these uprisings were a source of terror rather than of real danger. The meeting called by the tribune was probably to be prolonged until evening, and was to be the sign for concerted action. In the night two of the conspirators, with a great band of helpers, were to set the city on fire in twelve places. There were one hundred men assigned to this, each with his definite sphere of action, and others had been detailed to stop up the aqueducts and to kill those who should bring water to extinguish the flames. With the city in the chaos of universal conflagration, access would be easier, it was thought, to Cicero and the other leading men marked for death. Cethegus himself, the most dangerous and impetuous of the conspirators, was to be with his men at Cicero's door; other assassins had been appointed each for his man; the young patricians in the conspiracy, of whom there were many, were to despatch their fathers. Nobody was to be spared, says Plutarch, except the sons of Pompey. When the systematic murders had been perpetrated and while Rome was still burning, the conspirators were to break forth from the city and join Catiline, who would be near with his army, ready to follow up the bloody advantage. All this was to occur during the Saturnalia, the time of the great annual carnival, when the doors were usually left unguarded and the slaves, free for the short season, made up in license and holiday-making for the long year of servitude.

It was an excellent plan, worked out to the last detail, but it had one fatal flaw; and this reveals the absence of Catiline's guiding hand. While he was in Rome, as Cicero puts it, all the threads of the conspiracy were held by him; he knew everybody and directed everything; he not only delegated work to others, but he saw that it was done, always ready himself to step in. With Catiline gone, there was no one leader. Chief among the conspirators was Lentulus, who was of advanced age. He had been consul in 71 B.C., and, having later been expelled from the senate, he was now praetor; he was slothful and superstitious. But he was a Cornelius, and it had been prophesied by the

Sibylline books, which prophesied anything, that there would be three Cornelii who would rule Rome. Cinna and Sulla had been Cornelii; Lentulus was obviously the third. It was twenty years, moreover, since the Capitol had been burned, in 83 B.C., whether by the Marians under Carbo or by emissaries of Sulla; and it was ten years since the acquittal of the Vestal Virgins, in 73 B.C., perhaps when Cicero's sister-in-law was involved with Catiline; both of which events indicated, by Etruscan reliance on decimals, that 63 B.C. was the fated year for Cornelius Lentulus. Lentulus prevailed upon the conspirators to have the massacre and burning take place at the Saturnalia, a very suitable time except that it was three weeks off, and much might happen in the meantime, considering Cicero's vigilance. Cethegus, on the other hand, insisted that the situation required "deeds and not plans;" if only a few would assist him, he would make an attack on the senate-house; but Cethegus could not secure a following.

The conspirators made one other mistake. Not satisfied with managing matters in the city, they thought themselves capable of looking after things on the outside as well; of assisting Catiline, indeed, as if he needed their blundering help. Some envoys from the Gallic Allobroges happened to be in Rome; two of them, we are told, but these obviously had large retinues, as is seen in the account of their later departure from Rome. They had come to see about debts, public as well as private, and were not in a very friendly mood to the Roman government. The Gauls, furthermore, were constitutionally bellicose; they had often given Rome trouble and at this time, says Cicero, were the only people who could make war on the Romans and who were not unwilling to do so. To Lentulus and his accomplices, debating over their wine and with their women beside them, the presence of the Allobroges seemed providential. A war might be stirred up in Gaul, which would ease the pressure on Catiline and Manlius, and cavalry might actually be sent as an auxiliary to the

Catilinarian army. The conspirators therefore approached the envoys, through a certain freedman, Umbrenus, who had done business among the Gauls and who knew their prominent men. Umbrenus succeeded in bringing the envoys to the house of the clever Sempronia, whose husband was away, and there they were met by Gabinius, a conspirator. The latter talked about the wide extent of the conspiracy, claiming allegiance from many who had nothing to do with it; he set forth his plans for Gallic interference, and he made great promises.

At this juncture—according to Sallust, and also to Cicero, whom the historian is probably copying here as in many other places—Rome was saved by providence. The Gauls decided to refer the matter to their patron, Sanga; and the latter immediately communicated with Cicero. The Gauls, therefore, put themselves at the consul's disposal. Acting in accordance with his orders, they made a fine pretence of enthusiasm to the conspirators, but insisted that their compatriots at home could be persuaded only if the envoys brought them letters, that is, promises confirmed by oath, from Rome. The day of their departure homeward was set for the second of December. Letters to the men at home were given by Lentulus, Cethegus, and a third conspirator; a fourth, Cassius, when approached, said he would give them his letter shortly, and he then left Rome. Lentulus appointed a certain Volturcius to accompany the Gauls, and to take them to Catiline for further confirmation of the excellent pact. Lentulus also gave Volturcius an oral message for Catiline—everything was ready in the city; let Catiline come quickly; since he had been proclaimed a public enemy, why did he hesitate to enroll the slaves in the country districts?—and he added to the oral message a letter of much the same purport: "Who I am you will learn from him whom I have sent to you. See that you be a man; consider how far you have gone already. Make plans for everything that is necessary, and get help from all sources, even the slaves."

On the second of December Cicero summoned two praetors to his house, L. Flaccus and C. Pomptinus;[18] brave men, says Cicero, and devoted to the state. Cicero explained the whole situation, apparently knowing exactly when the Gauls would depart, and ordered the praetors to arrest them at the Mulvian bridge, which was a little less than two miles north of Rome, on the Flaminian Way. The praetors took armed men with them, none of whom knew the real nature of the undertaking; they were also assisted by several picked men from Reate, sent by Cicero. They arrived at the bridge toward nightfall, and hid themselves in the farmhouses on either side of the river. Toward three in the morning the Allobroges, with Volturcius and a large retinue, began to cross the bridge. Cicero's men rushed from their hiding places with loud shouts; swords were drawn, and used. Apparently the envoys had not been informed as to what would happen, another indication of Cicero's marvellous mastery of detail, but now they quickly realized the situation and surrendered to the praetors. Volturcius defended himself for a while and urged the others to resist, but, finding that the Gauls had deserted him, he too gave up his sword.

The praetors took both the arrested men and the letters directly to Cicero's house, arriving by daybreak. The latter sent for Gabinius, who had made the arrangement with the Gauls, and he came at once, suspecting nothing; the writers of the letters were thereupon summoned one after the other, and they obeyed the summons, the indolent Lentulus arriving last. One of the conspirators, Caeparius, who was not at home when Cicero's messenger arrived, fled from the city. Many prominent men in the meantime had gathered at Cicero's house; perhaps they had been notified by him, as on the morning after the meeting at Laeca's; perhaps the city was already stirred by the news that the consul had sent for certain men suspected of conspiring. Cicero's advisers urged him to open the letters;

---

18 Flaccus was later defended by Cicero in a lawsuit. Pomptinus accompanied Cicero to Cilicia; see below, pp. 309, 467–468.

it might seem overanxious, they thought, to bring them to the senate in case they should prove to contain nothing of importance; but Cicero decided for full publicity. The senate was called to meet in the temple of Concord, and they came together in large numbers, watched by the people in the forum. A praetor was sent to the house of Cethegus, where he found a large supply of swords and daggers, newly sharpened. The conspirators were taken to the senatorial meeting under a heavy guard; Cicero "leading by the hand" Lentulus, who was still a praetor. As the conspirators and the witnesses against them crossed the forum, the people who had gathered saw also that workmen were setting up a statue of Jupiter Optimus Maximus, the guardian of the city.

The investigation in the senate was begun with Volturcius, who was brought in alone. He was so overcome by fright that he could scarcely speak. At first he tried to lie, pretending ignorance of the conspiracy and giving a fanciful account of his connection with the Gallic envoys. When the senate promised him immunity, he revealed everything he knew, with the explanation, however, that he had been employed by the conspirators only a few days ago and really was no better informed than the Gauls themselves. The latter were then called, and described their relations with the conspirtaors; even mentioning Lentulus' prophesies, which may have strongly influenced the superstitious barbarians. The reckless folly of the conspirators was shown by the fact that the envoys had knowledge about the disagreement between Cethegus and the other conspirators; apparently the Gauls had been admitted to the meetings of the plotters.

The conspirators were then summoned; one at a time, it seems, but all those who had already been examined remaining. The letters, still sealed, were brought out. Cethegus, the first to be questioned, acknowledged his seal; the letter was opened—the string was cut, as Cicero more explicitly expresses it—and the letter was read aloud. It was addressed to the senate of the

Allobroges, and was in Cethegus' handwriting; he promised in
it that he would fulfill his part of the bargain and he urged the
Allobroges to do the same. Before the letter was read, Cethegus
had explained, in reference to the arms found in his house, that
he had always been a collector of choice weapons; now he no
longer insisted on this. Statilius came next; he acknowledged
his seal and his handwriting, and when the letter had been read
made a full confession. With Lentulus, the ex-consul and
praetor, whose examination followed, more ceremony was
observed. After he had acknowledged his seal, which was the
image of his grandfather, Cicero said a solemn word about the
latter; he had been a great patriot, first as consul and then as
leader of the senate. Cicero's backward glance may seem a little
strange to a modern reader; but it could not fail of effect
with the senate, who were always living in the presence of their
great ancestors. "This image, though mute," said Cicero,
"ought to have held you back from this great crime." When
Lentulus' letter had been read, he was given an opportunity to
speak. At first he denied everything; presently he rose and
began to question the Gauls, and then Volturcius. He was gifted
as a speaker, says Cicero, and had had much experience. But
he could not shake the testimony either of the envoys or of Volturcius. Suddenly, to the surprise of all present, he confessed.
Volturcius then asked for the reading of the letter that Lentulus
had given him for Catiline, and the anonymous missive was read.
Finally, Gabinius was summoned. It was he who had made
arrangements with the Gauls. He answered brazenly at first, but
after a while he too confessed.

When the examination had been finished, says Cicero, the
conspirators remained silent and dazed; they kept their eyes on
the ground, only occasionally looking up and exchanging furtive
glances; their manner was in itself a confession of guilt.

The senate, without a dissenting vote, passed various measures proposed by its leading members. Formal thanks, in most

THE EXAMINATION

laudatory terms, *amplissimis verbis,* were voted to Cicero, because his courage, wisdom, and foresight had saved the state from the greatest dangers. Flaccus and Pomptinus, the praetors who had made the arrests, were praised; so also was Cicero's colleague Antony, because he had "kept the conspirators from his own and the state's counsels"—whatever the senate intended that to mean. Probably it was only a formal recognition of the fact that Antony had given up his old associations. Arrest was decreed against the four conspirators that had been examined and against five others, including the freedman Umbrenus, who had brought the Gauls to Sempronia's house; nine in all. Lentulus was first to resign his praetorship; and it seems that he tendered a formal resignation in the senate and exchanged his purple-edged magistrate's toga for that of an ordinary citizen. The four conspirators were entrusted for safe-keeping to men of prominence; one was given to Caesar, and another to Crassus. To the four men under arrest was presently added Caeparius, who had been caught in the meantime.

The senate also decreed a thanksgiving to the gods, in the name of Cicero, "because he had saved the city from fire, the citizens from murder, and Italy from war." Such a thanksgiving, *supplicatio,* was a military honor, frequently given to successful generals in the midst of their campaigns as an earnest that a triumph would later be granted; it had never before been given to any one except a general, never to a man in the civil garb, *togatus.* Previously it had been the reward for slaughtering the enemy in the field, and so for serving the state well; now, for the first time, Cicero says, it was the reward for saving the state.

Ordinarily the minutes of the senate, kept by clerks, seem to have been of doubtful reliability, and as for the actual decrees, these were written out after the meeting, by or in the presence of the senators particularly interested in the measure. Cicero took extraordinary precautions that a full, exact, and trustworthy record should be made of everything that took place on this day, including the examination of the witnesses. He entrusted this task to four senators of unquestioned reputation, who also, as he says later,[19] found it very easy to follow the transactions because of their good memory, their learning, and their habit of writing rapidly. One of them, it is interesting to notice, was the scholarly Nigidius Figulus, considered the most learned man in Rome next to Varro; or the third most learned man, by those who assign the second place to Cicero. Usually, furthermore, the senatorial minutes, exclusive of the actual decrees, seem to have remained in the hands of the presiding consul, at least until the end of his year of office; but Cicero had copies made at once of the record kept by the four senators, and these copies were sent to all parts of Italy and the provinces. The whole Roman people were thus informed of the events that led to the arrest of the chief conspirators, and of the names of any others involved in the testimony of the Gauls; and this information was made as reliable as was possible. That Cicero's precautions were wise, was seen the very next year, when he was actually accused of having altered the records. The charge was advanced as an argument in court by a young man, Torquatus. Cicero, who was a friend both of Torquatus and of his father, treated the youth with much consideration, but the fact that a beginner in politics, personally on friendly terms with the ex-consul, could accuse him of forgery, and at the very time when Cicero was the most influential man in Rome, with an unsurpassed record for personal honesty, reveals the loose morality that governed public acts and public utterances; C. Verr-ucius was not a solitary phenomenon.

The meeting on the third lasted until late in the afternoon. When it was ended, Cicero went before the people in the forum and informed them of the recent events and of the senatorial decrees; in the *Third Oration against Catiline*. Sallust tells

---

[19] *Pro Sulla* 42.

us—perhaps from personal observation—that until this moment the *plebs urbana* had been only too eager for revolution and war, but that, when the full plans of the conspiracy were revealed, they veered about; they shouted curses against Catiline and praised Cicero to the sky. They were like men suddenly snatched from slavery; the greatest happiness a Roman could imagine. The ordinary deeds of war—and by these Sallust means the murder of the wealthy and the confiscation of their property—were prompted by a desire for booty, for the enrichment of those who have nothing, and were, by implication, in accord with the morals of the plebs; but the burning of the city planned by the conspirators was vandalism, striking at the plebs themselves, for where would the loafer find food and entertainment after Rome was in ashes?

The loud relief and enthusiasm of the people, as they listened to Cicero, is reflected in his speech. He was their hero, for the time being; their savior; and could, or must indeed, speak in this character. It was felt that the conspiracy was at an end, or very nearly so; and the end had come without bloodshed. There were only nine men to be punished out of the whole number of actual and potential conspirators, a situation that had no resemblance to the days of Marius, Cinna, and Sulla, as Cicero could not but point out. The day of a man's birth is the beginning of very uncertain fortunes, he said, and even if the newborn child is destined for happiness, he can have no realization of it; but the day on which a man is saved from danger gives him a gladness that is both certain and consciously enjoyed. Romulus had founded Rome and had been placed among the gods; Cicero has saved Rome after she had grown great and powerful, and asks only to be held in grateful remembrance. The juxtaposition seems extravagant at first, until we remember that Romulus was more than half a myth and that the Romans, Caesar among them, frequently made public boasts of their descent from the immortals. Far more is claimed when the speaker looks into the future and says men will remember that Rome had at one time two citizens, one of whom extended the empire to the very regions of the sky, while the other preserved the seat of this empire. That Cicero ranged himself even momentarily with Pompey, perhaps the greatest popular idol Rome ever had—and the victorious general's home-coming was near—indicates more than anything else the hilarious acclaim with which he was greeted. Cicero also appealed to the people for protection in the future, when he would have to live side by side with his vanquished enemies, but, compared with his references to Pompey, this appeal seems hardly more than a gracious reliance on the people's good will, an insinuating flattery of their power; but it was no doubt already serious in Cicero's mind, and was to be repeated. Nor was it anything but unselfishness that caused him to ask only for a grateful recollection; Roman politicians were rarely satisfied with such an unsubstantial reward. Cicero, however, told his audience that in attaining the consulship and in saving the state he had reached the goal of his ambition; his only concern would be so to conduct himself after he had returned to private life that men would attribute the present victory, not to chance, but to successful endeavor—*virtus*.

A tone of lofty solemnity, which lifts the speech above self-glorification, is imparted when Cicero, at considerable length and with fervid eloquence, attributes the saving of Rome to Jupiter, the guardian of the city. The populace of Rome lived beneath the eyes of their gods; Roman public and private life was filled with sacrifices, sacred games, and thanksgivings. There was no crisis in Roman history which was not foretold by strange omens, no victory and no defeat passed without religious observances. There had been many prodigies of late, which had stirred up the people. Lentulus had added his share by means of Sibylline responses and Etruscan computations. And this had not been confined to the last few months. Nearly three years before, in 65 B.C., at the time of the so-called First Conspiracy of Catiline, other prodigies had occurred; the lightning had descended on the Capitol; images of gods and statues of famous men had been thrown down, the bronze tablets that contained the laws had been melted, even the gilded group of the infant Romulus suckled by the wolf had been struck. The sooth-sayers, summoned from all Etruria, had prophesied slaughter and fire and civil war, even the destruction of the empire, unless the gods were placated; and, as a result, there had been games for ten days and a large statue had been vowed to Jupiter. This statue had at last been finished; it was the one that the workmen had been setting up at the very moment when the conspirators were being led to the senate. The synchronism was a palpable proof that Jupiter and no one else had saved the city, says Cicero; no man would be so rash or so insane as to deny it; if Cicero himself should claim the credit, he was not to be tolerated. It was the gods who had inspired Lentulus and his accomplices with the stupendous folly of entrusting their affairs to strangers and foreigners, and writing incriminating letters; and it was the gods who had turned the naturally hostile and warlike Gauls to a course of peace; the envoys might have destroyed Rome merely by keeping silent. The Romans, with their wives and children, had therefore good reason—they had never had a better one—for giving thanks to the gods. A thanksgiving of several days had just been decreed by the senate. The new statue of Jupiter was in sight of the people while Cicero spoke. Accordingly, almost his last word, as he dismissed the assembly, when night had already begun, was a request that they turn in worship to Jupiter before they depart for their homes.

The providential erection of Jupiter's statue was later described by Cicero in his poem on his consulship, and the description is quoted by Quintus in Cicero's essay on Divination.[20] Quintus is represented as endeavoring to convince the

---

[20] *De Divin.* 1, 17–22.

orator of the truth of such miraculous events by quoting from
the latter's own writings; but Cicero remains sceptical. As a
philosophical thinker, Cicero did not believe in prodigies and
omens; an attitude that, as previously indicated, was shared by
most educated Romans. And yet, when they spoke of or to the
gods in public, they were perhaps less insincere than seems at
first to have been the case. Intellectually they did not believe;
emotionally, however, they can not have been entirely beyond
the reach of the popular faith. Cicero seems to have been as
little affected by it as any one; certainly less so than many that
could be named; but in the presence of the people, who were
superstitious even if their feeling can not be called faith, he was
not consciously fabricating emotion.

In his private life, he was not much given to prayers; he
wrote to his wife that he had served men and she had worshipped
the gods.[21] But he believed in some kind of divine power in
the world, though it was not to be called by the names of the
ordinary gods; and in reference to the hurried events of his
consulship he seems in retrospect to have thought of himself as
having acted under a kind of divine inspiration. This thought
is expressed not only in this oration but also in some orations of
later date, and with considerable conviction.[22] In the year
61 B.C. Cicero, writing to Atticus,[23] refers to the state which
"you think was saved by my wisdom, though I think it was
saved by that of God." And yet this passage, apparently an
incontrovertible proof of Cicero's attitude, may after all be
nothing more than a playful reference to a previous conversation
or letter; Atticus, frankly an atheist and often twitted by
Cicero for his Epicureanism, may well have waxed humorous
about Cicero's public utterances about providence; the more so
as Atticus frequently edited his orations. It would be interesting to know what Cicero felt, but possibly he did not quite know

---

[21] *Fam.* 14, 4, 1.
[22] See, for example, *Pro Sulla* 40.
[23] *Att..* 1, 16, 6.

himself; all men, as they look back, find crises in their lives during which they acted without conscious foresight—under some mysterious guidance from the outside, as it were.

VIII
THE FOURTH CATILINARIAN

The disposition of the prisoners was now the paramount question. After addressing the people, Cicero did not return to his own house, for during the night the consul's residence was used for the annual sacrifice to Bona Dea, under the superintendence of Terentia, as wife of the consul, and the Vestal Virgins. Cicero, therefore, accompanied by the enthusiastic crowd from the forum, went to the house of a friend and neighbor; and there he and a few intimates anxiously discussed the future punishment of the conspirators.

The decision did not rest exclusively with Cicero. By passing the "last decree," the senate had placed all the government's resources in Cicero's hands, but he looked upon himself as their executive; as such, he had succeeded in saving the city and apprehending the chief conspirators, and he had throughout acted with the approval of the senate, though he had himself seen to all the details of execution. As he had said in the speech for Rabirius, it was the consul's duty to refer to the senate. Nevertheless this body, though ultimately the possessors of supreme power, would be strongly influenced by Cicero's recommendation, should he make any, or by his inclination, if as presiding officer he thought it his duty not actually to make a recommendation. Above all, the decision of the senate would have to be executed by Cicero, and he would be held responsible by the people.

Personal considerations obviously favored clemency. Cicero had already made numerous enemies, not only the secret sympathizers with the cause of Catiline, but also the men whom he had opposed in connection with the bill of Rullus and other matters during the past year. At present the senate was behind him, but he was a New man; the aristocrats would be very willing to throw him over if trouble should arise in the future. All these difficulties would be immeasurably increased if he allowed himself to become responsible for the execution of the conspirators, some of whom were nobles; and any agitator would always find it possible to raise the question of legality in reference to the "last decree," and the death-penalty, if it were inflicted. Cicero was naturally averse to harshness; all his writings show this. At this time, furthermore, there was a great temptation to act leniently, and so follow his natural inclination and stave off future trouble: his consulship was nearly at an end. In less than a week the new tribunes would take office, an event which virtually began the next official year; and in less than four weeks Silanus and Murena would be consuls. Failure to punish severely would probably lead to an ultimate renewal of the conspiracy; this had been the result of the laxness in 65 B.C.; but just as it had taken two years for the conspirators again to become dangerous, so it is not likely that the leading conspirators of 63 B.C., even if set free, could have gathered their scattered adherents so as to do anything during the next few weeks. The city, as Caesar pointed out on the fifth, was completely in the hands of the consul. Cicero could have continued his watch, and handed over the state to his successors on the thirty-first of December; he would have won the praise of the law-abiding citizens, and his enemies, neither so many nor so bitter, would have had no legal means of attacking him. Plutarch says that the multitude thought Cicero lacking in courage—naturally enough, perhaps, since he had for months found it necessary to utter accusations against the conspirators, in order to win the whole-hearted support of the people, and had been forced to act in the dark—but when Plutarch adds that

Cicero would have seemed cowardly and unmanly in case he had acted leniently, he can scarcely be describing the real situation. Caesar, when the question was finally discussed in the senate, moved for clemency; Cicero could have followed his lead without apprehensions about the attitude of the plebs.

But there were very grave reasons why Cicero should not consult his personal safety. Lack of severity would give danger-ous encouragement to the army of Catiline, whereas the death penalty would have the opposite effect; Cato expressed this opinion on the fifth, and later events proved the second alterna-tive correct. In the city, the situation was similar, but fraught with even greater danger, as was presently shown by the attempts made to liberate the arrested conspirators.

And now the gods again intervened. When the fire on the altar, at the sacrifice in Cicero's house, seemed to have died down, a bright flame suddenly shot forth. The Vestals interpreted this as a sign that Cicero ought to proceed bravely in whatever course he had decided upon; and Terentia at once carried the message to Cicero, urging severity against the conspirators. She was by nature neither gentle nor lacking in courage, adds Plutarch. Quintus and Nigidius Figulus seconded Terentia's advice; from what is known of them it seems probable that the sudden flame on the altar had more influence with them than it could have had with Cicero.[24]

There was need of immediate action. On the fourth, freed-men and a few clients of Lentulus tried to stir up artisans and slaves, and even applied to the recognized mob leaders in the city, who "were in the habit of disturbing the state for pay"; and Cethegus, though under arrest, was able to send messengers

---

[24] This story is told by Plutarch, who never omits the supernatural, and who attributes to Terentia an influence over Cicero which is not even hinted at in his large correspondence. Plutarch places the miracle on the night after the third, but assumes that the important debate about the punishment of the conspirators occurred on the next day, thus dropping the fourth of December from his narrative.

to his slaves and freedmen, trained fighters, to come in full force
and free him. Cicero, learning of these plans, increased the
guards.

.The senate also met on the fourth, but mainly to hear new
evidence. A certain Tarquinius had been arrested while on his
way to Catiline. . Brought into the senate, he turned state's
evidence, and gave very much the same testimony as had been
given by Volturcius. In addition, he asserted that he had been
sent by Crassus to tell Catiline not to be discouraged by the
arrest of Lentulus and the others, but to hasten with his army
to the city. The senate would not listen to the charge against
Crassus; it was voted "that Tarquinius' testimony was false, that
he be kept in chains, and that he be allowed to give no further
evidence unless he wished to reveal the name of the person at
whose advice he had told such a falsehood." An attempt was
also made to implicate Caesar. His enemies, Catulus and Piso,
tried to induce Cicero to have testimony brought against him
either through the Gauls or through some other witnesses, but
Cicero refused. Whether or not he believed Caesar innocent,[25]
he acted wisely, for the government was not in a position safely
to antagonize the leader of the people. Cicero had prudently
given a public proof of his belief in the loyalty of both Caesar
and Crassus, by entrusting two conspirators to them for safe-
keeping. Catulus and Piso, however, succeeded in stirring up
the knights against Caesar, so that some of them threatened him
with their swords as he was leaving the meeting.

---

[25] What Cicero actually believed in regard to Crassus and Caesar can
not be determined. Crassus later asserted that Cicero had trumped up the
charge on the fourth in order to humiliate him, but Crassus was not a
friend or admirer of Cicero, and he was eager to clear himself of suspicion.
Many interpretations were suggested of Tarquinius' appearance, but they
need not be discussed. Neither do we know whether Crassus or Caesar
secretly supported Catiline. There were many suspicious circumstances.
Nevertheless it is hardly probable that either of the men had allied himself
with Catiline. Since Pompey was soon to return, even success on the part
of the conspirators would not have furthered Caesar's or Crassus' ambitions
(see p. 244). Caesar, furthermore, if not Crassus, was probably too genuine a patriot to stoop to wholesale murder and destruction of property.

Rewards were decreed to the Allobroges and Volturcius, but nothing else seems to have been accomplished on the fourth.

On the fifth, at last, the senate met in the temple of Concord, which was well guarded, to decide the fate of the five conspirators under arrest as well as to pronounce judgment on the four who had not yet been apprehended. The reports of this momentous debate are conflicting; there were rival claims about the relative influence of some of the speakers even in the lifetime of Cicero, for Brutus, writing about Cato, his uncle, after the latter's death, assigned to him a larger share than Cicero considered proper.[26] It is certain that there were two main propositions before the house. One favored the death-penalty, chiefly advocated by Cato, though not originally proposed by him; the other, that of Caesar, would save the lives of the conspirators, but commit them to life imprisonment in suitable Italian municipalities, confiscate their property, and make it high treason ever to attempt to alleviate their punishment. Both these motions were of a degree of severity that the senate under normal conditions had no right to inflict, and consequently admitted, at least by implication, that the senate had a moral right to act at its discretion under the existing circumstances; but Caesar's motion took cognizance of the law that a citizen must not be put to death without an opportunity of appealing to the people—a right of appeal that he had indirectly championed in his prosecution of Rabirius. Cato, certainly a more law-abiding man than Caesar, said frankly that the occasion was extraordinary and required an extraordinary remedy.

Probably the debate proceeded somewhat as follows. Silanus, the consul-elect, was asked for his opinion first, and moved that the usual punishment be inflicted. This was universally understood to mean death, although this word was not mentioned. The next few speakers expressed their agreement, until Caesar, a praetor-elect, made his motion. This at once caused confusion.

---

[26] *Att.* 12, 21, 1.

Some of the previous speakers withdrew their agreement with
Silanus, in favor of Caesar; and perhaps others, who had not
spoken before, also sided with Caesar, for Quintus Cicero is
reported to have done so, and we can scarcely suppose that he,
though a praetor-elect like Caesar, would be called upon for his
opinion before the influential leader of the popular party.
Quintus, the night Terentia brought her message about the flame,
had urged severity; now he probably thought Caesar's motion
less dangerous to his brother, as several other senators seem to
have done. In the confusion that followed Caesar's speech,
Silanus made some retraction of his initial motion; perhaps
explained that by the usual punishment he had not meant death
but imprisonment, which was ludicrous. Another speaker had
proposed to postpone the decision to a later meeting, and Silanus
expressed his agreement with this. There was now a general
trend in favor of Caesar's motion.

At this time, either before or after Silanus' retraction, Cicero
took part in the debate. His speech is the *Fourth Oration
against Catiline*, which may also contain the remarks about the
general situation which he made at the beginning of the session,
when formally laying the matter before the senate. The main
thoughts in this speech are that the senators must not allow any
consideration for Cicero's safety to interfere with their decision;
that the conspirators have deserved the most severe punishment;
that they have forfeited the rights of citizens; that action must
be taken at once, because of the dangerous condition of Rome;
that the senate has the whole populace behind them and therefore
should act with courage; that Cicero entrusts his family to their
protection, in case of danger to himself; and finally, that he is
ready to execute their orders. Cicero, it would seem, had decided
for the death-penalty as the necessary course, and was willing
to take the consequences. As presiding officer, he did not openly
advocate one course to the exclusion of the other. Taken by
itself, the speech is inconclusive, and has led to various opinions;

but it could scarcely have been interpreted in more than one way by those who had listened to Caesar and had heard senators change their former opinions.

"I see," said Cicero, "that your faces and your eyes are turned toward me. I see that you are anxious not only because of your own danger and that of the state, but also because of mine. This is pleasant to me; but I entreat you by the gods to lay aside all thought of me. Give no heed to my safety; plan for yourselves and for your children. If my consulship is destined to bring me every kind of bitterness, and sorrow, and suffering, I shall bear all these not only bravely but willingly, provided my suffering may bring safety to you and to the Roman people. As consul, I have at no time been free from the fear of sudden death. I have been silent about much, I have endured much, I have yielded in many things. If the gods have willed that my consulship should rescue you and the Roman people from slaughter, let come whatever fate awaits me. Therefore take thought for yourselves and our country. Cease considering me. I ought to hope that the gods who protect this city will protect me; but should death come, I shall die with readiness and calmness. Yet my heart is not of iron. I am moved by the grief of my brother, who is present here, and by the tears of all these men who surround me. I am moved by the thought of my wife, my daughter, my little son; and of my son-in-law, who outside is awaiting the outcome of this day. But I wish them to be saved together with you, even though violence overtake me, rather than that we should all be destroyed with the state."

This, roughly, is the beginning of Cicero's speech; the rest, already indicated, and often resembling the *Third Oration*, could not have caused any one to believe that Cicero agreed with Caesar.[27]

---

[27] Cicero later (*Phil.* 8, 15) said: *Ego Catilinam perire volui.*

Cato, speaking shortly after Cicero, interpreted the latter as in favor of the death-penalty, praising the consul's words and proposing that they be spread on the minutes. Possibly other speakers between Caesar and Cato had favored the severer penalty; at any rate, some must have failed to withdraw their agreement with Silanus' motion, for Cicero makes it a point in his criticism of Brutus' account that many had urged capital punishment; a statement that would be meaningless if they had all retracted. The general opinion, nevertheless, was decisively in agreement with Caesar, until Cato made his speech.

It is not necessary to say much about the speech of Cato or that of Caesar; they are the only two reported by Sallust, but reported in the ordinary maner of an ancient historian. Each is a summary of the character of the speaker. Caesar's is extremely adroit. No punishment is too severe, but death is not the greatest evil, it is the end of trouble—a beautifully Epicurean thought. Don't act cruelly lest it lead to still greater cruelty, as in times past, though nothing of this kind need be feared while Cicero is consul. Don't act in excitement, but obey the laws[28]—meaning the right of appeal. To all of which Cato answers bluntly that Caesar evidently does not believe in a place of torment after death; that he seems to be the only one not afraid of the conspirators; that the death-penalty will break up the conspiracy; that the gods help those who help themselves; and that this help can be secured by acting in accordance with tradition, which bids that the criminals be put to death.

It was a stormy session, as some had foreseen it would be, for several men prominent in the popular party did not attend. When Cato had taken his seat, all the consulars, and a large part of the senate as well, expressed a boisterous admiration of Cato's courage; and charges of cowardice were hurled back and forth. Cato's motion was passed. Many also insisted on confiscation of the conspirators' property, which Caesar himself had pro-

---

[28] For a clear and brief statement of the legal situation, see Botsford, *On the legality etc.*

posed, but the latter was of the opinion that, since the senate had not adopted the milder part of his motion, they ought not to avail themselves of the rest of it. He appealed to the tribunes. the popular champions, some of whom at least were his strong adherents, but the tribunes refused to interfere. At last Cicero sided with Caesar, and the confiscation did not become part of the decree. It is said that the knights threatened Caesar at this meeting, actually brandishing their swords over him while he was still seated, so that some senators had to throw their togas around him for protection; and that Caesar was so frightened by the threat that he left the meeting and kept away from the senate-house for the rest of the year.[29] Cato was the hero of the meeting; at the end of it the majority of the senators escorted him to his house.

Again it was nearly evening. In view of the likelihood that an attempt to free the condemned conspirators would be made during the night, Cicero decided to carry out the verdict at once. Accompanied by the senate,[30] he first went to the house on the Palatine where Lentulus was held prisoner, and conducted him across the forum to the Tullianum, the state prison; and ordered the public executioners to do their duty. Similarly he brought the others, four of them, one after the other. Sallust, however, has it that Cicero conducted Lentulus only, and that the praetors brought the other four; which seems more likely, since this is what happened when the conspirators were brought to the senate on the third. In the Tullianum was a filthy, noisesome dungeon, into which the condemned men were taken, and there strangled.

The crowds in the forum were large. When Lentulus and the others were taken to the prison, the people had followed the guards in silence; they were overcome with the solemnity of the

---

[29] So Suetonius (*Div. Iul.* 14); but see the account given by Sallust (*Cat.* 49), which is followed on p. 278 above.

[30] This is Plutarch's description (*Cic.* 22). The senators must have hurried to join Cicero if it is true that they had first seen Cato home, as Velleius reports (2, 35).

proceedings, especially the young men among them; it seemed to them, says Plutarch, that they were taking part in some ancient aristocratic rites. After the execution, as Cicero recrossed the forum, he saw groups of conspirators scattered among the huge throng; they did not know what had taken place in the Tullianum and were waiting for the dark. Cicero turned to them and spoke in a loud voice: "They have lived." For, observes Plutarch, this is the way in which the Romans refer to death; desirous of avoiding inauspicious language.

Plutarch thereupon describes Cicero's return to his own house; relying no doubt on Cicero's later account of his consulship or on Tiro's biography. Evening had now come. The citizens were no longer silent nor did Cicero's guards encircle him in military array; men shouted and applauded, calling him the savior and the founder of his country. As he entered the narrow streets, which were usually dark, there were lights everywhere, and lamps and torches by the doors. The women were on the roofs of the houses, to see him and to do him honor as he passed. Around him were the chief men of the state, accompanying him in solemn procession. Most of these had won great wars and had entered the city in triumphal chariots; and they had carried the Roman sway to many new lands and seas. As they accompanied Cicero, they said to one another that the Roman people owed wealth, booty, and power to many commanders and generals, but to Cicero alone did they owe their security and salvation, for the danger from which he had freed them had been great and had lasted long. And the wonderful thing was not merely that he had held the conspirators in check, but that he had suppressed this the greatest conspiracy that had ever been attempted with the least amount of evil to the state, without riot or disorder.

Cicero appreciated the instability of popular enthusiasm. A few weeks earlier at the trial of Murena, he had reminded his friend Sulpicius that the populace is like the weather; a storm may arise at any moment, and it is only occasionally—as with a storm in nature—that the observer can discover its cause. Cicero knew well that some day the people might change their applause into shouts of hostility; but for the time being he was free from personal danger, which had not been the case for over a year, and he had indeed saved his country.

The fifth of December, the Nones, was always to Cicero the day when the conspiracy came to an end. After the execution, the malcontents in the city gave up all thought of violence; they disappeared in the crowd, from which a large number of them had never quite emerged. In the field, there were many desertions from Catiline's army; the majority of his men left him; of those who remained only a quarter had the arms of soldiers. The battle between Catiline and the government forces took place the next year, probably in January. The rebels fought bravely, and fell to the last man, most of them exactly where they had first been drawn up. Catiline himself, still breathing and undaunted, was found under a heap of corpses; he had rushed far ahead of his own battle line, and so met his death. Antony, Cicero's recent colleague, was the commander-in-chief for the state. Earlier, while acting as general, he had been watched by Sestius, a quaestor, for his loyalty was not above suspicion; now, facing Catiline, his old friend, he had an attack of podagra—trouble with his feet, says Sallust, without informing us how severe it was—and the command was taken by some one else.

It was fortunate for Rome in the year 63 B.C. that Cicero did not suffer from any indisposition, physical or moral.

CHAPTER X

THE TRIUMVIRATE

I

EMINENCE AND POLITICAL IDEAL

The consulship, as was pointed out at the beginning of this account of Cicero's life, was the turning point in his career. Having attained the highest office in Rome, he had no further political advancement to strive for; he was one of Rome's consulars. And since it had been his fortune during the consulship to champion the political stability of Rome, particularly by his successful opposition to the far-reaching scheme of Caesar proposed in the bill of Rullus, and since he had also saved the city from destruction and the country from civil war by suppressing the Catilinarian conspiracy, he was led to face political problems in which he would have played a very insignificant part if his consulship had consisted of the usual magisterial routine.

To the modern student of Cicero's life, there is also a peculiar contrast between the two periods separated by the consulship. Our intimate knowledge of Cicero is confined almost exclusively to the later years. All the letters except twelve were written then, all the essays except the autobiographically unimportant treatise on Invention, and thirty-four orations. Much of this information, however, has already been utilized to give a picture of Cicero's character, of his oratory, and of the Rome in which he lived. It would be interesting, perhaps, to observe Cicero's every little reaction to the shifting events of the last twenty years of his life, but a minute account would emphasize the later period far beyond its relative importance; it would involve much repetition, with new names and dates added, to no useful purpose; and it would often be less concerned with Cicero than with the disintegration of Rome, for he was the unconscious Boswell both of himself and of his contemporaries. A large number of these happenings, moreover, are of no individual importance. To describe them in detail would be like following the coils in a nest of snakes or the shifting currents and shadows in a dark whirlpool.

The consulship raised Cicero to a position of eminence that had not been attained by any Roman of his time who was not a general. He had defeated Caesar at his own game of politics, and he had saved the city. Catulus, the dignified and honorable leader of the aristocrats, and many others, among them Cato, who was not usually lavish of compliments, publicly hailed him as the father of his country. Plutarch thinks that Cicero was the first man so honored, and this was probably so, although Cicero himself had applied the title to Marius in his speech for Rabirius, and Livy later applied the term to Romulus and to Camillus. The title as an honor to Cicero lingered for generations in the minds of the Romans. When the emperors had arrogated it to themselves, the splenetic Juvenal recalled that it had been given to the consul of the year 63 B.C. by a Rome that was still free.[1]

Cicero's prominence is revealed to us in the two orations extant from the year 62 B.C. One of these was in defense of Sulla—P. Cornelius, one of the deposed consuls-elect for the year 65 B.C.—who was accused of complicity in the Catilinarian conspiracies. The defeat of Catiline had been followed by several trials of this kind, ending in verdicts of guilty. Cicero, with Hortensius, undertook the defense of Sulla and secured his acquittal. It is no longer possible to pronounce on the merits of the case; Cicero's main argument was that in 63 B.C. he had found no evidence against Sulla, and beyond this argument we can scarcely go. Hortensius spoke of the earlier conspiracy. The situation is involved, in a characteristically Roman fashion,

[1] Juv. 8, 246.

by the fact that at this time Cicero borrowed two million sesterces from Sulla, toward his purchase of the house on the
Palatine. The transaction became known, and Cicero promised
to admit it in case he should later buy the house. He bought
the house, after Sulla's acquittal, and turned off criticism as
well as he could by a jest: a man, he said, who wishes to buy
property must keep it secret for fear of competitors. And it
may be remarked that real estate deals, as appeared when Cicero
later wished to buy a place for his monument to Tullia, then as
now required shrewdness. But the loan was no indication of
Sulla's guilt.

Cicero's high station in Rome is shown by the opponent's
assertion that, unless Cicero had undertaken the defense, Sulla
would have been forced to go into exile. He also calls Cicero
a tyrant, *rex*, of the courts, as Cicero many years earlier had
called Hortensius. Cicero's whole speech is filled with the consciousness that, although he has enemies, Catilinarian sympathizers, he is now one of the leaders in Rome. Referring to the
conspiracy of 65 B.C., he remarks that at that time he had not
yet come to know the inner workings of the state; he had been
on the outside, as it were, which, by implication, was now no
longer the case. Much is said about the consulship, for Cicero's
honesty in reference to the senatorial records was questioned,
as has already been set forth,[2] and the case itself was concerned
with the year 63 B.C. Cicero claims no unusual honors, but he
reiterates that he has saved the state and that while he is alive
the wicked shall be powerless. He has earned his honorable
leisure, but is willing to exert himself in the courts for others.
He has not even time, he says, for recording his consular deeds
—an indication of his new eminence as well as a sign that it
would be proper for him to write about the consulship.

Even a stronger testimony to Cicero's new station is found
in the second speech extant from this year. It was in defense

---

[2] See above, p. 270.

of Archias, the Greek poet, whose citizenship had been questioned, probably to cause annoyance to the Luculli, the poet's
patrons, who were rivals and persistent opponents of Pompey.
Archias had been one of Cicero's earliest teachers, and had
inspired him with a love of reading. Cicero says very little
about the legal points involved, though evidently enough, since
he seems to have won the case. The presiding praetor was
Quintus, Cicero's brother; Archias' noble friends were also
present in court. Cicero, therefore, announces that he will plead
in a novel manner. He gives much high praise to the poet, who,
very likely, was the ordinary Greek chronicler of Roman greatness, but the speech as a whole is a eulogy of literature. Letters,
says Cicero, give inspiration and zest to men of affairs; they
contain the highest moral teachings, so that the greatest characters are those whose unusual talents have been fostered by
study; and, finally, literature, and nothing else, can give undying
fame, a thing which both individuals and whole nations rightly
desire. This eloquent eulogy, new among the Romans, though
perhaps trite to modern readers, is made to find its justification,
in a measure, in Cicero. He himself has enjoyed and profited
by literature, he says, never allowing it to take him from graver
duties, but finding in books both substance and inspiration for
his oratory. He has been moved by the desire for fame. Archias,
indeed, has already begun a poem on the consulship of 63 B.C.
It is this personal application, more often implied than expressed,
that reveals Cicero's consciousness of being one of the greatest
Romans: the Greeks, who wrote of Pompey and of the nobles
belonging to the old families, will now write about Cicero as
well; and Cicero, further, deems it proper to speak of his own
intellectual ideals as if these were now of interest to the Roman
people.

It should be added that the poet apparently failed to complete his account of Cicero's consulship. In 61 B.C., at any rate,
Cicero writes to Atticus that Archias, after finishing a poem

about the Luculli, will probably turn to the Metelli; as yet he has written nothing about Cicero. The reference to Archias, however, is purely incidental; very much as if a prominent statesman of today should say that a certain man was to have introduced him at a meeting, but had failed to appear. Archias' delinquency is coupled with that of another Greek, Thyillus, who is as little known as Archias would have been except for Cicero's oration.

Cicero was eager to have his serviecs of the year 63 B.C. commemorated in true Roman fashion, but he was not resting lazily on his prospective laurels. He was looking into the future. During the consulship he had succeeded in uniting the widely different elements of the nation in opposition to the revolutionaries; and that seemed to him significant. There had been no such union before.[3] If it could be perpetuated, Rome might have peace, and there was reason for thinking this possible in that this union had successfully withstood the accumulated shock of years of misrule. Out of his experiences in the consulship Cicero had thus been led to form a definite political ideal.[4]

This ideal is embraced in two phrases often used by Cicero. One, the harmony of the orders, *concordia ordinum*, refers to the union of opposing parties, particularly the senate and the knights; the other, the influence of the senate, *senatus auctoritas*, indicates that the senate was the traditional and rightful center of power. The influence of the senate recalls the great days when Carthage was defeated and the republic grew constantly stronger, but the ideal as a whole, while aiming at the grandeur and happiness of former times, was no blind reaching toward fallen gods. The knights, unknown in those days as a political party, were to be one of the pillars of the new order of things, and, far more important, so important as to make the ideal entirely different from anything that had preceded, there was to be large and

---

[3] *In Cat.* 4, 19.

[4] See above, p. 224, note 2.

honorable room for the representatives of the military power. Cicero had not failed to see that circumstances had changed. Rome was a military nation; the soldiers through their general, or rather the general through the soldiers, should have the first place, above the others, and yet acting with them. The general in question was Pompey. If the united orders would yield him this position of eminence, his character and his previous record gave ample hope that he would neither take too much power for himself nor endanger the new peace. By the side of Pompey would stand the leaders of the senate; not equal to him, but nevertheless with him the virtual rulers of Rome, through the influence which they had gained by honorable means. One of these leaders would be Cicero; he was already one of them. Harking back to the glorious days of Scipio Africanus the Younger, before the beginning of the internal troubles that seemed to have culminated in the conspiracy of Catiline, Cicero offered in a letter[5] to Pompey to become a minor Laelius, as it were, while Pompey would be even more than Scipio himself.

The new arrangement would give Cicero great prominence, but his hopes had no more personal ambition than those of a man who seeks the presidency of a republic or the premiership of a democratic monarchy, thinking that his own policies are the best for his country. He had indeed less personal ambition than the prospective president or prime minister, for there would be several men with influence like his own—a Catulus, a Hortensius, a Cato—each directing the affairs of state according to his ability and wisdom; and above them all would be Pompey. From the Roman point of view it was a singularly unselfish ambition, asking for none of the usual concrete rewards of immense wealth and the irresponsible rule over provincials. Cicero, for himself, thought only of the *otium cum dignitate,* which he would devote to intellectual pursuits and the cultivation of congenial

---

[5] *Fam.* 5, 7.

friendships, and of fame, contemporary and posthumous, which, as he said, had always been given in return for unselfish service.

The matter of fame is the point that offends modern modesty, whether real or assumed; the outspoken claim to fame in Cicero's writings also drew many wise comments from the Romans of the empire, who had lost the frank liberty of the republic, smugly flattering and deifying their emperors, many of whom were worthless. The Romans of Cicero's time, Caesar and Pompey no less than the Metelli and the Luculli, had their Greek poets and historians constantly in admiring and vocal attendance; and they sounded their own praises in the courts, the senate, at public meetings, and at aristocratic funerals. Even in the next generation the sensible Horace, the son of a freedman, sang that he had erected a monument more lasting than brass and higher than the pyramids, something that could withstand the corroding rains, the blasts of the winds, and the passing of innumerable years.

Cicero's ideal offered no remedy for some of the crying needs of Rome, such as the uneven distribution of wealth and the wretched condition of the provinces. This lack has been wearisomely insisted upon, in an attempt to prove that Cicero was not a statesman; and students have been reminded that the amelioration, for it was scarcely a complete change, came through autocracy. But no one in Rome was at this time thinking of helping the world by overturning the government. The destruction of the republic was the result of a series of unguided events; the work of fate, if you like. In the years that followed 63 B.C. many acts were done with an unselfish purpose, particularly by Cato, but they looked only to the temporary checking of nuisances; there was no thought of a larger reform. Men fought for their party or for themselves. Cicero alone aimed at something beyond this; the reëstablishment of peace to the state through a balance of its various powers. The question as to what he would have proposed had this harmony prevailed was never asked, for the harmony did not prevail. He had given a partial answer in his unselfish public service; the same answer would have been given by the Romans as a whole if they had adopted his ideal, for it demanded the sinking of personal ambition in an ambition for Rome, and so the regeneration of Roman public life.

But the powerful Romans of Cicero's time were not to be reformed. Better conditions came only after many years of civil war, which also brought violent death to all the leading statesmen of the period immediately after 63 B.C., except the few who had found their way to Charon by a kindlier road. Cicero, in imagining that Rome could be reformed, was thus more blind than those who did not see. He had been misled by the events of his consulship. Having succeeded in uniting the nation against Catiline, he supposed the union could be made permanent, and failed to understand that the conspiracy, despite its very real terrors, was the affair of a single year. The Romans were fond of comparisons drawn from the sea; they were poor sailors, but they all lived near the Mediterranean. One of their figures, coming from the Greeks, was that of the ship of state. Perhaps it can be used here. The Roman republic was a very leaky vessel, and the leaks were growing larger because the sailors were fighting among themselves, paying no attention to the danger of foundering. A storm had arisen, and the wrangling sailors, directed by Cicero, had forgotten their jealousies and with his aid had saved the old vessel from immediate destruction. But when the storm had passed, they immediately returned to their old quarrels, though not entirely forgetful of Cicero's recent leadership. It is not a very noble picture, that of a leaky old boat, but no comparison can do an indignity to the performances that had begun in Rome even before Cicero had laid down the consulship.

II

Ideal Fails

The ultimate power in Rome was still in the hands of the commander of her armies, provided he cared to use it. Pompey and Crassus had shown this by forcing themselves into the consulship of the year 70 B.C. Now Pompey had been away from the city for about four years, and city politics had run their own muddy course, but the thought of Pompey had been constantly present in men's minds, becoming more and more insistent as the day drew nearer when he and his army would return. And Pompey himself, a whole year before his arrival home, began to make plans for securing the kind of reception to which his power entitled him, and therefore sent an emissary to prepare the way. This emissary was Metellus Nepos, a member of one of the great Roman families. He arrived in Rome, from Pompey's army, toward the end of 63 B.C., and became a candidate for the tribuneship, the office which because of its close connection with the populace and its extensive powers would give its holder the best opportunity for political activity. Nepos' character as the tool of Pompey had from the first been so clearly understood in Rome that Cato, who had been on his way from the city at the time of Nepos' arrival, had turned back and also stood for the same office, in order to counteract the new Pompeian influence. Both Cato and Nepos were elected tribunes for the year 62 B.C.

Nepos' task was to make certain that Pompey had not been forgotten in the course of recent events in the city, and, if possible, to add fresh laurels to Pompey's fame. This could best be accomplished by rallying the voters to Pompey's support, a thing that was not difficult since the great general's achievements had long ago made him a popular idol; by antagonizing the senate, who claimed the right to guide Rome's fortunes and would therefore be opposed to the paramount influence of any single individual; and, finally, by humbling any one who was for the moment prominent in the city. One means of serving Pompey was therefore to attack Cicero, and this was the more easy because Catiline had always posed as the champion of the populace, whereas Cicero was naturally the representative of the more conservative elements of the population. After the execution of the conspirators, therefore, Nepos, as tribune, held violent public meetings at which he denounced the punishment as illegal, and uttered threats against Cicero; and, on the thirty-first of December, the last day of Cicero's term of office, when, according to custom, the latter was on the point of addressing the people at a public meeting, and would of course have given an account of his consulship, Nepos, by virtue of his tribunician power, prevented him from speaking. Cicero, however, took a solemn oath that he had saved the state, and was greeted with much enthusiasm; but this enthusiasm was not strong enough to prevent the hostile tribune from interfering with the retiring consul.

Nepos, aiming at the humiliation of the aristocracy and of any possible rivals to Pompey, and exerting himself for the glorification of the absent general, was joined in his endeavors by Caesar. The popular party had in a way been smothered by the events of the conspiracy. Caesar was now reëstablishing it, and he offered the chief place to Pompey. Caesar, after his rebuff in connection with the bill of Rullus, had decided to play second fiddle to Rome's military hero. Nepos proposed first to have Pompey called home to take the field against Catiline; he would thus appear as the true deliverer of Rome, filching other people's glory as he had done in the Servile War and in the war of Mithradates. But the armies already opposed to Catiline had the situation well in hand; and nothing came of Nepos' project. Caesar, as chief pontiff, also came forward with a proposal. The Capitoline temple had been rebuilt and dedicated by Catulus, the leading aristocrat, but it had not been quite finished. Caesar proposed that Pompey be entrusted with the completion of the work, but this measure also failed. There were public meetings addressed by Nepos, the tribune, and by Caesar, who had been praetor since the beginning of 62 B.C. Rioting ensued, led by the fearless Cato, and blood was shed. Nepos and Caesar were deprived of their offices; the tribune fled to Pompey, and Caesar retired to his house, but was presently reinstated in his magistracy.[6]

In the meantime Cicero was also making preparations for the all-important arrival of Pompey. He sent the victorious general a long letter, now lost, about the consulship of 63 B.C. The fact that Cicero published this letter at once, so that it was actually quoted at the trial of Sulla, reveals its real purpose. Cicero wished to win Pompey's approval of his position as the leader of the reformed state. As Caesar had made repeated bids for Pompey's favor, so Cicero bid for it; not, however, in the manner of a man willing to take the position of a mere political retainer, as Caesar had cleverly done, but as the savior of the state, who, now at the head of it, offered Pompey the place of honor. If Pompey had expressed his recognition of Cicero's services in his public letters to Rome, he would practically have sanctioned Cicero's political ideal, and this he was unwilling to do. He wished to be received in Rome as its one great man. He therefore said very little about the matter even in his private letter to Cicero, and the latter, in a reply still extant,[7] smooths over the situation, still hopeful, it would seem, of Pompey's support: your neglect, he suggests, was dictated by your wish not to offend any one—the reference probably being to Caesar

---

[6] The relations between Nepos and Cicero led Nepos' brother, who was a friend of Cicero, to write him a blunt and pompous letter, to which Cicero made an exceedingly adroit and dignified reply. The two letters (*Fam.* 5, 1; 5, 2) illustrate Cicero's superiority to the average aristocrat, and also show that his difficulties as a New man were by no means ended with the consulship.

[7] *Fam.* 5, 7.

and the popular party, Pompey's "old enemies and new friends," as Cicero calls them. It is in this letter that Cicero offers himself as a Laelius to Pompey's Africanus.

Pompey landed at Brundisium in December of the year 62 B.C. He disbanded his army, thus indicating to all that he had no intention of seizing supreme power through a direct use of the soldiers, and then he journeyed toward the city, where he arrived in January of the next year, 61 B.C. But in the very month of his landing an event had occurred which was to become of great importance to Cicero. Clodius, a young aristocrat of about thirty, had entered Caesar's house during the celebration of a festival in honor of the Good Goddess, *Bona Dea*. The ceremony was performed by women, and no men were admitted, but Clodius had gained access in the dress of a woman. He may have had an intrigue with Caesar's wife, though the religious festival scarcely seems to have been a favorable opportunity for a clandestine meeting; or he may have gone merely out of impudent curiosity. Whatever his motive, he was discovered, and the scandal was great. The senatorial leaders insisted on bringing the offender to trial; and Caesar divorced his wife, with the famous saying that Caesar's wife must be above suspicion, but he refused to urge punishment for Clodius, who was becoming a power among the common people.

In the midst of this confusion Pompey arrived at Rome, and was questioned in public as to his opinion about the sacrilege. He did not know what to reply. He had been too long with the army to feel at his ease amid the wrangling of Rome, particularly as he had no gifts as a politician. He praised the senate in general terms, but would express no definite opinion. "There is nothing straightforward, nothing courteous, nothing brave, nothing generous about this friend of yours," exclaims[8] the disgusted Cicero to Atticus. Nor did Cicero himself take an active

---

[8] *Att.* 1, 13, 4.

part in bringing Clodius to trial. This was done by Hortensius and Cato. But Clodius made his own preparations. He raved in public meetings against Lucullus, Hortensius, the consuls, everybody, incidentally taunting Cicero with the expression, "I have discovered," which Cicero had used in connection with the Catilinarian investigations frequently enough for his enemies to make it a byword. He also assembled street gangs, partly consisting of old Catilinarians, "the men of little beards." The case was at last tried; Clodius' gangs were in evidence; the parsimonious Crassus opened his money bags, as Cicero says, for the benefit of the poverty-stricken jurors; and Clodius was acquitted by thirty-one votes to twenty-five. The Roman worthies had to content themselves with leveling harmless gibes at the bribed jurymen; but Clodius, through his street gangs, had become a real menace to the state.

Though Cicero had not urged the trial, he had testified against Clodius' claim of an alibi; and as testimony was voluntary, this was a cause for hostility. The history of Clodius' hostile relations to Cicero can not be perfectly written. Plutarch says that Clodius' notorious sister Clodia, wife of Celer and the Lesbia of Catullus, had at one time desired to marry Cicero. The story is not accepted by some scholars. The proposed marriage may have been of a political nature, fostered perhaps by some admiration on the part of Clodia. If Cicero remained unresponsive, the situation would be made only more difficult. Plutarch assigns Terentia's jealousy as the reason for Cicero's testimony, but, whatever the reason may have been, Clodius was from that time Cicero's enemy. The two men waged frequent battles of words. The young aristocrat, though by no means lacking in gifts, was not quite a match for the satirical ex-consul, and it seems very likely that Clodius' enmity was due less to Cicero's testimony and the reported rejection of an alliance with Clodia than to Cicero's repartee. Some of this, by the way, was of truly Roman coarseness; scarcely befitting a consul, as Cicero himself writes to Atticus. Clodius called Cicero *cynicus consularis,* Tear-em the ex-consul.[9]

Cicero's position in the state was still excellent. During the trial of Clodius he received an ovation which he considered no less flattering than the one tendered him when he laid down his consulship; and after the trial, when the senate grew hopeless, he was the one to encourage them and to point out that the acquittal of Clodius served, after all, only to separate the sheep from the goats. Cicero's relations with the knights were satisfactory, as usual; and he tells Atticus that his partial defeat, in that his testimony failed to convince the jury, had won the common people to his side. They had been disgusted with his swelling popularity, he continues, but now that the swelling has been reduced by this little operation, he is received at the gladiatorial shows and the public games with remarkable signs of favor, unmarred by hisses and catcalls.

Pompey, though at first solemnly indifferent, was impressed by Cicero's popularity in the forum and among the talkative senators. Scenes were acted out like the one previously described,[10] in which Crassus—Pompey's enemy far more than anybody else's friend—orated tearfully about his gratitude to Cicero for saving Rome in the year 63 B.C., and Cicero himself, speaking for the first time in Pompey's presence, took up the subject with great fervor, as he later reported to Atticus. Gnaeus Pompey, not to be outdone by Crassus, came gradually to be so consistent and enthusiastic a herald of Cicero's virtues that the Catilinarians with the little beards called him Gnaeus Cicero.

By disbanding his army, Pompey had put aside his one means of coercion, and had descended to the ordinary level of the politicians. Among them he was helpless; he was like a

---

[9] Tyrrell's translation. See Tyrrell I², p. 23, note.

[10] See above, p. 21.

sleeping Gulliver ensnared by the Lilliputians. When he tried
to be politic, he was clumsily non-committal, satisfying nobody;
when he made flat statements, people suspected that he was lying.
His wish was, as of old, to be applauded as the first citizen of
Rome. He had no desire for supreme power, but he wished his
veterans to be rewarded and his arrangements in the East to be
ratified. If the senate had yielded in these respects, they could
very probably have won his good will, and there might have
been, not Cicero's harmony of the orders, perhaps, but a harmony
between Pompey and the senate, which would have been nearly
as effective. Instead of that, the usual political intrigues prevailed.

The senate, fighting blindly as always for supreme power,
opposed everybody. They antagonized the knights, who themselves were making shameless demands; they continued their
hostility to Caesar, Crassus, and the popular party; and they
put every conceivable obstacle in the way of Pompey. He
celebrated his triumph, to be sure, in September of 61 B.C.; it
was a splendid performance and lasted two days; but he was
unable to secure his two important demands.

Cicero's *concordia ordinum* was being shattered. He tried
to heal it by urging concessions to the knights, which he himself
considered shameful, but the senate remained obstinate. During
this year, 61 B.C., Cicero did not take much part in public affairs,
but he was exceedingly busy in the courts, in an attempt, as he
says, to retain his position by the same means by which he had
gained it. He wrote a little, but not much, revising some orations
and promising Atticus to write other things. In December he
wrote to Atticus that the state was in a miserable condition,
but that he himself managed to keep on the safe public road,
and was on intimate terms with Pompey, though not forgetting
the caution Atticus was urging upon him.

The next year, 60 B.C., was for Cicero very much like 61.
The friendship between him and Pompey seems to have grown

more intimate. Cicero frequently mentions it in his letters to Atticus, adding that he is proceeding warily and will not allow himself to be drawn from the honorable political path that alone can form a consistent continuation of his previous activity. He says that even though he himself may gain nothing by his intimacy with the vain general, the latter may be led into better ways of thinking and cease his hunt for popularity. But Cicero is not satisfied either with Pompey or with any one else. The state is doomed. The senators are amusing themselves with the tame fish in their ponds; *piscinarii* Cicero calls them. Crassus is friendly to no one. Pompey, who had received the right to wear triumphal insignia at the games, is "silently contemplating"—or "guarding," according to the interpretation—"his painted little toga;" a picture of the pompous dullard further hinted at by Cicero's frequent references to him under outlandish names suggestive of the Eastern conquest: Sampsiceramus, which has been rendered[11] Mikado; Hierosolymarius, the Jerusalemite; Alabarches, the Sheikh.

Only Cato is upright and courageous, says Cicero, but he spoils everything by his stubbornness; I am no fonder of him than you are, Cicero writes to Atticus; Cato the hero, who talks as if he were a character in Plato's *Republic*. Clodius, who has been in Sicily as quaestor since the time of his trial, has come back and is stirring up trouble. He is trying to secure adoption into a plebeian family, so that he may run for the tribuneship. Cicero meets him often and bandies words with him, usually getting the better of the argument.

Cicero's popularity, at least with the conservatives, remained undiminished. Catulus, the leader of the senatorial party, had died in the latter part of 61, and Cicero had succeeded him. The morning crowd at Cicero's house was great, and large escorts accompanied him to the forum. At the beginning of the year he received a singular tribute to his prominence. Trouble was threatening from Gaul, and lots were drawn in

---

[11] By Tyrrell.

the senate for consulars to go and settle it. Cicero's lot fell out
first, at which there was a universal demand that he remain in
Rome, a demand which was presently repeated in reference to
Pompey, so that the two were recognized as pillars of the state.

Nevertheless Cicero was heartbroken at the turn affairs were
taking. He left the city on a short trip early in the year, and
for a longer time on the first of June. When away from Rome,
he devoted himself to reading and writing; when in the city, he
busied himself in the courts and, as before, took as small a share
in the government as possible. His personal eminence gave him
no satisfaction. It was only in his family that he found any
contentment; in Rome he had no one with whom to joke or to
talk seriously, and he repeatedly expressed his longing for the
companionship of Atticus.

While the wretched politics in Rome were thus at a dead-lock,
in 60 B.C., neither the senate nor Pompey accomplishing anything, Caesar returned from his province of Further Spain,
which he had governed after his praetorship in 62 B.C. He
relinquished his claims to a triumph and became a candidate for
the consulship of 59 B.C. At this the senate gave one further
proof of the wretched condition of the state; with the incorruptible Cato at their head, they condescended to use bribery
in order to elect one of their staunchest men to hold office with
Caesar, and these two, Caesar and Bibulus, were elected.

But Caesar was not looking forward to an ordinary consulship. Pompey's ridiculous helplessness in the face of aristocratic
intrigues had opened the way to greater things. Shortly after
the election, therefore, acting with an adroitness that can only
be imagined, for there is no record, he succeeded in making a
private arrangement between Pompey, Crassus, and himself,
by which they agreed to work together. This was the so-called
First Triumvirate. Varro, in a Menippean satire of which only
the title remains, called it the Three-headed Thing, but there was
only one head, Caesar. Pompey was the body and Crassus was

the pocketbook. To their contemporaries, Pompey was the important member; the coalition, as it became gradually known, could have seemed only a union between the greatness of Pompey and the schemes of Caesar and Crassus.

Caesar asked Cicero to join the coalition. The three could prosper without the aid of Cicero, for they had the power; but their road would be much smoother if Cicero would level it. Next to them he was the most influential citizen. Caesar himself had had an unpleasant proof of Cicero's power in connection with the Rullan bill, and he could readily see that if there really was any leader among the conservative elements, that leader was Cicero. The latter's mere reputation for unselfishness in public life would have done much to put a fair face on the measures of the coalition; his ability as an orator would have been a shield against Cato and Hortensius, both uncompromising aristocrats. As a quattuorvirate, the coalition would have united in itself nearly all the elements of the state: the military power, through Pompey; the knights and many of the conservatives, through Cicero; much wealth and also a further hold on the knights, through Crassus; and the common people, through Caesar.

Caesar, the great political strategist, did not himself go to Cicero, but sent his trusted political agent, Cornelius Balbus. The latter was a Spaniard, who had been for many years a close friend of Pompey, having obtained the Roman citizenship through his assistance as early as 72 B.C., and who of late had been closely connected with Caesar as well. He was versed in the ways of the world; and it seems by no means improbable that Caesar had found him useful in first approaching Pompey. With Cicero, however, Balbus seems to have had no previous connection. He now called on the great consular to inform him that it was Caesar's desire to follow the advice of Cicero and of Pompey in all things and that he intended to bring Pompey and Crassus together. The letter to Atticus in which Cicero describes the interview was written at the end of the year 60 B.C., probably in December.[12] If the visit of Balbus occurred shortly before this time, as seems unquestionable, Caesar did not reveal the whole situation to Cicero, for he had already brought Pompey and Crassus together. The offer of partnership, however, was none the less genuine. Caesar had not needed Cicero for conciliating Pompey and Crassus; but he would need him when the plans of the triumvirs grew into overt acts. In fact, the particular reason for Balbus' visit was to win Cicero's support for the agrarian law which Caesar would propose on assuming office.

Cicero did not accept Caesar's offer, for he could not acquiesce in personal rule. He announces his momentous decision, one of his bravest and most high-minded acts, in a manner that is thoroughly characteristic. Atticus was always urging caution and prudence. Cicero, therefore, as was his wont, makes clear that he understands the situation: acceptance, he says, would give him the closest friendship with Pompey, and also with Caesar, if he should wish it. Cicero, furthermore, would be reconciled with his enemies, the Catilinarians; he would have peace with the multitude, and leisure in his old age. But he throws all this away, though realizing his personal danger. He had recently completed a poem on his consulship, with which Atticus was familiar. He therefore says that he will obey the advice that Calliope there gives him, that he increase the fame won in 63 B.C. and continue to earn the praise of good men. He also quotes a Homeric line to the effect that the best omen is to fight for one's country, and adds that he and Atticus will talk the matter over when they meet. And thereupon he promises to have the hot bath ready when Atticus comes to see him—as though he had been recounting some trifling experience instead of one of the most serious interviews of his life.

But the success of the triumvirs was not dependent upon Cicero. Their aims were carried out during the year 59 B.C.,

---

[12] *Att.* 2, 3, 3.

the consulship of Julius and Caesar, as the wits termed it. Under Caesar's management, which drew its strength from Pompey's military prestige and consequently swept aside all effective opposition, Bibulus was forced to retire from public business. He shut himself up in his house, and from there issued edicts condemning as illegal all of Caesar's propositions, which nevertheless became laws. On the surface, the year 59 B.C. ministered entirely to Pompey's desires; Caesar secured for him the legislation that the nobles had opposed. But when the results of the year are analysed, it becomes clear that only Caesar gained anything of real importance. He was appointed governor, for five years, of Cisalpine Gaul and Illyricum, to which was added Transalpine Gaul, at first only for one year. He thus had the opportunity of securing great wealth, to be expended mostly in politics, and of creating a large army, which was the one political weapon. In his ostensible service to Pompey, which very much resembled that of an intriguing minister to an indolent and short-sighted master, whom he is preparing to overthrow, Caesar carried out Pompey's harmless wishes by means of the latter's own military position, and, in return, received from him, potentially, a power that would in a few years rival his own. Crassus did not play an important part in the triumvirate. He obtained certain advantages for the knights, whose business interests were his own; but the reward for his willingness to support his old and hated rival Pompey consisted mainly in the discomfiture of the nobles, for whom his hatred was even greater than for Pompey. Crassus was little more than the supporter of Caesar, and still had his eyes on an indefinite future.

The military power had thus again made itself master of Rome, and this had come about because the senate had stubbornly insisted upon their traditional position of supremacy, unwilling to yield to the knights and to Pompey. There was no *concordia ordinum* and no *senatus auctoritas;* Cicero's ideal had proved impracticable.

III

DRIVEN INTO EXILE

When Cicero informed Atticus about his interview with Balbus, he wrote that by accepting Caesar's invitation to join the triumvirate he would have become reconciled to his enemies and secured leisure for his old age. The enemies were the Catilinarians and Clodius. As yet they were only annoying. Clodius, however, with his gangs was already a power in the streets, so that there might presently be real danger to Cicero's life. And Cicero was vulnerable in another way. By executing the conspirators in 63 B.C. without allowing an appeal to the people, he had exposed himself to attack. Metellus Nepos, the tribune, had inveighed against him for the execution even in the year 63, but had not carried the matter farther, being intent, not upon Cicero's ruin, but Pompey's glory. Another tribune, however, might arise who would make full use of Cicero's precarious position. Clodius was an aristocrat and therefore could not stand for the tribuneship, but aristocrats had before this secured adoption into plebeian families. If Clodius should succeed in doing this and then become tribune, he would have an almost certain means of bringing about Cicero's ruin. Pompey as consul, and, still more, Caesar as the chief pontiff, could scarcely fail to prevent Clodius from becoming a plebeian, and they could certainly protect Cicero whether or not Clodius ultimately attained the tribuneship, provided they would exert themselves, but Cicero's rejection of Caesar's overtures had made such exertion unlikely.

The state, in the meantime, was completely in the hands of the triumvirs, but this had not been accomplished without causing a disturbance. The change had been so rapid that men's fears were banished by their indignation. Outcries were raised in all quarters, even from the common people, who had been glad to see Caesar get office in opposition to the hated aristocrats. People showed their hatred in the theater, at banquets, and at gatherings of every kind. Actors were applauded when they repeated lines of old plays that could be interpreted as referring to the undoing of the state by Pompey. When Curio, an opponent of the triumvirs, entered the theater, the audience applauded; when Caesar entered, a moment later, he was received in absolute silence.

Most of this unpopularity was directed against Pompey, for he was the most picturesque figure of the three and it was apparently for his sake that the majority of Caesar's measures were carried. Pompey was profoundly unhappy. At first he tried to explain and justify the novel proceedings; then he tried to excuse them. There were rumors that the triumvirs were not in perfect agreement, and Pompey himself certainly spoke to Cicero as though he wished himself well out of the whole thing. Cato called him a private dictator, and Cicero wrote in a letter with his usual whimsicality that he had formerly been uneasy about his future fame, lest Pompey should seem the greater man, but that he is uneasy no longer.

Again Cicero left the city, and he wrote to Atticus that he had abjured politics forever and that he would now devote himself to reading and philosophy. He tried to find comfort in the writing of a geographical work suggested by Atticus, but geography failed to interest him. He called himself the laziest man alive. He traveled from one place to another, struggling with himself to forget matters of state and to acquire a philosophic indifference, but he did not succeed. "Tell me all about events in Rome," he wrote repeatedly to Atticus, "and especially about Clodius." And presently he was back in Rome, Atticus went to Epirus, and the correspondence was taken up again.

Cicero turned for occupation to the courts, as of old, and avoided politics. He was evidently willing to live according to the desire of the triumvirs, for even while away from the city

he had asked Atticus to procure for him a detailed statement
of how Pompey wished him to act. But he could not consistently
refrain from giving expression to his grief for the fallen state.
Encouraged to opposition perhaps by the unpopularity of the
triumvirs and the reputed likelihood of dissension among them,
he uttered some incautious words in reference to the political
situation during his defense of his former colleague Antony,
who was tried and convicted for extortion; his words were
reported to the triumvirs, and on the same day, only three hours
later, Clodius became a plebeian. Pompey acted as *auspex* at
the adoption, which was obviously carried out with the permission of Caesar, who, as pontifex maximus and all-powerful
consul, could easily have prevented it.

As the months went by, Clodius threatened to use violence
and to bring Cicero to trial for the execution of the Catilinarian
conspirators. At times, it seems, Cicero thought of avoiding the
impending struggle, but on other occasions he even longed for
it, convinced that he would emerge with enhanced glory. He
asked Atticus to come from Epirus. Atticus, he wrote, could
win friends for him; he could discover Clodius' real intentions
from Clodia, the demagogue's sister, with whom he was on
friendly terms; and if the blow should fall, he could help Cicero
with his sympathy. Clodius became a candidate for the tribuneship, giving it as his intention to undo the laws of Caesar. He
must have been sincere in his opposition to the powerful consul;
at any rate, it can scarcely have been merely a ruse to deceive
Cicero, as has been suggested, for Clodius had greater plans than
the undoing of Cicero. The truth seems to be that Clodius
tried to get himself into power by taking advantage of the
unpopularity of the triumvirs.

The adoption of Clodius had been a warning. Caesar, who
in a few months would set out for Gaul, was determined that
Cicero should not cause any trouble during his absence. At
the trial of Flaccus, nevertheless, which seems to have taken

place in August, Cicero gave another indication of what his future actions might be. Flaccus was accused of misgovernment in Asia. He had been praetor in 63 B.C., giving good service to Cicero against the Catilinarians; the accusation, probably ultimately due to Caesar, was in all likelihood one of the latter's numerous attacks on the man who had checked Catiline. Caesar was in this way giving proof of his popular attitude. Probably Flaccus had been guilty of extortion; but that was scarcely the question at issue. In his defense, which was successful, Cicero attempted to discredit the witnesses, and the audience was treated to much éxcellent fun at the expense of Greek popular assemblies and other Greek weaknesses.[13] Flaccus had also had dealings with Palestine, and the Jews are mentioned, not *honoris causa,* but as devoted to outlandish superstitions. Besides discrediting the witnesses, Cicero boldly declares that the prosecution is an attack on those who had suppressed Catiline and his accomplices; the attacks will mount higher until they reach Cicero himself, but he will know how to protect himself. Is it fitting, he asks, that the Catilinarian exiles be recalled and that punishment be inflicted on those who have saved the state?

Caesar was not yet ready to use extreme measures against Cicero. He undoubtedly liked the orator, and, realizing his influence, may have cherished a hope of winning him for the triumvirate cause. He offered him a legateship in Gaul, a free embassy, a place on the board of twenty who were to carry out the agrarian law. Though the acceptance of any one of these offers would have given Cicero security against his enemies, he refused them all, unwilling to be in any way bound to the triumvirs. Even at the end of the year Caesar promised that Clodius should not be allowed to indulge his desire for vengeance.

The same promise was made by Pompey, oftener, and in more detail. Pompey was neither gracious nor intellectual, so that

---

[13] In defending Fonteius, in the year 69 B.C., Cicero had used a similar argument against the Gauls. The account of the Gauls in this oration is one of Cicero's most vivid bits of description (*Pro Font.* chaps. 10 ff.). See also below, p. 335.

there could be no real intimacy between him and Cicero, but
the latter admired Pompey as a general and as a man, and even
had a personal liking for him. When Pompey had tried at a
contio to discuss the edicts of Bibulus, Caesar's sequestered colleague, and had made a wretched failure of it, Cicero wrote
that he could not restrain his tears at the pitiful sight; Pompey,
he adds, who used to be received with the greatest popular
enthusiasm, is now like one fallen from the stars. This was a
spectacle that could have given pleasure only to Crassus. As
Pompey had at that time been a party to Clodius' plebeian
adoption, Cicero had no reason for friendliness, so every one
thought, and yet he says: "so great was my love that no wrong
could destroy it."

Cicero believed Pompey sincere in his repeated promises that
he would hold Clodius in check, and he was not mistaken.
Pompey undoubtedly meant well. He even had a violent scene
with Clodius, in which[14] he insisted that he would be disgraced if harm should come to Cicero through Clodius, whom
Pompey himself had "armed" by allowing him to become a
plebeian; if Clodius would not give the required promise, Pompey would make it clear to everybody that nothing was so
important to him as Cicero's friendship. Clodius for a long
time refused to be moved; finally, however, he offered his hand
with the promise that he would do nothing against the wishes
of Pompey. Cicero's later comment on Pompey in this connection is that Pompey did not try to deceive Cicero, but was
himself deceived by Clodius.

Clodius, in the meantime, was elected to the tribuneship, but
Cicero remained in Rome. Both friends and strangers, so he
wrote to Quintus toward the end of the year, were offering to
defend him with everything they owned, even with their lives.
In December Clodius became a tribune. After he had passed
various bills destined to win popular support, he began to

---

14 *Att.* 2, 22.

declaim against Cicero, loudly boasting at the same time that he was doing it with the approval, even at the suggestion, of Pompey, Crassus, and Caesar. Finally he passed a law providing that "whoever had caused the death of Roman citizens without a regular trial should be forbidden fire and water." Cicero's name was not mentioned, but the law was obviously intended to send him into exile. At a *contio*, held by Clodius outside the city walls so that Caesar might attend, though already in command of the army he was to lead to Gaul, Caesar condemned the punishment of the Catilinarian conspirators as illegal, but said he did not approve of retroactive legislation. Perhaps he thought enough had already been done to muzzle Cicero.

The excitement in Rome became intense. Cicero, as was customary for a person under accusation, and he was really accused though not formally, put on mourning, left his hair untrimmed, and went about the streets to ask for the protection of the citizens. Clodius and his gang often met him and interrupted his appeal to the people by shouts of derision, says Plutarch; and even by throwing dirt and stones. Clodius also made preparations as for a serious riot or civil war. Free men and even slaves from all sections were openly enrolled in the forum and divided into military units; the shops were closed; the temple of Castor was filled with arms, and, to protect this "sacred arsenal," the very temple steps were torn away.

The whole equestrian order changed their dress; a crowd of twenty thousand accompanied Cicero on his round of entreaty. A large part of the senate also dressed in mourning; they tried to pass a decree that the whole people should wear mourning as at a time of public calamity; but the consuls forbade it. One of these was Gabinius, whose law in 67 B.C. had secured for Pompey the command against the pirates; the other was Calpurnius Piso, one of Caesar's fathers-in-law and a relative of the young Piso who had married Cicero's daughter. M. Lucullus, with a large number of others, waited on Pompey, but the latter said that without a public decree he could do nothing against a tribune in arms; if the consuls should undertake the defense of the state, Pompey would take up arms. The mediators, at Pompey's request, went to the consuls, to whom they had already appealed. The interview with Piso was stormy. He replied that there was no need of arms and strife; by yielding, Cicero could again save the state; if he resisted, endless slaughter would ensue; and Piso himself would support Clodius.

Cicero also made some appeal to Pompey. Plutarch has it that Pompey had gone to his Alban villa in order to avoid the man he was betraying. Piso, Cicero's son-in-law, first appealed to the shifty triumvir; Cicero later went to seek him, and Pompey is said to have escaped from the interview by a back door. At the time of the outbreak of the Civil War, when Cicero was on the point of throwing in his fortunes with his battered idol, he writes to Atticus that Pompey would not take him up when he lay at his feet, but said that he could do nothing against the wishes of Caesar. Perhaps Cicero did not literally lie at Pompey's feet; the expression may be figurative; but his appeal, in whatever form, was rejected. Pompey, in all likelihood, had no choice. By accepting Caesar's services he had placed himself in a position in which he must also yield to his wishes.

Caesar with his army was outside of Rome during these days; he was ready to start for Gaul, but waited, evidently to see that Cicero was sent away. "I will not call him my enemy," said[15] Cicero in public a year and a half later; "but he was silent when others called him my enemy." The "others" were Clodius and his partisans. But Caesar had managed things so well, having failed to win Cicero's support by peaceful means, that the danger threatening the orator seemed to come from Clodius.

Cicero decided to leave Rome. It can not be determined whether he could have remained. If he had submitted to a

---

15 *Post Red. In Senat.* 32.

trial, Clodius' power in the city would undoubtedly have secured a conviction. The only other way was to oppose force to the gangs of Clodius, and that was probably impracticable. As the next few months proved, Rome was in the hands of Clodius and his men; and behind Clodius was Caesar's army, one of the lieutenants of which was Clodius' brother.

Nor do we know whether Cicero ever thought seriously of making an appeal to arms. No such intention is found in his letters before the exile, as students have noted, but the last letter was written in October, so that the correspondence contains no evidence relative to the final crisis. It should be observed, however, both that Cicero mentioned the fact that men were ready to defend him "even with their lives," and that the incidents already described indicate that some sort of struggle was expected. Lucullus and some others, we are told, advised Cicero to remain in Rome; but many urged him to yield, as the people would soon demand his recall.

Among the latter was Atticus, whom Cicero later accused of weakness, as he also accused himself. Cicero's one great regret during the exile was that he had left Rome. Whether correctly or not, he thought it would have been less difficult to remain than to get back, once he had gone away. He also writes repeatedly of aristocratic envy and bad advice, especially on the part of Hortensius, his oratorical rival of many years. It may be that Cicero's view of things during the exile was distorted, but it is equally probable that Cicero's charges against Hortensius and others mirror his difficult relations as a New man with the haughty aristocrats, and that these, in their envy, urged Cicero to depart into exile even though he might have remained. In his speeches after his return, finally, Cicero consistently expresses the view that in withdrawing he had saved the city from bloodshed. This is no proof that Cicero had at any time thought of appealing to arms and still less that such an appeal would have been successful, but the fact that he continued making the claim may indicate that at least some men were ready to believe it. Cicero's going did save Rome from bloodshed, but he probably acted less from conscious patriotism than from his natural objection to violence, coupled with a feeling that resistance was neither advisable nor proper when men like Atticus and Hortensius advised against it. Clodius and Cicero's other opponents later said that he had fled because he was afraid.

Before leaving Rome, Cicero took a statuette of Minerva from his house to the Capitol, where he dediacted it to ''Minerva, the guardian of the city''; it was a symbolic act, doubtless observed with solemnity on the part of his friends and supporters. He departed from the city at night, with an escort of friends. It was toward the end of March, 58 B.C.

Clodius at once brought in a second bill, which formally exiled Cicero to a distance of at least four hundred[16] miles from Italy. The house on the Palatine was sacked and then burned; and its site was dedicated to Liberty. The villas at Tusculum and Formiae were also destroyed. Cicero stated later that the marble columns of his Palatine residence were taken to the house of Piso, the consul, in the very sight of the citizens; and that at Tusculum not only the furnishings of the villa were removed but even the trees were torn up and transplanted in the garden of the other consul, Gabinius, Cicero's neighbor. In order to prove Cicero's execution of the Catilinarian conspirators illegal in the view of his contemporaries, Clodius had a decree passed declaring that the senatorial decree of the fifth of December, which had ordered the execution, had been forged by Cicero. No admission of the recognized constitutionality of Cicero's act could have been plainer. Caesar departed for Gaul. Cato, like Cicero an unmanageable patriot, was entrusted with a mission to Cypress; Clodius had insisted on a commissioner of indubitable integrity, and the grumbling Cato had to go.

---

16 Plutarch says five hundred.

IV

Exile

Cicero went south, intending to go to Sicily, where he had many friends. He stayed for a while at the house of a certain Sica, near Vibo in Bruttium, which is in the toe of Italy; but, learning of Clodius' second law, with its four hundred miles, he decided to go east. The law could not have prevented residence in Sicily, provided the governor there had chosen to ignore it; the latter, however, though an old friend and twice a colleague of Quintus, wrote briefly that Cicero must not come. Cicero thought of Malta as possible, but this, too, was within the four hundred miles. He therefore set out for Brundisium, often threatened by enemies but protected by the towns along the way. Though Brundisium, thoroughly devoted to him, would gladly have received him, as he says, he did not enter the city, but stayed in its outskirts at the home of two Flacci, father and son; neither of them the Flaccus he had defended the year before. He was with them a fortnight, and then sailed for Greece, on the last day of April.

Atticus, writing from Rome, had suggested that Cicero go to his estate in Epirus; it was fortified and would be safe— reminding us that private gentlemen found it necessary, because of the prevailing violence, to protect themselves like mediaeval barons. Since Buthrotum, Atticus' estate, was within the four hundred miles, Cicero refused the invitation. Greece, after all, was full of Catilinarians, ready to even scores with their former conqueror. Cicero also gave up his desire to spend his exile in Athens; there, among others, was Autronius, whom Cicero had refused to defend in 62 B.C. and who, consequently, had been exiled as an accomplice of Catiline.

When Cicero landed in Dyrrhachium, coming from Brundisium, the quaestor of Macedonia, Gnaeus Plancius, immediately set out to meet him; dismissing his lictors and discarding the insigna of his office, as a sign of grief, and also changing his garb to one of mourning. Meeting Cicero, the quaestor wept and embraced the exiled consular, but in his grief he was unable to utter a word. Plancius escorted Cicero toward his province, Macedonia. On the way news was received about plots against Cicero's life, and he wished to go to Asia. This province was well disposed toward him; his brother Quintus had just been governor there, after the praetorship, and was now on his way homeward. Plancius, however, urged Cicero—practically forced him, Cicero says—to stay in Macedonia. The governor, though friendly, was too timid to take Cicero under his protection, but Plancius, resigning from his official duties, constituted himself Cicero's bodyguard. Cicero remained with him at Thessalonica from the first of June until the beginning of November. The months in Thessalonica seem to have been a period of real danger, for Cicero in his defense of Plancius four years later speaks of tearful vigils and sad nights, when Plancius stayed by his side to protect him. One occasion[17] was especially memorable, though for us the details are hidden. Plancius, as usual, was with Cicero; it was night; the quaestor was overcome with grief. Cicero, having some hope of being recalled, promised solemnly that he would repay Plancius for his friendship and protection; if death should intervene, he trusted confidently that others, in Rome, would not permit Plancius to remain unrewarded. The quaestor had hoped to accompany Cicero when the latter should leave Macedonia, but this proved impossible.

Cicero left Thessalonica in November, to be nearer Italy, in case the efforts for his recall should be successful, and to avoid Piso, one of the hostile consuls of 58 B.C., who had been appointed governor of Macedonia. Cicero went to Dyrrhachium, a letter to his family being written partly in Thessalonica and partly in

---

17 *Pro Plan.* 101. For Plancius' relations to Cicero during the exile, see esp. *Pro Plan.* 95–100.

Dyrrhachium. In this city he stayed from the end of November, 58 B.C., until the' fourth of August, 57 B.C., when he set sail for Italy.

Atticus remained in Rome, whence he wrote frequent reports to Cicero about the political outlook, sometimes chiding him for taking too hopeless a view. Atticus had put his resources at Cicero's disposal—according to Cornelius Nepos he gave him a gift of 250,000 sesterces, some 12,500 dollars—and he seems to have exerted himself in Cicero's behalf in many ways. And yet we can hardly determine whether his actions during this crisis were entirely admirable. Cicero, while journeying anxiously from one place to another in southern Italy, before sailing from Brundisium, had a great longing to see Atticus, and apparently really expected to do so, perhaps because of some half promise; he sent minute directions so that Atticus might find him, but Atticus did not come. Probably Atticus' business interests had interfered. And as Atticus left Rome at the end of 58 B.C., several months before Cicero's recall, he does not seem to have actually accomplished much, or even to have attempted very much, in the way of a termination of the exile. Cicero, regretting Atticus' failure to join him, calls it another sorrow added to the others, and entreats his rather self-centered friend not to be forgetful of their old affection; Cicero being still the same, as he writes, though his enemies have ruined him. Cicero shows no trace of ill feeling. Though he charges Atticus with being too hopeful of things in Rome, as others also seemed to him to be, he longs for no one else so much as for Atticus when he has finally returned to the city.

Terentia also stayed in Rome, partly because of poor health and partly to do what could be done. When the house on the Palatine was burned, she seems to have fled to the temple of Vesta; and from there Clodius forced her to come forth in public and make certain statements at a banker's in reference to the proscribed property of her husband—not a pleasant occa-

sion if Clodius and his gangs were her escort. In spite of the
serious situation there was apparently some quarrel between
her and Quintus, for Cicero entreats her to preserve harmony
in the family, "particularly since you are so few." Quintus,
who had been governor of Asia, had gone to Rome without seeing
his brother, at Cicero's own request. Cicero shrank from a
sad meeting, which would have had to be followed by an even
sadder parting; and it was unsafe for Quintus to remain with
Marcus inasmuch as he was threatened at Rome with a prosecution for maladministration in the province—entirely a political
act, for Quintus had been honest.

Cicero's correspondence during the exile consists of four
letters to Terentia and his children, two to Quintus, and twenty-
seven to Atticus. There is also one addressed to Metellus Nepos,
who as consul in 57 B.C. favored Cicero's recall, but this letter
is of the ordinary formal kind and does not reveal Cicero's
feelings. The other letters show us Cicero in his dark hour.[18]
His manner of expression is changed; the fluency and the finish
of his other writings are lacking—a thing he himself sadly
noticed and commented on to Atticus. His tears often interrupted his writing, whether the letter was to Atticus, or Quintus,
or Terentia. Friends, who had seen him, reported to Atticus
that there seemed to be danger of Cicero's mind giving way;
in reference to which, however, Cicero writes that his thoughts
are perfectly clear; he wishes they had been as clear when
he made the mistake of leaving Rome instead of staying to fight
it out. Nevertheless he did not know what to do with himself,
he could find no distraction for his thoughts. He grew thin,
and his health was not good. While still in Rome, he had come
near taking his own life. Atticus in some way had prevented
it; he had urged the claims of Cicero's family, and these had
prevailed. Now, in exile, Cicero speaks of his former thoughts
of suicide. Even in a letter[19] to Terentia he expresses the wish

---

[18] See esp. *Ad Q. Fr.* 1, 3.
[19] *Fam.* 14, 4.

that he had not clung to life, and adds that if there is no change for the better, his only desire is to see her again and to die in her arms.

Perhaps the grief and disappointment expressed in these letters are too great. Livy, according to Seneca the Elder,[20] said that Cicero bore none of his misfortunes as a man should, except his death, and Livy's judgment may be correct. To the calm reader who scans these letters for indications of Cicero's character, it will readily seem that Cicero was weak. But it should perhaps be remembered that the collapse of his fortunes was complete and apparently irremediable; it had been caused by the violence of a demagogue who had done nothing for the state and from whom the state could expect nothing; Cicero himself had saved Rome from Catiline, and now the only charge against him was connected with the conspiracy; and, finally, his exile had been due, or so it seemed, to weakness on his own part and the part of some of his friends, and to the envy and treachery of others.

Cicero's regret that he had failed to take his own life was probably not unseemly in the eyes of the Romans. Death was not for them surrounded with religious mysticism, even though they publicly avoided the word death itself as an ill omen. To die was a natural act; to take one's own life—to desert the post in which God had placed a man, as they expressed it—was not a normal or a proper thing to do; but there were occasions when nothing else seemed so thoroughly fitting. Suicide, in the next few generations, became common; men under the displeasure of the emperors were not executed, but were requested to take their own lives. And it is significant that Cato's great fame was very largely, perhaps almost entirely, due to his suicide at Utica; his name became Cato of Utica. And as for tears, they were not Cicero's alone. The whole senate had wept when the consuls refused to allow public mourning for Cicero; various individuals,

---

[20] Sen. *Suas.* 6, 22.

among them even Balbus, are said to have shed tears. Much of this was doubtless part of the usual public excitability; but it was not confined to the forum and the streets. Plancius' emotion was private; and Cicero writes to Atticus that the latter, at their parting, had broken down quite as much as had Cicero himself. And Atticus is scarcely to be thought of as much given to tears.

In the meantime the political situation in Rome was gradually preparing the way for Cicero's return. Clodius was mob king, and defied every one. The motives of his actions, in so far as they were not merely the headlong impulses of a leader of riots, were financial; he sold privileges right and left, even interfering with the measures of Caesar and Pompey. He fell out with Gabinius, and they had a clash in the street; with followers, of course. Pompey, finding the city unsafe, retired to his house, avoiding public affairs for a time. He was often out of Rome. Of Crassus we hear nothing; but of Pompey it seems true that he drew somewhat away from the absent Caesar and nearer to the senate, the logical opponents of Clodius. A coalition between the nobles and Pompey, it gradually appeared, was the only means of checking Clodius; and the battle cry of this movement was the recall of Cicero.

In August of 58 B.C. Cicero for the first time writes of his return as possible, but nothing was accomplished during that year. Pompey corresponded with Caesar, and the latter was found to have no objection to the ex-consul's recall. When the tribunes for 57 B.C. had been elected, one of them, Sestius, actually went to Gaul and had an interview with Caesar about the matter; and with the beginning of the new year there was constant speech making and other preparations for the return of Cicero. Metellus Nepos, now consul, but after all little else than the servitor of Pompey, forgot his enmity toward Cicero. Sestius and another tribune, Milo, formed gangs to oppose those of Clodius, who, though no longer a tribune, was by no means to be ignored. Some senators claimed that Cicero had never been legally exiled, and consequently did not need to be formally recalled, but only invited to return; others favored an explicit recall. The senate gave formal thanks to the states—that is, the cities and states—that had assisted Cicero, who "had deserved well of the state." Sentiment in all the orders was growing in favor of Cicero; his staunch supporters throughout Italy were bidden to come to Rome to assist, even Pompey making speeches outside of Rome in behalf of the friend he had deserted. It was all a tribute to Cicero's personal and political influence. In the next year a certain Vatinius, thinking to insult Cicero, said that the recall had been due not to Cicero's personal popularity but to his position in the state—*non mea sed rei publicae causa,* says Cicero; a curious indication of the man-to-man attitude in politics and also an unexpected revelation of the fact that Cicero's name was made the rallying cry against the anarchy of Clodius.

But all this agitation and enthusiasm would have accomplished nothing, had it not been for the new gangs of Sestius and Milo. Meetings of the senate were broken up, and there were frequent encounters, Clodius at first retaining the upper hand. The twenty-fifth of January was one of the noteworthy days.[21] A bill concerning Cicero was to be proposed. Fabricius, the mover of the bill, had arrived in the forum before daybreak, so as not to be excluded by Clodius and his followers. These, however, free men and slaves, were already encamped in the forum and around the public buildings; they made an attack on Fabricius, in which some men were killed and many were wounded. One of the tribunes arrived, and was driven off by force. The forum was now filled with slaughter; men, their swords dripping with blood, rushed about in all directions in search of Quintus Cicero, loudly shouting his name. He was

[21] *Pro Sest.* 75–76.

there, on the rostra. They pulled him down, wounded him, and left him for dead, but he was miraculously saved by the fact that he lay under a pile of corpses.

While in Asia, he had had a dream in which he seemed to see his brother crossing a broad river on horseback;[22] suddenly both Cicero and his horse disappeared in the water, and poor Quintus shuddered with terror; but presently Marcus and his horse reappeared, crossed the river, and the brothers embraced. Quintus had applied to "those who knew," and had learned that Cicero would be exiled and then recalled. Quintus had also heard of Marcus' strange dream about Marius,[23] in which the latter met the exiled Cicero and promised him aid. It was Cicero's only prophetic dream, as he tells us; he used to speak of it, and his freedman Sallustius often had its wonders on his lips. The interpretation, as in the case of Quintus' dream, foretold a recall. If Quintus, as he lay wounded on the street, thought of these cheerful prophesies, he must have had serious doubts about the efficacy of divination. He remained where he had been struck down until it was dark and then made his escape. The Tiber was strewn with the corpses of citizens, the sewers were choked up with them, and the blood was wiped from the forum with sponges.

Finally the gangs of Sestius and Milo prevailed. It was a tumultous time. Cicero's honorable popularity among the peaceable citizens in the districts of Italy and the justice of his cause would have been unavailing if they had not been enforced, at the capital, by armed bands, which were morally superior to those of Clodius only in that they fought, for the moment at least, for the restoration of some sort of government and order. The law that finally recalled Cicero was passed on the fourth of August. It was the triumvirs, particularly Caesar, who had caused Cicero's exile, and it was Caesar's permission and Pom-

---

[22] *De Divin.* 1, 58–59.
[23] See above, p. 32.

pey's exertions that made the return possible; but just as Cicero had been actually driven from Rome by the violence of Clodius, so he was restored by the superior violence of Sestius and Milo. Both the exile and the recall testify to Cicero's political and personal influence.

V

RETURN TO ROME

Cicero's return—the reception in Brundisium, the leisurely, stately journey northward, and the entry into the capital—was all that could be accomplished by the natural festive enthusiasm of the Italians and Romans, who were both southerners and ancients; and this enthusiasm was raised to its highest pitch by Cicero's own popularity and the thought of his undeserved misfortunes as well as by the systematic and widespread canvass in his behalf, which had been one of the chief means of his recall.

He had left Dyrrhachium on the very day when the law that reinstated him was passed; at a time when the law might yet be blocked by Clodius, as other similar measures had frequently been blocked. The reason for the particular date of Cicero's sailing must therefore be sought outside of the political situation. He landed on the fifth, the birthday of his dear daughter, who was awaiting him in the port; no day could have been more auspicious as marking the glorious ending if his long tribulations. This day was also, by a divinely ordered coincidence, the anniversary of the founding of the colony at Brundisium as well as of the dedication of the temple of Safety near Atticus' house. The details of the welcome in Brundisium, of old devoted to Cicero, are not told; but Cicero informs Atticus that the townspeople made Tullia's birthday the special occasion of their celebration—and Atticus needed nothing further to stimulate his imagination. Cicero, staying at the house of the faithful Flacci, who had harbored him when leaving Italy, remained in Brundisium some five days, on the third of which a messenger from Quintus brought word about the important law.

Of the journey to Rome Cicero later wrote that the people had brought him back on their shoulders, and, with more dignity, that he had come as in the golden chariot of a triumphator. And he did not hasten. The messenger from Quintus, undoubtedly traveling at his fastest, had needed four days. Horace in the next generation—he was born in the same year as Cicero's son—made a journey from Rome to Brundisium, as all the world knows. It was a very slow journey, and much delay was caused by muddy roads, so that even the never-hurrying poet found it long; and it took a fortnight. Cicero's progress consumed nearly a month. Congratulatory deputations retarded him on the road, and the cities along the way kept holiday because he was back among them.

The climax came in Rome.[24] People of all classes streamed out of the gates to welcome him. The nomenclator found his skill taxed to the utmost. All were there except those who could not even pretend to be friends of the returning statesman. Cicero entered Rome by the Capena gate, so that he had to pass through several streets to reach the Capitol, where, according to custom, he would offer thanks to the gods for his safe homecoming. The steps of the temples were filled with citizens, who wished to see him pass; and they shouted their welcome. A large crowd, large even by Roman standards, followed him to the Capitol; and in the forum the crowd was stupendous. It was a unique reception, and could be referred to as such several months later, though a few months in Rome at this excited period was a long time, when Cicero spoke for Sestius, prefacing his brief account with the statement that everybody knew about it. "In

---

[24] *Att.* 4, 1.

the midst of this great joy," he exclaims, "I had only one source of grief, that so grateful a city had once been so wretched and in such straits"—as during the domination of Clodius.

Cicero arrived in Rome on the fourth of September; on the next day he addressed the senate. The speech[25] is not a long one, comprising only fifteen chapters. Writing to Atticus, he speaks of it as the oration in which he returned thanks to the senate, for his recall, of course—*senatui gratias egimus*—and this phrase, variously worded, is the title by which the speech is known. It also reveals the keynote of Cicero's address. He begins with the thought that no speaker can do justice to the situation; and thereupon he soars into a long, balanced sentence that must have given intense pleasure to his eloquence-loving audience. "If I am grateful to our ancestors," he says in effect, though a paraphrase can not preserve the grandeur of the utterance—"if I am grateful to my ancestors, because they have given me life, liberty, and a country; if to the immortal gods, by whose kindness I retain these blessings and am increased in them; if to the Roman people, who have raised me to my position of dignity in the state; if to this senatorial order, who have passed the most flattering decrees in my honor: then great and almost infinite is the debt of gratitude I owe to you, whose friendship and agreement have in one single moment restored to me the gifts of my ancestors, the blessings of the immortal gods, the dignity received at the hands of the Roman people, and your own laudatory decrees; so that all the blessings due to you, to the Roman people, to my ancestors, and to the immortal gods—all these, which I formerly owed to these several benefactors, I have now recovered through you alone."

This is only the beginning, but, in the main, it will have to suffice. As Cicero proceeded, he singled out a few men—Pompey

[25] The genuineness of the four orations delivered immediately after Cicero's return from exile, and of some others, for that matter, has been questioned, but scholars no longer have serious doubts about any of the orations traditionally attributed to Cicero. See Schanz.

first of all, and some magistrates, who had been particularly
active in securing his recall. The praise lavished upon them
has a variety, a grace, and a sonorousness of language scarcely
paralleled in any of his other orations. He utters the doubt that
he will never be able properly to show his gratitude to Pompey,
who has traveled to the municipia and the colonies in his behalf;
and he calls Lentulus, the consul of the year, his parent and his
god. He does not forget the other consul, Metellus Nepos, his
old enemy, who has now laid aside his hostility and has not
allowed himself to be influenced by his relatives—the Clodian
family, of course. Cicero knew as well as any one that Nepos
followed Pompey, though he also might have had a change of
heart; but no such reflections could have a place on the present
occasion. Cicero's language has the exaltation of Roman political life, as we have frequently met it; and it may be worth
recalling, for our modern comfort, that the divinity assigned
oratorically to Lentulus was not such a transcending encomium
after all. The thought is found elsewhere among the orations,
the disagreeable Sestius being said to have revered his father as
if he were a god; and the word divine is applied to the study
of literature and philosophy to distinguish it, without emphasis,
from the pursuits of agriculture.

The speech has some expressions, not of gratitude, directed
against Clodius and the two consuls of the preceding year. The
attacks on these, very brief as compared with the rest of the
oration, had no importance in Cicero's mind, for in describing
the situation to Atticus he does not even refer to his enemies;
and to his audience these attacks, preceded and followed as they
were by Cicero's high expressions of gratitude, doubtless seemed
little else than the natural incidental thrusts at his political
opponents. Their virulence, however, has led some students to
the erroneous belief that the main object of Cicero's speech was
to empty the brimming vials of his wrath, and they have main-

tained that Cicero on this occasion revealed himself as a man of coarse mind and an unforgiving disposition. The point needs no argument if the amenities of Roman politics be kept in mind; one little matter, however, may be mentioned. The attack on Piso, one of the consuls, was repeated with much effective amplification in a later speech, *In Pisonem*. The speech is extant, and no modern can find it in his cultivated sensibilities to utter an exculpatory word in extenuation of its abuse. But the Romans thought differently. The speech was published, and a year after its delivery Cicero writes to Quintus that the school boys were learning it as a regular exercise. And yet the Romans guarded the virtue of their sons with an anxiety that we moderns reserve for our daughters; the Roman boy, to quote an example, passing through the street under the care of his *paedagogus*, was expected to keep his eyes duly lowered so as not to glance at the passers-by.

Clodius came off rather easily in the first speech to the senate, for Cicero's quarrel was not with him at this particular moment. The former tribune had, after all, only lived up to his previous reputation. He is frequently referred to, however, always with an opprobrious epithet; and a modern reader might compile a very comprehensive and impressive list of abusive nouns and adjectives from these incidental references. But Cicero's real vituperation is aimed at the former consuls, who had acted in a manner contrary to what "could reasonably be expected from their high office" and who had not had the excuse of political enmity. Before the main thunderous attack, there are little lightning flashes to indicate its approach. They have sold Cicero's safety; their minds are filled with murk and squalor; they are traders in provinces and vendors of the senatorial dignity; not consuls, but robbers. Cicero has been classing them together, but suddenly he launches into a description of them individually.

Gabinius, who had proposed the law which gave Pompey the command against the pirates, is himself an archpirate; he is a frizzly-haired frequenter of low resorts; he is besmeared with ointments. And this dignified gentleman addressed the people in the Circus though he was heavy with wine, sleep, and debauchery. His hair glistened with pomade; his locks were carefully arranged; his eyes were dull; his cheeks hung in pouches; and his voice trembled and was scarcely audible when he announced that he was much displeased that citizens had been punished without due process of law. Unsuspected and hidden for a long time, indeed, has been the worth and dignity of this dancing gentleman, whose forehead is scarred with the curling iron.

And Piso! He has frequented the forum since boyhood, remarkable only for his assumed seriousness of mien, and never displaying any wisdom, eloquence, knowledge of military affairs, friendliness, or liberality. Passing by this unmannered, bristling, long-faced individual, you might have thought him a boor, but not a debauchee. But you should see him indoors! He is the kind of man who is admitted by the back entrance. And this unwieldy brute philosophizes with Greeklings! He is an Epicurean; not a real one, whatever that may be, but one that is interested only in the one word, pleasure. His teachers are not the silly fellows who talk about virtue, hard work, and the facing of dangers for one's country—Cato knew these philosophers when he argued against Murena—but those who teach that no hour should be without pleasure, that every part of a man's body should at all times experience some delightful sensation. This philosopher, Piso, has deceived his senatorial colleagues and the Roman people, not by cleverness and eloquence, as will occasionally happen, but by his wise wrinkles and his eloquent eyebrows. And yet, despite those eyes of his, though there is no mind behind them; despite that fine forehead, though it is not a sign of noble living; despite those wonderful eyebrows, though Piso has never accomplished anything—despite all these, he could bring himself to make an alliance with Gabinius, and was not repelled by that fellow's redolence of ointments, his vinous breath, and his scarred forehead.

Such invective as this grew out of the same Roman soil of unrestrained license as that which nourished the political verses of Catullus, but the poet's feeble meannesses, though personally as insulting, are like pin pricks beside Cicero's demolishing artillery. And yet Cicero says, within the few minutes that the speech lasted, that this is not the occasion for personal strife and that he willingly forgives his enemies. Nor was his vituperation a matter of impulse, for he had not only written the speech beforehand but he even read it from the manuscript.

Indeed, the oration was a political manifesto. Pompey and the orderly elements—relatively orderly, it must be confessed, in view of the gangs of Sestius and Milo—had united in bringing Cicero back; law and order had been in abeyance during his absence; the union just formed, therefore, must be continued if Rome was to have peace. Cicero was well aware that ultimately his exile had been due to Caesar; Pompey's treachery had been, in a way, an enforced yielding. Cicero does not mention Caesar by name, but he refers to him in words that have already been quoted: "I will not call him my enemy, but I know that he was silent when others called him my enemy." Cicero, in this remark, daringly thrusts a wedge between the two chief triumvirs; his hope being, as before the exile, that disagreement in the triumvirate will lead to constitutional government, Pompey siding with the conservatives. And Pompey is reminded that he can not get along without support, for, acting alone, that is, in the interests of the triumvirate, he had been forced to take refuge in his house in order to escape the violence of Clodius. This was not a pleasant reminder to the great man. Critics have wondered at Cicero's lack of adroitness, and some have con-

sidered the statement an indication of the alleged spuriousness
of the oration. But Cicero had observed Pompey's irresolute,
fumbling city ways, and there is more than enough eulogy of
Pompey in the speech to counteract any little chagrin the
reminder of his weakness may have caused him.

VI

CICERO SUBMITS

Cicero did not have such high hopes for the future as this
speech and some later ones indicate. This is shown even by his
first letter to Atticus, written within a few days of his arrival.
Nothing, however, could be accomplished without a publicly
expressed confidence. But the situation was hopelessly like the
one that followed the consulship of 63 B.C. The union that
had restored Cicero was as weak as the one that had checked
Catiline, and of the same kind. The nobles were no more devoted
to Pompey than before. On the seventh of September, to be
sure, Cicero, prompted by the situation in Rome, made a motion
to place Pompey in charge of the grain supply, for the scarcity
of food was causing riots; and a law to this effect was passed.
Pompey received full proconsular powers for five years throughout the Roman realm, thus becoming virtual ruler, as he had
been before. But the nobles presently began to oppose him at
every turn. Nor were they for long inclined to follow the leadership of Cicero, the New man. The old envies quickly revived.
He was taunted with his present friendship for Pompey, toward
whom it was said he ought to feel nothing but enmity because
of the exile; and when he proposed any measures at all opposed
to the interests of the triumvirs, the aristocrats openly rejoiced.
Some of them, in their eagerness to thwart Pompey and make
Cicero's position even more disagreeable, openly favored Clodius,
who had quite revived from his defeat in Cicero's return. Of

the knights we hear nothing at this time; but Crassus, though he had been one of the many that welcomed Cicero on the fourth of September, showed friendship neither for Cicero nor for Pompey. The former situation was thus accurately reproduced, and Cicero, working for a coalition that involved mutual concessions, was like a neutral between belligerents, heartily supported by no one.

But there was still another difficulty. A return to constitutional government would be possible only in case the triumvirs disagreed. Of this there seemed for a little while to be some likelihood. Not only were Crassus and Pompey openly jealous of each other, but Pompey seemed to be drawing away from Caesar. On the fifth of April, in 56 B.C., Cicero proposed that Caesar's agrarian law be made a subject for discussion at a meeting to be held on May fifteenth. In some way the law had proved unsuccessful, and a speaker at a previous meeting had used against it the arguments formerly employed by Cicero against the bill of Rullus. Cicero's proposal, as he himself later phrased it, was an attack on the very citadel of the triumvirate, and yet Pompey made no objection. But the agrarian law was not discussed on the fifteenth of May. Caesar had created the triumvirate in the year 60 B.C. It had proved wondrously efficient, and now needed only to be restored. This was done at the famous conference at Luca, a small town in northern Etruria. Here, in April, Caesar succeeded in reconciling Pompey and Crassus, and new arrangements were made for the future. Pompey and Crassus were to become consuls for 55 B.C., each thereupon to receive an important provincial governorship, and Caesar's command in Gaul was prolonged so as to last ten years in all. Rome was in the hands of the reunited triumvirs, and their plans were carried out. After the consulship of 55 B.C., to anticipate, Crassus went to the East to fight against the Parthians, and was killed. Pompey received the two Spains as his provinces, and, remaining in Rome, governed them by lieutenants.

Pompey had shown no resentment, and probably had felt none, at Cicero's proposed attack on Caesar's land law, but after the conference with Caesar he expressed so strong a disapproval of Cicero's action that various men reported his words to Cicero. Pompey himself went to Sardinia. Meeting Quintus, who was one of his lieutenants, he severely criticised Cicero, recalling his own past services to the latter, such as they were, and said that in helping Cicero he had acted with the approval of Caesar. He reminded Quintus of conversations they had previously had in reference to Cicero's relations to Caesar, and told him that if Cicero could not be restrained, Quintus would be made to pay for his brother's behavior in accordance with promises he had given Pompey. These promises, evidently, had been to the effect that Cicero would not oppose Caesar's interests, but we know nothing further about them. Pompey also directed Quintus to request Cicero to show consideration for Caesar, or, at any rate, not to work against him if he was unwilling or unable to work for him. And finally, to make his altered view doubly clear, Pompey sent a friend to Cicero with the message that Cicero should refrain from committing himself in the matter of Caesar's land legislation until Pompey himself should come to Rome.

Pompey, again acting the part of a traitor to Cicero, had thus sent an ultimatum, and Cicero yielded. He was without a party and he was constantly opposed and insulted by those who were still inclined to offer a hopeless resistance to the triumvirs. The choice between Caesar and Pompey on the one hand and their powerless opponents on the other, who were friendly with Clodius, was a choice of evils, but the triumvirate offered him safety and some small chance to accomplish something, if not for the state, at least for his friends. Cicero's most dignified course would have been to retire from public life. This, however, seems to have been next to impossible. His prominence was too great; moreover, he had promised, in the first speech to the senate after his return from exile, not to forget the services of those who had aided his recall, and gratitude for such services was inevitably connected with public life.[26]

Cicero, having once decided to submit to the triumvirs, did so with frankness. Contrary to the advice of Atticus, he sent something written to Caesar which he called his recantation, his palinode. He had found the writing difficult, and "had nibbled around it for a long time," but he sent it. Just what it was, can not be determined with certainty; most probably it was the oration called *De Provinciis Consularibus,* though it may have been some other oration, or even a letter. In the speech mentioned, which was delivered at the end of May in 56 B.C., Cicero at any rate openly spoke for the necessity of retaining Caesar in Gaul, the very thing the triumvir's enemies wished to prevent; and reviewed his past relations to Caesar, concluding somewhat pathetically with the thought that he is no longer hostile to Caesar. They had been old friends, he says; Caesar had offered him a place in the coalition with Pompey and Crassus, and Caesar, though he had allowed Clodius to become a plebeian, had also favored Cicero's recall from exile. "Even if I were Caesar's enemy," he continues, "I would favor him, since he is a good servant of the state." Adroitly Cicero mentions how the senate had bowed to Caesar and voted him honors; but the public recantation was not easy. "I will say what I feel," Cicero says; "I will explain the whole situation."

The same necessity for explanation is present in nearly all Cicero's orations of this time; and we should undoubtedly find it, to the same degree, in the orations of other speakers, were they extant. These years were so full of new political combinations and recombinations that nobody can be said to have remained faithful to any one but himself.

Cicero delivered many orations after his return from exile besides those already mentioned. Fourteen altogether are extant

---

[26] *Fam.* 1, 9. contains a long account of Cicero's political attitude at this time. It is a very remarkable letter.

from the years 57–52 B.C. His first speech to the senate was followed by a speech to the people of the same tenor and much the same phraseology.[27] A little later, though still in 57 B.C., he spoke before the pontifices in a successful effort to regain his house lot on the Palatine. Soon after that strange sounds and the clash of arms were heard underground, and the soothsayers averred that sacred places had been desecrated. Clodius conceived this to refer to the rebuilding of Cicero's house on the Palatine, for the land, it will be recalled, had been dedicated by Clodius to Liberty. The matter was argued in court the next year. Cicero's speech[28] on this occasion sets before us the grotesque uses to which the national religion was put in partisan politics.

During the following years Cicero pleaded in numerous cases, all connnected with politics, whatever the occasion that prompted them. Attack on enemies and defense of himself and of his friends or political associates, therefore, form their main theme, the tone being that of his first speech to the senate. The consulship of 63 B.C. and the exile, with the events that preceded and followed it, were constantly brought up for criticism by Clodius and Cicero's other opponents, and Cicero replied. The same thoughts occur repeatedly, much to the wonder of the reader, until he remembers that the speeches are but echoes of the ceaseless talk and argumentation in the forum.

These orations contain passages of every kind. Cicero describes the circumstances of his exile with infinite pathos;[29] he gives an exalted definition of his ideal citizens, the *boni*, which is like a piece of noble music, leading the thoughts to distant places and half-forgotten resolves;[30] and on the occasion when he delivered this passage, which is one of his greatest, he

---

27 *Oratio cum populo gratias egit.* The next speech mentioned is *De domo sua ad pontifices.*

28 *De haruspicum responsis.*

29 *Pro Sestio* 36–52, *Pro Plancio* 72–100.

30 *Pro Sestio* 96–132.

descended to unrestrained vituperation of one of the witnesses, hurling insults at the man because of his personal appearance.[31] The step from grandeur to scurrility was not a long one in the Roman forum. An equally unrestrained attack was also leveled by Cicero at Piso,[32] one of the consuls in 58 B.C., in a speech that is scarcely more than an elaboration of the invective against the same man contained in Cicero's speech to the senate after his return to the city. The gaieties and gallantry of Roman society, with sordid financial transactions, disagreements, and poison charges in the background;[33] the propriety of sowing wild oats;[34] humor and seriousness mixed as effectively as in the speech for Murena;[35] the successful foreigner Balbus,[36] who finally secured the consulship; one Roman politician who demanded ten thousand talents from the king of Egypt to restore him to his throne, and another politician who lent the king the money and in return was put in charge of the taxes of the kingdom and scoured the country with Roman soldiers in the course of ruthless extortion;[37] and, of course, malversation in a province, with Cicero's assertion[38] in court that the foreign witnesses, who were Sardinians, could not be believed, just as previously Cicero had told the courts that no credence should be placed in the Gauls who testified against Fonteius and in the Greeks who appeared against Flaccus—all these persons and circumstances and opinions, and a great many more, are found in these speeches.

Taken together, these orations give perhaps the most vivid picture that we have of public life in Rome, its occasional nobility, its eloquence, its recklessness, violence, and selfishness. The

---

[31] *In Vatinium.*

[32] *In Pisonem.*

[33] *Pro Caelio.*

[34] *Pro Caelio.*

[35] *Pro Plancio.*

[36] *Pro Balbo.*

[37] *Pro Rabirio Postumo.*

[38] *Pro Scauro.*

real power was in the hands of Caesar and Pompey, but Caesar
was in Gaul and Pompey made no real effort to keep order in
Rome. The city was in a state of anarchy. The gangs of Clodius
and of his opponents, particularly Milo, filled the streets with
constant riots, and it was often impossible to elect the magistrates at the proper time. At last Clodius and his desperadoes
met Milo and his cutthroats near Bovillae, on the Appian Way,
on the eighteenth of January, 52 B.C., and in the fight that ensued
Clodius was slain. The events that followed were like those that
had been going on in Rome for years. The corpse was brought
to Rome and burned by the mob in the senate-house, which itself
was consumed by the fire, and all the evil passions of the mob
were let loose. Then at last the least disorderly elements in the
city elected Pompey sole consul. The motion for this unprecedented consulship was made by Bibulus, Caesar's former colleague and opponent in the year 59 B.C., and it was seconded by
Cato, though neither Cato nor Bibulus had any reason for favoring Pompey.

One hundred days after the murder of Clodius, Milo was
brought to trial. Cicero was in duty bound to defend the man
who had been among those most active in bringing about his
return and who also had been the mortal enemy of Clodius;
and he showed both independence and courage in persisting in
his course despite the violence of the Clodian mob and the evident
desire of Pompey to have Milo convicted. Milo, as has been
intimated before, was little better than Clodius; but it seems
probable that even Cato, when the trial finally took place, voted
for acquittal. Though Cicero had the courage to appear as the
only speaker for the defense, the sight of the soldiers with
whom Pompey had filled the forum and the angry shouts of the
Clodians so unnerved him that his speech was a failure.

Cicero's words were taken down, and published; but the
speech that he later wrote out and sent to Milo, which has won
praise even from Cicero's severest critics, is the one that we have.

Cicero argues that Milo had acted in self-defense, which may have been true, although it is of no consequence; and he also maintains that Clodius had amply deserved death. Only one little passage will be reproduced—a fitting commentary on the oratory of the times. Milo, like Clodius, was a typical leader of ruffians; he was absolutely without fear and at the trial had acted contrary to all Roman court propriety, for he had refused to dress in mourning, to let his hair and beard grow long, and even to shed tears. Cicero's description of him on the fateful day, however, is almost lyrical, and recalls Terence's account of the sensitive old gentleman in the *Self-Tormentor*. Milo, according to Cicero, attended the meeting of the senate and stayed until the end. Thereupon he went home, changed his shoes and clothes, waited a little for his wife to get ready, "as husbands do," and finally set out from Rome, having sacerdotal business in Lanuvium, which was beyond Bovillae. He traveled in a carriage, wrapped in a big cloak and sitting beside his wife. Many maid servants and slaves accompanied the peaceful couple. Then they were met by Clodius, on horseback, with his armed band, the famous struggle took place, and Clodius was killed.

But Milo was not saved by this touching description of his peaceable frame of mind, or, rather, by the part of this description which the orator was able to utter at the trial. He was sent into exile, and Rome, under Pompey as sole consul, enjoyed a brief period of comparative calm.

Cicero's own position throughout these years of frequent pleading was excellent. The lot on which his Palatine residence had stood was restored to him by senatorial decree in 57 B.C., despite Clodius' pious dedication of it to Liberty; and money was voted to Cicero both for the house and for the destroyed villas, though for the villas not quite as much as he had expected. In March of 56 B.C., he writes to Quintus that he is living rather more expensively than had been his custom, finding this necessary because his house had never been more crowded by visitors. At that time he was building in three places; and shortly before, he had been thinking of buying an estate at Tusculum, probably next to his own property and so intended for an enlargement. The senate, who had clipped his wings by exile, is not willing to let them grow again, he says; but even as late as October, 54 B.C., when Cicero's espousal of the triumvirate cause had taken open form in the courts, the senate rose with loud shouts when Gabinius dared to call him an exile. A highborn nobody, just previously to this, kept pressing dinner invitations upon him; this pleased Cicero, though he persisted in refusing them.

He had his troubles, to be sure. It became necessary more than once to defend political enemies who were the friends of the triumvirs. Sometimes the shifting political conditions made this easy, as in the case of Vatinius, a worthless Caesarian, whom Cicero had bitterly attacked in the oration that has already been mentioned. Unfortunately the defending oration is lost. At other times it was more difficult, as in the case of the ex-consul Gabinius, the man with the scarred forehead. Cicero reveals his annoyance to Atticus; but in public he has to pretend that Gabinius and he have been reconciled, explaining that Pompey is too noble a man to have required Cicero to act in behalf of an enemy. Occasionally Cicero, like every one else in Rome, was exposed to physical danger. He kept a body of armed men about him. Once, on the third of November, 57 B.C., Clodius and his followers drove away the workmen who were rebuilding Cicero's house; they also committed other outrages, and even set Quintus' house on fire. On the eleventh of the same month they attacked Cicero as he, with guards, was coming down the Sacred Way. Shouting ensued, stone-throwing, the use of clubs and swords; all unforeseen. Cicero retreated into the vestibule of a house nearby. In the mêlée Cicero's men seem to have had an opportunity of despatching Clodius, but, as Cicero writes to Atticus, he was opposed to violent methods: "I am dieting and object to surgery.'' But even in the midst of the daily uproar in Rome he was later held to be safe because of his friendship with Caesar and Pompey.

Many letters passed between Caesar in Gaul and Cicero; but only one is extant,[39] in which Cicero recommends Trebatius. ''You have indeed succeeded in persuading me,'' he begins, ''that you are my other self both in matters relating to me and to my friends.'' That Caesar has power is implied, but not expressed. Caesar had asked Cicero to send some one to whom he might show favors, and Cicero sends Trebatius, expressing his full conviction that Caesar will treat the young man as he himself would have done. And he does not forget to make graceful reference to a witticism in Caesar's letter. The letter is written ''as to a friend and yet with dignity''—the phrase employed by Cicero in characterizing, for his brother, his correspondence with Caesar.

Quintus had joined Caesar in Gaul as one of his lieutenants, and an able one, as every reader of the *Commentaries* is aware. Quintus' going to Gaul was an outward sign of the reconciliation between Caesar and the Ciceros. Caesar had welcomed it warmly. The letter in which Cicero announced Quintus' decision had fallen into the water and become almost illegible; Caesar, replying to it, writes that what it seems to mean is too good to be true. And that is the spirit in which he and Cicero met. Caesar expressed his prospective joy at renewing his old affection for the Ciceros through direct intercourse with Quintus; and he did Cicero various substantial services, even lending him eight hundred thousand sesterces. Cicero, on the other hand, writes to Quintus that, whatever Caesar's kind offices, his love is far more valuable. We know nothing of the early personal relations between Caesar and Cicero, but Caesar's words indicate that they had been intimate. The two great Romans, though different in many ways, were perhaps more alike than any other two; they

[39] *Fam.* 7, 5.

both had real culture, tact, kindliness, and, above all, genius. Probably their political differences in the past, radical though they were, had not seriously disturbed their mutual personal esteem.

Cicero's personal security and eminence is reflected in numerous letters of this period. To M. Fadius Gallus, an Epicurean friend, he writes at the end of 57 B.C. a humerous letter about having overeaten at a vegetarian dinner; Cicero, the vigilant politician, had been "entrapped by Mr. Beet and Mr. Mallow," and he moralizes about various sicknesses, of all of which he is afraid.[40] To Marius, another friend, he writes a beautiful letter, though it was doubtless very much of a rhetorical exercise, about the superiority of mental occupation to attendance at public games;[41] and he sends his brother an amusing account[42] of how this same Marius had once traveled with him toward Baiae. A friend had lent them a litter with eight bearers. As they were being borne along, Marius looked out and saw a troop of a hundred armed men behind them. "He almost collapsed with fear," writes Cicero, "and I with laughter, for the men were our bodyguard." And to the young lawyer Trebatius, finally, who had gone to Caesar in Gaul at Cicero's recommendation, he writes a whole series of letters,[43] full of legal puns, which at times call for elaborate exposition and are infinitely amusing. The basis of them all is that Trebatius, being a student, did not enjoy his stay in Gaul, but remained in order to make his fortune; often complaining, now of one thing and now of another. Thus Caesar, busy with fighting, did not always have sufficient time for social intercourse, though there seems to have been a good deal of this. Cicero attempts to cheer his depressed protégé, evidently to some purpose, for Trebatius apparently became

---

[40] *Fam.* 7, 26. Translations by Tyrrell.

[41] *Fam.* 7, 1.

[42] *Ad Q. Fr.* 2, 8 (10), 2.

[43] *Fam.* Book 7.

rich, through Caesar's bounty, before he returned to Rome. Trebatius, as a man of peace, did not go to Britain, at which Cicero expresses his joy: Trebatius has been spared much trouble by staying in Gaul and Cicero has escaped Trebatius' descriptions of the expedition. Trebatius lived long; and gave laconic answers to Horace when the latter had doubts about his own satirical manner.[44]

All of Cicero's cheerfulness, however, was no more real than had been his unconcern when he wittily defended Murena while the Catilinarians still infested the city. At the bottom of his heart lay a deadweight of inexpressible sorrow because the state had gone to ruin. Whether pleading in the courts or writing to his friends, he wore a mask. As every one could see, he had regained his lost position and he had become the honored and influential friend of the triumvirs; the house on the Palatine was restored and throngs filled it; such a man had every reason for happiness—and Cicero acted the part. But in this lay his dumb tragedy. He wore his mask even in his relations with Atticus and Quintus. To them, he could not pretend that the old republican god was in his heaven and that all was well with the political world; but he could profess no longer to care.

With Atticus this was easier. The latter had always given less thought to Cicero's principles than to his safety, and Cicero was now safe. Atticus, moreover, had never cared much what became of Rome, provided he himself and his friends could live a sheltered, comfortable life; if he had any passion beyond that of amassing wealth, it was for books and art. Cicero gave much of his time to writing, and he found much consolation in it. To Atticus, therefore, he could pretend, and successfully, that he found more than mere consolation, a happiness that satisfied the most intimate needs of his nature. "The state is lost," he writes.[45] "You ask if I take it easily? Certainly. I

am going back to my books—the life for which I am best fitted.''
And he also refers to the joy he takes in his private relations;
with Atticus, Quintus, and Tullia—Terentia being ominously
omitted, even just after Cicero's return, as though things were
not quite what they should have been.

With Quintus, to whom Cicero seems to have been even better
known than to Atticus, it was more difficult to wear the mask.
He does it bravely for a while. He counsels Quintus to be as
philosophical as Philoctetes, who, when wronged, could take
pleasure in the sufferings of his own country; and he writes
daily for a time, though most of the letters are lost, and enjoys
''rambling on as if conversing.'' But the letter in which he most
convincingly paraded before Atticus as happy, is followed in
the extant correspondence by one to Quintus[46]—both in 54 B.C.,
probably in October—in which he suddenly throws away all
torturing pretense. ''I keep away from public business and
devote myself to literature, but I will confess something that
I have wished to keep hidden, most of all from you. I am tormented, my dearest brother, I am tormented, for there is no
state, no law. This ought to be my happiest time, my *otium
cum dignitate*, but I am distracted by cases in court, often having
to defend my enemies; or else I have recourse to study. Only
Caesar, out of all men, has been found to give me the love I want,
or rather, to desire to love me. I have from day to day many
circumstances to cheer me; the greatest would be our being
together, but you are away.'' This confession—it is slightly
longer in the original—is not repeated afterwards; Cicero writes
later as he had written earlier, but no preoccupation with trifles
and no wit, after that, could deceive Quintus.

---

[46] *Ad Q. Fr.*, 3, 5 and 6.

CHAPTER XI

AUTHORSHIP

I

The Scipionic Circle and Literary Enthusiasms

The conference at Luca put an end to Cicero's independent political activity, and there was no prospect that it could ever be resumed. Immediately after the conference Cicero had considerable leisure; in the next few years he was at times distractedly busy in the courts, but he nevertheless seems to have had not a little spare time, certainly more than when he was working his way toward the consulship. He thus had his *otium*, and it preserved much of its outward *dignitas*, but the latter, now that the government was in the hands of individuals, was to Cicero only an empty shell. He would have used any leisure for continuing his reading and his studies; whether, under happier circumstances, he would also have written, is not certain. Now, however, seeking distraction even more than pleasure or improvement, he turned to the writing of long essays, and may be said to have become an author.

This step did not involve so great a change in his habits as would at first appear, for he had already written a great deal; but it did involve a new point of view. Beginning with his work on oratory in three books, the *De Oratore,* he turned his previous reading and experience into literature; he utilized his own past in a kind of writing that did not enhance his high position in Rome, but even detracted somewhat from it. The situation, however, can not be stated in modern terms; the position of Cicero or of any other Roman in reference to literary matters was wholly different from anything found in modern civilization.

Roman thought, when not concerned with the practical things in life, and sometimes even then, was largely borrowed from the Greeks, and the forms of Roman writing were almost entirely Greek. Rome during its period of great conquests, the third and the second centuries B.C., had become the mistress of a Hellenized world, and the Romans themselves had frequently come into close personal contact with individual Greeks. The Romans at that time had no literature of their own, no philosophy, and no system of education beyond a very efficient but unintellectual home training; they were soldiers and administrators, some of them also farming or engaging in business. The contact with Greece forced a new point of view upon them. They came out into the sun, as it were, into a wider, richer life. Not everything new was good, but much was pleasant and much appealed to the serious side of Roman character. Rhetoric especially was offered as something useful; philosophy, though suspiciously speculative and not so trustworthy a moral guide as the old Roman traditions, also made some headway. The Greek scholars discovered in Rome a large field for their activity, more glorious and more remunerative than Greece itself or the rest of the world; and they set about preparing their wares for the new market.

The beginning of this, in a definitely personal way, came with Scipio Africanus the Younger, the conqueror and unwilling destroyer of Carthage. Long before his time Greek influence, both for good and for evil, had been slipping into Rome. As early as 240 B.C. it had brought about what was later looked upon as the beginning of Roman literature, through the translation and acting in Rome of a Greek comedy and a Greek tragedy; a humble enough beginning, for the translator was a Greek slave. Africanus, however, was the first Roman noble who put himself under the tuition of a Greek.[1] During Scipio's

---

[1] See particularly Reitzenstein, and Schwartz (vol. 1, chap. 4). On the Greeks in Rome, see also Besançon, Reure, Buettner, Schneidewin, and Zielinski (both titles).

youth Polybius was living in Rome as a prisoner of war, free in every respect except for his enforced residence in the imperial city. He was an Achaean nobleman, long experienced in politics and war, a Stoic though not a professional philosopher, and thoroughly educated in the Greek way; he had traveled much and had a mind open to the political greatness of Rome, which in his large history he attributes mainly to the Roman aristocracy. In the year 166 B.C. Scipio, then slightly under twenty, appealed to Polybius for guidance, so that he might become a worthy member of the Roman nobility, fit to take the place of eminent predecessors. The Roman world was changing. The old nobles had led very narrow lives; they had looked in only one direction, toward politics; speaking broadly, they had been members of the Roman state and nothing further. To maintain in the new world a position equal to theirs in the old, Scipio had need of a wider training; and Polybius was ready to instruct him. The relation between the two became one of sincere personal affection, a source of pride to them both, and is nobly commemorated in Polybius' history.[2]

In later years, when Scipio had attained fame and power, he put himself under the tuition of the philosopher Panaetius. The latter, a Greek noble like Polybius, was a professional philosopher, a Stoic; but he was free from the typical Stoic dogmatism and contempt for beauty. The Stoics, to be sure, being Greeks, had heard of beauty, and proclaimed that goodness is beauty, but they were merely aiming at philosophical comprehensiveness; having made room in their scheme for beauty by calling it goodness, they quickly forgot its meaning. Such, at least, was their attitude as sectarians; but at this time orthodoxy had fallen on evil days; neither Stoics nor Epicureans nor even Sceptics were any longer of limpid purity. Panaetius was versatile, sensitive to social amenities, and inspired with the Greek joyousness and delight in art and literature. He was a lover of Plato, who said

---

[2] *Polyb.* 32, 9 ff.

that beauty is goodness, which has an emphasis opposite to that of the Stoic dictum. Both by training and personality Panaetius was a capable and winning interpreter to his enthusiastic Roman pupils and patrons of all that was best in Greek life; and these, Scipio and his friends, the so-called Scipionic Circle, became the definite nucleus of things Greek in Rome.

Though the Scipionic Circle flourished in the second half of the second century B.C., it was not distant in the eyes of Cicero and his contemporaries. Cicero himself, and those who with him frequented the house of Scaevola the augur, had almost a direct connection with it, for Scaevola was the son-in-law of Laelius, Scipio's bosom friend. Scipio and Laelius, as well as the other members of the Circle, were as intensely alive to Cicero as if they had belonged to his own time. He constantly mentions them. One bit of gossip may be repeated, for the light it sheds not only on Cicero's lively realization of these men but also on the character of these old nobles themselves. Scipio, according to Cicero, was of a less joyous, effervescent temperament than Laelius, but, though the conqueror of a third of the world, he could relax. Crassus, the great orator, the son-in-law of the augur, is represented by Cicero in the *De Oratore*[3] as repeating the remarks of Scaevola himself. Scipio and Laelius, so the old augur used to say, often went to the country, and, once away from the city, they became as hilarious as boys. Crassus is loath to gossip about great men, but Scaevola did say that Scipio and Laelius were in the habit of gathering shells and pebbles on the beach and that they, in Scaevola's dignified phrase, "stooped to all manner of games and mental relaxation."

Conquerors of the world who could stoop to games were ready to embrace the lighter side of Greek life, to become individuals as well as Roman citizens. Their ideal of a Roman noble was thus, first, a patriot thoroughly devoted to Rome and made more effective by the lessons of oratory and other things that the

---

[3] *De Or.* 2, 21–22.

Greeks could give, and secondly, an individual who was open to the finer side of life, especially art and literature. These nobles led, as it were, a double existence; they were Romans —always Romans—but also Greeks, their latter character being hidden from the nation as a whole, a private luxury to be cultivated when the business of the workaday political world of Rome allowed it.

Some men at the time of Cicero claimed to adopt only one half of this ideal, that of the Greek individualist; and we have already seen[4] how their claims were rejected, arguments against them being supplied even by the Greek philosophers, though these could themselves never realize more than one half of the ideal. Scipio's conception was thoroughly Roman, with the Greek qualities added, and had become the norm by the time of Cicero. The Roman nobles were Stoics, Epicureans, or Academics; and the books in which they studied philosophy were Greek. Their physicians were Greek, and consequently also their diseases, in name. Greek words and proverbs were introduced in their conversation and their correspondence, though this habit did not always meet with full approval. All educated Romans knew Greek, after a fashion; many took considerable pains to master the Greek idiom and accent, and were inordinately pleased with compliments on their success, nor were the subtle Greeks chary of compliments. It was the fashion, the one mark of good breeding, to be interested in things Greek; but, as with other intellectual fashions, submission to it was occasionally mostly external. The lazy or dull or pleasure-loving Roman noble would content himself with collecting Greek works of art and Greek books, with having clever Greeks about him, and with giving dinners of exquisite Greek cookery, enlivened by the talk and the poems of Greek celebrities.[5] But even a pretended obedience to an intellectual fashion has its uses.

---

[4] See above, pp. 37 ff.

[5] An example is Piso, as described by Cicero, *In Pison.* 64–75.

The Roman boy of good social position now grew up in an intellectual atmosphere that was Greek. The cleverest of his father's slaves and freedmen were Greeks. Often highly educated, they were their master's business agents and private secretaries. In many cases they were among his closest friends, though not his social equals. Greek tutors gave the young Roman noble or knight almost his earliest instruction; or, if they were not Greek, the material of instruction was overwhelmingly Greek; and when the boy advanced to the higher and more specialized training of rhetoricians and philosophers, his instructors were Greek almost to a man. A Greek philosopher was a permanent member of many Roman households—Diodotus, the Stoic, was the one in Cicero's home—and performed very much the same duties as a spiritual father confessor; thus holding a position like that of Panaetius in the home of Scipio. Many Greeks of artistic and intellectual eminence, such as Archias, lived in Rome on intimate terms with the great; others, like Molo, came to the world's capital occasionally and were entertained at the city houses or the suburban villas of leading Romans. These visitors, as well as those living constantly in Rome, gave lectures, readings, and private instruction, and conversed with the young Romans and with their fathers on the meaning and the beauty of life.

One result of these close relations between the Greeks and the Romans was literary. Scipio and Laelius were said to have aided Terence in his reworking of Greek comedies for the Roman stage; a statement that gave rise to much scholarly argument, in which, however, it was always taken for granted, that Roman nobles could not with propriety have put their names to a literary product intended for public performance. The interest in literary creation displayed by Scipio and Laelius had by the time of Cicero become almost an obsession. The nobles, however busy with practical affairs, whether in the forum or on foreign battlefields, were always scribbling. There was literary letter writing, as has already been mentioned; and dialogues, descriptions of travel, epigrams, tragedies, discussions of grammar, and translations were also written. To do these things was a sign of culture; it was also frequently a means of training; but, above all, it was the blind groping of the Roman upper classes to become citizens of the Greek intellectual world. To these literary performances belong such things as Caesar's tragedy *Oedipus*, which Augustus later considered unworthy of publication; and also Caesar's work on grammar, his so-called *Praise of Hercules*, his collection of noteworthy sayings, his epigrams, one of which is addressed to Terence, and his poetical account of his journey· from Rome to Spain, in 46 B.C., when he went to fight against the sons of Pompey. Here, too, belong the four tragedies of Quintus Cicero, written in sixteen days while he was Caesar's lieutenant in Gaul; as well as a number of things by Marcus Cicero himself.

These literary exercises of Cicero, which belonged mostly to his youth, are of little importance; the more so as only fragments of them are now extant, and in some cases not even fragments. There was a youthful poem in tetrameters called *Glaucus*, known to Plutarch; Glaucus was a divinity of the sea. which may suggest the content of the poem. *Alcyone*, in hexameters, was probably an account of a metamorphosis; *Nilus*, the Nile, was obviously descriptive; *Uxorius*, the Uxorious Husband, may have been satirical; *Limon*, the Meadow, had to do, partly at least, with literary criticism, for four hexameters, still extant, praise Terence as an excellent translator of Menander; an elegy, finally, seems to have been entitled *Thalia Maesta*, the Sad Thalia, and it is known that the nymph Thalia, beloved by Jupiter, was not in favor with Juno. Cicero also wrote epigrams; rather naughtily, it would seem, for they lured the middle-aged Pliny the Younger to descant in verse on his mild passions, which he had until then kept hidden. But most interesting of all these

poetical essays must have been Cicero's poem on Marius, for in
this he could draw from his knowledge of Arpinum and his
enthusiasm for his famous fellow-townsman.

Cicero also made a good many translations. The essays contain numerous passages from Greek poets, particularly from the
tragedians; and there are long fragments from Cicero's translation of Aratus' astronomical poem the *Phaenomena* and his
meteorological *Prognostica*. Aratus was a didactic singer who
was popular both in Rome and elsewhere; St. Paul quoted him
in Athens, as we learn from the *Acts*.

Cicero as a poet was probably neither better nor worse than
his literary contemporaries. Perhaps the most interesting later
comment on this subject comes from Tacitus. "Caesar and
Brutus wrote poems," he says,[6] "not better than Cicero, but
more fortunately, for fewer people know that they did it."
Cicero did not think of himself as divinely inspired; in his letters, he always takes for granted that Quintus was the poet of
the family, though it should be stated that the fragments of
Quintus' verse are not superior to those of his brother's. Verse
writing was one of the things the Romans learned in school, under
Greek influence; as practised, it did not differ essentially from
prose. Lucretius, however, who was a real poet, borrowed several
turns of phrase from Cicero; the great orator's poems were
known for centuries after his death; and Plutarch says that at
one time he was considered not only the best orator but also the
best poet of Rome. At that time, however, whenever it was, the
Roman poets must have been as uninspired as their Greek contemporaries, of whom Archias is an example. The latter gained
great literary fame, according to Cicero's speech in his defense,
even when he was hardly more than a boy; and Cicero had himself heard him deliver "a large number of very excellent verses"
on the things that were happening at the very time of Archias'
declamation, and thereupon Archias had started all over again

---

[6] Tac. *Dial.* 21.

and treated the same subject "in new phraseology and new thoughts"—all, of necessity, extemporaneously. Cicero could do almost as well; according to Plutarch,[7] when he really tried he made five hundred verses in a night.

But these literary enthusiasms were not limited to verse. In 44 B.C. Cicero wrote to Atticus that there was not yet a collection of his letters, but that Tiro had gathered together seventy and that probably Atticus also had some. Cicero ought first to look them over and make corrections, whereupon they would be published. It has been well conjectured that these letters were intended as models of letter writing; that is, they would be another contribution to the purely literary productions of the period. Their small number alone indicates that the aim could have been neither political nor autobiographical. There is no evidence, however, that such a collection as this, or any collection of Cicero's letters, whether revised or not, was published during his lifetime. Cicero also wrote a work called *Admiranda,* Things to Wonder At, of uncertain date and now lost; and in 59 B.C., while casting about for a literary distraction, he was for a time at work on a book on geography. He found the subject difficult and uninteresting; but he seems to have accomplished something, then or later, for there is a quotation from a work of his probably entitled *Chorographia,* Geography. Still extant, finally, are the first two books, probably all that were ever completed, of a systematic work on rhetoric. They are called either *Libri Rhetorici,* Books on Rhetoric, or *De Inventione,* Invention, which is a rhetorical term and describes the content of the books. Cicero wrote them while still a student, when about twenty years old; as has already been mentioned, the character of the work is that of a student's thesis.

---

[7] Plut. *Cic.* 40.

II
FOR GLORY

But the endless scribbling practised by the leading men of
Rome was not entirely for the purposes of training, giving
pleasure to friends, or testifying to the personal culture of the
authors; it also found a very frequent, though a very modest,
use in the political world. This was an age of pamphleteering,
as has already been explained in connection with the publication
of Cicero's orations. Not only orations, however, whether or
not originally delivered, were written and given circulation;
all the forms of literature were employed, in verse as well as
in prose.[8] There were letters, dialogues, epigrams, historical
accounts, long poems, biographies, and even autobiographies;
anything in writing might be a political argument, an apology,
or a glorification; the glorifications, because of the intense factional strifes, being at times little else than either argument or
apology. The line between the distinctly ephemeral and that
which had hopes of a longer existence can not always be drawn.
Cato, after his suicide, became the subject of a veritable literary
warfare, in which Caesar, Cicero, Brutus, and many lesser lights
took a hand. The writers may be divided into eulogists and
detractors of the departed Stoic, or, more specifically, of the
aristocratic republic that he had championed; and yet some of
these numerous effusions, being biographies, could lay claim to
the character of history. Caesar's own *Commentaries on the
Gallic War*, apparently a most sober history though not concealing the fact that the author was a great general, was probably
a strong argument in Rome; and this is true to an even greater
extent of his *Civil War*. In the latter, after winning the battles,
he was proving to the Roman world that all blame for the war
belonged to his opponents. And eulogistic autobiography was

---

[8] See Peter, *Geschichtl. Litt. etc.*, pp. 163 ff.

not limited to men of real eminence; even Varro, the petulant
scholar, seems to have celebrated his modest military performances in the so-called *Legationes;* not to mention his Autobiography, *De Sua Vita,* which was probably concerned with
his literary activity. Nor was this writing confined to Latin.
Rutilius Rufus, consul in 105 B.C., wrote about himself and his
times both in Greek and in Latin.

In this field of literary production the Greeks found a very
suitable and remunerative occupation, particularly as eulogists
who claimed to write for posterity. The poets of Mytilene who
warbled about Pompey have already been mentioned; Pompey's
Greek historian, Theophanes, became for a time one of the influential men in Rome, acting as his patron's mouthpiece. Archias
belonged to this class, though he sang of Pompey's rivals. And
a long list of these prose and verse writers could easily be drawn
up. They clamored for an opportunity to do this work, knowing
that it would not go unrewarded. They, and their Roman or
Italian rivals, pressed their services upon the great. On one
occasion,[9] when Sulla was superintending a public sale, probably
of confiscated property, he ordered that some of it be given to
a poet who had written an epigram in his honor; but, as the
epigram was poor, Sulla added the condition that the bard should
not write in the dictator's honor in the future. When Caesar
was fighting in Spain, to mention only one other instance,[10]
Cicero sent him a freedman with a commendatory letter; the
freedman, it appears, possessed literary ability and had previously written about Crassus; now that Crassus was dead, he
had been fired with enthusiasm for Caesar and was "wonder-
fully eager to do justice to the undying fame of Caesar's
exploits."

Sometimes the deathlessness of fame might be secured when
a man of literary ability gave finish and rhetorical ornament to

[9] *Pro Arch.* 25.
[10] *Fam.* 13, 16.

the recital of facts executed by the great man himself. For this
purpose Sulla may have dedicated his *Memoirs* to L. Lucinius
Lucullus; and Q. Lutatius Catulus, who with Marius had fought
against the Cimbri, wrote an account of his consulship, the
glories of which had been absorbed by Marius, and sent it to a
certain A. Furius, who was writing an annalistic poem on Roman
history. Caesar's *Gallic War,* because of its lack of rhetorical,
that is literary, ornament, was in danger of being mistaken for
such a recital of facts; but Hirtius, who continued the account
of the war in Gaul, intimates that historians had better refrain
from attempts to improve on Caesar's work; and Cicero was of
the same opinion. The very title of Caesar's account, however,
lent some color to the theory that he was supplying material
for more ornate historians, for Commentaries, the Latin equivalent of the Greek *hypomnemata,* was the name given to such
historical material.

The three men of this period who most frequently became the
subjects of biographies were Pompey, Caesar, and Cicero. When
the Catilinarian conspiracy had been suppressed, the Greeks, as
Cicero wrote to Atticus, were annoyingly insistent about getting
something that they could convert into fine history. One of
them seems to have been Posidonius, who was a sort of scholarly
and literary dictator of the times; at any rate, Cicero sent him
a *hypomnema* in Greek about the consulship of 63 B.C., and he
could scarcely have done so without solicitation from the Greek
literary man. But Cicero, with his long experience in publishing oratory of a high literary finish, made his account as brilliant
as was within his power; and Posidonius wrote back that he had
no stomach for an elaboration. This, Cicero observes,[11] put an
end to the Greek insistence. It may be supposed that Posidonius
was unwilling to glorify Cicero and that his excuse was a pretext,
but this presupposes that Cicero had made the first advance, and
it ignores the fact that Cicero as a great Roman statesman was

---

[11] *Att.* 2, 1, 1–2.

infinitely higher in the social scale than any Greek, however learned, and that Cicero himself was one of the greatest literary men of all times; the works of Posidonius, despite all his contemporary reputation, were allowed to perish, whereas Cicero's extant works are voluminous. Cicero's Greek account of the consulship was published; he tells Atticus, in case he should approve of the book, to see that it is put on sale in Athens and other Greek cities. The account is lost, but it was probably used, at least indirectly, by Plutarch.

Of other Greek enthusiasts, Archias and Thyillus have already been mentioned. There was also a certain Herodes, who apparently wrote a letter to Cicero, and applied directly to Atticus in connection with an account that he had made, evidently wishing to read it to Cicero; and the latter informs Atticus that he would rather have been a conspirator himself than to have had to listen to Herodes. Probably the eager Herodes was no great literary light. Atticus, too, wrote an account. As a compliment from his friend, it pleased Cicero, but he found that it was an unadorned performance compared with his own. Atticus, indeed, had an excellent critical judgment, but his writings seem to have been concerned with the bare collection and recital of facts; he was timid, as Cicero wrote to Tiro,[12] and as his frequent political advice to Cicero indicates.

The account sent to Posidonius was written in 61 B.C. Before that time Cicero had despatched to Pompey the long letter about the year 63 B.C., which, as has already been remarked, was strongly in the nature of a political pamphlet. It is possible that this letter is referred to in a statement to Atticus,[13] in which Cicero promises to let him have an account of the consulship in Latin. If anything else is referred to, it has been lost, leaving no traces. In December of the year 60 B.C., however, Cicero had completed a Latin poem in three books on the same topic; and

---

[12] *Fam.* 16, 23, 2.
[13] *Att.* 1, 19, 10.

in 54 B.C. he completed another, also in three books, on which
he had been at work, off and on, since 56 B.C. It was concerned
with the period surrounding his exile, and seems to have been
entitled *De Temporibus Suis*, On His Times. As early as 59 B.C.
he had begun a historical work, which he refers to as *Anecdota*,
Secret Memoirs. Apparently he was still at work on it fifteen
years later; it was strongly polemical, after the fashion of the
Greek historian Theopompus, and revealed the inner machinations of the time. Atticus seems to have liked it, probably referring to it in 44 B.C., after Caesar's death, when he urged Cicero
to "collect all the crimes of his enemies" in a history. It was
not published during Cicero's lifetime; Dio informing us that
Cicero gave the book, sealed, to his son, with orders neither to
read it nor to publish it until after Cicero's death; it was too
outspoken in its criticisms of Crassus and Caesar. When published posthumously, very likely under the title *De Consiliis Suis*,
On Cicero's Plans or Political Attitude, it made a great stir.

This is a formidable list of autobiographical writings,[14]
though in the number of books, and probably in actual extent,
far from rivaling the twenty-two books of Sulla's autobiography,
and has caused many modern exclamations about vanity and
babblements. Cicero had of course the confidence in his own
powers that invariably accompanies genius, and he took the
delight in applause and praise that is equally inseparable from
the ability to sway great multitudes, whether it be by word or
by song or by acting. He knew this, and laughed about it with
Atticus. But his so-called vanity went no further. He had
done a great service to Rome; he had been made to suffer
through political terrorism and had been gloriously vindicated;
he was one of Rome's greatest men, and owed this to his own
ability and tireless efforts; and he was conscious of having performed unselfish public service. His contemporaries, except

---

14 On ancient autobiographies, see the excellent work of Misch. He has
a great deal about Cicero, for which see his Namenregister.

those who were his pronounced enemies, admitted this, and there
is no sign that any one of them thought that he wrote or spoke
too much about himself.

It is all a question of the Roman point of view. If the literary
situation in Rome has been adequately presented; with its
immense amount of eulogy, as well as of detraction, and with
the profound insignificance of the written word as compared with
the practical Roman life of battles, triumphs, public meetings,
money-getting, quarrels in the forum, hisses and applause in the
theatre, bribery, proscriptions, and bloodshed; then it will
scarcely be necessary to insist that Cicero's writings did not
shock his contemporaries. Atticus read these things, one after
the other, as they were finished, but even Atticus' caution and
sense of propriety found nothing to remark; rather he urged
Cicero on, both by writing an account of the consulship himself
and by his expectations in reference to the *Anecdota*. Cicero
sent his second poem, the one that embraced his exile, to Caesar
for criticism, while Caesar was fighting in Gaul; but he could
not conceivably have submitted to Caesar a piece of inordinate
self-assertion after openly admitting, in the palinode, that he
was now in the latter's political camp. Caesar, we find, criticised
it without comments on its propriety. And ten years after the
publication of the second poem, Cicero quoted poetical extracts
in his essay on Divination; a thing that he could not have done
if the poems, when published, had aroused hostile criticism from
any except those who would attack everything that Cicero did
and whom Cicero attacked similarly in his turn.

Indeed, these poems were to a considerable extent a part
of political life. When Cicero asked Quintus for Caesar's criticism, he wished to know not merely what Caesar, as a literary
friend, thought of the execution, but also what he thought of
the content; the latter request obviously referring to the political
attitude. Writing[15] in 54 B.C. to Lentulus, the consul of 57 B.C.,

---

[15] *Fam.*, 1, 9, 23.

who had made great exertions for Cicero's recall, Cicero mentions
the poem *On His Times*, hesitating about publishing it, less
because he has attacked his enemies, which he has done sparingly,
than because he may have failed to name all those to whom
he owes gratitude in the matter of his recall; considerations that
occur frequently in the orations after the exile. It is not necessary to gather further indications of the political character of
the poems. The manner in which they were viewed, however,
is indicated by another incident. Piso, the consul of 58 B.C. and
the one with the eloquent eyebrows, maintained[16] that Pompey
had been alienated from Cicero by the latter's statement, in the
poem on the consulship, that "arms had yielded to the toga";
a reference to the bloodless suppression of Catiline, which
Cicero's opponents tried to interpret as an assertion that Cicero
was greater than Pompey. Such attempts at creating ill feeling
between Cicero and Pompey, as has already been shown, were
common during these years.

If Cicero's friends meditated on his autobiographical writings they probably felt, not that he was indulging in too much
self-laudation, but that he as a consular lowered himself somewhat in thus putting himself on the level of scribbling Greeks
and self-confessed Roman devotees of a literary *otium*.

The mythological machinery, with gods in council and gods
as well as muses addressing Cicero, was used in these poems;
which recalls the *Aeneid* and several of the epics of the empire,
and would probably be found in the epics of such poets as
Archias, were they extant. Omens and supernatural events, such
as filled Roman public life and are found throughout Livy, were
also introduced; and, for a parallel, we know from Plutarch that
Sulla's *Memoirs* teemed with these things. They, like the kindly
muses, were obviously a part of the customary paraphernalia.
Nevertheless, Cicero looked upon these poems as historical in
character, and not eulogistic. And this was doubtless equally

---

16 *In Pison.* 72 ff.

the case with the works in prose. But it was the kind of history exemplified in Xenophon's account of Cyrus, which has less resemblance to a modern biography than to a historical novel. The *Cyropaedeia* of Xenophon is, indeed, compared by Cicero,[17] though not to its advantage, with the autobiography of Scaurus, consul in 115 B.C., who like Cicero had risen from humble beginnings; Scaurus' work was rather neglected in Cicero's day, but he considered it worthy of more attention.

A very full characterization of this kind of historical monograph is given by Cicero in a letter[18] to Lucceius, written in the year 56 B.C. Lucceius, an intimate friend, was at that time just finishing a history of the Social and civil wars, and had intentions of going on. Cicero, however, wished him to treat of the period from the year 63 B.C. through the return from exile in a separate monograph; there was no certainty, otherwise, when Lucceius would get to these years. The request is couched in the most formal and polite language, with references to poets, historians, and painters, and with numerous general observations; all of which, when we remember the friendship between the two men, marks it as largely a rhetorical exercise, not unlike a letter of the next year to another friend, Marius, on the subject of gladiatorial shows. Cicero was writing a composition on the customary historical monograph, though his desire for Lucceius' services was very genuine. The most pertinent statement is to the effect that Lucceius had said in his history, just as Livy later said, that he would not be influenced by favoritism, "no more, indeed, than Hercules had been influenced by Pleasure," but Cicero urges him not to scorn the voice of Friendship, if she should commend Cicero, and to yield somewhat more to affection than was in strict accord with truth. It might seem as if Cicero were asking Lucceius to manufacture historical fame; but it did not appear in that light to Lucceius

---

[17] *Brut.* 112.
[18] *Fam.* 5, 12. See Misch, 147 ff.

or to Cicero;[19] certainly not in a way to cause the latter to feel
ashamed.   Cicero thought that he had written a very excellent
letter; *valde bella est,* he writes a few days later to Atticus, advis-
ing him to get it from Lucceius and read it.   As for the historian
himself, he promised to comply with Cicero's request; he had
once appeared as the prosecutor of Catiline; but there is no
evidence to show that the monograph was written.   Probably it
was not, but this in no way disturbed the friendship between the
two men.

III

FOR ROME

There were, however, other literary possibilities than the
dilettante scribblings and the glorifications and apologies connected with the workaday world. These, from the larger point
of view, were ephemeral, and have perished almost entirely; and
the student of ancient times may feel with justice that he has
escaped at least as much as he has lost. The scribbling, once it
came into the hands of a master, produced real literature, and
we have Catullus; later still we have Horace and Vergil, and
a host of others, both small and great; but that happened when
Rome had become an empire and the attitude toward literary
creation had changed. The prose and poetry of this period more
or less directly subordinated to political needs—the biographies,
autobiographies, dialogues, or whatever they were—did not
deserve to live, and their place has been taken, for us, by the
letters and orations of Cicero, which were the direct expression
of his private and public life and had little or no connection
with literature. If the former productions had survived, we
should probably know very little more of any real value, but we
should possess countless products of a literary convention that
was on the whole perverted. All of which is true, of course, only

---

[19] A similar request is addressed to Cicero by Trebonius (*Fam.* 12, 16).

in its broader application. Caesar's *Commentaries*, for example, have survived, because of their intrinsic merit and the political 'and martial greatness of their author; some good things have undoubtedly been lost, and others, not very good, are still with us.

The same fate has overtaken the Greek productions of this period, and for the same reason. The Romans, in these works, largely imitated or emulated their Greek contemporaries, and these may have done better work, or it was at 'least easier for them to do so, particularly because they had a highly developed language; but the Greeks of this time, and for a considerable period preceding it, were pygmies, when placed side by side with their own early giants. They lived on their inheritance. They studied, explained, and taught, to each other and to the Romans, the great books that had come down to them; they combined, elaborated, twisted and straightened out again, the ideas of the great authors and thinkers of the fourth and the preceding centuries; but they added very little that was new, and they wrote no books comparable for originality or charm to the early literature. Their task in their relation to Rome was that of teaching, and they were good teachers, but the subject of their teaching was mainly the Greek past. The Romans were becoming coheirs with them, as it were; but, being Romans and not Greeks, they could not rest satisfied merely with this.

As scholars or investigators, the Romans turned to their own language and to their own past, trying to do for these what the Greeks had done and were still doing for theirs; in these efforts they often worked side by side with the Greeks, who indeed did nearly as much for Rome in this respect as the Romans themselves. The Romans also gave expression to one of their own peculiar gifts, in their writings on jurisprudence; and, as purely literary men, they added a new type, that of satire. But these productions, except the satire, were concerned. with material things, and had no literary value; the great books of literature, no less for the Roman than for his Greek contemporary, were still Greek, and the Latin language remained inadequate for expressing many of the thoughts that fashioned the lives of the educated Romans. If they had gone no farther, they would not have created anything much worth while, and they would not have become an essential link in the spiritual evolution that reaches from the great Greek period to modern times.

Roman patriotism, impatient of vassalage to Greece, here stepped in; and the Romans strove to emulate the early Greeks. In poetry and history this was not done until the age of Augustus. In oratory, however, it was accomplished by Cicero, for no one would even think of comparing him with a contemporary Greek orator; his Greek rival—some would say his superior, though that is debatable—was Demosthenes. In his writings on rhetoric Cicero surpassed his Greek predecessors, at least in so far as literary form is concerned; and in the field of political science, naturally an important subject in Rome, he created a body of literature that did for the Romans very much what Plato had done for the Greeks. His greatest service, from the historical point of view, however, was his contribution to philosophy. Varro said[20] that if the Romans wished to read philosophy, they could go to the Greek books, and that was true; but contentment with Varro's attitude would have meant a continuance of intellectual dependence. Philosophy, even if political science be excluded, though the philosophers claimed it for their own, formed, after all, the very texture of ancient thought. Cicero, with the originality and robustness of character that had already made him a leader in public life, rejected Varro's dictum; he transferred to Latin, and interpreted, the Greek philosophy of his time, which meant the philosophy since Aristotle; and he did it so well that the Greek philosophical writings of this period were allowed to drop into oblivion. In doing this, he made Latin into a new language; not single-handed, to be

[20] *Ac. Post.* 4.

sure, for we need only remember Lucretius; but it was nevertheless Cicero who created the instrument which Seneca and later writers used.

These statements need modification for perfect exactness; he did both more and less than has been indicated; but they define the spirit in which he worked and roughly describe his accomplishment. He by no means began with a complete plan; he moved from one thing to another, yielding to various influences; and he also made plans that were never carried out. He thought of writing a Roman history; and some students, with the letter to Lucceius in mind and other similar expressions referring to historical writing, have dismissed him as incapable. Cornelius Nepos regretted that Cicero did not become a historian. It may be said that Cicero's view of history was that of nearly all ancient historians. To them it was a part of literature; its chief aim was to give aesthetic pleasure and moral teaching. This is the ideal that inspired Livy, who himself chose Cicero for his model in many things; and it is worth remembering that Livy had no experience in public life, whereas Cicero had had more experience than perhaps any Greek or Roman historian. But all this is speculation, useful only as indicating Cicero's energy and wide interests.

Given Cicero's genius and capacity for hard work, the extent and variety of his results should cause no surprise. If rhetorical training and practise in the forum accomplished nothing else, it gave fluency in speaking and writing; and Cicero had this to an extraordinary degree. He was a complete master of the Latin language before he began his first long essay. As for the content, it was already very largely a part of his acquisition; he made some investigations about details and he applied his own mature point of view, most extensively in connection with rhetoric and least with certain parts of philosophy, but his task was in the main that of the literary worker: what he did not know already, he found in books.

Cicero did not turn to this kind of writing quickly. In
59 B.C., during the detested consulship of Julius and Caesar, he
was still fumbling about for a literary distraction, and found
little comfort in geography. The change came after Luca, when
he was fifty years old. He began with rhetoric, in the *De
Oratore;* perhaps prompted by Quintus, as he tells us in the
preface. But he did not give all his leisure time to such authorship even after he had begun it. In 54 B.C., the year after the
De Oratore was finished, he wrote an epic poem about Caesar's
expedition to Britain; it was one of the courteuos acts between
two literary friends as well as a public sign of their friendship.
This poem is lost; not a fragment remains; but the loss can
not have been serious, for Quintus supplied the local color,
and Marcus was often interrupted, which was unfavorable to
the inspired mood. In later years, too, Cicero took part in
pamphleteering activities, and he continued publishing his
orations.

But while engaged on the essays—and he gave more and
more of his leisure to them as the years went by—he experienced
a greater satisfaction than he could procure from anything else.
They were of a more permanent nature and could seem like a
real service to Rome, and at the same time they were far removed
in spirit from the toppling republic. Cicero returned, in them,
to the studies and enthusiasms of his hopeful youth and early
manhood, and carried these studies farther; he was concerned
with greater questions than personal success or failure, and
at times, chiefly in the later years, he was able to view his whole
life from a larger point of view than that of a Roman.

Nevertheless Rome was always near. His literary occupation,
however congenial and inspiring, did not satisfy his most insistent craving for honorable public activity, and it offered no
remedy for the fallen republic. It was only an anodyne. During
the first years he disguised this fact and pretended to be satisfied, revealing the truth only to Quintus, and not even to him

except for a moment; but later, when private sorrows as well as public disappointment drove him to writing, he says to Atticus that he was the first to write for his own consolation. Though this statement[21] refers to a little book technically styled *Consolation,* it is applicable in a wider sense.

Cicero's Roman friends were surprised, as time went on, at his preoccupation with rhetoric and philosophy. Others had written a little on either subject, but neither should be the serious occupation of a consular. Cicero answers their criticisms. In the *Orator,*[22] published in 46 B.C. and addressed to Brutus, he proclaims it as proper for a man in his position to write a good deal on the art of oratory, provided he does not do it in the spirit of an ordinary teacher, but in the way of friendly advice and encouragement. After giving this and various other good reasons for authorship, he concludes by urging that, since he has nothing to do in the forum, he ought not to be criticised for writing. In the next year, when he was busy with philosophy, he answered his friends again, in the preface to the *Academica.*[23] Here, too, he gives several reasons for his activity, sufficient, and indeed quite superfluous, from the modern point of view; but his last words are these: "I see nothing else that I can do."

---

[21] *Att.* 12, 14, 3.
[22] *Or.* 140–148.
[23] *Ac. Post.* 11.

CHAPTER XII

RHETORIC

I

THE WORKS

It was natural that Cicero should begin his more ambitious literary productions with a treatise on rhetoric. He had long been recognized as the leading orator of Rome. Like all conscious artists, he was interested in the theory of his art as well as in its practise; an interest, however, that was shared to an almost incredible degree by his contemporaries. Oratory, having been his chief political weapon, had received his most constant and passionate attention; throughout his intellectual development, except for a little while in his youth when it seemed that there would be no opportunity in Rome for a political career, it had been, as it were, the subject toward which all his other studies were made to contribute, so that an exposition of his oratorical ideal would be almost a statement of his intellectual ideal, and his own work on the subject would take him back through all his former thoughts and plans. He would live his life again. Rhetorical writing was also in a measure a practical thing, something in which he could feel that he was serving Rome. His third treatise, the *Orator,* was not intended for young men, so he wrote to a friend,[1] but even so it might be useful to the latter's son, if only to accustom his ears to good Latin. Rhetorical authorship, if not carried to excess, was not altogether unworthy of a consular; M. Antonius, Cicero's great exemplar, had set a precedent. The teaching of oratory, furthermore, was the means by which the Greeks, whether rhetoricians or philosophers, contributed most directly to Roman practical ends; to do

---

[1] *Fam.* 6, 18, 4.

in Latin what the Greeks had for centuries been doing in Greek, and had thereupon sold to the Romans, would be a step toward the intellectual emancipation of Rome. Cicero might hope to do it better,[2] or at least from a saner point of view, because of his practical experience; few of the Greek writers or teachers of rhetoric were orators, none of them rivaling Cicero.

Whether oratory, with its obvious dependence on native talent, could be taught at all, was to be sure a matter for philosophical discussion; but while the question was being debated by students, and perhaps by a few somewhat indolent gentlemen like Quintus,[3] the teaching continued without interruption. It was almost entirely in the hands of the Greeks. Some Romans were beginning to offer instruction in Latin, and naturally received many pupils, for it was, after all, ridiculous that young men who expected to speak in the forum should receive all their theory and practise of oratory in Greek, but the Latin rhetoricians were not highly favored by men of prominence. Crassus, in his censorship in 92 B.C., closed the Latin rhetorical schools, his reason being that the Latin teachers did not know their subject.

Their schools were schools of impudence, Crassus is represented as saying in the *De Oratore*.[4] This may indicate, as has been conjectured, that the Roman rhetoricians, though incompetent, made large claims as to practical usefulness. Possibly the subjects of their declamations were taken from the forum, thus arousing in the pupils a feeling that they were doing real things, declaiming in a way that was significant as a contribution to political questions. This is by no means certain. The oratorical exercises contained in the Latin books of the next century are as remote from actual political life as the Greek; nor does the work dedicated to Herennius, presently to be mentioned, indicate such a procedure. Whatever the methods of instruction, the

---

[2] *De Or.* 1, 23.

[3] *De Or.* 1, 5.

[4] *De Or.* 3, 93–95.

Roman rhetorician was not as yet nearly so prosperous as his Greek rival, though his time was coming. The theory of rhetoric, however, was already being set forth in Latin. The extant example of this is the treatise in four books addressed to a certain Herennius, which was certainly composed during Cicero's youth.

Cicero had wanted to attend rhetorical instruction in Latin as well as in Greek, but was deterred by Crassus, so that all Cicero's training under teachers of rhetoric was in Greek. Despite its obvious drawbacks, this method had substantial advantages: the teachers knew more and were pedagogically more capable, and the literature of Greece, oratorical and otherwise, as well as the Greek language itself, had reached a far higher state of excellence than the Latin. "By declaiming in Greek," Cicero said, "the student acquires many things that can be transferred to Latin."

Cicero was throughout life interested in rhetoric. He practised declamation, for his own benefit, until he was forty, and late in life he directed his young friends in it. As for the theory, parts of which he considered too abstruse for practical application, he found it pleasant to know; it was, after all, a whole system of education, hallowed by centuries, and he thought the learning of it a good discipline for the young. Indeed, as regards the young, he approved sufficiently of the whole rhetorical system, theory as well as practise, to have his own and his brother's son receive the traditional instruction, explaining to Quintus that this was what he himself had received and that its objectionable effects could be eliminated by Cicero himself when he should find leisure to take the boys in hand.

He also wrote on rhetoric. His works are of two kinds, entirely different both in form and in content. One group sets forth rhetorical theory, and contains three works. The first of these is the early *Libri Rhetorici*, Books on Rhetoric, or *De Inventione*, Invention. It was the direct outcome of his interest as a student. His intention, never carried out, seems to have been to give a complete account of rhetoric like that in the work addressed to Herennius. In character it is of a piece with the ordinary works on rhetoric, setting forth the theory with its almost innumerable classifications, carefully defining and illustrating everything. Cicero's avowed claim to originality is that he is not following any other rhetorician, meaning of course that he is not translating or adapting a Greek author, but that he has read the authorities, and is giving the essence of the whole matter. He modestly compares his method to that of the painter Zeuxis when the latter was making a picture, necessarily imaginary, of Helen. The painter asked the people of Crotona, his employers, to bring him their most beautiful girls for models. The Crotonians, moral beyond all others, brought their most beautiful boys, at which Zeuxis said: "But these boys surely have sisters." The handsome sisters were thereupon brought, after the authorities had taken a vote on the question; and Zeuxis chose five of them, from whose combined charms he created his famous picture.

Cicero's work has no other resemblance to Zeuxis' Helen than the asserted variety of its sources. What use he made of these can not be determined, since they are lost. Probably he worked very much according to the method of a modern student writing an expository account of an intricate subject that has been much discussed. The work is clear and systematic, but hardly attractive except to students interested in rhetorical theory. As such, it was much read and praised by later generations. It contains a discussion of the importance of oratory, and thereupon takes up the subject in detail. But the two books of which it consists do not get beyond *inventio,* the first division of rhetoric. If the work had been completed, it would have been a very illuminating exposition of rhetoric as taught during Cicero's youth. Probably Cicero never finished it. In later life, as has already been mentioned, he regretted that he had allowed its publication; it seemed too youthful.

The other two works of the same group as the *De Inventione*
are very short, and were written many years later. One, the
Topica, treats of the theory of Topics so-called, an intricate and
difficult part of rhetoric. Its difficulty was the reason for Cicero's
exposition. While visiting Cicero, Trebatius, a friend, had happened upon a work on the subject by Aristotle. He borrowed the
book, but was unable to understand it. He then applied to a
famous rhetorician, but the latter knew nothing about the matter; a circumstance by no means surprising to Cicero, who said
that even the philosophers, with few exceptions, were equally
ignorant. At Trebatius' request, therefore, Cicero undertook
to write a brief account of Aristotelian Topics whenever he had
leisure, and he actually did this, according to his preface to
the book, while traveling by boat. Being away from his books,
he wrote from memory. The exposition is not much like the
theory as found in Aristotle; probably it represents the contemporary teaching that went under Aristotle's name.[5] Like
the former rhetorical work, it consists entirely of classifications
and definitions. The *Topica* was written in 44 B.C.

The third work, of uncertain date, but probably written
shortly after 54 B.C., is the *Partitiones Oratoriae,* Oratorical
Divisions. In 54 Cicero's son Marcus and his nephew Quintus
were receiving instruction from a Greek rhetorician, whom the
boys liked but of whom Cicero did not quite approve. He therefore writes to the elder Quintus that he will try to do something
for them; and this work may be one result of Cicero's promise.

It is a complete account, brief and with extremely few illustrations, of rhetorical theory. The form is that of a dialogue
between Cicero and his son, the former answering the latter's
questions. It is thus a rhetorical catechism, obviously intended
to teach young Marcus, and probably his cousin, the theory and
technical language of rhetoric. In the preface Cicero says that

---

[5] See Laurand, *De M. Tulli etc.,* pp. 35 ff. and notes. See also below,
pp. 377–378.

he had been in the habit of questioning his son in this way in Greek; now Marcus may question him in Latin. Marcus shows a very commendable eagerness to profit by his opportunity, but our knowledge of the young man makes this eagerness seem at least doubtful, particularly in the light of the difficulty and intricacy of the subject. The little book was apparently intended merely as a help to Marcus and perhaps to a few young friends, the old Romans often having written their children's textbooks. It is not mentioned by Cicero in his other works and may not have been published by him. Though possibly founded directly on an Academic work on rhetoric, it may be more independent, being the result of Cicero's own knowledge of rhetorical theory; but it certainly is not intended to set forth any new views.

The other group of Cicero's rhetorical works does set forth new views, or rather expresses Cicero's mature opinions about oratory without any intention of making additions to rhetorical theory. Taking for granted that the reader knows this theory and has received the customary training, Cicero discusses the subject from the point of view of the successful orator, as distinguished from that of the teacher of rhetoric.

In the *De Oratore,* the first and most important of these works, he describes the education that he considers necessary for the orator, and also discusses the theory and the declamatory exercises of rhetorical teaching. The work is therefore not a textbook, to take the place of those already in use; it is critical in intent, condemning some practises of the schools and praising others, and it is above all constructive, in that it puts before the reader the ideal toward which he ought to aim after he has gone through the regular training. Being the outcome of Cicero's own experience and of his thinking about the subject, it contains numerous suggestions that might help the reader both in his further study of rhetoric and in his actual practise of oratory.

The *Brutus,* the second of these works, is a history of Roman
oratory. It discusses the individual orators, taking them in
chronological order and grouping them into oratorical periods;
and shows how public speaking in Rome had developed gradually until it reached its climax at the time of Cicero—indeed, in
Cicero himself. As the criterion used in criticising the individual orators is the ideal set forth in the *De Oratore,* this
treatise, aside from its historical character, becomes an attempt
to justify Cicero's own views by showing how the historical
development of oratory had constantly tended toward Cicero's
ideal.

In the *Orator,* the third work in this group, Cicero portrays
the ideal orator. In the *De Oratore* he had described the orator's
ideal education and training; in the *Brutus* he had criticised
the whole list of orators in the light of his ideal requirements;
in the *Orator* he gives a picture of his ideal orator, what he is
and what he can do. This work has therefore mainly the same
content as the *De Oratore,* but differently expressed. Both the
Brutus and the *Orator,* furthermore, contain a polemical element,
which need not be discussed here, but which adds something to
the previous theory and introduces a new emphasis.

In addition to these two well-defined groups there are extant
two bits of rhetorical writing, very brief and in themselves very
unimportant. They illustrate, however, Cicero's continued interest in the subject and are rather pleasant reading. Cicero had
intended to publish a translation of Demosthenes' oration *On the
Crown* and Aeschines' oration *Against Ctesipho,* which would
indicate what the best Attic oratory had been, and, consequently,
what Roman oratory should be. It is uncertain whether he made
the translation; he almost certainly never published it. But
he wrote a brief preface for the intended translation, and this
is extant under the name *De Optimo Genere Oratorum,* On the
Best Kind of Oratory. Being a part of the polemic already
mentioned, it need not be further discussed here. It indicates,

however, another way—that of comparison with recognized oratorical classics—in which Cicero defended his oratorical ideal. Apparently it belongs in or near the year 46 B.C., when the *Brutus* and the *Orator* were published.

In 46 B.C. the other work, the *Paradoxa,* Paradoxes, was also composed. It is merely an incidental result of Cicero's preoccupation with oratory. Generalizations of various kinds were constantly introduced into all sorts of speeches. Cato, whose correct Stoicism met with scant popular favor, was in the habit of enlivening his orations, or weighting them, with meditations on such subjects as death, morality, and patriotism. Now Cicero, as he says in his preface addressed to Cato's nephew, Brutus, had in mind to discover just how far this sort of thing was possible. It was merely a playful exercise, the result of oratorical inquisitiveness, so to speak, and was not intended to furnish matter for the forum. Cato had confined himself to thoughts of a general application. Cicero, on the other hand, puts into oratorical form six of the famous Stoic paradoxes: that which is honorable is alone good for a man; virtue is sufficient for a happy life; every fool is insane—and others. The very perversity of these assertions offered excellent practise to the orator, for the latter's business is, among other things, to make the incredible seem credible and to express interestingly that which is dry.

II

THEORY

Rhetorical theory,[6] as it can be gathered from the first group of Cicero's rhetorical works and from similar expositions, is dry almost beyond alleviation; much of it is incredible as a means for creating actual oratory fit for the forum; and it is

---

[6] For this and the following section I have made use of the books and articles on rhetoric mentioned in the bibliography, but my account is founded directly on the ancient authorities, particularly Cicero's *Partitiones* and *De Oratore.*

not always easy to understand. The books in which it is set forth, as has already been indicated, contain little else than classifications, definitions, and illustrations. The whole theory is the result of centuries of study, during which many scholars, whether philosophers or rhetoricians, seem often to have lost sight of their only proper aim—oratory—and to have expended an almost tireless ingenuity in redistributing and redefining the old material, sometimes improving, no doubt, on the logic of the system, but quite as often making the confusion only more pronounced.

It will nevertheless be necessary to attempt to give some sort of an idea of it. It is not merely that Cicero was trained in it for years, kept his interest in it, and wrote about it; nearly all the educated Romans of his time received a similar training and shared his interest. Indeed, the method pursued by the rhetoricians was largely adopted in the lower grades of instruction and it also reached up into the sphere of the philosophers, so that it contains within it practically the whole pedagogical theory followed by the ancient Greeks and Romans; the aim being always to give the student an oratorical style, literary, we might say, and the ability to make the most of his case. Furthermore, as has just been indicated, the rhetorical works of the second group, interesting, significant, and frequently read, take a knowledge of the theory for granted; without such knowledge they can be only half comprehended, nor can the reader appreciate the wonderful skill with which Cicero managed to treat this intractable subject.

The system is not entirely devoid of interest. Being avowedly founded on public speaking, it contains many shrewd comments, naively enough expressed, on human nature as it had been observed among ancient jurors and audiences; and it furnishes a useful commentary on Cicero's orations. Students are constantly told to do the very things for which he has frequently been criticised.

But it is a monstrously difficult theory, as involved as mediaeval theology. Poor Marcus and the other little Romans probably never understood why the word for game, *ludus,* also meant school.

Roughly stated, there are two things to which the orator must attend in preparing his speech, namely, the thought and the expression. These, though theoretically distinct, are frequently fused in practise. Certain thoughts are included in an oration merely because they offer an opportunity for effective expression; and it is true, generally, that we think in words. The distinction nevertheless remains. In the *De Oratore,* which is not arranged with an uninspired observance of rhetorical system, Cicero groups his material with a regard for this distinction; and it is the basis of the *Oratorical Divisions.* All matters of expression were grouped by the rhetoricians under *elocutio,* Style; the rest belonged to the so-called *inventio* and *collocatio.*

Inventio means discovery or finding. As the word might apply to the finding of the proper vocabulary quite as readily as to the finding of the proper thoughts, the rhetorician said that it was concerned with words and things, *verba* and *res;* but it was in practise restricted to the latter. The term itself is significant. The student, having received from his instructor the subject of a discourse, must decide what effect he should aim at, and thereupon choose or find his material accordingly. *Inventio* taught him how to do this.

Besides finding his material, the student must know how to arrange it effectively. This is taught in *collocatio,* Arrangement. Like the term *inventio,* the word *collocatio* may refer to words as well as things, but as a technical part of rhetoric it is limited to the content of a speech. A speech naturally has a beginning, a middle, and an end. The middle, which is by far the most important part of a speech, was divided into two or more parts. If two, these were called the Narrative and the Argumentation.

Rhetorical theory in reference to the composition of an oration thus consists of three divisions: *inventio, collocatio,* and *elocutio.* But as the student was instructed in delivery as well, there is a fourth part, *actio* or *pronuntiatio,* Delivery, which had to do with the management of the voice, facial expression, and gesture. But since these matters could be taught only orally, very little was written about them. As students, furthermore, were trained in memorizing[7] as well as in a science of mnemonics, *memoria,* Memory, was sometimes added as a fifth part of rhetoric. Real rhetoric, however, in so far as it was a scientific subject, consisted of the three divisions first mentioned.

But theory without practise is much like faith without works, a truth thoroughly grasped by the teachers of rhetoric despite occasional lapses into pedantry. A large part of their teaching, possibly the greater part when the student had attained a fair amount of adroitness, consisted in the writing and reciting of speeches, and even in extemporaneous speaking. It will therefore accord tolerably well with the ancient pedagogical method and it will also be least obscure, first to give some general conception of rhetorical theory as it falls under its three large divisions, and then to indicate briefly how this doctrine was applied to actual speech making. There is no order of presentation possible which will keep together all the details that belong together. The fields themselves overlap even when viewed merely from a theoretical point of view, and when the actual composition of a speech is considered, all the fields work together. The order proposed is to a considerable extent the one used by Cicero in outlining rhetoric for his son Marcus in the *Oratorical Divisions,* and even slight experimentation will show that Cicero's arrangement of an expostion is usually the best. But as he wrote for Marcus, who already had a Greek acquaintance with rhetoric, some changes will be necessary.

---

[7] See *Ad Herennium,* 3, chaps. 16–24, for an interesting account.

Invention, being concerned with the subject matter of a speech, undertook to give the student both general and detailed guidance. Like the rest of rhetoric, it had to do mainly with oratory in the courts, which was considered the most difficult. It showed him how to determine the main issue in the case presented to him; guided him toward a clear understanding of the aim he must pursue in order to secure a favorable verdict; gave rules as to the proper appraisal of the known facts by pointing out, among other things, their relative importance for the prosecution and for the defense; it informed him how to make use of testimony and how to treat the witnesses; and, in addition, it trained him generally in adroitness of presentation.

Adroitness of presentation, which is not a phrase from ancient rhetoric, is intended to cover a multitude of devices. Thus, in the famous case of Norbanus, which has already been cited, Norbanus was accused of high treason for taking part in a riot. The riot had occurred in connection with the trial of Caepio, who by insubordination had caused the Roman army to suffer a defeat in Gaul, and who had been brought to trial by Norbanus. Now, to commit high treason is, according to Latin phraseology, to diminish the majesty of the Roman people. The orator for the defense might therefore say that if the majesty of the Roman people is its grandeur and dignity, he diminishes it who surrenders a Roman army to the enemy, as Caepio had done, and not he who hands over to the Romans for trial the man who has so surrendered a Roman army—as Norbanus had done when he took part in the riot. In other words, a proper definition of the term high treason shows that Caepio was guilty of this offence, but not Norbanus. In speaking like this, the orator, as the rhetoricians put it, argued from the definition of a word.

In the same way, an orator was said to argue from things similar if he said that, inasmuch as wild beasts love their young, human beings ought to be even more devoted to their children; and from things dissimilar: while barbarians live with no

thought of the morrow, civilized man ought to lay his plans with
a view to eternity; and from a comparison, thus: if good repute
is better than riches, and if riches are considered highly desirable,
then fame is even more to be desired.

In these examples the orator's arguments were drawn from
a definition, from similars, and dissimilars. Other considerations
from which they might be drawn are genus, species, whole, part,
cause, effect, disparates, contraries, relates, privatives, contra-
dictories, greater, less, and equals. These considerations were
called *loci*, Places, or Topics, from the Greek word for place;
the doctrine concerned with them was named Topica. The list
of Topics varies not only with different writers on rhetoric, but
even within the works of Cicero. The whole subject was exceedingly obscure, and it was for this reason that Cicero wrote his
short *Topica* for Trebatius. The list of Topics there expounded,
called Aristotelian, includes those given above and a few others,
and is practically the one that Cicero gives in the *Oratorical
Divisions* and in other works. But there are slight variations,
doubtless due to the fact that these topical lists were frequently
modified by teachers of rhetoric. Cicero had no ambition to
add to rhetorical theory, but the professional teacher had,[8] and
Cicero, as a student, probably became familiar with more than
one list. Whatever the details, these lists gave logical training
to the student. Cicero considered them very helpful to an orator,
provided he had mastered them thoroughly, by means of constant
practise, and displayed good sense in applying them.

The above Topics were perhaps called Aristotelian because,
like those still found in Aristotle's works, they had to do with
the consideration of a case in the abstract. They might be used
anywhere.

But the rhetoricians, in their eagerness to supply their pupils
with more detailed help, drew up lists of Topics that applied to
the concrete phases of a case as well. They might be something
like this: as to the persons concerned—his name, sex, nationality,

---

[8] *Ad Herennium, passim.*

age, education, teachers, friends, property, social position, and numerous other kindred matters; and as to the deed under consideration—the place where it was alleged to have happened, the time, the means by which it was accomplished, its motive, and a great deal more. These Topics, concrete as distinguished from the abstract, are mentioned by Cicero in his early work on Invention, but he thought poorly of them in later life. He found them too numerous for easy memorizing, and, in any case, too obvious to be of much help. Cicero's attitude, though doubtless founded largely on his own experience, was the attitude of the philosophers who taught rhetoric, while the opposite view was held by the professional rhetoricians.

The word Topic—or rather, *locus,* its Latin equivalent—is constantly used by Cicero in his rhetorical works. Topic is the seat of an argument, the place in which the student can find a proof or a thought. If there are fifteen ways of arousing anger, these fifteen ways might be called the Topics of anger; and are so called in Cicero's *Invention.* In the same way almost any suggestion contained in the theory of Invention was a Topic, so that Invention, which shows the pupil where he can find his material, does so by indicating Topics. *Topica,* the theory of Topics, is thus, largely speaking, the same as *inventio;* technically, however, and as used by Cicero, it has to do with the abstract Aristotelian Topics.

This brief and incomplete discussion of Topics has been introduced here because it is so thoroughly characteristic of the whole ancient rhetorical attitude, indicating exactly the manner in which the teacher attempted, in Invention, to assist his student in thinking. It is, furthermore, of so general an application that it can not be readily considered in connection with the actual composition of speeches. The other parts of Invention can, however, he treated there most profitably.

The question of Style, *elocutio,* is so largely a matter of language that only a few general observations can me made without detailed reference to Latin. The acquisition of a good style was considered of supreme importance. It was the object of nearly all the instruction that the Roman boy received before he came under the teachers of rhetoric, and these, in their turn, gave much attention to it. A large part of rhetorical theory, as seen in the extant textbooks, was concerned with stylistic matters of many kinds. The rules given, like those of modern rhetoric, though to an even higher degree, may seem pedantic and useless; they contain, however, some hints about the method pursued.

Instruction in Style consisted in the critical study of classical authors—orators and historians under the rhetoricians, and poets under the teachers that preceded the rhetoricians—and in composition. It was therefore much like our instruction in rhetoric and composition, including training in the ordinary stylistic devices, such as the use of figurative language, in numerous subdivisions, the repetition of words, and the proper use of conjunctions. Considerable attention was given to word order, an extremely important matter to the Roman boy, since Latin allows almost any arrangement; and to the acquisition of a vocabulary.

In connection with the latter there is one circumstance particularly noteworthy. Latin words, the Roman boy was told, are the result either of natural growth or of conscious formation. This distinction, of no practical stylistic importance in such a language as English, is a reflection of the fact that Latin was still largely in the making, so that it was no doubt a frequent duty of the orator, as of the literary artist in other fields, actually to coin his own words. Such words, as Cicero tells Marcus in the *Oratorical Divisions,* may be formed according to the laws operative in Latin, that is, a new abstract noun may be made from an old adjective in the way that similar nouns had already come into existence; they may be imitated from the Greek; they may be Greek words inflected according to Latin accidence; or they may be compounds of two Latin words. All of these methods, except the first, show the influence of Greek, for even the formation of compounds was often in direct imitation of a process natural to the Greeks, but never fully accepted by the Romans. The Latin vocabulary was thus being constantly increased, more or less according to methods characteristic of the Greek, and the question of old words and new had a peculiar significance.

Perhaps it is not unreasonable to imagine that the Roman boy received instruction in the formation of new words. Most of the rhetorical teaching in Rome—all that Cicero received—was in the hands of Greek teachers, but, though these knew little or no Latin, they may well have suggested methods of word formation. As they apparently were none too modest, their very ignorance of Latin may have made them only the more willing to formulate rules; to them, Latin could always be improved by imitating Greek.

However that may be, Latin was at this time growing very fast; whole fields of thought, like rhetoric and philosophy, were for the first time finding expression in Latin; so that the question of vocabulary was far more important to the Roman orator than it would be to a modern writer. Cicero himself did perhaps more than any other one man to enrich Latin in this very respect.

The study of vocabulary as well as of everything else connected with style aimed not merely at correctness, clearness, precision, and similar matters, with which the modern prose writer is mainly concerned, but also at rhythm and musical effects. This was not a casual search for grace, a thing to be decided by an uninstructed feeling for sound; it was as complex as the question of sound and rhythm in verse. Prose, according to the current teaching, must be like verse, and yet unlike it. The balance of phrases and clauses; their just length; the making of the long period, ending with suitable metrical combinations and divided by pauses that would contribute to the clearness of its contents and also enable the speaker's voice to have its full effect without danger of straining or breathlessness; the avoidance of hiatus and other harsh combinations—all these were matters for careful training.

It is probably no overstatement to say that rhythmical and musical effects were as important, or nearly as important, to the ancient orator as they are to the musician.[9] Latin, like Greek, was not a language of sharp accents, but of well regulated long and short syllables rigidly observed. The Romans were exceedingly sensitive on this point. If an actor dragged or clipped a syllable, the whole audience shouted with disgust; and yet the theatrical audiences in Rome were very large and consisted almost exclusively of uneducated citizens. They did not know, as Cicero said,[10] what was wrong, or why; they had no knowledge of rhythm; but they were offended by the slightest failure to observe the proper quantity. And it was the same with the actual sounds of the words and the inflection of the voice.

The whole subject, however, is rather foreign to modern English; it is certainly not conscious enough with us to be reduced to stylistic rules. Our use of alliteration, anaphora, and other musical means, which were employed and much discussed by the ancients, scarcely touches the matter. The reader of English can perhaps most easily get some impression of it from the renderings of the *Psalms* and similar works in the *Old Testament;* the Hebrew parallelism and the delicate sense for sound on the part of the English translators have produced a similar effect. But Latin oratorical prose, as seen in Cicero, is far more varied and subtle than this English.

The attention to sound and rhythm is indicative of the care with which the orator endeavored, and was taught to endeavor, to please his audience. Another indication is the surprising

---

[9] Norden, *Die Antike Kunstprosa,* 1, 212 ff.; Laurand, *Études etc.,* pp. 107–213; Clark.

[10] *De Or.* 3, 196.

statement in the *Oratorical Divisions* about the stylistic quality
of clearness. It is divided into two kinds. There is the ordinary
clearness, addressed to the intellect, the thing that any person
would aim at merely for the sake of being understood; and there
is a heightened degree of it, brilliance or lustrousness, which, in
Cicero's words, puts the thing spoken of before the very eyes
of the listener. These two kinds of clearness are given as separate stylistic qualities, but Cicero remarks that all the characteristics of the former are to be found in the latter.

This appeal to the aesthetic or emotional side of the audience
was considered highly important. It is reflected in the customary list of qualities that a good style should possess. As given
in the *De Oratore,* this list contains correctness and clearness,
which are to be acquired in boyhood, and which are necessary, though of no positive value; and literary distinction, and
appropriateness. The last quality is of varied application, but
has always for aim the proper impression on the audience.
Literary distinction, an approximate rendering of the untrans-
latable adverb *ornate,* is called sweetness or grace in the
Oratorical Divisions. It has nothing, or should have nothing,
to do with purple patches—the quality of appropriateness would
guard against them—but indicates everything that gives aesthetic
pleasure or appeals to the emotions. And so, going beyond the
sphere of mere language as opposed to thought, the rhetorician
can say that this quality is also to be attained by the mention
of things strange and remarkable. Drawing his method from
public life, he frankly recognized that the aim of oratory is
twofold: it must convince the audience, but it must also please
them and move them. And throughout his system he kept
these two points of view before his pupils.[11]

Arrangement—*collocatio, dispositio*—teaches the orator how
to distribute his material, and to that end divides the oration

[11] They were sometimes expressed as three; see below, p. 440, note 51.

into four or more parts. Like Invention, it is concerned mainly
with speeches in court. These, according to the theory of
Arrangement, must have at least four parts: the Introduction or
Exordium, *initium, principium, exordium;* the Narration, *nar-
ratio;* the Argumentation, *confirmatio;* and the Conclusion or
Peroration, *conclusio* or *peroratio.* The twofold appeal that the
orator must make to his audience serves as the basis for characterizing these divisions. The Argumentation is, of course,
directed primarily to the intellect. The Narrative, which precedes this and supplies the facts from which the arguments are
to be drawn, is thus also addressed to the intellect. The other
two parts have to do with the emotions of the audience. By
means of the Exordium the orator must secure a favorable
hearing for his speech, must get into proper relations with his
audience; whereas in the Peroration he must so stir them that
they give the desired verdict. Obviously the emotions may be
appealed to in the course of the Narrative and the Argumentation, and the listener's judgment must not be ignored in the
course of the Exordium or the Peroration, but the distinction
nevertheless is true in the main.

The fourfold division of the speech suggests everything
essential and really helpful, and is the one most frequently used
by Cicero. But he was no doctrinaire on the subject, and considered the addition or omission of other parts a matter for
personal preference. Thus the Argumentation is called *confirmatio,* which means merely confirmation or the proving of
your own view. Another part of the Argumentation consists
in refuting the opponent's arguments, and was therefore called
refutatio or *reprehensio;* and the two might be considered independent parts of the speech. A sixth part was created by giving
a name, *partitio,* to a passage frequently beginning the argumentation, which enumerated the proofs that were to follow,
and so indicated the parts, as it were, of the most important
sections of the speech. As a seventh part, finally, was often

counted a digression of almost any kind; and as these frequently occurred at the end of the Narrative, Digression as a division, if counted at all, was placed here.

In connection with the study of Arrangement, the teacher could suggest both the thoughts and the style suitable for the different parts of a speech, thus borrowing from Invention and Style. Cicero does this in the *Oratorical Divisions,* but, before discussing the different parts of the speech, he mentions the so-called Amplification, *amplificatio.* As the name indicates, this was a device by which the orator dwelt on a certain thought, enforcing it, and so bringing it home to the audience. It is very efficient in the way of persuasion, Cicero says, and may be called a kind of vehement proof. An Amplification is most natural in the Peroration, when the orator makes his final appeal, but it may also be used in any other part of the oration. From the point of view of rhetorical theory as a whole, the elaboration of such a device is another, and a very significant, recognition of the fact that the orator must endeavor to stir the emotions.

These Amplifications would most naturally be generalizations on a well-known subject, such as patriotism, the love of kindred, the wickedness of murder, and the wretchedness of exile. In the language of Invention, patriotism would be a Topic or Place, since it contained a thought or argument; and as thoughts of the kind indicated might be used in connection with any trial, these generalizations were called Commonplaces, *loci communes.* Perhaps nothing is better known in the whole field of rhetoric, and certainly nothing is more characteristic of the literary manner of the ancients, both in and out of rhetoric, than these Commonplaces. They are found everywhere, not merely in oratory but in history, poetry, and philosophy. Students were trained in composing them, and seem to have carried their training into every field of literary activity.

Commonplaces suitable for various purposes and the advice as to the style to be employed in them will be given later, but it may be useful here to note the brief classification of them that Cicero inserts in the *De Oratore*.[12] Some, he says, contain an attack against a clearly recognized vice, such as theft, treachery, and parricide; others contain a plea for mercy, and move the audience to pity; and still others are arguments on one side or another of some abstract question, as: Is rumor to be believed or not? It is obvious that Commonplaces would be much practised by the philosophers who taught rhetoric, for they were concerned with the interpretation of life, with which all these things would be connected. Especially was that the case with the arguments about abstract truths, since philosophical efficiency, in the eyes of the Academics and Peripatetics, may be said to have consisted largely in the ability to argue on both sides of a question.

As for the rhetorical directions in reference to the different parts of the speech, they are stated most briefly in the *Oratorical Divisions*. The account of Argumentation, however, will be treated later. It contains an elaborate theory about the methods to be employed in different sorts of cases, and is really a subject by itself.

The Exordium, as already defined, is intended to secure a hearing for the rest of the speech. Such a hearing, according to the exposition in the *Oratorical Divisions,* must be friendly, intelligent, and attentive. Friendliness can be attained by proper attention to the persons concerned in the trial. The orator should speak of his own past deeds, of his position in the state, and of any virtues be may possess, particularly those that have a public usefulness, such as liberality, devotion to duty, justice. and reliability. He should attribute the corresponding failings to his opponents, at the same time denying, or as much as possible minimizing, any charges they may have made. And, finally, he should convince the jurors either that he is already

---

.12 *De Or.* 3, 106–107.

of their way of thinking or that such may readily become the case in the future. In other words, the orator should from the start make the trial a personal matter between himself and the opposing counsel on the one hand, and between himself and the jurors on the other—a thoroughly Roman method of procedure.

A proper understanding of the case on the part of the jurors, and consequently an interested attention, will result, the student is told, if the orator begins his Exordium with a clear presentation of the facts, making careful use of definitions and divisions. But he must avoid confusing his listeners or overburdening their memories with minute recitals of things which will later be set forth in the Narration.

The jurors can further be made attentive, the rhetorician goes on to say, by showing that this case is important, or necessary, or in some way of intimate concern to the jurymen themselves—another method of arguing beside the point! In conclusion, the student is advised to profit by every adventitious aid: the time of the trial, the political situation in Rome, the place of the trial, the accidental arrival in the court of some prominent man, and any other interruption. He must be alert to take advantage in the Exordium of anything said by the opposing counsel, particularly if it occurred at the end of his speech. All these matters make the jurors attentive and interested.

The Narration, which comes next, sets forth the facts of the case, and is thus, as it were, the foundation on which the orator will later build to convince his audience. All the stylistic qualities previously mentioned are useful here, but two of them are absolutely necessary. The Narrative must be clear and brilliant, using the latter term in its technical meaning; and it must be appropriate, that is, convincing, inasmuch as appropriateness involves the adaptation of style to the audience. Clearness is greatly aided by brevity; and, indeed, brevity is especially to be recommended in the Narration. To carry con-

viction, the Narrative must be inherently probable—a characteristically naive bit of advice!—as regards the persons, times, and
places mentioned; the motives as well as the results of an action
must be given; the account must be substantiated by witnesses
and be in accord with the opinions and convictions held by men
in general; and the narrator must give the impression of being
a man of honor, of good standing in the community, truthful in
speech, and reliable in action. The quality of charm, though
not absolutely necessary, is desirable. This is attained by exclamations of astonishment and expectation on the part of the
narrator, by unexpected happenings in the course of the narrative, by emotional passages, and by the introduction of dialogue.
The emotions advised for special cultivation are sorrow, anger,
fear, joy, and, without particularization, the instinctive human
desires, *cupiditates;* and thus a field is opened for various
Commonplaces.

The Peroration concludes the speech, and must therefore
endeavor to impress the audience as strongly as possible in favor
of the speaker's view. One part of the Peroration is therefore
the so-called *enumeratio,* or Recapitulation, of the facts and
thoughts already set forth. This serves either to remind the
audience of things they are in danger of forgetting. or to
strengthen the final appeal by marshaling all the arguments in
one place. Recapitulation is obviously of frequent service to
the accuser; but not to the defendant. The latter has been
repelling specific charges, but as he would not have time to repeat
his defense in detail, he would only hurt his own cause by restat-
ing the charges and so bringing them again before the minds
of the jurors. The student is advised that in recapitulating
he must avoid the appearance of pride in his own powers of
memory; he must not go into much detail, but confine himself
to the main points.

The chief part of the Peroration, so the theory continues,
is in the nature of an Amplification, and is actually called by

that name. The character of Amplifications, which usually contained Commonplaces, had already been described; but a few observations are added. In the matter of language, the orator, while avoiding everything offensively unusual, must make his style brilliant and graceful. He must pay great heed to the musical and rhythmical side of his expression, along the various lines previously indicated. He must be ready to use figurative expressions, and he will find it profitable to omit conjunctions, it is said, for his words will then seem more numerous, since they press one upon the other. But, in this whole connection, he must carefully consider whether his case is important enough to admit of this lofty treatment, for Amplification misplaced is the extreme of absurdity.

As for the thoughts, they will naturally be suggested by the Argumentation that preceded. The student is told that he may well assign speech to fictitious characters and to mute objects in nature—a reference to such frequent oratorical prac-tises as the introduction of deceased ancestors pleading with degenerate descendants and of a personified Rome exhorting, encouraging, or reproaching the Romans. If the case permits, the orator should make use of things that are in any way remark-able or noteworthy, *magna*. These, briefly mentioned under Style, are now divided into two groups. One of these groups consists of things that are naturally or essentially remarkable, and embraces the heavenly bodies and their courses; things divine, such as omens, prophecies, and oracles; and any mar-velous or inexplicable occurrences in nature. The objects in the other group are noteworthy as a result of experience. They are the circumstances or relations of life that greatly assist or harm a man, and can be classified in their relation to the loving reverence, *caritas*, men feel toward the gods, the state, and their parents; the love, *amor*, they have for husband or wife, children, and friends; and the sense of honor, *honestas*, shown in human intercourse. In this systematizing the philosophic rhetorician

made Topics out of his ethical meditations. The orator thereupon is told to exhort his audience, by means of Commonplaces,
to retain the happiness resulting from these three virtues, and
to inveigh against those who destroy it. He is also to express
pity for the man who has lost it or is in danger of losing it, for
nobody is more pitiful than the man who has once been happy.
The arousing of pity was, indeed, important enough to have a
name of its own: *miseratio,* Commiseration, or *conquestio,* Complaint; it would give an excellent opportunity for Commonplaces. The Topics of pity, as given in Cicero's *Invention,* are
sixteen. But the student is counseled not to indulge in minute
details, for the tears shed for other people's misfortunes are
soon dried.

As a last suggestion in reference to the Peroration, the
rhetorician repeats his caution that the amount of Amplification
must be carefully adjusted to the character of the case; and we
surmise here, as often elsewhere when similar warnings are given,
that the students trained in rhetoric might readily be led to
make mountains out of molehills, or, in Horace's phrase, they
would be like mountains in travail that bring forth a mouse.

Turning from the exposition of theory to its application in
the preparation of speeches, the Greek rhetoricians said that the
latter were of three kinds. This classification is due to Greek
public life. If the orator pleaded in court, his speech belonged
to the Judicial class—*genus iudiciale;* if he discussed a question
of public policy, his speech was of the Deliberative kind—*genus
deliberativum;* if he spoke merely for purposes of display, without a practical aim, his oration was Epideictic or Demonstrative
in kind—*genus demonstrativum.* In their search for completeness of description, the rhetoricians further pointed out that the
listener is a judge in the first two cases; he gives a verdict as
to the past in the Judicial class, when he serves in the courts,
and he decides about the future in the Deliberative class, when

he listens in the forum or in the senate-house; whereas his only concern with an Epideictic speech is aesthetic—he is expected merely to enjoy it. The speaker, therefore, has merely to please his audience, and nothing more, in an Epideictic speech, but in the other two kinds he must both convince them, by proving his assertions, and please them or win their favor, and move them, so that they will give the desired verdict.

Teaching in Rome, the Greek rhetoricians preserved this classification, and the Roman rhetoricians followed them, although it is not quite in accord with Roman conditions. Judicial oratory there was the same as in Greece, and Deliberative oratory was practised both in the senate and in the forum; but there was no real Demonstrative speaking. The Romans of the republic were too practical and too busy—or too inartistic, according to the point of view—to tolerate purposeless harangues, however perfect in form.

They had, however, one kind of oratory that avowed no practical aim and was very much in the nature of display—the Eulogy, *laudatio*, delivered at aristocratic funerals. The display was one of family pride rather than of oratorical skill, but the speech was Epideictic enough to be classed as Demonstrative oratory; and the rhetoricians could say that the speaker's sole aim was to give pleasure, even though the pleasure of the ordinary listener might be less than that of the mourning relatives and the bereaved speaker himself. It was perfectly true, however, that the orator did not need to prove his assertions—as is amply indicated by the early records of Roman history. Neither did a speaker prove his assertions when, in the course of a trial or a debate, he launched into eulogy or denunciation; and, as a result, such laudatory or invective passages were looked upon as examples of Epideictic oratory. This class of speaking was therefore said to be concerned with praise or blame, but actually it included only funeral eulogies, and was often called merely *laudatio*.

Obviously Demonstrative oratory, requiring no proofs, was
the least difficult; and may therefore be treated first. The
rhetoricians paid scant attention to it. It was easy; it was not
very important, especially in Rome; and it was, after all, nothing
but an emotional Narrative. The student, in his study of Style,
was first trained in Narration. The theory of style, therefore,
has nothing particular to add in reference to Laudations. What
has been said about Narrative in general and about Amplification
and Commonplaces, is applicable here. The aim of a Eulogy, so
far as the audience was concerned, was to give pleasure. The
student, consequently, should profit by stylistic advice toward
making his speech aesthetically pleasing, the *ornate* of Cicero's
list of stylistic qualities; he should also attempt to inspire his
audience with the emotions of expectation and wonder—to use
the rhetorical phraseology—according to the rules already laid
down.

In the matter of Arrangement, rhetorical theory has but
little to offer. The division into four parts of a Judicial speech
is of little value here. There is no need of an Exordium to
secure a favorable hearing, for the mere presence of the audience, we are told, indicates a receptive mood; there is no call
for Argumentation; and there is no necessity for a Peroration,
as defined by the standards of legal oratory, inasmuch as the
orator does not endeavor to secure an agreement with his views
that will result in action. It is all Narration, and has a beginning and an end merely in the sense that all things must begin
somewhere and end somewhere. Some general, and rather
obvious, observations were nevertheless made. The speaker may
proceed chronologically, it was said; or he may arrange the
deeds narrated according to subjects, suggested by the virtues
from which they spring, as will be shown later, or he may go
from lesser to greater things, or from the greater to the lesser,
or, finally, he may weave together great things and small, simple
and complex, clear things and obscure, joyful and sad, incredible
and probable.

It is only in the field of Invention that more definite suggestions are given. Starting with the initial observation that Demonstrative oratory relates to matters deserving of praise or of blame, the teacher divided these matters into three groups, naturally thinking of Laudations and therefore putting the emphasis on things praiseworthy.

First, there are the man's external circumstances, those which relate to the position of his family. If they are deserving of commendation, they should be mentioned with brevity and moderation; if base, they should be passed by; if humble, the orator should either pass them by or indicate how the subject of his Eulogy rose above them. Something may also be said, in this connection, about his wealth and other worldly advantages. Secondly, the eulogy may take up his appearance. In discussing this, it is well to speak particularly of his facial expression, in case it mirrors excellent mental or moral qualities. Lastly, there are his good deeds, which result from his virtues. It is here that the speaker must look for most of his thoughts; and Invention endeavored to assist him by a classification of the virtues. The philosophers who taught rhetoric, connoisseurs in virtue, here stepped in with a long list of moral excellencies, carefully subdivided and defined, thus drawing up a veritable Topica of praise.

Virtue—as Cicero tells Marcus in the *Oratorical Divisions,* and Marcus was probably in need of the information—virtue is a large subject, much debated. Briefly it comes to this: virtues have to do either with knowledge, knowing what is right, or with action, doing it. Virtues of knowledge are concerned with a man's private affairs or with the state. Great aids toward them are the sciences of dialectic and rhetoric, the former teaching a man how to judge, and the latter, how to express himself. Evidently a Eulogy might well be based partly on a man's dialectic or oratorical efficiency. As for the virtues of action, they, too, relate either to a man's private affairs or to the state.

They are summed up in the one word *temperantia,* which causes a man to be moderate in using the advantages within his reach and to refrain from demanding others, and which gives him courage to oppose evil, and patience to endure it. It is in fact spiritual greatness, *animi magnitudo,* the source of all good qualities. In matters of the state, it leads to justice, piety, kindness, reliability, and everything else of good repute.

There are many more virtues, which need not be given, and there are equally many vices, opposed to them. The vices are not treated in the same detail, but the student is warned against misapprehending vices that parade as virtues. A list of parallels then follows, such as generosity and extravagance, courage and rashness, moderation in the enjoyment of pleasure and rigid abstemiousness, which is called brutishness or enormity, *immanitas,* and, finally, eloquence, as opposed to an empty flow of words!

In praising a man, therefore, and this is the summing up of the whole matter, it is proper to speak of his family, his education, and the influences that formed him; to mention anything strange or incredible that happened to him, especially if it came from the gods; to describe his praiseworthy thoughts, sayings, or deeds, referring them to their several virtues; and also to speak of his death, provided it was in any way noteworthy or was followed by remarkable events.

A Deliberative speech urged the acceptance or the rejection of a proposal, and was also called *suasio,* Urging, which is primarily applicable to a speech that favors acceptance. Such speeches were delivered at the meetings of the senate or of the people. In the matters of Style and Arrangement, ordinary rhetorical theory contained very little specific advice about Deliberative speaking, as it did about Demonstrative speaking; the reason being that he who had learned, in Judicial oratory, how to present his own side of a case would need no instruction in presenting his view of a proposed action. It was observed, however, that the style should be simple and weighty, deriving its distinction rather from the thoughts than from the expression.

As to the four ordinary divisions of a speech, the rhetoricians said that here, as in the case of Demonstrative oratory, there was no need of an extended Exordium: the presence of the audience indicated a willingness to listen. The speaker should, therefore, state his subject and his attitude briefly, and also promise to observe brevity in his discussion. The Narrative, too, should be brief, since Deliberative oratory has to do with the future and not with the past or the present. The Argumentation, on the other hand, and the Peroration, both of them important, received considerable attention, but only from the philosophers.

The method of treatment employed by the philosophers was analogous to that used by them in Demonstrative oratory. The philosophical rhetorician had there drawn up a list of virtues and vices, practically giving a Topica of praise and of blame; here he informs the student that all deliberations are concerned with the question of utility. Invention as applied to this kind of oratory therefore consisted, in the first place, of a philosophical discussion of this term.

Before really arriving at a discussion of the usefulness of a proposal, the orator was taught that he must consider its practicability and its necessity. If the proposal is impossible of execution, the discussion ceases, however useful the proposed action may be. And if it is absolutely necessary, then, too, all discussion ceases, and questions of utility as well as of morality are not in place. In the matter of practicability, the orator should discuss the relative difficulties involved, for very difficult things are often to be treated as impossible. Similarly, as to necessity, the importance of the proposed action must be investigated, for supreme importance is equivalent to necessity. The mode of procedure is therefore simple: if a thing is useful and practicable, let it be done; if useless or if impracticable, let it not be done. The man who favors a proposal must thus prove two things, the utility and the practicability of it; his opponent need disprove only one of the two.

Utility has to do with the good and the bad things in life. Of the former, some are essential, such as the preservation of life, a good character, liberty, children, husbands or wives, relatives, and parents; others are desirable. Those desirable are so either because of their ethical excellence or because they are advantageous. The different kinds of advantages have to do with a man's physical well-being or with his worldly position; some of them are connected with morality, such as glory and friendship; others are not, as, for instance, bodily strength, health, good birth, wealth, and political influence. The student is further informed that it is easy, knowing the good things, to discover what is bad, and that he must possess a knowledge about these matters because in this kind of speaking there is often a conflict between utility and honesty. This conflict was much debated by the philosophers, as appears in Cicero's own work on Duty, and would supply the orator with numerous Commonplaces.

The speaker, however, must take into account, here as elsewhere, not merely his subject but also his audience. Men are of two kinds: some are high-minded and unselfish, others are base and selfish. The speaker must suit his reasons to both classes, at times even praising pleasure, though nothing is more hostile to virtue. In this connection it is profitable to remember that those who are base are eager to avoid disgrace even though they care but little for virtue.

As to the question of practicability, the orator will consider the means for accomplishing the proposed action, some of which are direct and some indirect, and also the obstacles in its way, striving to show that it is not merely possible of execution but also easy and pleasant. His opponent will argue in the opposite direction. Both should cite precedents, recent ones because they are best known, those more distant because they are hallowed by tradition and therefore have more weight.

All these matters are intended primarily to prove the speaker's point of view. He must also, especially in the Peroration, appeal to the emotions of the audience. His purpose here may be to inspire them with hope, and thus stir them to action by showing them that they will be able to attain their wishes, satisfy their hatred, or wreak vengeance; or it may be to rouse their fears, and then calm them so that they will refrain from action, by pointing out that the present is at best uncertain and the future doubtful; if they are prosperous, they should not imperil their prosperity by rash action, and if they are in misfortune, they should not court needless dangers. All of which could be enforced by the introduction of Commonplaces and other forms of Amplification.

But it was on Judicial oratory that the teachers of rhetoric expended most of their efforts. The theory of Arrangement was elaborated entirely with reference to legal speeches, and everything that was taught in Invention and Style was applicable to them. The writing and declamation of orations intended to teach this kind of oratory were the final and most difficult parts of the training.

The first step toward the mastery of a case is to reduce it to its lowest terms, by the omission of all personal and circumstantial details. The main issue will then appear as an abstract question. Thus, in the case of Norbanus, the question will be: Did he commit high treason who, in accordance with the wishes of the Roman people, by violence performed a deed which was pleasing and just? All cases can be reduced in this way, and it will be found that the main issue is a question of fact: Is this so or not? Did this happen? Or, if the deed is admitted, a question of definition: Norbanus took part in a riot; did he commit high treason? Or, thirdly, if the deed is admitted and has been correctly named, a question as to its morality: Was the defendant justified in committing the deed which he admits?

As the form of question which the main issue assumes will determine the orator's attitude, *status*, every judicial case can be referred to one of three *status: coniecturalis*, Conjectural, where the fact has to be ascertained; *definitivus*, concerned with defining the admitted deed; and *rationis* or *qualitatis*, a question of reason or character, which has to do with the justification of the deed.

This, very briefly, is the theory of *status*, which was much elaborated by the teachers of rhetoric. Thus the *status qualitatis* had thirteen divisions, and these were further subdivided. The three *status* mentioned are those most often used by Cicero; a fourth may be referred to. The orator might claim that the case did not belong to the court before which the prosecutor had brought it, and so try to have it transferred. But this *status* does not apply when the case is actually being tried, and need not be further examined. It was of course possible for an orator to assume more than one attitude toward a case; he might argue that Milo did not murder Clodius—*status coniecturalis*—and at the same time maintain that, if he had done it, he would have been justified—*status qualitatis*. At least one position, however, had to be assumed. Most cases in the Roman courts, as in ours, belonged naturally to the Conjectural class, in which the accused pleaded not guilty.

The essential part of a Conjectural speech is the Argumentation. The theory of Invention, therefore, endeavored first of all to supply the student with the means of proving or disproving the question at issue. By means of the abstract Topics, which consist of such considerations as definition and comparison, he had received logical training and had learned how to present his side of the case with adroitness. The concrete Topics, on the other hand, directed his attention to the various phases of the case, whether personal or circumstantial.

The subdividing and defining of these Topics were carried to a degree of minuteness that could not have been very helpful. It will be sufficient to cite a single example; taken from the *Oratorical Divisions,* a work that, on the whole, is relatively concise. As to the question of time, one of the concrete Topics, the student was informed that there are two kinds of time: that due to nature and that due to chance. Natural time comprises the conceptions of present, past, and future, and the two latter may of course be more or less distant; also the four seasons of the year; the different time measurements of year, month, day, night, and hour; and finally the weather. The time that results from chance has to do with special occasions such as sacrifices, festal days, and weddings.

A word should· be added about the motives and the traces of an alleged crime, both of them concrete Topics. A man's motives are due to considerations of utility; a statement that directs the student to the philosophical exposition of that term, already given in connection with Deliberative oratory. As the audience of a Deliberative speech was to be inspired with hope or with fear, so the defendant here is alleged to have committed his crime either with the hope of attaining something desirable or because of his fear of something undesirable. There are many things that may have influenced him; such as recent anger, an old hatred, a desire for vengeance, ambition, love of money, debt. He may have expected to keep his crime hidden, or, if found out, to defend it successfully in court. He may have decided that the eventual punishment was of less account than the benefits his crime would secure.

A discussion of the motives, the theory continues, is of less importance than the unearthing of traces of the alleged crime. Several kinds of damaging evidence of this nature are given; and it is thereupon observed that, if the accuser can find none of these, he should resort to a Commonplace, declaring that the culprit was not so foolish as to leave any traces. The defendant will rejoin with another Commonplace, to the effect that a man who was bold enough to commit the alleged deed could not have been prudent enough to hide all traces of it, for criminal boldness is usually coupled with carelessness and rashness, and not with prudence. Other Commonplaces may also be used: you can not expect a man to confess; wrongs must be proven and not merely argued about as likely—and the student is advised to strengthen these generalizations by the citation of analogous cases.

All these arguments, whether abstract or concrete, are ·to be evolved, as it were, from the case itself. They require ingenuity, rhetorical skill, for their discovery. There are also other kinds of arguments, which are supplied, as it were, from the outside. They consist of laws, contracts of all kinds, and testimony. These can be discovered without rhetorical ability, it is said, but they can be best managed by the man who knows rhetorical theory.

The most important of these is testimony, and the *Oratorical Divisions* has something to say about the way to treat witnesses— a reflection of the treatment actually accorded them in the Roman courts. Witnesses, it will be recalled, were of two kinds, free men and slaves. The former gave testimony if they chose. Their connection with a case was like that of the orator and of the friendly supporter, and their testimony was in the nature of help given to a friend or of attack directed against an enemy. Slaves, on the other hand, were offered to the courts by their owners, and gave testimony only under torture.

Since a free man gave testimony voluntarily, he might readily be looked upon as partisan, and was treated accordingly. Every suggestion, therefore, that has been given in connection with praise or blame as the subjects of Demonstrative oratory, may be used in reference to the character of the individual witness. According to the needs of the case, the orator will mention previous occasions on which such and such a witness has failed to secure credence for his testimony; or, on the other hand, the orator may claim belief for a bit of testimony because of the prominence of the witness. If the witness be of humble station, the orator should say that his words are reliable, not in proportion to his worldly position, but in proportion to his opportunity for knowing the truth.

The speaker is also advised to speak of witnesses as a class. The defendant, the prosecutor may say, has succeeded in obliterating the traces of his crime, but he has not succeeded in escaping the observation of true and good men; material proofs are obscure, but not so the spoken word. To which the opponent may rejoin that material proofs are incontrovertible, whereas testimony is conditioned by personal predilections or antipathies, and, in any case, depend on human powers of observation.

If the testimony be that of slaves, the individual characters of whom were scarcely considered, the orator may, according to his need, defend or attack the whole system of torture. The desire to avoid the momentary pain of torture, he may say, has very often caused slaves to lie and even to court death. Many slaves have imperiled their own lives in order to free their masters, whose lives they prized more highly than their own; others, naturally insensible to pain or inured to it by previous experiences, or fearful of punishment and death, have borne up under torture, refusing to give damaging testimony; and still others have lied against their enemies. Torture may be defended as a traditional practise. It may be observed that the Greeks allow even children and free men to be tortured, whereas the wiser Romans employ torture merely as a means for getting the truth from slaves, who are naturally unreliable, and, furthermore, do not admit a slave's testimony against his master except in cases of incest and conspiracy. Examples should be cited to prove the truth of all these generalizations, but the orator should be careful, for they point in either direction.

Finally, in his treatment of all witnesses, the speaker should avail himself of any ambiguity, inconsistency, or improbability inherent in the testimony, as well as of contradictory depositions.

In presenting evidence, the orator may pursue one of two courses. Since he aims at establishing something doubtful by means of that which is certain or likely, he can proceed either analytically, stating his desired conclusion first and then giving the proofs, or synthetically, stating the proofs first and then drawing his inference. He must be clear and he must vary his manner. He can do the latter by addressing questions to himself or to his opponent—a very frequent trick—or by using any other rhetorical device. Obvious matters may be stated briefly, without proof; nor is it necessary always to draw the inference, provided it be evident.

The problem of the prosecutor, it is needlessly observed, is different from that of the defendant. This appears in connection with the four main parts of the speech. The prosecutor aims, in his Exordium, to rouse suspicions against the defendant and generalizes on the danger threatening everybody if crimes go unpunished; whereas the orator for the defense tries to gain the good-will of the jurors and generalizes on the danger to the state from trumped up charges. In the Narrative, the prosecutor sets forth the facts step by step, taking care to hint a suspicion wherever possible, and mingling his own proofs with rebuttal of the points of the defense.' The opposing lawyer makes his Narrative brief, omitting it entirely if it is likely to damage his case; and he tries to minimize the suspicious character of the events narrated. In the Argumentation proper the prosecutor states his case clearly, drawing his conclusions with certainty; he shows how his statements are supported by proper evidence and takes care to elaborate the individual points. The speaker for the defense denies everything, if possible; if this is impossible, he argues that the prosecutor has relied on that which is uncertain or even false, and that his premises do not warrant his conclusions; he attacks a single link in the prosecutor's argumentation, thus breaking the whole chain. If he can not meet the latter's arguments, he tries to obscure and overwhelm them by Digressions. In the Peroration, finally, the prosecutor sums up his whole case, and then, by means of Amplifications, endeavors to rouse the audience to anger. The orator for the defense, as has already been noted, omits the Recapitulation, unless he has met the charges convincingly; in any case, he concludes with a *miseratio*—an appeal to the sense of pity.

In general, the prosecutor is advised to use little Digression, but to advance step by step, piling proof on proof, until he reaches the Peroration, in which he will exert all his emotional powers to enhance the horror of the deed he has attempted to prove. The defendant's lawyer, on the contrary, is told to obscure and mitigate the situation by means of generalizations of every kind, causing the jurors to forget their righteous indignation, and leading them gradually to a pitying view of the whole matter.

The cases that belong to the other two classes, being concerned with the definition or with the justice of a confessed deed, were necessarily rare, nor is the distinction between them of any real importance. Theoretically, it is satisfactory to the student's conscience, and it is also clear, to say that in the cases of Definition the orator maintained or denied that a certain deed, for instance, was treason, while in the cases involving a question of justice he admitted the treasonable character of the deed and merely maintained or denied that the treasonable conduct was justifiable.

In practise, however, the two fused. When Antony defended Norbanus, he asserted that his client's actions were not treasonable, inasmuch as they were for the glory of Rome; in other words, they were justifiable. He could not have argued otherwise if his avowed aim had been to justify Norbanus' confessed actions. Under the former conception of the case, he argued that, inasmuch as Norbanus was justified, he did not commit treason, and consequently should not be punished; under the latter conception of the case, his conclusion would have been that, inasmuch as Norbanus was justified, he should not be punished. The distinction between the two, therefore, seems to exist mainly for the sake of logical precision and also, no doubt, for pedagogical reasons. The student could be trained first in one view of the case and then in the other, and the aids offered by rhetorical theory could be grouped under one or the other view.

Cicero, when describing this case in the *De Oratore*, represents Antony as saying that he gave little attention to defining high treason, this being a matter for the theoretic rhetorician, but directed his efforts toward proving that Norbanus' actions did not lead to such results as would come from treasonable conduct; in short, that they were justifiable. In the technical treatment of the *status definitius,* as set forth in the *Oratorical Divisions,* this procedure is also one of those suggested.

Stated technically, the problem of the prosecution and of the defense is the same in cases of Definition: to define the term in such a way as to satisfy the jurors. There is no room for evidence. The orator will most easily arrive at such a definition, theory says, by classifying the term under discussion as a subdivision of a larger conception. He may also argue about the essential qualities of the term, drawing his arguments from definitions of terms that are contrary, similar, or of equal importance. He will use description; he will enumerate the results that should have come from a certain deed if it was really that which it is alleged to be, as Antony did, and he will especially rely on etymology—a favorite device of the pedantic Stoics in all philosophizing—in order to arrive at the real meaning of the term.

The discussion will of course readily center about the interpretation of the law against the crime which is defined. One side will maintain a literal interpretation, and the other an interpretation according to the intent of the lawmakers. Both will use Commonplaces. If the prosecutor maintains that the confessed deed is punishable according to the law in question, while the defense relies on a literal interpretation to exclude the deed, the prosecutor will say that a confessed criminal should not be protected by technicalities. He will declaim about the real aims of justice, for which, as Cicero says, there are many Topics. The defense will insist on literalness of interpretation as the only means of securing reliable verdicts, and he will also take the larger view, that lawless prosecutions are dangerous to the people as a whole and must be stopped. Or the situation may be reversed, in which case the rhetorician merely reverses his advice. Whatever the line of argument, the prosecuting orator is counseled to arouse the indignation of the jurors, and the orator for the defense, to stir their sense of pity. But here, as elsewhere, the case must be important enough—the old advice —if glowing Amplifications are to be used.

In the *status qualitatis,* the fact that the issue is concerned with a question of justice, suggests as Topics for arguments the whole field of moral philosophy. Use the Topics, says theory, that have to do with nature, laws, tradition, the repelling of injury, and vengeance. If it can not be shown that the deed is in itself a just one, then show that it was committed to avert or avenge a wrong, or that it was dictated by a feeling of reverence or modesty, by religion or by patriotism. If this is not possible, defend it as unavoidable, as due to lack of knowledge or to chance. In the latter group belong actions due to temporary excitement, which, without being technically the same, is very much like the modern plea of temporary insanity.

Since justice is often concerned with law, the *Oratorical Divisions* contains here a discussion of legal interpretation. It is pointed out distinctly that this discussion has nothing to do with cases of Definition, since there the issue centers on a word and not on a law; but we have already seen that the distinction is arbitrary. The mere insistence on it shows that the rhetoricians used emphasis because they were not very certain of their ground.

There are three kinds of doubt that may arise in reference to a law; and these were called *status legales*—another use of the protean term *status*. The wording of a law may be actually ambiguous; it may be faulty, so that the speaker can claim that one thing is said and another intended; or one law may be in disagreement with another law. The discussion of these legal tangles given by Cicero, though long, has nothing to say about actual laws; it merely suggests, in many words, the obvious remarks available to the orator. He may say, of his own interpretation, that any sane and just man will agree with it; he may amplify praises of law in general, attacking those who undermine law by perverse interpretations. In case he is supporting a literal interpretation, he will ask if the opponent dares maintain that the lawgivers, wise men of old, were so stupid that they said one thing and meant another; while the opponent will wonder whether criminals ought to go free because lawgivers were careless.

III
PRACTISE

This huge and complex theory was not allowed to slumber ingloriously in the rolls of the rhetoricians and philosophers. It was very much in evidence, as the strong backbone of the whole educational system, and it is easy to comprehend how years would be needed for its mastery. Some ways in which it was imparted to the student have been suggested in connection with the account of the theory. Our information in this regard is somewhat incomplete, in so far as it applies to this period, but it is very full for the middle and the latter half of the next century, and the method is not very likely to have undergone considerable changes. Much, however, perhaps all that is significant, can be gathered from the theory itself; and further light is thrown on the subject by various references and especially by Cicero's incidental criticisms in the *De Oratore*.

In the first place, the student was undoubtedly expected to know and understand the theory as a matter of mere knowledge. Marcus asks: "Are we to use all the arguments that can be found in these Topics?" And Cicero replies: "No. We must discover all, and then with judgment choose the best." This particular question, with its answer, suggests indeed that there was a good deal of meaningless recitation, all for the purpose of learning the theory, and Cicero tells[13] us elsewhere that there was much singsong delivery of rules. Apparently the theory was committed to memory very much in the manner formerly used in connection with Latin grammar; but even Latin grammar was easier.

The theory was explained by means of lectures. The comfort-loving young Marcus, while studying rhetoric in Athens, wrote to Tiro for a trained slave to copy out his lecture notes, adding that a Greek slave would be preferred. The ambitious student was possibly encouraged to study and compare disagreements in detail as they could be gathered from the lectures or textbooks of different rhetoricians. At least, Cicero's own work, the *De Inventione*, treats the subject with an eye to various rhetoricians, and takes sides for or against them. Cicero was doubtless more ambitious in this matter than his son Marcus or the average student; but it is very likely that the lecturing rhetorician had something to say about the erroneous teaching of his brother-lecturers; certainly if they happened to be philosophers.

---

[13] *De Or.* 1, 105. See also above, p. 370.

Composition and declamation, however, constituted the main part of the instruction. Here the rules could be applied. Training in writing seems to have followed very much the different types of writing indicated by the main parts of the speech, and the rules for each part were here made effective. Thus the student wrote Narratives, and no doubt, Exordia, Arguments, and Perorations. This method, similar to modern training in narrative, exposition, and argumentation, had its drawbacks. Brevity was, according to the rule, very desirable in Narration; and here attention was paid to it, but not elsewhere, as Cicero hints. Emotional language belonged particularly in the Peroration, and it was forgotten that the orator must appeal to his audience throughout his speech. Exordia had a character of their own; and, as a result, orators wrote and delivered Exordia which had little to do with the rest of the speech. They were equally suitable, or unsuitable, to several speeches. This way of insisting for a time on one thing, and then neglecting it as if it had been mastered, is well enough in learning a subject like law, Cicero says, thinking no doubt of a mastery of the various statutes; in rhetoric, it is pernicious.

Writing is onerous, whereas extemporaneous speaking, with a little practise, becomes easy. Students spoke extemporaneously, to get fluency and presence of mind; but Cicero thinks there was too much of it. Speaking is not like swimming. Students do not learn to speak well merely by speaking, said Cicero, for bad speaking, as extemporaneous speaking often is, leads to more bad speaking. He would have the learner take time for thinking before he speaks, and especially for writing. Silent thought, to Cicero, is better than speaking; writing is better than either. If an orator has written with care in preparing a case, he will speak well, using as far as possible what he has written and then being able to go on, extemporaneously, in the same manner.

But most of the practise consisted in the writing and declaiming of whole speeches. These were of two kinds. In some, the question at issue was stated without personal or circumstantial details: What shall be done about captives? In the other kind, the details were added. An abstract question was thus like the main issue of a real case, which the student discovers by the elimination of all details; whereas the concrete question was like the whole case. But the resemblance between actual oratory and these declamations was very slight.

The abstract propositions, called by the Greek word *theses*, had not been evolved from real cases. They were almost exclusively concerned with philosophical questions. According to the *Oratorical Divisions,* they had to do either with questions of knowledge or with questions of action—a division that was also applied to the human virtues. The questions of knowledge, like Judicial cases, belong to the three *status* of Conjecture, Definition, and Morality. Thus, under Conjecture, it is asked whether justice is derived from nature or from tradition; under Definition, whether justice is that which is useful for the majority of men; and under Morality, whether or not it is useful to live justly. The questions of action bear the same general resemblance to Deliberative oratory that the questions of knowledge do to Judicial oratory. They either discuss in a general way how to attain or avoid something—How can glory be attained? How can unpopularity be avoided?—or else they point out what men should do or how they should behave under certain conditions: How is the state to be governed? How is a man to live in poverty? There are further definitions and classifications, which need not be repeated. All the subjects quoted as examples are of a very general nature; they are the very subjects about which the philosophers, as philosophers, argued for and against.

The value of these abstract declamations consisted in the training they gave in Amplifications, Commonplaces, and the stirring or allaying of emotions, which form so large a part of ancient oratory. Cicero says, to be sure, that their aim is to

establish an abstract truth, and that consequently they are
addressed to the intellect and have none of that emotional quality
which is used for persuading an audience; but their whole
content was of a general, usually philosophical, nature, and general and philosophical meditations were the very material out
of which the orator wove his Amplifications.

Cicero, who was no doubt partly attracted to these declamations by their philosophical content, found them useful, and
engaged in them long after he had made his reputation.[14] They
are also the ones he recommends to the orator who has been
through the regular drill and has had some actual experience
in the forum. If we remember that the orator's effects, and
consequently his success, depended to a very great extent upon
his ability to please and to move his audience, to impart to his
speech a largeness of view that touched upon life in all its
multifarious complexities, and to stir the audience with winged
words about patriotism and morality, it is easy to see how
these declamations would keep his hand in, as it were. They
had very much the same relation to actual oratory as the singing
of scales has to the public performances of a concert singer.

The declamations about concrete questions—*hypotheses,* in
the Greek—were different. The abstract questions, as has been
shown, had rarely any real resemblance to actual cases, despite
the fact that every real case can be reduced to an abstract question. The resemblance was even less in the case of the concrete
declamations.

Theoretically, the concrete declamations were real cases. A
situation was given with its attendant circumstances, and the
students argued for the defense and for the prosecution. If
the teachers had taken cases that had actually been argued in
the Roman courts and if the students had been required first to
study the orations concerned with these cases—there were apparently enough orations available for this purpose—and then to
write and declaim speeches on the subject, the result would have

---

[14] Sihler, Amer. Journ. Phil., 1902, 283 ff.

resembled the case method of modern law schools. But the teachers of rhetoric did not do this. They invented their own cases or used those that had already been invented. The situations put before the students were unreal. Cicero gives an example, probably typical, in the *De Oratore:*[15] there is a law to the effect that foreign residents in Rome must not mount to the top of the city wall; a foreign resident does this, however, during a siege, and repels the enemy; he is thereupon prosecuted for having disobeyed the law. This kind of a subject is not only entirely foreign to the cases actually tried in court, but it is also too easy; and the students, according to Cicero, did not acquire the habit of mastering the details of a real case.

Such a subject as this might presumably give the student the same opportunity for generalization as the abstract declamations, and so it undoubtedly did, to some extent. The objection to it, from this point of view, seems to have been that the student was kept in an atmosphere where laws and conditions prevailed that had never been heard of on either land or sea. The subjects were chosen from history, distorted and simplified, and also from mythology and the imaginings of comic poets. Did Ulysses kill Ajax? Can the Fregellani be friendly to the Roman people? If the Romans had not destroyed Carthage, would she now cause trouble to Rome? These three examples, taken from Cicero's *De Inventione,* have been supposed not really to represent these concrete declamations; being opposed to the use of *hypotheses,* he is said to have manufactured ridiculous examples. But the later development indicates that the hand of pedantry and tradition lay heavy upon these exercises. And to pedantry was added a perverse ingenuity. The exercises preserved from the next century show what these concrete declamations became, and so indicate, at least in part, what they were.

To take a single example, that of the Ailing Twins.[16] Two little brothers who were twins fell sick. The physician said

---

[15] *De Or.* 2, 100.
[16] Quintil. *Declam.* 8.

they had the same illness. When they grew worse and everybody had relinquished hope of their recovery, the physician said that he could cure one of the twins if he were allowed to examine the vital organs of the other. The father gave his permission. The physician killed one of the infants and performed an autopsy. When the other boy had been cured, the mother of the twins prosecuted the father for allowing the murder of his son.

These concrete questions were used mostly by the rhetoricians, while the philosophers favored the abstract questions; but they borrowed from each other, incidentally making charges of professional theft. From the modern point of view, there are objections to both kinds of declamation; neither makes a real attempt to instruct the student in a legal mastery of actual cases. But that was to be learned by observation in the forum, by consulting older advisers, and by actual experience. The emotional side of speaking, in most cases more important by far than legal knowledge, could probably be best acquired by means of the abstract declamations. It is, at any rate, not difficult to see why Cicero objected to a mature man declaiming about sick twins.

IV

DE ORATORE

The first of Cicero's three chief treatises on rhetoric, the *De Oratore*,[17] literally, On the Orator, was finished toward the end of the year 55 B.C. In a letter to Atticus written in November Cicero mentions its completion, and also says that he has been at work on it for a long time. The long time can not have been more than about one year and a half, the period since the conference at Luca; for he had certainly not begun the work before the exile, or, at least, there is not the slightest indication that he had. He wrote nothing during the exile, and the few troubled months between his return to Rome and the conference

---

17 On the *De Oratore,* see esp. Kroll, *Neue Jahrb.* and *Rhein. Mus.*

at Luca were filled with public activities. But eighteen months, even though not given exclusively to writing, was a long time for any work of Cicero's; and yet the *De Oratore* contains about two hundred and fifty ordinary pages. Ten years later, after many had read the work, Cicero was still pleased with it, as appears from another letter to Atticus; and he had good reason for his satisfaction.

It is not easy to give a conception of the infinite variety, the sanity, the charm, and the enthusiasm of this work. In the *Rhetorici Libri* Cicero had written, or begun to write, a painstaking, orderly account of rhetorical theory; in the *De Oratore,* taking for granted that his readers have received the ordinary training and are familiar with the technical terms and the details of the theory, he throws system to the winds, chooses the dialogue for his artistic form, and lets the talk of his characters wander back and forth over the whole field. The conversation, as in all of Cicero's dialogues, begins with a general discussion; the speakers are, as it were, gradually drifting into their subject, and make broad statements of their opinions. The whole content of the work is thus indicated at the beginning, as would happen in a real conversation, and it is only later, when criticisms have been suggested, that each speaker settles down, one might say, to his own particular part of the subject, enlarging and supporting the views he has previously expressed.

No conversation can be accurately produced in writing and at the same time convey to the reader exactly what was said as well as what was meant. Some degree of artificiality must be employed. The writer must add something, by way of comment or explanation, in order to suggest the things that in real life remain unspoken; and as for the actual conversation, if he makes the attempt to reproduce it in dialogue, he must make his characters more logical and more articulate than ordinary human beings. Perhaps written dialogues can be divided into two classes; some proceed by means of comparatively brief utterances on the part of the speakers, while others consist largely of monologues. Both methods may give the reader a vivid impression of conversation, for both, the former no more than the latter, contain the elements of real talk.

The dialogue of brief utterances, made precise and carefully articulated, is found in Plato's early treatises, and is supposed to have developed from an attempt to reproduce Socrates' dialectic talks with young men.[18] An assertion was to be overthrown; a bit of truth was to be arrived at; and the young follower of Socrates was to be taught clear thinking, by a careful watching of every statement that he made. When the aim of a dialogue is like that of Socrates with his young interlocutors, the brief utterances, the rapid give and take, will best suit the writer's purpose. But as Plato came gradually to use his dialogues as vehicles for the setting forth of a theory or the conveying of information, the short utterances necessarily yielded to the monologue, until a monologue might fill the greater part of ten books, as in the *Republic,* and be more like a lecture or a series of lectures than a part of a conversation. Quite as often one monologue might follow another, for the sake of introducing different points of view.

It seems likely that Aristotle, who had no such dialectic aim as Socrates, used the latter form of dialogue in his popular treatises, which have been lost. Cicero, in the *De Oratore* as well as in his other dialogues, uses this method. He calls his own manner the Aristotelian.

The meaning of the term has been much discussed.[19] In one place, writing to Atticus,[20] Cicero characterizes it as introducing several speakers but leaving the main discussion in the hands of the author himself. This does not apply literally to the *De Oratore,* for Cicero is not one of the speakers; but it is never-

---

[18] On the whole question of the dialogue, see Hirzel. Cicero's dialogues are fully discussed, pp. 457–552.

[19] Hirzel, p. 276, note 3; Watson, p. 219, note on *"Aristotelio more;"* Reid, p. 25.

[20] *Att.* 13, 19, 4.

theless true that in this work, as in his other dialogues, the reader
is rarely left in doubt as to Cicero's own opinion, even though
Cicero himself is not an interlocutor. The use of long monologues, however, particularly if they set forth opposing views,
may be the decisive characteristic of the Aristotelian method.
In the *De Oratore*[21] Cicero, at all events, uses the term in reference to the ability to speak at length—make orations, are his
words—both for and against a proposition. Plato having also
the dialogue of rapid give and take, Aristotle's name may well
have been applied to the other method although Plato used this
also.[22]

The name is of relatively small importance. Its mention,
however, recalls the fact that Cicero, in choosing this dialogue
form, was consciously rivaling the ancient Greeks. It is not as
if dialogues had not been used recently even in Latin for the
discussion of rhetorical questions. Lucilius and Varro, in their
satires, wrote of rhetoric, but these satires were very brief. It
has also been surmised, though not proved, that the work on
oratory by M. Antonius was a dialogue. But neither in Latin
nor in the Greek that was either contemporary with Cicero or
somewhat earlier, is there any sure trace of an extended literary
treatment of rhetoric in dialogue form such as that of the *De
Oratore*.

The Aristotelian dialogue was adapted to Cicero's aim of
giving a critical exposition of a large subject. The Socratic
manner of rapid give and take, being more realistic, made an
increasing appeal to him, but it was not suitable except in short
passages introduced here and there[23] for the sake of variety.
These show that Cicero was well able to manage this kind of
dialogue; a statement of which there are further proofs in his
orations and in the introductory scenes of his treatises.

---

[21] *De Or.* 3, 80.

[22] Cicero imitated Heraclides Ponticus. Reid, p. 25, and Hirzel, esp.
pp. 321 ff. and 464.

[23] A good example in *De Fin.* 2, chaps. 1 ff.; see below, p. 550. Hirzel,
p. 317.

In a few works Cicero uses the essay form, addressing himself to some definite person, his son or Brutus; but the Aristotelian dialogue, the long monologue, had all the advantages of the essay and several others peculiar to itself. It removed the appearance of dogmatizing, enabled Cicero to shift readily from one phase of the subject to another, to omit insignificant details, to introduce criticisms freely and naturally through the different points of view of the speakers, and to relieve the strain on the reader's attention—a thing Cicero, the accomplished pleader, always remembered to do—by the use of small bits of conversation, usually humorous.

But there was still another reason for Cicero's choice of the dialogue. By means of it he could place his treatise in whatever historical atmosphere he chose. The principal speakers in the *De Oratore* are thus Crassus and Antony, the two orators who had inspired him and directed his early studies. The spirit of the work is therefore that of Cicero's youth, the time when he formed the ideal which he had later realized and is now setting forth. The discussion is supposed to have taken place in the year 91 B.C., shortly before the death of Crassus; Cotta, one of the less prominent interlocutors, is represented as having reported the conversation to Cicero.

Through Cicero's historical imagination and his vivid consciousness of personality the old orators are made to live again, and their talk is filled with references to their own time and reminiscences of men and events. Cicero poured into the dialogue both what he had heard and what he had read.[24] Scaevola's recollection of Scipio and Laelius, and the cases of Norbanus, and of Brutus against Crassus, have already been mentioned; they are only a few of the many passages that give vividness to the presentation. To the modern reader the treatise gives a glimpse into the Roman world, seen through the eyes of the great nobles, who are the speakers. And this is what perhaps constitutes the main charm and the main value of the treatise.

---

24 See Hendrickson.

In the matter of the accuracy of Cicero's historical picture, in this treatise as well as in others, it is known from his letters that he took considerable pains to inform himself; he frequently made inquiries about details from Atticus, who was a searcher after facts. Occasionally there is a lapse from historical truth, but it is slight; the atmosphere seems to be extraordinarily correct even to minute details, and it is always vivid.

The persons in the *De Oratore*, especially Crassus and Antony, are made into living personalities. Whether these are portraits or fictions can not be determined. Crassus is suspiciously like Cicero, and Antony, though perhaps not changing from Book One to Book Two, at least adopts a new attitude. Cicero's aim in this connection resembled that of Shakespeare or of a writer of historical novels. He tried to make his characters consistent and convincing. In order to accomplish the latter, since his Roman readers already had a conception of the historical personages he introduced, he explains how Antony and Crassus were better educated than was popularly supposed, or how Cato the Elder, when speaking of old age, had profited so much by his Greek studies that he could speak as a philosopher. Sometimes the character Cicero had created, or recreated, became extraordinarily real to him, so that he could say that in rereading the essay on Old Age he seemed to be listening to Cato himself. On other occasions, however, he felt that he had made his interlocutors too accomplished. This would most naturally occur in the case of contemporaries, who were known to Cicero's readers, and he actually changed the interlocutors in the *Academica* after the treatise had been published. Lucullus was one of the speakers in the earlier edition; the book[25] in which he appears is still extant, and contains in the introduction a long account of Lucullus' supposed training in philosophy; an account that seems to have misled Plutarch.[26] But Cicero, writing to Atticus,[27] says

[25] *Ac. Prior.* 2 ff.
[26] Plutarch's *Life of Lucullus*, chap. 42.
[27] *Att.* 13, 16, 1.

that Lucullus no less than Catulus and Hortensius, the other
speakers, was, if not illiterate, at least not sufficiently versed in
philosophy to carry on the discussion in the *Academica,* and
that he has therefore assigned the parts of these three men to
Cato and Brutus.

Whether or not Cicero has represented Crassus and Antony
as more learned and more conscious of their art than they were
in reality, they had certainly been the two foremost orators of
their generation; no speakers could therefore be more suitable
for a dialogue on oratory.

The thought with which they begin their conversation and
which inspires the whole work, binding all its parts together and
constantly lifting it above the plane of an ordinary technical
discussion, is that eloquence is a noble thing, extremely difficult
of attainment and consequently requiring the most comprehensive training. Oratory being the chief visible activity of men
engaged in public life, whether they were petty politicians or real
statesmen, the orator is made equivalent to the statesman as well
as to the advocate, with the result that education for oratory
becomes the education for public life in its widest sense. Cicero
does not put forward this claim without taking note of the
narrower view that the business of an orator is speaking and
nothing further, but inasmuch as the entire training of the
Romans aimed at speaking, the larger conception of the orator
is not invalidated.

Our rapid survey of the intricacies of rhetorical theory and
of its application has shown at least one thing, that the ordinary
training aimed only at the ability to extract from a subject all
its possibilities of treatment and to make use of these possibilities
in speech. The training gave ingenuity and stylistic ability.
This narrow view is enlarged by Cicero in two directions. Wishing the orator to be better acquainted with the facts that he
uses, Cicero would have him learn law, political science, and
history. The two latter, however, had a far less technical nature

than with us, for political science was a branch of philosophy, indulging almost exclusively in ethical meditations and in utopias, and history, distinctly a part of belles-lettres, scarcely professed to serve any utilitarian purpose beyond that of giving inspiration by means of noble examples. The knowledge of law, on the other hand, was a professional matter; but the advocate's attitude toward it and Cicero's insistence on it have already been set forth in considerable detail, and need not be repeated. The other way in which Cicero wishes to enlarge the training of the orator is in the direction of a liberal education. Political science and history belong here, at least in part; more clearly general are literature and philosophy, though, as we have seen, the philosophers made their subject partly professional for the orator by manufacturing rhetorical Topics out of their ethics, and the Stoics also put forth large practical claims for their instruction in dialectic. Cicero had received such training from the Stoic Diodotus, who lived in his home.

Cicero was not blind to the fact that many men have reached great heights without any formal education whatever. The boast of the self-educated man has probably been heard as long as there have been teachers; in Rome it was even more natural than elsewhere, since education, as a Greek thing, was readily brought into contrast with the old Roman traditions and the old Roman virtues. In speaking for Archias,[28] Cicero had tempered his eulogy of literature and reading by the admission that great men without training had been numerous, and he had added that natural endowment is far more important than education, but he had also insisted that education brings natural talents to their highest fruition. The last statement, incidentally, was less open to attack among the Romans than among us, since formal education had not yet been widely enough accepted to lay a paralyzing hand on men's originality.

---

[28] *Pro Arch.* 15.

But oratory, like the writing of poetry, is so obviously a matter of inspiration that it can not be taught; at least so a man could urge, even if he believed in education. Cicero's reply to this is dictated by sanity and experience. Law needs no defense in this connection; it has to do with facts, and a pleader either knows the facts or he does not. As for the training in rhetoric, though it has never made an orator, as he expresses it, declamation nevertheless gives a helpful fluency, and the theoretical instruction is suggestive and serves as a useful check; the orator who, for example, has made the theory of Topics his second nature sees the possibilities of a case more quickly and more clearly, and if he can extract the main issue from a mass of material, as he has been trained to do in connection with the *status* of Conjecture, Definition, and Morality, he is likely to avoid pitfalls. Inborn common sense, experience, and constant vigilance, however, Cicero observes, are of course far more potent for success than any training.

In the matter of a liberal education, Cicero makes no extravagant claims. Its effect is general; without it the orator is likely to be a tinkling cymbal—to have only empty sounds, is the phrase. A general education puts substance behind his words, which was true in Rome where orators spoke in a human way to exceedingly human jurors; it also gives tone, a charm that seasons the whole oration, as salt seasons food. An orator, often choosing to introduce scientific matters, will also derive benefit from a knowledge of technical science; and in general it is true that knowledge of anything increases his vocabulary, his *copia verborum,* and it is to be remembered that the orator's business is mainly with words.

Mere knowledge does not give the ability to speak. Socrates, Cicero recalls, said that a man could speak well if he was thoroughly informed; but that, according to Cicero, is only a half-truth. The rhetorical philosophers, on the other hand, made pompous assertions. They contended that, since the orator's aim is to influence the emotions of his auditors, he should have the philosopher's knowledge of human emotions—an assertion that recalls the study of child psychology for teachers. Cicero's observation on this point is that the study of philosophy, especially of ethics, is useful in many ways, but that, as Antony is allowed to say, an orator can move his auditors if he is instinctively in sympathy with them, is *en rapport*, and this is not a matter of training in ethics.

The informing thought of the whole discussion, then, is this: natural endowment, both mental and physical, is essential; without it nothing can be done; but the orator, to reach his highest development, must be inspired with a noble enthusiasm for his profession and be always willing to work; and in this work he must not be narrowly preoccupied with mere rhetoric, but he must reach out far, remembering at all times to observe real life and to use common sense in applying his knowledge. To this ideal one objection is inevitable: there is not time. Antony expresses this thought, and Cicero's answer is that the orator can not be expected to know a subject as well as the professional student of it. This is not even desirable; some Greek students have so buried themselves in the details of a science that they have made it unprofitable. Nor is it for the orator's advantage to make a display of knowledge; he must not talk like a philosopher. If he has a good memory, he must not indulge in mnemonic pyrotechnics.

The ideal of a liberal education as opposed to vocational training is not a thing of recent growth. At present the apostles of vocational training, with their eyes on the busy world, rejoice in the novelty of their message and lead the attack on the old stronghold of liberal studies. The sophists in the time of Plato did the same; they would prepare young men for practical life, since the philosophers, according to them, taught but useless prattle. As time went on, the place of the practical sophist was taken by the rhetorician, who taught eloquence, the most practical of accomplishments, whereas the philosophers professed to teach wisdom; it was *dicere* opposed to *sapere*.

With the collapse of Greece as a great democratic nation, oratorical eloquence wandered into lean pastures, and the philosophers had very much their own way. Then Rome was discovered by the Greeks. The rhetoricians polished and sharpened their old weapons and brought them for sale to Rome; Hermagoras of Temnos, the founder of the rhetoric current during Cicero's time, lived in the second century B.C. But the philosophers, who had even formerly attended to rhetoric, now appeared as rival teachers; presently they began to teach rhetoric, but, keeping also their old subjects of philosophy and allied studies, they asserted that they, and not the narrow rhetoricians, gave the most suitable preparation for life. The situation was thus the reverse of that which exists today: the champions of a liberal education were the aggressors.

The battle was carried on with much lecturing and much writing, of which we still have traces. The two sides stole from each other, each accusing the other of theft. The philosophers had an inalienable right to the discussions of abstract questions, *theses,* and the rhetoricians to the concrete questions, *hypotheses;* but now both sides gave training in both, or at least asserted their profesional right to do so.

The arguments employed must have been familiar to Cicero; and very likely he reproduced some of them. This does not make it necessary to imagine that he borrowed all of his arguments or that he took them from books; the thoughts must have been in the air; but it seems almost certain that he did follow some book in certain places, as, for example, when he supports his advocacy of a liberal training by a minute historical account, studded with Greek names, of the growth through the centuries of this ideal.[29] What book he used, or what philosopher, rather,

---

[29] On the pedagogical struggle between the rhetoricians and the philosophers, see von Arnim, pp. 4–114; also Kroll's two articles.

he followed, can not be determined.[30] The two most learned modern investigators give different names, Philo and Antiochus, two Academic philosophers under whom Cicero studied and whom he frequently mentions. They are, indeed, among the four Greek philosophers that, according to Cicero himself, had the greatest influence on him, the others being Diodotus and Posidonius.

But the identity of Cicero's source for such passages as the one referred to is not important for our knowledge of Cicero. He often mentions the authors from whom he draws; as will be explained later, his aim as a writer made such mention natural. Where no name is given, it may be said in general that the inevitable procedure for identifying his sources is to arrive, by careful piecing together of innumerable references, at an opinion about the attitude or actual teaching of some Greek from whom Cicero might have borrowed, and then to declare that a certain thought or passage in Cicero comes from the Greek who has been thus uncertainly characterized. The main result of source study in Cicero is, indeed, as one prominent investigator[31] has admitted, the reconstruction of the intellectual Greek atmosphere in which he lived. If Philo said some of the things found in the *De Oratore*, then Philo is the source; if Antiochus said them, he and not Philo is the source. Cicero obtained his information somewhere, from somebody, and he was undoubtedly familiar, in considerable detail, with the pedagogical arguments of rhetoricians and philosophers; everything else is of relative insignificance.

But Cicero's incidental use of these arguments does not make his work a contribution to pedagogical controversy.[32] It might

---

[30] Von Arnim says Philo; Kroll, Antiochus.

[31] Kroll, *Neue Jahrb.*, p. 685.

[32] Kroll, *op. cit.*, p. 682, criticises Cicero for his inability to withstand the strong tradition of Greek rhetoric; as though Cicero had ever thought if initiating a new system of pedagogy. See above, p. 371, and below, pp. 425–426.

turn some noble Romans to the lecture halls of the rhetorical philosophers, and the latter would have reason for rejoicing, but it might also turn them to the study of law or to the reading of history, with which the philosophers had little to do. Neither is the treatise directed against the Latin rhetoricians, as has been suggested, for the latter are barely mentioned; nor is it intended to prove, as has also been imagined, that Greek rhetorical instruction was superior to Latin—a thing that in Cicero's time needed no proof. The work is on too large a scale for controversy; Cicero is writing for men who have received their training and have already had some experience in actual pleading, intending, in so far as his purpose is didactic, to suggest along what lines they may go farther; and, above all, besides various other matters that could be suggested, it is unthinkable that he, one of the two or three most famous ex-consuls of his time, should stoop to participation in the jealous squabbles of dependent Greeks. His aim, now that he had nothing better to do than to write, was to create a literary work; as the recognized leader among orators, he had also a strong autobiographical tendency, the stronger because his political influence had been greatly diminished; and he was interested, as a student, in the theory of his art.

Perhaps it does not greatly matter whether any one—Crassus, if he was such as he appears in the *De Oratore*, or Philo, or Antiochus—suggested this ideal to Cicero, or whether he evolved it himself. Every man is, after all, self-educated; and this is true particularly of a literary artist. It is not difficult to suggest ways of development; the difficulty consists in traveling along those ways and reaching the goal. Of some importance in this connection is Cicero's account of his training in the *Brutus*, a passage that has already been quoted. He says that he was constantly in the forum observing the various orators; and he attributes his success very definitely to the fact that his was a new kind of oratory, the result of observation and of studies that no other orator had pursued. One might say, therefore, not too seriously, that if the philosophers explained to him the ideal that he later realized, either they explained it to him alone or else they had no success with their other pupils. In the *Brutus,* moreover, Cicero mentions both Philo and Antiochus among his teachers, but only as teachers of philosophy, not of rhetoric.

Crassus and Antony, reflecting the Roman unwillingness to be confused with the Greeks, are at considerable pains to make it clear that they speak as Roman gentlemen and not as Greeks. The latter are said to care more for an argument than for truth. They have no tact;[33] indeed, their language has no word for the Latin *ineptus;* which, as it happens, is not always easy to translate into English either; it means wanting in tact, impertinent, and includes awkwardness and officiousness. The Greeks, so Crassus maintains, do not even give a thought to their shortcomings; wherever these Greek scholars happen to be and in whatever company, they always start some subtle argument about things that are exceedingly difficult or at least quite unnecessary.

They are never troubled by doubts about their own knowledge. Catulus, one of the speakers, recalls the story[34] of Phormio, a Peripatetic philosopher who is otherwise unknown. and Hannibal. The great soldier had been exiled from Carthage and was staying at Ephesus. Here Phormio, invited to speak before the assembled company, discussed the duties of a commander and, for that matter, military affairs in general. Everybody applauded except Hannibal. When the latter was asked how he liked it, he replied, in imperfect but very frank Greek, that he had seen many foolish old men in his day, but nobody quite equaling Phormio. Antony remarks by the way that he has seen many Phormios. The Greeks show their self-complacency not merely in their intercourse with young pupils, he says; not one of them thinks a Roman knows anything. But Antony is not ruffled by their behavior; either they have some-

[33] *De Or.* 2, 17 ff.
[34] *De Or.* 2, 75 ff.

thing worth learning, he observes, or else they are such persons that the mere sight of them makes Antony glad that he has not spent very much time in study.

Cicero's Roman speakers, however, find much that is useful in rhetoric, while they also have some things to criticise; as has already been pointed out. Eager not to be didactic, they introduce their references to rhetorical theory in a casual way, often summing up a long and abstruse part of the science in two or three sentences. The work consists of three books; the first of which contains a general discussion of Cicero's oratorical ideal, the second an account of *inventio,* everything in fact that is not purely stylistic, and the third the treatment of style; but it is impossible to say beforehand in just what book any particular topic may be found, because of the conversational and carefree method of the speakers. A rhetorical subject is sometimes referred to more than once, a later speaker indifferently remarking that he happens to state it in a new way; which reminds the reader how the complex theory varied infinitely in matters of detail.

The two qualities most needful to an orator, which could have been inferred from Cicero's orations as well as from the performances in the courts, are wit and pathos. The forms which they took have already been amply illustrated. The laughable receives an exhaustive technical treatment.[35] Wit, it is explained, originates in that which is disgraceful, pointed out in a manner not disgraceful. It turns either on the form of the expression or on the substance of the thought; and there are seven types of the former kind and six of the latter. Personal defects are mentioned as proper subjects for jokes, if these avoid scurrility, a term the Romans did not understand in the modern Anglo-Saxon sense, though they would have agreed with our forbears. The expounder of wit almost saves the pedantry of his long exposition by observing, in his first remarks, that wit, being a natural gift,

---

[35] *De Or.* 2, 217–290.

can not be taught and that the systematizers of jests have invariably made him laugh at their own lack of humor; but the reader
can scarcely follow him when he says that he intends merely to
give some rules derived from observation.

The account must have been inserted in deference to current
handbooks. Besides these, the ancients made collections of witty
sayings; Cicero's were thus collected—a matter not to be taken
too solemnly, in the light of the scribbling propensities of his
age. Many jokes he had never heard of were fathered on him,
and he makes it known in one of his orations[36] that he has no
objection to this, provided the jokes are good. Caesar had so
keen a sense for Cicero's manner that he could infallibly distinguish between the genuine and the spurious.

The disquisition in the *De Oratore* abounds in examples,
which almost make the reader charitable toward the system.
Most of them come from public life. One little story worth recalling, not from the forum, is connected with the poet Ennius and
his noble friend Nasica. It might have happened today. Nasica,
calling at Ennius' house, was told by the maid that the poet
was not at home. The caller, however, suspected that his friend's
absence was purely social. A few days later Ennius called at
Nasica's residence, and heard a voice shouting that Nasica was
not at home. "Don't you think I know your voice, Nasica?"
the poet called. To which, Nasica: "You are an impudent fellow,
my friend. You expect me to believe your maid, and yet you
won't believe me."

Stories like this one, and observations of many kinds, are
numerous throughout the treatise, revealing the sanity and wisdom of the author or flashing a sudden light on the thoughts
and actions of the Romans. We learn that the best Latin accent
was to be found in Rome, as the best Greek accent was found
in Athens; and this despite the fact that the residents in the
country districts and the towns were more given to study than

---

[36] *Pro Plan.* 35.

the city dwellers. Good habits of speaking are best learned in youth. The ladies speak the purest Latin, for they do not go to the forum and listen to careless speech—an observation that de Quincey read. Laelia, the daughter of Scipio's friend Laelius and the mother-in-law of Crassus, spoke such wonderful Latin that her son-in-law might think he was listening to Plautus or Naevius; though one must hope the worthy Laelia did not indulge in Plautine jokes. Orators are counseled to avoid affectation in speech; and various affectations are named, one of them being the assumption of a brusque, churlish manner in order to seem honest and rugged—a trick not unknown in modern times.

The manner of delivery, as has been indicated before, is said to be of very great importance, and it is recalled how Demosthenes declared it to be the first requisite of good oratory, and the second, and the third; his preference for it resembling old Cato's preference for grazing. Aeschines, Demosthenes' rival, when in exile, aroused great enthusiasm among his hearers by reading Demosthenes' speech *On the Crown;* but his comment on their applause was that they should have heard Demosthenes himself deliver it. Excessive violence of delivery is deprecated by Cicero; it must be reserved for the great moments. The eyes are important; but the voice most of all. It is absolutely essential for an orator to take care of his voice; he must not strain it. And the reader is informed that C. Gracchus, when speaking in public, had in the vicinity a slave with an ivory pipe, who gave the proper pitch when his master let his voice rise or fall more than was desirable.

Exuberance in young men is, on the whole, a good sign; it can be pruned down. But the orator must endeavor to observe a measure in all things. Strong effects pall quickly, for they produce satiety; so the old paintings, free from the modern extravagance in color, Cicero says, retain their hold on us when the new favorites are forgotten. This does not mean that orators should aim to be all alike. Orators, like artists, are of many kinds; each should develop his own possibilities, and so Crassus, speaking for Cicero, says that he will mention the things that have been useful to him; they may not be useful to every one else. And even in doing this, he is modest, confessing that every man knows himself least.

Crassus discusses style, and describes his own early exercises, which obviously are to be taken as Cicero's.[37] He used to read a bit of verse or a part of an oration, just long enough for him to remember the thought in detail, and then he would write it out in his own best form. But there was one objection to this method; Ennius or Gracchus, his models, had already used the best expressions, so that Cicero's language either fell below theirs or was identical, neither of which seemed very profitable to him. Thereupon he turned to free translation from the Greek orators, taking care with his language and using familiar words, but also coining words on the analogy of the Greek. He also translated from other Greek writers, though they are not mentioned in this connection. Imitation, in matters of style and in other things, is recommended, but the reader is warned not to imitate faults or non-essentials; it is easy to walk or to wear the toga as somebody else. Nor does every one need to practise imitation in order to make progress.

Crassus gives many technical rules about writing, and Cicero, both through Crassus and other speakers, lays strong emphasis on the orator's need of constant writing; but much of this is for the clarification of thought, and it is never forgotten that substance and expression can not be separated. Indeed, it can not be stated too strongly that in the case of Cicero the style was the man. He worked hard to acquire his style, but his work looked toward greater powers of self-expression, the releasing of his natural gift, as it were, and not to the acquisition of stylistic ornaments or peculiar turns of phrase. No style could be clearer than Cicero's, or more natural. The musical element is observed,

---

[37] *De Or.* 1, 154 ff.

but it is not obtrusive. In his arrangement or in his choice of words, he never visibly strives for effect; everything is there merely for the greater clearness. Macaulay resembles Cicero in the unimpeded flow of his language, but he is more formal and lacks Cicero's humor. Perhaps Thackeray bears a closer resemblance to Cicero than does any other English writer; but Cicero has more power and a wider sweep.

The discussion of style is in the mouth of Crassus; Antony, speaking technically of Invention, gives[38] several hints of a broader nature, some of which were apparently more necessary to Roman orators, who often ranted senselessly in the forum, than to modern lawyers. Antony—Cicero, that is—took very great pains to master the facts of a case. He interviewed each litigant privately, letting him tell his story in his own way. Thereupon he thought out the various points of the case, and did not consider how to present them until later. He tried to put himself in the position of his adversary, to see the case with his eyes; and when he came to arguing, he tried as much as possible to omit the latter's strong points, covering up his retreat with pompous and fine talk, so as to seem not to be running away but to be yielding in order to take up a better position; making a strategic retreat, in other words. Some orators placed their weakest argument at the beginning of their speech; not so Antony. He placed his best arguments first, put the weaker points in the middle, and then he concluded with a repetition of his best arguments.

He always aimed at variety. If he attacked an opponent, he gave himself the appearance of doing it against his will; and he resisted all advice to inveigh against an angry witness, if the latter was a man of sense and influence. When speaking of the fame of a client, he tried to show that the latter took no proud delight in it, and he enlarged on the client's hard work, which had earned his fame. Antony did not hurry into emotional language, and, once there, he did not hasten past, for it takes

---

[38] *De Or.* 2, 99 ff.

time to stir an audience. He felt the emotion he expressed, for a man can not rouse others to anger if he seems calm himself. On the other hand, he tried to have the appearance of one who with difficulty restrained his feelings. And, finally—a bit of advice sorely needed in Rome—in preparing his speech he wrote his Exordium last of all, having it grow out of the thoughts of the speech as a whole; for an introduction must not be like a musical prelude, lacking connection with that which is to follow. He wondered at the method of Philippus, his contemporary, who, when rising to speak, never seemed to know how to begin, but trusted somehow that he would presently warm to his subject.

Philippus is not one of the interlocutors in the dialogue, but the harmless fun at his expense is frequently paralleled in the remarks exchanged by the speakers themselves. Antony had urged frequent writing as an exercise, observing at the same time that Sulpicius would have been a better orator if he had written more. Sulpicius, while admitting the truth of the criticism, retorts that Antony was not known to have practised writing very extensively; to which Antony replies that they must do what he says and not what he does. Crassus is praised both for his charm and for his power, and Antony finds such ample praise intolerable. As for Crassus' power, he remarks that he shivers when his friend mounts to the high altitudes. Crassus, speaking of careful pronunciation, says that Cotta drops his i's and enunciates his e's too carefully, and is imitated in this by Sulpicius; "for," he adds to the latter, "if you insist on my speaking, you will hear something about your own failings." Crassus had wandered into a discussion of the political attitude of the Gracchi, and is interrupted by one of the speakers: "Never mind that, Crassus; come back to the ivory pipe."

The speakers are also very modest and much given to self-depreciation. Crassus recalls how he never wanted the grave Scaevola to be near while he was canvassing in the forum; Scaevola's presence would have made it difficult for him to act

the fool. And they pay each other extravagant compliments.
The work itself ends with such a compliment, neatly addressed
by Cicero to Hortensius. One of the speakers expresses the regret
that young Hortensius, young in 91 B.C., is not present, and
prophesies that in time Hortensius will excel in all the good
qualities that have been described, very much as Plato in the
Phaedrus represented Socrates as prophesying about the young
Isocrates.[39]

And yet it is not all jest or compliment; the tragedies of
political life also are present. In the preface to the work, Cicero
recalls in a few eloquent sentences how his own life had been
passed amid almost constant turmoil. His youth had come in the
ʼbloodstained days of Marius and Sulla. During his consulship,
when everything hung in the balance, he had voluntarily entered
the strife. Ever since that time he had battled against the waves
that threatened to overwhelm him, as he expresses it; he had
turned them from the state, and they had recoiled upon him.

At the beginning of the third book Cicero describes Crassus'
last speech, which in every one's opinion had surpassed all his
previous efforts, though people always thought that Crassus'
latest oration was his best. Even while speaking, Crassus had
been seized with a pain in his side; he was taken home, and fever
set in; a week later he died from pleurisy. Cicero, sixteen years
old at that time, and his brother had often gone to the senate-
house as if still expecting to hear the voice of the great orator,
who had been their friend. His death was a serious loss to his
country and to those who loved him, says Cicero, but death was,
after all, a kindly gift, since Crassus was thus spared the sight
of Italy in flames. Antony was murdered, and his head nailed
to the rostra; and one of the other speakers in the dialogue,
Catulus, took his own life, to avoid the cruelty of Marius.

The thought of what Crassus had escaped is suggested again
at the beginning of the *Brutus*. Hortensius had died in 50 B.C.

---

[39] See *Or.* 41.

Cicero, who had ended the *De Oratore* with a compliment to Hortensius, begins the later work with a sad reference to his death; but this death, too, had been merciful, for Hortensius did not live to see the Caesarians warring with the Pompeians. It will be remembered that some three years before Cicero published the *De Oratore* he had come very near following the example of Catulus, the father of the Catulus whom he had succeeded as the leader of the senate.

V

BRUTUS AND ORATOR

The *Brutus* and the *Orator* can be looked upon as amplifications of certain parts or characteristics of the *De Oratore*. They were written nine years later; the former in the early months of 46 B.C. and the latter in the second half of the year, after the practical establishment of Caesar as the ruler of Rome. Despite the long interval between the composition of the *De Oratore* and these two works, Cicero looked upon them all as forming one whole; in the essay on Divination,[40] after mentioning the three books of the *De Oratore*, he lists the other treatises as books four and five.

These do not possess the literary charm of the earlier work. There is less humor in the *Brutus* than in its predecessor, and almost none in the *Orator;* there are also fewer winged words of wisdom and not so much of the lofty inspiration that illumines the *De Oratore*. These things are not lacking, to be sure, but the purpose of the later books was somewhat different; they are more didactic and expository; and it would not be profitable to compare them with the earlier work as a whole. The *Brutus* is read more, and certainly more edited, than the *De Oratore*, but this is due to its shorter compass and its highly systematized historical content; it is decidedly a bird of a smaller spread of wing.

---

[40] *De Divin.* 2, 4.

The composition of the *Brutus* was largely suggested to Cicero by a little book written by Atticus. In 51 B.C. Cicero had published his large work on the State, and Atticus had discovered in it certain slight inaccuracies of historical statement. These led to a discussion between the friends, some traces of which can still be seen in the correspondence; and finally Atticus, always a patient delver for facts and already something of an authority in Roman antiquities and genealogy, drew up what might be called a chronological outline of Roman history. It was brief, covering seven hundred years in one book, but it contained a large amount of information about magistrates, laws, wars, and political events, and it also had references to other nations. This book, called *Liber Annalis*, in its turn gave Cicero the thought of his history of Roman oratory; and it supplied a backbone, as it were, around which Cicero could put his extensive knowledge about the Roman orators. Its main service, however, seems to have consisted in its inspiration to write the *Brutus* rather than in any actual help toward doing so, for if the *Brutus* be compared with the *De Oratore*, it will be seen that the later work does not contain very much, and nothing of any real importance, that is is not found in the *De Oratore* and yet could have come from Atticus. Many statements about dates and other historical matters are introduced, but they are irrelevant, and were felt to be such by Cicero, who explains their presence by his interest in Atticus' work; in other words, they were taken from the *Liber Annalis* in compliment to Atticus.

Being a history of Roman oratory, the *Brutus*[41] is Cicero's most original treatise in so far as the content is concerned. He was unusually well equipped for the task; probably better equipped than any other man in Rome. Aside from his experience and his knowledge of rhetorical theory, his own preparation for his profession, coupled with his love of Rome and his inquiring spirit, had given him an extraordinary command of the facts

[41] On the *Brutus*, see particularly the introduction to Martha's edition.

to be employed. He had always been a close observer of his own contemporaries; and he had heard, and remembered, as is shown by the *De Oratore*, what his older friends had to tell about the men who had gone before, as far back as the time of the Scipionic Circle. In addition to this, he had collected and read all the speeches of these and of earlier orators that he could procure, even making investigations as to their authenticity. Thus he was familiar with one hundred and fifty orations of Cato the Elder. Cato's were the earliest orations extant, he tells us, with the exception of the speech delivered by Appius Claudius the Blind against Pyrrhus, and some early eulogies. For the earliest orators, whose speeches had been lost, he had recourse to historical annals and similar works. Of the orators of his own time and for a generation or two before, he therefore can write fully, not merely criticising their speeches but also describing their manner of delivery; in the case of the orators just preceding these, he formed his judgment from their orations, and has rarely anything to say of their delivery; of the earliest orators, he can say only what he could infer from history.

To write a history of Roman oratory was in itself highly congenial to Cicero; it was a patriotic act, like the writing of political history, and tended to show that Rome, no less than Greece, with its long list of orators, had to its credit a solid accomplishment in this, the most difficult of arts. The whole character of the *Brutus* indicates that the main purpose of the treatise is that of history—literary history and criticism. But it had also another purpose, already noted, which binds it to the *De Oratore*. In discussing the orators in chronological order, —both the famous ones and others, though the sub-title later invented for the work is *De Oratoribus Claris*—it shows how Roman eloquence gradually improved, many men contributing, until it reached its climax at the time of Cicero, and practically in Cicero himself. It becomes thus a restatement and a justification of the ideal expressed in the *De Oratore*. This historical

justification had already been put forward in the earlier work;
now, however, it is given with greater clearness and much greater
detail.

The criterion for judging the orators is therefore the ideal
expounded in the *De Oratore:* Did the orator in question have
native talent, a broad education, experience? For detailed criticism, the orator is brought to the bar of rhetorical theory;
Cicero's language, whether informal or actually technical,
derives its meaning from the theory, so that the full force of
Cicero's criticisms can not be understood without a knowledge
of Greek rhetoric. He asks in how far an orator fulfilled the
requirements of the five parts of rhetoric, Invention, Arrangement, Style, Delivery, and Memory; whether he accomplished
an orator's three aims, to teach or convince, to please, and to
move; and as the style of a speaker had of old been classed as
simple, temperate, or grand—*tenue, medium, grande*—for which
also other terms occur, Cicero uses this classification in his
characterizations.

These characterizations, however, are not lacking in insight
and fine distinctions, though these are found only in the more
detailed criticisms. Cicero discusses the early life of an orator,
whether, for instance, he had the opportunity of learning good
Latin in his youth; he also takes into account the political conditions of his time, the stage of development reached by the
Latin language when he spoke, the kind of education then accessible. The criticisms thus become personal evaluations, and are
made from the two points of view of an absolute standard, that
of the *De Oratore,* and of a relative standard, that of an orator's
own time. The recognition that the times were changing is an
important part of Cicero's attitude. He divides the history of
Roman eloquence into seven periods, and shows how the conditions for good oratory improved from one to another; and
this, in its turn, becomes an argument for his thesis that the
best oratory belonged to his own time, as had been set forth in
his earlier work.

Cicero himself is the main speaker, Atticus and Brutus being his auditors. In order to bring the account down to Cicero's own time, which was necessary, the expounder had to belong to this time; and nobody was as suitable as Cicero himself. He is, after all, giving his own frank opinions.

He excludes living orators, on the alleged ground that Brutus had heard them. There are only two real exceptions,[42] namely, Caesar and Cicero himself. As for the dramatic propriety of including Caesar, Brutus remarks that he has not had an opportunity to hear him speak; but the real reason is obviously a desire to compliment the dictator. And it was largely a literary compliment. Caesar had written his work on grammar, concerned with the choice of words, and he had dedicated the work to Cicero, with high praise of Cicero's services to Rome because of his oratory. Atticus is represented as recalling Caesar's eulogy of Cicero, and thereupon he gives a very laudatory account of Caesar's oratory.

The book, though devoted to exposition and criticism, was indirectly didactic, for the recognition of former orators' failures was intended as advice to Brutus, who still had to win his spurs. Cicero can therefore rather naturally end the book, or very nearly end it, with an account of his own training and the description of his own new style of oratory. Cicero traces his growth through the ten years before the journey in Greece; the journey, with the description of his physical condition and the changes wrought by the teaching of Molo; and, finally, the period prior to his consulship. He mentions his teachers and the conditions in Rome that influenced him, and also the speakers whom he observed or emulated. It is not a long passage, only some three or four pages, but it is probably better known than any other in all his treatises. Its analytic insight has been highly praised[43] as marking a distinct step in the gradual evolution of

---

[42] A few lines are also given to Marcellus (248–251).
[43] Misch., pp. 196 ff.

autobiographical writing toward the complete psychological self-expression found in St. Augustine. An important part of it is Cicero's account of his friendly rivalry with Hortensius. The passage therefore merges into a criticism of Hortensius, which both closes the book, except for some concluding conversational remarks, and is also Cicero's final jugdment of his great contemporary.

One of the orators discussed in the *Brutus* is Calvus, who had died in 47 B.C., the year before the *Brutus* was composed. Calvus had been a prominent member, probably the most prominent, of a group of young orators and poets, which included Brutus and Catullus. In poetry they sought their models among the Alexandrine writers; in oratory they harked back to Lysias, and even to Thucydides and Xenophon. Their ideal in oratory, put briefly, was clearness and simplicity, the avoidance of emotion and of literary artistry, especially the use of rhythm. As a sign of the purity of their tastes, they called themselves Attic orators. These new Atticists, *Novi Attici*, were opposed to the verbosity and euphuism that had flourished in Asia Minor, represented conspicuously in Rome by Hortensius, as well as to the less extravagant manner taught at Rhodes, of which Cicero can be said to have been the representative.

It is no longer possible to decide upon the relative merits of Cicero and the New Atticists, for no orations of the latter are extant. Quintilian, Seneca in the *Controversies*, and Tacitus, all decided in favor of Cicero, though there were some men who held Calvus to have been the greatest of Roman orators. A thought perhaps worthy of consideration is this, that Cicero looked at oratory from its practical application, making the people, the listeners, the final judge; whereas Calvus and his associates set up a theoretic ideal—always a deadening thing to do in any art.[44] Calvus, says Cicero in the *Brutus*,[45] watched himself too closely; in his anxiety to avoid everything faulty, he lost all real strength.

---

[44] See Norden, *Die Antike Kunstprosa*, 1, 221.
[45] *Brut.* 283.

Cicero, in his characterization, takes no note of Calvus' vehement power as it had been displayed, and later became known to the Roman critics, in his speeches against Vatinius, the Caesarian whom Cicero attacked and later defended; but the vehemence in these orations was not a part of Calvus' expressed oratorical ideal, and one may conjecture that he was more sensible as an orator than as a theorist. Cicero's quarrel, however, was with the theorist. It should be added that, according to Tacitus,[46] the second speech against Vatinius, the best known, had the usual rhetorical ornaments of style and rhythm.

The differences between Cicero, on the one hand, and Calvus and Brutus, on the other, had been discussed in private letters, and these letters were still read in the time of Tacitus. To students of the empire, the more as they lived in an age when real oratory was dead, these epistolary discussions assumed an importance which they very probably did not have in the eyes of the original correspondents. The intellectualists of Cicero's time disagreed about all sorts of things, rhetorical as well as philosophical; but these disagreements were of slight contemporary significance. Calvus, furthermore, was dead when Cicero wrote the *Brutus;* and neither Brutus nor any other adherent of the New Atticism could rival Cicero either as an actual orator or as a writer about the theory. At this time, too, the domination of Caesar had banished real oratory from Rome, as Cicero feared and regretfully expressed when he thought of Brutus' future, so that the surviving New Atticists would have slight opportunity for practising their theories. It may safely be conjectured that Hortensius had caused Cicero much more worry than Calvus and Brutus.

As a theoretical quarrel, however, it led Cicero to insert in the *Brutus* a brief controversial passage in connection with Calvus, and very likely to write the *Orator*. In the preface to this treatise, he represents Brutus as having urged him to give a picture of the ideal orator; and at the end of the book he says

---

[46] Tac. *Dial.* 21, 6.

that Brutus may follow the ideal just described if he should approve of it; if not, he may retain his own opinion, and Cicero will not undertake to decide between them.

Cicero in this literary controversy displays all his cleverness as the foremost pleader of Rome.[47] The New Atticists, he says, might win the favor of students and those who take care to listen, but they make no appeal to the people; why, not only ordinary loiterers about the tribunal but even the *advocati* leave them;[48] and this had at least a measure of truth, despite Calvus' speeches against Vatinius. Cicero repeats it later, and Tacitus[49] says that almost no one read the other orations of Calvus, and as for Brutus, all testimony seems to show that he aroused no enthusiasm.[50] The New Atticists, Cicero continues, imitate what seems easy of imitation, clearness, but wisely deprecate the higher flights. They also choose for their models not merely Lysias, but also Thucydides and Xenophon, who were not orators at all. And, altogether, they make an erroneous claim to Atticism, for though Lysias is truly Attic, no less so are others, especially Demosthenes, the greatest of them all, and Demosthenes uses the grand manner and pays much attention to rhythm. It was in connection with the last argument that Cicero projected a translation of Demosthenes' oration *On the Crown* and Aeschines' oration *Against Ctesipho,* of which only the preface seems to have been written.

But Cicero goes farther in the *Orator.* As has already been remarked, scholars recognized three kinds of style: the simple, the temperate, and the grand. The rhetoricians, furthermore, gave it as the duty of an orator to prove or teach, to please, and to move.[51] These two concepts are brought together by

---

47 See Kroll's edition of the *Orator,* Einleitung.

48 *Brut.* 283, 289.

49 Tac. *Dial.* 21, 10.

50 See below, p. 599 and note 4.

51 These three tasks are often stated as two: (1) to prove or to teach, which is addressed to the intellect; (2) to please and to move, which are addressed to the emotions. See above, p. 383, note 11.

Cicero, and as the New Atticists cultivated only the simple style, they fulfilled, according to him, only one of the duties of an orator, that of giving information or proving their point, and neglected the other two, which were far more important in real life, to win the favor of the hearers and to stir them to the desired action.

Though the controversial purpose influences both the arrangement and the content in the *Orator*, this work reaches far beyond controversy. Cicero, at Brutus' request, had undertaken to give a picture of the ideal orator, and he professes to undertake the task with much misgiving, hinting, as Crassus had done in the *De Oratore*, that perhaps he has never seen the perfect orator, who, indeed, may be like one of the incorporeal ideas of Plato, something to be aimed at, though not quite attainable. Nevertheless the *Orator* is virtually a description of Cicero himself; he writes in the first person, and draws numerous illustrations from his own orations. He states again the oratorical ideal of the *De Oratore*, his own attainment of which had at least been implied in the autobiographical passage in the *Brutus;* and as the style of an orator is his most important quality, at least from a literary point of view, his manner of delivery and his grasp of argument being concerned exclusively with practical success, he devotes nearly one half of the book to questions of the choice of words and rhythm.

The treatment of style, indirectly, is an argument against the New Atticists, but it is much more an exposition of Cicero's own stylistic theories; it repeats and enlarges the account in the third book of the *De Oratore*, and is indeed almost the only source from which modern scholars derive their knowledge of Cicero's theoretical attitude toward these matters. Cicero himself said that this book contained a fuller treatment of style than had previously been attempted; a statement that perhaps should be interpreted, though by no means certainly, as referring to writers in Latin.

The *Orator,* therefore, becomes Cicero's final statement not only of his oratorical ideal but also of what he conceived himself to have attained. It is as if the discussion begun by Antony, Crassus, and their friends, in the *De Oratore,* had been carried farther, first by Cicero in the presence of Atticus and Brutus, in the *Brutus,* and then by Cicero alone, speaking no longer as a character in a fictitious conversation but in his own person.

CHAPTER XIII

ON THE STATE

I

DE RE PUBLICA

The *De Oratore* was followed by Cicero's second large treatise, the *De Re Publica,* On the State. He began actual work on it in May, 54 B.C., as is indicated by two letters[1] to his brother Quintus, who was then in Gaul. In May he speaks of being engaged in writing on politics, which he finds slow and laborious, adding that if he succeeds, it will be labor well expended; if not, he will throw the book into the sea that he is looking upon while writing. He was then at Cumae. "I shall in that case go on to something else," he continues, "for I can not rest." In October or November he refers again to the work, stating definitely that it was begun in his villa at Cumae. The task had proved difficult.

It was an Aristotelian dialogue, the speakers being Scipio and some members of his Circle, and consisted of nine books, the conversation of each book filling one day. Cicero had read his manuscript to a friend, Sallustius, who suggested that Cicero should himself be the main speaker. This would be fitting, Sallustius thought, inasmuch as Cicero was not a theorist, but a man of consular rank, who had been much engaged in politics. Assigning the discussion to people long dead, men whom Cicero had never seen, would make the work seem too much like fiction, mere imaginings. Aristotle, too, had made himself the chief speaker. The change in plan proposed by Sallustius seemed attractive, Cicero adds, particularly because it would enable him to treat of events that had happened since the time of Scipio. He had previously chosen the early dramatic date, he explains,

---

[1] *Ad Q. Fr.* 2, 12 (14); 3, 5.

for the very purpose of avoiding giving offense to any one by comments on contemporary matters, but now he thinks he will be able to avoid the offense and yet be the main speaker himself. He promises that when he gets to Rome he will send Quintus the first draft, of which he himself is still rather fond.

The work progressed slowly. Probably the treatise was not published until just before Cicero's departure for his province, in the year 51 B.C. On his way thither, after leaving Athens, he writes to Atticus that the latter must, by Hercules, send full news of the political situation, the more as he is now turning over Cicero's own books on a similar subject. Atticus had evidently been attending to the publication of the treatise, for in May, immediately after Cicero's departure, Caelius had written to Cicero that the work was having great success with everybody.

As finally published, the work consisted of six books, and not of nine, as in the first draft; but the early speakers were retained. The conversation is supposed to have lasted three days, instead of nine, two books being assigned to each day. But the treatise has not come down to us in complete form. The first three books have been fairly well preserved, though much has been lost; thus the preface and the introductory scene contain two thirds of all that remains of the first book. The three remaining books are represented only by fragments, which are disconnected and, with one exception, very short, not one of them filling one page. The exception, from the sixth book, is the Dream of Scipio, *Somnium Scipionis,* which, because of its beauty, was chosen for a special commentary by Macrobius in the fifth century, and so preserved. References to the last three books by later authors, however, especially by St. Augustine and Lactantius, as well as the contents of the first three books, enable us to understand the general trend of thought in the latter half of the work, but practically all details are lacking. Even the general thought is at times beyond sure inference. The fragments of the whole treatise cover about one hundred pages.

As a companion work to the *Republic*, Cicero began a treatise on the Laws, *De Legibus*, which, however, as has been noted before, was almost certainly not published in Cicero's lifetime, and possibly had not received the last touches when he died. There are three books extant, with gaps in them; but a fifth book is quoted. While the *Republic* describes the ideal state, the *Laws* discusses its statutes, so that the later work sometimes repeats the thought of the former. Thus the first book of the *Laws* lays as a foundation for the whole treatment of laws the thesis that all law is derived from God, through our inborn sense of justice; and this is also the subject of the third book of the *Republic*. The second and third books of the *Laws* are concerned with religion and with magistracies; two topics that in some form or other were touched upon in the latter half of the *De Re Republica*.

As the laws proposed and discussed are very much those actually found in Rome, the *De Legibus* was less dependent on Greek sources than its companion treatise. The relation between the two works is thus much the same as that between the *De Oratore* and the *Brutus;* Cicero's discussion of the laws corresponding to his former account of the Roman orators. This similarity is further borne out by the fact that in the *Republic*, as in the *De Oratore*, the speakers belong to a past age, whereas in the *Laws*, as in the *Brutus*, Cicero himself is the chief speaker. He has two interlocutors in both treatises; Atticus occurs in both, whereas Quintus in the *Laws* corresponds to Brutus in the work named for him. Cicero had almost certainly made considerable progress with the *Laws* before he went to Cilicia, prompted in his researches by his election to the board of augurs in 53 B.C.; when he again turned to composition, after the Civil War, his first work was the *Brutus*.

Scipio, in the *Republic*, begins his discussion with a formal definition of the term state. A state, he says, is its people, and a people, or nation, is not any fortuitous aggregation of human beings, but a body of men joined together by a common recog-

nition of what is right and by a community of interests. The
reason why men have thus come together is not their sense of
weakness, and so a desire for mutual help and protection, but
rather an innate human instinct which urges the individual to
seek fellowship with other men.

A state, Scipio continues, must have a governing power, just
as a human being is governed, or should be governed, by his
mind. As this governing power may be in the hands of an individual, an aristocratic minority, or the people as a whole, there
are three kinds of government: monarchic, aristocratic, and
democratic. Of these the monarchic is most to be preferred;
it might indeed be considered as fashioned after the divine rule
in the world, the king corresponding in his love and care for his
subjects to Jupiter, the divine father.

But no one of these three forms of government is the best.
The basis of all rule must be justice, and justice is not humanly
attainable in an individual or in any group of individuals,
however large. Human beings tend to deteriorate. The king
becomes a tyrant; the rule of the aristocracy becomes a rule by
factions, *factio*; and the rule of the people becomes mob rule.
The three simple forms of government, therefore, can not make
a good state; but their advantages may be retained in a mixed
form, as in Rome, where the consuls, the senate, and the popular
assemblies together wield all power, supplementing and checking
one another. This kind of a government is therefore the best,
and, since it makes the most adequate provision for the rule of
reason and justice, it contains an element of perpetuity. Its
foundation is as stable as that of the universe itself; they are
both governed according to the same principle.

A government is evolved by the people themselves after they
have come together in accordance with their instinct; it is a
natural growth; but, being the work of human beings, it is
exposed to changes, both good and bad. There is thus a natural
evolution. Polybius in his history, and he was Scipio's teacher,

has a complete series,[2] which illustrates the transformations of the simple forms of government and shows how they make a circle. First arises the single ruler, who most completely represents the human need of a ruling power. While good, he is a king; when deteriorating, he becomes a tyrant. He is driven out by the revolt of an aristocracy, which in its turn changes into a wicked oligarchy. The latter is expelled by the people, who set up a democracy. The democracy, having become mob rule, gives rise to a single ruler. And thereupon the evolution begins again.

Polybius had not made this theoretical account tally with the development of Rome. Cicero, therefore, while including Polybius' series as scientifically satisfactory, and no doubt humanly possible, or even likely, tries also to show other forms of development more nearly in accord with Roman history. But the fragmentary condition of the book makes it impossible to follow his treatment in detail. He recognizes, however, that changes are inevitable, and gives it as the highest achievement of a statesman to be able to foresee them, so that he may check or anticipate them as the case may require.

Of all the states that have ever existed or been imagined, so Scipio concludes at the end of the first book, Rome is most nearly perfect; humanly speaking, it is the perfect state. In the second book, therefore, Scipio traces the evolution of the Roman government, which serves both as an illustration of the theory and as a picture of the ideal state.

He begins with a statement of Cato the Elder, whom he greatly admired, to the effect that the constitution of Rome has not been given by one person but is a natural growth, the work of many men. This growth is thereupon shown in detail by a rapid review of Roman history, in the course of which Scipio frequently stops to point out how political theory agrees with actual facts. But, as Laelius observes, the facts of Roman history are difficult to ascertain; and this difficulty is even greater for

2 See Schmekel, pp. 75 ff.

us because of the gaps in the book. Cicero's account, as we have
it, ends about the time of the Decemviri and the writing of the
Twelve Tables.

There are, however, many passages of considerable interest,
which can only be touched upon. The site of Rome, to begin
with, was chosen with much wisdom. Placed on a river but
away from the coast, Rome has the advantages, Scipio says,
without the disadvantages, of a seaport. It can not be so readily
attacked by sea-roving enemies, and it is less exposed to the
deleterious moral influences at work wherever sailors congregate.
Its hills are healthful and afford protection in war. The kings
of Rome were usually elected. This is the preferable way, for
only thus the best men become kings. Rome, though developing
naturally within itself, acquired much from other peoples, and
improved upon these acquisitions. It was in the time of the
Tarquins that the Greek influence became a mighty river; formerly it had been but a trickling brook. Servius Sulpicius saw
to it that the greatest power in the state was given not to the
majority but to those who owned property; and this should always
be done, for the people of means have naturally the greatest
interest in the prosperity of the state. When the republic had
been established, the political wisdom of the Romans became
increasingly apparent. The right of appeal was granted to the
ordinary citizen, so that he might not be flogged or executed at
the mere bidding of a magistrate, and the tribunes of the plebs
were created to give still further protection to the common
people. But a proper moderation was observed; only a little
power was given to the ordinary citizens, most of it being in
the hands of the aristocracy, and the old regal power was perpetuated in the consuls, who, however, are two in number and
hold office for only one year.

There is a lofty enthusiasm in Scipio's account of Rome;
he finds it very congenial to prove that Rome is the best state
that ever existed; but suddenly he is interrupted by Tubero.

"You are talking about Rome," says the latter, "and not about the perfect state." Scipio admits that Rome, though best, is not perfect; and Philus suggests that they discuss justice in its relation to the state, which forms the subject of the third book.

Justice, according to the Stoics, is inborn in man and derived from God; it is one and unchangeable; laws and morality come ultimately from it. This subject, as has just been mentioned, is also treated in the first book of the *Laws*, and it is no longer possible to determine the amount of repetition. In the *Laws* Cicero meets one criticism of this theory, based on the differences in morality and convention that can be observed among different peoples; and we do not know in how far this criticism was met in the *Republic*. The Stoic answer is that the differences are due to external circumstances; the motive impelling good men is invariably their innate sense of justice.

There was another criticism, that of the sceptic Carneades, who said that states can not be governed without injustice; that utility, or selfishness, is the impelling motive. According to St. Augustine, who gives an outline of this book, this question of utility as opposed to justice was the chief topic of the book. The reply to Carneades must have been that nothing is useful if it is not just, that it is better for a man to suffer losses, even to die, than to depart from the dictates of his soul. At least, this is the Stoic answer given by Cicero in his later work, the *De Officiis*, where the same subject is discussed, though from the general point of view of a man's whole duty.

Perhaps Carneades was not to be taken very seriously. His aim seems to have been merely to show the Stoics that dogmatizing is dangerous. When in Rome as an ambassador from Athens, he is said to have discoursed one day with much fulness on justice, and on the following day he disproved everything he had previously maintained. Carneades, nevertheless, had the unregenerate world with him. Justice is folly, he said. If a man has a slave who is inclined to run away or a house that is unhealthful, he naturally wishes to get rid of them; but shall he tell the truth to a prospective buyer? If a ship has been wrecked and a man has found a plank to float on, shall he surrender it to some one who is weaker?

Lactantius, who reports these and other questions of Carneades, says that when Cicero championed justice, he was unable to answer them and passed them by as pitfalls. Cicero's answer, however, has already been indicated; but the Stoics did not quite agree about such cases as that of a man trying to sell a house. The whole matter is put briefly, though not altogether convincingly, in a fragment of this book: that only a madman would fail to prefer justice to personal advantage. Or, as in a fragment of the next book: a man would rather die than have his body transformed to that of a beast, even though he be allowed to retain his human soul. How much worse it is to retain the human form and get the soul of a beast!

But this discussion is a part of ethics and not of political science, as Cicero himself observed in the *Laws*.

The contents of the last three books can not be made out with any fulness. In the fourth, Cicero seems to have discussed various topics connected with morality in the state. Speaking of education, he says that Rome had pursued the correct policy in leaving the training of the young to the family, instead of making it a concern of the state. In this view he opposed Polybius and the practise generally current among the Greeks. Cicero also disapproved of the socialism advocated by Plato, and, in a less advanced form, by Lycurgus. He believed it the duty of the state, indeed one of its main purposes, to protect each citizen in the possession of his property. A man should prosper or suffer according to his own deserts. And socialism, if extended to a community of wives and children, is utterly subversive of morality, the basis of which is the home. The drama, too, seems to have been discussed in some detail. In the extant fragments, Cicero says that it is a mirror of life, so that the Greek comedy is indecent because of the indecency of the Greeks themselves. The Greeks had also allowed political criticism in their plays. Cicero maintains that lapses from morality should be punished by the censors and not by the poets. Naevius, as we know from report, had leveled his verses against the powerful family of the Metelli, and had been sent into exile for his pains.

The fifth book, and probably to some extent the sixth as well, gave a picture of the true statesman, the man who guides, moderates, steers the state—the *rector, moderator, gubernator.* He is the very opposite of the tyrant. There is nothing baser in the sight of gods and men than the tyrant, whether he be a king who has become tyrannical or a citizen who has sought to overthrow the republic after it had been established in freedom. The good statesman, on the other hand, is honorable and wise ; he protects the state ; his aim is the happiness of the citizens, the strength, prosperity, glory, and virtuous character of the state ; he trains himself by experience and reading, rouses others to imitate him, and is by the nobility of his character and his life a mirror to his fellow-citizens. He needs training no less than men in other walks of life, but the kind of training that Cicero set forth is not known to us. Perhaps we get more than a glimpse of it in the *De Oratore,* for the orator should be a statesman as well as a speaker, and in the *De Officiis,* which, though treating of Duty in general, never loses sight of the citizen.

II
SCIPIO'S DREAM

A somewhat complete account of the extant fragments of the *Republic* has been given because this work and the *De Oratore* were probably Cicero's most important literary undertakings. He spent more time on them than on any others ; with their sequels, they certainly contained far more of his Roman spirit and his thoughts about practical matters than was the case with the philosophical treatises, the *De Officiis* excepted. An indica-

tion of the care and imagination that went into the making of
the *Republic* is contained in the introductory scene, which professes to reproduce a conversation between several members
of the Scipionic Circle. There is nothing more vivid or more
pleasing in the *De Oratore*. For this scene, and undoubtedly for
the artistic side of the whole work, Cicero drew upon his reading
about these men, and even more, one may conjecture, on his
recollections of Scaevola's and Crassus' reminiscences.

The artistic care expended upon the work and its wide scope,
together with its philosophical substructure and its large historical view, mark the treatise as a comprehensive treatment of
government and at the same time an ambitious contribution to
literature, such as had not been previously attempted in Latin.
Cicero frankly puts it side by side with Plato's *Republic*. This
is indicated not merely by its sequel, the *Laws,* which parallels
Plato's work of the same name, but by numerous resemblances
to Plato in the fragments and by frequent references to him
both in them and in the *Laws*. *The Dream of Scipio* recalls
Plato most of all, perhaps, for it is clearly suggested by Plato's
account of Er, even though the content of *Scipio's Dream* is
different.

Plato had described a utopia. Cicero, on the other hand,
makes Rome his ideal state; a difference that he insists upon both
in the *Laws* and in the *Republic* itself. Scipio, in the second
book, explains that he can more easily attain his object if he
shows how the Roman state came into being and grew to fulness
of strength than if he discoursed on an imaginary republic, as
did Socrates in Plato's work; he will not deal with a shadowy
image, he remarks later, but with a real state. Socrates was a
philosopher, whereas Scipio was a statesman. It is of course
unthinkable that Cicero should express any contempt for Socrates or Plato, such as he often puts in the mouth of Crassus
and Antony in reference to the presumptuous and inexperienced
Greek rhetoricians, but the contrast between the attitude of

Cicero's speakers in the *Republic,* who are practical men of affairs, and that of Socrates or Plato is nevertheless very much the same.

But however thoroughly Cicero believed in a practical way that Rome was the best of all states, it was not he who discovered that Rome fulfilled the theoretical requirements of the philosophers. When the Greek commonwealths had lost their political importance, and in many cases also their independence, the Stoics turned their eyes from individual governments, whether real or imaginary, and began to think of men as citizens of a world-embracing community. Men were no longer Spartans, or Athenians, or even Carthaginians, but human beings, all brothers; they could find their duties in their relations to individual men and not to a government. But when these Stoics came into close contact with the Romans, who were conquering the world, Rome became in their eyes this world state of which they had been dreaming, and men were again citizens under a definite government.

Polybius almost certainly initiated this view. Rome is represented in his history as deservedly the ruler of the world; he explains how this had come about, and he never tires of praising Rome as he knew it. But Polybius was a politician and a soldier rather than a philosopher; his work is a political history and not a philosophical treatise on government. In describing the Roman constitution, he is much more concerned with its practical excellencies than with its correspondence to a Stoic ideal. But others must have treated of this; particularly Panaetius, who, as Cicero says in the *Republic,* was in the habit of discussing political questions with Polybius and Scipio. Both the purely philosophic parts of the book, therefore, and the conception of Rome as the philosopher's ideal state come from the Stoics. We do not know, however, whether any book had been written by Panaetius or by any one else from which Cicero derived the plan of his work; very likely it was original with

him. He does not succeed in the *Laws*, and probably did not in
the *Republic*, in connecting the philosophical meditations very
intimately with the real Rome; a fault that is inherent in all
speculation; but, as shown above, he seems to have done better
in this respect than Polybius.

In spite of Cicero's dependence on Polybius, Panaetius, and
other Greeks, there must have been a great deal in the *Republic*
which came from Roman thought, largely from Cicero himself.
His very intention at one time of appearing in the dialogue
indicates this. Some differences of opinion between him and the
Greeks have already been pointed out. In the *Laws*—the first
book of which is dependent on Panaetius or Antiochus, a disputed matter—Cicero is constantly expressing his own political
opinions; he dwells particularly on such matters as the tribuneship and the free embassies, in which he was interested, and
he refers to political events that he had himself observed or in
which he had taken part.

Cicero's borrowings from the Greeks supply, nevertheless, the
leading thoughts in the work; its aim is largely to transfer, with
criticisms, Greek philosophical meditation. This aim makes the
treatise only incidentally, as it were, a statement of Cicero's
political ideal. That had been expressed in his own life, in the
orations after his consulship, particularly after the exile, and in
his autobiographical writings. This is a very important consideration. Students have been inclined to take for granted that
Cicero lived in an atmosphere of books, that his eyes looked upon
real life without seeing it.[3] His political ideal is supposed to
have been Scipionic Rome,[4] toward which he was always reaching

---

[3] How far this belief has led scholars is seen in Zielinski, *Cicero im
Wandel etc.*, pp. 186–188, where Cicero's difference in attitude toward
Caesar and Pompey is attributed to his psychological idiosyncracies, with
very little thought of the difference between the two triumvirs. Zielinski,
189 ff., finds a reason for Cicero's alleged inability to see things as they are
in his rhetorical training, as though nearly all other prominent Romans were
not similarly trained.

[4] Cauer maintains that Cicero's political ideal was Scipionic Rome and
then he seems to criticise him for not upholding this ideal in practical
politics.

back. He had striven, and was later to strive, for the retention of the republican form of government; but it has already been shown that nobody, not even Caesar, was consciously planning to destroy it. The march of history destroyed it. And it has also been indicated how Cicero, in making a place in his ideal for Pompey, took cognizance of the changing times, in a way that the aristocrats did not—and the aristocrats included most of the prominent politicians of the day. They wished to retain the old oligarchical government as it had been legalized by Sulla.

As for Scipio himself and the other representatives of Scipionic Rome, though it is true that Cicero mentions them very frequently, he refers quite as often to other Romans. Cato the Elder was constantly on his lips; Cicero indeed makes Cato of Utica notice this; and the old Cato was no friend to the Hellenized Rome of Scipio. Marius occurs in Cicero's writings at all periods, and Marius was the least bookish of all Romans.

Indeed, Rome was much governed by tradition; the *mos maiorum* was the strongest argument on every occasion. If we still had the orations and other writings of Cicero's contemporaries, we should undoubtedly find as frequent references to the old worthies in them as in Cicero. Cato, for one, was unceasingly giving an impersonation of his ancient relative the Censor. In his private letters, to be sure, especially to Atticus, Cicero very often comments on current events, with references to ideas contained in books he was reading or had himself written. But this is no proof of a bookish blindness to actual life. As Atticus was intimately conversant with Cicero's literary occupations, nothing was more natural than a literary reference.

In publishing the *Republic*, therefore, Cicero did not utter a vain cry for the return of Scipionic Rome, nor does it seem likely that he tried in any way specifically either to influence or to justify the political situation. The work made an appeal to readers of different political persuasions. "Everybody likes it,"

wrote Caelius. In the years 54–51 B.C., when the work was
written, Cicero had no hope of a change to a more constitutional
government; and he had himself openly sided with Caesar and
Pompey. On the other hand, it seems very unlikely that by an
anachronism or by prophecy he made room for their new power
in his ideal state. If he had done so, it must have been in
connection with his account of those who guide the state, the
rectores. This account is extant only in fragments. In the year
49 B.C. Cicero writes to Atticus that Pompey is not acting in
accordance with the advice given by Scipio to such directors
of the state; and this might indicate that Scipio's statements
were prophetic of the two surviving triumvirs. But the reference
is probably one of that general kind just mentioned. Indeed,
the *rector* or *moderator* of the state was any statesman who had
risen to great influence. Even in the *De Oratore* the term is
used of several men, and in the *Republic* itself Scipio, Laelius,
and Philus are mentioned as unequaled examples of such statesmen.

In so far as the *Republic* contained an expression of Cicero's
practical ideal of politics, which is not the same as incidental
opinions about details, and in so far as Cicero did at all expect
it to influence actual conditions, this is to be sought in its enthusiasm for public service and in the high ideal of unselfishness that
is set before his fellow-citizens. This was the very thought that
had governed Cicero's political life. In the preface to the
Republic, speaking in the first person, he proclaims it the duty
of all who can to take part in political life—some of his words
have been quoted before—and at the end of the last book he gives
in the *Dream of Scipio* a lofty, though somewhat transcendental,
expression to the thought that not only is public service the
highest of human activities but it must be guided by virtue; fame
and other earthly rewards are of little value.

Laelius had asked what were the rewards of unselfish statesmen if statues and triumphs were not to be considered, and Scipio

replied by narrating his dream. Er of Pamphylia, incidentally, had been represented by Plato as coming to life again after death, a literary device much ridiculed by the materialistic Epicureans; Cicero, to avoid criticism, makes Scipio dream. The philosophic thoughts in the dream are Greek; Stoicism combined with the mystic attitude of Pythagoras and Plato; but through it all shines Cicero's own character and his striving for philosophic calm.

At the beginning of the Third Punic War, so Scipio tells, he had come to Africa as a military tribune. He was about thirty-six years old at that time. He was eager to visit Masinissa, the aged king of Numidia, now eighty-nine, who had been a staunch ally of the Roman people and a friend of Scipio's family. The old king embraced his Roman visitor, shed tears, and, raising his eyes to heaven, gave thanks because he was still alive to receive P. Cornelius Scipio. The very name of Scipio, he said, seemed to inspire him with new life; never for a moment did he forget the Elder Scipio, the adoptive grandfather of the Younger.

During the day the two men conversed much, Masinissa asking about Rome, and Scipio inquiring about Numidia. In the evening, too, they talked, when the old king would speak of nothing but the Elder Africanus, his deeds, and his conversation.

It was late when Scipio retired. The talk about the Elder Scipio still filled his thoughts, so that, when he had fallen asleep, he seemed to see his grandfather. His face was such as it was represented in the portrait bust in the family atrium rather than as Scipio himself remembered it. The dreamer recognized his grandfather, but trembled with awe, at which the latter bade him not to fear but to listen to his words.

From some high place in heaven, it seemed, the Elder Scipio pointed to Carthage, visible below, and foretold that the grandson would conquer and destroy it. He would carry on other great wars, but, returning to Rome, he would find the city plunged in civil strife because of Gracchus, the speaker's own grandson. The Younger Scipio, the Elder continued, would have been chosen dictator, had it not been his fate to die at the hands of his own relatives.

At this moment in Scipio's narrative Laelius uttered an exclamation and the other friends groaned, but Scipio said: "Hush! don't wake me!"

"Those who have struggled well for their country," pursued the Elder Africanus, "have a place reserved for them in heaven, where they will enjoy unbroken happiness."

The young Africanus, terrified less by the thought of his own death than by the treachery foretold about his relatives, asked whether his grandfather, his father, and others considered dead were really alive, and Africanus replied that they were. True life comes after the soul has shaken off the trammels of the body. The existence on earth, though called life, is death.

And at the same moment Scipio's own father, Paulus, was seen to approach. Scipio burst into tears, but Paulus embraced him and kissed him, telling him not to weep.

Exalted by the thought that real life was to be attained through so-called death, Scipio expressed his desire to leave the earth, but his father corrected him. Until God should free him from his bodily chains, he could not proceed to the other life. Men are placed on earth to care for it. Their souls are sparks from heaven, but these can come to the abode of happiness only after performing their mortal duties, the greatest of which is service to their country. The final home of the souls is the Milky Way; and as Paulus said this, Scipio seemed to be among the stars. He could see many great stars, the very existence of which he had never suspected. The earth was farthest away, deep down, and around it revolved the moon. The other stars were far greater than the earth, so that when Scipio considered its small size, he was grieved at the thought of the still smaller extent of the Roman empire.

The grandfather urged him not to turn his eyes in regret to the insignificant planet, but to contemplate the nine spheres, one within the other. On the outside was the sphere of the ether, the supreme god that encloses all. Within it were the spheres of Saturn, Jupiter, Mars, the Sun, Venus, Mercury, and the Moon. Within the sphere of the Moon, so the Elder Scipio explained, all things are mortal except the human soul. The earth itself, the ninth sphere, lies immovable at the center; at the bottom, as Scipio and his guides looked down.

Scipio then heard a sound of music, loud and yet sweet, more harmonious than anything that had ever come to his ears before. Africanus explained that it was caused by the movement of the heavenly bodies he had named; it was the music of the spheres. There are seven tones, for Mercury and Venus move with the same note. These are the seven that earthly musicians have copied, and have thus opened a way, as it were, by which they can return to heaven. But it is so powerful that it overwhelms the human sense of hearing, just as does the sound of the cataracts of the Nile, or just as the sun is too strong for human eyes to look upon.

Still the young Scipio turned his eyes toward the earth, and the Elder Africanus asked him to consider its insignificance when compared with the heavens. Reputation and fame among men, he said, were not worthy of much struggle. Even on the small earth men lived in widely distant places, with great stretches of desert between them, these different sections having no intercourse with one another. How could fame be gained by them? And he directed his grandson's attention to the five zones, of which only two are inhabited, and these two widely separated. "The earth as the Romans know it," he said, "is but a small island surrounded by the ocean, which men call great, but which is very small. Roman fame can not go beyond this little section of the earth."

And how long do men speak of one of their great heroes? The earth is periodically ravaged and life destroyed by floods and conflagrations, so that human fame, far from being everlasting, does not even endure for a long time. In earlier ages better men lived than those now living, and yet they have been forgotten. How can Scipio expect to be remembered among the generations to come? Human memory is, indeed, even briefer than a year, a real year. Men count a year by one revolution of one single heavenly body, the sun, but a real year is counted by the revolutions of all the heavenly bodies; when these return to the relative positions they have previously occupied, then one year is completed. It can scarcely be stated how many human generations such a year embraces. The time from the death of Romulus to the moment when the Elder Africanus is addressing his grandson, is not even a twentieth part of a great year.

Remembering all this, Scipio should fix his eyes on the eternal home and neither heed the talk of men nor place in them his hope of reward. Virtue alone should be his guide; let men talk as they choose, for talk they will. But all their talk is limited to a small region and is soon forgotten.

As the dreamer heard this, he avowed his purpose to strive for the eternal reward, and the speaker encouraged him. "Remember that only your body is mortal. Your soul moves of its own accord; nothing from the outside gives it motion; but as movement is life, that which is in its very essence movement has never been born and can never die. Your soul, being eternal, is therefore a god; as God rules the world, so your soul rules your body."

By good deeds, therefore, Scipio should hasten his way to the heavenly regions; and the best deeds are those done for one's country. His time of waiting will be the shorter, the more his soul can, as it were, rise above the body. The souls of those who have been slaves to the body are destined after death to flit restlessly about the confines of the earth, and it is not until after they have been tossed about for aeons that they at last find their way to heaven.

The Elder Africanus then departed, and Scipio awoke.

Such was the *Dream of Scipio,* with which Cicero concluded his chief political work. Knowing Cicero, we can easily imagine that he had often gazed toward the stars in heaven during the years when his beloved Rome was drifting into anarchy and autocracy, and that he had tried to comfort himself, now that his own unselfish attempts to restore peace and harmony had come to nothing, with the thought that the greatest thing in the world is love of one's country and a high-minded striving for its happiness, with no yearning for fame, power, or other earthly rewards.

find their way to heaven.
The Elder Africanus then departed, and Scipio awoke.
Such was the Dream of Scipio, with which Cicero concluded
his chief political work. Knowing Cicero, we can easily imagine

<h1 style="text-align:center">CHAPTER XIV</h1>

<h1 style="text-align:center">IN CILICIA</h1>

<h2 style="text-align:center">I</h2>

<h3 style="text-align:center">CIVIL WAR IMPENDING</h3>

Cicero was governor of Cilicia for a twelvemonth, beginning
on the last day of July in 51 B.C. He left Rome for his province
in May of that year and returned to Italy on the twenty-fifth
of November in the year 50 B.C. A law had been passed to
the effect that ex-praetors and ex-consuls should no longer
administer a province immediately after their year of office, but
after an interval of five years; and, in order that there might
be the necessary number of magistrates available for the provinces, it was further ordered that ex-magistrates who had not
already held provincial governorships should do so now. This
law sent Cicero to Cicila.

As the provinces in Roman eyes existed for the sake of Rome
—a view that dominates even the Verrine orations, in which the
provincials had a more capable and a more devoted protector
than at any other trial in Rome known to us—the Romans went
to administer these dependencies for one or both of two reasons.
They sought wealth, by legal means or by extortion; or they
sought military renown, with which, in the case of a few, was
coupled military power to be used in the city. Neither of these
motives appealed to Cicero. Like several other political leaders
of praetorian or consular rank, he had not taken a province as
a reward after a year of office in Rome, and he had no desire
to do so now. His joys as well as his sorrows were centered in
the city; he gave it very much the same preference as French-
men give to Paris, and such seems to have been the attitude of
the great majority of Romans.

At best, to the Romans who had no personal needs or ambitions to be served, the government of a province was a duty to be performed. It was an exacting duty, as Cicero knew, and one not altogether easy for an honest man, since the conception of the provinces as providential bonanzas both for those who went to them and those who stayed at home placed the upright governor between a Scylla and a Charybdis. All political activity is a compromise, but the compromise thrust upon an honest provincial administrator was exceptionally harassing; the provincials, whom he would protect, were strangers as a rule and not supposed to have any rights, whereas the bloodhounds he felt it his duty to keep away were Romans, usually his own political associates and even personal friends. "Don't promise any one anything from me," Cicero wrote to Atticus after he had been in his province about half a year, "unless you are certain that I can with good conscience grant the request." In this little sentence lies the kernel of many of Cicero's provincial tribulations, the greater because even Atticus, whom Cicero calls his conscience, failed to take the lofty view that Cicero attributed to him.

Cicero's natural disinclination to be away from Rome was greatly strengthened by his desire to watch the political situation in the city. The eve of the Civil War had set in before he departed; while he was away, the air grew darker and ever darker. The future of Rome hung visibly in the balance as it had not done since the year 63 B.C., perhaps not since the time of Marius and Sulla. Cicero's part in the turmoil, had he been present, would probably have been largely that of a very anxious spectator, anxious for peace in Rome, which had always been his one object; but there might have been some opportunity for counsels of moderation, for mediation even, between the contending parties. It is well enough to say, as has been said, that Cicero should have gone to his province with the eager desire of a modern philanthropic statesman, bent on instituting reforms and ready to take a student's and investigator's interest in the antiquities of his large province, but a far more important matter was under way in Rome, the question of world war or world peace, and Cicero was keenly aware of it. He was like a general sent from the battle front to some insignificant locality far behind the lines, where he had certain work to do that normally might have seemed rather interesting and important but that had no connection with the issues at stake.

Caesar was now at the head of a powerful army in Gaul; by princely gifts of many kinds to the people in the city and by bribery of individuals on a larger scale than had perhaps ever before been known, even in the forum, he was weaving a net of exceedingly strong and fine threads around the blind, buzzing politicians of Rome; he was also recognized as a man of unbounded ambition; and he had throughout his career been an adversary of the traditional senatorial government. Now that his term in Gaul was drawing to a close, it was clear to the senate that either he must be checked once for all or else supreme power would in no distant future be in his hands. Some of the aristocrats were unselfishly patriotic, and Caesar had no doubt already conceived some of the thoughts for Rome's betterment that he later tried to carry out, or actually did carry out, but both Caesar and the aristocrats were in the main fighting a selfish battle for their political existence and for everything of a social and financial nature dependent upon it. In the means that they employed both sides were equally immoral.

The natural and only available champion of the senate was Pompey. He was in Rome, he had an army in Spain, and in the view of the aristocrats he was not only less dangerous than Caesar but scarcely dangerous at all. A victory won through Pompey would be a senatorial victory. There had been several indications that Pompey was no longer in harmony with Caesar. In 54 B.C. Julia had died. The daughter of Caesar and the wife of Pompey, and devoted to them both, she had been a strong bond between them, immeasurably stronger than could have been expected from a political marriage. After her death Caesar had proposed new family connections to Pompey. Caesar would marry Pompey's daughter—she was already betrothed to some one else, but this was no obstacle—and Pompey was to take for wife Caesar's grandniece. Pompey had refused both connections, and in 52 B.C. had contracted another marriage. In 53 B.C., furthermore, Crassus had been killed; he had never done anything to cement the friendship between Caesar and Pompey, quite the contrary, but his death reduced the triumvirate to a union of two, making discord more likely. And in the year 52 B.C. Pompey as sole consul had not always taken thought for Caesar, one instance of which will presently be mentioned.

As always in Rome, the skirmishing that preceded the resort to arms was carried on along supposedly constitutional lines, each party claiming to demand only what was legal and professing to be acting in defense of the republican form of government. Rome was filled with oratory, bribery, the making and disregarding of laws, and with pretense of every kind.

Most probably, though the question can not be settled definitely, Caesar's government of Gaul would come to an end on March 1, 49 B.C. As he had held the consulship in 59 B.C., he could not hold it again until the year 48 B.C., an interval of ten years between two similar magistracies being required by law. Caesar's desire was to secure the consulship of 48 B.C. By remaining governor of Gaul until he became a consul, and then by receiving a consular province at the end of his year in Rome, he would be in office continuously. This was necessary, for if he once became a private citizen, the aristocrats would immediately institute proceedings against him—for maladministration, obviously—and would put an end to his political career, there being no doubt that their influence in the city would procure a verdict of guilty. His fate would thus be exile or worse.

His projected canvass for the consulship would take place in
49 B.C. If he could be a candidate while absent in Gaul, everything would be well; if he should relinquish his command in
order to become a candidate, he would be a private citizen, and
his aristocratic opponents would see to it that he was not elected.
A prosecution, and Cato was ready with one, would debar Caesar
from candidacy. It was about this question of candidacy that
the political maneuvers turned. Sometimes the question was
directly in debate, at other times it took the form of recalling
Caesar from Gaul; Caesar was asked to give up his army and
Pompey was asked to give up his; but all through the eighteen
months of Cicero's absence from Rome the aim of the senate
and Pompey was to make Caesar a private citizen just long
enough to be able to undo him, while Caesar, seeing his danger
and unwilling to recede from his ambitions, intrigued to keep
his army and at the same to secure the consulship.

Though the factional game was played mostly during Cicero's
absence, it had begun before his departure. In 52 B.C. Pompey
had had a law passed requiring candidates for any magistracy
to present their names in person; a thing that had not always
been done, and it will be recalled that this very requirement had
been a part of the Rullan bill in 63 B.C., to exclude Pompey from
the proposed commission. Under pressure from Caesar's supporters, Pompey later resorted to his usual tergiversation, and
is said to have inserted in the law a clause to the effect that
the requirement should not be valid in the case of those already
specifically exempted by the people, and such exemption had
actually been secured by Caesar shortly before Pompey's consulship; but the law, though thus crippled in reference to the
very man against whom it was aimed, nevertheless gave more
than a hint of the approaching struggle.

The very law that sent Cicero to Cicilia, also passed in 52 B.C.,
may have been partly directed against Caesar, though its avowed
aim was to curb reckless politicians. It decreed that **provinces**

should not be administered, as before, immediately after the holding of the consulship or praetorship, but after an interval of five years. Pompey himself was not bound by this law, for at the end of 52 B.C. he became governor of the two Spains; but the law, if carried out so as to compel ex-magistrates to take provinces if they had not done so before, might be made to work against Caesar. A governor remained in his province until the arrival of his successor; this law would find a successor to Caesar in March of 49 B.C. or shortly thereafter. The law might have looked farther still. If Caesar should succeed in obtaining the consulship for 48 B.C., the end of this year would find him a private citizen. All this did no harm to Caesar, but Cicero, as one of the available ex-consuls, was chosen for Cilicia.

He took care to have the news of the city sent him regularly, his chief correspondent being the young Caelius whom he had defended against the onslaught of Clodia. Caelius wrote some letters himself, and he had others written for Cicero's information; he was a shrewd observer and not averse to expressing his opinion. As a large part of his correspondence is extant and as Cicero himself wrote frequently, both to Atticus and to others, including Caelius, our knowledge of Cicero's administration and of contemporaneous events in the city is very considerable.

II
CICERO IMPERATOR

As governor of a province, Cicero was the commander in chief of the forces detailed for its protection. His lieutenants of military experience were his brother Quintus, who had fought with great bravery and resourcefulness under Caesar in Gaul, and C. Pomptinus. The latter had been one of the two praetors in 63 B.C. who made the arrest at the Mulvian bridge. His delay in leaving Rome on this occasion—apparently there was a lady of charm in the capital—made Cicero's slow journey to the province even slower. How much Cicero owed to Quintus and Pomptinus is only a matter of surmise, but his military record, with or without them, as the case may be, seems to have been distinctly good. He carried out successfully what had to be done, and he took all possible precautions to ward off a danger that threatened but did not materialize.

The threat came from the Parthians, who since their victory over Crassus were hovering on the edge of the Roman empire. In the year before Cicero's arrival, Cassius, formerly the lieutenant of Crassus, had driven them out of Syria. Syria lay between the Parthians and Cilicia, but even the latter was not considered safe. There was every likelihood that the Parthians would make another attempt in 51 B.C. Cicero's troops were insufficient in number for extensive fighting, though he hoped they would prove loyal. He saw to it that they were properly equipped, and marched toward the eastern frontier, having made arrangements for auxiliaries from client kings, especially his personal friend Deiotarus, king of Galatia. The Parthians were reported to have crossed the Euphrates, and it was known that Cassius, acting for the governor of Syria, who had not arrived in his province, was at Antioch with all his forces, awaiting the enemy. Cicero moved farther toward the enemy, but learned presently that Cassius had beaten them back.

It is probable that Cicero depreciated Cassius' services, and we do not know whether his own preparations would have been sufficient to protect his province. To Atticus he wrote that Cassius took heart and the Parthians were frightened at Cicero's approach, and that his name was great in Syria.

The danger, however, was not past. Most likely the Parthians would return in 50 B.C., for an annual incursion was to be expected. Cicero wrote officially to Rome for more troops, and the situation seemed so serious that the question was raised of sending either Caesar or Pompey against the enemy. Pompey himself wrote to Cicero that he might take charge of the campaign. But nothing was done; the intrigues against Caesar were too engrossing; and Rome was saved by the gods, for the Parthians were prevented by internal dissensions from making an attack the following year. Bibulus, the governor of Syria, received a thanksgiving, and asked for a triumph, on the strength of the success of his lieutenant Cassius; and Cicero says that Bibulus no more left his camp during his pretended military activity in Syria than he had left his house in the year 59 B.C.; Bibulus having been Caesar's sequestered colleague of that year. Cicero's anxiety about the Parthians was not relieved until the summer of 50 B.C. was well advanced. Some conception of his army may be gathered from his statement that in the year 50 B.C. he expected 12,000 infantry and 2,000 horse from Deiotarus.

There was, however, some real fighting, though not of a very serious or spectacular kind. It took place in the fall of 51 B.C., and was directed against the rebellious mountaineers on the border. Several fortified places were taken and many rebels were captured or slain. Finally, after a siege of fifty-seven days, the fortress of Pindenissus surrendered. Cicero sold the prisoners into slavery and took care that the proceeds were properly recorded, the money being destined for Rome; the rest of the booty he gave to his soldiers—all according to the accepted traditions of Roman warfare. The soldiers hailed Cicero as *imperator*. Pindenissus fell about the eighteenth of December, and the army was thereupon placed in winter quarters, under the command of Quintus. Cicero himself went away to attend to his duties as a judge.

From a letter[1] to Atticus describing these and other events, we learn that Cicero on one occasion made his camp at Issus, where Darius had been defeated by Alexander, "quite a better general than either you or I." "Who in the world are those Pindenissitae of yours? I never heard their name," Atticus is supposed to exclaim; and Cicero admits that they are not on

---

[1] *Att.* 5, 20.

Atticus' map. And yet, adds Cicero, Pindenissus is the best
fortified town of the Eleutherocilices—which, possibly, may not
have enlightened Atticus.

Cicero's witty friend Paetus had written,[2] with much display
of military knowledge and with some advice. Replying, the
conqueror of the Eleutherocilices promises to follow his coun-
selor's directions, noting that Paetus has given much time to
the writings of Pyrrhus and Cineas on the military art. As for
himself, Cicero intends to have a little fleet near his coast, ships
being admittedly the best weapon against the Parthian cavalry;
he has also read Xenophon's *Cyropaedeia* "to pieces," and is
following its precepts in every department of his administration.

But the victory over the rebels had also a political or ornamental side. Cicero was granted a thanksgiving, and expected
a triumph, which he probably would have obtained if the Civil
War had not filled Rome with other thoughts, for Caesar was
favorable. Cicero had not shaped his career toward riding to
the capitol in a golden chariot, but he seems to have deserved
such an honor as much as some others who secured it, or at least
claimed it; certainly more than Bibulus.

The thanksgiving was opposed by Cato, who had adopted the
singular view, and also expressed it in the senate, that Cicero
both as an administrator and as a military leader merited the
highest praise, but that there was no propriety in thanking the
gods for services to the state which were entirely due to Cicero.
Cato, incidentally, was a Stoic, and the Stoics believed in a
providence. The letter[3] in which Cato sets forth his views to
Cicero is a model in many respects; even in its stiffness of style,
for every sentence ends most properly with a verb. A thanksgiving, *supplicatio*, was usually the forerunner of a triumph;
but Cato expresses an opinion to the contrary, and observes, by
the way, that it is a much more glorious thing to have the senate

---

[2] *Fam.* 9, 25.

[3] *Fam.* 15, 5.

praise a governor's gentleness and unselfishness than to celebrate a triumph because of military success. This also Cato had said in the senate. He concludes with an explanation that his desire to persuade Cicero of his good intentions toward the latter has led him to write at great length—though the prim epistle scarcely covers a small page.

Cicero's reply[4] to this remarkable missive is as clever as his reply to Metellus Celer in 62 B.C. He begins with quoting a poet to the effect that it is a joy to be praised by a man himself worthy of praise, and he thereupon assures Cato of his appreciation. But he did not write everything that was in his mind, as other letters inform us. Cato voted for the thanksgiving decreed to Bibulus, but that great warrior was an unswerving aristocrat and Cato's son-in-law. It should not be forgotten, however, that after the thanksgiving had been granted to Cicero, Cato showed his personal interest in it by being one of the men who attended when the resolution was drawn up formally. Caesar rejoiced at Cato's clumsiness; the sight of conservatives at loggerheads gave him no pain.

III
BETWEEN SCYLLA AND CHARYBDIS

Though Cicero made no attempt to hide his martial glories under a bushel, he did conceal several measures which he took for the alleviation of the provincials—a more damaging bit of evidence against the usual Roman treatment of the provincials than long lists of actual crimes. But the morality of his time made it impossible for him invariably to follow his good impulses.

Appius Claudius, his predecessor in office, was the brother of the tribune Clodius who had caused Cicero's exile. Appius had behaved like a wild beast in the province, Cicero writes to Atticus; but Appius was a fellow augur of Cicero, his daughter was married to the son of Pompey, and Pompey himself was

---

4 *Fam.* 15, 6.

expected to come out to Cilicia to fight against the Parthians. Consideration on Cicero's part was therefore dictated both by personal and political reasons and by thought for the provincials, who were eager to stand well with Appius in case Pompey should come to rule them.   They sent embassies to Rome to praise Appius.   Cicero, also, though finding almost everything in Appius' administration deserving of criticism when he writes to Atticus, praised him publicly, and even in letters to Appius himself he is not very outspoken, though at times he does not conceal his opinion.   Probably Appius was no worse than the average governor.

It is not possible to give in detail very much of that which Cicero did or failed to do for the provincials. In everything that related to his own person, he was scurupulously unselfish, not merely refraining from enriching himself in the ways thoroughly approved by honest men, but also forbidding the grateful provincials to spend money in his honor. He insisted that his subordinates should follow his example; they know, he wrote to Atticus, on what conditions I have taken them with me; and he took what care he could to prevent overbearing behavior toward the provincials; a moderation of temper he had strongly urged upon Quintus when the latter governed Asia. The home government allowed certain moneys for a governor's administration.   Cicero did not use it all, and returned the remainder. This was demanded by no code of honor, and his staff did not approve of it, but they could not change his resolution. Nevertheless, he found himself at the end of the year richer by two million two hundred thousand sesterces, which he deposited in Ephesus, and lost during the Civil War.[5]

He allowed the provincials to settle their controversies in their own courts, which seemed to them like a gift of independence. Scaevola, the former pontiff, had governed Asia forty-two years before.   Cicero followed his edict in several respects;

---

[5] See above, p. 216, note 19.

in others he used the rules that guided the praetors in Rome. He discovered, among many other sources of trouble, that even the Greek magistrates had been robbing the communities. He forced them to pay back their peculations of the last ten years, promising immunity from further proceedings; and in this way he helped both the provincials and the farmers of taxes, for the latter had begun to despair of getting back the money they had invested. As he himself wrote, he took care that the Romans doing business in the province should not practise extortion; when the publicans made less money than they had expected, Cicero consoled them with courtesies, so that "each one thought he was Cicero's particular friend."

He was indeed steering between Scylla and Charybdis. Caelius, his correspondent, was an aedile, and asked Cicero to send him some panthers for his games in the city. The matter is mentioned in several letters, and Caelius himself writes that he had spoken of it almost every time he wrote. A Roman knight, doing business in Cilicia, had sent ten panthers to Curio, a brother politician, and Caelius thinks Cicero ought to be ashamed if he can not do better than that. Obviously, Cicero was unwilling to put unnecessary burdens on the provincials and considered Caelius' request impudent. He promised to employ the ordinary hunters for the purpose, if they could be engaged; Caelius thought a more general hunt should be made; and many months after the request was first made Cicero explained that the scarcity of panthers in his province was remarkable, and that, according to report, the few remaining panthers, with very loud complaints to the effect that snares were laid for nobody but them in Cicero's whole province, had decided to migrate to Caria. Caelius also asked Cicero to impose a tax on the provincials for the purpose of defraying the expenses of Caelius' games, but to this Cicero replied that it was fitting neither for him to comply with the request nor for Caelius to make it.

Cicero's province was large—nearly forty thousand square miles on the mainland, it has been estimated,[6] and also the island of Cyprus—so that he was much occupied in refusing impudent demands and in-checking attempts at extortion. Only one more of his predicaments, the most famous, need be described; but it throws light in many directions.

When Cicero reached Ephesus, just before entering his province, he was informed by ambassadors from Cyprus that a certain Scaptius had been prefect in Cyprus under Appius, Cicero's predecessor, and in this capacity had commanded a troop of horse, with which he had shut the senate of the town of Salamis in the senate-house, because of debt, and had kept them there until five died. Probably, though this is not stated, the rest of the senate had complied with Scaptius' demands. Cicero at once ordered the horsemen out of the island.

Later Scaptius came to Cicero, who was then in camp, and, introducing himself as the friend of Brutus, explained that the people of Salamis owed him money. Cicero promised, for Brutus' sake, that the debt should be paid. Scaptius expressed his gratitude, and then asked to be made prefect. Cicero said no; he would not give a prefecture to any one doing business in the province. He had already refused a similar request to representatives both of Pompey and of others, even to his own friends, and had secured approval of his action; though apparently such appointments were not unusual. Scaptius went away, ostensibly satisfied with Cicero's promise that the debt should be collected.

Not long afterwards representatives from Salamis and also Scaptius came to see Cicero, and he asked the islanders to pay the debt. The Salaminians began to complain both about the bond and about Scaptius' harshness toward them. Cicero refused to listen; he begged and urged the debtors, in consideration of his kind rule over them, to settle the matter; and finally he even threatened. They said they were willing to pay, and that in

6 Tyrrell III, p. xv.

fact they were paying out of Cicero's pocket, for their usual contribution to the governor was larger than their debt to Scaptius. The amount was thereupon to be fixed. Cicero's edict for the island had limited the interest on debt to twelve per cent, which seems to have been considered very reasonable; Scaptius wanted forty-eight.

The situation was this. The people of Salamis, who had been made destitute by taxes and requisitions, had sent an embassy to Rome in 56 B.C. to raise a loan. Foreigners were by law, and for their own protection, forbidden to borrow money in the capital, but the loan was nevertheless made by Scaptius and another man. As the transaction was illegal, the lenders insisted on forty-eight per cent. Decrees of the senate were passed, at the instance of Brutus, the friend of the money-lenders, which not only exempted the latter from punishment for their illegal transaction but also made the debt recoverable by law.

Cicero, however, refused to let the forty-eight per cent stand. Scaptius took him aside, expressed his willingness to comply, but added that the Salaminians thought they owed two hundred talents—roughly two hundred thousand dollars. They really owed a little less, said Scaptius. Cicero then spoke to the Salaminians, who said the debt was one hundred and six talents. At this Scaptius began to shout, but when the papers were produced, the sum was found to be one hundred and six. Scaptius then asked that the matter be dropped, thinking he would have better success with the next governor of Cilicia. Cicero, to please Brutus, granted this. The Salaminians then offered to deposit their payment in a temple, an act that would cut off further interest, being like depositing the money in a bank to Scaptius' credit. This Cicero also did not allow; but he issued a decree that the Salaminians had made a legal tender—in other words, that their payment to Scaptius was good at law. Cicero knew, however, that his decision might be reversed by his successor.

Then came the revelation. Brutus, and not Scaptius, was the creditor. He wrote many letters to Cicero about the matter, insistent to the point of insolence, but Cicero would make no further concessions. Atticus took a hand, begging that Cicero would give Scaptius a little troop, some fifty; and at this Cicero exclaims against his friend, who had constantly been praising Cicero's honest administration. Cicero is ready to wash his hands of the whole business; but many letters were written about it. To the modern reader it would seem that Cicero had favored Brutus altogether too much, but his long explanations are to the effect that if he has been too inconsiderate of Brutus' demands. he can not help it. He is willing to submit the whole situation to Cato, hopeful that the great Stoic, Brutus' uncle, will find that he has not acted with harshness toward Brutus.

This was not the only financial transaction in which Brutus insisted on his Roman rights. And yet Cicero can write to Appius Claudius, his predecessor in office, that Brutus has for a long time been the chief light among the Roman youth and will soon, Cicero hopes, be the chief man in the state. Atticus had written, and Cicero recalls his words in connection with the activity of Scaptius, that if Cicero should gain nothing by his administration beyond the good will of Brutus, he ought to consider himself rewarded. When Cicero left Rome, Atticus had also, with tears of emotion, urged him to take care of his good reputation.

IV

GOING AND COMING

A governor could not in his one year of office change the provincial policy of the Romans; at most, he could only give some relief, leaving many matters undecided. Cicero, at the end of his twelvemonth, was glad to set out for Rome. He felt that his administration had been unique in its honesty; he had pleased his own conscience, as he writes to Atticus, even more than he had ministered to his reputation for uprightness, though the good reputation was also pleasant to contemplate. As he turned toward the city, his spirits rose with the thought of soon being back, and even after his arrival, though the hopelessness of the political situation made him deeply anxious, his letters reveal a surprising buoyancy.

His journey to Cilicia had taken between two and three months, delayed mostly by the dilatoriness of his military aid Pomptinus. Cicero and Quintus had stayed in Athens nearly two weeks, giving much of their time to conversations with philosophers. While there, he wrote one[7] of his best known letters, addressed to the exiled politician C. Memmius, then at Mitylene. The latter, it seems, had possession of a ruined house that had belonged to Epicurus, which the head of the Epicureans at Athens wished to acquire. Cicero therefore intercedes with Memmius, prompted by his respect for Patro, the Epicurean leader, and above all by his affection for Atticus, who belonged to the sect. The remarkable circumstance about Cicero's letter, carefully written, he said later, as he had also said about the letter to Lucceius, is that he takes for granted that Memmius can have no patience with the Epicureans as a sect, a sentiment with which Cicero stands ready to agree, but that nevertheless Memmius is in all probability the man to whom Lucretius, the great poet of Epicureanism, dedicated his poem.

Cicero's journey home seems to have taken about one half the time he had needed to reach Cilicia. While in Rhodes, he learned of the death of Hortensius; the great orator had been seriously ill for a considerable period. The news was a serious blow to Cicero, as he wrote to Atticus; he had intended on his return to Rome to live on the closest possible terms of intimacy with his old rival. In 55 B.C., it will be recalled, he had written in the *De Oratore* of Hortensius' greatness; in 46 B.C., in the *Brutus,* he was to refer to the news about his death that he had

---

[7] *Fam.* 13, 1.

just received. During the exile, Cicero had been bitterly conscious of Hortensius' artistocratic jealousy; but he had forgotten
his bitterness. The death of Hortensius was the first among those
of Cicero's famous friends who were very nearly of his own age.
Cicero was then fifty-six years old.

Tiro, Cicero's secretary and favorite freedman, fell sick
during the journey home, and had to be left behind. Cicero
wrote letters to him at almost every place where he stopped and
later when he had landed in Italy. They are full of anxiety
about Tiro's health, overflowing with appreciation and affection.
Everything will be done for Tiro's comfort. The doctor shall
be paid, whatever his charges, so that Tiro is not to worry; gifts
will be given to the doctor to secure greater care; no expense is
to be spared; a faithful slave is sent to wait on the sick man;
arrangements are made for his journey to Italy, though he must
not hurry; when he arrives in Brundisium, a horse and a mule
will be at his disposal. Lyso, at whose house Tiro was staying,
had given a large musical party, and Tiro had been present,
to the injury of his health; he must not again neglect himself
in order to be polite. Everybody in Cicero's family and among
his friends is looking forward to Tiro's arrival. When a messenger came that might have brought word from Tiro and brought
none, Cicero was much troubled; presently another messenger
brought at note from Tiro, and Cicero was delighted that he was
well enough to write, but Tiro's hand had trembled.

Cicero's son Marcus, now about fifteen, and Quintus' son,
a trifle older, had accompanied Cicero to the province, attended
by a Greek teacher, of whose instruction Cicero approved, while
the boys found him very short of temper. The two young
Ciceros visited king Deiotarus, and later, during the winter, they
studied under the supervision of Cicero. Tullia was at home.
She had been divorced from her second husband, if the marriage
had really taken place,[8] and now, during Cicero's absence, she

---

[8] See below, p. 524.

married Dolabella, younger than herself. Cicero disapproved
of the marriage, for Dolabella was not noted for stability of
character, and at this particular time he was bringing proceedings against Appius Claudius, Cicero's predecessor in Cilicia,
and Cicero did not wish to have the appearance of countenancing
such a lawsuit.

Terentia also was at home. There is one letter[9] addressed
to her extant from all the eighteen months, written in Athens
when Cicero was returning home. Apparently she had written
often, with reports about many things. Cicero is grateful, but
as Terentia feared that he had not received all her letters, it is
to be feared by us that he had not been careful about replying.
His one letter, however, is very affectionate and contains many
terms of endearment. He hopes that she will come as far on the
road to meet him as her uncertain health will allow; and we
know that she was at Brundisium when he landed, on the twenty-
fifth day of November. She reached the city gate at the same
time as Cicero's ship came into the harbor, as he informed
Atticus, and they met in the market place; her first news was
political.

---

[9] *Fam.* 14, 5.

CHAPTER XV

UNDER CAESAR

I

CIVIL WAR

The Civil War began on the twelfth or thirteenth of January, 49 B.C., when Caesar at the head of one legion crossed the Rubicon, which formed the boundary between his province and Italy. It was illegal for a provincial governor to retain command of his troops on Italian territory. War against Caesar, however, had been declared by the senate, when, on the seventh of January, they passed the "last decree."

A few events preceding these two should be mentioned, since they lead rather directly to the final action through a long period filled with illegalities, mutual recrimination, and specious proposals. In May, 50 B.C., during a debate about the threatened invasion of Syria by the Parthians, the senate decreed that Caesar and Pompey should each give a legion for service in the East. Pompey had previously lent Caesar one of his legions; this he now asked back. Caesar returned it, and also, in obedience to the senatorial decree, sent one of his own. Both legions had thus been taken actually from Caesar's army, and both were stationed at Capua and were never sent to Syria; but Caesar had wisely given generous gifts to the officers and soldiers.

In September of the same year, after the complete conquest of Gaul, Caesar held a military review in the northwestern part of his province. Here he determined to send one of his legions, the thirteenth, to Cisalpine Gaul to take the place of the one released for service in Syria. This was a proper and natural arrangement, though also wise. By the time the report had reached Rome, rumor had increased the single legion to four.

This would be practically equivalent to a march across the Alps with a large army, and would contain a serious threat of war. In October, therefore, the consul Marcellus, who was a determined opponent of Caesar, moved in the senate to have Caesar declared a public enemy. It was a violent meeting. The outcome, since the senate did not pass Marcellus' motion, was that the latter, sword in hand, rushed out of the city to Pompey, and, on his own authority and that of the two consuls-elect, ordered the former triumvir to take command of the two legions at Capua and also to levy more troops. Pompey, though without enthusiasm, accepted the task, and began to make arrangements for the new levy.

War had thus almost begun before the end of the year. On the first of January the senate, according to custom, met to consider matters of general policy. This meeting lasted until the seventh; suspended, however, on the third and fourth, which were comitial days. Caesar's latest offer, presented during the meeting, was to the effect that he would lay down his command if Pompey would do the same; otherwise, he would come at once and defend his country and himself. This was a declaration of war; and the senate, as noted above, passed the ''last decree.'' The tribunes Marcus Antonius—Mark Antony—and Cassius, who had been working for Caesar, fled to their leader; thus incidentally giving him an opportunity of maintaining that he was defending the constitution in defending them, for they, it seems, had been declared public enemies. With the tribunes went Caelius and also Curio, a young friend of Cicero, who as tribune of the preceding year had been extraordinarily active. Caesar had bought his services.

After crossing the Rubicon, Caesar on the thirteenth of January seized Ariminum, an important town on the road along the eastern coast of Italy. Within the next few days he occupied three other towns, all on the coast, and also despatched Mark Antony westward across the mountains to Arretium, a strong fortress in eastern Etruria, and Curio to Ignuvium, in central Umbria. His success in these undertakings gave him a strong foothold in northern Italy and also put him in possession of roads leading to Rome.

When the news of these movements reached the city, the senate met in consternation. A *tumultus*, or state of war in Italy, was declared; and Pompey, announcing that he would be unable to hold Rome, called upon the magistrates and the senators to follow him southward. This was on the seventeenth of January. The consuls, many of the other magistrates, a majority of the senators, and numerous rich knights followed Pompey's advice.

Pompey sent two ambassadors to Caesar, mainly, it seems, to inform him of the declaration of the *tumultus* and to explain that Pompey was acting for the good of the country and not from personal enmity against Caesar. Apparently the embassy was entrusted with no definite terms; their mission was to indulge in moral suasion. Caesar sent back the ambassadors with a proposal. Pompey should go to Spain, where of course he belonged as governor; the armies on both sides were to be disbanded, and the levies in Italy to be discontinued; Caesar would then give up his two Gallic provinces and come to Rome to stand for the consulship. Most important of all, Caesar wished all these matters to be arranged in detail at a conference with Pompey. Both Caesar and the aristocrats knew from long experience how such a conference would result. On the twenty-fourth of January the ambassadors reached Pompey, and a written message was at once sent back to Caesar. His terms would be accepted if he would first evacuate the towns in Italy and return to his province. This would have left things very much as they had been before the outbreak of hostilities. Pompey's proposal was delivered to Caesar on the twenty-eighth, but he was unwilling to relinquish his military advantages in return for such an indefinite promise. The terms were rejected, and the war went on.

During the days consumed in these fruitless negotiations Caesar had further strengthened his position in the north; more towns had been taken and men had deserted to him. Presently he left the coast, and on the fourteenth of February he was before Corfinium. Here, almost due east from Rome but two-thirds of the distance toward the eastern coast, nearly all of Pompey's forces in this part of Italy were gathered under Domitius, a determined opponent to Caesar and the man who had been appointed to succeed him in Gaul. Pompey was at Luceria, in northern Apulia. Domitius wrote to Pompey to come north, to assist him against Caesar; Pompey wrote for Domitius to leave Corfinium, and on the seventeenth he ordered his own troops to retreat to Brundisium, for an eventual embarking for Greece. Corfinium surrendered on the twentieth. Caesar dismissed Domitius and the other senators, and the soldiers enlisted in his army.

Cicero's letters are almost daily from the eighteenth of January. He had landed at Brundisium on the twenty-fifth of November the preceding year; on the fourth of January he arrived in the vicinity of Rome. As he retained his *imperium*, in expectation of a triumph, he was able to avoid taking part in the momentous meeting of the senate that declared martial law. In connection with this decree Italy had been divided into military districts, for the prosecution of the war, and Cicero had been assigned to Capua. He soon offered his resignation; the garrison was quite insufficient for defending so important a place, and if Cicero once took part in the war, he would be unable afterwards to mediate for peace. Apparently the senate accepted his resignation, but Pompey asked Cicero to have general charge of Campania and the coast.

On January the seventeenth Pompey left Rome. On the next day, before it was light, Cicero went away, secretly so as to cause no talk; his lictors would be conspicuous, as he writes to Atticus. He had no plans; everything seemed uncertain. If

Pompey should decide to remain in Italy, all his partisans would join him; if not, then the future would have to decide. On the nineteenth, going south, Cicero again writes to Atticus. Cicero has learned that Labienus has abandoned Caesar. Is Caesar to be considered a Roman general or a foreign invader like Hannibal? Again, no plans and no certainty about Pompey.

Atticus, in Rome, fears that Caesar will prove to be a tyrant of the worst sort, a Phalaris.

Cicero reached his villa at Formiae about the twentieth. On the following day he had an interview with Lentulus, one of the consuls, and also with another man, and on the twenty-second he writes to Atticus. Cicero fears that Caesar will be a Phalaris; the lictors are a nuisance. What ought Cicero to do? Shall he join the Pompeian side openly? He is not afraid of the danger, but he is overcome with grief, for everything is being mismanaged and Pompey's plans are uncertain. Ought Cicero to put off a decision and try to remain on good terms with both sides? Even if his duty as a citizen did not deter him from this, his duty as a friend to Pompey would do so. But the thought of his children makes him hesitate. On the same day he wrote to his family to leave Rome while they could.

He arrived in Minturnae that evening, and on the next day he writes to Atticus. Labienus is a hero; his desertion, if good for nothing else, will give Caesar pain; there is fear and confusion everywhere; men are unwilling to enlist. Should the two young Ciceros be sent to Greece for safety? Tullia and Terentia, at Rome, will be in danger if the barbarians, Caesar's Gallic soldiers, come to the city. And on the same day, also to Atticus: Cicero has heard of Caesar's terms, and finds them absurd. To Terentia and Tullia, also on the twenty-third: let them determine their future action by conditions in Rome; find out what other ladies will do; there is fear that if they stay too long they may be unable to get away.

On the twenty-sixth and the twenty-seventh Cicero was in Capua, and wrote to Atticus and to Tiro. There was a general desire, so Cicero wrote to Atticus, that Caesar might be serious in the terms he had offered; even Cato was ready to accept them, only the irreconcilable Favonius opposing. Cato was unwilling to go to Sicily, which was to be held against Caesar, and wanted to be in Rome when the discussion of Caesar's terms should take place. Cicero feared that Cato might obstruct action. Most of the senators are afraid that Caesar is negotiating merely to gain time and to induce the Pompeians to discontinue their preparations for war.

To Tiro Cicero explains the political situation, and urges him to take good care of his health; Cicero has recommended Tiro's comfort to a certain Varro, not the great scholar, who is devoted both to Cicero and to Tiro himself.

On the twenty-eighth of January Cicero started back toward Formiae, reaching Cales in the evening, when he wrote to Atticus. Pompey, we learn, is saying that in a few days he will have a strong army, and that if Caesar goes into Picenum, the Pompeians may all return to Rome soon. Labienus has raised Pompey's courage by his report that Caesar's forces are very weak.

On the second of February Cicero writes to Atticus that he is still waiting to hear about Caesar's reply to Pompey's terms; Caesar is a madman if he does not accept, but Caesar is going on with his preparations. Trebatius has asked Cicero, from Caesar, to be in Rome when Caesar arrives, but Cicero replied that he did not think he could do it. Cicero fears that there will be war throughout Italy.

On the same day Cicero's family and also Quintus with his family arrived in Formiae, so that Cicero is in good spirits when he next writes to Atticus, before daybreak on the following morning. He is pleased that people in Rome have approved of Pompey's terms to Caesar; Caesar will be ruined if he rejects them.

Which would Cicero prefer? He could tell Atticus if he knew
what forces the Pompeians really have at their command. Caesar
is desperate to go on with military preparations while actually
engaged in negotiations. Cicero is willing to yield to circumstances and accompany Pompey to Spain; that would be the
lesser evil, considering that Caesar was so foolishly prevented
from becoming a consular candidate. But on the same day Cicero
inferred from a letter from Curio that Caesar would not accept
Pompey's terms, and he was persuaded that the war would continue, with no hope of success for the aristocrats. Cicero will
start for Capua to learn something about Pompey's plans.

In this way the letters continue day after day, and week after
week. When the Pompeians forced matters with Caesar to a
serious issue, they had not been prepared for war and they had
utterly misjudged the situation. The inhabitants of Italy had
no interest in maintaining the senatorial power against Caesar,
who had always, though perhaps mostly for personal reasons,
been a champion of the so-called popular party. Recruiting was
not enthusiastic, and the officers in charge of it were often in fear
that their active opponent, with his forced marches, would be
upon them while they were actually enrolling their lukewarm
soldiers. The two legions that had been filched from Caesar,
who were the only trained soldiers on the aristocratic side, were
not to be depended upon. If placed face to face with their old
comrades in Gaul, they might decide, it was feared, that there
was no good reason for bloodshed.

Caesar's power was underestimated. Labienus, by his desertion, did no good, and possibly considerable harm, to his new
allies. He talked about Caesar's weakness, and yet he ought to
have known, and perhaps did know, that Caesar's legions, of
which more presently arrived from Gaul, were thoroughly devoted to their considerate and brave commander. And Caesar,
perhaps the most important circumstance of all, was the sole
leader on his side; it was his war; all who had been with him

from the beginning or who had joined him since his arrival in Italy were his subordinates.

On the aristocratic side it was different. It was not Pompey's war. The several aristocrats considered themselves free to act according to their own judgment. Domitius in Corfinium had ordered Pompey about and had refused to obey the latter's command, although Pompey was the military leader; and this division of authority was to last until the end of the war. No doubt Pompey did the best he could. He had been sickly of late and perhaps he was not as good a general as of old, for it was now a long time since he had been in a campaign, but his difficulties were insuperable. He had to retreat. Perhaps Cicero's criticisms should be forgiven, for his information was often both late and unreliable, as has been seen; it was natural that discouragement and then almost contempt for Pompey should lay hold of Cicero, who had not wanted the war and who saw that the aristocrats were not prepared. But Pompey, so far as can be judged, could not have acted differently.

He fell back on Brundisium. He had a fleet, which Caesar lacked, and he was strong, presumably, in the eastern part of the empire, in which he had won his great victories and created new provinces. Caesar, having taken Corfinium, hastened toward Brundisium. He arrived on the ninth of March, and immediately began negotiations, renewing his request for a personal interview. The negotiations lasted in vain until the thirteenth, and on that day Caesar began the siege. Pompey had replied that he could not negotiate because the consuls had already gone to Greece; indeed, they and the bulk of the army had sailed. Caesar tried to block the harbor mouth, but was unsuccessful. Pompey went away on the fifteenth of March, having burned the ships he did not need, and Caesar entered Brundisium on the next day. He had mastered Italy in five weeks, but Pompey and a republican army were in Greece, and there was also a Pompeian army in Spain. The war, after all, had only begun.

With Pompey's departure from Italy the war might well seem desperate to Cicero. Up to this time Caesar's frequent attempts at negotiation had given good hope of a peaceful settlement. No doubt Caesar wanted peace, provided he could have it with safety to himself and with the practical certainty of election to the consulship. Few men could have been more suitable for mediation than Cicero, and the latter had acted from a true instinct when he abstained from seriously committing himself to the Pompeian side. With the going of Pompey and the consuls, the hopes for peace became more distant, but they did not altogether fade.

Even before returning from Cilicia, Cicero had been convinced that in case of war his duty lay with Pompey, and in his letters of that period he often speaks of his desire to repay his debt to Caesar, since it would be unbecoming to owe money to a political opponent. Caesar was a more charming and far more considerate man than his rival, and his personality had a great many more points of pleasant contact with that of Cicero than had Pompey's unintellectual and unappreciative ponderosity; but, as Cicero himself wrote to Atticus, he had become the friend of Caesar for Pompey's sake—though possibly also for his own sake, as we have seen. Pompey, however, had been Cicero's hero, somewhat clouded on occasion, since the year 66 B.C., at the time of the Manilian law, and it was Pompey who, though responsible for the exile, had made possible the return. Roman politics being intensely personal, Cicero was required both by his own conscience and by popular opinion to side with his old idol.

The idol and his supporters had of late given little reason for eager adherence. Before their departure, many aristocrats had talked loudly about bloody reprisals and conscriptions after they should have conquered; they had deserted Italy in five weeks; and now, when they were abroad but had the fleet at their disposal, there was a fear in Italy that they would cut off the grain ships and starve their own country into submission. Caesar, on the other hand, had throughout acted with surprising leniency and gentleness. He did not say that those who were not with him were against him, as did the aristocrats; he was satisfied with a benevolent neutrality on the part of those who could not whole-heartedly support him. And he was victorious.

Though the war was at bottom a personal contest and though politics had an avowedly personal complexion, it was nevertheless true that Caesar could readily be looked upon as the aggressor. The constitutional government of Rome centered in the senate; opposition to the senate was rebellion. Cicero, four years later, in speaking for king Deiotarus, could say openly that the Galatian king's championship of the Pompeian cause was pardonable; to him, justice had properly appeared to be on the side of Pompey. Cicero could say this before Caesar, who had for a long time been the ruler of Rome, and he could also publish the oration. In March of 49 B.C., after the flight of the aristocrats, Caesar's position was even more than later in need of moral sanction. Most men of the great names were opposed to him: even the consuls were among the fugitives.

This situation caused Caesar to make repeated efforts to win Cicero, if not to active approval, at least to neutrality. Not merely Trebatius but other Caesarians had interviews with Cicero for this purpose, or wrote letters, and Caesar himself communicated directly with him. Personal liking for Cicero may now, as before, have contributed to Caesar's attitude, but this was no time for a yielding to personal feelings. Caesar was fighting the great battle of his life, diplomatically as well as with the sword. What Cicero had said of himself in connection with the Catilinarians was now true of Caesar: as victor, he would have to live with the conquered. He was therefore gentle by policy and not merely by nature, and he saw that the approval of Cicero would be a great moral asset.

Of Cicero during this period of daily anxiety and daily letters only a brief glimpse need be given. On the eleventh of March Atticus seems to have suggested, or Cicero himself had come to the conclusion, that he should have an interview with Caesar. The time was near for putting the man's toga on his son Marcus, and Cicero had thought of hiding himself, as he expresses it, in Arpinum, the ceremony of the *toga virilis* serving as an excuse; but he now decided, at Atticus' advice, to remain at Formiae. That place would be the most suitable for an interview with Caesar. On the same day he had word to the effect that Pompey had left Italy. The rumor was false, but Cicero, believing it, writes: "I have been anxious before, now I am distraught with grief."

On the next day, and that is the more significant letter,[1] he writes to Atticus that, in order not entirely to yield to his grief, he is practising declamation; his subjects are general propositions, *theses*, and he is speaking "both for and against," in Greek and in Latin; and he finds some consolation in it. He gives in Greek several subjects that he is thus debating; they are. connected with the thoughts constantly in his mind, he says, so that, while they relieve his anxiety, they yet do not take him entirely away from the political situation. Should a man remain in his country when it is governed by an autocrat? While it is governed by an autocrat, should we strive in every way to destroy the autocracy, even if this should bring great danger to the state, or should we be on our guard against him who is trying to overthrow the autocrat, lest this second man in his turn gain supreme power? And other questions of the same kind; the last one referring directly to Cicero himself: If a man has done great services to his country, which have been repaid with intolerable evils and with envy, ought he again to expose himself to danger for his country, or should he be permitted to think of himself and his dear ones, ceasing to struggle against those in power?

[1] *Att.* 9, 4.

There is something infinitely sad, and to modern feelings also strange, in the picture of Cicero at fifty-seven loudly declaiming in order to silence his harassing thoughts. But he was, after all, somewhat like the man who seeks relief in the routine of a busy office, and still more like the musician who plays his old pieces, noisily and restlessly, to avoid thought.

After taking Brundisium, Caesar had set out for Rome, and on the twenty-eighth of March he saw Cicero at Formiae. This was the third of Cicero's four great days, though like other great days it was by no means free from pain. The first had been the fifth of December in 63 B.C., when he took the responsibility for the execution of the Catilinarians; on the next,[2] in the year 60 B.C., had occurred his interview with Balbus, when Cicero refused to join the triumvirate. The fourth was to come five years later.

Cicero describes his interview with Caesar in a letter of the next day to Atticus.[3] He had been anxious during the preceding weeks, as his letters indicate, but now he is firm. "I followed your advice in both respects," he writes. "My words were such as to gain Caesar's respect rather than his gratitude, and I persevered in my refusal to go to Rome. You and I had made a mistake in thinking he would be easy to deal with; he was quite the contrary. He said that my resolve involved a condemnation of him, that others would be less willing to attend the senate if I did not come. I replied that their situation was different from mine."

"We talked for a long time, and then he said: 'Come then and urge peace.' 'According to my own conviction?' To which, Caesar: 'Should I prescribe to you?' And I: 'Then I shall move in the senate that they disapprove of your going to Spain' —to fight the Pompeians—'and of taking an army to Greece,

---

[2] Tyrrell IV, p. xxxv, hints at Sept. 4, 57 B.C., when Cicero arrived in Rome from exile, as Cicero's second great day.

[3] *Att.* 9, 18.

and I shall express great sympathy with Pompey.' 'I do not want you to say that.' 'I thought so,' I returned, 'and that is my reason for not wishing to attend the meeting. I must either speak in this way, and utter many things about which I could not keep silent, or else I cannot be present.'

"The upshot was that Caesar, as if trying to find a way of ending the interview, asked me to think the matter over. To this I could not say no. And so we parted. His last remark was to the effect that if he were not to avail himself of my counsels, he would use the counsels of those he could, and that he would stoop to anything. I am afraid he is not pleased with me, but I am pleased with myself, a thing I have not been for many a day."

Cicero did not go to Rome, and Caesar himself stayed there only a few days. He held a meeting of the senate, asking them to coöperate with him, and when they showed a recalcitrant spirit, he exclaimed that if he could not manage things with them, he would do so without them. He proposed to enter on negotiations with Pompey, but no envoys could be found. The senate did grant him the reserve fund in the treasury; a tribune, however, offered resistance, and Caesar had to take the money by force. Thereupon he hastened away, by land, to meet the Pompeian army in Spain.

Every possible effort was made, from friendly as well as political motives, to restrain Cicero from joining Pompey. Caesar himself wrote to Cicero that he appreciated his reasons for not coming to the city; hinting, however, that he was acting more generously toward Cicero than toward certain others; and when he was on his way to Spain, he wrote again to Cicero, asking him to stay in Italy. Antony, not a friend to Cicero but a devoted Caesarian, and during Caesar's absence in general charge of Italy, asked Cicero by letter not to go away; he ought to think of his daughter and his son-in-law. And later, on the third of May, he informed Trebatius, who already had attempted to win Cicero for Caesar's cause, that Caesar had left orders about Cicero. This meant that Cicero was to be prevented from going away.

Curio, to show Cicero the hopeless position of the Pompeians, wrote that Cato, who had been holding Sicily, or intending to hold it, had sailed from Syracuse on the last of April. Caelius had formerly advised Cicero to adopt the cause of Caesar, as the safest; and he had done so himself. Now he urged Cicero at least to put off a decision until news came of the fighting in Spain. Young Caesarians, like the son of Hortensius, visited Cicero, ostensibly to pay their respects, in reality perhaps to spy on him.

Atticus had been charmed with Cicero's firmness at the interview of March twenty-eighth, but he had also made a formal call on Caesar during the latter's brief stay in Rome; for Atticus was a consummate neutral. Now he inquired of Balbus whether Cicero might retire to Malta, but Balbus did not think this proper. Quintus, Cicero's nephew, had displayed Caesarian sympathies by having an interview with Caesar in Rome, which prostrated his father with grief and caused Cicero himself to give the young man a piece of his mind. Tullia begged her father to wait until the end of the Spanish campaign; and so did Terentia, weeping.

Cicero, however, remained firm to what he considered his duty both to Pompey and to his country; and on the seventh of June he sailed from the harbor of Caieta, near Formiae, accompanied by Quintus and the two boys.

But there had been no need for Cicero to give anxious thought to his duty or to imperil his position, and perhaps even his life, in the fulfilment of it. Though the Pompeians had a kind of abstract justice on their side, they were chiefly concerned with the details of the war and their own prospects after it. One of the most patriotic and unselfish among them was Cato, and yet, when Cicero arrived in Dyrrhachium, it was Cato who took him aside to explain, with his usual candor, that Cicero would have done better to remain in Italy, so that he could have mediated between Caesar and the Pompeians. Plutarch, who tells the story, says that Cicero was welcomed by the rest, but that Pompey had no task for him—a statement that is amply borne out by Cicero's letters.

It was not a happy time. Except for Pompey and a few others, Cicero says two years later, the leaders indulged mostly in threats against the Caesarians, and the forces were neither numerous nor eager for war. Cicero found relief in witticisms, but they were not well received. "Where is your son-in-law?" asked Pompey, referring to the Caesarian Dolabella. "With your father-in-law," replied Cicero. Pompey wished Cicero might go over to the enemy. Cicero was not well; he worried about the financial position of his family in Rome, and had fears that his house on the Palatine might be confiscated.

He had arrived in Dyrrhachium in the autumn or early winter of 49 B.C., having first spent some time on Atticus' estate in Epirus; on the ninth of August in the following year was fought the battle af Pharsalia. Cicero, Varro, Cato, and a number of others had been left at Dyrrhachium; Plutarch explaining that Cicero was prevented by sickness from fighting at Pharsalus, an explanation that carries little conviction. After the battle, Pompey fled to the East; and the Pompeians went to Corcyra, where they held a general council. At this Gnaeus Pompey, the son of the triumvir, threatened Cicero because the latter proposed surrender; he even came near killing him, it seems, but was prevented by Cato. Cicero, as highest in rank, had been asked by Cato to take the chief command, but had refused. Ultimately most of the Pompeians went to Africa. Cicero and Quintus went first to Patrae, whereupon Quintus and his son set out for the East, to make their peace with Caesar; and Cicero himself returned to Brundisium, where he staid about eleven months, until Caesar returned from the East.

II

The Dictatorship

Neither the eleven months of Cicero's dreary waiting at Brundisium nor the subsequent years in Rome and its vicinity until the assassination of Caesar on the Ides of March, 44 B.C., are significant in Cicero's life except for the domestic tragedies that befell him during this time and the essays that he produced as a result of his political inactivity and disappointment. Our information about this period, as well as about the months of indecision after the outbreak of the Civil War and the fruitless tarrying in Dyrrhachium, is immense. There are only three orations, to be sure, delivered in 46 and 45 B.C., but the correspondence for the five years contains about four hundred letters as against the one hundred and seventy odd of the eleven years between the consulship and the administration of Cilicia. This large correspondence includes letters to and from many people, and it has sometimes daily letters to Atticus for considerable stretches of time. It is possible to observe Cicero's thoughts and plans and activities in considerable detail; many of the letters are of great charm and, taken together, they are of wide diversity; new friends come into view, or old friends of whom the previous correspondence has given little or no information; and yet we learn almost nothing new about Cicero's personality and manner of life, and as for historical information of importance, the letters, broadly speaking, do little more than supply a background for the great figure of Caesar.

To the student of Roman history these years belong to Caesar. In the matter of the fighting, and it continued until well into 45 B.C., he obviously dominates the time, for he was not only ultimately victorious but he was present in nearly every campaign. His notable opponents came to a quick end. Nor is the fighting seen in Cicero's correspondence except by way of brief comments, which reflect the manner in which the news was received in Rome. And in the city itself Caesar's preponderance was even greater. It was often exercised through his adherents, for Caesar was in Rome only about one year and a half during this whole time, but his adherents were his subordinates, only executing his commands. Neither Cicero nor any one else of the many who had submitted to the new power accomplished anything politically, or even tried to do so; they lived in the shadow of the conqueror. Caesar's great work—his numerous measures to meet pressing needs and the initiation of his large plans for a new kind of state—was carried out without their participation, without their approval, usually, though also without their opposition, for they were helpless; but it is only these measures, whether put into effect or only planned, that have a permanent interest. They are the kernel of the later developments during the empire, both for good and for evil.

Caesar's struggle for complete power was long, but his hold on Italy was never questioned after Pompey's flight in 49 B.C. In Rome, therefore, the situation was a repetition of the conditions under the triumvirate, except that there was now only one ruler and that he faced no opposition. Cicero's experiences were also a repetition; he reacted as he had done formerly. Indeed, this whole period was for him even externally like that of the earlier years: first, a time of indecision, followed by a hopeless attempt at opposition, if his espousal of Pompey's tottering cause can be called an attempt; then, a period of virtual exile, much like the real exile in Greece; and after that, some years of submission to a personally favorable ruler, during which Cicero again turned to authorship. It is because of this similarity in Cicero's outward fortunes and because of his enforced submission that the large correspondence of these years contains but few new revelations about Cicero; it only heaps up further incident and illustration.

Since everything at Rome revolved around Caesar, his movements should be rapidly traced. He had crossed the Rubicon
in January of 49 B.C. In April of the same year, after Pompey's
flight, he had spent a few days in the city, and had then set out
for Spain, whence he had returned victorious at the end of the
year. For eleven days he remained in Rome, and again he
departed for the war, this time to go east. Cicero in the meantime had joined Pompey at Dyrrhachium. On the fourth of
January, 48 B.C., Caesar sailed from Brundisium. The battle
of Pharsalus was fought on the ninth of August, and thereupon
Caesar followed Pompey to Egypt, learning on his arrival that
his great rival had been murdered. Egypt and Cleopatra occupied him for nine months, and these were followed, from June,
47 B.C., by more fighting in the East and in Asia Minor. Pharnaces, the son of Mithradates, was conquered, and Caesar wrote
briefly *veni, vidi, vici* about him, though his father had been
one of Rome's most dangerous enemies. About the twenty-
fourth of September Caesar landed at Tarentum. For some
three months he remained in Italy, almost entirely in Rome, and
then he set out for Africa. Here the Pompeians were defeated
at Thapsus, on April the sixth, 46 B.C.; and Cato, a few days
later, took his own life. In July of the same year Caesar was
back in Rome, to remain about five months; and again he went
to Spain, to meet the sons of Pompey. The battle of Munda,
on the seventeenth of March, 45 B.C., decided this campaign.
For the last time, in September, Caesar returned to Rome.
Measures for the present and the future, now as before, and
preparations for a new campaign—this time against the Parthians—filled his days, but at the end of six months he was
murdered.

Cicero's greatest anxiety during his long stay in Brundisium,
while Caesar was fighting and dallying in Egypt and conquering
Pharnaces, was concerned with the treatment he would ultimately
receive at the hands of Caesar. Young Caesarians in Italy,

devoted to the old ex-consul now as they had been before he
decided for Pompey, not only showed their devotion in their
ordinary relations with him but also communicated to him their
conjectures and their rare words from Caesar; they were asked
by Cicero to write in his behalf to Caesar, and no doubt did so.
Word from Caesar, who was busy with other things, did not
reach Italy often, but messages did come, and even a letter to
Cicero himself, allowing him to keep his imperator's trappings.
This was an unequivocal sign that Cicero's high position in the
state would not be altered. He never celebrated a triumph. We
do not know exactly when he abandoned the thought. Probably
he had kept his prospective hold on a triumph during the early
part of the war as a sign that he still claimed to be one of the
prominent statesmen of Rome, ready to act with independence
in favor of peace; but he could have no pleasure in celebrating
a triumph under the auspices of a conqueror. The honor would
clearly have been a personal gift, and, as we shall see, Cicero,
though he submitted, never gave either public or private approval
to the new regime except in so far as it held promise of a return
to constitutional government.

Perhaps Cicero had no very great reason for concern about
Caesar's attitude to him. The war was largely a personal matter;
many men had transferred their allegiance to Caesar both immediately after Pharsalus and at other stages of the struggle.
Caesar always forgave. Nevertheless he had made unusual
efforts to win Cicero, at least for neutrality, and his failure in
these attempts had involved almost a public condemnation of
his actions. In his interview with Cicero he had admitted this.
And the matter was the worse because Cicero had formerly,
after Luca, given his open approval to Caesar's policies and he
had been known as Caesar's personal friend.

All doubts in Cicero's mind as to Caesar were solved at the
interview near Tarentum. Plutarch's picturesque pen, prompted
perhaps by Tiro, records that Cicero was a little in advance of

his companions, and that Caesar went forward to meet him, and saluted him, whereupon the two, conversing, walked along the road, side by side, for some stadia.

Cicero at once returned to Rome. During the rest of this year and during the next he wrote numerous letters, sparkling with wit and filled with light-heartedness. The vagaries of Epicureanism, pen pictures of people and events, quips and quirks are there. To one of his friends, Paetus, he is always threatening to arrive for dinner. Poor Paetus had gout, as many Romans seem to have had, and Cicero hopes that Paetus' cook is not suffering from the same complaint. Cicero even pretended now at last to have become a devotee to high living; some young Caesarians, who declaimed under him in the morning, in the evening taught him how to dine. "I have already mourned for my country more deeply and for a longer time than any mother ever mourned for her only child," he writes to a friend;[4] and this sentence, with its implication of gaiety, characterizes well his attitude during these years.

These letters, though about new things, are of a kind with those written after Luca. Now, as at that time, Cicero pretends to have found happiness at last in writing and study. Particularly is this the case in his correspondence with Varro, the aged scholar, who was ten years older than Cicero. On his return to Rome, Cicero had made distinct advances to the old student; evidently determined on a closer relation, as he had been in reference to Hortensius when setting out from Cilicia. The two men, however, do not seem ever to have become intimate; they were too different. Thus in July, 45 B.C., Cicero wrote to Atticus: "We were talking about Varro. Talk of the devil," or, as the Latin puts it, "the wolf in the story! He arrived, and it was so late that he had to be kept over night. Well, I kept him, but I did not quite tear his cloak off his back in my efforts to retain him." Nevertheless there grew up between them a sort

---

[4] *Fam.* 9, 20, 3.

of literary friendship, signalised by the dedication[5] to Varro of the second edition of the *Academica,* in which Varro was himself an interlocutor, and by numerous compliments in the later treatises.

Many prominent men of Cicero's own age had now died; Hortensius by a natural death, Pompey by murder, Cato by suicide; and there were others. Cicero was fifty-nine when he met Caesar near Tarentum. A new generation was coming to the front. These were largely on Caesar's side, worshipers of the new sun, but they admired Cicero. Many of them had acquired their oratorical ability from him, mostly by imitation no doubt, but some of them, as just mentioned, by direct teaching. And one at least, Brutus, shared Cicero's interest in philosophy. A picture of Cicero's daily life is contained in a letter to Paetus,[6] dated August, 46 B.C. He holds a reception in the morning, to which come many conservatives, who are sad, and many Caesarians, cheerful victors and yet very courteous and devoted to Cicero. After the reception, he buries himself in his books, writing or reading. Some men later drop in to hear him talk, listening to him as though he were a learned man; the real situation being merely, as Cicero explains, that he is a little better informed than they. Thereupon he takes his exercise.

Though Cicero's outward position was excellent and the young Caesarians honored themselves in honoring him, there must have been many moments when men on the victorious side flaunted their new glories. In 46 B.C., while Caesar was conquering in Spain, Cicero writes to Varro that the Caesarians look upon others as upon enemies in defeat, and that it is impossible even for a man of the sharpest sight to avoid stumbling upon disagreeable experiences. There were always men about Caesar ready to slander Cicero and present him as dangerous, though, as he said himself, he had no fight in him.

---

[5] The dedicatory letter is *Fam.* 9, 8.
[6] *Fam.* 9, 20. 3.

When he was out of Rome, the friendly Atticus, more friendly
than tactful, reported Caesarian talk about Cicero that was not
pleasant to hear. Such talk was at one time concerned with a
certain Tigellius, who imagined that he had a private grievance
against Cicero. Tigellius was a Sardinian and a musician, ord-
narily quite beneath the notice of a Roman consular. Atticus,
however, and also another friend of Cicero's, thought differently,
and even tried to mollify the irascible Caesarian. Cicero became
impatient with their efforts. "I am receiving as much honor
from all the Caesarians but Tigellus," he writes, "as I ever
received when I was considered to be at the head of the state.
It is a clear gain to be free from the society of this fellow. I
won't be a slave to everybody any more than Cipius would shut
his eyes for everybody." And Cipius had become proverbial.
Having a frail wife, he was supposed to have pretended sleep for
her greater liberty, but when a slave saw his master's eyes closed
and started away with a stolen cup, Cipius looked up, with the
remark that he did not sleep for everybody.

Sometimes, during Caesar's frequent absences from Rome,
there was even danger to Cicero, or at least a threat of it. Two
days after Cicero had retired from Rome in the spring of 45 B.C.,
after the death of Tullia, Antony arrived unexpectedly in the
city, and immediately the prominent Caesarians, Oppius and
Balbus, who were always devoted to Cicero, wrote that he need
have no fear in connection with Antony. Atticus wrote the
same, and would not believe Cicero's reply, to the effect that he
was giving no thought to Antony. At this time, indeed, Cicero
was overwhelmed with grief for the loss of his daughter and
he was meditating and writing on death, as will presently be
seen, so that he probably held his own life as valueless; but the
letters of assurance addressed to him give a clear indication of
what might have happened. It would have been easy for Antony
to send a detachment of soldiers to Cicero's house. The violent
Caesarian, however, had at this time come to Rome for other

purposes than to cause mischief; he was in debt and also wished
to visit his wife.[7]

No such stir could have been caused when Caesar was in
Rome. Cicero was credited with considerable influence with the
dictator. Vatinius, for example, whom Cicero had once bitterly
attacked and later defended, was one of Caesar's most ardent
supporters, and apparently very able. He had received a *supplicatio* for his military services in Dalmatia, and had thereupon
continued his successful career, capturing six towns, one of
which he had been forced to retake three times. Finally the
snows, the cold, and the rains had caused him to abandon it.
Caesar was a hard taskmaster, and Vatinius knew he would have
to render an account. He therefore writes[8] to Cicero to explain
the situation, in December of 45 B.C., a little over three months
before Caesar's death, and asks Cicero to intercede in his behalf
if the need should arise. Earlier, Cicero's influence with Caesar
had been of considerable service to several exiled Pompeians.
He recommended them to Caesar's mercy, just as in the years
after Luca he had recommended friends to Caesar's generosity.
Many letters from Cicero to such exiles are extant, of infinite
variety, although the contents are necessarily limited to consolation, hopes for the future, and assurances that Caesar would
not be cruel.

One of Cicero's speeches, *Pro Ligario,* was delivered in behalf
of such a Pompeian in exile, perhaps the only one to be regularly tried. It was considered one of Cicero's notable orations,
but the case is scarcely important enough to call for much consideration. The main plea is frankly for forgiveness; not such
a weak plea, after all, inasmuch as the crime was merely that of
having taken the opposite side in politics and as Caesar's desire
was to be known as a gentle ruler. The external circumstances
of the trial are more noteworthy. It took place in the official

---

[7] For Cicero's later account of this visit, see below, p. 640.
[8] *Fam.* 5, 10a.

residence of Caesar, and only a few persons were present, so
that the trial resembled a private interview; indeed, as Cicero
writes to Ligarius himself, he had had some difficulty and had
suffered some humiliation in securing access to Caesar. In the
same letter Cicero describes the favorable acceptance of his
plea, a matter further described by Plutarch. According to him,
Caesar's color came and went during the progress of the speech,
and when Cicero spoke of the battle at Pharsalus, Caesar shook
with emotion, even dropping from his hand some papers that he
held. Caesar, says Plutarch, had observed previously that he
knew Ligarius to be a wicked man and an enemy, but he would
grant the trial for the pleasure of hearing another speech by
Cicero; and now Caesar acquitted the defendant.

But intercessions like those in favor of Vatinius and of exiles
were largely private matters; they had nothing to do with the
government. In his management of the state Caesar neither
asked for nor listened to advice. Cicero and every one else were
subjects. Thus, when Cato had committed suicide, Cicero wrote
one of several eulogies, but he found the task as difficult as a
mathematical problem worthy of Archimedes; praise of the late
Stoic necessarily involved praise of his political attitude, and
such would not readily appeal to Caesar. As has already been
mentioned, Cato became the subject of a literary warfare; Caesar
praised Cicero's work, for its style, but said nothing about the
content.

At one time, in 45 B.C., Cicero cherished the hope of actually
influencing Caesar, and wrote a formal letter of advice, such as
Aristotle had addressed to Alexander. Atticus had suggested
that the letter be submitted to Oppius and Balbus for approval
before it was sent to Caesar, so doubtful a procedure was it even
for Cicero to address the dictator, and this was done; but when
these, after a considerable correspondence, had finally made all
the necessary alterations, Cicero found the letter so changed that
he decided not to send it. If he could not give the kind of advice

he considered good for Rome, he said, he had no intention of
sending eulogies or meaningless verbiage to a man who would
brook no interference.

The relations between the two great Romans were very cordial,
Cicero himself writes in 46 B.C., but that they were of a strictly
social nature, divorced from politics, Cicero reveals in a letter
to Atticus of the following year; the very next, indeed, in the
correspondence after the note from Vatinius. When refusing in
49 B.C. to come to Rome, Cicero had assumed a position of non-
participation in Caesar's rule, and Caesar had taken him at his
word. The letter to Atticus was written in December, the day
after Caesar had paid Cicero a visit at his estate at Puteoli.

Caesar was a formidable guest, Cicero wrote,[9] and yet Cicero
had no reason to regret the visit. Caesar had been very pleasant.
On the evening of the eighteenth he had stayed with Philip,
Cicero's neighbor. The latter's house had been filled with the
soldiers that escorted the dictator, two thousand of them, so that
Philip's house had scarcely had a room in which Caesar himself
could dine. Cicero was anxious as to what would happen on the
following day, when Caesar would visit him, but Barba Cassius,
one of Caesar's friends, came to Cicero's assistance by placing
guards around the villa and making the soldiers encamp in the
fields. Caesar stayed with Philip until about twelve on the nineteenth, and would see no one, probably going over his accounts
with Balbus. Then he took a walk on the beach, and afterwards
had his bath. Some news was brought about Mamurra, his
notorious adherent of Catullan fame. Perhaps it had to do with
Mamurra's death, but he received it without comment, or without
a change of expression, according to the reading of the text.
He was rubbed down, and then took his place at Cicero's table,
eating and drinking heartily and with enjoyment. It was a
good dinner and a pleasant one. Caesar's retinue were well
entertained in three dining-rooms, even the less refined freedmen

---

[9] *Att.* 13, 52.

and slaves wanting for nothing. Caesar seemed to enjoy himself; his attitude was free and natural. But he was not the kind of man to whom you might say: "Look in again when you come this way." Once was enough! There was a good deal of literary talk, but not a single serious word, nothing, that is, about matters of public policy. In this remark Cicero reveals the sting of the visit.

A little more than a year earlier than the dinner at Puteoli, Cicero, and doubtless others, had hoped that Caesar would restore the constitutional government. He had not been much in Rome, so that his autocratic measures might well have seemed temporary, intended to keep the power in his hands until he should have an opportunity to make permanent arrangements; and he had been consistently lenient toward his defeated opponents. One of these was Marcellus, the consul of 51 B.C., a staunch and active aristocrat, who after Pharsalia had retired to exile in Mitylene; he was too proud to make formal submission and beg for restoration, but had been prevailed upon by Cicero's entreaties to return to Rome, thus virtually acknowledging Caesar's right to power, if pardon were extended to him. At the intercession of the exile's relatives Caesar granted the pardon. This happened at an excited meeting of the senate; the brother of Marcellus fell on his knees before Caesar and all the other senators rose to enforce the supplication of the kneeling ex-consul. Caesar at first replied with a recital of the exile's numerous acts of hostility, but concluded by leaving the matter to the senators. They all voted in the affirmative, one after the other expressing his opinion and at the same time giving thanks to Caesar.

One of the senators was Cicero. During Caesar's absences from Rome Cicero ordinarily stayed away from the city, but when the dictator was personally at the head of affairs, Cicero could not avoid an ostensible participation in public business. He attended the meetings of the senate; his only concession, however, for he took no part in the deliberations. In his letters he does not disguise the fact that the decrees of the senate were mere forms, and mentions how he himself was stated both to have witnessed the formal writing down of decrees and actually to have made motions about which he had not even expressed an opinion; in return for which he received grateful letters from favored monarchs of whose very existence he had until then been unaware. But in the matter of Marcellus Caesar really left the decision to the senate; and this seemed to Cicero an indication that Caesar would in the future allow himself to be governed by their opinions—that he was assuming for himself such a position of eminence and yet of obedience to the constitution as Cicero had once intended for Pompey. In the midst of the enthusiasm Cicero's thanks took the form of a glowing eulogy, later published under the name *Pro Marcello*.

The eulogy is extravagant, as has been pointed out to satiety, especially by critics who accuse Cicero of insincerity in his utterances, but, as others have observed, Cicero was perfectly sincere, for he expected a return to constitutionalism. Nor was his praise of Caesar considered extravagant at the time. Indeed, it attains no higher flights than Cicero's repeated laudations of Pompey; not so high, it would seem, as his words to Pompey and even to the consuls of 57 B.C., in the first address after the exile. More significant still is the fact that the main emphasis of the speech is laid on the things that are still to be accomplished by Caesar for the good of the state.

His life, Cicero exclaims, is more precious than that of any other man, and he must not say, as report has it, that he has had enough of years and glory. Nobody would be so mad as to make an attempt on his life, and yet he should not expose it recklessly, for the state needs him. His martial glory is great, but his clemency is greater. He must live with a thought of future ages; otherwise, there will be much disagreement among men, as there already is, some lauding his martial success to the sky, while others perhaps want something more, and that something is the restoration of peace and safety to his country. The Latin phrase used by Cicero, *salus patriae,* meant the return to a stable, constitutional government.

The words of Cicero were a true prophecy of the contrary opinions about Caesar pronounced by history, but his hope was quickly shattered. Caesar was determined to retain absolute power, and he made this clear within a few weeks of the pardon of Marcellus, for, on setting out for Spain, he left the government in the hands of his subordinates, who thus took the places of the ordinary republican magistrates. Side by side with the speech in recognition of Marcellus' pardon, therefore, should be placed Cicero's defense of Deiotarus, which was delivered a year later, after many things had occurred to render Caesar's intentions unmistakable. It was Cicero's third and last speech under Caesar, and it was also his last plea for a defendant, spoken, like that for Ligarius, in Caesar's own house. Once when Cicero was waiting for an audience in one of Caesar's anterooms, the latter is reported[10] to have said: "I have no doubt that people hate me cordially when Marcus Cicero has to sit and wait, unable to see me at his own convenience. If any man is good-natured, it is Cicero, and yet I have no doubt that he hates me thoroughly." The speech for Deiotarus expresses no hatred, but many passages read like an indictment of the great dictator, and answer the question whether Cicero's speech for Marcellus was dictated by sincere hopes for the future or by cringing flattery.

Deiotarus at this time was an old man, so weak that he could not mount a horse unassisted. He had fought on the Roman side against Mithradates, and had throughout his life done many services to Rome, in return for which he had been honored by several Roman generals, particularly Pompey. During Caesar's consulship in 59 B.C. he had received the title of king. He had

---

[10] *Att.* 14, 1, 2.

joined Pompey before the battle of Pharsalus, bringing him a troop of six hundred horsemen. After the defeat, he had accompanied Pompey as far as Lesbos, and had then returned to his own country, Galatia. When Pompey had been murdered and Caesar had come to the East, Deiotarus had submitted to the conqueror, assisting him with money and other things in the Alexandrine war, and later with troops against Pharnaces. Caesar had allowed Deiotarus to retain his royal title, but he had deprived him of part of his territory. While in Deiotarus' kingdom, Caesar had been sumptuously entertained and had received numerous costly presents—as was in accord with the usual ruinous generosity of dependent potentates.

Now, two years later, Caesar's visit supplied the enemies of Deiotarus with the means for accusing the old king. There was strife, both private and political, in the family of Deiotarus. A grandson, Castor, was in Rome with an embassy; ambassadors were also present from Deiotarus. In order to ruin the grandfather, Castor accused him of having planned to assassinate Caesar during the latter's visit in Galatia, and asserted that only chance had saved him. The charge itself could be readily disposed of, and need not be discussed; the real difficulty for the defense consisted in Caesar's well-known hostility to the old Pompeian and in the fact that Deiotarus could hardly have been expected to love the man who had shorn him of power. Cicero, however, took the case. Deiotarus was an old friend; he had entertained Cicero's son and nephew during Cicero's governorship of Cilicia, and at that time he had also brought troops to Cicero himself.

"Despite my advanced age and my long experience in the courts," says Cicero, "I am always agitated at the beginning of an important plea, but in this case I have special reasons for agitation. In the first place, I am speaking in behalf of a king. It is not injustice on your part to try him, particularly since the case involves danger to yourself; nevertheless the trial of a king on a capital charge has never been heard of before. Formerly, in the senate, I have often had occasion to praise Deiotarus for his great services to our state; now I must defend him against the most impudent charges, which proceed from a cruel grandson and from a man who belongs merely to the retinue of an embassy and who, as a slave, should not give testimony except under torture, and then never against his master. It is a difficult matter, furthermore, to plead before you, against whom Deiotarus is accused of having plotted, for almost every man will believe such an accusation. Only your own noble character can insure justice, and I am glad to forget what your opinion of Deiotarus may be, while I remember what you wish others to think of you. And finally, I am speaking within the walls of a private house. I have to turn to you alone, address you alone. Though this may make it easier to establish the truth of my plea, it nevertheless takes away the support that a speaker always finds in a large audience. If you were trying this case in the forum, I should be hearteend by the large gathering of Roman citizens, all of whom are in favor of this king, who has spent his life fighting for them in their wars. I should turn to the senate-house, the forum, even to the sky. In recalling the benefits heaped upon Deiotarus by the immortal gods, by the Roman people, and by the senate, I should find it easy to plead in his defense. But these walls cramp me. You, who have spoken in behalf of many defendants, can appreciate my difficulty, and should lessen it by impartiality toward my client and a willingness to hear the arguments.''

After this earnest introduction, which by implication condemns Caesar both for conducting the trial under the circumstances described and for holding the trial at all, Cicero turns, not to the charges against Deiotarus, but to Caesar's supposed hostility toward him and the grounds for it. And in this passage Cicero's criticism of the dictator's rule is again visible through the compliments of the pleader.

"The accusers are relying on your well-known dislike of Deiotarus. But you have partaken of his hospitality. You have pardoned him, and you have never been known to harbor ill feeling against a man whom you have forgiven. Nor was Deiotarus guilty of any crime. He sided with Pompey, as many of us did, and with even more excuse. He heard that the senate had issued a call to arms, that the magistrates had been ordered to defend the state, that the consuls and all the ex-consuls, for such was the report that went to the East, had left Italy. He knew nothing of your situation, of the opposition to you, and of your attempts at conciliation. He thought Rome was in danger. What was he to do, especially after he had been summoned by letter from Pompey? We all followed Pompey, on whom gods and men had heaped honors, you yourself most of all. Deiotarus was a personal friend of Pompey as well as an old comrade in arms. He is to be forgiven for obeying Pompey's command. Even if your great deeds have thrown those of all others into obscurity, we have not forgotten Pompey. He had reputation, wealth, military renown, and every kind of honor, given him by the people, the senate, and by you yourself. He was as much superior to all that preceded him as you are to every one. We used in wonder to count his wars, victories, triumphs, and consulships; yours we can not count."

After discussing various charges against Deiotarus, Cicero comes to the assertion of the prosecutor that Blesamius, the head of Deiotarus' embassy, was in the habit of sending his master reports about the state of things in Rome—a sign of hostile interest in Caesar's fortunes, according to Castor, who may have been right. The contents of these reports, however, could not be charged to Deiotarus, and might readily have been omitted by Cicero. They contain in a few lines a description of the very circumstances that caused the assassination of Caesar. And yet Cicero not only repeats the reports but professes, in an exceedingly weak manner, to explain away their disparaging character.

"Blesamius writes," says Cicero, "that you, Caesar, are unpopular, that you are considered a tyrant, that men are offended because your statue has been placed among those of the old kings, and that people do not applaud you in public. But that is clearly only the low talk of enemies about the city. How can Blesamius call you a tyrant? You have not acted like all other victors in civil strife. No heads of citizens have been set up on the rostra, people have not been worried, beaten, and killed, houses have not been robbed or destroyed, the forum is not filled with armed men. You are the only conqueror in whose victory nobody has been killed except with arms in his hand. If we who have been born free do not consider you a tyrant, how can Blesamius do it, he who is the subject of a king? And your statue? Do we not see statues of generals all about us? Your trophies of various kinds are not unpopular; why should your statues be? Is it because of the place they occupy? But can there be a more honorable place for statues than the rostra? And what about the lack of applause? The need of it has never been felt in your case; men have remained silent because overcome with admiration of your greatness, and perhaps they have felt that nothing ordinary was worthy of you."

Coming to the end, Cicero makes no peroration. "The usual impassioned appeal," so he concludes, "is not necessary; your own sense of justice must decide. Your clemency will be your greatest monument in the years to come, especially clemency toward a king."

King! The word permeates the speech, contrasting Caesar and Deiotarus, to be sure, and yet Caesar was publicly addressed as king, regal intentions were attributed to him, and it was because of them, whether genuine or not, that he was to die. On August the second Cicero, in a letter to Atticus, had spoken of him as king. Honors of every kind were showered on him when no new powers could be given. The question of Caesar's assumption of royalty was in the air; his supporters favored it, to please him, and his secret enemies were active for it, to stir up the unpopularity which Cicero mentioned in his speech, and had the temerity to publish. Many incidents pointed toward kingship, culminating in the famous scene at the Lupercalia, in February of 44 B.C., when Antony offered Caesar the crown; but nothing could so arouse hatred in Rome, among aristocrats as well as among common citizens, as the name of king—the name far more than the power.

The governmental changes initiated or contemplated by Caesar were dictated by the wide vision of a statesman. They have been held responsible for many of the evils of the empire, and it is perhaps possible that better things could have been done, but the possibility is debatable even in the minds of academic critics, though to them nearly all things, in the past, seem possible. It is certain that no one else in Rome looked so far into the future or saw the present so clearly as did Caesar. But the aristocrats were not ready for a king.

Caesar knew that there was bitter discontent, and he allowed his knowledge to become known, but he took no measures to insure his safety. Perhaps he thought that his compatriots, finding him a gentle ruler, would acquiesce in the rule since it was for the betterment of Rome. He dismissed his Spanish bodyguard and refused to accept the senatorial offer of a bodyguard consisting of senators and knights. He was never afraid. He may also have felt a contempt for the men who had submitted, and accepted his pardon. Possibly he did not much care whether his life was to be long or short; his remark that he had lived long enough indicates weariness. His life had been exceedingly arduous, and he had but lately come to a position of power, only to find himself confronted with a new and more difficult task, that of remaking a world empire and persuading its people that the changes were for their good. It has been said, and probably with truth, that the wonderful balance of his great nature was breaking down from ill health or from too much work. Cer-

tainly, during the last months of his life, he committed many acts
of deliberate insult, or of equally insulting indifference, to the
aristocrats. Whatever his feelings, and they can never be known,
he misunderstood the Roman aristocrats, for it can scarcely be
supposed that he clearly foresaw and desired his own death.
Cicero had imagined that these aristocrats could be made like
the Romans of old, which had proved impossible; Caesar thought
that they could forget their former freedom and acquiesce in
the rule of an individual, but this was equally impossible.

Though it was the Roman hatred of an autocrat that made
the conspiracy possible, this feeling was more a matter of personal opposition than of patriotism. Love of Rome there doubtless was, as in the case of Brutus; but even Brutus' patriotism
was sadly adulterated with personal vanity and pompousness.
Some conspirators were malcontents; their rewards, at the
hands of Caesar, seemed to them too small. Others were his
enemies, personally as well as politically. And it must not be
forgotten that political assassination had been by no means rare
in Rome ever since the days of Scipio. The murder of Caesar
was one of the great tragedies of history, but not even his most
ardent admirers could have seen in him the towering figure that
he appears to us. To his contemporaries he was a great soldier
and a very able but also a very unprincipled politician; he was
not allowed to live long enough for his reforms to become really
fruitful.

Cicero's utterances, both public and private, and his whole
political attitude can be looked upon as part of the ground out
of which the conspiracy grew; and he would have considered the
death of an individual as no great price for the liberty of his
country. He had himself walked in the valley of death, when
in exile; he had recently lost Tullia, and he had been living in
the contemplation of the brevity of human life, as his essays
of this time indicate. Many of the conspirators were his personal
friends. Nevertheless there is no indication that he knew of the

conspiracy. Indeed, after the assassination, his political ardor
led him to wish that he might have had a share in it; so that he
certainly would not have thought of denying complicity, had it
existed. But Cicero could not have aided the conspiracy. The
latter was not a popular revolution, in which his well-known
patriotism could have been of avail, but a secret banding together
of individuals. Cicero, furthermore, was a personal friend and
in many respects an admirer of Caesar, and he was sixty-two
years old.

Of Cicero's movements and thoughts during the last months
of Caesar's life we have no detailed knowledge, though it is
known that he was busy with his philosophical writings. The
last letter to Atticus of this period was written at the end of
December, 45 B.C. There are later letters to others, but they are
few in number and of insignificant content.

To Curius, a banker of Patrae, he writes[11] in January of
44 B.C. that he is not urging the latter to come to Rome. He
would like to go away himself. Nor can Curius appreciate
Cicero's feelings of mortification at the doings in the city. They
are bad enough to hear about, but worse to witness. Curius, says
Cicero, was not present in the Campus Martius when the following incident occurred. The election of quaestors was being held.
At the second hour, in the early morning, the chair of Maximus
the consul had been brought, when word came that he was dead,
and the chair was taken away. Caesar presided. At the seventh
hour he announced the election of a new consul, who, as Curius
might see, would hold office until the first of January, or, in
other words, until the morning of the next day. And so nobody
took lunch during the consulship of Caninius. No evil was done
during his term of office, for he was a man of such wonderful
vigilance that he never closed his eyes while consul. "All this
may seem laughable to you," Cicero concludes, "for you are not
here; but if you saw these things yourself, you would not be able
to restrain your tears."

11 *Fam.* 7, 30.

Possibly Caesar had formal reasons for seeing to it that the year did not end without a consul; but it could only give offense to the Romans, who looked upon their high office as something more than a distinction to be thrown at a nobody for the space of a few hours. Epigrams and jokes were made about the event, and other sayings of Cicero are quoted in this connection. The election, or appointmnet, rather, of Caninius was one of the many reminders that Caesar was king.

In another letter to Curius, written in February, Cicero urges him to return to Rome. The fountain of wit has run quite dry, Cicero says, and Curius must come back. Otherwise the very seed of wit will perish as has perished the freedom of the state.

This is the last datable letter before the assassination of Caesar. On the fifteenth of February the crown was offered to him at the Lupercalia; on the fifteenth of March, the Ides, he was struck down. It is practically certain that Cicero did not witness the assassination. Later in the day he despatched a note, the shortest in the correspondence, to Basilus, one of the assassins. "Congratulations!"—so it runs[12]—"I am happy. I love you and watch over your interests. Send me your love, and let me know what you are doing and what is happening."

III

DEATH OF TULLIA

The Civil War and the autocracy of Caesar wrought a great change in Cicero's life, but their effect was politically only an intensified repetition of the situation that had resulted from the formation of the triumvirate, as has already been shown, and they did not cause him any personal humiliation equal to that of the exile. Nevertheless this time tested him with greater trials. In the earlier period he had been upheld by the affection of his

---

[12] *Fam.* 6, 15.

family, though also saddened by the realization that he had
brought ill fortune upon them as well as upon himself. During
the three years subsequent to Pharsalia his family life was
shattered; there was treachery, divorce, and death.

The treachery came from Quintus. Together they had joined
the Pompeian side in the Civil War, and after the battle of Pharsalia they had gone to Patrae. Here, after about a month, they
had a quarrel, and separated; Marcus departed for Brundisium,
and Quintus accompanied the Pompeian fleet eastward, soon,
however, repairing to Caesar and obtaining pardon for his
opposition in the war. People had expected that he would also
intercede for Marcus, but, quite on the contrary, he seems to
have done everything to make Cicero's relations with Caesar
difficult, and, indeed, to blacken his character in the eyes of
others as well. He almost carried on a campaign of vilification
against his brother, for he wrote bitter letters about him not
only to Caesar but also to Atticus and to a number of people
who were scarcely more than mere acquaintances. Some of these
letters were brought to Cicero's notice by the addressees, and
some fell into his hands by accident, and he opened them, as has
already been mentioned.[13] A whole year after the separation
of the brothers, when Cicero had succeeded in overcoming much
of the sorrow caused by it, Atticus sent him such a letter, which
he himself had received, and Cicero's comment is that it has
served only to reopen the wound.

Atticus could have spared himself the trouble, for Quintus
made no secret of his feelings. Both he and his son wrote coarse
and insulting letters to Cicero. The younger Quintus, like his
father, also took others into his noble confidence. In Ephesus,
so Cicero learned, he displayed to a friend a long account he had
drawn up about his uncle and intended to read to Caesar. It
is to be presumed that Caesar never listened to it. Young
Quintus, incidentally, was a worthless rascal, and caused trouble

---

[13] See above, p. 17.

to his father as well as to his uncle. The elder Quintus, after a while, wrote to Marcus in Brundisium in a somewhat conciliatory spirit, but his excuses, as Cicero told Atticus, were more bitter than accusations. Among other things Quintus wrote that he regretted having written to people about Marcus, since it had displeased Atticus, but that the letters themselves had been justified.

We do not know very well what caused Quintus' enmity to Marcus, whom he had always admired and to whom he very probably owed much of his public success. It was not a passing quarrel, such as abounded in Quintus' life. In all likelihood it was due to the political situation. Quintus, because of his legateship in Gaul, had been nearer to Caesar than to Pompey. Either from a natural tendency to imitate his brother or because of persuasion, but of such persuasion we hear nothing, Quintus had followed Marcus when the latter joined the Pompeians, and when the Pompeians failed at Pharsalus, he seems to have held his brother responsible for his own political mistake. This would explain his repeated criticisms of Marcus, for, once embarked on an attempt to disparage the latter in the eyes of Caesar and Caesarians, he could not readily change his attitude while Caesar's opinion of Marcus was still uncertain; and we know that Quintus sent hearty congratulations to Marcus on learning that Caesar was well disposed to him. While still hostile, Quintus thought of everything in which his elder brother had supposedly wronged him, and so he complained of having failed to receive a share of the money made in Cilicia; apparently he had not asked for it before.[14]

It was a one-sided quarrel, with all the honor and kindness on Cicero's side. After reaching Brundisium, Cicero wrote to Caesar about Quintus.[15] He could no longer venture to recommend Quintus to Caesar, he says, but he wished to make it clear

---

[14] *Att.* 11, 13, 4.
[15] *Att.* 11, 12, 2.

that Quintus had been more opposed than favorable to Marcus'
decision to leave Italy for Dyrrhachium; Quintus had been a
companion and not a leader; and Cicero hoped earnestly that
his own relation to Caesar would in no way be detrimental to
Quintus. And later, in the many references to Quintus' treachery that are found in the correspondence, Cicero's only feeling is
one of grief. Quintus' actions caused him more sorrow, he wrote
to Atticus, than anything else—and yet this was written while
Cicero was still in Brundisium. On his birthday, the third of
January, in 47 B.C., he ends a pathetic letter[16] to Atticus with
the wish that he had not been reared or that his mother had
not had another child.

Quintus apparently returned with Caesar to Italy. We have
no information as to when and how the brothers were reconciled.
Quintus, after all, was affectionate; he had never received anything but benefits from his brother; and he had a very excellent
reason for being thoroughly ashamed of himself. And as for
Marcus, he was always ready to forgive. They were now about
sixty, old men, as the Romans counted it. In July of the following year, 46 B.C., Cicero speaks of Quintus' foolish delight
at young Quintus' appointment as one of the Luperci, a favor
received from Caesar; and in November he visited Quintus. But
it does not seem that even then the old relation had been quite
reëstablished, for shortly afterwards, at the death of Tullia, it
was Atticus and not Quintus who gave comfort. As for the
nephew, he remained a nuisance for a long time.

Less harrowing probably was the divorce from Terentia,
which took place at the end of 47 or the beginning of 46 B.C.
Apparently Cicero and Terentia drifted apart, and nobody now
can assign the blame.[17] The first letter extant from Cicero's long
stay in Brundisium is addressed to Terentia. She had offered
to join Cicero, it seems, but Cicero replies that it would be a long

---

[16] *Att.* 11, 9.
[17] See Tyrrell, IV, p. xlviii, note.

journey from Rome, that travel is not safe, and that her coming
would do no particular good. It is a brief note, only a few lines,
but it is not unfriendly. The fact still remains, however, that
Cicero had no desire for her company. Later, we learn, she had
made a will in such terms that Cicero asked Atticus to interfere;
apparently some evasion of debt on her part was involved, for
Cicero urges that the condition of the times demands that she
make arrangements to pay her debts. The report of her financial
doings was such that Cicero could scarcely believe it.

There are several notes, always brief, to Terentia from Brundisium. He asks her, as of old, not to neglect her health, and
he occasionally gives a bit of news, referring her for details,
however, to somebody else. And when he is finally on his way
to Rome again, he informs[18] her of the date when he can be
expected at the Tusculan villa and asks her to have everything
ready. There may be several people with him and they may
stay for a considerable time, he writes; if there is not a large
basin in the bathroom, he wishes her to have one put in. This
letter, the last to Terentia that has come down to us, may owe
its matter-of-fact brevity to haste, but such can not have been the
case with the other letters. It was written on the first of October
in 47 B.C., and the divorce soon followed.

There are only two or three further matters to be noted, and
then Terentia passes out of his life. The repayment of her
dowry, always a slow process in Rome, as many cases indicate,
was still under discussion in the year 45 B.C. Terentia had
entrusted the matter to Balbus, the Spanish Caesarian. This
may have been done to insure prompt payment, but it may also
have been intended to bring Cicero into a humiliating relation
with the Caesarian, since Terentia possibly feigned that her
divorced husband either could not or would not pay. Cicero was
annoyed, and calls Terentia's action domineering. But he is
not greatly worried about it, for he had a more profound sorrow

[18] *Fam.* 14, 20.

then. He refuses to see Terentia for the purpose of coming to
a settlement, and asks Atticus to make the necessary arrangements. He would rather be overreached by Terentia, he explains, than insist on his own rights; it is a matter of honor with
him.

Terentia was active also in another way. Cicero had recently
made his will, the witnesses to which, according to Terentia,
were not such as would protect the rights of Lentulus, the son
of Tullia. Cicero explains to Atticus how the witnesses came to
be chosen. He adds that he is willing to let any one read the
will; if Terentia will do the same with her will, it will be discovered that her provision for the grandson is no more generous
than Cicero's. Dolabella, the father, was in Spain; he was a
spendthrift, furthermore, and had been divorced from Tullia in
the late autumn of 46 B.C. Tullia herself had died early the
following February. It would seem that Cicero looked after the
child's support, for in the letters of this year he asks Atticus to
assign the slaves necessary to care for the child.

The identity of Lentulus is not certain. In the year 49 B.C.
Tullia had given birth to a son, born in the seventh month and
very weak; and in 45 B.C. she bore another son. The child mentioned was one or the other of these two. Since nothing is
known about the boys beyond the statement of their births and
Cicero's thought for Lentulus, they probably died in childhood.
Cicero had no other grandchildren, so that only four generations
of the family are known to us. His portrait bust, therefore,
never gathered smoke in an aristocratic atrium.

It is scarcely conceivable that Terentia could have believed
Cicero capable of neglecting Tullia's child. Her avowed reason
for anxiety was the fact that one of the witnesses to Cicero's will
was Publilius, the brother of the young girl whom Cicero had
married early in the year. After Cicero's divorce from Terentia,
his friends immediately interested themselves in the possibilities
of a new marriage; particularly the wife of the jurist Servius

Sulpicius. Cicero considered the daughter of Pompey, and another lady of whom he writes to Atticus that he had never seen anything uglier. He was in need of money, and finally, at the advice of friends and relatives, if Plutarch is to be trusted, he married Publilia.

Cicero's second wife is scarcely more than a name. She had a widowed mother and a brother; she was very young and very rich; and she was Cicero's ward. A few weeks after the wedding Tullia died, and Cicero, seeking solitude, sent Publilia back to her mother, perhaps at first merely for a visit. Plutarch explains that she had rejoiced at the death of Tullia; but no such explanation is needed for her return home. Cicero at this time shrank from every one, even from Atticus, and the young wife—a child, in Plutarch's phrase—could have been no companion to him. Apparently Cicero never saw her again, and they were divorced, for the letters mention the dowry which was to be repaid.

The fact that Cicero had married her so soon after his separation from Terentia and had thereupon divorced her, was held up to scorn by his political opponents of the next year, but in the light of the Roman attitude it does not seem that he could be held to blame. His friends had taken a prompt marriage for granted, and after the separation Caerellia, Cicero's old literary friend, had visited him, to be sure, for the purpose of urging him to take Publilia back, but, as he himself writes to Atticus, she was not urgent and was readily persuaded that there was no reason for a continuance of the marriage. She had been sent by the brother and mother, who apparently were loth to lose the honor of a connection with the illustrious statesman. The young Publilia does not seem to have been considered in the matter. If we knew more about her, we might have reason to pity her.

The divorce led to a ludicrous incident. Publilia, so Cicero informs Atticus,[19] had written that her mother and brother were

---

[19] *Att.* 12, 32.

coming to visit Cicero, and she had proposed that she accompany them. Cicero had sent word back to Publilia not to come, but we are not told what he had written to the relatives. Being unwilling to see them, he asks Atticus to discover the exact date of their proposed visit, in order that he himself may be away. He will come to Atticus. Publilia, he remarks, could not herself have composed the letter. As Cicero presently left Astura, where he had been staying, it is likely that he succeeded in avoiding the unwelcome relatives.

Marcus, Cicero's only son, was at this time making preparations to go to Athens to study, though, as we know, he did not exert himself, and Cicero was arranging for a generous allowance. Marcus had been with his father in Dyrrhachium and Brundisium. After their return to Rome, he had proposed joining Caesar in Spain, but his father, in a serious conversation, reported to Atticus,[20] had pointed out the political unseemliness of such a course, and he had also adroitly hinted that Marcus would be annoyed to find his cousin Quintus high in Caesar's favor. Though Cicero had left the decision in the hands of Marcus, the latter had yielded. The young man had also had a desire of setting up a bachelor establishment in Rome, but this plan, too, had come to nothing; and now he was leaving for Athens. This saved his life, for in the next year his father, his uncle, and his cousin were proscribed and murdered, and he himself was proscribed. Before he went away, Terentia made it known that she might remember him in her will. Apparently he had sided with his father; indeed, he had been Cicero's companion almost constantly since the year in Cilicia. Cicero did not greatly credit Terentia's kindly professions, but he considered it wise for the son to observe a prudent decency toward his mother. It is doubtful whether Marcus was rewarded. He survived his father by at least thirty years, but Terentia lived to be one hundred and three, if the report is true.

---

[20] *Att.* 12, 7, 1.

The departure of Marcus, however, though it left Cicero alone, and the tribulations with Terentia and Publilia seem to have had little effect upon Cicero; Atticus was asked to manage them all. Cicero was grieving for Tullia. In January he had been staying in Rome with her. She was expecting to be confined, and about the fifteenth her son was born. At first she seems to have done well, but presently her strength gave way. Cicero had taken her to his Tusculan villa, the one he loved best, from which they could look down upon the city where his whole life had centered; and there, a month after the childbirth, Tullia died.

With the death of Tullia all joy went out of Cicero's life, or all solace in affliction, rather, for his moments of joy had been rare of late. Only a few incidents are known in the relation between the father and his daughter, but it is abundantly clear from numerous references that no one else had responded so fully to Cicero's extremely affectionate nature. She resembled him both in appearance and in character, and was devoted to him. In joy as well as in sorrow she was with him. When he returned from exile, she met him in Brundisium, and they celebrated her birthday in the first happy hours of his restoration. When he came again to Brundisium, to wait for Caesar, she visited him; though only for a little while, as circumstances forced her soon to return to Rome. And Cicero's love for her seems to have been even greater. He was impetuous, ready when disappointed to find fault both with himself and with his dearest friends; but he found no fault with Tullia. She had become engaged to Dolabella against her father's wishes, but he acquiesced in her choice; and when the political extravagances and the faithlessness of the young husband made the marriage unhappy, and at last impossible, as Cicero learned when in Brundisium, he laid the blame for the marriage on himself; he ought to have prevented it, he thought. The little Tulliola who scribbled her greetings to Atticus in Cicero's earliest extant letters had fulfilled her promise, and now that she was dead, his heart was like a house gutted with fire.

A little more is known about Tullia's marriages than about
anything else connected with her, and they were not altogether
fortunate. With her first husband, Calpurnius Piso, she was
happy. They had been married in the year of Cicero's consulship, or shortly before it. During the time of Cicero's exile he
died, and not long afterwards, the haste being truly Roman, she
became engaged to a certain Crassipes, a man of good birth.
It is not certain that they were married. If the marriage took
place, it ended in divorce, for Crassipes was still living when
Tullia, in 50 B.C., became the wife of Dolabella. The latter had
been divorced within the year in order to marry Tullia, and he
brought her no happiness. It is therefore a strange commentary
on Roman marriages that meets us in the famous letter[21] written
to Cicero by Servius Sulpicius after Tullia's death. She had
been happy, says Sulpicius, in many ways; she had lived to see
her father attain the praetorship, the consulship, and the augur-
ship, and she had been married to young men—not to one young
man!—of the first rank. Her death, after a life of good fortune,
had come opportunely, for she was spared the sight of a fallen
Rome. And what could further years have given her? Cicero's
high station could easily have secured for her a husband among
the foremost youths of Rome, and she might have become the
mother of children, but these would have had no opportunity
of continuing the tradition of public service begun by their
grandfather; they would not have been free men. This was
written by Sulpicius, who was one of the most high-minded men
of his generation, and yet he found a source of comfort to Cicero
in Tullia's marriages and prospects of further unions.

After seeing how Sulpicius looked upon marriage, we should
not be surprised on learning that Cicero's relations with Dolabella were not altered by the divorce of his daughter; marriage
was, after all, a simple contract; and we need not imagine, as
some have done, that Cicero remained friendly in order to secure

---

[21] *Fam.* 4, 5.

the repayment of Tullia's dowry, which never was repaid, or because Dolabella was influential with Caesar. Cicero needed no such mercurial mediator between himself and his old friend. Dolabella took Cicero's part when men about Caesar slandered him, but, as Cicero writes himself, he received no services from his son-in-law.[22] Cicero, like Tullia, submitted, despite a better knowledge, to the spell of the young rascal's personality. When Tullia had died, Dolabella sent Cicero a letter of consolation, unfortunately lost. Cicero, in reply,[23] says that although he is not a broken man, he has lost that gaiety and charm which used to delight Dolabella above all others.

After Tullia's death, probably immediately after the funeral, Cicero went to Atticus in Rome, having sent Publilia to her mother. He stayed with Atticus about three weeks; but many people came to the house, and Cicero could not refuse to see them, though he was in no mood to receive their condolences. Finally the strain became too great, and he left Rome, on the sixth of March, for his villa at Astura, some miles down the coast. Solitude had become necessary to him, though immediately on arriving in Astura he writes to Atticus that his longing for the latter is almost unbearable.

The villa at Astura had probably been recently acquired by Cicero, for it is not mentioned in his earlier letters; perhaps he had bought it during his stay with Atticus, in order to have a refuge free from all associations with Tullia. He certainly avoided the Tusculanum because of its wealth of reminiscences. Astura, furthermore, was far enough from the city to make visits unlikely. Three days after his arrival, Cicero writes with concern that a friend of his, who owned a villa near by, is reported to be coming down, and it is with a sigh of relief that he can write the next day that the threatened destroyer of his solitude had merely called and had thereupon departed for Rome.

---

[22] *Fam.* 6, 11, 1.
[23] *Fam.* 9, 11, 1.

Astura had wild and dense woods, and it had the beach. Sometimes Cicero goes into the woods in the morning, and does not emerge until evening. He is busy with his books all day, and even in the night, for sleep will not come; and this statement about his sleeplessness is dated two weeks after he came down.

The books with which he was busy during the first days were philosophical works that spoke of sorrow and how to meet it. While with Atticus, he had read all the books on this subject in the latter's library, and there were many. These books and the numerous visitors are the only things mentioned in reference to Cicero's three weeks in Atticus' Roman house, except that Cicero did not utterly sink under his grief, but struggled against it, as he calls upon Atticus to testify. The character of the books indicates the nature of his struggle, which continued in Asturia. He wrestled in solitude, not with the Angel of the Lord, as Jacob had done, but with Fate, which, by taking away his daughter at a time when he most needed her, threatened to shatter the very foundation of his whole being. Though the crisis through which he passed was different from that of a man who believes in a personal god, there was nevertheless an element of mysticism in his experience which made his struggle almost religious.[24]

To the ancient Romans, as Panaetius had phrased it for them, there were three kinds of religion, that of mythology, found mostly in Greek literature, that of the Roman state, and that of the philosophers. But the mythological gods were mostly dead by this time. Perhaps they had never been quite alive in Rome. They had lent some of their attributes to the members of the Roman pantheon, making the latter a little more human than they had been before the Greek gods arrived; but beyond that their sole office was to adorn a tale, though rarely to point a moral. We cannot imagine a saddened Roman going into his closet to pray to Zeus or to Aphrodite.

The religion of the Roman state was still in existence, but this existence was mainly an external one. Jupiter and the other

---

[24] Fowler, *Religious Experience etc.*, 383 ff.

gods were a part of the Roman social order; they received sacrifices, they had their priests to minister to them, and they were
often apostrophized in the forum; when the Roman state was in
trouble, it turned with gifts and promises to Jupiter; Roman
life, indeed, both private and public, was filled with the worship of these gods; but the individual Roman, facing the crises
of his life, was not likely to ask for strength and courage from
Jupiter Optimus Maximus. Even if he believed in the actual
existence of the gods of his state, and there were countless grades
of unbelief, these were, after all, merely the gods of his state
and not of his own individual self. There was nothing vicarious
in his religion. No Roman god, however anxious for the glory
of Rome—and Roman history pointed proudly to numerous
events tending to prove the existence of this anxiety—no Roman
god had ever died for the sins of the Romans nor had any
divinity whose temple adorned the forum promised to take men's
burdens on his shoulders. If properly worshiped, the Roman
gods might refrain from doing harm, and might even give
assistance, to the Roman people or its great men, but under no
circumstances did they love the individual Roman.

The uneducated Roman was at this time turning to the
religions of the East; religions that abounded in shouts, ecstacies,
and dreams; forms of worship that benumbed his consciousness
of the living world and transported him to a new atmosphere.
And if he embraced a philosophy, it was that of the Epicureans,
which said that the gods had nothing to do with men, that the
soul died with the body, and that, as the uneducated interpreted
it, pleasure, mainly physical pleasure, is the chief end of life.

To the educated Roman the Eastern religions were too blind
to the facts of life and too noisy. There were too many cymbals
connected with them, and too little sobriety. If the man of reading and culture was of a trusting temperament, he no doubt
crept closer than his sceptical neighbor to the religion of his
state, but the result was likely to be little else than a belief in

omens and a constant anxious interpreting of good and bad
dreams. And so the only religion left for him, if he wished to
have one at all—and many had none—was that of the philosophers.

But the philosophers were human beings. They observed
the heavens and they watched their fellows, and then they
reasoned about what they had seen, or thought they had seen,
and drew inferences; but, being men, they did not always agree.
Some said there was a providence and others said there was
not. Some believed in a life after death and others denied it.
Some insisted that man was endowed with a free will, while
others made him part of a large soulless machine called the
universe. Some admitted that their own inferences might be
erroneous, for, after all, the premises were doubtful; and others
asserted that they alone were right and everybody else was wrong.
If Pythagoras had said that a thing was so, his followers believed
him; and the *ipse dixit* of Pythagoras was heard occasionally
through the centuries of the Roman republic, though few men
heeded it. The Epicureans, scornful of others, if they were
true Epicureans, shouted that Epicurus was always right. He
was like a god, nay, he was a god, as Lucretius had sung; but
that scarcely added to his authority.

The Stoics were no less certain of the truth of their own
teachings than the Epicureans, and they believed in a divine
providence; but they assigned its workings almost entirely to
the external world.[25] The world was beautiful; therefore a god
must have made it. The world continued well-ordered and
beautiful; it was a cosmos; and so the creator of it must still
be watching over it. He no doubt watched also over the individuals, but only incidentally, as it were. Placed in a beautiful,
well-ordered universe, the individual human being need have no
apprehensions. All was well with the world; consequently, if
he was wise, he would see that everything was well with him.

---

[25] See below, pp. 567–568.

If things seemed not to be well with him, he was after all not wise, and it was his duty to get wisdom, to follow duty, and to be strong. The god who was looking after the world did not come down to help him. Man, in the face of his troubles and his sorrows, was alone. If he broke under them, this only proved that he did not have the true wisdom. But even the Stoics had human weaknesses. Chrysippus, one of their greatest, had taught that there was nothing to do for fresh grief. It must be left alone. Time would cure it. It was the old human cry that time heals all wounds.

Cicero, however, was not made of the stuff that left things to the kindliness of time. He had never let himself drift. He was always terribly, courageously honest with himself, and he faced his problems. While a question was still debatable, he debated almost endlessly, for he saw clearly, so that his letters to Atticus are filled with the long and anxious weighing of one side against the other; but when the decision had to be made, he decided for himself. If a blow threatened to fall and there was still hope of escape, his appeals and his regrets were sometimes numerous. After the blow had fallen, he hid his grief as best he could, fighting with it by himself. This he had done after Luca; and this he did also now. Writing to Atticus shortly after he had reached Astura, he says that no one can help him as yet, but whenever he shall be able to receive help, it will be from Atticus. He also says, a day later, that he will show his grief to nobody, not even to Atticus, if he can avoid it. And he did avoid it in a remarkable degree, for in all his daily letters to Atticus during the first month's stay in Astura, except in those of the first three days, he makes no mention of his loss except when some word in a letter from Atticus calls forth a reply.

On his second day in Astura he informs Atticus[26] that he has written, and is sending him, an essay On Grief and How to Meet It, *Consolatio* or *De Luctu Minuendo,* which he has

---

[26] *Att.* 12, 14, 3.

addressed to himself. In this he had brought together the arguments of various writers on the subject, following mainly, as we learn from Pliny the Elder, Crantor, who lived in the fourth and third centuries. Nobody had ever before addressed such an essay to himself, Cicero says; adding that he finds unusual comfort in this kind of treatment.

The thoughts were not new. Indeed, it would be difficult to find new reasons for consolation after generations of philosophers had pondered the subject. Nor did Cicero innovate in combining various people's thoughts, for the philosophers of Greece were always borrowing from each other.[27] But to address it to himself was new. This was not like the satires of Varro and of others, in which a man carries on a discussion with his other self. The *Consolation* of Cicero may have been in dialogue form, but this is not likely, and we have no hint of a divided personality, as in Varro's satires. What Cicero seems to have done, was to step away from himself, and, looking upon his position with the eyes of the philosophers whom he had been reading, gather together what applied to him and address it to himself as if it were an exhortation to endure.

The essay has been lost. It was much read, however, so that later writers quote from it and refer to its thoughts, and Cicero himself, in treating of death and the endurance of pain in the *Tusculan Disputations,* written some four months later, both refers to it and in one instance quotes from it. It could not have been a very long essay. Apparently it was written during Cicero's first two days in Astura, unless we are to suppose that he had been working on it in Rome without informing Atticus. It seems likely that after reading the philosophers in Atticus' library, filling himself with their thoughts as he staggered under his fresh grief, he suddenly, on reaching Astura and its solitude, having perhaps taken with him Crantor's book, which most appealed to him, threw himself into composition, following Crantor when possible and adding things of his own.

---

[27] *Tusc.* 3, 76; *De Fin.* 1, 6.

It was an effort to clarify his thoughts. It was also the act of the born writer, who never reads without an impulse to write; and he had long ago discovered the solace of constant occupation.

One weapon against grief was the realization that others had suffered in the same way, and had endured. The Greek philosophers were fond of citing examples to prove their theories; it was one way of bringing their philosophy close to life. Cicero cites many instances of prominent Romans who had lost their children. He speaks of numerous deaths shrouded in great sadness. While in the heat of composition, he did not stop to insert all the cases parallel to his own that he wished to include, so that, after finishing the essay in the rough, he writes to Atticus for further information. The remarkable thing is that he wishes to include people about whom he did not know whether they had died before or after their children; people, therefore, about whose manner of enduring their loss, if they had had any, he could have known nothing. "Did Caepio die before or after his father?" he writes. "Did Rutilia survive her son?" And other cases. This reveals the author, who writes for others even while he is writing for himself, but it is also probable that the mere length of a list of sufferers had in it a considerable amount of comfort. Cicero certainly did know that most of these men and women had led brave lives and done noble deeds; and that was a call to him also to live bravely and act nobly.

But these men and women had had one source of comfort denied to Cicero. Q. Marcius Rex, colleague of the Elder Cato in the consulship, lost his son, and went directly from the funeral services to the senate-house, to preside at a meeting. Aemilius Paulus lost two sons while he was celebrating a triumph, and he was able in public to refer to his loss with such courage that people might have thought he was speaking of somebody else. Cicero, on the other hand, could not have recourse to the state. The state that he had been able to serve was fallen, apparently never to be restored, and his political opponents, some of them also personal enemies, lorded it over the ruins. In the *Consolation* he declares that he had always fought against Fortune and had conquered her, repelling the attacks of his enemies; that he had not lost heart even when he was driven into exile; but that now, after losing Tullia, his beloved daughter, he confessed himself defeated. "I yield," he cried, "and raise my hand."

Owning himself defeated in the unequal fray—basely defeated, he wrote—he turns to the transcendentalism that some years before had inspired his *Dream of Scipio*. Life is sad, he wrote, enlarging on it with such conviction that the speaker in the *Tusculan Disputations* can say that when he read it he wished for nothing except to leave this world. The best thing for a man is never to have been born, so as not to fall upon the rocks of life; the next best, to die as soon as possible, and so escape, as it were, the fierce fire through which Fortune makes men pass. Indeed, men are born to earth in order to atone for the crimes they have committed in a previous life. After death, the souls that are laden with crimes and wickedness are thrust into darkness and lie in filth, whereas those that are pure and innocent and have improved themselves with suitable meditation rise naturally and easily to the gods, who are like themselves. The soul, he takes care to prove, is not of the earth earthy. Its wonderful qualities prevent such a belief. It is heavenly, divine, and so eternal. And God himself can be understood only as a spirit, free from all earthly admixtures, knowing and directing all things, and endowed with unceasing motion, that is, life. This passage about the nature of the soul is the only one he quotes in his later writings, which is perhaps an indication of the importance he assigned to it.

But Cicero, in this transcendentalism, was thinking less of himself than of Tullia. He may have cherished the hope of meeting her in a future life, as he later makes Cato hope in reference to his son in the essay on Old Age; but this hope does not occur in the fragments of the *Consolation*. It is for Tullia that he writes. His father's love would not allow him to think of her as dead. The gods that men worship were at one time human beings, he says, combining in his mysticism, as the Stoics had done, the belief in immortality and the current religion. And he wishes to give Tullia the glory of deification that had been given to the children of a Cadmus, an Amphitryo, and a Tyndarus; and the gods, he says, will gladly receive her into their midst, while mortals will always remember her.

Lactantius, the church father, who quotes this passage, says that people might suppose that the great grief had made Cicero unbalanced, and proceeds to show that the excellence of the whole essay makes this impossible; it was the work, he says, of one whose soul and judgment did not waver. From the point of view of the Christian Lactantius, this is true; but it is only partly true when we consider Cicero's· own character. He was not unbalanced, but his yearning for Tullia caused him for a time to embrace a belief of which under ordinary circumstances he knew that there was considerable uncertainty. He willed to believe. Presently, as the days pass by, he writes in his ordinary manner about the eternity that begins with death, calling it the time when he will be no more. He may be less certain than he was at first about Tullia's deification; no more certain, indeed, than he was about the existence of the gods; but he seems nevertheless to cling to the exalted belief, and he desires at least that Tullia shall not be forgotten on earth.

Even before leaving Atticus, he had determined to build a memorial to Tullia. It was to be a shrine, *fanum,* such as had been erected to others before her, as he had learned from his Greek philosophers. This shrine would perpetuate her memory; it would also be a reminder to Cicero himself, and an encouragement to believe in her continued existence. Three days after reaching Astura, he writes of it to Atticus, and from that time on it is much in his letters. He has set his heart on it. If Atticus wishes to do anything to please him, he must do his

best to further Cicero's plan. Cicero has determined to do it;
an architect has made the drawings; there is nothing left except
to find a suitable place and to procure the money. Atticus
must see to these two things.

The place was important. The shrine must have a conspicuous situation, so that people will see it. It must be erected in a
spot where it will remain untouched, even if the land on which
it is built should in the future change owners. It must not be
too far from Rome, for Cicero should like to visit it without
having to take a whole day to do it. Many places are considered,
and difficulties arise. Some owners will not sell. Others ask
too much. One piece of land is too small; another too remote
and hidden, though this would add to the sanctity of the shrine.
And Cicero writes about it almost daily, desiring reports from
Atticus as to what he is doing about the matter and what the
prospects are. He asks Atticus not to weary at his importunity,
for it is the one thing that he desires. It appears to him almost
in the light of a vow to Tullia; he owes it to her.

And Atticus seems to have done his best. Being an Epicurean,
he could not doctrinally take much interest in deifications, but
he and Cicero never quarreled about doctrine. He reports daily
about the place for the shrine. For months the matter is under
discussion. Gradually it ceases in the letters, as Atticus and
Cicero meet, and after that there is no reference to it. But
we do not learn that the shrine was ever built. Probably the
assassination of Caesar, which convulsed Rome, putting an end
to many men's plans and starting others, put an end also to
Cicero's plans for deifying his daughter.

But neither the thoughts of Tullia's shrine nor Cicero's own
Consolation could remove the pain from his heart. Nor were the
letters he received from friends more successful. Many of his
friends had seen him in Rome; one of them, the son of Sulpicius,
is mentioned; but some of them were away. Brutus wrote from
Cisalpine Gaul, where he was fighting for Caesar. It was the

letter of a friend. It arrived on the second day of Cicero's stay in Astura, when his loneliness was most profound; and he wept when he read it. But it brought no comfort. Brutus probably talked mainly of firmness in the face of grief, for Brutus never forgot that he was a Stoic. Caesar wrote from Spain, where he was settling matters after Munda, and, as has already been mentioned, there were letters both from Sulpicius and Dolabella.

Sulpicius' letter is the only one extant. The great jurist, now sixty years old, did not have much iron in his nature. At the outbreak of the Civil War, during an interview with Cicero, he had been thoroughly upset, fearing everything and everybody, and shedding so many tears that Cicero, describing the incident to Atticus,[28] wondered that Sulpicius' eyes had not become dry with his long grief. His one wish, whatever happened, had been that he might die in his bed. Now, writing of Tullia's death, he has no thoughts of consolation to offer besides those Cicero had found in Atticus' books, and the letter has, indeed, something of the character of a philosophical essay; but the gentleness and the delicacy of the old jurist are no less apparent. It is one of the best letters in the correspondence. Cicero's reply[29] is nearly as good, and it is more personal. It shows, however, that Sulpicius had not succeeded in taking away his grief.

Nothing could take it away. Cicero was from now on a changed man. His *dolor,* as he calls it, meaning the pain at the bottom of his very being, the knowledge that he was destined to remain a desolate man—this sense of loss could not be eradicated. What he strove to do was to get control of his facial expression and his voice, and at first even this effort seemed like disloyalty to Tullia. He was conscious of retaining his strength of character, his *constantia* and *firmitas,* as he writes both to Atticus and to others. Some friends had said that he grieved too much, that he behaved like a broken man. ''Why,'' he exclaims

---

[28] *Att.* 10, 14.
[29] *Fam.* 4, 6.

impatiently in a letter to Atticus, ''I write more than they even read.'' They would find nothing in him of which to complain when he mingled again with the politicians of the forum. But they would nevertheless find him a changed man. He would not be the pleasant, witty companion, who could relieve a dark situation with a little joke.

His main source of comfort from others was an occasional meeting with Atticus, after which he was likely to write that now that he was alone again he realized better than during the time of the visit how much Atticus' presence had meant to him. He discouraged visits from others, although he wrote to a few men, like Brutus, Dolabella, Lucceius, and Sulpicius, that it would be a satisfaction to see them. He remained as much as possible alone; when friends insisted on coming to see him, he left them for a while, to pour out his heart to Atticus in a letter.

During this time he read and wrote constantly. Immediately after finishing the *Consolatio,* or perhaps even earlier, he began to make plans for his comprehensive presentation in Latin of Greek philosophy. He had thought before of writing on this subject and had even made a sort of announcement to that effect in the *Orator,*[30] but the *Consolatio* was his first work. · The writing, as he said, did not diminish his sense of loss, but it kept his thoughts from dwelling on it; and it is interesting to note that while much time had to pass before his letters regained even a little of the former light-heartedness, the philosophical treatises are from the first as witty as his earlier works. He wrote in feverish haste, with very few interruptions, until the assassination of Caesar, and later at intervals, until the end of 44 B.C. The mere bulk of this writing is marvelous, but when we consider the difficulty of the subject and the excellence of the results, as well as his many disappointments and sorrows, which could have sapped the vitality of almost any man, this period of production becomes one of the miracles in literary history.

---

[30] *Or.* 148.

CHAPTER XVI

PHILOSOPHY

I

HORTENSIUS

The *Hortensius* was the second of Cicero's philosophical treatises.[1] It has been lost, but later references to it and a number of brief quotations give a pretty complete idea of its content. It was an exhortation to the study of philosophy, in dialogue form, Hortensius being one of the chief speakers and also giving his name to the treatise. The conversation doubtless proceeded much as in the *De Oratore*, one interlocutor advancing and defending one view while another criticised it; and consequently the dialogue became a defense as well as a eulogy of philosophy, just as the *De Oratore* had been a defense and a eulogy of Cicero's oratorical ideal.

There was need of defense. Aside from the difficulty of writing about philosophy in Latin and the questionable propriety of a Roman ex-consul undertaking the task, matters discussed in nearly every one of the prefaces to Cicero's later philosophical works, it could well be maintained by the practical Romans that other intellectual pursuits ministered more directly to the needs of life. Such were oratory, which scarcely required defense; history, which inspired by noble examples and supplied information useful in public life; and even poetry, which among other things provided the means for stylistic instruction. Philosophy, on the other hand, taking the place of religion, professed to discuss life, to give rules, as the objector held, where no rules were needed. There had not always been philosophers; and after

---

[1] On Cicero as a philosophical writer, see esp. Zeller, pp. 648–668; Reid, *Acad.*, Introduction; Goedeckemeyer, pp. 130–200; Zielinski, *Cicero im Wandel etc.*, pp. 44–106. Goedeckemeyer gives numerous references to Cicero's philosophical works.

this hair-splitting tribe had appeared, they had often failed to agree among themselves, they had been pedantic, and they had not made their lives tally with their teachings.

In replying to these strictures, Cicero apparently said little or nothing about the usefulness of philosophical study for the orator, a thing the *De Oratore* had set forth at length; nor does he seem to have drawn any arguments from the part of philosophy that was concerned with government, a field which, next to rhetoric, needed less defense in Roman eyes than any other kind of didactic writing. He seems to have confined himself to philosophy in its narrower, modern sense, putting the emphasis on its claim of being a guide and comforter, but also saying something about its literary form.

Philosophy as practised by the old masters, the consular philosophers, as Cicero calls them, and also by many later writers, was a part of literature. Like history, it was intended to give aesthetic pleasure as well as to teach; and Cicero at least touched upon this conception here in the *Hortensius*. In the philosophical series that he was introducing, he wished to appeal to those who loved literature for its own sake; if once attracted by the form, they would be led to consider the substance.

It was with the substance that he was most concerned. In the *Consolatio* he had urged the need of philosophy in grief; now he enlarged the thought so as to apply it to life in general. But the main contention remained the same. Life on earth is full of errors and unhappiness, and needs direction and comfort. We must learn to look upon it with exalted contempt. Man consists of a body and a soul, of which the latter is by far the more important. Certain Etruscan robbers, so he wrote, tortured their captives by closely tying them to corpses, so that they would rot with the dead bodies. The soul is like one of those captives; it is tied to the body as to a corpse, and needs to be freed by philosophy.

But he went beyond this. Philosophic contemplation, mere knowledge without a practical bearing, would be most open

to attack at the hands of the objectors.   Cicero, however, glorifies
it as the best fruit of philosophy.   If there is no life after this,
man needs philosophy to make this life tolerable; but if there
is a future existense, his need of philosophy is even greater.   In
the Isles of the Blessed, Cicero says, men do not require eloquence,
for there are no law courts, nor even the four cardinal virtues.
Fortitude is not demanded in a place that has no troubles and
no dangers; nor justice, where no one tries to cheat his fellow;
nor self-restraint, where there is no lust; nor wisdom, where no
one is called upon to choose between good and evil.   These virtues
are necessary on earth, but in the Isles of the Blessed men find
happiness only in contemplation.   They must therefore prepare
themselves here for a life of thought.   The joy of knowing, without extrinsic advantages, is what makes blessed the lives of the
gods, he says.   Perhaps, by the way, no statement sheds a
stronger light on the difference between the ancient philosophical
and the Christian attitude; to the Greeks and Romans, God was
Intellect; to the Christians, He is Love.

The intense feeling with which Cicero wrote, not many weeks
after Tullia's death, and his power as a writer of impassioned
prose undoubtedly made this treatise one of the most brilliant
and effective of his works.   It was a glowing introduction to his
projected series of philosophical writings; a portal to the temple,
as it has been called.[2]   Four hundred years later it had not lost
its power of appeal.   St. Augustine, in his *Confessions*,[3] describes
how he came upon the book in the ordinary course of his study,
and how thereupon his purpose in life changed.   Vain hopes
became worthless to him; he was filled with an incredible longing
for wisdom, and turned to God.   He adds earnestly, for he had
been reading Cicero to become a speaker, that it was not for the
sharpening of his tongue that he later employed the book, but for
the content.

---

[2] Zielinski, *op. cit.*, p. 45.

[3] St. Augustine, *Confess.* 3, 4, 8.

II

ACADEMICA

Though St. Augustine found inspiration in the *Hortensius,* he could in later years have felt no agreement with the doubt that caused Cicero to refer to a future life as a mere possibility. This doubt, or unwillingness to decide, when no proofs could be adduced was the most marked characteristic of Cicero's philosophical attitude. He explained it in the next treatise, the *Academica,* thus informing his readers of the spirit in which he intended to proceed. The question propounded relates to human knowledge: Can we know absolutely, or can we not?— and would properly lie at the foundation of any philosophical system. Cicero, however, ignores one of the three theories held at this time, the Epicurean, and devotes the treatise to an examination of the views of the Stoics and of the so-called New Academy, or of Antiochus and Philo, rather, both of whom claimed to be true followers of the Old Academy. He discusses the question less as a philosopher in search of the truth than as a member of the Academy who would explain how the question had been treated within this school and why one view was better than another.

The work has come down to us in a peculiar condition. The first edition of it consisted of two books, named Catulus and Lucullus, after two of the principal speakers. Of this edition the second book is extant, except for the loss of a considerable portion at the end. There was also a second edition, undertaken both because Cicero felt that the two men of affairs, as well as Hortensius, who also appeared, would not be convincing in an abstruse discussion, and also because Cicero wished to compliment Varro by making him a speaker. This edition consisted of four books, of which the first has come down. Though the work is thus far from complete, quite enough is left to make clear the whole matter.

The ancients agreed that all knowledge is derived from the senses, but they held varying views as to the reliability of sense impressions. The Epicureans asserted that the senses were infallible. If the eyes tell us that the sun is about a foot in diameter, it is a foot in diameter, or very little more or less, despite astronomical theories to the contrary. If we push an oar into the water, it looks crooked, to be sure, but the reason for this does not lie in any fallibility of the eye but in some obviously mistaken reasoning about the impression received from it. The Stoics, on the other hand, maintained that sense impressions may be erroneous, but that man possesses a certain innate criterion by which he can correct them. This criterion resides in his soul and comes from the Creator. The wise man, therefore, whose soul and judgment have been trained, by Stoic teaching of course, can never be in doubt. Both Epicureans and Stoics were thus dogmatists, believing, for different reasons, in the human ability to attain absolute knowledge. Antiochus had adopted the Stoic view.

The sceptics, on the other hand, who were represented in Cicero's youth by Philo, and now by Cicero, held with the Stoics that the senses were fallible, but denied the existence of the Stoic criterion. To them absolute knowledge was humanly unattainable, so that the proper philosophical attitude was one of doubt or indecision. Probability, a conviction that certain things are more likely to be true than others, could be attained, and this would serve as well as any alleged absolute knowledge both for speculation and for practical life.

The philosophical question at issue, however, namely, the sources of human knowledge and their reliability, receives relatively small attention. The Epicureans are dismissed with a single sentence. "Let them look to their assertions," it is remarked; and no attempt is made to prove the senses fallible any more than the Epicureans themselves had tried to give proofs as distinguished from mere assertions. Perhaps this was natural. Ordinary observation constantly shows that men see, or think they see, what does not exist; and beyond that the ancients could scarcely go.

The modern scientist, with his delicate instruments, has created psychology and chemistry; and though he must ultimately theorize if he wishes to make fundamental statements about the processes of the human intellect or about the structure and creation of the world, he nevertheless bases his theories on an almost infinite number of observations or experiments of constantly increasing exactness, and, more important still, he realizes clearly where experimentation stops and theorizing begins. The ancients, on the other hand, had no instruments for sharpening the senses or differentiating their impressions. If speaking of sight, they reasoned about unaided vision. They had neither microscopes nor telescopes, and they did not know that the eye is a camera, nor that this camera may be out of focus.

The discussion, therefore, is limited to the question of the Stoic criterion, which, by correcting the fallible senses, would yield a knowledge of the truth; but even here the arguments are puerile. The Stoics themselves, in their eagerness to confute their arch-enemies, the Epicureans, had collected whole books of instances to prove that the senses make mistakes. These instances are now laid at the door of the Stoics by the sceptics; and it is further pointed out that dialectic, by which the Stoics professed to train their alleged criterion, is a useful enough science in some ways, but it does not lead to certitude. It gives rise to fallacies, admitted even by the dialectician. If you say that it is daylight, and if you are speaking the truth, then it is daylight; but change the verbs thus: if you say that you are a liar and if you are speaking the truth, then you are a liar; and yet, how can a liar speak the truth?

Quite as interesting as the epistemological part of the discussion, however, both to Cicero and to his contemporaries, was the question of the historical justification of the sceptical attitude. Zeno, in the third century B.C., had founded Stoicism. The Greek world, politically at least, was out of joint, and men turned from the state to the individual. There was need for a philosophy that assisted and comforted the individual. Philosophers, therefore, addressed themselves to ethics as eagerly as Socrates had done, but they became dogmatic, for speculation only raised questions without answering them. Stoicism thus arose, and it was rigidly dogmatic; and the later Stoics looked upon their system as an independent philosophy. Arcesilas, however, somewhat younger than Zeno, and probably in protest to the latter's dogmatism, asserted that nothing could be known, and he claimed that this was also the attitude of Socrates and of Plato. Socrates professed to be sure of only one thing, his own ignorance, and even this certainty was denied to him by Arcesilas; and as for Plato, he discusses various topics in his dialogues, but approaches them, so Arcesilas and his followers held, in a spirit of inquiry; he does not dogmatize. Arcesilas, therefore, insisted that he was a follower of Plato, a true Academic.

The sceptical attitude was thereupon notably represented by Carneades, and later by Philo, Cicero's teacher; but these added something positive to the doctrine of the school, particularly Philo, though the exact extent of his positive teachings can not be determined. Then came Antiochus, once a pupil of Philo, who abandoned scepticism, and would have it that he, and not Arcesilas, Carneades, or Philo, was a true disciple of Plato. In his eyes these three philosophers had been heretics. There was thus a struggle for the name of Academic, a matter never settled; and we have as many as five Academies: that of Plato and his immediate followers, of Arcesilas, of Carneades, of Philo, and of Antiochus; or else two Academies, the Old and the New, the New being the sceptical school, and the Old being that of Plato, to which Antiochus returned.

The historical squabble renewed by Antiochus is significant as an indication of the lack of originality that had come upon philosophy. If a new view had appeared, but none did, it would probably have been considered little less than damnable heresy. Philosophers were forever stretching their hands, for justification, to their old gods, Socrates, Plato, and Aristotle, and the writings of Plato and Aristotle had very much the same relation toward philosophizing as the Bible has, or had, toward protestant theology. Philosophy was largely a matter of interpreting Plato and Aristotle; men wished to prove themselves orthodox. Even the Stoics, although they considered Stoicism an independent philosophy, and though proud of their system, constantly appealed to the early philosophers; only the Epicureans stood aloof. They were the Ishmaelites; but they were more orthodox than any one else—in their acceptance of Epicurus.

All this babble about ancient worthies would not have arisen if men had been really orthodox, willing unconditionally to yield to ancient authority. On all sides there was a falling away from grace. Even the Epicureans, though doctrinally of chemical purity, had allowed the practical spirit of the times to invade their ranks. They took sides for and against rhetoric, with which properly they should have had no concern. They wrote about things that ought to have lain beyond their sphere of interest, as conceived by Epicurus; some of them, like Lucretius, cultivated a literary style, at which Epicurus would have shaken a sad head; and nearly all the professing Epicureans among the Romans, Atticus excepted, and he did not act from doctrinal motives, allowed Roman instincts to get the better of their philosophical profession, and took part in political life.

The Stoics, though to them all others were fools, did not agree among themselves; their greatest had doubts. And when Antiochus abandoned the sceptical attitude, becoming practically a Stoic, he insisted that the Stoics were nothing but followers of Plato, disguising their dependence under a cloud of words—as appears from Cicero's next treatise, the *De Finibus.* The Stoics, according to Antiochus, were thieves; but the opponents to Antiochus asked whether his objection to being called a Stoic was not due to a desire to be looked upon as the founder of a new school. Thus hairsplitting and recriminations were abroad in the philosophical lecture rooms. Varro announced that there were two hundred and eighty-eight different philosophies; he had examined them all, and had rejected two hundred and eighty-seven, clinging to the two hundred and eighty-eighth.[4]

But philosophy is a power in the world, or it is nothing. No philosophers could be more conscious of this than those who taught the practical Romans. The discussion in the *Academica,* therefore, becomes largely a series of assertions and denials relative to the effects of the sceptical attitude. Antiochus, for the dogmatists, maintained that the result of scepticism is inactivity of every kind, both physical and mental. Logic, memory, art, and morals can not exist side by side with scepticism, for they depend on certainty of knowledge. The sceptics can not be considered philosophers at all if they lack confidence even in their one dogma of scepticism. Man is made for the attainment of certitude; the denial of its attainability throws all life into confusion. The probability of the sceptics is random guesswork. Even if they profess to decide after careful pondering, a decision that may be false is useless. Their doctrine even does away with probability, and leads to that suspension of judgment which Arcesilas announced as the result of the sceptical attitude, and such suspension of judgment is inevitably fruitless. Cicero may praise philosophy, so he has his opponent say in this dialogue, but he is the one person in the world who ought not to consider knowledge unattainable. If nothing can be known, how could he in the senate give utterance to the notorious expression that Clodius found so delightful, namely, that he, Cicero, had discovered all about the Catilinarian conspiracy?

4 St. Aug., *De Civ. Dei* 19, 1, 2.

The charge of the dogmatists was palpably weak, and Cicero points out that the difference between sceptic probability and dogmatic certitude is a mere matter of assertion, in so far as they relate to an active life. Even dogmatists act on probability. People can remember things that are false, as, for instance, the doctrines of Epicurus, no less readily than those that are true. In the sphere of thought, however, the difference is considerable. The sceptics are open-minded, the dogmatists are not. They follow somebody else's lead. Is not their position, after all, due to laziness? Or can any one of them claim—Varro excepted— that he has completely examined everybody's every opinion, and on the basis of that examination has come absolutely to agree with every single tenet of one particular philosopher? And, finally, the dogmatists do not agree among themselves. Not all of them, indeed, only one of them, can be right; and he, very likely, is wrong. The dogmatic attitude itself, therefore, makes dogmatism impossible.

All this, though very fine, goes in a circle. The point of it all is this, that the sceptical attitude is not one of mere criticism, as it had been. The New Academy leaves its adherent free to choose the good things wherever he may find them. Philo advised his hearers to attend the lectures of other philosophers. And so a New Academic, like Cicero, when he turns to the one subject of importance, ethics, is not merely free, but feels it his duty, to examine various views, whereupon he has the right to adopt the best. He may borrow from the Stoics, of varying degrees of orthodoxy, from Antiochus, and even from the Epicureans. He is not hampered by a proud desire for consistency, and he is not trying to build up a complete system, a thing for which dogmatism is necessary, but he moves from revelation to revelation, as it were, always realizing that he does not know, and only finding one thing more likely than another. In modern phraseology he might be called a pragmatist.

III

De Finibus

This is the attitude Cicero at once exemplified in the *De Finibus Bonorum et Malorum,* his next treatise, in which he discussed the fundamental question of ancient philosophy: What is happiness? The search was for the chief end of human action, and this explains the title. *Finis* is the aim or end. To this was added *Bonorum et Malorum,* of good things and bad, for an inquiry into the theories of the chief end or good in life involved a consideration of the evils as well.

The work is in five books. In the first, the Epicurean doctrine is set forth, and in the second, it is criticised. The third and fourth books are similarly devoted to the Stoic view. The fifth book gives an exposition of Antiochus' version of the Old Academic and the Peripatetic doctrine, which he conceived to be the same—Plato and Aristotle and their immediate followers, in other words, or the Ancients—and this is followed by a brief criticism. In including an account of the Epicurean teaching, with which Cicero had no sympathy, he is obeying the dictates of his New Academic conscience, which demanded an examination of all things, but he is also carrying out the purposes that inspired his philosophical writings. One of these, though not very important it would seem, was to confute the Epicureans and counteract their growing influence; another, his paramount purpose, was to transfer to Latin, with criticisms, all that was significant in contemporary philosophical thought.

Though the *De Finibus* is a long work, for the peculiar manner of each philosophy is reproduced, the substance of it can be stated briefly.

Turning to unsophisticated nature for guidance, Epicurus had observed that every living thing, as soon as it is born, seeks pleasure and avoids pain. A child has no need of intricate

arguments to know that honey is sweet. Nature herself thus
indicates that the one thing toward which all creatures strive,
the one criterion by which all things are tested, the chief end in
life then, is pleasure; whereas the great evil, its opposite, is pain.
All the nonsensical disparagement of pleasure and praise of
pain—so the Epicurean continues contemptuously—arise from
faulty reasoning. No one scorns pleasure because it is pleasant,
but because some men lack sense in their pursuit of it, and so
are made to suffer; nor does any one love pain because it is
painful, but because the endurance of pain at times brings
pleasure. So, too, the Epicurean philosopher rejects some pleasures that he may enjoy others which are greater, and he is willing
to suffer pain that he may avoid still greater pain. But when
there are no effects to be considered, all men choose pleasure
and avoid pain.

Epicurus does not understand pleasure in a narrow sense.
The ceasing of pain, as all will admit, is positively pleasant, a
fact that points to the true interpretation of Epicurus' term:
that pleasure is freedom from pain, freedom from every desire for a change. The Stoics, Cicero's Epicurean spokesman
observes, are fond of asking whether the raised hand of a statue
can be said to enjoy pleasure. No, not if pleasure is merely a
pleasant titillation of the senses, as the hedonistic Cyrenaics
maintained, but yes, if pleasure be rightly understood as the
opposite of pain, which is the great evil. Pleasure is thus painlessness, absolute contentment. It can be varied, but never
increased.

The Stoics set up virtue as the chief end in life, but, the
champion of Epicureanism continues, the practise of their four
cardinal virtues, wisdom, temperance, courage, and justice, can
easily be shown to aim at nothing but a happy life, that is, at
pleasure. They are in their essence selfish. Even justice is not
altruistic, for, however well a wrongdoer may insure himself
against discovery, he can never be certain that he will not be

found out. Men may be deceived, but not the immortal gods. And so, in the last analysis, a man is just because he is afraid of being unjust. The virtues are means to an end, and not an end in themselves.

All pleasures, to be sure, are ultimately derived from the senses, but the pleasures of the body are by no means so great as those of the mind. Physical sensations, whether pleasurable or painful, are confined to the present. The mind, on the other hand, looks both into the past and into the future. This can be easily shown. Physical pain becomes immeasurably more irksome if the sufferer learns that he will never be free from it, that it is chronic. Fools are always torturing themselves by thinking of past injuries, whereas the wise man forgets these and turns his thoughts to the pleasant things that have befallen him.

"Oh, what a clear, open, simple, straight road to happiness!" Cicero's Epicurean finally exclaims; whereupon he launches into an ardent eulogy of Epicureanism, in which the sentences follow one another in breathless exaltation, mingling praise of Epicurus with contempt and ridicule for every one else, but particularly for the Stoics, who are said to prattle about virtue, a thing sublime in name but empty of substance; showing how a pleasant life is always virtuous, and a virtuous life always pleasant; pointing out the uselessness of logic, which is of no assistance either to happy living or clear thinking, and extolling the study of natural science, which teaches that the atomic world has nothing to do with any gods, but is formed and will be dissolved according to natural laws, so that man, fearing nothing, can calmly await death, which will bring utter extinction, beset by no hopeless longings, and suffering no tortures; lauding friendship, for which the Epicureans were noted, as the greatest blessing in life, and insisting that their assertion that its basis is selfishness does not weaken their friendships, for, having once won a friend, the Epicurean forgets his own advantage and sacrifices all for his friend; and finally exclaiming, somewhat weakly it would seem, that Epicurus, having found the one road to happiness, was right in neglecting, as many Epicureans in their cultured weakness did not neglect, both poetry, which is unpractical and mere child's play, and other arts and sciences, such as music, geometry, arithmetic, and astronomy, on which Plato had wasted his time; for these can not be true, since they are founded on erroneous premises, and, even if they were true, they would not be helpful to a happy life; they are taught as a matter of convention, and it is a disgrace not to know them.

The ardor of the Epicurean speaker, who is no less fervid than Lucretius himself, is suddenly abated by Cicero, who proves by Socratic dialectic that Epicurus has attempted to unite under one term two different conceptions—that of pleasure, whether physical or mental, and painlessness. This attempt, it is pointed out, was due to a desire on the part of Epicurus to avoid being classed with the pure hedonists. It led him to the assertion, furthermore, that pleasure, though variable in kind, can not be increased. The error of this is demonstrated by a simple dilemma: if a man mixes a drink for another, without being thirsty himself, does he get as much pleasure from his action as the thirsty man who receives the drink? The confusion of terms also vitiated Epicurus' manner of reasoning. He had started from the premise that the new-born child seeks pleasure, but he had abandoned it when converting pleasure into painlessness. Nor, indeed, is it true that pleasure is the one object of instinctive appetition; there are many such objects, the chief of which is self-preservation.

The principal objection, however, to Epicurus' theory is that he excludes virtue from his definition. Such a doctrine is rejected, Cicero maintains, both by human reason and by human endeavor, for all good men strive to live virtuously. And virtue, or morality, is not a matter of convention, as Epicurus would have it, but is founded in the very nature of man.

In this statement, which Cicero had already made in his works on the State and on the Laws, Cicero is on Stoic ground; and it remains for him only to give the Stoic explanations and arguments connected with it. But the Stoics, despite their nobility, were a proud, contentious, logical sect, abounding in nicely differentiated terms, which, Cicero admits, were sometimes difficult to understand and frequently hard to turn into Latin. Cato, with his faults and his virtues, was a fit representative of these philosophers, and Cicero makes him the speaker.

Like the Epicureans, the Stoics based their theory on the primal instinct, Cato says; but this, according to them, is self-preservation. The earliest actions of a new-born creature are aimed at acquiring things that are good for it and avoiding things that are bad for it. The former minister to physical and mental health, not to pleasure, and may be called excellent or preferable. The others are neither excellent nor preferable. When a man reaches years of discretion, his duty, as derived from his unadulterated instinct, that of self-preservation, is to choose properly between the preferable things in life and their opposites. The systematic exercise of this proper choice constitutes virtue, which is thus the chief or sole good.

Since the aim of philosophy is to make men happy and since, therefore, a perfect philosophical system must be able to make men perfectly happy, the Stoics further explained that perfect happiness consists in this proper choice. Happiness is not the possession of the preferable things, for a man might not succeed in acquiring them; it is the choice itself, which is always within the power of the philosopher. The true Stoic, therefore, the *sapiens* or wise man, is always perfectly happy.

The preferable things and their opposites are neither good nor bad. Only virtue is good, and only vice, its opposite, is bad. Some things are more or less preferable than others, or more or less to be avoided; but they are of importance only as objects among which the philosopher chooses rightly when the choice is presented to him. And since all wise men are perfectly happy, they are of necessity equally happy. There are no degrees. Neither is there any difference between them due to time. Happiness being the proper choice, an hour of virtuous action is as good as sixty years. On the other hand, those who are not wise— the foolish, the *stulti*—are also alike in their unhappiness.

The Stoics condescended to make their assertions a little less obscure by the use of comparisons. The preferable things in life, over which the Stoic has no control, like wealth, health, friendship, are as insignificant when compared with virtue as the light of a lamp beside the sun, a drop of honey in the Aegean Sea, a penny among the millions of Croesus, a single step on the long road to India. There are no degrees in happiness. If the virtue of a shoe is to fit, many shoes can fulfil that purpose no better than one; nor are big shoes better than small ones. Time has no influence. It is folly to instance good health, and how it is better to be well for a long time than for a short time. It is, of course, but that comes from the fact that good health is valuable just in proportion to its continuance. Virtue is different; it is an action. To say that virtue, perfect happiness, is increased by continuance is no better than saying that the act of dying or being born is made better by being made longer. All fools are equally unhappy. If you are above the water, you can breathe; if you are not, you can not breathe, and it does not matter whether you are near the surface or near the bottom.

Cicero was at one with the Stoics in exalting virtue. His criticism, therefore, is not very serious; he has not a good case against them, as he makes Cato say, but he has won worse cases. His objections, those of Antiochus, are directed against Stoic pedantry and assumption of logical precision.

Zeno, the founder of Stoicism, took his ideas from the Ancients, Cicero contends, and, to cover up the theft, he invented a technical vocabulary professing to express differences on which he laid much emphasis but which in reality do not exist. Zeno has thus poured the good old wine into very poor new bottles. The Ancients made the claims of virtue paramount, just as do the Stoics, but they did not say that happiness depends entirely on virtue. Good and bad things they called good and bad. Pain is bad, and the Stoics do not mend the matter by saying that it is not bad, but hard, irksome, hateful, contrary to our nature, difficult to endure. It is true that a man who is rising to the surface is no more able to breathe than the man at the bottom of the sea, but he is more likely to recover his breath; and that constitutes a difference which should not be neglected. There is also a difference between the man who beats a slave and the man who beats his father.

The Stoics had reared a system so consistent and logical, they proudly claimed, that not a word could be changed without causing the whole structure to collapse. They based their theory on the instinct of self-preservation, which applies both to the body and the soul, and thereupon they abandoned all thought of the body and said that happiness depends entirely on a man's spiritual attitude. You might think that man consists only of soul, that he is a disembodied spirit. And, even worse, some of their preferable and not preferable things, like good and bad health, have a demonstrable influence on a man's spiritual condition, but the Stoics, stating such things to be negligible, had thought of the soul only in so far as it was concerned with right and wrong. Their so-called instinct of self-preservation was thus made to preserve nothing but a man's morality.

The matter had now been threshed out. The attitude of the Ancients, which was also that of Antiochus and of Cicero, had been given in the criticism of Stoicism, and Cicero makes his speaker repeat it, only adding some praise of the wider intellectual interests and the attention to literary form displayed by the Academics as opposed to the narrow and uncouth Stoics. As a motto for Cicero's attitude stands the old reply of Apollo: "Know thyself," and this is interpreted as applying to the body as well as to the soul. Of this view Cicero has necessarily no criticism to make; he only reminds his readers that they must realise that they are dealing with probabilities and not with demonstrated verities. The last word of all, none the less, is that a man's moral attitude is the only thing really important for his happiness; it is justifiable to call a man happy who is on the whole happy, and that depends on virtue. M. Crassus, the father of the rich Crassus, was called laughterless, and this was proper, in spite of Lucilius' report that Crassus did laugh once in his life.

IV

TUSCULAN DISPUTATIONS

Although the whole discussion in the *De Finibus* is concerned with the question of happiness, it is only a theoretical examination of the term, and offers but little assistance to the struggling individual. The individual, however, was to be helped, or else philosophy had failed of its aim. In the next work, therefore, the *Tusculan Disputations,* Cicero approaches the question of happiness from the other side, and inasmuch as life is full of trouble—a circumstance that is not always admitted, particularly by the Stoics, but nevertheless taken for granted—philosophy becomes in the *Tusculans* a defensive armor.

In the first book, which treats of death, this defensive character is scarcely more than a pretense. The ancients, with rare exceptions, did not worry much about death. The possibility of punishment in a future life for sins committed on earth was not vivid to the Greeks and Romans, and is usually dismissed by the philosophers as absurd. Cicero often expresses this thought, even in his orations. The alternatives connected with death, therefore, were to the ancients either absolute extinction or else a future life of happiness, for it is only in poetry that we have the ghostlike existence after death which Achilles found so unsatisfactory. And extinction, the more troublesome alternative, did not cast a veil of gloom over human existence; Prometheus, according to Aeschylus, had taught men not to think of it. It is therefore only theoretically that the fear of death was considered one of life's troubles, which needed to be dispelled by philosophy. But the consideration of death, with which goes an attempt to determine the nature of the soul, has always been of absorbing interest, and it is consequently one of the most remarkable illustrations of Cicero's philosophical method, and of that of his contemporaries, that this metaphysical question, which they wished to discuss, was introduced under ethics.

It would be possible—and it has been done[5]—to construct, approximately at least, a philosophical system from Cicero's writings, or to discuss his writings from the point of view of a system,[6] under the three ancient fields of physics, logic, and ethics. Either of these methods contributes to clearness, but it tends to obscure the main characteristic of Cicero's philosophical attitude,[7] and that of his contemporaries, that only one field was important, namely ethics. Philosophy was after all religion, and mainly a religion of the intellect, on the whole concerning itself with this life; philosophers followed Socrates, who had directed his fellow-men to turn their eyes to earth.

Physics, the science of the whole world, included mathematics, the natural sciences, and metaphysics. Though technically a part of philosophy, it becomes a matter of real concern to the philosophers of Cicero's time only in so far as it can be brought under ethics. The Epicureans emphasized their theories of the structure of the world, because these explained that the world is governed by physical laws, without a providence, and that the human soul is mortal. The other philosophers, when they treated these subjects, did so in the spirit of the modern scientist. Posidonius, the Stoic, was thus a tireless investigator. Cicero

---

[5] By Goedeckemeyer.

[6] By Zielinski.

[7] Zielinski, *op. cit.*, p. 45, thinks otherwise.

had an interest in these matters; his philosophical works refer to them, especially to the atomic theory of the Epicureans, which is also frequently mentioned in his letters. There is likewise still extant a partial translation of Plato's *Timaeus,* which treats of creation. This translation was made by Cicero for use in a projected dialogue, since it is preceded by an introductory scene; but this dialogue was not finished. The only parts of ancient physics, properly metaphysics, that he treats of in extant dialogues are the questions of the existence and nature of the gods, and of divination, providence, fate, and free will, which grow out of the former; and his reason for discussing them was ethical.

As for logic, that had little connection with philosophy of an ethical trend. One part of it, *inventio,* or more specifically, *topica,* was neglected by the Stoics, but received much attention from the Academics. It had become a rhetorical subject, and was treated as such by Cicero, though cursorily and without any claim to originality, in his smaller rhetorical works.

The other part of logic was dialectic. The Stoics cherished it as leading to the precise definitions in which they took delight. Cicero had studied the subject with Diodotus, who lived in his house, and he frequently speaks very highly of it; but we have already seen, in the *Academica,* that Stoic dialectic was not considered useful by the New Academy for the attainment of sure knowledge; and it was only in this connection that it could have found a place among Cicero's philosophical writings. As an aid to the orator, however, it seemed to him very valuable, and probably the Stoics cultivated the subject largely for a didactic purpose. In the year 44 B.C., while writing the *Topica,*[8] Cicero himself thought of treating the subject, but this was never done.

The ethical purpose of the philosophers resulted in numerous books that seem to have had very much the character of modern lectures or sermons, being, in reality, something between these

---

[8] *Topica,* 7.

two. As Cicero himself says, at the end of the third book of the *Tusculans*,[9] philosophers treated of poverty, of disgrace, of exile, of the destruction of one's country, of slavery, of sickness or weakness, of blindness, and indeed of everything that could be called a calamity. They delivered lectures on these subjects and then published the lectures in separate books. These books Cicero found interesting, but he adds with a smile that the Greeks certainly do look for work, or, as we might say, for trouble. Since the arguments would be drawn from the basic conceptions of philosophy, there was necessarily much repetition from one book to another, as would not have been the case if the philosophers had been intent, as modern philosophers usually are, on expounding a system.

This repetition is also seen in Cicero. Thus the arguments for the immortality of the soul are given most completely in the first book of the *Tusculan Disputations,* but one or another is frequently mentioned in other works, as in the *Dream of Scipio,* and in the essay on Old Age they are set down systematically. Old age was one of the troubles in life that had to be combated; it was thus properly the subject of one of the many little books of consolatory meditation. But one of the troublesome circumstances about old age is its proximity to death; and so the philosophical lecturer or preacher at once leads forth his metaphysical arguments.

The *Tusculan Disputations* is a sheaf of such consolatory meditations. By Cicero's own avowal,[10] indeed, it came about in the same way as such books among the Greeks, for Cicero professes to have lectured to several friends who were visiting him in his Tusculan villa, hence the name, and later to have put these lectures into book form. As the lecturing lasted five days, there are five books. The listeners propounded a thesis, and Cicero, in the manner of a philosopher of the New Academy,

---

[9] *Tusc.* 3, 81.
[10] *Tusc.* 1, 7–8.

controverted it. The first book discussed death; the second, physical pain; the third, grief; the fourth, other mental affections, such as fear, desire, and unrestrained joy; and the fifth book, instead of meeting some definite trouble, gives unity to the work by addressing itself to life as a whole and maintaining the Stoic thesis that virtue is sufficient for happiness.

There might have been other books. Cicero's own essay on Old Age might have been included; but possibly old age was not obviously enough one of the drawbacks of human existence. Cicero preferred to treat it separately, addressing it to his old friend Atticus and giving his treatment a wide character by making Cato the Elder the speaker. Cicero later wrote on Glory, two books, which are lost, and on Friendship, and these books might have been a part of the *Tusculans,* for philosophy consoles by pointing out the blessings of life; but glory was such an important subject in the Roman view of things, and friendship was so well adapted to a separate treatment addressed to Atticus, that they became subjects of special treatises.

There might also have been fewer books. The third book, on grief, and the fourth, on other mental affections, are so much alike that they could easily have become a single book. Even the second book, on physical pain, might have been incorporated with them, though less readily. And it should be remembered that in the *Consolatio* Cicero had already treated of grief, the subject of the third book, and, to some extent, of death and a future life, the subject of the first book. The treatment in the *Consolatio,* however, was obviously less calmly philosophical than in the *Tusculans,* and it had a wider range, in that it discussed the sadness of life in general.

That man consists of a body and a soul was recognized by philosophers generally, even by the materialistic Epicureans. To the latter, however, the soul was composed of atoms, which separate at the death of the body, so that the soul dies, though its fragments wander about the universe, ultimately entering into new combinations. The soul of the Epicureans consisted of a higher and a lower part, and they were modest enough not to give a name to the highest constituent element of the soul, but this element was material nevertheless, and not spiritual; the two parts of the soul correspond surprisingly to our brain and our nervous system, even though the higher part of the soul was placed in the chest.

To others the soul was spiritual. The scattered references to it in Cicero's works make it clear that he did not try to determine its composition, its form, or its place in the body. He says that men know little enough about the body, and still less about the soul. It comes from the outside, being of divine essence, and is placed in man, as Cicero says in the *De Senectute,* so that the earth may have inhabitants to govern it, guided by their contemplation of the heavenly order, or, rather, by their recollection of it. The soul consists of two parts; the lower, vegetative part, which feels, moves, and desires, and the higher part, which thinks and wills. This soul is immortal, and immortality involves pre-existence as well as post-existence.

Cicero willed to believe that the soul was immortal, as has already been noticed. It was the nobler doctrine; more convincing, too, according to the *Tusculans,* than the view of the Epicureans. Not all men or philosophers, even among the loftiest, agreed with Cicero. Some Stoics, he says, maintained that the soul lived longer than the body, but not eternally; and Panaetius even gave arguments for thinking the soul destructible. Nor does Cicero himself wish to seem certain of the matter. His questioner, in the first book of the *Tusculans,*[11] explains that, while reading Plato, who argued for immortality, he agrees with the latter's doctrine, but, after putting away the book, he has doubts. Cicero also allows Cato to say, in the *De Senectute,*[12] that he would rather err in his belief in the soul's immortality

---

[11] *Tusc.* 1, 24.
[12] *De Sen.* 85.

than give it up; if death should end all, there is at least some consolation in the thought that the philosophers whom he had opposed, and who will thus be proved right, will also be dead, and consequently unable to laugh at him.

The arguments for immortality are drawn from reason, Cicero says, and from the natural human attitude. Reason, necessarily only inference, leads us to believe that the soul is light, and so is of divine substance and will naturally rise to heaven, its true home, after death. It is swift and always in motion, and consequently has had no beginning and will have no end, for motion, which is life, is its very essence. Being of a simple and indivisible nature, furthermore, it can not be destroyed, for destruction means disintegration into component parts, as in the case of the atomic soul of the Epicureans. Finally, and here the philosophers become a little more concrete, the wonderful human powers of memory, foresight, expression, ability to study and to create artistically, indicate both that we have a soul and that it is divine—immortal, in other words. This last inference, as will be seen in the *De Natura Deorum*, is exactly like the one by which the existence and the nature of the gods can be gathered from the excellence of the world itself.

In addition to these reasons, men have always believed in the immortality of the soul, as is indicated by their care of the dead, deifications, and their interest in events that will occur after their death. The noblest men desire posthumous fame; they have an instinctive longing for immortality. Indeed, the souls of dead men continue to exert an influence on human affairs, without which their fame could not be perpetuated, so Cato in the *De Senectute*[13] quotes from the supposed last words of Cyrus in Xenophon's *Cyropaedeia;* but how this is done, Cicero unfortunately does not undertake to explain.

But if the arguments to prove the soul immortal are weak, those to the contrary, Cicero says, are even weaker. He men-

---

[13] *De Sen.* 80.

tions two, advanced by Panaetius, who disagreed with his master, Plato, only in regard to this one subject. One of Panaetius' thoughts was like that of the Epicureans. The soul, he said, can feel pain, and pain is equivalent to sickness, but that which can be sick can also die. To which Cicero returns that it is only the lower part of the soul that is exposed to pain; the higher part, not so exposed, neither falls sick nor dies. The soul, furthermore, still according to Panaetius, has been born, and that which has been born will die; and the fact that the soul has had a beginning is indicated by the resemblance of a child's soul to that of the parent, as though the soul of the child had been born from that of the parent. The reply to this contention is the explanation that this similarity is due to inherited physical characteristics, which influence the soul.

The question before Cicero, however, is whether death is an evil. If there is a future life, it is happy, as has already been stated, and death is in that case a blessing. Indeed, what we call life is really death, whereas real life begins after physical death; while on earth, the soul is shackled and held to unavoidable, heavy tasks, sunk to earth from its heavenly home, as it were. But even if death means extinction, men have no reason for anxiety. Having ceased to be, the soul can feel no regret for the loss of its wonderful powers. Even if life be considered a blessing, there can be no longing for it after death. Nor can we ever say with certainty that death deprives a man of any happiness awaiting him on earth; fortunes are too uncertain; Priam would have been happier if his life had been shorter. The first thought, however, is that human existence is an evil; and, in that case, death is a deliverer. As Cicero had written in the *Consolatio*, it is best never to have been born; after that, the most fortunate thing is to die young.

Death, then, is either a blessing of a somewhat uncertain nature, or it is, sadly enough, a release from human misery, actual or threatening. If these thoughts fail to bring conviction, then a man can merely realize that death, being decreed for all, can not be an evil—provided he believes that the world is ruled by a kindly providence. The man who has lived a good life should be ready to die. As for the act of dying, which also might be a cause for anxiety, the thought is thrown out that the death struggle lasts at the worst only a few moments. But the philosophers' consolation for this falls under the question of the endurance of physical pain, just as the further phase of the question, the sorrow caused by death to the survivors, belongs under the treatment of grief.

Physical pain, Cicero says, in the second book, is, Stoically speaking, not an evil, but he adds that a mere assertion to that effect is of little value. We have to endure pain by getting accustomed to it, and still more by keeping our mental balance, realizing from our philosophical meditations that praiseworthy actions are the greatest good in life and that our higher nature must govern the lower. It is only philosophical meditation that enables us to endure all kinds of pain; without it, we become inconsistent. Thus the Greeks endure sickness with fortitude, but they lack the courage to look an enemy in the face, and barbarians exult in battle, but wail in sickness. Physical pain, however, is a real evil; bodily medicines do not always help. If the pain becomes too great, there is always an escape through suicide.

Sorrow and other mental affections differ from physical pain. If a man really wishes to cure himself, he can do so, says Cicero in the preface to the third book; later in the book, however, he recedes somewhat from this position, as he remembers the death of Tullia. There are many considerations that may bring help; different philosophers urge one or another, but Cicero, in agreement with still other philosophers, thinks that all means of assistance should be used. Our imagination is the chief cause of suffering, and as a riotous imagination is philosophically a sick condition of the soul, it is our duty to eradicate it. In other words, it is bad for us to grieve, to fear, to rejoice overmuch. The imagination also at times makes it appear that grieving is our duty, as Cicero had experienced not many months before writing this treatise, but our real duty is to endure all things with calmness. We must be prepared for anything that may happen, realizing that trouble comes to all men. Time, though working slowly, is a great comforter; and Cicero confesses[14] that he was unwise when he tried to hasten his own cure by writing the *Consolatio*. A man must lift up his soul and forget his sufferings in the contemplation of the grandeur of the universe. But some part, at least of sorrow, may still remain, and for that philosophy has no cure.

The Epicureans would have a man forget his sorrows by turning to thoughts of pleasure. Cicero rejects this advice, repelled by the introduction of the word pleasure, which he gives as the reason for his opposition to the Epicureans. And yet it was the Epicurean counsel that he had virtually followed, working out the solution for himself. In Astura he summoned philosophy to his aid, but even then his main comfort lay in mental occupation, one of the pleasant things in life; and earlier, after Luca, he had found comfort, not in philosophical contemplation, but in writing about rhetoric. Aside from the cure effected by time, occupation with other matters than the grief itself was the thing by means of which Cicero had preserved his mental balance and his usefulness, but such occupation is not given by him as a help in sorrow. Perhaps it seemed too much like running away.

Nearly all of Cicero's arguments necessarily come back to the one thought that life must be met with calmness and nobility; man must rise above his fate. The last book of the *Tusculans*, therefore, maintaining that virtue is sufficient for a happy life, fitly concludes the work; and the spirit of the book is unavoidably one of exultation.

---

[14] *Tusc.* 4, 63.

The potency of virtue, Cicero exclaims at the beginning of the book, is difficult to prove because of the many and varied blows of fortune; but we must strive toward it with our best effort. Nothing in philosophy deserves to be announced with more exphasis or with more enthusiasm. If we once admit that chance or fate is stronger than virtue, then there is nothing left except prayer, and prayer, we thus see, is a confession of defeat. Cicero himself, so he says, has faltered, not because virtue is weak but because he and others have been weak. Philosophy is the guide of life. Without it, human existence would be impossible. One day spent in accordance with the teachings of philosophy is better than an eternity of error. And Cicero goes on to describe philosophical contemplation as the highest of human activities, comparing life, with Pythagoras, to a fair.[15]

This unwavering belief in the efficacy of virtue was Stoic, and Cicero explicitly renounces his New Academic attitude, which he had expressed in the *De Finibus*. The book becomes thus a hymn, with much argument such as had been used by the Stoic in the earlier treatise; but suddenly, in his enthusiasm, Cicero reverts to the previous teaching, and even goes farther. The Old Academy and the Peripatetics, he repeats, thought as highly of virtue as do the Stoics. The power of virtue over fate may indeed be illustrated from other philosophies; and the book which had begun with an insistence on the Stoic view, ends with a eulogy of Epicurus. He was better than his teachings. He cared neither for pain, nor death, nor wealth, nor popularity, nor exile; mental pleasure was paramount in his eyes; and if life should become too difficult, he considered suicide justifiable.

It is a far-reaching commentary on the ancient attitude that even in this book almost the last word should be a justification of suicide. It is an indication, however, not of weakness, but of independence—the final argument to prove that man is master of his own fortunes.

---

[15] See above, p. 38.

V

METAPHYSICS

After finishing the *Tusculan Disputations*, Cicero turned to the part of metaphysics, already mentioned, that dealt with the gods and their relation to the world. This subject is treated in three dialogues. The *De Natura Deorum*, in three books, is concerned with the gods and their nature as well as with providence; the *De Divinatione*, in two books, treats of prophecies of every kind; and the *De Fato*, in one book, of which only a part is extant, discusses the question of fate and free will.

The *De Natura Deorum* follows the arrangement of the *De Finibus*; the Epicurean and the Stoic doctrines are stated and criticised from the New Academic point of view. No conception of the gods, however, is put forward as that of the New Academy. Cicero, as we have seen, believed in a divine power in the world just as he believed in a future life, a religious attitude seeming to him essential to lofty living, but beyond this he did not go. Though he says later[16] that the work on the gods was not intended to destroy religion, both the preface to the treatise and the whole tenor of the work is destructive of Epicurean and Stoic doctrines alike. This was probably not so very iconoclastic, after all, for the Romans who read his philosophical works do not seem likely to have believed the ridiculous theories advocated by either of the two important schools. The reason for Cicero's treatment of the subject, ethical though it was, must have been his overwhelming desire to transfer to the Latin Greek philosophic thought, or rather, in this case, philosophical vagaries. The whole subject, even more than that of the *De Finibus*, was theoretical.

The Epicureans, it is explained by their spokesman, based their belief in the existence of the gods upon the universal

[16] *De Divin.* 1, 8.

opinion of mankind, but the critic points out that this opinion
has not been ascertained and that many men deny that there
are any gods. The Epicurean deities have the most beautiful
form conceivable, the human; but it is only prejudice, so the
critic says, to claim such preëminence for the human form.
They are made of a finer texture than men, and consequently
can be perceived only by the mind. But the Epicureans asserted
that the world was made of atoms and void. What then are the
gods made of? What is quasi-blood? These gods, enjoying the
Epicurean happiness of painlessness, take no thought for mortals
and do them no harm, so that men need not grovel in superstitious awe. But, retorts the critic, can inactivity make any
beings happy? And if the gods did not create the world and
have nothing to do with it now, then there is no reason for
worshipping them. Posidonius, therefore, was correct in asserting that Epicurus professed to believe in the gods merely to
avoid the charge of atheism.

With the Stoics the problem is less simple, though their
pedantry and logic led them into extravagances that could readily be dismissed as ridiculous. Like the Epicureans, they found
reason for their belief in a divinity in the universal opinion,
a singularly unfortunate argument in their case, since they
called all men but themselves fools. They also adduced various
epiphanies, but these could scarcely be well established. They
were pantheists, and explained at great length how the universe
was all-sufficient, consequently perfect, and therefore pure intellect, the essence of which is fire. And yet fire, or heat, is no
more essential to life than many other things, as for example,
moisture.

They individualized this pantheistic deity, and asserted that
the divine form is the most beautiful. But as they had already
announced that the sphere is the most perfect form, as seen in
the universe and the heavenly bodies, the anthropomorphic Epicureans inquired whether the Stoic gods were round. Some of

them were round, for the heavenly bodies, being pure ether or heat, Stoically also intellect, were gods. As the Stoics considered it man's duty to worship according to the popular religion, the popular gods are also included among their divinities, and are explained by much etymology and allegory to be mainfestations of the one pantheistic deity. These popular gods, so they said, are names for benefits received from the divine power, personified virtues and passions, the spirits of departed benefactors of mankind, or, finally, personified forces of nature. Thus Concord, Liberty, and Victory are gods, or rather, goddesses; and an endless series of gods is made possible, which the Academic critic immediately places side by side with the deities of mythology, inquiring why there are so many Jupiters, one in each of several localities, or why Hercules had so many parents.

The main contention of the Stoics, however, was that the world is perfect, and that this indicates both that there are gods and that these rule the world with kindness. They saw the wonder-working hand of providence in everything, from the stars in heaven to the flowers on earth, and particularly in man, with his erect position, his ingeniously capable hands, his delicate senses, his reason, his power of speech, and his capacity for meditation and worship. Throughout nature, according to them, there is a perfect adaptation, and everything exists for the sake of man.

This raised the old question about the happiness or unhappiness of human life, with endless arguments, which can easily be imagined. One matter, however, should be noticed. The Stoic gods, we are told, have created and rule this perfect world; they care for the human race; they protect whole nations and cities; they give wisdom and strength for great deeds, like those of a Fabricius, a Cato, and a Scipio; but when the enthusiastic Stoics, in their long account, finally reach the ordinary individual, not the exceptional man engaged in the performance of great national deeds, but the man in the crowd, living his daily

life, then their eloquence dwindles to two sentences. Sometimes,
they say,[17] storms cause damage to the crops, and in the same
way misfortunes come to men; but let us not infer from this
that the individual is either hated or neglected by the gods.
The gods, and here is the root of the matter, the gods take
thought for great things; little things they neglect—*magna di
curant, parva neglegunt.*

These Stoic gods, however, vouchsafe to men a view into the
future; indeed, the gift of prophecy to mankind is one of the
Stoic proofs of the existence of the gods, as it is also an inference
from the belief in a divine providence. Here, as in all the Stoic
reasoning about the deity, their arguments go in a circle. The
world is perfect, therefore there must be gods who have created
it and who maintain it; since the gods created this perfect world
and are maintaining it, they must be all-powerful and kindly,
and consequently there is a beneficent providence. Transferred
to the matter of prophecy, the argument becomes this: if the gods
do not foretell the future, either they do not love us, or they do
not know the future, or they think that prophecy would not be
useful to us, or they consider prophesying beneath their divine
dignity, or they have no means of communicating their knowledge to us. Since all these suppositions, in Stoic eyes, are
obviously erroneous, either there are no gods or else there is
prophecy; but there are gods, therefore there is also prophecy.

The answer to this manner of reasoning is not difficult to find.
Prophecy, or divination, is possible only if everything happens
according to the unchangeable decrees of fate; but if nothing
can be changed, no evil avoided, then divination can give no
help in a sad world. Would it have profited Pompey to know
that after three consulships and three triumphs he would be
murdered in Egypt, and that his death would be followed by
events to be spoken of only with tears? What assistance or joy
could Caesar have derived from a knowledge that he was to be

---

[17] *De Nat. Deor.* 2, 167.

murdered at the foot of Pompey's statue, in the midst of a
senate appointed largely by himself, by nobles some of whom
he had honored?

The real reason for a belief in divination, however, and also
the reason for discrediting it, is found in experience; and
Cicero's two books on the subject are a veritable encyclopedia
of dreams, omens, portents, soothsaying, fortune telling, oracles,
strange visions, the whispers of Socrates' demon, the answers of
the Sibylline books, and the ceremonious mummery of Roman
augurs. There is a story about nearly every prominent Roman,
and countless experiences of common people. The whole mantic
art is set forth, from its large part in the state religion to the
wandering tricksters that penetrated to every cranny of ancient
life. Philosophical books had been written, we learn, to prove
that a knowledge of the future would be useless; other books,
countless in number and also by philosophers, interpreted dreams.
Nothing was so absurd, says Cicero, that it was not maintained
by some philosopher. And every kind of ridicule and sarcasm
and criticism is leveled against a belief that seems to have
influenced many men of whom it could hardly have been
expected. Pompey, Caesar, and Crassus, constantly objects of
prophecy, had been told that they would live glorious lives, and
then die in their beds. During the Civil War many answers
of haruspices came from Greece to Rome, and Pompey was
inclined to heed them; but they were nearly all wrong. Apollo
at Delphi once gave a reply in Latin, but it is well known that
he knows only Greek. How can the position of the stars at a
child's birth have any influence, and yet twins be different both
in character and fortunes? Prophesying gods, since they need
interpreters, resemble Spaniards or Carthaginians struggling
with idiom in the Roman senate. Why do the gods hover about
a man's cot, ready to begin their whispers when the man begins
to snore? Why is it that an omen in Galatia often has a mean-

ing entirely different from what it would have in Rome? Cicero
himself had discussed divination with Deiotarus and found this
to be the case.

Cicero also wrote a treatise on auguries, now lost, which was
probably of a technical content. His view of the whole situation
has already been stated in many connections, and it seems to have
been the general view among educated men. Appius Claudius,
his predecessor in Cilicia, was an augur; and he was nicknamed
by his colleagues for believing in augury. He had a quarrel
about the matter with Marcellus, and Cicero sided with the latter,[18] to the effect that the art of augury was practised for the
good of the state, not because it could foretell the future. Cato
the Elder used to wonder, so Cicero also reminds his readers,
that a soothsayer could meet a colleague without laughing.[19]
They were both in the precious secret.

Closely connected with the treatise on Divination is the *De
Fato*, which discusses fate and free will. If fate rules the
world, if everything is preordained, then a man is morally irresponsible, for not only his character has been given him but
his every smallest action is in accordance with an outside decree.
Chrysippus, the great Stoic, who believed in divination, would
have it so; and it is, indeed, also obvious that there is a cause
for everything that happens. On the other hand, we feel that
we exercise a free will.

The Epicureans tried to solve the dilemma. Though they
did not believe in fate as an outside power, their philosophy was
thoroughly fatalistic, in that they considered the world an aggregation of atoms, which move unconsciously according to physical
laws, and they made man a part of this huge machine, himself
an aggregation of such atoms. In order to save human free will
in the midst of these whirling atoms, the Epicureans broke their
own physical laws of atomic motion, and introduced what they

---

[18] *De Divin.* 2, 75.
[19] *De Divin.* 2, 51.

called the swerve: the atoms, for no known reason, sometimes veer from their regular course, they said, and this swerve—itself not dictated by human consciousness, it must be remembered— results in certain impulses and desires in the human soul which constitute what men call free will.

This was not very satisfactory. Carneades, the New Academic, whom Cicero follows, had another explanation. There is a causal connection in the world, according to him, but this does not extend to every detail of life. Causes are of two kinds. The so-called natural causes bring about a certain condition, but before human action takes place, another cause, the accidental, must intervene. Thus fate, through natural causes, preordains that an athlete will, or rather may, win in a contest, but he cannot win unless he himself decides to enter the contest. Men may have an inclination to viciousness; for example, Socrates was said by a physiognomist to be fond of women, at which Alcibiades laughed, but Socrates, and any one else, can determine, in virtue of his free will, not to yield to his natural propensities. It is absurd to imagine a minute concatenation of cause and effect in the world. Ennius wrote: ''Would that this fir beam''— to make the Argo—''had never been cut with axes in the Pelian grove!'' He should have written: ''Would that the tree had never grown!''—or: ''Would that there had never been a Mount Pelion!''

VI

OLD AGE AND FRIENDSHIP

Cicero's philosophical authorship was drawing to a close. The *De Divinatione*, in both books, contains expressions some of which were obviously written before the assassination of Caesar, and others after it. Apparently the work was composed before the Ides of March, but published later, after a revision. In the preface to the second book Cicero bids farewell to writing; his time must be given to the state. Shortly before the death of

Caesar, it seems, he had written the essay on Old Age; it certainly came before the preface to the second book of the *De Divinatione*, in which it is mentioned. Conditions, however, presently forced him into leisure again, and he composed his works on Fate, Augury, Glory, Friendship, Duty, and the Virtues. Those on Augury, Glory, and the Virtues have been lost.

The brief dialogues on Old Age and on Friendship, perhaps most often read of all Cicero's treatises, have a character of their own. Like the rest, they were no doubt modeled upon Greek works on the same subjects, and yet they seem to contain, not more of Cicero's philosophical opinions than those that preceded, but more of his own personality. This is due to some extent to the fact that they were addressed to Atticus; Cicero writes as one old friend to another, not as either a teacher or an expounder. The essays, indeed, stand outside of his philosophical series. They could have been included in the *Tusculans*, as has already been observed, but, written as they were, they became less technical, more directly founded on ordinary human experience. This is fitting since Atticus was an Epicurean, presumably in doctrinal opposition to Cicero. The other treatises could not so properly have been addressed to him; but these are like personal gifts. Cicero, in the preface to the *De Senectute*, says that while writing the little dialogue, he had thought of Atticus as the person to whom it should be naturally dedicated; the composition of the *De Amicitia* he attributes to a request from Atticus.

The *De Senectute,* called also *Cato Maior,* after the principal speaker, who practically delivers a monologue, has a firm philosophic substructure, once the conversation is under way. The method is that of the New Academy. Objections to old age are advanced, in this case by Cato himself, and they are thereupon shown to be baseless, or nearly so. Cato, with sanity, refrains from proving too much. Old age is said to take men from active life, to deprive them of strength, to take from them almost all pleasures, and to be near death. Each one of these charges points to a real obstacle to happiness; but even while Cato admits this, no reader can feel that old age is a burden. Cato's replies are familiar to all students of Latin, and need not be repeated. The old man gossips on, and on, excusing himself for his garrulity, but not mending his ways. He weaves into his discourse precise statements about men and events, with many dates, always correlating them with happenings in his own life, as an old man would; and yet the learned reader suspects that much of this information came from Atticus' scholarly *Liber Annalis.*

Cato's character shines through his whole monologue; he praises farming with an enthusiasm that neither Cicero nor Atticus shared, except as a matter of patriotism and of the past; he is pompous, which Cicero never was; he seems older than Cicero could ever have become, despite his sorrows. And yet, though the manner is Cato's, or what would have been Cato's if he had truly profited by the late study of Greek which Cicero attributes to him, the sentiments are very much those of Cicero. When rereading the book, Cicero said[20] that he seemed to be listening to Cato himself; and the modern reader has the same feeling; but it is a Cato thoroughly admired by Cicero, though also treated with an eye to his eccentricities.

Laelius speaks in the *De Amicitia,* giving his name to the treatise. He is represented as having Scipio in mind as the model of a true friend; but Cicero, in the preface, says that Atticus may recognize himself in the picture. Indeed, some of Laelius' expressions are found almost word for word in Cicero's letters to his friend. The philosophical skeleton of the treatise is less rigid than that of the *Cato,* but Laelius, on the other hand, speaks more as a student than the old censor. The essay is neither so gossipy nor so light-hearted as its companion work; the troublesome conditions after Caesar's death have set their mark upon it, although there is no direct reference to them.

---

[20] *De Amic.* 4.

PHILOSOPHY

A few remarks may be recalled, for the book is Cicero's public recognition of Atticus' long friendship. Friendship consists in a complete agreement about all things, human and divine, to which are added good will and affection; next to wisdom, it is the greatest gift of the gods to man. What is better than to have some one with whom you can speak as with yourself? A friend increases the joy in success, and makes adversity easier to bear. It is not true that a man should avoid friendship, so as not to take up the burdens of others, as though each one should think only of his own difficulties. Nothing is more foolish than for a man to give all his energies to the acquisition of horses, servants, clothes, and furnishings, and not to win friends, for without friendship life can not be happy. Do not treat a friend, as some would have us do, as if you were some day to hate him. Ambition is opposed to friendship; it is therefore difficult to find true friends in public life. Confidence is the basis of friendship; friends do not listen to malicious gossip. Friends can not always remain equally intimate, for we outgrow some of them, but that is no reason for neglect. Sometimes external events make it necessary to break with a friend; in such a case, it is only the weakling who clings to the old relation. Such a weakling can not be a true friend.

True friendship can exist only between good men, and friends must neither ask from each other nor do for each other anything base. Do not be hasty in making friends. We all need friendship. The misanthrope, though he avoids and hates men, wants some one on whom he may vent his bitterness; and if a man should rise to heaven and view all its splendors, he would find no pleasure in it unless he could communicate his joy to a friend. Old friends are best, but new friendships are not to be rejected. Nothing is more desirable than to keep a friend through life, setting out with him from the starting point, as it were, and reaching the goal still by his side.

VII

DUTY

The *Laelius* was Cicero's tribute to the lifelong friendship
between Atticus and himself. In the *De Officiis,* on Duty, he
wrote, as it were, his spiritual testament. It stands as his last
comment on life, and so fitly concludes his philosophical writings.
In a later work, the *De Virtutibus,* which has been lost, he discussed the four cardinal virtues; but this treatise comprised only
one book and was in the nature of a more particular statement,
more philosophical perhaps, of the matter already treated in the
De Officiis, and can therefore be looked upon as a mere appendix
to the longer treatise. The *De Officiis* was thus to Cicero's
readers, as it is to us, his last word.

It is Cicero's Roman view of life that is here set forth. The
first two books, far more important than the third, were taken
largely from Panaetius, Scipio's Stoic friend and teacher, but
Panaetius, whether from conviction or policy, had adopted the
Roman attitude. Probably very much of the detail in Cicero's
first two books comes from him. We have already seen,[21] for
instance, how Panaetius had maintained that it was proper to
defend in court a man known to the pleader to be guilty, provided the defendant was not personally base. It would therefore
seem that Panaetius, living in the atmosphere of the Scipionic
Circle, had commented on the various phases of Roman life, fitting his comments into a philosophical frame. Where Panaetius,
that is the Stoics, expressed views that won Cicero's assent, the
latter incorporated them, but in other cases, as he himself says
in the preface, he reserved the rights of criticism and selection.
"In this work," so runs Cicero's explanation,[22] "I shall follow
the Stoics in particular, not as an interpreter"—a translator, we
should say—"but, according to my wont, borrowing from them

---

[21] See above, p. 122.
[22] *De Off.* 1, 6.

that of which my judgment approves." That Cicero was not overawed by Stoic authority appears in his witty manner of introducing Panaetius' observation about the defense of a guilty person. Cicero would not have dared to say such a thing, he remarks, if it had not also been the opinion of Panaetius, the strictest of the Stoics. The theory of the good Stoic, in other words, was no stricter than the practise of the forum.

It is a curious work, fortunately deceptive in the apparent philosophical character of its content. The first book discusses moral goodness, *honestum*. Moral goodness, we are told, consists of four principles: a regard for the welfare of others, a desire for knowledge, a desire for prominence and independence, and a sense of propriety. These are the four cardinal virtues: justice, wisdom, courage, and temperance. They are treated, one after the other, and then, briefly, their various claims are compared. In the second book Cicero takes up the question of expedience, *utile*, or the duties that arise out of our needs in life. These duties are thereupon compared in a single paragraph, or rather it is merely stated that comparisons will arise. Since the matters discussed have to do with man in his relations with other men, they might well have been included in the first book, under the headings of justice, courage, and temperance; and the material of the second book is, indeed, treated to a considerable extent in the first. The division, however, is justified by a slight difference in the point of view, and by the greater ease with which the extensive material can be handled in two books. That the two belong together in content appears in the third book. Here, investigating the supposed conflict between moral goodness and expedience, Cicero first discusses the question in general, and thereupon points out under what circumstances expedience may come into conflict with the virtues of justice, courage, and temperance.

This outline is formidably philosophical, and Cicero did pride himself somewhat on its theoretical completeness. Panaetius had failed to discuss the relative claims of the four virtues and also of the obligations connected with expedience, and Cicero, with some surprise at this failure, does discuss them; very briefly, however, and yet not altogether fruitlessly, for it gives him an opportunity to insist on the paramount claims of social duties. Panaetius had also intended to write on the conflict between moral goodness and expedience. He seems, however, to have been one of those whose plans are larger than their performance. According to his pupil Posidonius, he lived thirty years after completing his work on Duty—in three books, corresponding to Cicero's first two—but he never carried out his intention in reference to the moral conflict.

If the dictates of expedience be rightly, that is, Stoically, conceived as demanding those things from us which contribute to spiritual health, and not to worldly success, then there can be no conflict between expedience and moral goodness. The mere conception, however, of expedience as a source of action introduces worldly advantage; and the conflict becomes inevitable. Cicero had doubts about the wisdom of discussing the question at all. He does so, nevertheless, drawing from various philosophers, and states that in this book he has exercised unusual independence. The treatment, however, is scarcely useful except to show into what casuistries philosophers may fall. A typical case is that of a man wishing to sell a house. Ought he to inform the prospective buyer about its hidden defects? The philosophers disagreed, but Cicero decides for absolute honesty.

But the work is not so innocuously speculative as this dilemma might indicate. Purely abstract statements are constantly illustrated by references to Cicero's long record of public service and to persons and events that were still the subjects of acrimonious disagreement in Rome.

The references to Caesar may be mentioned, being perhaps the most important. The treatise was written toward the end of the year 44 B.C., within a few months of Caesar's death.

Cicero, speaking of the civil war between Caesar and Pompey, says that there was too much crime on one side and too little good fortune on the other. Injustice, according to Cicero, is caused particularly by a desire for power and glory. Thus Caesar broke every law, human and divine, in order to attain the rule on which he had wrongly set his heart. And the tragedy consists in the fact that such overweening ambition comes especially to the greatest and most gifted men. Caesar, so Cicero observes in another place, did not confiscate the property of private citizens, but he placed whole provinces and regions under a rule of destruction—a reference to his land laws and to his government of the provinces, which he took from the senate and assigned to political supporters. To abolish debts, says Cicero, is to enable one man to buy something with another man's money. Caesar abolished debts from the mere desire of doing wrong, at a time when such action could bring him no benefit—a statement that reveals Cicero's unwillingness, perhaps his inability, to see anything good in Caesar's rule, since the rule itself had overturned the state. Of tyrants, though without a mention of Caesar, Cicero remarks that there can be no intercourse with them; it is honorable to kill a tyrant, and to exterminate the whole race of tyrants from society. Can the base and wicked murderer of his country, so he asks elsewhere, be useful to any one even if he be called the father of his country? This name had been given to Caesar. And, finally, personal affection is the strongest foundation for power, fear the weakest; no resources can withstand the hatred of the many; and even if this was formerly unknown, it has recently been illustrated.

The treatise, however, is no more a political pamphlet than it is a series of abstract speculations. Cicero gives in it an account of the goals which a man may set for himself, his duties in the forum and in the courts, toward his enemies and his friends, and how he should behave under various circumstances; and Cicero goes into great detail. Nearly every important expression of opinion on his part that has already been quoted can be found in the *De Officiis*, at least in some indirect form, as well as many of the incidental comments that have been used to indicate the Roman attitude both in politics and in private intercourse. It is therefore unnecessary to repeat them. The governing thought is duty toward Rome, greater than all others, even than the duty toward a parent or a child. But, beside it, is the demand that a man be his own self, and that he observe the proprieties of life. Indeed, the virtue of temperance is concerned with the so-called *decorum*, that which is suitable and fitting; and, according to Cicero, it must permeate a man's whole existence. Cicero's treatment of this duty becomes thus a statement of the *humanitas* that was first created in Rome when Scipio and his friends listened to Panaetius. It demanded that a man be an individual, a scholar, and a gentleman; but since he was already a Roman, he must first of all devote his energies to the service of his country. This Scipionic ideal has already been mentioned. The most complete expression of it is found in the *De Officiis;* no one was a better exponent of it than Cicero.

Philosophically, Cicero speaks throughout this work as a dogmatist. But it is a dogmatism, as he explains at the beginning of the second book, which clearly realizes that intellectually it is founded on probability. How Cicero's New Academic attitude enabled him to transfer and criticise Greek philosophy has already been explained and illustrated. It was inevitable that he should be a follower of Philo. The Academics gave far more attention to the esthetic side of philosophical study and writing than either the Stoics or the Epicureans, and they were active teachers of rhetoric. Cicero, furthermore, had an extraordinarily alert, inquisitive, and all-embracing intellect, and his long practise at the bar had accustomed him to seeing both sides of a question. He abhorred posing; and it is posing, unless it be blindness, or laziness, or a conscious surrender of individual judgment, for a philosopher to assert that he and his fellows alone know, and that their knowledge is absolute. But Cicero's moral convictions, on the other hand, were as strong as those of the most rigid Stoic. Where a question arose in reference to a man's duty in the world, Cicero would have no hairsplitting. And he also saw clearly that a man is good or bad quite independently of his intellectual opinions. Thus he frequently observes that the Epicureans are better than their doctrine. In the *De Finibus*, therefore, he treats the question of human happiness as a proper matter for debate, even criticising what we know to have been his own preference; but when, as in the *De Officiis*, the question no longer is what a man states in philosophical language to be his goal, but what he actually should do, then Cicero leaves no room for the Epicurean teaching, for instance, that men should avoid public life, but makes a definite requirement.

This is not like the momentary dogmatism in the fifth book of the *Tusculan Disputations*, which was due to moral enthusiasm and presently ended in a eulogy of Epicurus. It is not emotional, but comes from a very matter-of-fact desire to make clear the motives of his own actions and to influence the actions of others. This division of the philosophical field · into a part in which scepticism is proper and a part in which dogmatism is required, is the most marked, and perhaps the most original,[23] characteristic of Cicero as a philosopher.

The *De Officiis*, being on the whole a serious sermon, naturally keeps young men in view, and was therefore fittingly dedicated to young Marcus.

VIII

CICERO'S ORIGINALITY

Cicero's position as a philosophical thinker may thus be defined as that of a doubter and an investigator. He rightly called himself a New Academic. He also had the noble transcendental yearnings of Pythagoras and Plato, shared by others,

---

[23] Zielinski, *op. cit.*, p. 81.

even by Stoics like Panaetius, and he was thoroughly sympathetic with the best aspirations of the Stoics, but he did not attempt to demonstrate the truth of these yearnings and aspirations by fitting them into a system, and he had no patience with the etymological explanations or the logical self-sufficiency of the Stoics. It would therefore be a misrepresentation to cull from his works the statements from the Stoics and the Old Academy toward which he is more sympathetic than toward those of the Epicureans, and to construct from them a complete philosophical system, as if it were his.

Cicero's attitude was human rather than philosophical. While he laughs at Stoic dogmatism, he also, both in his letters and in his philosophical treatises, ridicules the agnosticism of the New Academics. They give forth an uncertain sound, he says in the *Fifth Tusculan;* and at the end of the *De Finibus* he has one of the speakers suggest that if young Lucius Cicero should follow the opinions of Marcus and master the New Academic doctrine thoroughly, then it would result in his knowing nothing at all.

In practical matters, however, Cicero had very definite convictions, and these had been most insisted upon by the Stoics. It must be remembered, however, that they were claimed for the Old Academy by Antiochus, who differed in ethics from the Stoics only in his assertion that virtue, while the one important element in happiness, was not the only one. And Cicero agreed with Antiochus, for when he addressed the work on Duty to his son, the latter was studying under a Peripatetic philosopher, and Cicero observes, in the preface to the first book, that the Peripatetics like himself claimed to be Socratics and Platonists, so that they did not much differ from him. Cicero also, as has already been pointed out, reserved the right to choose and to criticize while he followed the Stoics, and the Stoic whom he followed was Panaetius, himself an admirer of Plato and a renegade from Stoic dogmatism. Cicero, therefore, can not be called a Stoic in ethics, except with reservations.

Whether Cicero's attitude would entitle him to be called an
independent philosopher, depends ultimately on the relation
between his own works and those of the Greeks that had written
on the same subjects, and here our information is slight. What
has already been said in general about the sources of his treatises,
particularly of the *De Oratore,* need not be repeated in detail.[24]
The sources have to be reconstructed largely from Cicero's own
works, and the results are far from trustworthy. In connection
with nearly every work—except where Cicero, as in the first two
books of the *De Officiis,* expressly indicates his main source—
there is the greatest diversity of opinion. Sometimes we have
practically nothing to guide us. Thus in the *De Senectute*
Cicero says that he will not assign the conversation to the mythological Tithonus, as Aristo has done, and this statement is the
only starting point for an inquiry. Does it indicate that he
followed Aristo in other respects, as, for instance, in the four
charges against old age? Who was Aristo? From Ceos or from
Chios? In any case, his work is lost. Cicero in his treatise
quoted passages both from Plato and Xenophon. Did the unde-
termined Aristo do likewise? Cicero was certainly familiar with
the books from which these passages came; he wrote to Paetus
that he had read his copy of Xenophon's *Cyropaedeia* to pieces;
so that there was no need of Aristo's mediation.

When Cicero gives an outline of a part of a definite
philosophy, as of the Epicurean doctrine of the chief good, he
undoubtedly followed some philosophical handbook; but when
he writes on less clearly defined topics, as in the *Tusculans,* the
sources were numerous and must remain debatable. Cicero constantly refers to the opinions of Greek philosophers, but though
he seems often to be repeating somebody else's citation of these
opinions, that need not always be the case. The books that he
may have read were extremely numerous, ranging from large
works to published lectures; and, in addition, he may have
incorporated thoughts that had never been written down at all,

24 See above, pp. 422–423.

but had been merely expressed in lectures and conversations. It was difficult to obtain books. The books that he actually used while composing a treatise, therefore, are sometimes indicated by a request to Atticus in a letter for a certain book, or for an outline of a book, with which Cicero himself may, or may not, have been familiar, but these indications only give names of authors and titles, the books in question being lost, and, indeed, the names of some of the books as well. The Greeks themselves, furthermore, were constantly copying from one another, as Cicero says; we have seen in connection with Antiochus that they called one another thieves.

Cicero frequently mentions his sources, but not always, for he was, after all, transferring a whole field of thought, and his readers were not interested to know the exact books or lectures from which he had received the various details of his information. It was enough to know that one opinion was Epicurean and another Stoic, or that one came from Carneades and another from Philo; and often even that amount of knowledge was unnecessary.

Once Atticus wondered anxiously at the rapidity of Cicero's composition, and Cicero replied[25] that he was only making transcripts—*apographa*—only supplying the words. This expression may well describe his method in parts of such a book as the *De Finibus*. In other works his task was less easy. He selected, and he criticised, as he himself said in the *De Officiis*; and this expression, found also even in the *De Finibus*, is made to apply to his method in general. It is his formal statement, whereas the words of Atticus—whether humorously self-depreciatory or not, and scholars take them both ways, sometimes with much solemnity—are not intended to tell the whole story.

There is one other consideration. Since originality among the Greeks in Cicero's time was a very small quantity, he may have been as original as many another who made philosophy a

---

[25] *Att.* 12, 52, 2.

profession. The sceptical attitude had been in abeyance[26] since Philo, who died about 79 B.C., and Cicero in a manner revived it, and went farther than Philo on the constructive side. One of the noteworthy characteristics of Cicero as a philosopher, furthermore, is his separation of practical from theoretical ethics, in the *De Officiis* and the *De Finibus*. This may be a sign of originality, but it is not to be forgotten that in the work on Duty he was following Panaetius. The latter also was responsible for another element in Cicero's ethics, namely, the emphasis on the individual, in the *De Officiis*. This very emphasis, though the earliest extant philosophical expression of it is found in Cicero, must have been the very essence of Panaetius' message to the Scipionic Circle.

These somewhat uncertain marks of originality, and others like them, have been brought forward as proofs of Cicero's independence as a philosopher, and he has been considered an important member of the New Academic school, even having Greek followers.[27] Usually, however, Cicero is held to be merely a translator. Only one thing is absolutely certain, that Cicero, the Roman consular, had no ambition to be classed among Greek philosophers. He experienced a certain satisfaction when he could improve upon their works, or add to them a little, as in the *De Officiis*, but his claims to philosophical fame went no farther. Cicero's Roman attitude to Greek pursuits has been stated before; but one of his expressions of it may be recalled. In the preface to the first book of the *De Officiis*, he writes of his philosophical works that they seem to have given much assistance to the Romans, so that not only those who are not Greek scholars but also the educated think they have gained a good deal from them, both as speakers and as philosophical thinkers. This is a reference to very gratifying results, and yet, in the preface to the third book, Cicero compares his own leisure

---

26 *De Nat. Deor.* 1, 6 and 11.

27 Goedeckemeyer, p. 201.

to that of Africanus, with a confession of weakness because Africanus could enjoy his leisure in calm meditation, whereas Cicero found it necessary to resort to writing.

Cicero's claim to originality, and it is a very real claim, consists in the fact that he alone saw the possibility of creating a philosophical literature in Latin. Other Romans had written and were writing on philosophy. Lucretius' poem had been published, but systematic philosophy in verse was an anachronism. Lucretius, despite his ardent enthusiasm, worked in the spirit of a recluse, and, therefore, need scarcely be considered in the general trend of things. Indeed, Cicero does not mention the poem in his philosophical writings, though he was acquainted with it, as a letter to Quintus indicates; and the character of the poem makes it amply clear that it could not make converts, nor lead to imitation except as poetry.

Brutus wrote on Virtue, and Cicero, in the *De Finibus,* says that this work inspired his own philosophical writing. But Cicero is obviously only complimenting his young friend, for in the *Tusculans,* though they are dedicated to Brutus himself, Cicero practically ignores him as a philosophical writer, when he says that little or nothing had been done in philosophy by the Romans except by certain Epicurean propagandists. Brutus also wrote on Duty and on Patience. But while such works as these were doubtless much like Cicero's own essays on Friendship and Old Age, or like one of the consolatory meditations in the *Tusculans,* they were no part of a complete presentation of philosophy and could not have suggested Cicero's comprehensive plan. They left the philosophical situation unchanged; the chief books and the vocabulary were still Greek. Cicero could have satisfied his need of mental occupation by such writings, but he saw better things to do.

Neither was he satisfied with making mere translations from the Greek. This he would have considered a worthy enough thing to do, and he even hints[28] that he may yet undertake it;

---

[28] *De Fin.* 1, 7.

but translations, and philosophically Lucretius was a translator,
would not have answered his wider patriotic purpose. There was
need of critical interpretation and of comparisons.

Even the ethical aim of Cicero was subordinate to the
patriotic. Of course, if he had not considered philosophy important morally, he would not have written at all; but if ethical
instruction had been his principal aim, he would scarcely have
given so much attention to the presentation of debatable matter,
and he would certainly not have presented this matter in so
impartial a way. So far as we can judge, he does full justice
to Epicureanism, and in reference to the *Academica*, about which
we have his own private comment, he says[29] that in assigning
the dogmatic side to Varro he had treated the latter honorably,
not exhibiting him in the character of a defeated combatant.
The preponderance of ethics in his treatises was obviously due
quite as much to its similar position in contemporary philosophy
as to Cicero's personal appreciation of its importance.

Cicero's ethical purpose was perhaps active to some extent
in reference to the Epicurean propagandists just mentioned.
These had set forth their doctrine, particularly the physics of it,
without any literary finish. As they were easy to read, says[30]
Cicero, and as the common people would be attracted by the
doctrine of Pleasure as the chief end of life, and as there was
no other philosophy in Latin, they had conquered all Italy.
Cicero, though explaining that he had not read them, mentions
them frequently enough to show that he had them in mind. To
counteract their influence may no doubt have been one of Cicero's
purposes, but it can easily be overestimated. Cicero's writings
are not at all of a character to appeal to the people who were
attracted by the bald Epicurean tracts. Cicero wrote for the
educated, or, at least, for those who appreciated literary style.
He was opposed to Epicureanism, but his opposition was not

---

[29] *Att.* 13, 25, 3.

[30] *Tusc.* 4, 6–7. For further references, see Schanz, p. 339.

of a missionary kind. The educated Epicureans in Rome were no better and no worse than the Stoics; even the publisher of Cicero's essays, Atticus, was an Epicurean. Cicero would gladly have admitted, as he did admit in reference to Epicurus, that they were better than their doctrine. He hints at that pleasant fact more than once.

Cicero's philosophical aim is obvious, from the treatises themselves, but it also finds frequent expression in the prefaces. These prefaces—nearly every book has one, and not merely every treatise—are very remarkable documents. Cicero informed Atticus that he had a book—a *volumen*—of them, and it is clear from Cicero's use of the same preface twice[31] that they were, sometimes at least, written without any thought of a particular work. They contain Cicero's thoughts about philosophical writing, jotted down apparently from time to time, as well as his answers to criticisms. They thus belong together, and constitute a history of the philosophical situation in Rome, just as the prologues to Terence's comedies give a history of the theatrical situation. The same thing is naturally said more than once, for not every reader would have all his works, nor would a single reply convince all objectors. The expression, nevertheless, is infinitely varied; the emphasis shifts according to the fortunes of his works as they were published and also according to the content of the books to which they were prefixed, for, whatever form they may have had in Cicero's *volumen,* he only once, to our knowledge, made a slip in using them; so that, as we have them, they are adapted each to its particular book. In this respect, too, they resemble the Terentian prologues.

It is clear from these prefaces that Cicero's readers did not approve of his self-imposed task, and failed to comprehend its full signficance. He was an intellectual pioneer, and met with the usual fate; but he gradually won his critics to his own view of the matter, or at least he did so to a considerable degree. As

---

[31] See below, p. 615, note 14.

he says in the *De Officiis*, both the educated and the uneducated
admitted that they had learned something. He convinced nobody, neither himself nor others, however, that philosophical
writing was quite worthy of a Roman consular, but that was to
be expected; nor does it really touch the situation.

Any study of philosophy, some contended, was useless. To
these Cicero had already replied in the *Hortensius*, but the reply
is enthusiastically repeated in several of the prefaces. Others
wished him to indicate his own beliefs, and Cicero explained
that he was not interested in preaching a dogma. He wished
to arouse interest, and was glad of philosophical opponents. It
was through controversy that philosophy had flourished in
Greece, and he could add that he had had some success in
turning other Romans to philosophical writing. It was observed
that Cicero wrote too much. But, he retorts, it is not enough
merely to make men interested, which can be done with a little
writing; they must also be taught. Nor is it possible to exercise
temperantia in so noble a subject. Why, some asked, had he
so suddenly turned to philosophy? And he replies that in his
youth he had given much time to it, and later he had been even
more busy with it, as was indicated by the frequent references to
philosophy in his orations and by his friendships with learned
men, many of whom were often at his house.

Greek, it seemed to his critics, was the only language for
philosophy. Latin was inadequate; and even if philosophy were
written in Latin, it would be useless. Those who knew Greek
would prefer to read their philosophy in Greek, and the others
would not understand even the Latin. Cicero replied that he
had no objection to anybody reading Greek, provided he really
read it. A contempt for Latin, however, was hypercritical and
unpatriotic; and, for that matter, Latin was as good a language
as Greek, better at times, as he tried to prove by pointing out
in the treatises themselves, now and then, how certain conceptions could be more precisely expressed in Latin than in Greek.

But the real answer to all these criticisms was given by the character and the success of Cicero's works. They contain mistakes and inconsistencies. Some of these are doubtless due to Cicero, and were caused by rapidity of composition and, at times, by misunderstanding, but many of them must have come from the Greek sources. It was an age of constant shifting and borrowing, and the modern critic must not forget that his own professed knowledge of the Greeks is often only uncertain inference. But it is not possible to discuss minute details. Cicero's task was a difficult one, and he solved it with signal success. His style saved his treatises when those of all the Greeks of this period, and of the centuries that lay between him and Aristotle, were lost, with fragmentary exceptions; and Cicero's treatises were so well conceived and so well executed that our knowledge of post-Aristotelian philosophy, as derived from him, is very considerable. It is not likely that anything of real importance was omitted.

The assertion has been made that Cicero's philosophical treatises have had a more profound influence than any other works belonging to ancient Greece and Rome, with the single exception of Plutarch's *Lives*. Whether this be so or not, the power and the fascination that they exercised upon later generations for centuries are attested in almost countless ways. St. Augustine's acknowledgment of indebtedness to the *Hortensius* has already been mentioned. One other instance, equally well known, is worthy of mention—that of St. Jerome.[32]

He had determined to leave his house, parents, sisters, and relatives, and even to change his mode of life and go to Jerusalem, making all these sacrifices that he might save his soul, but he had not been able to give up the books that he had succeeded in collecting in Rome. He fasted, he says, in order that he might be justified in finishing his day with the reading of Cicero. Once he was seized with a fever, and his condition became critical. Even preparations for his funeral were being

[32] Zieliński, *op. cit.*, pp. 112–114.

made. Suddenly, during his sickness, he seemed to be translated to heaven and stood before the judgment seat of God. Asked who he was, he said, "A Christian." "No," was the reply, "you are not a Christian, but a Ciceronian, for where your treasure is, there will your heart be also." St. Jerome was overcome with his transgression. Those present, it seemed to him, interceded in his behalf, for he was still young. Finally, he cried aloud and took an oath that he would not again keep worldly books in his possession, nor read them. He was released, and returned to earth. Regaining consciousness, he wept so bitterly that all who saw him were convinced of his repentance and change of heart.

But he could not keep his oath. He continued reading Cicero, quoting him repeatedly in his writings. When he later became involved in religious controversy, an opponent, Rufinus, charged him with his continued love for Cicero, and even spoke of it as perjury and sacrilege. St. Jerome tried to defend himself. His promise had referred to the future, he said; he had not promised to forget all he knew. And, indeed, where had Rufinus acquired his own copiousness of expression, his brilliance, and his variety, if not from Cicero? Either St. Jerome was mistaken or else Rufinus, too, read Cicero—in secret. But Rufinus had made no promise, and St. Jerome was forced to resort to causistry. He had given his promise while in a dream. Rufinus should heed the prophets, who tell us not to believe in dreams.

Cicero could not have foreseen St. Jerome's devotion and agony; nor, most likely, did he have his eyes turned to a very distant future. His task seemed to him a very modest one, despite his moral and literary enthusiasm and his conviction of its Roman usefulness. He was writing for a relatively narrow circle of contemporaries, with some thought of further results. As he said himself in the *De Divinatione*,[33] he hoped to reach, not all young men, but a few, whose influence, however, might be con-

---

[33] *De Divin.* 2, 5.

siderable in the state. He also found some pleasure in the knowledge that even older men read his books; they were more numerous than he had expected. It seemed glorious, so he said, still in the same connection, to think that the Romans would no longer need the Greeks.

It is therefore interesting to remember how Caesar and Cicero, the two greatest Romans of their time, were occupied in the early months of the year 45 B.C. Caesar was conquering in Spain, and so establishing his power, which would result in the Roman empire. Quite unknown to him, the empire would become the bridge, as it were, over which would be carried the numerous gifts that the ancients had been preparing for the modern world. Cicero, in the meanwhile, sorrowing at Astura, was seeking consolation in writing, and, with a lack of foresight like Caesar's, was making ready one of the most precious of these gifts.

CHAPTER XVII

THE LAST BATTLE

I

AFTER THE IDES

Caesar was murdered, in the senate-house erected by Pompey in the Campus Martius, on the Ides of March, the fifteenth, in the year 44 B.C. Though we do not know where Cicero was at this time, it is almost certain that he did not witness the assassination. Neither is it likely that he was in the forum. He had not been in the habit, for a long time, of mingling with men in public; it was too humiliating an advertisement of his political helplessness. Most probably he was at home, whether in his Palatine residence or in his Tusculan villa. During the days when the plot against Caesar was being matured, and perhaps on the very day it was executed, he may have been collecting instances of ancient superstition for the *De Divinatione* or writing his essay to Atticus on Old Age. News of the assassination was probably sent to him by Basilus, one of the assassins;[1] and he wrote in reply his famous two lines: "Congratulations! I am happy. I love you and watch over your interests. Send me your love, and let me know what you are doing and what is happening." Later in the day he repaired to the Capitol for a conference with the assassins; he was ready to take his place in the political turmoil.

---

[1] If Cicero had been present in the senate-house or in the forum on the Ides, he would undoubtedly have referred to it in his letters or in his *Philippics*, but these contain no such reference. Basilus was far less intimate with Cicero than were several of the other conspirators. Cicero's note to Basilus can therefore scarcely be explained except on the supposition that Basilus, who was not an important member of the conspiracy, was either delegated to communicate with Cicero or else did so out of a greater thoughtfulness. This letter (*Fam.* 6, 15) is the only one in the correspondence addressed to Basilus.

The relief and the unpitying exultation at Caesar's death which inspired Cicero's note to Basilus is a sad testimony to the hatred the great dictator had drawn upon himself during the last months of his life. Cicero had been his friend; he had admired his talents probably more than those of any other man in Rome; Cicero himself was not cruel, though he could on occasion be surprisingly stern; but Caesar had made himself a tyrant. The murder was dastardly, for many of the conspirators owed their whole political existence to Caesar and some had been on very intimate terms with him. All men did not condone it. The soldiers did not forget their great commander. Though some of the prominent Romans made their devotion to Caesar's memory a cloak for their own ambitions, others were moved by profound grief. Matius was one of these. The letter[2] to Cicero in which he discussed his relations to Caesar bears witness, as does nothing else, to Caesar's lovable personality, and is one of the most pathetic things in history. To the modern student who has learned to know Caesar the murder can not but be inexpressibly sad. But this feeling did not predominate in Rome. Matius thought that all men should mourn, and yet he continued on terms of intimacy with such men as Cicero, who supported the assassins, and publicly praised the deed. Indeed, political assassinations were not rare in Rome; Caesar's death did not seem to raise a moral question. Matius was actually criticised for not concealing his grief, which, it was claimed, argued a lack of patriotism. It was felt to be a noble thing to have had a part in the murder; men who were innocent wished to be known as conspirators. Cicero made no such claim, but when Antony, a few months later, accused him of having instigated the murder, he replied that Antony was giving him more credit than he deserved. Trebonius was one of the conspirators. It had been his duty to detain Antony outside the senate-house while the

---

[2] *Fam.* 11, 28. It is a reply to *Fam.* 11, 27.

assassins crowded around Caesar. In a letter[3] to Cicero, who
was expected to write something about Caesar's death, he
expressed the hope that Cicero would not assign to him too small
a part in the deed.

There is something almost appalling in the suddenness and
the energy with which Cicero changed the whole tenor of his
life. It was almost eight years since he had last appeared in the
courts of Rome. Then had come the wearisome administration
of Cilicia; the Civil War, with Cicero's many anxieties and disappointments, including the long humiliation in Brundisium and
the years of submission to Caesar's dictatorship. Once, when
Marcellus was pardoned, Cicero had broken his silence in public;
but otherwise he had been absent from public life or silently
present. Terentia had been divorced, Publilia had come and
gone, Quintus had been treacherous, and Tullia had died. Cicero
had composed the *Brutus* and the *Orator*, and several minor
things; and lately he had been immersing himself in the disputes
of the Academy, and the ethical and metaphysical meditations of
Stoics and Epicureans. He took an active part in the doings
of the first few feverish days of chaos after the assassination,
but after that, for several months, there was nothing that he
could do. During these months, however, he held himself in
readiness, and when his opportunity at last came, at the end of
the year, he acted with an energy, vigilance, courage, and wisdom that he had not surpassed in his prosecution of Verres or
in the trying and perilous activities of his consulship.

The assassins had counted on Cicero's support. His name was
therefore the first to be mentioned in public after Caesar had
been slain. While the dictator was still lying in his blood on
the floor of the senate-house, Brutus brandished his dagger in
the air and, shouting the name of Cicero, congratulated him on
the restoration of Roman liberty. This was a summons to
Cicero to come forward and labor for his country, but it was

[3] *Fam.* 12, 16.

also an announcement that the murder was a patriotic act. And this claim was in the main true. There is necessarily a multiplicity of motives wherever men band themselves together for good or for evil, but the one thought that animated the conspirators against Caesar's life was the desire to get rid of a King and to reëstablish the republic. They sought no power greater than would fall to their lot as senators or magistrates. In their eagerness to avoid even the appearance of aiming at more than this, they spared Antony, Caesar's colleague in the consulship.

The tyrannicides made a mistake in allowing Antony to live. Some of them had urged that he should fall with his master, but Marcus Brutus, we are told, had objected to what he considered useless bloodshed, and he had carried his point. The conspirators made other mistakes, which could less easily have been avoided, but the hope that the assassination would restore the republic was not altogether chimerical. Indeed, among the sixty or more conspirators were many men who had had quite enough experience both in war and in politics not to strike down Caesar without a thought of the consequences. Marcus Brutus himself was unfortunately a theorizer and a dreamer, but even Marcus showed later, in the East, that he was not a man of contemptible ability. Decimus Brutus and Cassius were, with Marcus Brutus, the leaders of the conspiracy; Decimus had proved himself a very capable soldier under Caesar, and Cassisus had fought with great success in the East. These men and their accomplices had reason for expecting that, with Caesar gone, the republic would immediately revive. Rome had not been changed into an autocracy by Caesar; the new order had not been so well stabilized that at Caesar's death another man would automatically take his place. Caesar's power had been something over and above the republican constitution, but that constitution still remained. The senate and the assemblies still met, though their decisions were dictated by Caesar. There were still magistrates:

Antony was Caesar's colleague, and Dolabella, Cicero's son-in-law, had been selected to take Caesar's place till the end of the year after Caesar himself should have departed on his intended campaign against the Parthians. The expectation of the conspirators, therefore, was that the agencies of the republic—the magistracies, the senate, and the assemblies—which had not ceased to exist, should now become effective. The senate, which had lost all its power through Caesar, might well be counted upon to hail with eagerness the restoration of its ancient supremacy; the people of Rome, who on the whole seemed to care but little for anything except their own livelihood and amusements, had of late shown indifference and even hostility toward the deceased dictator, and would not be likely to make any serious attempt to put some one else in his place. Everything might be well if the conspirators could only persuade the senate and the people that no man's life was in danger and that the death of Caesar was not intended to secure unusual powers for the conspirators themselves.

It was necessary to start the republican government at once, or rather, to make sure that it continued in operation under the new circumstances. The tyrannicides tried to do this. Caesar was slain in the senate-house. The assassins endeavored to calm the senators, evidently hoping that the fathers might be induced to take immediate action; Brutus' apostrophe to Cicero, which proclaimed the liberation of Rome, indicates what the assassins wished to announce; but the senators dared not stay to listen. The unexpected fall of Caesar had come upon them with the shattering force of a thunderbolt. No one would trust himself to the men who had been bold enough to strike the great Caesar. The senators fled, leaving the expostulating assassins beside the bloody corpse of their victim.

The conspirators decided to appeal to the people in the forum. Adjoining the curia, from which the senators had just fled, was the theatre of Pompey, where a performance was being given.

The news of the murder scattered the large audience, and the word was carried through the city. Decimus Brutus had some gladiators at hand, perhaps kept in readiness for the eventuality that had now occurred. Guarded by these, the assassins marched to the forum. They had their bloody swords in their hands, but on a spear one of them carried a cap of liberty. But the excited people in the forum would not listen to their assurance that all men were safe, and that a tyrant had been slain. Violent scenes ensued, in which many were accidentally killed. The conspirators seem to have held some sort of public meeting, but they could arouse no enthusiasm. There were many Caesarian veterans among the people. They were in Rome awaiting their rewards from the state, which Caesar had been expected to procure for them. The veterans were a class by themselves, and could not be won by grandiloquent phrases about Roman liberty. They wanted concrete recompense for their services; they had at no time preferred the senate to a general, and many of them had been devoted to their great leader. Whether or not any violence was now attempted by them, the conspirators found it desirable to retreat. They mounted to the Capitol, where they could best protect themselves; they had no soldiers, only their personal attendants and Decimus Brutus' gladiators.

Though the assassins had failed both in the senate and in the forum, and were actually on the defensive, their failure had been largely due to the tumult that resulted from the murder. The rioting was certain to come to an end, and they could then have made another appeal to the senate and the people, as well as to the veterans, and might have been more successful, if they had not made the mistake of sparing Antony. The latter had fled when Caesar was struck down. Disguised as a slave, according to the story, he had first remained hidden in a friend's house, and had later reached his own dwelling, which he garrisoned with his slaves and clients. He was soon able to make arrangements looking to the future. From Caesar's widow he secured possession of the late dictator's papers and official accounts, as well as of his private moneys, which are said to have amounted to four thousand talents, or approximately four million dollars. He also seized the state treasure of some thirty-five million dollars, which had been kept in the temple of Ops. His prospects both of safety and power were now far better than those of the assassins. As consul, he was legally at the head of the government; as the representative of Caesar, he could appeal to the veterans, strengthening his appeal with his immense treasure. And he was presently aided by one other circumstance. The only soldiers stationed in Rome were under the command of Lepidus, who had been Caesar's master of horse. Appointed by Caesar to the governorship of Hither Gaul, Lepidus had enlisted a legion for service in the province. With this legion he occupied the forum, probably during the night following Caesar's death, and thus became for the moment master of Rome. He was intensely hostile to the assassins, and, being a man of weak character, he allowed himself to become the tool of Antony.

The conspirators in the meanwhile had accomplished nothing. Several prominent men had come to consult with them in the Capitol, willing in this way to express their public approval of the assassination. Dolabella was among these. He had been chosen by Caesar to hold the consulship during the months of. this year that would remain after Caesar should have departed for Parthia, but Antony had as augur interfered with Dolabella's election. As consul-elect and the opponent of Antony, Dolabella was therefore an important adherent. Cicero also had joined the assassins. Seeing the need of immediate action, he had urged that the senate be summoned to meet on the Capitol. Though Antony, as sole consul, was the only person who could constitutionally summon such a meeting, this was not a time for the observance of legality. Dolabella might have issued the summons with a fair appearance of decency; it could have been done by Brutus or Cassius, who were praetors. The senators, as later events showed, were in sympathy with the conspirators. They might have come together, and so given their sanction to the new order of things, and this action might have had some influence with the populace; but the senate was not summoned. Cicero also insisted on a new appeal to the people; and such an appeal was made on the next day. But Brutus, the orator, declaimed about the tyranny of Caesar, which had not borne very heavily on the veterans; he compared Caesar's death to the expulsion of the tyrants; he demanded the return to Rome of those Caesar had exiled, for whom the people could scarcely he expected to care; he very nearly identified his cause with that of a mere political party by championing the rights of Sextus Pompey, who had remained in revolt against the state since the death of his father, Pompey the Great; and, above all, Brutus failed to put any patriotic ardor into his speech, such as would have answered to the needs of the moment. He spoke like a philosopher, and we are told that the people listened with deference, but without enthusiasm.[4]

There was now nothing to do but to negotiate with Antony and his supporters; but the result of these negotiations were not comforting. Decimus Brutus had by Caesar been appointed to Cisalpine Gaul and wished to go to this province. The assassins, having failed to gain a following in Rome, must look abroad; if Decimus Brutus could hold Cisalpine Gaul with an army, this would give strength to the tyrannicides, for, with the exception of Lepidus' legion, Decimus' army would thus be the military force nearest Rome. But Antony declared that Decimus must not go to Gaul. Antony also gave it as his opinion that in

---

[4] Brutus later wished to publish this oration as a pamphlet and asked Cicero first to criticise it "candidly," but Cicero found it too tame and could do nothing with it (*Att.* 15, 1b, 2). About the same time Atticus asked Cicero to write a speech for Brutus to deliver at a public meeting, but Cicero would not undertake it, and mentioned that when he had written an edict for Brutus, at Atticus' request, Brutus had preferred his own (*Att.* 14, 20, 3). These two letters contain other matters as well which are interesting as comments on Brutus' "Attic" oratory.

view of the attitude of the veterans and the populace in Rome the city was not a safe place for the assassins. Other matters were discussed, all indicating that the assassins were not only on the defensive but even in danger.[5]

After two days of chaos the senate met, on the seventeenth, but it was Antony who had issued the summons. Outside the temple of Earth, in which the meeting took place, were the populace, Caesar's veterans, and Lepidus' legion. The assassins were not present. Antony presided. By his side sat Dolabella, also in consular garb; and Antony wisely made no objection. Among the senators was Cicero, but he had come unwillingly, not expecting anything very favorable to the republic. The debate was long. Some of the senators ventured to move that the assassins receive thanks and rewards for their deed, and the people outside, it is said, when an attempt was made to enlist their sympathies for Antony and his partisans, refused to interfere; two circumstances which indicate that a more strenuous effort on the part of the assassins to win support, as Cicero had urged, might have altered the situation to a considerable degree. Now, however, it was too late. The assassins could hope for nothing beyond their personal safety, and were glad to make a compromise. Nor was this rejected by Antony. He and Lepidus had the upper hand, but they were not sufficiently sure of their power to dictate harsh terms. Cicero acted as the mediator. The assassins were not to be held accountable for their crime, but Caesar's acts were to remain in force, while his will was to be opened and read in public and his body was to receive the honor of a public funeral. The veterans were not forgotten, for both the Antonians and the liberators hoped for their ultimate support; it was decided that the colonies planned for them by Caesar should be founded. In passing these measures, the two hostile parties pretended to be actuated by a desire for peace

---

[5] A very vivid picture of the situation is found in a letter addressed by Decimus Brutus to Marcus Brutus and Cassius, probably on the morning of March 17 (*Fam.* 11, 1).

and concord, and the touching act of patriotic conciliation was celebrated in the evening when Brutus dined with Lepidus, and Cassius with Antony. The two tyrannicides, however, had not thought it safe to descend from their fortified aerie on the Capitol until they had received hostages; Antony's son is reported to have been one of these.

The compromise had, in Cicero's words, laid a foundation for peace, but neither he nor any one else expected ever to erect a temple on it. The republic had been restored, but it was under the shadow of Caesar's dictatorship; Caesar himself had by the honor of a public funeral been declared the benefactor of Rome. Antony had the favor of the veterans and the support of Lepidus' legion; he had money; he was at the head of the state; and he had possession of Caesar's papers, of which he presently made good use. He had also strengthened his position by recognizing Dolabella as consul and by securing to Lepidus the office of chief pontiff, made vacant by Caesar's death. The assassins, on the other hand, were safe from criminal prosecution, but their lives were in danger. Antony had already advised them that they were remaining in Rome at their own risk. The truth of his advice became alarmingly clear at the reading of the will and at Caesar's funeral. When the will was opened, it was discovered that Caesar had left three hundred sesterces to each and every citizen and had donated his gardens on the right bank of the Tiber to the public for a park. Octavius, his sister's grandson, had been adopted as his son and was the chief heir, but among the second heirs, those who were to inherit in case the first or real heirs failed to accept, was Decimus Brutus, who had been one of the chief plotters against Caesar's life. Emotions of gratitude to the late dictator and of intense hatred against his assassins were thus aroused, and these were cleverly fanned into flame by Antony's dramatic management of the funeral and his exceedingly astute eulogy of Caesar. A serious riot ensued. The crowd rushed through the streets with firebrands to ignite the houses of the assassins. Brutus and Cassius had enough armed men to protect themselves, but the house of one assassin was burned, and a harmless citizen, who was mistaken for an assassin, was murdered.

The fate of the tyrannicides was now sealed in so far as the city was concerned. Decimus Brutus departed for Cisalpine Gaul, and Trebonius set out for Asia, to take possession of these provinces, for which they had been destined by Caesar. The other assassins slipped out of Rome, and skulked about in various hiding-places. The senate continued to meet, but though Antony was not unquestionably supreme, there was no opportunity for independent action by republicans like Cicero. For some three weeks Cicero lingered in the city, but on the seventh of April he was on his way to his Tusculan villa. From this time on, for several months, there was nothing that Cicero could accomplish. He lived now at one villa and now at another; he wrote a good deal, but no longer professed, as he had done during the period of Caesar's sovereignty, that he was finding happiness in writing; the wonder is that he could write at all. All his thoughts were engaged with the rumors and messages that came to him from Rome, from other places in Italy, and from the provinces. He also had meetings with many men, always discussing the political situation, and he was in direct, though not in frequent, communication with the assassins. The extant letters written by him or to him were very numerous; one quarter of the whole correspondence belongs to the year and a half after Caesar's death. But the letters of the first few months after the assassination are only a record of disappointments, hopelessness, and disgust.

These months witnessed the gradual but constant rise to power of Antony. At first he had need to be conciliatory, and we hear that he made a motion to abolish the dictatorship, which was, of course, unanimously carried. His real power, nevertheless, was not disguised. It rested on the veterans, who seem to have been devoted to him, whereas they detested the assassins and had no confidence in those who championed a republic with the senate in the chief place. When riots occurred in Rome, Antony seized the opportunity to declare that his life was imperiled, and by this means he seems to have secured permission to enroll a bodyguard. This troop, which consisted of veterans, was gradually increased to six thousand men. With them Antony ruled Rome. The constitutional means by which he established and extended his power consisted of Caesar's papers. There can be no doubt that these contained plans for making changes, but, what they did not contain, Antony seems to have inserted. Caesar's former secretary is reported to have made any additions Antony desired. The senate tried to interfere, interpreting the confirmation of Caesar's acts as referring only to those that had actually been published before the Ides; they also decreed that on June first a commission should examine Caesar's papers, but their decree led to nothing since the commission consisted of Dolabella and Antony himself. With a show of piously carrying out Caesar's intentions, Antony plunged into an orgy of legislation. Immunities from taxation were granted, forged decrees were passed, exiles were recalled, Roman citizenship was given to whole communities, petty sovereigns in distant countries were confirmed; and for all this Antony received money. "Caesar is dead," wrote Cicero, "but Rome is ruled by his nod." And when Antony felt tolerably secure of his power in the city, he departed on a tour through Campania, where he founded colonies for veterans and won the favor of those who were already settled there.

Antony thus dominated Rome and central Italy, and there was no means of opposing him. The senate was overawed by his bodyguard. It also contained a minority who were his supporters, while its more independent members had left the city. The populace occasionally showed a preference for the friends of the assassins, but, as Cicero put it, they used up their energy in applause. Outside of Rome things were scarcely better. There was exultant joy in some of the municipal towns; people rushed eagerly to hear Cicero speak of the regained liberty of the state. Cicero had many visitors. Some of these, like Hirtius and Pansa, the consuls-elect for the next year, were not friends of Antony, but they would, or could, do nothing; they desired peace, so that they might without molestation enter upon their offices at the end of the year. Nor were they heartily in favor of the assassins. They were Caesarians, but neither Antonians nor republicans. Cicero was on intimate terms with them, even giving them lessons in declamation; and he did his best to win their adherence for the assassins. The latter both Cicero and others praised highly. Cicero called them heroes, liberators, tyrannicides; but presently he was punning on the name of Brutus as though Marcus and Decimus had acted like stupid brutes. Perhaps this appellation was partly deserved. Brutus and Cassius issued edicts, which had no effect. Brutus published the uninspired oration he had delivered to the people shortly after the assassination. He was forever hoping for peace with Antony. One day he thought he might safely return to Rome; on another, he was meditating exile. Neither he nor any other republican had reason for a cheerful view of the future. While Antony was in Campania, riots took place in Rome; Dolabella suppressed them with severity, and this was looked upon by Cicero as a good omen for future peace. At Atticus' advice, he wrote his congratulations to his former son-in-law; he was very complimentary,[6] for there was yet a forlorn hope that Dolabella would side with the republicans against Antony.

A new element was injected into the situation by the landing in Italy of Octavius, the adopted son and chief heir of Caesar. During nearly six months before Caesar's death the young man had been living in Apollonia in Macedonia. He had been sent

---

6 Letter to Dolabella, *Att.* 14, 17a (*Fam.* 9, 14). For Cicero's comments on it, see *Att.* 14, 19, 4; 14, 18, 1.

there, by the order of Caesar, his great-uncle, to continue his studies, for he was only eighteen years old, and to get some military training. Caesar had stationed six legions in Macedonia, which he meant to employ in his campaign against the Parthians. When the news of Caesar's death reached Apollonia, the people of the city offered their support to Octavius, and the officers and some soldiers of the legions volunteered either to protect him or to assist him in avenging the murder. Octavius refused their assistance for the time being, but asked them not to forget their offer in the future. He then went to Italy to claim his inheritance. He did not dare to land at Brundisium, which was the busiest Italian harbor on the Adriatic and had a garrison, but when he had received more complete information about the murder, after he had landed, he visited Brundisium, and here the soldiers, like the soldiers in Macedonia, greeted him as the son of Caesar. This was important for the future. Octavius thereupon started slowly toward Rome.

Cicero did not fail to realize the political possibilities involved in Octavius' arrival. Hearing of his landing, he wondered anxiously whether a great number of Caesarians were flocking to meet him and whether he would be likely to attempt a coup. For the moment this did not seem likely. Octavius in the meantime traveled northward. Cicero heard that he had arrived in Naples on the eighteenth of April, and a few days later Cicero himself met him. Octavius, who was born in the year of Cicero's consulship, treated the old consular with every mark of respect, but Cicero could not bring himself to look upon the young man as the heir and successor of Caesar. By accepting the adoption of Caesar, Octavius would take his adopted father's name, only retaining a modified form of his own, thus becoming Gaius Iulius Caesar Octavianus. Following the lead of Octavius' stepfather, Cicero nevertheless addressed the young man as Octavius. To address him otherwise would have been virtually to acknowledge any claim to power that Octavius might put forward in his capacity of Caesar's son. And Cicero had his fears, for Octavius was surrounded by a large number of avowed Caesarians, who threatened the assassins with the severest reprisals. Octavius gave indication that he meant not to renounce the position offered him by Caesar, saying that "the present state of things was intolerable." Cicero's only consolation was the thought that Octavius would cause trouble to Antony; and he wondered what would happen when "the boy" came to Rome.

Octavius proceeded slowly to the city, probably forming connections on the way with veterans of Caesar settled in the region, and after reaching Rome during Antony's absence in Campania, he made a public declaration, according to law, before the praetor that he would accept the inheritance. This he did contrary to the advice of his mother Atia and his step-father Philippus. In order to get the adoption completed, it was necessary to have a law passed by the curiate assembly. He was therefore introduced to the people at a public meeting as Caesar, by a tribune, and made a speech in which he eulogized Caesar, and promised to pay Caesar's legacies to the people. He was extremely well received.

Antony now returned to Rome from his tour among the veterans in Campania, and it is very likely that his return was hastened by the presence in Rome of the young Caesar. What-ever Octavius' natural attitude of hostility might be toward the assassins of Caesar, who were Antony's chief opponents, Octavius had arrived in Rome to claim his inheritance, and Antony had already inherited Caesar. He had taken Caesar's money, and he had taken as much of Caesar's power as he could lay hands on. He was neither able nor willing to pay Octavius Caesar's money, and he had no desire to give Octavius an oppor-tunity to become his political rival. Cicero had called Octavius a boy; Antony treated him as a boy, and even threatened him. Octavius could get no concessions from Antony; Antony hindered the passing of the curiate law, which would complete Octavius' adoption, and he caused him annoyance in other ways. But Octavius, whose resources seem to have been considerable, and who was assisted by friends and relatives, paid Caesar's legacies, and gave games in Caesar's honor, thus increasing his popularity among the people and the veterans. On the tenth of June Cicero wrote[7] to Atticus about Octavius, for the first time giving him the name of Caesar's son, that is, Octavian. Cicero remarked that Octavian had talents and spirit, and that he seemed as well disposed as could be wished to the "heroes." But Cicero thought it well worth considering what trust could be placed in him, in view of his youth, his name, his inheritance, and his education. Cicero quoted Octavian's own stepfather to the effect that the young man could not be trusted, and he ended his brief but shrewd characterization of the young Caesar by saying that efforts must be made to keep him on the side of the republicans, "to foster him," and above all to separate him from Antony.

Antony's position, while for the present unassailable, was precarious. In the city he was master by means of his body-guard, and perhaps did not greatly fear Octavian's growing popularity; and the tyrannicides who were hiding in Italy, were not dangerous. Trebonius, the assassin who had gone to Asia, would doubtless secure a military force, but Asia was far away. Decimus Brutus, however, was growing powerful in Cisalpine Gaul, and in the western Mediterranean was Sextus Pompey. The latter seems already to have won some successes against Asinius Pollio, the governor of Further Spain; he had a navy and threatened Italy with invasion. Indeed, the interference by Sextus had been feared since the days immediately after Caesar's death; and the war cloud had been growing darker. Sextus was in communication with the assassins, but he was also negotiating with Antony. Though the latter had earlier in the year per-suaded Lepidus to go to his provinces, Narbonese Gaul and

[7] *Att.* 15, 12.

Hither Spain, for the purpose of winning over Sextus, the result of Lepidus' undertaking seems still to have been uncertain. Antony, on the other hand, had no army. It seems likely that Macedonia had been intended for him by Caesar, and Syria for Dolabella, but even if they secured these provinces at the end of the year, their position would be far from favorable; they would be farther from Rome than Decimus, and the tenure of their governorships would be only two years. Antony therefore determined to take drastic measures. His first acts after the assassination of Caesar had been dictated largely by a sense of self-preservation, though, as was seen from the conspirators' decision to spare him, he had been in no real danger. The way to unbounded power had suddenly opened before him, and he had followed it. During the subsequent months he had made so many enemies that, even if he had been inclined not to seize more illegal power, he could not draw back now.

On the first of June and the days following he carried out his plan. Rumors of his intention to seize Cisalpine and Transalpine Gaul had long been heard; immediately after the assassination he had forbidden Decimus Brutus to go to Cisalpine Gaul. He now filled the city with veterans; neither the assassins, nor Cicero, nor even Hirtius dared to come to Rome. As the senate seems still to have shown some signs of independence, due perhaps to the presence of Octavian, Antony acted through the assembly. The two Gauls were assigned to him for the illegal period of six years, including the current year. This gave him a legal excuse for making war on Decimus. The six years, furthermore, would establish him in a position not unlike that held by Caesar after his Gallic campaigns. Dolabella received Syria, also for six years; and was thus won over definitely to the side of Antony. As governor of Syria, which bordered on Parthia, Dolabella might claim the six legions stationed in Macedonia for Caesar's Parthian campaign. Arrangement was therefore made so that Dolabella should be satisfied with one legion, another should remain in Macedonia, and the four remaining legions should be given to Antony for service in the Gauls—that is, to fight against Decimus. Marcus Brutus and Cassius were assigned each to an insignificant province, though, according to one story, Caesar had destined them for Macedonia and Syria respectively. They were also appointed to have charge of procuring grain for the city, Brutus in Asia and Cassius in Sicily, but without such sweeping powers as would place them above the governors of these provinces. The intention was obviously to get them out of Italy with the least amount of trouble.

By these measures Antony proclaimed without dissimulation that he meant to make himself master of the Roman world. The situation of the assassins became utterly hopeless, and was presently made worse, if possible, by the rumor that Sextus Pompey had sided with Antony. It is, therefore, from the first of June that Cicero later dated the beginning of Antony's usurpation. Many of his acts before that date had been subversive of law and order, but, compared with the measures which were passed on the first of June—so Cicero said in the *First Philippic,* which was delivered on the second of September—they had been harmless; Antony and Dolabella had until then almost deserved to be called law-abiding.

The immediate effect of Antony's measures on the leaders of the republicans, Brutus and Cassius, is seen in a conference[8] Cicero had with them at Antium on the eighth of June. Several persons were present, including three ladies of Brutus' family, his mother, his second wife, and his half-sister, who was married to Cassius. Brutus talked about going to Rome, and Cicero had to remind him that he could not do so with safety. As·praetor, Brutus was to give some games, from which he expected much in the way of popular enthusiasm, but it was finally settled that Brutus should stay away from Rome, though the games would be given at his expense. The grain commission to Asia at first

---

[8] See *Att.* 15, 11 and 12.

seemed to Brutus an insult, but he presently came to look upon
it as his only respectable opportunity for leaving Rome; indeed,
two days after the conference he was busy collecting vessels for
the voyage, though he talked tragically about the matter. Cassius, more fiery than Brutus, angrily rejected his commission,
which would have taken him to Sicily, and proclaimed that he
would go to Achaia. This plan, on which he did not seem
absolutely determined at the end of the conference, meant preparation for future war against Antony. Both Brutus and Cassius
were bitter in their regrets and their reproaches; many opportunities for opposing Antony, they said, had been missed;
especially had Decimus Brutus been negligent, who ought to have
come to Italy with his northern army. As a matter of fact,
Decimus was waging war against native tribes, doubtless to give
his legions some very essential training, for a large number of
his soldiers were raw recruits; altogether it seems that Decimus
was the only conspirator who thus far had acted with promptness, prudence, and a certain measure of success. In the course
of the long conversation at Antium there was much talk of the
past. Cicero observed that nothing could be gained by harping
on the past, thus making use of an expression that characterized
his later efforts;[9] but he did say that one great mistake had been
made at the beginning, in that the senate had not been
summoned and no adequate effort had been made to profit by
the popular enthusiasm which ensued upon the assassination,
whereas it had been of supreme importance to get the governmental machinery running at once. Cicero refrained, however,
from repeating a remark with which he had earlier put his
finger on the weakness of the conspirators' plans: that Antony
should have been taken out of the way at the same time as
Caesar; all the trouble had come from Antony. It was a discouraging conference, Cicero wrote to Atticus. Going down to
Antium, Cicero had been considering carefully what he ought to
say; after the conference was finished, he could only feel that

---

[9] See below, pp. 633, 645.

he had done his duty as a friend and an adviser: "I found the ship of state going to pieces or rather already in fragments."

The discouraging interview with Brutus and Cassius revived in Cicero a thought that he had had for a long time, that of going to Greece. As early as the middle of April he had written to Atticus that he wished to go away in July. He was now in a position to leave Italy with all the dignity of a Roman of high rank. Dolabella had appointed him a legate on the second of June, at the very time when Antony's revolutionary measures were being pushed through in Rome; and the legateship was in every way suitable. Its terms left Cicero free to leave Italy and to return whenever he should choose; it imposed no duties upon him; and it would last for the whole period of Dolabella's governorship of Syria. The relations between Cicero and his former son-in-law had been on the whole satisfactory during the year. · Dolabella was inexcusably dilatory in repaying Tullia's dowry, and Cicero, whose circumstances were straitened, had written to the young man very sharply about this. Dolabella had also disappointed Cicero's hope that he would side with the republicans. There had, nevertheless, been no break between the two men, and Dolabella had now shown his friendliness in the matter of the legateship.

Nor did Antony make any objection to Cicero's departure. He and Cicero had known each other for several years, not always pleasantly, but without open enmity. Though after Caesar's death they were inevitably on opposite sides, they had preserved their old relation of outward respect and friendship. Both Antony and his brother had gone out of their way to please Cicero. On one occasion, for example, Antony had in the most polite language requested Cicero's approval of his intention to recall from exile a freedman of Cicero's late enemy, Clodius. Antony had married Clodius' widow. He explained to Cicero that Cicero's friendliness in the matter, which would be a sign that old enmities were forgotten, would give great pleasure both

to Antony and to Clodius' son; Antony would not recall the
man if Cicero objected. Cicero gave his approval in the most
cordial terms. But all this mutual politeness and flattery was
only a farce; Cicero wrote to Atticus that he was certain that
Antony would have carried out his purpose under any circumstances.[10] Antony's deference was due to a realization of Cicero's
political influence; he could scarcely hope to gain Cicero's support, but he was determined not to break with him openly. In
all likelihood Antony welcomed Cicero's desire to go to Greece;
it would remove one possible source of trouble.

Cicero had long wished to visit his son in Athens. The young
man was spending his generous allowance as befitted the son
of a great consular, but it was not so obvious that he was working
very hard. Early in June, to be sure, Cicero received a letter
from him which showed an improvement in style, and was indeed
well written, as Cicero informed Atticus. There were, however,
varying reports both from friends and from the son's teachers;
in reference to one account of Marcus, which was highly eulogistic, Cicero said that, even if he was deceived, he was glad
to be credulous. It should perhaps be added that young Marcus
was glad to profit by his father's willing credulity. Two or three
months later he wrote a letter[11] to Tiro, obviously for careful
transmission to Cicero. Marcus, Tiro is told, has just been greatly
delighted by a letter from his affectionate father, and now his
joy has been made complete by a few lines from Tiro. He thanks
Tiro for publishing his good fame, and will strive to increase it
as the days go by. And much more to the same effect, including
a most entrancing picture of Marcus' industry and his intimate
relations with one of his admirable teachers. Evidently Marcus
might profit by a visit from his father.

The political situation in Rome, however, was Cicero's chief
reason for planning his trip, as it was also his chief reason for
hesitating to go. While it was still possible that Sextus Pompey

---

[10] *Att.* 14, 13a; 14, 13b. See also 14, 13, 6; 14, 19, 2.
[11] *Fam.* 16, 21.

might invade Italy, Cicero had desired to be out of the way; he could do nothing in a civil war, and this war promised to be such that nobody would be allowed to remain neutral. "I go away," he wrote to Atticus, "to meet a better kind of death than would come to me here." He had remained in Italy with a vague hope that an opportunity would present itself for him to take some part in politics; if anything was to be done, he would be ashamed to be absent from his post. But the changes brought about on the first of June precluded any possibility of political action. The first of January, when Antony would no longer be consul, would present the earliest opportunity, and Cicero, in deciding to leave Italy, made clear to every one that he meant to return before that date. Atticus and other friends approved thoroughly of his decision. And yet, since nothing could be accomplished on the first of January, except through war, Cicero found it ridiculous that he was going away while Rome still had peace, only to return when there would be war.

Cicero also shrank from the fatigue of a sea voyage at his time of life; he heard with some apprehension that the pirates were still hovering about Italy; and he was very loath to be separated from Atticus. Up to the last day before his going he would have preferred to remain, provided, as he wrote to 'Atticus, he could have remained in safety; and when he learned from his friend that the latter had wept after bidding farewell to him, he wrote back that, if Atticus had wept in his presence, he would perhaps even then have given up his trip. He thought for a little while of accompanying Brutus, who was preparing to go to the East, but Brutus could not get ready; he was still expecting some favorable turn in the political situation. And when Cicero was at last about to go, one of his freedmen caused a delay by some mismanagement of his affairs.

Cicero's perplexity arose from the fact that he could see no clear path of duty before him; he loved Rome too much to leave her while there was the slightest chance of his accomplishing anything for her betterment, and he decided to withdraw in order to escape the sight of an arbitrary and lawless government. But no worries quite deprived him of his inexhaustible resiliency. Going to Astura, toward the middle of June, he found great enjoyment in the natural beauty of the little place, the more as he could there be alone and write, if he pleased. He was at that time deeply vexed by the appointment of Brutus as a grain commissioner, which he looked upon as a deliberate insult, and yet he wrote to Atticus that it would perhaps be better for Brutus to undertake the commission than to sit idly by the banks of Eurotas, explaining that Eurotas was a stream on Brutus' estate in Lanuvium. "Can you laugh in reference to such matters?" he makes Atticus ask. "What shall I do? I am tired of finding fault." While in the midst of preparations for his voyage, he turned to philosophical writing, probably the *De Officiis;* and he was planning further work. On the day of his departure he sent Atticus a revised copy of his essay on Glory. "Have it copied on large paper," he wrote,[12] "and read it to your guests, but if you love me, make them first cheerful with a good dinner, so that they do not vent their spleen on my writing when they are really annoyed with you." Atticus was parsimonious, and had been known to serve cheap dinners on expensive plate. This letter, however, is not all equally light-hearted. It ends with love and kisses for Atticus' wife and daughter.

Cicero departed from Pompeii on the seventeenth of July with three ten-oared vessels. Like Octavian when he landed in Italy, Cicero in leaving had decided to avoid Brundisium, though the voyage from this port would have been shorter; he did not wish to encounter the legions that were expected from Macedonia. The voyage down the coast was slow, for, as there was little wind, the oars had to be used. In Velia he borrowed a

---

[12] *Att.* 16, 3, 1.

Greek book *On Overeating,* and remarked in a letter[13] that
he was an apt pupil of the teaching it contained. He was staying at the house of Trebatius, the jurisconsult, who was then in
Rome. Trebatius had been thinking of selling his house in
Velia, and Cicero urged him not to do so. Another house belonging to Trebatius had a lotus tree which attracted tourists. Cicero
advised that it be cut down, so as to improve the view. He had
once promised the young lawyer to explain to him the nature of
Aristotle's Topics. As he coasted down from Velia, therefore,
he wrote the *Topica,* which is still extant. It was a habit of
Cicero's to glance over his own books. On board ship he now
read his *Academica,*[14] and discovered that the third book was
introduced with a preface which he had recently prefixed to
the essay on Glory. He wrote a new preface and despatched it
to Atticus. Cicero was trying to forget his unwillingness to leave
Rome. Atticus had written that his departure was being
"lauded to the skies" on the understanding that he would return
before the first of January. "That I shall certainly try to do,"
he answered. "I would rather be in Rome in fear, than in your
beloved Athens without fear."

II

Philippics

Cicero was not destined to reach Greece. He arrived in
Syracuse on the first of August and put to sea on the following
day, but contrary winds drove him to Italy. He set out a second
time, and was again driven back. While he was waiting for
better weather at a friend's house not far from Rhegium, a
number of prominent citizens came from this place to visit him.
Some of them, who had just returned from Rome, brought with
them a copy of a speech delivered by Antony at a public meeting,

---

[13] *Fam.* 7, 20. See above, pp. 97–98.
[14] *Att.* 16, 6, 4. This preface is not extant.

which was very satisfactory from Cicero's point of view, and they also enthusiastically informed Cicero that everything in the city held promise of a return to peaceful methods. Antony, they said, had given up his plan of taking the Gallic provinces and would bow to the authority of the senate. It was expected that the meeting of the senate scheduled for the first of September would be of extraordinary importance; Brutus and Cassius were requesting all ex-consuls and ex-praetors to be present.

Cicero started at once for Rome. He had intended under any circumstances to be back in the city by the first of January, when, under the presidency of the new consuls, Hirtius and Pansa, the senate would be freed from Antony's military tyranny and might take measures for the reëstablishment of normal conditions. If the opportunity for senatorial action was to come on the first of September, Cicero felt that it was his duty, as it was also in accord with his desires, to be present on that date. His absence, furthermore, might arouse unfavorable comment, for he was recognized as a leader and a patriot. The unfavorable comment had indeed already begun. At this time he received a letter from Atticus. This prudent gentleman, who always counseled caution, and who with others had thoroughly approved of Cicero's projected visit to Greece, now wrote about his absence in a petulant spirit, accusing Cicero of abandoning his country and requesting him to draw up a formal statement of his reasons for leaving Rome. Evidently things looked for the moment so bright that people began to wonder why Cicero was going to Greece, and Atticus, in his anxiety for Cicero's good name, came to think that Cicero ought not to have gone away. Cicero replied to Atticus while traveling toward the capital.[15]

On his way, he also met Brutus, who was delighted that Cicero had not proceeded to Greece. His absence would have indicated that he despaired of the republic, or was so indifferent

---

[15] *Att.* 16, 7.

that he thought only of his own amusement, for, according to one rumor, he had intended to go to Olympia for the games. Brutus regretted that Cicero had not been in Rome on the first of August, for on that day opposition to Antony had been voiced in the senate by Piso, the consul of 58 B.C., against whom Cicero had delivered one of his most bitter invectives. Brutus' news was by no means altogether encouraging. He did not know whether Piso had secured a following, nor whether he had subsequently dared to face Antony in the senate. Neither was Cicero heartened by the activities of Brutus and Cassius, the republican leaders, who were expending their energy in issuing edicts, which seemed futile to Cicero, since they had no physical force behind them. This was the last time that Cicero saw Brutus, who left Italy for Greece a few weeks later. Cicero went on to Rome. He had little hope of finding it possible to accomplish anything there, but he told himself that he would look after his financial obligations. The money market was getting tight, and Cicero's affairs were in a wretched condition.

Cicero reached Rome on the last of August. Though he did not expect at once to take a prominent part in politics, he could not have failed to realize that his mere arrival in the city would have a remarkable effect. He had not been in Rome since the few days of tumult that ensued after the assassination of Caesar, and by setting out for Greece he had virtually announced that for the time being he had renounced politics, and yet it was he who had proposed the compromise between the Antonians and the republicans early in the year, and he was known not only as the most distinguished ex-consul living but also as an avowed friend of the assassins. His arrival caused the commotion that he must have foreseen. The people flocked to meet him in such numbers, we are told, that it took him nearly the whole day to make his way from the city gate to his house; and Antony decided at once to have it clearly understood whether Cicero was to be counted among his enemies or his friends.

Antony was not in a mood for conciliation or for submission to senatorial authority. Any slight signs of yielding that he may have shown, as well as the temerity of Piso in his fruitless opposition to Antony on the first of August, had been due no doubt to the popularity of Octavian, which for a little while may have made Antony's position seem precarious; but when Cicero returned to Rome, Antony still had the upper hand. He was expected soon to go to southern Italy to take command of the four legions that had been summoned from Macedonia, which, with his large bodyguard, would make him the undisputed master of Rome, and he was bidding for popularity by the introduction of two important measures, which seem to have been passed in September. One of these measures, intended to win the support of the veterans, provided that one third of the jurors in the standing courts should be drawn from a panel consisting of the centurions and soldiers of the legion Alauda; the other measure, which was addressed to the prejudices of the common people, allowed an appeal from the courts to the popular assembly in cases of public violence and of treason. Besides these subversive proposals, he was going to bring before the senate on the first of September, the day after Cicero's arrival, a motion that in all public thanksgivings a day should be added in honor of the deified Caesar. This proposal had for aim to attract the Caesarians.

Cicero decided not to attend the meeting on the first. He was opposed to the extraordinary honor proposed for Caesar, and he was probably unwilling to appear in the senate, where he would be forced to take sides for or against Antony, while he was tired from his journey and before he had had time to inform himself thoroughly in regard to public opinion. As a matter of courtesy, he sent word to Antony that he would not attend; he needed rest after his journey. A consul had the right to coerce senators to attend meetings if the occasion seemed to require their presence. Antony, therefore, who was determined to force Cicero to make a political decision, declared[16] angrily in the senate that he would take some carpenters with him and go to tear down Cicero's house if he did not come to the meeting. Antony's outburst was the first act of open hos-- tility during the year between the two men.

Cicero did not attend the meeting of the first, but he was present on the following day, when Dolabella presided and Antony had gone to his villa. Cicero explained[17] the reasons for his departure from Italy, remembering perhaps Atticus' advice that he draw up a formal statement. He said that the events in Rome up to the first of June had made him hope for the restoration of the republic, but that Antony's measures in June had shattered this hope. The senate had been frightened into inaction, the populace had become revolutionary, and the veterans had become insolent. Cicero had therefore left Rome, finding no opportunity for accomplishing anything for the state, but he had intended to return by the first of January, when the senate would meet under new magistrates. After he had been accidentally prevented from continuing his journey, good news about Antony had led him to set out for Rome, he said, and he had proceeded to the city in spite of later information from Brutus, to the effect that Antony had not fulfilled his promise to yield obedience to the senate on the first of August.

Cicero protested against Antony's violence of the day before. Fatigue had prevented Cicero from attending the senate; the meeting was not so important that Antony had a reason for

---

[16] *Phil.* 1, 12.

[17] In the *First Philippic*. The *Philippics* seem to have received their name by accident. The *Fifth* and the *Tenth* had been sent to M. Brutus, and Cicero had in jest referred to them as Philippics, the name given to Demosthenes' speeches against Philip of Macedon, which were held to be masterpieces of political invective. Brutus approved of Cicero's reference (*Ad Brut.* 2, 3 (5), 4; 2, 4, 2), and the name became attached to all the speeches delivered during Cicero's struggle with Antony. Fourteen of them are extant, but there were others. Fragments are quoted from a *Sixteenth Philippic.* See also below, p. 653, for a lost *Philippic.* Gellius refers to them as *Orationes Antonianae* in a way that might indicate this to have been the accepted name.

indulging in threats; and, indeed, if Cicero had been present, he would not have voted for Antony's motion. Cicero complimented his old enemy Piso on the stand he had taken against Antony on the first of August, expressing his regret that he had not been present; in that case, he said, there would have been at least one consular whom fear and personal considerations could not prevent from upholding the senatorial dignity. He hoped that the senators would listen with their usual consideration to what he had further to say, even though they should lack the courage to adopt his views; and he thereupon gave it as his opinion that Caesar's acts should be maintained, not because he approved of them but because they were essential to peace. But by Caesar's acts he did not mean the subversive measures published by Antony; he could in no way approve of Antony's proposal to establish a jury panel of soldiers and to allow an appeal from the courts to the people.

Cicero avowed feelings of friendship for the two consuls; he still believed that they had acted from a mistaken desire for glory, he said, and not from an unlawful craving for money and power. He complimented Dolabella warmly on the fact that he had restored order in Rome during Antony's absence in Campania; and he praised Antony for his behavior after the assassination, particularly because he had abolished the dictatorship. But as he approached the end of his speech, he warned Antony against adopting for a motto the line from an old play which read to this effect: "Let men hate, provided they fear." This line Cicero was soon to quote in his work on Duty, where he wrote of Caesar that it is the most gifted men who are particularly tempted to do wrong by a desire for fame. He called upon Antony to remember his grandfather, the famous orator Marcus Antonius, who had befriended Cicero in his youth, and about whom Cicero had often spoken to Antony. And especially, Cicero continued with sudden grimness, ought Antony to be warned by the fate of Caesar; no man is happy if his murderers are able not merely to remain unpunished but even to reap glory from their deed. Cicero finally concluded with the promise that he would speak again in the senate if that could be done with safety both to the senate and to himself. He had had enough of years and glory, he said, just as Caesar had said before him; any time still remaining to him he would devote to the senate and the state.

Cicero's speech was calm and dignified; he had come to the senate, as he also declared while speaking, to put his political attitude on record. From the Roman point of view, he had not broken with Antony, for he had refrained from personal vituper-ation, and he had professed himself ready to remain on a friendly footing. But he had spoken with a frankness and a determina-tion that could not fail to indicate his readiness to undertake the leadership in any opposition to Antony that should prove practicable, provided Antony persisted in his autocratic rule. Antony's irritation now flared into open enmity. He formally renounced his friendship with Cicero, and challenged him to appear at a session of the senate which he set for the nineteenth. When this day arrived, however, Antony's soldiers were present to overawe the meeting and Cicero wisely remained at home. Antony delivered a bitter speech against him, in which he reviewed Cicero's whole political career from the conspiracy of Catiline, and accused Cicero of having instigated the assassina-tion of Caesar. The last charge, as Cicero correctly interpreted it, had for aim to turn the veterans from Cicero.

Cicero had done wisely in remaining away from the meeting of the nineteenth. He declared later that Antony had intended to murder him, and this may well have been the case. Antony ruled Rome by means of his huge bodyguard; he had consider-able influence with Caesar's veterans, and he was on the point of starting for Brundisium to take command of the four Mace-donian legions, two of which had already arrived, it seems, while the others were expected at any time. The senators, therefore, who were known as Antony's opponents, did not dare to attend senatorial meetings, and some of them left the city. Brutus set sail for Greece at the end of the month, hoping to create a military force in the East before Antony's growing power should make that impossible. Cicero wrote at this time to Cassius that conditions in Rome were desperate and that no change could be looked for unless Cassius should be able to do something, but that Cicero expected nothing from him; and Cassius was power-- less. He left Italy, also for the East, shortly after Brutus had gone away.

There was still some slight opposition to Antony in the city. On the second of October, a tribune of the people called upon him at a public meeting to express his views about the assassins, and he declared that they were to be punished. It was an embarrassing situation, thus to be forced to break openly with the republicans; and Antony in his anger exclaimed that it was Cicero who had caused the tribune to put the question, and that it was Cicero, indeed, who was also directing the activity of Cassius, that is, of the republicans. On the fifth of October, Antony charged openly that Octavian had tried to bring about his death. The common people, Cicero wrote of this, considered the charge false, and intended merely to justify Antony in taking possession of Octavian's property; but the more prudent believed the charge well founded, and approved of Octavian's attempt. It is no longer possible to decide as to the truth of the matter, but Antony's accusation indicates that the rivalry between him and Caesar's heir had by this time become open hostility. Antony was in a state of extreme irritation. Before starting for Brundisium, he declared publicly that only the victor in the impending struggle would escape death, and he announced that even after the expiration of his consulship he would enter and leave the city at his pleasure. Since Antony would at that time be in command of a provincial army and consequently could not legally enter the city, this declaration was tantamount to an avowal that he meant to make himself absolute ruler. On the ninth of October he left Rome. Cicero remained a little longer and then departed for his villas. He was finishing the so-called *Second Philippic,* his reply to Antony's speech of the nineteenth.

And then a dramatic change came over the situation. Octavian started on a journey through Campania for the purpose of appealing to the Caesarian veterans settled there, and he sent agents to work among the Macedonian legions at Brundisium. Antony's declared enmity, which had culminated in his charge that Octavian had plotted against his life, had made Octavian's position impossible; either he had peacefully to await Antony's return to Rome at the head of a powerful army, and then, with every one else, to submit to whatever treatment Antony should accord him, or else he must seek a decision by arms. He was the only man in Italy for whom the latter alternative was possible; as the heir of Caesar, he had the affection of the soldiers, both of the veterans and the legionaries from Macedonia, and besides, he had the money with which to buy their support.

Octavian's success was phenomenal. The Macedonian legions had offered him their services early in the year, at the time when the news of Caesar's death arrived in Apollonia. Now they were readily influenced by his agents, who distributed pamphlets and promises among them, adding the information that in Campania Octavian was giving each soldier five hundred denarii, about one hundred dollars, whereas Antony was offering only one fifth of this amount at Brundisium. As a result of Octavian's machinations, Antony had trouble with the legions and was forced to resort to military discipline. According to one report, the ringleaders among the mutinous soldiers were arrested, and finally every tenth man was executed. Cicero said that three hundred of the bravest men were cut down. In the meantime Octavian prospered even better in Campania. Everybody was joining his standard; he was received with shouts of

joy, the people of one place coming in procession to meet him as
he was approaching. As early as the first of November, Cicero
heard from him that his force amounted to three thousand.

But Octavian was acting like a rebel in mustering an army
with which to oppose Antony, who was after all consul of Rome.
He could not hope for ultimate success unless the people and
government of Rome gave him their support. He needed an
alliance with the large party who wished to see the reëstablishment of a free republic and who were disgusted with Antony.
But this could be secured only through action of the senate, and
nobody was more likely to succeed in winning the senate for
Octavian than Cicero. Octavian therefore turned to him. He
wrote to Cicero constantly, sometimes more than once a day,
and he sent messengers to him, one of whom was Oppius,[18] the
former adherent of Caesar, who was a friend of Atticus and
who had always had cordial relations with Cicero. But Cicero
had serious apprehensions in reference to the new political situation. He recognized Octavian's high spirit and he appreciated
his influence among the all-important veterans, but he also saw
that these had been won over by the large money reward and
that Octavian was very young and without prestige. In addition
to Cicero's doubt as to Octavian's ability to accomplish anything,
his chief concern was caused by his suspicion of Octavian's good
faith. Octavian was almost inevitably an enemy to the assassins
of his adoptive father, and his political aim could scarcely be the
restoration of the republic since he himself had been chosen by
Caesar to be his successor. Oppius explained that Octavian
would not merely refrain from hostility against the tyrannicides
but would actually become their friend. Cicero, however, was
not persuaded.

Octavian professed his eagerness to follow Cicero's advice.
When he had gathered together three thousand veterans, and it

---

[18] Oppius has been called the shadow of Balbus (Tyrrell, IV, p. lxix).
It was Balbus who acted for Caesar in offering Cicero a place in the triumvirate; now Oppius acts for Caesar's son.

had become known that Antony was on his way from Brundisium with the faithful legion Alauda, while three of the Macedonian legions were marching northward along the Adriatic, Octavian wrote to Cicero inquiring whether he should go to Rome, or hold Capua against Antony, or set out to meet the three legions. Cicero advised him to go to Rome, on the ground that he would secure the support of the people, and possibly of the republicans. Octavian wished to have a secret interview with Cicero at Capua, but Cicero considered secrecy impossible. Apparently Octavian realized that Cicero would not consult with him in a public manner, being unwilling in this way to give his approval to Octavian's position, and he therefore suggested secrecy; but Cicero, who could not have traveled about without causing comment and political speculation, refused to confer with him in person. Octavian also urged Cicero to go to Rome, to lead the senate, but Cicero replied that the senate could not act before the first of January. The reason was, we may surmise, that there were no consuls in Rome to preside; and for the senate to meet under another presidency when one consul, Antony, was on his way to Rome, would be tantamount to a proclamation of civil war. Cicero, indeed, had not sufficient confidence in Octavian to act; he wanted some proof of Octavian's proclaimed change of heart in favor of the assassins, and thought that some proof might be contained in Octavian's attitude toward Casca, one of Caesar's murderers, who would enter on the tribuneship on the tenth of December.

Cicero held himself in readiness to go to Rome, both because he wished to be present if anything of importance was to be undertaken, and because he feared to be cut off in the country by Antony's troops. But in spite of Octavian's urgent messages and in spite of Octavian's success among the veterans, Cicero did not look forward to a prompt participation in politics. Some days after hearing that Octavian had three thousand men, he wrote to Atticus wondering whether the day would ever come

when the *Second Philippic,* his attack on Antony, could be freely
circulated in Rome. He gave much of his time to writing; he
discussed the name of his essay on Duty as well as other literary
matters, in the very letter in which he expressed his view of the
political situation. His opinion, which agreed with that of
Atticus, who urged caution, was that if Octavian should get
much power, the situation would be bad for Brutus, that is, for
the republicans, whereas, if Octavian should be beaten, Antony
would be intolerable. Cicero did not consider Octavian a champion of the republic, although the latter was making efforts to
assume this character, but looked upon the situation as presenting a choice between two evils, submission to Antony or to
Octavian, of which submission to Antony was of course the
greater.[19]

Octavian, in the meantime, went to Rome, perhaps as a
result of Cicero's advice. He addressed the people at a public
meeting, and was well received. He appealed to them as the
successor of Caesar, for he raised his hand to the dictator's
statue, and prayed that "he might attain to the honors of his
parent." Cicero read Octavian's speech, with the comment[20]
that he hoped he would never owe his safety to such as Octavian;
after that, Oppius' arguments had no effect. It is also reported
of Octavian's visit to Rome that when the veterans heard that
they were expected to oppose Antony, there was much grumbling
and many of them returned home under one pretext or another,
but that their places were quickly filled by new men. If this
really occurred, it only proved the truth of Cicero's interpretation of Octavian's success among the veterans: they had sold
their services; at heart they were friendly to Antony no less
than to Octavian.

Antony was hastening toward the city. On the way he had
exacted contributions of money from the municipal towns. He
was marching in military array, and Octavian, who was not

19 *Att.* 16, 14. See also 16, 11.
20 *Att.* 16, 15.

strong enough to meet him, retired to Arretium in Etruria, where he made his camp, his officers training his soldiers and enrolling new recruits. Antony took possession of Rome, but his stay was brief and nothing of importance was accomplished. First came the news that the Martian legion, one of the four from Macedonia, had revolted to Octavian; and soon afterwards it was learned that the Fourth legion had done the same. Antony succeeded in keeping the two remaining Macedonian legions, by offering them the same pay that Octavian was giving his soldiers, but he was not in a position to take stringent measures against his enemies. He had summoned the senate for the twenty-fourth of November, threatening death to the tribunes hostile to him if they attended, and proclaiming that he would consider as an enemy any senator who stayed away. As Antony found it necessary to go to Tibur in order to confirm the loyalty of the soldiers who were stationed there, the meeting was postponed until the twenty-eighth. On that day many prominent senators were present; one of them, an ex-consul, brought a written motion to declare Octavian a public enemy, but the motion was not made. A thanksgiving was decreed in honor of Lepidus, because he had dissuaded Sextus Pompey from making war on Italy, and late in the evening various provinces were assigned to new governors. Antony's brother Gaius received Macedonia, and was thus chosen to wage war against Marcus Brutus. Mark Antony himself hastened from the city late at night, and, after making a vain attempt to win back the loyalty of. the Martian legion, marched north to Ariminum, which was situated near the boundary of Cisalpine Gaul.

Antony's purpose was to drive Decimus Brutus from this rich and populous province; if he succeeded, he would be in a position to raise new armies, and Rome would be at his mercy. Civil war, which had been smoldering since the Ides of March, had now begun, and it had begun in the very manner in which it had threatened to break forth in the beginning. While Caesar still lay unburied, Antony had forbidden Decimus Brutus to take possession of Cisalpine Gaul; Brutus had disobeyed Antony's injunction, and had raised an army in the province; and now Antony, with far larger forces than he could have put in the field early in the year, was attempting to expel Brutus.

The situation in Italy was one of utter chaos. All the prospective combatants were in the wrong, and all could claim to be in the right. The law was on the side of Antony and his supporters. Cisalpine Gaul had been assigned to Antony himself. If Decimus Brutus refused to give it up, it was both the prerogative and the duty of Antony to take forcible possession. His brother Gaius had been appointed to Macedonia. The generals and armies stationed in Greece and Macedonia were in duty bound to give their allegiance to him, and Marcus Brutus, who had gone thither to organize a military force, was acting in opposition to the legally constituted authority. The same situation prevailed farther east. Dolabella had received Syria, and neither Cassius nor any governor in that part of the world had legal justification for opposing him. Antony and Dolabella, furthermore, were the consuls of Rome. They, and they alone, had the right to levy and command armies in Italy. Praetors also possessed the so-called *imperium,* the right to command an army, and Brutus and Cassius were praetors, but no armies had been entrusted to them, whereas Antony had received permission to raise his famous bodyguard and had actually had the Macedonian legions transferred to him. Octavian was a rebel; the Macedonian legions that had gone over to him were deserters; the veterans who had joined him could not even pretend that they had acted legally. And yet it was true that the laws and decrees which justified Antony had been passed under coercion; they were the result of Antony's unjustifiable domination. He was consul, to be sure, but he had neither spoken nor acted as befitted a consul; quite to the contrary, he had announced that he would rule Rome, and to this announcement he had added threats of future reprisals against any one who should oppose him. His opponents, therefore, though legally in the wrong, could lay claim to the moral justification that they were defending Rome herself against an avowed usurper.

The legal confusion was no greater than the weakness, the mutual distrust, and the lack of harmony which prevailed among Antony's actual and prospective opponents. On Antony's side, everything was clear and unanimous. He and his two adherents, Gaius and Dolabella, had set out to secure military dominance; they had chosen different spheres of action, and there was neither rivalry nor secret suspicion to divide them. The legions of Antony also, though their services had been bought, knew against whom they were arrayed, and they were also perfectly conscious of the fact that victory would make Antony ruler and would bring them extraordinary rewards and privileges. There was no such unanimity of purpose or of feeling on the other side. The restoration of the republic, in the character which it had had before the First Triumvirate, would make the senate the chief seat of authority. But the senators, though they knew and admitted that Antony had acted arrogantly, violently, and illegally, nevertheless did not all believe, or at least they did not all admit their belief, that Antony was a serious threat to the republic. It was said that Antony could be won over from his unlawful practises by proper and yet safe concessions, and there was a disinclination to adopt strong measures against him. Perhaps a few senators were sincere in their attitude. Some, however, favored Antony openly, even excusing themselves on the ground that they were bound to him by ties of friendship or relationship. Many others were timid, particularly the more prominent members of the senate, who, in their character of leaders, would be especially exposed to Antony's vengeance in case they headed an unsuccessful opposition.

And there was reason for timidity. Antony had so long dominated Rome that men had not yet learned to breathe freely.

The armies of Octavian and Decimus Brutus, furthermore, could scarcely be considered a match for Antony's legions; as later events proved, two additional armies had to be sent against him. Nor could the generals or the soldiers opposed to Antony be relied upon to act together or to yield obedience to the senate. Decimus Brutus would undoubtedly remain faithful to the republic, for he was in danger from Antony, but his forces, which consisted largely of recruits, were not to be trusted to face Antony's veterans. Cassius and Marcus Brutus would not willingly make terms with Antony, but if they acquired great power in the East, it was by no means so certain that they would obey senatorial orders. The tyrannicides could not view Octavian without suspicion. If the senate honored and rewarded him, they would be jealous; if Octavian became very powerful, they would fear him. Octavian himself, though an enemy of Antony, was not a friend of the tyrannicides; and his troops abhorred them, whereas they had no serious quarrel with Antony. In addition to these generals and armies, there were the governors and legions stationed in the provinces, the more important of whom held Gaul and Spain. Though these were not likely to become immediately involved in the impending struggle, nothing but the annihilation of Antony would prevent them from having a decisive voice in the final settlement. None of them, however, had any reason for opposing Antony except a possible desire to restore the republic; and one of the governors, Lepidus, who had a large army in Southern Gaul and Hither Spain, was a notorious turncoat and had early in the year sided with Antony. But whatever the disposition of the generals and the soldiers, whether in the East, in Italy, or in Gaul and Spain, armies needed not only pay but also gifts and rewards, and the treasury had been rifled by Antony.

These difficulties, however, insuperable though many of them might seem, and these conflicting moral claims neither deterred nor confused Cicero. Antony was actually marching against

Decimus Brutus. Unless a powerful opposition to Antony were organized in Rome and in the provinces, Decimus would be crushed and Antony would return to establish an intolerable tyranny. Perhaps Antony would be victorious under any circumstances. Cicero saw this possibility; and he also feared that the defeat of Antony, if it did take place, would result merely in establishing Octavian as a dictator. He had had no reason for changing his opinion about the young Caesar; the latter, so far as is known, had done nothing in reference to the tribune Casca which could convince Cicero that he was well disposed to the tyrannicides. By raising an army, however, Octavian had made it possible for the first time since the death of Caesar to oppose Antony. Cicero had not embraced this opportunity at the time when the conflict was not absolutely inevitable. He had said that Octavian might not be strong enough, and Octavian had shown his lack of strength by leaving Rome at Antony's approach. But now there was no choice. The question of victory, as well as the question of the future disposition of Rome, had to be dismissed. Neither could Cicero ask himself, as some modern students might ask, whether it was worth while to attempt to reëstablish the republic. During the republican form of government, there had been license, perhaps, rather than freedom; the senate had been selfish and corrupt, the assemblies had been equally selfish and corrupt, and the provinces had suffered grievously; but the situation created by Antony's march against Decimus offered a choice not between a faulty republic and a less faulty monarchy, but between the only kind of freedom the Romans knew and slavery under a man who had already acted with violence and brutality and who had uttered the most violent threats.

Cicero could have evaded the struggle. He had drawn upon himself the enmity of Antony, as had others, and he had written the *Second Philippic,* which would mark him as Antony's declared opponent, but he had not yet published it. If he had held back this speech and if he had followed the example of other prominent leaders, either abjuring politics or taking a vague and conciliatory attitude in his opposition to Antony, he might have earned Antony's gratitude, for it was Cicero of all men in Rome that Antony feared; he certainly would have exposed himself to no especial enmity. He was nearly sixty-three years old, and might well have felt that the younger men should do the fighting. But in spite of his advanced age and his personal danger, and despite his own misgivings about the outcome, he determined to take the lead in Rome.

Cicero's task was to unite the nation in unswerving opposition to Antony, in order that moral and legal support might be given to the armies and generals already in the field against Antony, and that new armies might be equipped and sent against him. Since the senate was the chief possessor of power in the republic and could most readily initiate action, it was mainly as the leader of the senate that Cicero exerted his influence. He was not technically its leader, for he was not called upon to give his opinion first, though, as one of the few ex-consuls, he spoke very early at the meetings. Neither did the senate always obey his advice. The measures advocated by him were sometimes voted down and sometimes postponed, and measures that he opposed were adopted, but Cicero's policy of unconditional warfare with Antony prevailed in the end. In his capacity of leader, he could not confine his activities to the senate. It was he who generally addressed the people, informing them of important senatorial action, inspiring them with zeal for the war, even appealing to them for support when the senate had failed to uphold his policy. And it was he who more than anyone else kept in touch with the various generals and provincial governors on the loyalist side, and to whom they turned with requests for aid and for senatorial recognition of their numerous claims to distinction.

Cicero has been called the prime minister of Rome, but his activities were more varied than those of any prime minister.

He guided and often coerced the senate, he explained and defended policies at public meetings, he had countless interviews with private individuals, and he wrote countless letters; and through it all he kept his faith, uniting discordant elements, praising and criticising, and always inspiring the nation with courage and enthusiasm and love of Rome. His speeches and his letters contain many wise and energetic sayings, but nothing is more characteristic of his attitude than his frequent advice, which is found both in his public utterances and in his private messages, that past mistakes or misfortunes must be forgotten and all thoughts turned to the future.[21] He thus became the conscience and the nervous center of Rome. In his work entitled the *Republic* he had given a description of those who should guide the state. He was now such a *rector* and *moderator;* he waged the longest, the most violent, and the most brilliant parliamentary battle that was ever waged in Rome; his successes and his failures show in just how far Rome could yet be directed by reason and patriotism.

Cicero entered Rome on the ninth of December, eleven days after Antony's hurried departure. Though the city was free from the immediate domination of Antony, everything was disorganized. Nor did it seem possible for the senate to meet until the first of January. In the absence of the consuls, a meeting could legally be summoned and presided over by the praetors or the tribunes, but the senators, who even in the midst of violent civil upheavals clung pertinaciously to old forms, seem to have felt that they could not take energetic action under any but consular presidency, and as the levy of an army was the duty of a consul, they may also have been of the opinion that if a senatorial decree could not lead to a levy, then it was useless to meet at all. No doubt some of them were also glad to postpone action as much as possible. The tribunes, however, did summon a meeting for the twentieth of December, announcing that they

---

[21] See above, p. 610, and below, p. 645.

would make a motion for the protection of the consuls-elect, or, in other words, devise measures so that the senate might meet in safety on the first of January. This proposal of the tribunes may have had for object to create some military guard to over-awe those supporters of Antony who were still in Rome, for there seem to have been a number of these, but a meeting like this one held out no promise that anything of importance would be attempted, and may, indeed, have been considered as merely a routine matter.

Cicero did not look forward to taking a prompt part in politics. The date of his coming to Rome seems to have been due to business reasons. But his mere arrival indicated, as it had indicated on the last of August, that he was prepared to do his share. This was further shown by the fact that he called at once on the consul-elect Pansa, to inquire about the situation in Cisalpine Gaul, for Cicero could not visit Pansa without the knowledge of the citizens. During these days Cicero urged the need of immediate action, but he seems to have had no success. A large attendance was not expected at the meeting summoned by the tribunes for the twentieth. But on that very day an edict of Decimus Brutus was put up in the city, in which Brutus announced that he would hold his province ''for the senate and people of Rome.'' This was a declaration of war against Antony, and Cicero, who feared that the timid and disorganized senate would take no cognizance of it, decided to attend the meeting. He went early; and when this was observed, the senators came together in large numbers.

Cicero led the debate. In the speech he delivered, the *Third Philippic,* he urged that war must be waged against Antony, and that the action of Brutus and Octavian must be approved; the people of Cisalpine Gaul who had joined Decimus in oppo-sition to Antony must be praised, the veterans who had deserted from Antony must be praised and rewards must be promised to them, and the other provincial governors must be instructed not to surrender their provinces to those to whom Antony had assigned these provinces. Fear and hatred of Antony and enthusiasm for Octavian were the two emotions that Cicero aimed to inspire; and these two, rightly interpreted, meant patriotism, the determination to make Rome free from tyranny.

When all were apprehensive of Antony's return from Brundisium, Cicero said, then Caesar, a young man, or almost a boy, put himself in Antony's way. Nobody had expected him to do this, nor had any one even dared to wish it. The young Caesar had spent his patrimony in securing the services of the invincible veterans. No, he had not spent it, Cicero exclaimed, he had invested it for the safety of the state. At Brundisium Antony had massacred three hundred gallant men; it was known that his wife had been present and that her face had been besprinkled with blood. The victorious return to Rome of such a man as Antony would have meant slavery, and though it is true that all slavery is wretched, it would have been intolerable to bow to a man who was profligate, immoral, and effeminate, a man who did not keep sober even when he was afraid.

Octavian had saved the city. Antony had formerly insulted the young Caesar, taunting him with the fact that his mother came from the small town Aricia; but when Antony had last returned to Rome, he had not dared to make a motion, as he had prepared to do, that Octavian be declared a public enemy. Antony, who could not write an edict in decent Latin, had threatened death to the tribunes opposed to him in case they attended. In his fear, he hurried through some legislation. Certain provinces had been assigned by lot, and the kind gods had favored him, so that his friends secured just the provinces they wanted. Two provinces, however, had strangely fallen to men who were not his supporters; evidently the gods had been negligent.

Nothing but misery, Cicero said, could be expected from the rule of Antony. His brother Lucius, who was leading a force to join the tyrannical consul, was destroying provisions and slaughtering cattle, wherever he found them; his soldiers were feasting, and Lucius himself, in imitation of his brother, was intoxicated; fields were laid waste, farms were plundered, matrons, girls and boys were carried away and given to the soldiers. But Lucius was only doing what his brother had done everywhere. Now the opportunity had come to the senate to exert their mighty influence. It was their last opportunity. Caesar was protecting the city; Decimus Brutus was holding Gaul; Cicero was ready to undertake any task. Let the senate therefore approve of Decimus, of Octavian, and of their soldiers, and instruct the consuls to prepare for forcible action at the beginning of next year.

The senate passed the resolutions moved by Cicero. Though Antony was not decreed a public enemy, war was declared against him, for the senate, acting for the nation as of old, commended and promised rewards to his opponents. And the people approved. Cicero was received with unbounded enthusiasm when, appearing before them after the meeting, he explained[22] what the senate had decided, and urged war against Antony.

As the leader of debate in the senate and as the spokesman of the senate before the people, Cicero was now unofficially at the head of affairs. He had reëstablished the republic, as it were, in that he had caused the senate to take action with old-time independence, and he had succeeded in committing this reëstablished nation to war with Antony, the consul of Rome. He had also given legal sanction, through the decrees of the senate, to the position of Brutus and of Octavian; and he had secured authority for loyal governors to retain their provinces in defiance of Antony's recent legislation. But he realized that there was both fear and treachery in Rome. "We wage war," he wrote[23] to Cornificius in Africa, "against the most abandoned

---

[22] *Fourth Philippic.*

[23] *Fam.* 12, 22.

cutthroat in the world, but not on equal terms, for it is words against arms. Rome is a scene of universal depression. The loyalists have no leader, and the tyrannicides are far away.''

It was probably during his first days in Rome that Cicero published the *Second Philippic,* which he had polished with great care. We have no record of its publication or of the manner in which it was received, but Cicero's assumption of leadership and the need of arousing enmity against Antony made this the most suitable time for issuing the oration. It would have been suicidal, as well as useless, to publish it while Antony held Rome under military sway; to publish it later would have served no purpose.

The *Second Philippic* was Cicero's reply to the speech that Antony had delivered on the nineteenth of September. On that day Antony had taken much care to explain that he and Cicero had formerly been on intimate terms, and that Cicero had been the recipient of many services at Antony's hands. Cicero, therefore, according to Antony, had had no justification for opposing him on the second of September, the day when Cicero delivered the *First Philippic.* Antony's argument was due to the Roman feeling that politics was largely a personal matter, but it may also have been an effort to give Cicero's opposition the appearance of personal enmity, in order to obscure the fact that Cicero had in reality attacked Antony's arrogant and illegal behavior. To show, however, that Cicero was not a safe person to follow, Antony had thereupon reviewed Cicero's political career, reviling and ridiculing him with the violence customary in Rome. Cicero replied to Antony's charge of lack of gratitude, saying among other things that in a certain sense he did owe his life to Antony, inasmuch as Antony had not murdered him during the civil war between Caesar and Pompey; he answered the criticisms levelled against him as a statesman; and he gave a picture of Antony's preparation of the speech. Antony, so Cicero said, had spent seventeen days in Scipio's villa, which he had seized illegally. He had declaimed assiduously, though, according to his friends, he usually declaimed to work off the effects of too much wine. He had engaged a witty rhetorician to teach him jokes, and had rewarded this unsuccessful teacher with a gift of two thousand acres of land, exempt from taxation. The result of this expensive teaching had been merely to make Antony a fool.

After thus meeting Antony's charges in the spirit in which they had been made, Cicero continued with an account of Antony's own life. Antony's father, he wrote, had been bank-rupt. Antony himself was in his youth so dissolute that the details must for shame's sake be omitted. He was a friend of Curio, and Curio's father often had to turn him out of the house. Later he was with Caesar in Gaul, and came from that province to stand for the quaestorship. At Caesar's request Cicero supported Antony's candidature, and the latter showed his gratitude by trying to murder Clodius. As soon as he had been elected, he went off to Gaul, without waiting for the neces-sary authorization of the senate. The reason for his haste was his insolvency; only in a camp could he hope to restore his shat-tered fortunes. Then he became a tribune. Though still a young man, he had the assurance to oppose the senate at every turn, until finally he fled to his ambitious patron, who thus got a pretext for beginning civil war. It was Antony's tribunician rights, forsooth, that Caesar was defending. What Helen had been to Troy, Antony was to Rome: a cause of war, trouble, and ruin.

Caesar went to Spain and left Antony in charge of Italy; and now Antony's behavior became scandalous. Everywhere men talked about him. He traveled back and forth over the country, and this was the mode of his progress: though a Roman magistrate, he rode in a barbarian carriage, such as only women use; though he was only a tribune and as such had no right to the use of lictors, he was preceded by lictors, and these were

crowned with laurel wreaths, as though Antony had won a
vitory. But this was not all. The lictors surrounded the open
litter of his mistress, an actress; her name was Cytheris, but as
she had been manumitted by her former paramour, a certain
Volumnius, she was hailed as Volumnia by the citizens of the
municipal towns, who were forced to come out and greet the
cavalcade. Behind Volumnia came a carriage filled with pimps;
behind them were a crowd of Antony's worthless boon companions; and finally Antony's own mother followed. You would
have thought that she was doing honor to the actress as a legitimate daughter-in-law. In the course of these peregrinations
Antony despoiled the cities of Italy; he stole their gold, their
silver, and especially their wine. Even on public occasions he
so overloaded himself with food and wine that he became sick
and disgraced himself. It was during these performances that
he showed the great goodness of not taking Cicero's life.

In the meantime Caesar had gone to Egypt, and on his
return the house of Pompey was put up for sale; but among all
Caesar's reckless followers there was only one who had the
effrontery to bid for it, and this man was Antony. He began
to act like a buffoon in a farce. Pompey had been a very rich
man; his house contained a large supply of wine, of plate of
exquisite workmanship, expensive clothes and furnishings.
Antony wasted it all in an incredibly short time. No, there was
nothing incredible about it, after all, for he had filled the house
with actors, actresses, gamblers, and drunkards; nothing was
kept under lock and key; and Antony himself gambled away
enormous sums. Even the slaves had their share in the ruinous
doings; their quarters were adorned with the precious tapestries
of Pompey. And all this took place in the house of Pompey, a
house which for a long time men could not pass without shedding
tears, a house adorned with the beaks of captured ships and
other trophies of war. But Antony had not paid for all this
luxury. Caesar asked him to settle, and finally had to send

soldiers to collect. But there was nothing to collect. Forced to sell at auction, Antony brought out what he alleged to be the property he had bought, some wretched old clothes, covered with stains, a few silver vessels, all nicked, and a few meanly clad slaves. As nothing could be done with such a miserable collection, the auction was stopped; Caesar actually discussed the disgraceful proceeding in the senate.

In the course of time Antony became Caesar's master of horse, and was thus next in dignity to the dictator, and this is the way in which he supported that dignity. While Caesar was absent in Spain, Antony was once on his way to Rome. Arriving late in the afternoon at a little town called Red Rocks, he spent the rest of the day drinking in a public house. At night he hastened to Rome in a gig, with his head veiled, and knocked at the door of his own house. "Who are you?" asked the porter. "A messenger from Marcus Antonius." He was at once admitted to the presence of his wife, to whom he handed a letter in which he promised not to have any further connection with the actress. It was a real love letter, and his wife wept with joy. Her emotion so affected the susceptible Antony that he made himself known, and they embraced. But Antony had not come to Rome merely to comfort his wife. He had come also to prevent a creditor from selling his sureties. As soon as it was learned that Antony was in town, the city was alarmed. He was asked at a public meeting to explain the reason for his presence in Rome, and he informed his auditors that he had come on private business. Everybody thought this a good joke, and the wits had much to say about it.[24]

Antony had always professed to be a friend of Caesar's, but this was only a pretense; and Cicero, coming to the end of his bitter review of Antony's life, gave an account of Antony's lawlessness during the time before and after Caesar's death, especially insisting that not only was Antony in every way

24 See above, p. 502.

inferior to Caesar, whom he resembled only in his love of power, but that his protestations of reverence for Caesar's memory were merely a cloak to cover his own greed and ambition. Cicero concluded with this attack on Antony's alleged devotion to Caesar in order to weaken Antony's hold on the Caesarians, and he instituted the comparison between Antony and Caesar to remind his readers, it would seem, that, if they had found Caesar's rule tolerable, they must not imagine that Antony would be like Caesar. Antony posed as the upholder of Caesar's laws, Cicero said, but he had upheld only those which served his own purposes. On the Ides of March he had been in debt to the amount of forty million sesterces; two weeks later he was free from debt.

This invective against Antony was far coarser and venomous, and also far more powerful, than can be represented; but it was quite to the taste of Cicero's contemporaries. So far as Cicero's relations with Antony were concerned, it proclaimed that Cicero was now his enemy, but it did not go much beyond that. Antony's attack on Cicero had been equally bitter, as we can infer from Cicero's quotations from Antony's speech, and Cicero himself had inveighed with no less virulence against several political opponents, with some of whom he had later made his peace. Others, furthermore, had attacked Antony with even less restraint. Of Cannutius, the tribune, it was later said[25] that his speech, when compared with the divine brilliancy of Cicero, seemed like the snarling of a mad dog. The *Second Philippic*, nevertheless, was not looked upon as a tame performance. Pliny the Younger, evidently referring to it, said that, just as it was Cicero's longest speech, so it was his best; and Juvenal, who had an eye for satire, called it heavenly.[26] The enemies of Antony must have relished it, but it was not Cicero's chief purpose either to vent his personal chagrin or to amuse

---

[25] Velleius, 2, 64.
[26] Pliny, *Epist.* 1, 20, 4. Juv. 10, 125.

his readers. In publishing this speech, Cicero was striking a mighty blow against Antony. In view of the greed, the violence, and the baseness of Antony, so Cicero would have it understood, the Romans had no choice but to oppose him to the end; to make terms with him was impossible, and to submit to him meant shameful slavery. This thought Cicero constantly repeated in his later orations, and there was constant need of the repetition.

But it was not enough that Antony should be looked upon with abhorrence; the people of Rome must also be made to feel that they could trust Cicero, that he was unselfish and courageous, aiming at nothing but the liberation of Rome and fearing nothing, not even death. The *Second Philippic* therefore contained Cicero's justification of his own political career; and it is very probable that, as a further appeal to the Romans, he published his long essay on Duty at this time. He had been at work on it while writing the *Second Philippic;* two of its three books were finished on the fifth of November. This essay set forth Cicero's view of life, with frequent references to his own career; it was addressed particularly to young men; and it taught that a man's foremost duty is to serve the state. In the *Second Philippic* itself, as well as in the speech that preceded it and in all those that followed it, no less than in Cicero's letters to generals and governors, he repeatedly insisted that nothing was dearer to him than Rome, and that for Rome he was willing to lay down his life. "No one for the last twenty years has been an enemy to the state who has not at the same time declared war against me," he wrote at the beginning of the *Second Philippic*. And, at the end, he expressed two wishes: one, that dying he might leave Rome free; the other, that every one might fare as he had deserved of the state.

It was in this spirit of unhesitating devotion to Rome and of undeviating opposition to Antony that Cicero took up the burden of leadership, and he carried it to the end in the same spirit. The senate met on the first of January under the presi-

dency of the new consuls, Hirtius and Pansa. Quintus Cicero,
who had been with them in Gaul, had recently written of them
that they were both immoral and slothful; and Cicero's opinion
of them was very much the same. They were too fond of wine
and sleep; and at this time Hirtius was also in poor health. In
the senate, however, they spoke loyally and energetically enough,
but they called first upon Calenus to deliver his opinion, and
Calenus, who was Pansa's father-in-law, was known as an
opponent to Cicero and as Antony's most devoted partisan. The
latter's wife and children were actually staying at Calenus'
house. With a show of moderation and leniency, Calenus proposed that an embassy be sent to negotiate with Antony.

Cicero, who was called upon after two other consulars had
spoken, at once took issue with Calenus. If Antony wanted
peace, Cicero exclaimed, he could get it by laying down his arms
at once and imploring pardon; he would find nobody more reasonable than Cicero. But Antony did not want peace. At the most,
he wanted an opportunity for bargaining, and the bargain was
already being prepared, Cicero said, for it was understood that
one of the senators, who had not yet spoken, intended to propose
than Transalpine Gaul be handed over to Antony in case he
would desist from his attempt to expel Decimus Brutus from
Cisalpine Gaul. But this exchange, it may be remarked, would
have placed Antony in as favorable a position as Caesar had
secured after the formation of the First Triumvirate.

The speech which Cicero delivered, the *Fifth Philippic,* was
violent and acrimonious, and led to a debate which lasted four
days. Cicero pointed out that the negotiations, even if the terms
proposed to Antony were made exceedingly severe, would have
the effect of lowering the martial enthusiasm which was abroad
in Italy. Men had already begun to enlist; if it was learned
that the senate, which on the twentieth of December had virtually declared war on Antony, was now sending embassadors
to him, then it would be impossible to continue effective prepara-

tions. The partisans of Antony insisted that these preparations could go on, irrespective of the embassy, but Cicero retorted that great events are frequently the result of very trivial causes; that in civil war common gossip is a powerful factor; men would say that the senate was afraid. Cicero therefore proposed that the "last decree" be passed; the declaration of martial law, he said, would once and for all put the opposition to Antony on the right footing. For three days Cicero held his own, but when the matter came to a vote on the fourth, it was decided to send the embassy.

A dangerous step backward had thus been taken. Something, nevertheless, was gained during the long debate. Decimus and the inhabitants of Cisalpine Gaul, as well as Octavian and his veterans, who had been accorded praise two weeks earlier, were commended again; Octavian was also given a seat in the senate and was in other ways made a privileged person, and his veterans were promised greater rewards than had ever been given to soldiers. Even Lepidus was not forgotten; he received the unprecedented honor of a gilt statue for his services in dissuading Sextus Pompey from making war on Italy. Lepidus had negotiated with Pompey for the benefit of Antony, but the senate, under Cicero's guidance, eagerly made this attempt to bind the shifty general to the loyalist side.

The decrees in favor of Octavian and his soldiers were the most important. It was well known to Cicero that the two legions from Macedonia which had gone over to Octavian, as well as a number of deserters to Octavian from the other two Macedonian legions, had not acted from patriotism; yet Cicero described them as high-minded patriots, even proposing and carrying a motion for rewards to the quaestor who had commanded one of the deserting legions. An amnesty was also offered to those of Antony's soldiers who should join the republican forces before the first of February. The ultimate decision, as every one knew, rested with the veterans.

In order to win support and honors for Octavian, whom the senators distrusted, Cicero pledged himself formally for Octavian's future conduct. He professed to know the young man intimately, and averred that nothing was dearer to this new champion of liberty than the true glory that comes from service to one's country. Octavian had already saved Rome from Antony; in order to insure this safety for the future, he had renounced any enmity he might have felt toward the liberators. It was not rashness to trust Octavian, said Cicero, knowing necessarily that Octavian had not acted from patriotism, and still doubting the sincerity of his proclaimed friendliness for the assassins. By announcing publicly that Octavian was the savior of Rome, Cicero hoped perhaps that he could win the young man to a generous and patriotic state of mind.

At the end of the meeting Cicero addressed[27] the people. He made no secret of his disappointment at the decision to open negotiations. The ambassadors were to order Antony to desist from his attempts on Cisalpine Gaul and to place himself under the authority of the senate. The purpose of the embassy, properly speaking, was therefore to deliver an ultimatum, but even an ultimatum was at this time unnecessary, Cicero said; he knew that the people must be disappointed no less than he was himself. "But we will say nothing of the past," he urged.[28] "Let the ambassadors hasten their return! In the meantime there must be no slackening of effort in prosecuting the war, for war is not to be avoided." Everybody was opposed to Antony, Cicero exclaimed; all the orders of the state, as well as the municipal towns, the colonies, and the whole of Italy. After all, the embassy would accomplish one thing: the negotiations would fail, and this would prove to every one that Antony was no longer to be thought of as a Roman citizen, but as an enemy. "Hereafter," said Cicero in conclusion, "if any disaster happens to us, it will be of our own making."

---

[27] *Sixth Philippic.*
[28] See above, pp. 610, 633.

The ambassadors departed for Antony's camp, and the preparations for war continued in Rome and Italy. A levy was held, but men volunteered with such enthusiasm, so Cicero wrote to a friend, that it could scarcely be called a levy. The municipal towns furnished soldiers in large numbers and promised sums of money; one town voted that any one who evaded military service should be branded with infamy. A wave of martial ardor swept over Italy.

But Cicero's moral guardianship was not allowed to relax. Traitorous propaganda was still active. Antony wrote letters filled with confidence in ultimate victory, and these letters were copied and distributed in the city. Rumors were also started to the effect that Antony was ready for negotiations. And while these things were going on, the senate met to wrangle about trivialities. At one meeting of such a nature Cicero arose. "We are talking about matters of small import," he said,[29] "though perhaps they have to be considered. It is not possible, however, to forget the grave crisis which we are facing;" and with this brief introduction, he launched into a vigorous attack on those who were whispering about peace. "I too am for peace, but there can be no peace unless we first wage war; if we shrink from war, we shall never have peace. I dread war disguised as peace." To treat for peace was shameful and inconsistent, he said; it was dangerous; and it could lead to nothing. The mood of Antony's opponents, and they comprised the whole people, was such that they could never come to an agreement with Antony. "As to the matter under discusison," Cicero said, as he prepared to take his seat, "I agree with Servilius." Three lines at the beginning of Cicero's speech and less than one line at the end constituted his references to the object for which the senate had met. Just as Cato had been in the habit of demanding at every senatorial meeting that Carthage should be destroyed, so Cicero demanded that Antony should be destroyed.

---

[29] *Seventh Philippic.*

The ambassadors proceeded to Antony. Hirtius, one of the consuls, had by that time led an army against Antony, and some fighting had taken place. Decimus Brutus, unable to face Antony's forces in the field, had shut himself up in the fortified city of Mutina, where Antony was besieging him. When the Roman ambassadors reached Antony's camp, they were invited to view his measures for reducing the town, and as the siege was prosecuted with undiminished vigor during their presence, they actually witnessed the bombardment. They were not allowed to proceed to Decimus, as they requested, nor did Antony listen to their ultimatum. He sent them back with terms of his own, and these were the terms of a man who already considered himself victorious. Antony wanted full pardon for himself and his followers for the proceedings of the past year; no inquiry was to be made about the money he had taken from the temple of Ops; all his laws, as well as his distributions of land to his soldiers, were to remain in force; and, in return for his willingness to raise the siege of Mutina and surrender his claim to Cisalpine Gaul, he was to receive Further Gaul. It was chiefly in his proposal in reference to Further Gaul that Antony revealed his true state of mind, for he demanded the province for a period of five years, and he asked for six legions; these legions were to be brought up to their full complement with soldiers from Decimus Brutus' army, and they were to remain under Antony's command as long as Brutus and Cassius kept possession of their provinces in the East.

Cicero's prophecy as to the outcome of the negotiations had thus been justified, and the indignation in Rome at Antony's proposal was intense; but Antony's supporters were not abashed. They treated Antony's envoy Cotyla with notorious courtesy and friendliness, and succeeded, despite Cicero's objections, in having him admitted to the senate. This body met on the second of February, the very day when the ambassadors arrived. Cotyla kept his pen busy recording for Antony's perusal the words of the various speakers, and he seems even to have actually canvassed among the leading senators, for Cicero says that these "sold themselves to him in utter disregard of their dignity." Pansa proposed, properly enough, that war should be declared against Antony, but it was immediately moved that the term war should be avoided, and he replaced with the word for civil disturbance; it was to be a *tumultus* and not a *bellum;* and Pansa acquiesced. By this change in terms Antony was saved from being declared a public enemy, but the state nevertheless committed itself to war; the toga was to be exchanged for the military cloak.

But the partisans of Antony had further plans. At the meeting of the senate which took place on the following day, the third of February, they began to agitate in favor of a second embassy; but, before a motion was made to this effect, Cicero intervened. He had urged the declaration of war on the preceding day, and had been outvoted. Now he appeared in the senate dressed in military garb; as an ex-consul, he was not required to lay aside the toga, but he wished by his change of dress to emphasize the fact that all loyal Romans were at war with Antony. He was not in a mood to spare those who were influenced by timidity, or greed, or disloyalty. On the day before, he said,[30] things had been managed in a spirit of confusion that was unworthy of the way in which Pansa had begun his consulship. Pansa himself had been too lenient. Lucius Caesar, the ex-consul who had moved to substitute the term *tumult* for the term *war,* and whom Cicero knew to be genuinely devoted to the republic, had had some excuse, so Cicero seemed to feel, for his action. While admitting that the more severe expression was deserved, Lucius Caesar had justified his preference for the other by pleading his relationship to Antony. He was Antony's uncle. "But," Cicero exclaimed, "are you all Antony's uncles?" The question of the exact term, however,

---

[30] *Eighth Philippic.*

was of minor significance, Cicero continued; the senate should not waste its energies in quibbling about words. Indeed, a *tumult* is a more serious thing than war, for it does not allow exemptions from military service, Cicero said, which are allowed in war. The one circumstance worthy of consideration was that, whatever the name used, Rome was actually at war with Antony.

Calenus, Antony's chief supporter, suggested that what was really wanted was peace. "Yes," retorted Cicero, "I could speak in praise of peace as well as Calenus, were that suitable, but slavery is not peace." Calenus, in the course of the debate, complained that Cicero was speaking in anger. "I do not readily get angry with my friends," Cicero replied, "even when they deserve it." And later: "I speak without anger, but not without profound indignation." And he inveighed against the ex-consuls; in sorrow, as he explained, for they were all his friends. Their actions, however, had been disgraceful; they, who should have guided the senate, had deserted it. Nor had the ambassadors done their duty. While their inability to influence Antony was pardonable, they had had the callousness to report his demands without any signs of indignation. And yet these demands, if acceded to, would make Antony all-powerful! Cicero therefore moved that pardon should be given to those who deserted from Antony to the republican forces before the fifteenth of March, that rewards should be given to those among them who should perform any signal service to the state, and that, while Antony's envoy, Cotyla, would be allowed to return to his master, any one else who should go to Antony was to be adjudged a traitor to Rome. By this motion, which was carried, Cicero tried, as he had tried at the first meeting of the year, to draw the veterans from Antony, and he also, for the time being, prevented the sending of a second embassy.

Scarcely had the agitation in favor of further negotiations been successfully combated by Cicero when he had to face new difficulties, this time from the East. Marcus Brutus had done well in Greece and Macedonia. He had raised an army, consisting partly of old Pompeians and some cavalry which were on their way to Dolabella in Asia Minor; he had secured additional ships, money, and arms; and the governors of Macedonia and Illyricum had submitted to his authority. Antony's brother Gaius, who had come to take possesion of Macedonia, was unable to resist him; some fighting took place, in the course of which some distinction was won by Cicero's son, who had joined Brutus in Athens; and finally Gaius, whose troops deserted, was forced to retreat to Apollonia, leaving Brutus in command of the whole Balkan peninsula. Nothing except the actual annihilation of Mark Antony and his army in Italy could have been more favorable to the republican cause; the success of Brutus not only cut off all danger to Italy from Gaius Antony or from any other possible sympathizer with Antony in the near East, but it also gave the republicans a large army close at hand, to which they could retreat, or which they could summon to Italy, in case the campaign of Mutina should end disastrously. Brutus, however, like Decimus and like Octavian, had acted without authorization from the senate; and this body, on the reception of news from him, very properly met to consider whether he should be confirmed in his position.

Pansa laid the matter before the senate in an enthusiastic address, but Calenus saw his opportunity for embarrassing the republicans and moved that Brutus be removed from his assumed command. An acrimonius debate ensued. Cicero defended[31] Brutus' position, not on the ground that he had acted legally or had any claim to the overlordship of the Balkan peninsula, but on the ground that he had acted for the best interests of the state, and was not a person who would in the future rebel against the authority of the senate. Calenus' objections to Brutus were

---

[31] *Tenth Philippic.* For the *Ninth Philippic,* see below, p. 665. According to Appian (3, 2), Caesar had intended that Brutus should govern Macedonia, and Cassius Syria.

obviously partisan, and it was finally voted to give formal thanks to Brutus and to recognize him as the commander in general charge of Macedonia, Illyricum, and Greece, with power to use public moneys, to contract for loans, and to levy supplies. He was also directed to remain as near the eastern coast of the Adriatic as possible, evidently for the purpose of lending aid, if necessary, in the struggle in Italy.

A situation analagous to that of Brutus arose almost immediately afterwards in connection with Cassius. Dolabella, who had gone to the East early in the year to take possession of his province of Syria, had by treachery captured Trebonius, one of the assassins, and had put him to death. Trebonius had been scourged and otherwise tortured for two days, Cicero said; his head had been cut off and fixed on a javelin; and his mutilated body had been dragged through the streets and then thrown into the sea. Cassius in the meantime had secured a considerable following among the armies stationed in the East, and was very favorably placed for opposing Dolabella. There was a strong likelihood that Brutus and Cassius would presently hold the eastern part of the empire. When the reports of these events reached the senate, Dolabella was declared a public enemy, but on the following day it was moved to deprive Cassius of his command, and to entrust the inevitable war with Dolabella to some one else.

The chief opponent to Cassius was, of course, Calenus. He had seen that nothing could be done to save Dolabella in the eyes of the senate, and had therefore himself moved to declare him a public enemy; but, Dolabella failing, it was clearly his duty as a partisan of Antony to have the senate appoint some one, any one, to the eastern command who would be a less able or a less determined opponent to Dolabella than Cassius. Calenus was supported by Pansa. The consul wished an eastern province for himself, and was willing to endanger the precarious harmony among Antony's opponents in his eagerness to provide for his own future. It was proposed that the eastern command should be given either to a certain Servilius, who was not a magistrate, or to the consuls Pansa and Hirtius, after they had first aided in the defeat of Antony. Cicero wanted Cassius. He argued[32] against Servilius, on the ground that it was not customary for the senate to appoint a private individual to a proconsulship; and against the consuls, on the ground that, as they could not go against Dolabella at once, their power would have to be exercised by lieutenants, and this was always unsatisfactory. He also showed that the appointment of the consuls would make it seem that they were thinking less of Antony's defeat than of their own future, and he assured their supporters that, once victory had been gained over Antony, the senate would see to it that Hirtius and Pansa were well provided for in the provinces. Cicero defended the irregular position of Cassius in the same way that he had defended that of Decimus Brutus, of Octavian, and of Marcus Brutus: Cassius had acted wisely and patriotically, and such action was better than mere obedience to law, for the highest law comes from the gods and bids us do that which is right. He pointed out that no man was so well prepared to carry on the war in the East as Cassius, who was already there, and that no decree of the senate could deprive Cassius of his command; he had a devoted army and would go on as he had begun, with or without the approval of the senate. Cicero's arguments were wise and just, but the senate followed the lead of Calenus and Pansa. Some of them were probably mere partisans of Antony; but that a majority favored Pansa's ambition must have been due not merely to the influence of Pansa but also to a feeling that the republicans could get along without Cassius. The loyalty of Marcus Brutus had been secured; he and the armies in Italy, it was felt, would be able to take care of Antony; it was better not to put too much power into the hands of the assassins. Hirtius and Pansa were therefore appointed to the provinces of Asia and Syria.

---

[32] *Eleventh Philippic.*

Having failed to persuade the senate, Cicero appealed[33] to the people, who listened with great enthusiasm to his praise of Cassius and to his declaration that Cassius would act for the best of the state, even without the authorization of the senate. Cicero at once wrote to the same effect to Cassius, urging him to "defend the constitution in his own way." Cicero had written in this manner to Decimus Brutus before the senate met on the twentieth of December, and, indeed, it was the attitude that he generally assumed in his correspondence with the republican commanders. The position in which Cicero found himself was a strange one. His aim was to prevent Antony from becoming a military dictator and to restore the republic, but this restoration consisted chiefly in the reëstablishment of the senate's authority. The senate, however, was often influenced by treachery, or timidity, or selfishness to such a degree that Cicero, while laboring for senatorial ascendancy, urged loyal republicans to ignore the decrees of the senate, and openly announced to the senate and the people that these decrees both should and would be disobeyed. The necessity for such action on the part of Cicero was a bad omen for the future.

An omen of even greater seriousness appeared when Cicero's opponents argued that he must not carry his advocacy of Brutus and Cassius so far as to offend the veterans. This thought, to judge from Cicero's reply, was constantly brought forward to paralyze action in Rome and to create dissension among Antony's opponents. "Why, in the name of mischief, is the name of the veterans always introduced to prevent every good undertaking!" Cicero exclaimed, while defending Brutus. Proclaiming himself attached to them when they acted patriotically, Cicero refused to tolerate them if they should put on airs. There were others besides the veterans, he said, who were devoted to liberty. The senate ought to be grateful to the youth of the country, who were everywhere enlisting. "And this one thing I must say: if the senate is to be governed by the nod of the veterans and if all our

---

[33] This speech is lost. The situation is described in *Fam.* 12, 7.

words and actions are to be referred to them, then it is time to wish for death; true Romans have always chosen death in preference to slavery." And in his speech in behalf of Cassius, Cicero divided the veterans into three groups: those who had sided with the republicans, those who remained neutral, and those who were fighting under Antony; insisting that, whereas the well-disposed veterans should be properly rewarded, they were not to be feared. Indeed, the day of the veterans was passed, he said; success now depended on the young soldiers.

Cicero could not have failed to realize that the final outcome of the war depended on the veterans; every Roman knew that young recruits could not face seasoned soldiers, and Cicero had already heaped unprecedented praise and promises on the veterans. But Calenus and his supporters had no tender regard for the veterans; they were using the weakness inherent in the republican cause in order to strengthen Antony, and Cicero answered as best he could. It was also wise to stimulate enthusiasm among the troops who were gathering under Pansa. As for the veterans, Cicero said justly that they were fighting under Octavian to free Decimus, who was an assassin. Hirtius and Octavian were also exerting themselves in behalf of Decimus, and yet they, too, were devoted to Caesar's memory. It was neither possible nor profitable to alienate the assassins and their supporters by ignoring their claims in an effort to bind the veterans more closely to the republican cause. Each element of the republican coalition must be humored, so that Antony might be promptly defeated. The veterans cared less for Antony than for themselves. They could be trusted to carry through the present campaign under Octavian and the consuls; if Antony was utterly undone before Mutina, neither the veterans nor Octavian, nor any other Caesarian, would be greatly tempted to make common cause with him from any love of Caesar's memory.

But it was by no means certain that Antony would be defeated. Though Hirtius and Octavian had written to Cicero in a spirit of hopefulness, they were as yet too weak to attack their powerful opponent; severe winter weather may also have impeded the movement of their armies. Antony blocked the road to Mutina, where provisions were running low. The partisans of Antony took advantage of the anxiety about Decimus which prevailed among the republicans, and again began to urge the propriety of sending an embassy. They hinted that Antony, uncertain of ultimate success, was eager for peace; they assumed an air of dejection, for the benefit of such as Cicero, who, according to his own statement, was always observing them; and they circulated a report that Antony's wife, who was staying with Calenus, was overcome with apprehension. A motion to send an embassy was finally introduced in the senate; Pansa supported it; and Cicero as well as his staunchest followers allowed it to be passed. Five ambassadors were appointed, including Cicero himself.

A night's meditation, however, convinced Cicero and the loyal republicans that they had made a mistake; and the question of the embassy was revived in the senate on the following day. Cicero obviously directed the discussion. Servilius, one of the newly appointed ambassadors and a determined opponent of Antony, made a speech in which he explained that his approval of the embassy must not be interpreted as an act of treachery; but Cicero's speech, the *Twelfth Philippic,* makes it clear that the reconsideration was due to his efforts. He frankly admitted that he had made a mistake on the previous day, influenced both by his anxiety for the safety of Decimus Brutus and by the behavior of Antony's partisans. Good men, he said, had properly wondered at his action, and loyal friends had criticised him for hoping that there could be peace. The Antonians themselves had helped him to regain his correct view of things. Thinking the senate unalterably committed to the embassy, they had openly rejoiced as though they had won a victory; they had discussed the character of the ambassadors, calmly declaring that three of them were friends of Antony; they had criticised Servilius for his past antagonism to Antony, and had insisted that a prejudiced man like Cicero should not be on the embassy at all. In other words, they had made no secret of their opinion that, since the appointment of the embassy was intended as a favor to Antony, the ambassadors should have been chosen accordingly. Now they were questioned in reference to their former hints about Antony, and admitted that there had been no news from him; there was no reason for supposing that he would lower his demands.

Starting from this admission, Cicero urged vehemently, as he had urged throughout this period, that the embassy could at best only defer the inevitable war. It would weaken the ardor and martial preparations of Antony's opponents, and it would be a breach of faith with such men as Hirtius and Octavian. The situation was exactly what it had been when the first embassy had been sent; and in one respect it was worse: the ambassadors had not been intrusted with a definite message for Antony, that is, they were not to ask for his submission. Cicero added a new argument. After showing that his undisguised enmity toward Antony quite incapacitated him for carrying on negotiations, he declared that it would indeed be impossible for him ever to reach Antony's camp. He gave a picture of the violence and the lawlessness that prevailed everywhere. In the city he had constantly to be on his guard; outside the city the dangers were even greater. His life had frequently been threatened; only a few days before, he had not dared to leave Rome for the suburbs and to return on the same day. But even if he was able to reach Antony's camp, he could not trust himself to Antony's good faith. And supposing he reached the enemy's camp safely and was allowed to leave it, he would be set upon before he could return to Rome. He was willing to go if he could go safely, but that was impossible. Nor was it likely that Antony would come to the camp of the ambassadors. The negotiations, therefore, would have to be carried on by correspondence, and this could be done equally well directly from the city. Cicero dwelt at great length on these personal arguments, the effect of which must have been profound, for they came to this: if it was impossible for a loyal republican even to negotiate with Antony, how could loyal republicans expect to be able to live side by side with Antony after patching up a truce? Against Cicero's opposition to the embassy it was argued that the veterans wanted peace. Cicero met this reference to the veterans as he had met it before, by insisting that the senate must act independently. Many calumnies of him, he said, had been circulated among them, but, as every one could bear witness, he had always exerted himself for their good. The senate followed Cicero's lead, and the embassy was abandoned.

We do not know just when this debate took place; probably it was in the last days of February or early in March. On the twentieth of March, exactly three months after Cicero had first led the senate against Antony, Pansa left Rome with his army. He had not been zealous in prosecuting the war with Antony, and he had been willing, for the sake of his own advantage, to oppose Cassius and so foster discord among the loyalists; but, once in the field, he coöperated loyally with Hirtius and Octavian. With his departure for the north Cicero's task was finished: he had given to the nation whatever union was possible, and two armies had been sent against Antony. The outcome of the war rested now with the armies.

But the successful completion of Cicero's labors did not procure him any rest. Rome was seething with hopes and fears; speeches, meetings, and disturbances still continued. Even the efforts to make peace with Antony had still to be combated. They came this time from Lepidus and Plancus, who commanded armies in Gaul and Spain. Cicero argued the question in the

senate, in his *Thirteenth Philippic*. His reasons were those that
he had used before, but, as a further argument in favor of war,
he produced and read a letter from Antony to Hirtius and
Octavian, which Hirtius had forwarded to him.

In this letter[34] Antony expressed his joy at the murder of
Trebonius, because he was one of the assassins of Caesar, and
bitterly denounced the senate for declaring Dolabella, the murderer, an outlaw. He pointed out that, although Hirtius and
Octavian owed everything to Caesar, they were acting in a way
that could have but one result, the supremacy of Brutus and
Cassius. He called the republicans Pompeians, as though they
were merely a political party, and referred to Cicero as their
defeated leader. Under this leadership, Hirtius and Octavian
had made friends with the assassins, Antony maintained, and had
acted exactly as Pompey would have done if he could have come
to life again. On the pretext of destroying the assassins, they
had collected an army of soldiers who legally belonged to Antony
himself, and had then led them against their commander and
fellow-soldiers. In a letter to Antony, Hirtius and Octavian had
written that there could be no peace unless Antony either raised
the siege of Mutina or supplied Decimus Brutus with provisions.
In reply to this, Antony asked if they were in this matter voicing
the opinions of the veterans who were still neutral. If Hirtius
and Octavian should answer that it was really Decimus' soldiers
they wished to relieve, then Antony avowed his willingness to
have this done, provided Decimus paid the penalty of death,
which he richly deserved. Hirtius and Octavian had informed
Antony that five consulars had been appointed to negotiate with
him. Antony asserted that he expected nothing from a senate
that had already refused his moderate terms, which indeed he
had been thinking of making even more moderate; a senate
that had declared Dolabella a public enemy would not spare
those who agreed with Dolabella.

---

[34] This letter is given by Cicero in *Phil.* 13, chaps. 10 ff. It is not contained in the correspondence.

There were two courses open, Antony continued: either he and the republican commanders must fight against each other, and so put the Pompeians into power; or they must come to terms, and so avoid making themselves ridiculous. The death of Antony or of his opponents would only profit their common enemy, the Pompeians. The armies facing each other at Mutina were like gladiators, and it was Cicero who had pitted them against each other. He had deceived Hirtius and Octavian by the same awards of honors by which he boasted of having deceived Caesar. Antony, however, would uphold his own dignity and that of his friends; he would not desert those whom Pompey had hated; he would champion the rights of the veterans; he would not abandon Dolabella, nor break the agreement he had made with Lepidus and Plancus. After thus insinuating that the two generals in the west were on his side, and after declaring that he would take some satisfaction even in his own eventual defeat and death, inasmuch as that would be followed by disaster to Hirtius and Octavian, Antony concluded to the effect that he was willing to forgive the injuries inflicted upon him by his own partisans, in case they would forget that they had themselves inflicted them and were ready with him to avenge Caesar's death; as for the five ambassadors, he did not believe they would come, but if they did come, he would then learn their demands.

Cicero accompanied his reading of this letter in the senate with attacks on Antony which for bitterness and scorn had not been excelled by any of Cicero's utterances during the long parliamentary struggle. Antony had put his finger on the weakness of the republican cause; from the point of view of a man who had no thought of the republic, his diagnosis was absolutely correct. And the correctness of it was not hidden from Cicero, who had constantly battled against dissension within the republican ranks. The letter showed, however, as Cicero had intended that it should show, that no peace could be made with

Antony; unless Antony was defeated, the republic, which the assasins of Caesar had hoped to reëstablish, would not become a reality, nor would the assassins themselves and their supporters be safe.

The reports from the north were still disconcerting. About the seventeenth of April rumors reached the capital that Antony had won a victory and was marching upon Rome. The city was thrown into confusion; large numbers of citizens with their wives and children departed to seek safety in the camp of Marcus Brutus across the Adriatic. The chaos lasted for a period of three or four days. The partisans of Antony did not conceal their exultation. They gathered openly at the senate-house, made plans for the massacre of their opponents, and even assigned men to seize the capital, the rostra, and the city gates. Knowing that in this crisis the citizens would look to Cicero for leadership, they started a rumor that Cicero was planning to make himself ruler. According to Cicero's assertion, they even made arrangements to bring lictors' fasces to his house, intending to use their presence as evidence of his alleged design, whereupon, when the people should have turned against him, they meant to begin the massacre in Rome with the murder of Cicero. At this juncture a tribune of the plebs, who had been devoted to Cicero since the year 63 B.C., intervened by calling a *contio;* the people surged to the meeting, and when the tribune in the course of his speech was entering upon his vindication of Cicero, the whole assembly shouted with one voice that Cicero's one aim had always been the welfare of the state.

Within less than three hours after this meeting, messengers arrived announcing that Antony had been defeated; and the people, streaming in multitudes to Cicero's house, escorted him to the Capitol and thence to the forum, where they placed him on the rostra, acclaiming him as their savior. "This," Cicero wrote on the next day to Marcus Brutus, "was the abundant reward for my labors and my many sleepless nights. I have no vanity about it," he added; and on the same day, speaking in the senate, he referred to the tumultous demonstration in his honor as in reality a compliment to the victorious generals, for whom he recommended signal distinctions.

The defeat of Antony was reported in Rome on the twentieth of April. The arrival of Pansa in the north had threatened Antony's position before Mutina, and had led to an engagement[35] on the fifteenth of April at Forum Gallorum, which was situated on the road to Mutina, not far from this city. Pansa had been defeated and had been seriously wounded. But Antony had immediately afterwards been defeated by Hirtius, and Octavian had at the same time successfully defended his camp against an attack of Antony's brother, Lucius. Six days later, on the twenty-first, Antony was completely defeated by the republican armies under the walls of Mutina, and fled toward the west. In this battle Hirtius was killed, and shortly afterwards Pansa died from his wounds.

The authentic news of the first battle thus reached Rome on the day before the second battle was fought; it was discussed in the senate on the very day when Antony suffered his second defeat. Servilius, the tribune, moved that the military garb should be laid aside and that a public thanksgiving should be celebrated in honor of the victory. Cicero's speech in reference to this motion, the *Fourteenth Philippic*, is the last of his extant speeches, though it was not the last speech that he delivered. Both in its noble expressions of joy at the victory and in its sane recognition of the fact that the war was not ended, it is worthy to stand at the end of Cicero's long career as an orator. Reminding his auditors that the siege of Mutina had not yet been raised, he opposed the motion to lay aside the military garb, and while he favored the public thanksgiving, even proposing to have it extend for fifty days, which was unprecedented, he

---

[35] An account of this battle was sent to Cicero by a certain Galba (*Fam.* 10, 30).

pointed out that his approval of the proposed thanksgiving rested
largely on the fact that, as thanksgivings were not celebrated
for victories over citizens, this particular celebration would indicate that Antony from now on was looked upon as an enemy of
his country.

Cicero saw the difficulties that would arise within the ranks
of the republicans after the elimination of Antony. Writing to
Marcus Brutus on this very day, he expressed a somewhat doubtful hope that it might be possible to restrain and guide Octavian
in the hour of triumph no less than he had allowed himself to
be guided in the past. Octavian's share in the battle of Forum
Gallorum had been insignificant, but Cicero, seeing the necessity
of retaining his loyalty by rewarding him in the same way as
the other generals, proposed in the senate that all the commanders should receive the title of *imperator* and that the
thanksgiving should be celebrated in the name of all of them.
Nor did Cicero forget the soldiers. He concluded his speech with
a eulogy of their valor and patriotism, with a proposal to erect
a monument in honor of those who had fallen, and with the
request that the honors and rewards due to the dead heroes
should be given to their surviving relatives.

There was no light-hearted rejoicing in Cicero's oration. He
began by reminding the senators that Decimus Brutus was still
in danger, and he went on to urge the necessity of declaring
Antony a public enemy, which even yet the senate was unwilling
to do. It was only in connection with the senators who still
favored Antony and opposed Cicero's leadership that he made
mention of the task which he had carried to the very threshold
of a successful completion. He noticed "with grief" that some
were opposed to the interests of the state, that others were utterly
indifferent, and that those who were well-disposed lacked perse-
verence, and were swayed, now by hope and now by fear.
Having referred to the envy and the enmity that had tried to
discredit him by alleging that he was seeking supreme power,

he declared that the leadership which had come to him was not of his own seeking, but was the result of his attitude throughout the long crisis, whereupon he briefly reviewed the recent events. "The people remember," he said, "that I on the twentieth of December took the initiative in recovering our freedom; that from the first of January until this hour I have not ceased watching over the state; that my house and my ears have been open night and day to the advice of all men; that it is by my letters, my messages, and my exhortations that all men in every part of the empire have been roused to the defense of their country; that I have not voted for negotiations with Antony; that I have always called Antony a public enemy, and this a war, so that, though at all times favoring genuine peace, I have refused to give the name of peace to an arrangement that could bring nothing but disaster."

These words contained a just characterization of Cicero's position and efforts; they were spoken by way of argument, without the feeling of triumph that might well have been inspired by the thought that his task had been practically completed by the defeat of Antony. A few days later there arrived the report of the second battle. The news, which no one thought of doubting, was excellent: Antony had fled with a small body of men, who were without arms, panic-stricken and demoralized; the republican armies were in pursuit. On hearing this, the senate declared Antony and his followers public enemies. Cicero's speech in the senate on this occasion has not been preserved, nor have we any record in his correspondence of the feelings with which he received the word that he had succeeded in making Rome free.

Indeed, we know very little about his thoughts or his private doings throughout the period that began with his arrival in Rome in December. He was a very busy man, sometimes finding no other time for writing his letters than when his house was actually crowded with morning callers. It is not likely that he

had much leisure for the talks with such friends as Atticus which
he loved so well. We do not know whether Atticus was in Rome
during this time; he is not mentioned in Cicero's letters, nor are
there any extant letters addressed to him. Quintus seems to have
been in Rome. He is mentioned once, in February, when Cicero
wrote that he had had a talk with him and two other men about
a matter of politics. Cicero's son was in Greece, and did good
work in Brutus' army; they wrote to each other, but the letters
have been lost.

Apparently Cicero's thoughts as well as his time were
occupied with his struggle in behalf of Rome. Only one letter
is extant—and probably there were not many—in which we see
his old ability to jest in the midst of the gravest anxiety. "I am
sorry you have stopped going to dinners," he writers[36] to his
witty friend Paetus, "for you have deprived yourself of much
gratification and pleasure. And I also fear, for I am allowed
to tell the truth, that you will unlearn and forget something
that you once knew, how to arrange pleasant little dinner parties.
For if in former times, when you had some one to imitate, you
did not get very far in that art, what will you accomplish now?
Spurinna thinks it a serious matter for the state if you do not
go back to your old habits when the West wind begins to blow.
But, joking aside, nothing brings greater happiness than to
associate with good, pleasant, and fond companions. I am not
referring to excellent dinners, but to good talk, which is always
best at a dinner table. But don't think because I am joking,"
he adds, "that I have thrown away all thought of the state.
Day and night I do nothing and think of nothing except for the
purpose of making my fellow-citizens safe and free. My thought
is that if I have to lay down my life in these efforts, I shall feel
that my end has been a glorious one." This thought, that his
day was nearly done, which he uttered in his speeches as well,
crept into one or two other letters, accompanied by a passing

---

[36] *Fam.* 9, 24.

confession that the strain was almost too heavy to bear. "I shall continue to protect the interests of the state, if the strength is given me," he wrote after learning of the deaths of Hirtius and Pansa, "and yet I am by this time very tired. No weariness, however, must stand in the way of a man's duty."

Cicero was living in a new generation. Antony could have been his son; Octavian, his grandson. The men with whom he had begun life had nearly all died, most of them violent deaths. One of these friends, Servius Sulpicius, the great jurist, died at this time. He was one of the three ambassadors sent to Antony early in the year, but he had succumbed to sickness on the way to Antony's camp. When it was moved in the senate to honor the deceased with a gilt equestrian statue and a public funeral, Cicero spoke in favor of the motion, in the *Ninth Philippic.* This is one of his shortest orations, but it is one of the most impressive. Though spoken during the days immediately subsequent to the return to Rome of the embassy, and both the appointment of this embassy and its report drew forth Cicero's most violent invective, still this speech is free from partisanship, calm and elevated; it is like a bit of blue sky suddenly revealed amid an angry welter of dark storm clouds.

Sulpicius had been the greatest of jurists, Cicero said; his knowledge of law had never been equalled. But the principles that had guided him were those of kindness and justice; he was no more eager to manage a lawsuit properly than to prevent disputes altogether. Such a man needed no monuments; but in honoring him the senate would honor itself. Cicero here spoke out of his long friendship with Sulpicius, and it will be remembered that it was Sulpicius who wrote the noble letter to Cicero after Tullia's death, and that it was his son who visited Cicero in Rome during the first days after the funeral. Sulpicius, Cicero said, had traveled through snow and over bad roads, in the middle of winter, in order to reach Antony's camp, and had not stopped for rest on the way, though he knew that the exertion might cause his death. He had sacrificed himself to his duty. When appointed on the embassy, he had pleaded illness, but when the senate and the consul had insisted, he had yielded. His son and Cicero had attempted to dissuade him, but he had answered that the wishes of the senate were more important than his life. And early in the morning on the next day the young Sulpicius and Cicero had accompanied him as he set out; his last words had seemed like a prophecy of his end.

The increasing loneliness of Cicero's life, his advanced age, and the mental and physical weariness that occasionally beset him, had not relaxed his energy; he had fought on, with the one wish of seeing Rome free. The news of Antony's defeat must therefore have brought him an intense feeling of relief and of triumph, but this feeling was quickly dissipated. The war had been all but lost in the hour of victory. It was learned in the next few weeks that, while Antony had indeed been defeated, he had not been crushed, and, what was of even greater import, the republican armies were not in united pursuit. The flight of Antony had raised the siege of Mutina, but the troops of Decimus Brutus were in a deplorable condition on account of their long investment, and Brutus lacked both cavalry and pack animals. Even if his forces had been fit and well equipped, it would have been highly desirable for him to arrange for the pursuit with the generals who had relieved him; now it was necessary. Hirtius, however, was dead, as he soon discovered, and Pansa, who summoned him to a conference, died from his wounds while Brutus was actually on his way to see him. Octavian remained, but neither he nor his soldiers would coöperate with the assassin of Caesar, and the legions of the deceased consuls also sided with Octavian. Brutus thus lost two days in fruitless efforts to organize a pursuit, and when he started, on the third day, he had a feeble army and was unable to proceed with the despatch of Antony. The latter, whose cavalry was powerful, marched rapidly westward; he enrolled in his army the slaves quartered in the barracks along his way; and presently he was joined by Ventidius Bassus, a praetor, who had enrolled three legions of veterans, with whom he had come up from Italy. The force of Antony was now considerable, and might readily become even more formidable if Lepidus, who was stationed nearest to him in the west, should make common cause with him. The war, therefore, was far from won; it had only been transferred to another region, and the prospects were less promising than they had been at any time since Cicero assumed the leadership.

Nothing short of a defeat of the republican armies could have been more disastrous to the republic than their failure to unite in pursuit of Antony. The refusal of Octavian and the armies to join Decimus was partly due to policy. While Antony was still in command of a large army, he had in vain urged upon Hirtius and Octavian that an agreement between them all was to their mutual advantage; now, with Antony no longer in a predominant position, there was a greater likelihood that Octavian might secure favorable terms from Antony. But more important than any policy of Octavian and his soldiers was the death of the consuls. What would have happened if both or one of them had survived, can not be determined. By their death, however, Octavian and the soldiers were brought into immediate relations with Decimus; and with him, the assassin of Caesar, any association would be intolerable. Octavian himself might not have found it more difficult to act in unison with Decimus than with Antony, who had insulted and robbed the young man, had actually prepared to have him declared a public enemy, and had forced him to fly to arms; but it is unthinkable that the armies should coöperate with Decimus, especially in an effort to destroy Antony. The veterans had rallied to Octavian, or had deserted to him from Antony, as the case might be, largely because of his generous pay; while devoted to him as the heir of Caesar, they had no quarrel with Antony, and may indeed have been in as friendly a frame of mind toward

him as toward Octavian himself. Antony, no less than Octavian,
had been faithful to Caesar's memory; and Antony, the dashing
general, was the idol of the army, whereas Octavian had not
shown himself a great commander. The veterans, indeed, according to one account, had expected to be led by Octavian against
the assassins, and had mutinied when told that they were to go
against Antony. Both the interests and the sentiments of the
veterans and of Octavian therefore prevented a union with
Decimus.

To the student who remembers Octavian's adroitness as displayed in his later life, it may readily seem that the young man
caused the rupture with Decimus in a farsighted view of the
future, but such a conception leaves out of account the fact that
in times of revolution the leaders of a party keep their position
only by following the men whom they seem to lead. The Roman
legions had learned independence; their likes and dislikes had
been a frequent argument in the forum; it is inconceivable that
they would have obeyed Octavian if he had ordered them to
march with him and Decimus in pursuit of Antony. They had
fought against Antony while the consuls were still with them,
representing the loyalist element which bound together the followers of the assassins and of Octavian; and they had fought,
less, it would seem, to free Decimus than to free the legions shut
up with him in Mutina; but after the death of the consuls and
the relief of the legions in Mutina, the veterans were not willing
to carry the fight any further.

The fateful antagonism that kept Octavian and his soldiers
aloof from Decimus was presently increased by the perversity
of the senate. When the news of the second victory at Mutina
reached the capital, the senate, believing that the state had been
saved, at once set about ordering the affairs of Rome as though
all power had again come into its hands. Marcus Brutus and
Cassius were given special powers in the East, for the purpose
of holding the provinces and of crushing Dolabella. Sextus

Pompey was made commander of the fleet. Decimus Brutus was directed to take command of all the forces in the north; and this order applied not only to the legions of the deceased consuls but also to the Fourth and Martian legions, which had in the previous year gone over to Octavian and so made opposition to Antony possible. A triumph was decreed to Decimus; the lesser honor of an ovation was granted to Octavian. The preference for Decimus over Octavian might be explained on the ground that Decimus had by the death of the consuls become the ranking officer in the north; he was older than Octavian, and it was for his relief that the campaign about Mutina had taken place; but the senate had nevertheless shown that they no longer considered Octavian's assistance of supreme importance, and thought that he could be safely ignored.

The senate went even further. A committee of ten was appointed to revise the acts of Antony's consulship. The decisions of this committee would inevitably be of far-reaching importance; it would practically remake the political situation, which included the assignment of land to the veterans; and yet neither Decimus nor Octavian was made a member of this committee. In its determination to exercise complete control, the senate thus managed not only to intensify the antagonism already existing between the northern generals but also to indicate that, as these generals would have nothing to say about the rewards due to the veterans, the latter would have to depend entirely on the senate. By these measures, and others like them but of less importance, the senate once for all gave proof that they could not to be trusted to recognize the claims either of Octavian or of the veterans. The republican coalition had been held together for a few months by the eloquent patriotism of Cicero, aided by the threatening position of Antony; the restoration of a peaceful republic would have meant supreme power for the senate, and now the senate, in its supposed hour of triumph, had proved itself unfit for such power.

A period of intense activity now set in for Cicero; in June he wrote to Cornificius that he could not choose his own time even for letter-writing; on the twenty-seventh of July, when he wrote the last letter that has been preserved, he was in the midst of the political turmoil. Everything depended on the attitude of the generals and the armies in the field, and Cicero did what he could to retain their allegiance to the doomed republic, but it was not much that he could accomplish. He had not been a party to the high-handed behavior of the senate. During the first debate, he had not advocated severe measures. Though he had undoubtedly welcomed with eagerness the branding of Antony and his followers as public enemies, for on this he had insisted from the beginning, the only measure proposed by him in which an individual was mentioned by name related to Antony's brother, Gaius, who had been taken captive by Marcus Brutus and had been treated by him with a consideration that had already caused a scandal among Brutus' friends. It was due to Cicero, it seems, that Octavian received even as much as an ovation. And when the senate was considering the appointment of the important board of ten, Cicero spoke vehemently for the inclusion of Decimus and Octavian, but he was silenced with shouts, and outvoted. Cicero was thus powerless while the senate believed Antony hopelessly defeated and in danger of prompt capture; nor was he more successful after the first news had been contradicted. The city became a prey to fear and anxiety. There were meetings of the senate and Cicero spoke, but by the end of May he wrote that he seemed like one beating the air, for he no longer had his "old weapon" the senate.

The disorganization of the senate merely reflected the confusion prevalent in Rome. Rumors and guesses filled the air. Even as late as the end of May there were people who were surprised that the war in the north was not ended. Criticisms were leveled at Decimus for having allowed Antony to escape. Writing to Marcus Brutus, Cicero himself expressed the opinion that Decimus had blundered fatally; writing to Decimus, he made light of the general's detractors, but added that care must be taken to avoid criticism. The partisans of the various generals were active; there were enemies in the city, according to Cicero, no less than in the field. Nobody knew for some time exactly what had happened in the north, and nobody knew what was going to happen. The attitude of Lepidus and of Plancus was most important. Lepidus had seven legions, and was stationed nearest Antony. Plancus, a little to the north, had a good army, apparently consisting of three veteran legions and one of recruits. When a loyal message was delivered from Plancus, the senate shouted with joy; no dispatch within the memory of man, wrote Cicero, had been more welcome. The senate had just been alarmed by a shifty letter from Lepidus. Though Antony's former supporter was distrusted, yet people felt that he might, after all, remain loyal to the republic. On the twenty-second of May he sent Cicero his professions of loyalty, surmising with regret that the political situation must have given rise to unfavorable rumors about him; and on the twenty-ninth he joined Antony.

On the next day Lepidus despatched a letter[37] to the magistrates and senate of Rome, informing them that his army had mutinied and forced him to make peace with Antony. The soldiers had been averse to shedding the blood of fellow citizens, Lepidus wrote; and he himself, adopting their point of view, urged the senate not to condemn the action that had been taken. This account of Lepidus' defection seems on the whole to be correct. It is certainly beyond doubt that there had been a question as to the loyalty toward the republic among Lepidus' troops even before the final crisis arrived, for Plancus in his correspondence with Cicero refers to this, and it is also reported in some detail that when the armies of Lepidus and Antony were encamped near each other, there was fraternizing among the

---

[37] *Fam.* 10, 35.

troops. The attitude of Lepidus' veterans is worthy of note, not as a means of clearing Lepidus of double dealing, for he would under any circumstances have acted for his own advantage, but as another indication that the soldiers had perhaps an even greater influence than the generals in bringing about the fall of the republic. When the army had first become a power in Roman politics, it had been the instrument of its leaders; it was now beginning to speak for itself, directly; the time was approaching when the soldiers would make and unmake Roman emperors.

The other general of importance in the west was Plancus. He had perhaps not been whole-heartedly on the side of the republicans at the beginning of the war, but he had been won over by Cicero's example and letters, and he had, no doubt, also been influenced, earlier in the year, by Antony's proposal to take his province, Further Gaul, in exchange for Cisalpine Gaul. Plancus had done his best, by letters and messengers, to secure the loyalty of Lepidus; and two weeks after Lepidus' desertion he joined forces with Decimus Brutus. Their armies seem to have been of about the same size as the combined armies of Antony, Bassus, and Lepidus. The latter had approximately ten full legions and six fragmentary legions, whereas the two republican commanders had about fourteen legions. But the proportion of recruits was very great in the armies of Plancus and Decimus, so that they could not confidently offer battle. Nothing therefore was done. As late as the twenty-eighth of July, when Plancus wrote the last extant letter to Cicero, which is also the last in the correspondence, Plancus recalled the fact that experience had often shown that raw recruits could not be trusted to oppose veterans, and he pointed out that the only hope of safety lay in reinforcements from Africa or from Octavian. Plancus had written constantly to Octavian, and the latter had always replied that he was coming straightway, but now, by the end of July, Plancus understood that Octavian was pursuing a policy of his own.

The senate, in the meantime, had on the thirtieth of June declared Lepidus a public enemy. The decree, though voted unanimously, had been long delayed, and may in the end have been chiefly due to the new hope inspired by Plancus' junction with Decimus. Writing of the decree to Cassius, Cicero said that the courage of the senate was founded mainly on the expectation that Cassius would bring aid to the republic. There was still some hope that Lepidus' soldiers might desert, for an amnesty was offered to those who "returned to their senses" by the first of September.

As the decree against Lepidus made his property forfeit to the state, the senate may also have been influenced by their lack of money. The treasury was empty, and yet money was needed in all directions. Cassius seems to have been the only republican general who was able to pay his own legions. Decimus had begun the war with more than forty million sesterces, about two million dollars, and by the fifth of May he had not only spent this but had been forced to "load all his friends with debt." What the senate could gather together, was decreed to him. A property tax, the first for over a century, was declared, but the wealthy made fraudulent returns, and no more was realized than was needed for two legions.

Armies were needed quite as much as money. Troops were summoned from Africa, and two legions ultimately arrived, but too late to alter the situation. Cassius was called from the East, but Cassius was clearly too far away. Marcus Brutus was repeatedly requested to come from Macedonia. Whether he could have aided the state is not certain. The task of transporting a large army across the Adriatic was considerable; he had reason for doubting the loyalty of Octavian, whose army would stand between him and Antony; and he could not be confident that his legions would remain loyal if brought face to face with an opposing army. But Brutus did not wish to come. He did not refuse to obey Cicero's insistent summons; for reply, he merely paraded his own grievances. He bitterly criticised Cicero's praise of Octavian and the ovation that Cicero's efforts had secured for him, not seeming to realize the necessity of binding Octavian and his army to the state by every possible means; and he objected strenuously to the threatened confiscation of Lepidus' property. Lepidus was married to a half-sister of Brutus, and the latter was eager to protect her and her children. Cicero had at first been inclined not to interfere with the course of the law, but he later spoke in the senate in favor of Lepidus' family, and assured Brutus that the settlement of the question would be left to him. No concession, however, had any effect on this philosopher who had turned politician. Indeed, Brutus had from the beginning of the struggle believed in the possibility of an amicable arrangement with Antony; he had not yet learned that there could be no peace between the assassins of Caesar and those who revered Caesar's memory and desired to inherit his power.

While these events were slowly shaping themselves for the destruction of the republic, Octavian remained in the north with his army. His refusal to join Decimus had brought on the new phase of the war; his possible intervention on one side or the other was still of supreme importance. Cicero and he corresponded frequently, and Cicero kept in constant touch with his friends and partisans in Rome. The personal relations of the two men seem to have been cordial and even intimate. Octavian is said to have called Cicero "father," and this may be true, but there is no evidence for the further statement that the young Caesar deceived Cicero by the use of this name, and by the deference and affection it implied. Neither did Cicero attempt to deceive Octavian. On one occasion he said that the young man must be "praised, distinguished, and extinguished."[38] There is no indication in Cicero's public acts that this epigram,

---

[38] *Laudandum, ornandum, tollendum.* Shuckburgh's translation. For his conjecture as to the circumstances under which it was uttered, see Shuckburgh, *Augustus*, p. 52, footnote 3.

which was reported to Octavian by a busybody, represented Cicero's real attitude to Octavian. It is not unlikely that the words were a diplomatic reply to Octavian's numerous detractors, against whom Cicero was constantly urging Octavian's claims. Cicero understood that Octavian's attitude to the state would inevitably depend on the way in which the senate treated him; since his power for good and for evil was unusual, his loyalty had to be secured by unusual concessions. The ultimate position intended for Octavian by Cicero seems to have been that of a man held in high esteem and generously rewarded by the republic. Cicero was known as Octavian's champion. When Octavian desired the consulship, after the death of Hirtius and Pansa, Cicero opposed it. There were constitutional difficulties about a consular election in 43 B.C. and Octavian was very young. Cicero urged Octavian to desist from his intention; he reasoned with Octavian's friends in Rome, and he spoke of the matter in the senate; but there was nevertheless a rumor to the effect that Cicero and Octavian were planning to make themselves consuls, and Brutus actually was informed that Cicero had been elected. While Cicero therefore seems to have been sincere as well as prudent in his advocacy of Octavian, the latter, on the other hand, may not have attempted to deceive Cicero. If circumstances had allowed him to receive the honors intended for him by Cicero, he might have been satisfied. But the hatred felt by the soldiers for Caesar's assassins and the perversity of the senate made this impossible. Cicero speaks again and again of Octavian's numerous bad advisers, who might at any time turn his loyalty to enmity. Perhaps there is more truth in Cicero's view of the young Octavian and his position than is usually supposed.

On the twenty-seventh of July Cicero wrote the last letter[39] which has been preserved from his hand; it was addressed to Marcus Brutus. At that time Cicero still expected Brutus to come to Italy, and he hoped, though with very little confidence,

---

[39] *Ad Brut.* 1, 18.

that Octavian would remain loyal to the extent of protecting the
city. The crisis followed shortly after this date, but our knowledge of it comes from later historians, and can not be trusted in
all its details. Rumors, guesses, and partisan assertions constituted much of the evidence for these narratives. The main
facts, however, are clear. Octavian needed the consulship, in
order that he might meet Antony on somewhat equal terms when
the deadlock in the north should have come to an end, and also,
it would seem, in order that he, as consul, might take measures
for the reward of his soldiers. For some months Octavian
remained quiet, watching events, but in the month of August
he sent a deputation of soldiers to Rome with two demands:
that Octavian receive the consulship, and that his soldiers receive
the money due them. They also asked for the repeal of the
decree declaring Antony a public enemy. This deputation was
not successful, and Octavian marched on Rome with his army.
The senate, we are told, sent him word, offering to yield in everything, but when two legions at last arrived from Africa, they
changed their minds, and decided to defend the city with the
African legions and one other legion, which had been left in
Rome by Pansa. They also made preparations to flee to Marcus
Brutus. Octavian came nearer, and the three legions deserted to
him. The senate had now no choice; and we are informed that
among those who sought pardon from Octavian was Cicero, who,
however, was received with scorn.[40]   Again the senate had a
moment of hope, for it was reported that the Fourth and Martian
legions had refused obedience to Octavian. The fathers met,
Cicero standing at the door of the senate-house to welcome them,
we are told, but when the rumor was exploded, Cicero vanished
in a litter. About the truth of these stories we can no longer
decide.

---

[40] Cicero had a successful interview with Octavian during this time.
There is still extant a fragment from a letter addressed by him to Octavian,
perhaps the last words of Cicero which have come down to us. It reads:
''Touching your grant of leave of absence to Philippus and myself, I feel
a twofold pleasure; for it implies pardon for the past, and indulgence for
the future'' (Tyrrell, VI, 298).

Octavian, however, and his half-brother Pedius became consuls on the nineteenth of August, and several measures of importance were passed. The soldiers had already been paid: Octavian had secured possession of public moneys, it is said, but the treasury was empty, and no explanation is given of the origin of this treasure. Octavian was put in command of Decimus Brutus' army; the assassins were condemned and their property declared forfeit; even Sextus Pompey was included in this sentence; the decree of outlawry against Dolabella was repealed, for it was not known that Dolabella had committed suicide when his struggle with Cassius had grown hopeless; later the decrees against Antony and Lepidus were also repealed. Octavian thereupon marched north. His avowed purpose was to carry out the verdict against Decimus Brutus, but he went away really to make terms with Antony. He had begun to prepare a way for reconciliation with Antony immediately after Mutina, when, in addition to remaining aloof from Decimus, he released Antonian soldiers, who had been captured, and allowed some officers to join Antony.

Antony in the meantime had prospered. Pollio, who had held Further Spain with three legions, had come up from the south. Though conceited and ill-tempered, he was a patriot and would doubtless have preferred to remain loyal to the republic, but his three legions were no match for the large forces commanded by Antony. He therefore made common cause with him. The armies of Decimus Brutus and Plancus were thus made still more inferior to the forces of Antony, and there was no prospect of relief. Pollio is said to have managed the negotiations with Plancus, who went over to Antony. His army, like that of Pollio, could not have been in a mood to fight against unequal odds with less reward in prospect than if they joined the superior forces of Antony. It is at any rate reported that the army of Decimus refused to stand by their commander, and his army had been as loyal an army as the republicans had had. They joined Plancus in his desertion to Antony. Decimus tried to escape to the East, but the few troops that had at first accompanied him melted away, and he was finally killed by a Gallic chieftain, at the command of Antony. Antony, Lepidus, and Pollio then marched eastward with a large part of their forces, and were met by Octavian.

The result of this meeting was the establishment by Antony, Lepidus, and Octavian of the military dictatorship which has been called the Second Triumvirate. The duty of the triumvirs, according to the very phrase under which they took office, was to settle the constitution. This settlement took twelve years of almost constant warfare. Brutus and Cassius were defeated at Philippi in the year 42 B.C.; Sextus Pompey, who had hovered on the edge of things since his father's death, was conquered, and executed in 35 B.C.; Lepidus was thrust aside, to live on to an inglorious old age; the inevitable rivalry between the two remaining triumvirs, which was patched up twice, led to the battle of Actium, in 31 B.C., where Antony was defeated; and finally Antony stabbed himself, and Octavian remained the undisputed master of the Roman world. When Octavian first took up arms against Antony, Cicero had surmised that the outcome would be supreme power either for Antony or for Octavian, and he had preferred Octavian. His ineffectual efforts to restore the republic had put Octavian in a position in which he could ultimately bargain with Antony, and had thus had the result which Cicero had foreseen but had hoped to avoid. He had served Rome in a way that he had not intended, but the service was considerable; Antony, as dictator of Rome, would not have created an empire like that of Augustus.

For the purpose of settling the constitution, in the meantime, the triumvirs decided upon a proscription. It was the prudent thing to do, for the republic could be destroyed only by destroying her defenders; it was necessary, for the triumvirs needed the money of the proscribed with which to pay the soldiers; but it was also an act of vengeance, so that each triumvir agreed to sacrifice some relative or friend to the hatred of the others. Before the triumvirs themselves reached Rome, where they published a large proscription list, they sent soldiers in advance with orders to put to death twelve or seventeen of their most conspicuous opponents. Cicero was one of these.

III

The End

The death of Cicero has been described by many ancient writers. It took place on the seventh of December, 43 B.C.; but as to the truthfulness of the various descriptions, it must be recalled that Cicero's last days became early a subject for declamation in the rhetorical schools. The rhetoricians discussed such topics as that of the Ailing Twins; and they also made use of historical, semi-historical, and mythical episodes. Agamemnon was made to deliberate whether he should sacrifice Iphigenia, for Calchas had foretold that without the sacrifice the Greek fleet would not be allowed to depart for Troy. Alexander the Great deliberated whether he should enter Babylon in spite of the augur's response that it would be dangerous. The Athenians deliberated whether to destroy their Persian trophies, Xerxes having threatened that otherwise he would invade Greece again. In the same way Cicero deliberated whether he should beg Antony for mercy; and also whether he should burn his writings, for Antony had promised that if he did this, his life would be spared. And, finally, this situation was suggested, for its ethical bearings: Cicero had successfully defended Popillius on a charge of parricide; when Cicero had been proscribed, Popillius was sent by Antony to murder him; this he did, and returned to Antony with the orator's head.

For these exercises the rhetoricians suggested every conceivable thought and detail, eagerly embroidering the event and arguing as to the probability and effectiveness of their points. A few of these will illustrate their character.

The state could be a slave to Antony, it was said, but not Cicero. How could Cicero have entered the senate, to beg for mercy, when this body had been cruelly depleted and its ranks thereupon filled with Antony's base adherents? Cicero would no longer see Pompey there, nor Cato, the Luculli, Hortensius, and others. What, O Cicero, have you to do with a new age? Your day is past. If you, Cicero, consider the longing for you on the part of the Roman people, then your life, whenever you die, has been too short; if you consider your own great deeds, then you have lived long enough; if the injuries inflicted by fortune and the condition of the state, then you have lived too long; if the memory of your deeds, you will live forever. All the murders of the proscriptions were perpetrated in order that Cicero, too, might die. When you come before Antony, you will ask for death. It was just that Cicero should give satisfaction to Antony, whom he had himself declared an outlaw and a public enemy. Cicero, finally, could not be so cowardly as to ask for mercy, nor so stupid as to expect it.

No one but Asinius Pollio thought so, says Seneca the Elder, from whom these details come,[41] and even he did not dare to put his charges against Cicero into his history. Pollio, continues Seneca, was the only one to assert that Cicero died a coward's death. In the reign of Augustus he was a literary light, exceedingly jealous of Cicero's fame. Once he was present at the house of Messalla when a certain Sextilius Ena won applause with a poem on Cicero, in which one line was to the effect that men must weep for Cicero and for the silence of the Roman tongue. Pollio became angry, and said to his host, "It is for you to decide what may be allowed in your house, but I shall not listen to a man who makes me out to be a mute."

---

[41] Sen. *Controv.* 7, 2; *Suas.* 6 and 7.

Livy said[42] that at the time of the proscriptions Cicero left Rome for Tusculum, and thence by devious ways he went to Formiae to take ship from Caieta. Contrary winds arose, Cicero became seasick, and he was also disgusted with the thought of flight and of living any longer. He therefore returned to his upper villa, more than a mile from the sea, saying, "I shall die in my country, which I have so often saved." It is well known, says Livy, that his slaves were both brave and faithful, ready to defend him, but he, when pursued, ordered them to set down the litter and quietly to allow an unjust fate to take its course. He bent out of the litter and, without wincing, received the blow that severed his head from his body. His head and hands were taken to Rome, and nailed, a hand on either side of the head, to the rostra, where his voice had often been heard. The citizens could scarcely raise their tearful eyes to look at the sight.

One author, Seneca adds, tried to describe the expression on the dead orator's face, but found the task too difficult.

And it would be difficult, indeed impossible, to ascertain the truth about Cicero's ending. The broad outlines are known, but we can not be certain of the emotions with which he met death or of the events that surrounded the murder. The influence of the rhetoricians is everywhere present. The details that could be gathered are very numerous. Only one more, because rather well known, need be set down. Fulvia, the widow of Clodius and the wife of Antony, it is said, took Cicero's severed head in her lap, addressed insulting words to it, pulled out the tongue and pierced it with a sharp hairpin. St. Jerome, who tells[43] the story, compares these indignities to those inflicted by Herodias on the head of John the Baptist.

The most complete account of Cicero's last days is found at the end of Plutarch's Life. Many of his details doubtless come from Tiro; but when he speaks of Popillius and Philologus, it is

---

42 Sen. *Suas.* 6, 17.

43 St. Jerome, *Contra Rufinum*, 3, 42.

necessary to remember the rhetoricians. He represents Cicero as considering suicide, but that is exactly like the rhetorical deliberations about his books.[44] Plutarch never omitted anything, however incredible, provided it was picturesque, pathetic, or useful to point a moral. Nevertheless his account is the best that we have, and may well be cited.

"Whilst these things were contriving,[45] Cicero was with his brother at his country-house near Tusculum; whence, hearing of the proscriptions, they determined to pass to Astura, a villa of Cicero's near the sea, and to take shipping from thence for Macedonia to Brutus, of whose strength in that province news had already been heard. They traveled together in their separate litters, overwhelmed with sorrow; and, often stopping on the way till their litters came together, condoled with one another. But Quintus was the more disheartened, when he reflected on his want of means for his journey; for, as he said, he had brought nothing with him from home. And even Cicero himself had but a slender provision. It was judged, therefore, most expedient that Cicero should make what haste he could to fly, and Quintus return home to provide necessaries, and thus resolved, they mutually embraced, and parted with many tears.

"Quintus, within a few days after, betrayed by his servants to those who came to search for him, was slain, together with his young son. But Cicero was carried to Astura, where, finding a vessel, he immediately went on board her, and sailed as far as Circaeum with a prosperous gale; but when the pilots resolved immediately to set sail from thence, whether fearing the sea, or not wholly distrusting the faith of Caesar,[46] he went on shore, and passed by land a hundred furlongs, as if he was going for Rome. But losing resolution and changing his mind, he again

---

[44] Gudeman, pp. 27–29.

[45] Clough's translation. The quaintness of the style accords well with the legendary character of the content.

[46] i.e., Octavian, later Augustus.

returned to the sea, and there spent the night in fearful and perplexed thoughts. Sometimes he resolved to go into Caesar's house privately, and there kill himself upon the altar of his household gods, to bring divine vengeance upon him; but the fear of torture put him off this course. And after passing through a variety of confused and uncertain counsels, at last he let his servants carry him by sea to Capitae, where he had a house, an agreeable place to retire to in the heat of summer, when the Etesian winds are so pleasant.

"There was at that place a chapel of Apollo, not far from the seaside, from which a flight of crows arose with a great noise, and made towards Cicero's vessel as it rowed to land, and lighting on both sides of the yard, some croaked, others pecked the ends of the ropes. This was looked upon by all as an ill omen; and, therefore, Cicero again went ashore, and, entering his house, lay down upon his bed to compose himself to rest. Many of the crows settled about the window, making a dismal cawing; but one of them alighted upon the bed where Cicero lay covered up, and with its bill by little and little pecked off the clothes from his face. His servants, seeing this, blamed themselves that they should stay to be spectators of their master's murder, and do nothing in his defence, whilst the brute creatures came to assist and take care of him in his undeserved affliction; and therefore, partly by entreaty, partly by force, they took him up, and carried him in his litter towards the seaside.

"But in the meantime the assassins were come with a band of soldiers, Herennius, a centurion, and Popillius, a tribune, whom Cicero had formerly defended when prosecuted for the murder of his father. Finding the doors shut, they broke them open, and Cicero not appearing, and those within saying they knew not where he was, it is stated that a youth, who had been educated by Cicero in the liberal arts and sciences, an emancipated slave of his brother Quintus, Philologus by name, informed the tribune that the litter was on its way to the sea through the close and shady walks. The tribune, taking a few with him, ran to the place where he was to come out. And Cicero, perceiving Herennius running in the walks, commanded his servants to set down the litter; and stroking his chin, as he used to do, with his left hand, he looked steadfastly upon his murderers, his person covered with dust, his beard and hair untrimmed, and his face worn with his troubles. So that the greatest part of those that stood by covered their faces whilst Herennius slew him. And thus was he murdered, stretching forth his neck out of the litter, being now in his sixty-fourth year. Herennius cut off his head, and, by Antony's command, his hands also, by which his *Philippics* were written; for so Cicero styled those orations he wrote against Antony, and so they are called to this day.

"When these members of Cicero were brought to Rome, Antony was holding an assembly for the choice of public officers; and when he heard it, and saw them, he cried out, 'Now let there be an end of our proscriptions.' He commanded his head and hands to be fastened up over the rostra, where the orators spoke; a sight which the Roman people shuddered to behold, and they believed they saw there, not the face of Cicero, but the image of Antony's own soul. And yet amidst these actions he did justice in one thing, by delivering up Philologus to Pomponia, the wife of Quintus; who, having got his body into her power, besides other grievous punishments, made him cut off his own flesh by pieces, and roast and eat it; for so some writers have related. But Tiro, Cicero's emancipated slave, has not so much as mentioned the treachery of Philologus.

"Some long time after, Caesar, I have been told, visiting one of his daughter's sons, found him with a book of Cicero's in his hand. The boy for fear endeavored to hide it under his gown; which Caesar perceiving, took it from him, and turning over a great part of the book standing, gave it to him again, and said, 'My child, this was a learned man, and a lover of his country.' And immediately after he had vanquished Antony, being then consul, he made Cicero's son his colleague in the office; and under that consulship, the senate took down all the statues of Antony, and abolished all the other honors that had been given him, and decreed that none of that family should thereafter bear the name of Marcus; and thus the final acts of the punishment of Antony were, by the divine powers, devolved upon the family of Cicero.''

If it is true that no man should be accounted happy before his death, then it is also true that a man may be accounted happy because of his death. Cicero's death was happy, despite its tragedy. He died, as he had lived, for Rome; after the republic had fallen, he would not have chosen to live. It is not possible to conceive of Cicero as finding rest or contentment hidden away in a Roman villa or in a Greek city while the Roman world was convulsed by the ambition of her masters, or even later, when the rule of Augustus gave peace, for the peace of Augustus would have seemed like a pall of death to the old champion of the free republic.

SELECT BIBLIOGRAPHY

This bibliography contains only the books and articles that I have found particularly useful or that treat in greater detail some of the topics not usually much attended to in biographies of Cicero. For a classified and very full bibliography, see Schanz; also Heitland, Laurand, and Niese.

ABBOTT, F. F.

A history and description of Roman political institutions; ed. 3. 1911.

ARNIM, H. VON.

Leben und Werke des Dio von Prusa. 1898.

BERNOUILLI, J. J.

Roemische Ikonographie. 1882.

BESANÇON, A.

Les adversaires de l'hellénisme à Rome pendant la période républicaine. 1910. A very interesting book. Discusses Cicero's attitude both to things Greek and to the Romans in their connection with the Greeks. Like other writers, Besançon takes Cicero's characterizations of Crassus and other Romans as true to history; but see above, pp. 416 ff.

BERTRAND, ÉD.

Cicéron artiste. 1890.

Cicéron au théatre. 1897.

BIRT, TH.

Abriss des antiken Buchwesens; ed. 3. 1913. *In* Mueller's *Handbuch.*

BOISSIER. G.

Cicéron et ses amis (1865); ed. 13. 1905. A classic, and needs no praise. This book is not superficial, as has sometimes been maintained.

BOTSFORD, G. W.

"On the legality of the trial and condemnation of the Catiline conspirators," *Classical Weekly,* VI, 130–132 (March 1, 1913).

BOTSFORD, G.

The Roman assemblies from their origin to the end of the republic. 1909.

BUETTNER, R.

Porcius Licinus und der literarische Kreis des Q. Lutatius Catulus. 1893.

CAUER, FR.

Ciceros politisches Denken. 1903. See above, p. 224, note 2.

CLARK, A. C.

Fontes prosae numerosae. 1910.

COWLES, F. H.

Gaius Verres; an historical study. 1917. Published after I had written the chapter on the prosecution of Verres.

CUCHEVAL, V.
  Cicéron orateur; analyse et critique des discours de Cicéron. 1901.
    2 vols. Has many excellent observations on the details of Cicero's
    orations.
  Histoire de l'éloquence latine depuis l'origine de Rome jusqu'à Cicéron.
    1892. 2 vols.
DRUMANN, W.
  Geschichte Roms. 1834 ff.; ed. 2, 1899 ff. 6 vols.
FOWLER, W. W.
  Social life at Rome in the age of Cicero. 1909.
  The religious experience of the Roman people. 1911.
FRUECHTL, A.
  Die Geldgeschäfte bei Cicero. 1912.
GASQUY, A.
  Cicéron jurisconsulte. 1887. See above, p. 115.
GOEDECKEMEYER, A.
  Die Geschichte des griechischen Skeptizismus. 1905. This is the most
    complete account of Cicero as a philosophical writer. See Zielinski's
    criticism. *Cicero im Wandel etc.*, p. 374. See also above, p. 555.
GREENIDGE, A. H.
  Roman public life. 1901.
  The legal procedure of Cicero's time. 1901. See above, p. 115.
GUDEMAN, A.
  "The sources of Plutarch's life of Cicero." *Publ. Univ. Penna. Series
    in Philol. and Lit.*, VIII, no. 2 (1902).
HEINZE, R.
  "Cicero's politische Anfänge," *Abh. d. sächs. Ges. d. Wiss.*, XXVII
    (1909), 947–1010. See above, p. 140, note 10.
HEITLAND, W. E.
  The Roman Republic. 1909. 3 vols.
HENDRICKSON, G. L.
  "Literary sources in Cicero's Brutus and the technique of citation in
    dialogue." *Amer. Jour. Phil.*, XXVII (1906), 184–199.
HIRZEL, R.
  Der Dialog. 1895. See above, p. 414.
KROLL, W.
  "Cicero und die Rhetorik," *Neue Jahrb. f. d. klass. Alt.*, XI (1903),
    681 ff. Founded on investigations given by Kroll in *Rhein. Mus.*,
    LVIII, 522 ff. See above, p. 423.
  Ed. Cicero's *Orator*. 1913.
LAURAND, L.
  De M. Tulli Ciceronis studiis rhetoricis. 1907.
  Études sur le style des discours de Cicéron. 1907.
MARTHA, J.
  Ed. Cicero's *Brutus*. 1907.

Misch, G.
   Geschichte der Autobiographie, Erster Band, Das Altertum. 1907. See
      above, p. 356.
Niese, B.
   Grundriss der römischen Geschichte nebst Quellenkunde; ed. 3. 1906.
      In Mueller's Handbuch.
Norden, Ed.
   Aus Ciceros Werkstatt. 1913.
   Die antike Kunstprosa, I. 1898.
Peter, H.
   "Der Brief in der römischen Literatur," Abh. d. sächs. Ges. d. Wiss.,
      XX, no. 3 (1901). 258 pages. Full of suggestions.
   Die geschichtliche Literatur über die roemische Kaiserzeit. 1897.
Plaumann, G.
   "Das sogenannte senatus consultum ultimum, die Quasidiktatur der
      spaeteren roemischen Republik," Klio, XIII (1913), 321–386. See
      above, p. 238, note 8.
Reid, J. S.
   Ed. Cicero's Academica. 1885.
Reitzenstein, R.
   Werden und Wesen der Humanität im Altertum. 1907.
Reure, C. O.
   Les gens de lettres et leurs protecteurs à Rome. 1891.
Schanz, M.
   Geschichte der roemischen Literatur, I, 2; ed. 3. 1909. In Mueller's
      Handbuch.
Schmekel, A.
   Die Philosophie der Mittleren Stoa. 1892.
Schmidt, O. E.
   Cicero und Terentia. 1898. Neue Jahrb. f. d. klass. Alt., I, 174–185.
   Ciceros Villen. 1899. Also in Neue Jahrb. f. d. klass. Alt., III, 328–
      355, 467–497.
   Der Briefwechsel des Marcus Tullius Cicero von seinem Prokonsulat in
      Cilicien bis zu Caesars Ermordung. 1893.
Schneidewin, M.
   Antike Humanität. 1897.
Schwartz, Ed.
   Charakterköpfe aus der antiken Literatur. 1903–1910. I, 4 (Polybius
      und Posidonius); I, 5 (Cicero).
Sihler, E. G.
   Cicero of Arpinum. 1914. The most useful reference book on Cicero
      in a single volume. Very little effort to treat the broader aspects of
      Cicero's life, though many golden thoughts can be found by the
      reader who will search for them.
"Θετικώτερον, Cicero ad Quint. Fr. 3, 3, 4," Amer. Jour. Phil. XXIII. (1902).
   283 ff.

STRACHAN–DAVIDSON, L.

Cicero and the fall of the Roman Republic. 1894. Excellent. As the title indicates, the book is concerned largely with the history of Cicero's times.

TAYLOR, H.

Cicero, a sketch of his life and works. 1916. Mentioned here principally because it is the latest biography of Cicero. Constructed on broad lines, but shows little evidence of independent study of Cicero's works.

TYRRELL, R. Y., *and* PURSER, L.

The correspondence of M. Tullius Cicero, arranged according to its chronological order. 7 vols. 1879 ff.; I, ed. 2, 1885. Indispensable to the student of Cicero or of his times. The introductory essays are of very great value. The publishers would do a real service to classical scholarship by issuing them separately, so as to make them widely accessible. The index volume contains in brief a critical biography of nearly every person mentioned in the correspondence.

VOLKMANN, R. E.

Die Rhetorik der Griechen und Römer; ed. 2. 1885.

Rhetorik; ed. 3, by C. Hammer, 1901. *In* Mueller's *Handbuch.*

WATSON, A.

Cicero, Select letters; ed. 4. 1891.

WILKINS, A. S.

Ed. Cicero's *De Oratore.* 1892.

ZELLER, ED.

Die Philosophie der Griechen. Dritter Teil, Erste Abt., ed. 3. 1880.

ZIELINSKI, TH.

"Antike Humanität," *Neue Jarb. f. d. klass. Alt.*, I (1898), 1–22. Mainly a criticism of Schneidewin's *Antike Humanität.*

Cicero im Wandel der Jahrhunderte; ed. 2. 1908. A third edition, which I have not seen, in 1912. Probably the most brilliant book written on Cicero. Though Zielinski is concerned primarily with Cicero's influence in later times, he has made a very earnest effort to grasp Cicero's personality and at the same time to express it in brief compass, but his account, though very interesting and suggestive, explains too much. A human character is not a skeleton, the bones of which can be taken apart and labeled. Zielinski too often assumes that Cicero's actions were dictated by conscious motives, and he fails to give due consideration to the private or political circumstances that lie behind many of the passages on which he founds his judgment. See also above, p. 454.

Transmitted February 14, 1919.

INDEX